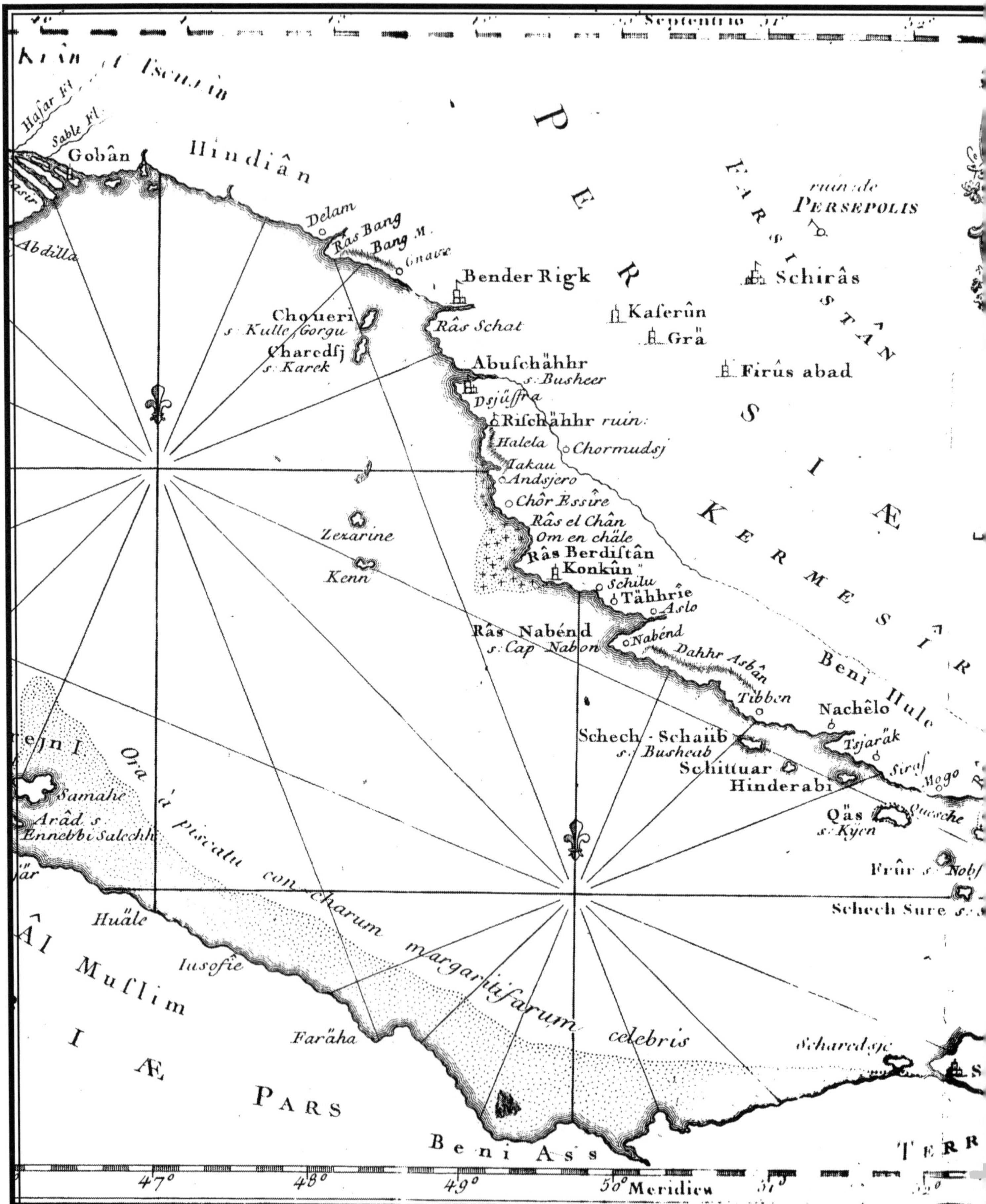
Septentrio
Hasar Fl.
Sable Fl.
Gobân
Hindiân
PERSIÆ
FARSISTÂN
ruin: de PERSEPOLIS
Delam
Râs Bang
Bang M.
Gnave
Bender Rigk
Schirâs
Kaserûn
Grä
Abdilla
Choueri s. Kulle Gorgu
Charedsj s. Karek
Râs Schat
Abuschähhr s. Busheer
Firûs abad
Dsjüffra
Rischähhr ruin:
Halela
Chormudsj
Takau
Andsjero
Chôr Essire
Râs el Chân
Om en chäle
Râs Berdistân
Konkûn
Schilu
Tähhrie
Aslo
Zezarine
Kenn
KERMESIR
Râs Nabénd s. Cap Nabon
Nabénd
Dahhr Asbân
Tibben
Beni Hule
Nachêlo
Schech Schaiib s. Busheab
Tsjaräk
Schittuar
Hinderabi
Siraf
Mogo
Samahe
Arâd s. Ennebbi Salechh
Ora à piscatu conscharum margaritifarum celebris
Qäs s. Kyen
Quesche
Frûr
Schech Sure
Huäle
Al Muslim
Iusofie
IÆ PARS
Faräha
Scharedsje
Beni Ass
TERR
47°
48°
49°
50° Meridies
51°
52°

THE PERSIAN GULF

The Rise of the Gulf Arabs

The Politics of Trade on the Persian Littoral, 1747–1792

WILLEM FLOOR

MAGE PUBLISHERS

Library of Congress Cataloging-in-Publication Data

Floor, Willem M.
The Persian Gulf : the rise of the Gulf Arabs : the politics of trade on the Persian littoral, 1747-1792 / Willem Floor.
p. cm.
Includes bibliographical references and index.
ISBN 1-933823-18-6 (pbk. : alk. paper)
1. Persian Gulf Region--History. I. Title.
DS326.F64 2007
956--dc22
2007036054

ISBN: 1-933823-18-6
ISBN 13: 978-1933823-18-8

Printed and Manufactured in the United States

Mage books are available at bookstores,
through the internet, or directly from the publisher:
Mage Publishers, 1032 29th Street, NW, Washington, DC 20007
202-342-1642 • as@mage.com • 800-962-0922
visit Mage Publishers online at
www.mage.com

CONTENTS

CHAPTER FOUR

CHAPTER FIVE

FIGURES AND TABLES

INTRODUCTION

Arnold Wilson in his study *The Persian Gulf* characterized the eighteenth century as the century of the growth of English influence; in fact, it is the title of his twelfth chapter. It is my intention to evaluate whether he was correct in his assessment of the situation. At face value it would seem that he was right, for the Dutch, the main commercial rival of the English, withdrew from the Gulf in 1766, while their main political rival, the French, were absent from the Gulf between 1763 and 1793. The English thus had the Gulf all to themselves after 1766, or did they? That is one of the main questions that this study aims to answer and the result may surprise you.

The eighteenth century was one of great upheaval, for after (i) the breakdown of the central government in Persia in 1722, resulting in four decades of warfare; (ii) the occurrence of the same phenomenon in Oman in 1719, resulting in civil war and the Persian invasion (1737-47), causing much havoc and destruction, and (iii) the weakening, if not the breakdown, of Ottoman rule over Basra, the Persian Gulf countries suffered from an increase of poverty, insecurity, oppression and war, both at sea and land. Due to the improvement of security in upcountry Persia after 1753 as well as the re-establishment of a strong Imamate in Oman under the new Al Bu Sa'id dynasty after 1747 (although in both cases it took another decade to establish greater security in the respective countries), trade revived and there was increasing competition between the various Persian Gulf ports. Whereas Basra remained thriving as the main port for the upper part of the Persian Gulf until 1775, Bandar 'Abbas gradually but surely lost its leading commercial role in the lower part of the Persian Gulf, in particular after 1750. On the Arab side of the Gulf the role of Masqat increased significantly after 1750 as did that of Zubara after 1775, both acquiring much, if not most, of the trade of Bandar 'Abbas and Basra respectively. On the Persian side Bushire became the main port of entry after 1760, although Khark for a short time tried to challenge its position. There were many other small ports on the Persian littoral (Bandar-e Rig, Deylam and Ganaveh) that sometimes also saw a temporary increase in their commercial activities, but none became as important as Buhsire and they only continued to play a traditional local distributive role.[1] The main reason for Bushire's success seems to have been the presence of a critical mass of Persian and 'country' merchants as well as a relatively secure hinterland. The presence of first the Dutch (1737-53) and later of the English (1763-68, 1775-78) East Indies Companies also contributed to its importance.

1 For example in 1758, a small English ship (two-master) named the *Triumvirate* from Bombay sold its entire cargo of rice, Mallabar cinnamon, Bengal gum-lac, curcuma and ginger at Kangan and Taheri. A large French ship, the *Bristol*, on its return from Basra bought wheat at Bandar-e Rig and Ganaveh. VOC 2968, Khark to Batavia (16/11/1758), f. 29.

Another important change in Persian Gulf politics was that of the reluctantly enforced use of violence by the European Companies in local conflicts. Both the Dutch and English Companies wanted to remain neutral as to the local conflicts and military exploits that occurred after 1735 in the Persian Gulf. However, the use of economic and military blackmail, first by Nader Shah and later by Karim Khan, often left them no choice but to support military adventures initiated by the central government in Persia, when the Companies decided to stay and trade in Persia rather than abandon its unprofitable trade. Basra had suffered from internal problems between 1730 and 1750, while in 1753 the Dutch decided to abandon their factory (i.e. trading station) there. Due to the inability of the Ottoman government to provide security in the Basra area and its maritime and river routes, the EIC was more or less forced to intervene militarily to protect the city and the Shatt al-Arab, so that trade might be carried on unimpeded. In fact, the pasha of Baghdad hired the EIC to supply ships to do so. Very important also was the rise in the interference with the shipping lanes in the Persian Gulf, often through piracy and due to poverty, caused inter alia by the lack of responsible government in the hinterland ruling the coastal areas and its concomitant oppression of the coastal population. The increasing piracy by Arab coastal dwellers interfered with the interests of all merchants whether Asian or European, local or foreign. Unlike their Asian competitors, the European Companies had an armed force at their disposal and they, therefore, were forced to use violence against such pirates on occasion. Despite the high human and financial cost that both Companies incurred as a result of these military activities, they were not decisive at all from a military point of view. In fact, both the Dutch and the English suffered humiliating defeats against the Arab coastal dwellers and their larger ships were at a disadvantage with the much smaller, but shallower and nimbler, Arab vessels. Moreover, even when Europeans acquired local vessels, which used both sails and oars, they still were at a disadvantage, because their Arab opponents had larger crews and thus more power, which allowed them to outmaneuver and, if need be, to outrun the European vessels. This development of insecurity had the pernicious result that the Persian and Ottomans governments abandoned their responsibility to provide protection to trade in the Gulf, a vacuum that perforce was filled by those who felt they had and were able to play a role there.

Despite these important developments, the history of the Persian Gulf during the eighteenth century is still little known, for relatively few studies have been published so far on this subject dealing with this time period. As a result, not only has the chronology of events that unfolded during this era not yet properly been established, but also many of the issues that are pertinent to this century have not been analyzed in detail. The Arab side of the Persian Gulf has received most of the attention so far, in that there are monographs on the history of Masqat/Oman, Kuwait and Basra, which were the two main maritime Arab powers in respectively the lower and upper Persian Gulf and the major Ottoman port in the upper Persian Gulf.[2] The role of the Qavasem Arabs of Jolfar (Ra's al-Khaymah) and Lengeh has also received little attention, although they were a main contender for power in the lower Persian Gulf.[3] On the Persian side of the Gulf the state of our knowledge is much less detailed and there is no published monograph for any of the Persian ports. The dissertation by Thomas Ricks fits that bill where Bandar 'Abbas is concerned, but it remains unfortunately unpublished, while it is mainly based on English sources.[4] The same holds for the dis-

2 Patricia Risso. *Oman & Muscat: An Early Modern History* (New York, 1986); Ahmad Abu Hakima. *History of Eastern Arabia 1750-1800: The Rise and Development of Bahrain and Kuwait* (Beirut, 1965); Thabit A.J. Abdullah, *Merchants, Mamluks, and Murder: The Political Economy of Trade in Eighteenth-Century Basra* (Albany, 2001); Hala Fattah. *The Politics of Regional Trade in Iraq, Arabia and the Gulf 1745-1900* (Albany, 1997).

3 The best study on the Qavasem, although it concerns a later period, is that by Charles E. Davies. *The Blood-Red Arab Flag: An Investigation into Qasimi Piracy 1797-1820* (Exeter, 1997).

4 Thomas Miller Ricks. *Politics and Trade in Southern Iran and the Gulf, 1745-1765*. unpublished dissertation Indiana University, 1975. The history of Bandar 'Abbas by Mohammad 'Ali Sadid al-Saltaneh, *Bandar 'Abbas*

sertation by Stephen Grummond, while its main focus is on Bushire after 1800.[5] The role of Bandar-e Rig in the second half of the eighteenth century has been analyzed by John Perry and me,[6] while the history of the other ports on the Persian littoral basically remains unknown. The most comprehensive study, covering both sides of the Gulf, is that by Ben Slot, which although mainly based on Dutch sources, for the period after 1750 also draws on English sources.[7] In the last two decades a number of monographs of varying quality have appeared in Persian that deal with the history of a number of the smaller ports such as Kong, Lengeh, Ganaveh, Deylam, and Qeshm but their main focus is on the nineteenth and twentieth century as there is little information on the history of these ports in the eighteenth century extant in the available Persian sources.[8] The role of the English East India Company has been analyzed by Amin for the second half of the eighteenth century (1757-1780) and provides a useful framework highlighting the English interests in the Persian Gulf.[9] I myself have analyzed the role of the Dutch East Indies Company (*Verenigde Oost-indische Compagnie* or VOC) in the Persian Gulf during the second half of the eighteenth century in a number of articles.[10] In addition, I have published a number of studies concerning the relationship between the VOC and Safavid Persia during the first part of the eighteenth century.[11] Finally, I

---

va Khalij-e Fars ed. Ahmad Eqtedari (Tehran, 1342/1963) is a very important source, but its main focus is the nineteenth and the early twentieth century, although it has some useful information concerning the eighteenth century.

5 Stephen R. Grummond. *The Rise and Fall of the Arab Shaykhdom of Bushire: 1750-1850 (Iran, Persian Gulf)* unpublished dissertation Johns Hopkins University (Baltimore, 1985). It has been translated into Persian by Hasan Zanganeh as *Chalesh baraye qodrat va thervat dar jonub-e Iran az 1750 ta 1850 miladi* (Bushire, 1378/1999).

6 John Perry, "Mir Muhanna and the Dutch: Patterns of Piracy in the Persian Gulf," *Studia Iranica* 2 (1973), pp. 75-95; Willem Floor, "The Dutch and Khark Island: The Adventures of the Baron von Kniphausen," in: Européens en Orient aux XVIIIe siècle. *Moyen Orient & Ocean Indien* (1994), pp. 157-202. For an enlarged version of the latter study see chapter three in this publication.

7 Ben J. Slot, *The Arabs of the Gulf, 1602-1784: an alternative approach to the early history of the Arab Gulf States and the Arab peoples of the Gulf mainly based on sources of the Dutch East India Company* (Leidschendam, 1993) translated into Arabic by 'Ayidah Khuri muraja'at Mohammad Mursi 'Abdollah as *'Arab al-Khalij, 1602-1784: fi daw' masadir Sharikat al-Hind al-Sharqiyah al-Hulandiyah* (Abu Dhabi, 1995). It is strange that the Arabic version of this book is more readily available in libraries than the original English version, of which even the Library of Congress and the Widener Library (Harvard) have no copy.

8 Iraj Afshar Seystani, *Nehagi beh Bushehr* 2 vols. (Tehran, 1369/1990); 'Alireza Khalifehzadeh, *Bandar Deylam va Haft Shahr-e Liravi* (Bushire, 1382/2003); Hoseyn Nurbakhsh, *Bandar-e Lengeh dar Sahel-e Khalij-e Fars* (Bandar 'Abbas, 1358/1979), Ahmad Nur-Darya'i, *Marasem-e Ayini va Fulklur-e Mardom-e Bandar-e Kong* (Tehran, 1384/2005).

9 Abdul Amir Amin. *British Interests in the Persian Gulf* (Leiden, 1967).

10 Willem Floor, "Pearl fishing in the Persian Gulf in the 18th century," *Persica*, vol. 10 (1982), pp. 209-222 (reprinted here as Appendix II); Ibid., "Dutch trade with Masqat in the second half of the 18th century," *African and Asian Studies*, vol. 16 (1982), pp. 197-213 (reprinted here as chapter six); Ibid., "The Bahrein Project of 1754," *Persica*, vol. 11 (1984), pp. 129-148 (reprinted here as Appendix I); Ibid., "Dutch East India Company's Trade with Sind in the 17th and 18th centuries," *Moyen-Orient & Ocean Indien*, vol. 3 (1986), pp. 111-144; Ibid., "The Decline of the Dutch East Indies Company in Bandar 'Abbas, 1747-1759," *L'Ocean Indien & Le Moyen-Orient*, vol. 6 (1989), pp. 45-80; Ibid., "The Dutch and Khark Island, 1753-1770, A Commercial Mishap," 24 (1992) *IJMES*, pp. 441-460 (reprinted here as chapter five).

11 Willem Floor, "The Revolt of Shaikh Ahmad Madani in Laristan and the Garmsirat (1730-1733)," *Studia Iranica*, vol. 8 (1983), p. 63-93; Ibid., "The Iranian Navy during the Eighteenth Century," *Iranian Studies* 20 (1987), pp. 31-53 (reprinted here as chapter one); Ibid., *The Commercial Conflict between Persia and the Netherlands, 1712-1718*, Durham University, Occasional Papers no. 37. (1988); Ibid., *Hukumat-e Nader Shah* (Tehran: Tus, 1367/1988), translated by Abu'l-Qasem Serri; Ibid., *The Afghan Occupation of Persia, 1722-1730* (Paris-

have published a VOC report concerning the peoples inhabiting the Persian Gulf in the 1750s[12] as well as a comprehensive study of the political economy of trade in the Persian Gulf and of the economy of Safavid Persia, which also deal with the first quarter of the eighteenth century.[13]

Not only are studies concerning the Persian Gulf in the eighteenth century limited in number, but most of them are almost exclcusively based on English sources, despite the fact that Dutch sources (until 1766) and to a much lesser extent French sources also are very relevant to the events then developing in the Gulf. In fact, most of our information on the Persian Gulf during the eighteenth century and about the various ports comes from the mostly still unpublished records of the Dutch and English East-Indies Companies. These two Companies had been in the Gulf for a long time and it may therefore be of interest to give a short overview of their presence there. The *English East India Company* (EIC) was created in 1600 and started trading with Persia in 1617, when Shah 'Abbas I granted it attractive privileges. It had a factory in Bandar 'Abbas, where it had the right to the moiety of the customs revenues, and one in Isfahan. After having suffered a defeat against the Dutch in 1653 the EIC experienced a downturn in its commercial activities in Persia, but after the 1680s it turned around its weak performance and slowly but certainly began to get even with the VOC and eventually even surpass it. In the 1680s, the EIC established a trading station in Kerman to buy goat wool, an activity that it had been engaged in since 1660 and in which it continued to trade until 1763. The EIC also started trading in Basra. It made its first voyage there in 1636 and a second one in 1641 and thereafter continued trading there, with interruptions due to war or other impediments.

The *Vereenigde Oostindische Compagnie* (VOC) was founded in 1602 and began its trading activities in Persia and the Persian Gulf in 1623, when factories (trading stations) were established in Bandar 'Abbas and Isfahan, after a favorable commercial treaty had been concluded with Shah 'Abbas I. This was the beginning of a very profitable trade for the VOC, which throughout the seventeenth and in the beginning of the eighteenth century was Persia's most important foreign trading partner. VOC activities in Persia were not restricted to Bandar Abbas and Isfahan: the VOC also had a trading station in Kerman (ca. 1690-1739) for the collection of goat's wool, and in 1738 its sphere of activities was extended to Bushire. The VOC also intermittently had a factory in Basra as of 1645, while it also had a small station in Masqat between 1672 and 1675.[14]

It was silk that initially drew the European East Indies companies (English, Dutch, and French) to the Persian Gulf. Their decision to start trading there was not based on the availability of that one commodity, however. Before oil was discovered, the Gulf itself neither constituted a major market for goods nor a major source of export commodities suitable for the European or Asian markets. Consequently, the Gulf trade remained marginal. Companies began trading there only after they were securely established in Southeast and West Asia and could decide whether or not the Gulf trade would fit into their existing trading pattern. Other factors that played a role in that decision

---

Cahiers Studia Iranica, 1998); Ibid., "Dutch Trade in Afsharid Iran (1730-1753)," *Studia Iranica* 34 (2005), pp. 43-93.

12 Willem Floor, "A Description of the Persian Gulf and its inhabitants in 1756," *Persica*, vol. 8 (1979), pp. 163-86; reprinted here as chapter two.

13 Willem Floor, *The Persian Gulf 1500-1730. The Political Economy of Five Port Cities* (Washington DC, 2006); Ibid., *The Economy of Safavid Persia* (Wiesbaden, 2000).

14 Floor, *The Persian Gulf*, pp. 386-406, 532-45; Ibid., "First Contacts between the Netherlands and Masqat," *Zeitschrift der Deutschen Morgenlandische Gesellschaft* 132 (1982), pp. 289-307; idem, "Masqat Anno 1673," *Le Moyen-Orient et l'Océan Indien* (1985), pp. 1-69. For trade relations in the eighteenth century see chapter six in this publication.

were the opportunity cost of the Gulf trade, activities by the major competitors, and the market, of course.

The availability of silk and the need for cash were the deciding factors that led the VOC to embark on the Persian Gulf trade. In exchange for spices—for which it had a virtual monopoly—and pepper, the VOC obtained silk and cash. Because of the very high marginal profits that the VOC realized on spices and pepper, the Gulf trade was very profitable during the first 100 years. The hard cash earned in Persia was invested in India in commodities that could be sold at high profits in Europe. After 1664, silk became a minor export commodity and was replaced by specie and to a much lesser extent by Kerman goat wool, although interest in Persian raw silk would occasionally flare up. The increased exports of specie served to finance the VOC operations in Ceylon, Bengal, and Coromandel. The English East India Company (EIC) was driven by similar considerations, and Persia constituted a major market for English woolens. Both companies also realized considerable earnings by transporting cash and goods to and from Surat for the account of local merchants.

The profitable EIC and VOC trade with Persia ceased to exist after 1722, as a result of the occupation of the Safavid state by the Afghans in that year. The defeat of the Afghans by the future Nader Shah in 1729 did not lead to the restoration of internal security and to economic revival in Persia. In fact, the downward trend continued and appeared to be irreversible. Nader Shah's reign (1736-47) did not improve the situation, for his continuous wars and demands for increasing taxes to pay for these wars crippled the country. Nader Shah's assassination in 1747 did not bring a change either. For until 1763, there was an interregnum during which the various contenders fought over the throne and caused anarchy in Persia.[15] The VOC factories in Basra and Bushire received their orders from the VOC director in Bandar 'Abbas. When in 1747 the VOC decided to close down its factories in Persia and to maintain only its coastal factories in Bandar 'Abbas and Bushire, it was decided that Basra would henceforth be an independent factory to which the Bushire factory would be subordinate. It was the reorganization's objective to boost the VOC's commercial position in the Persian Gulf. The establishment of the Khark factory in 1753 must also be seen in the light of the VOC's efforts to improve the performance of its trading operations. The EIC's situation was not that much different. As in the case of the Dutch, its Basra factory was subordinate to its Bandar 'Abbas Agency. Trade was dismal for the English as well, and after Nader Shah's death the English also searched for other and better options and locations to improve the profitability of their commercial operation in the Gulf.

Information in Arabic, Persian, Indian and Ottoman sources concerning trade and political events in the Persian Gulf during this period is scant and almost non-existent compared with the wealth of information in Dutch and English sources.[16] This dominance of European sources in the available information raises, of course, the danger of a euro-centric approach to the analysis of the events unfolding in the Persian Gulf. Also, it has been suggested for the case of India, that the Dutch and English authors of the letters and reports written to Batavia and London were not always entirely truthful in presenting their information. This may have held, for example, where prices of both merchandise and food necessities were concerned, because under-reporting the former and over-reporting the latter provided additional income to the chief of the factory and his immediate collaborators. However, in case of the Persian Gulf trading stations, this only worked if the members of a factory's council were all part of the conspiracy to defraud,

15 On the situation in Persia during this chaotic period, see John R. Perry, *Karim Khan Zand: A History of Iran, 1747-1779* (Chicago, 1979); Michael Axworthy, *Sword of Persia: Nader Shah, from Tribal Warrior to Conquering Tyrant* (London, 2006); Floor, *Hokumat-e Nader Shah (Tehran, 1367/1988).*

16 For a discussion of the dearth of data from these sources see, for example, the studies by Abdullah (Basra), Abu Hakima (Kuwait; Bahrain), Risso (Masqat) and Perry (Persia).

while the reality was that often members of the council cast aspersions on one another, in particular the chief. This mis-reporting of market prices was even more difficult in the Persian Gulf where both the EIC and VOC had more than one factory, which 'competed' with one another and might be hurt by price schemes of the other factory. Also, the cause and nature of problems with and between local authorities may not always have been reported in a truthful fashion, certainly when the chief of the factory wanted to hide or highlight his own role therein. However, that danger is also less problematic than it appears to be in the case of political events, because the English sources act as a check on Dutch accounts and vice-versa as these commercial rivals were constantly reporting on each other's activities and the same political events. Also, whenever local sources report on events in the Gulf they invariably bear out the events as described in European sources. For example, it is now quite popular in modern Persian historical studies (e.g. Ra'in, Hamidi, Eqtedari) to describe Mir Mohanna, the chief of Bandar-e Rig and Khark, as an anti-colonialist and defender of Persian national interests.[17] Contemporary Persian sources, however, are as negative about his moral character and the destructive nature of his raiding activities on trade as are the European ones. He may have been a Persian anti-colonialist *avant la lettre*, according to some modern Iranian scholars. But to the Zand and Ottoman authorities as well as to his neighbors Mir Mohanna was nothing but a murderer, pirate and robber of the worst kind, and the Ottoman governor beheaded him when he was arrested in Basra, where he had sought refuge from his surviving relatives and other fellow countrymen who were also hell-bent to kill him.

Chapter one serves as an introduction to the major events that took place between 1730 and 1747 in the Persian Gulf, which centered on the Persian invasion of Oman and the related formation of a Persian royal fleet, one of Nader Shah's major projects. It is the slightly extended version of an article that has been published in the journal *Iranian Studies* in 1982. Chapter two provides an overview of all the local players in the Gulf by way of the translation of a Dutch report on the peoples of the Persian Gulf in 1756, a translation that I have published earlier in the journal *Persica*. In chapter three, I discuss the reasons for and dynamics of the fall of Bandar 'Abbas. This chapter contains all the material of an article that I have published earlier, in the journal *Moyen-Orient et Océan Indien*, which article had an exclusive focus on the role of the VOC. In this chapter I have incorporated that earlier material, but have put the focus on the political economy of Bandar 'Abbas rather than exclusively on the VOC by adding new materials and expanding its size and scope. In chapter four, I analyze the quick rise and fall of the island of Khark as a trade emporium due to the establishment of a Dutch factory on that island, as well as the commercial and political causes of that rise and fall. This chapter also benefits from an article that has been published earlier, in *Moyen-Orient et Océan Indien*, but much new material has been added so that this chapter is more than double the size of the earlier publication. Chapter five is an analysis of the trade results of the Dutch settlement on Khark, which is an article that has been published earlier in the *International Journal of Middle Eastern Studies*. In chapter six I discuss the reasons why the Dutch did not return to the Gulf, but resumed only voyages by private traders to Masqat, which is a republication of an earlier published article, in the *Journal of Asian and African Studies*, although new material has been added. In chapter seven I describe the rise of Bushire as the main port of entry to the Persian market, which is based on hitherto unpublished

17 Some of these claims are discussed in e.g. Sayyed Qasem Ya Hoseyni, *Mir Mohanna - ruyaruye inglisiha va holandiha dar khalij-e Fars* (Bushire, 1375/1994), pp. 145ff and Khorshid Faqih, *Zaval-e Dowlat-e Holand dar Khalij-e Fars ba Zohur-e Mir Mohanna Bandar-e Rigi* (Bushire, 1383/2004), pp. 12ff. Needless to say that Ra'in, Hamidi, Eqtedari and others did not bother to define what they meant by 'anti-colonialist' and 'nationalist', terms they used to refer to individuals in a time that colonialism did not exist and Persia was most definitely not a nation state. Their use of this and other similar terms (like the term 'spy' for Sir John Malcolm, the first British ambassador to the Qajar court) reflect current personal and/or governmental political objectives rather than historical reality. Mir Mohanna's upgrade from villain to national hero began already in an early Qajar chronicle (ca. 1840). Mohammad Hashem Asaf, *Rostam al-Tavarikh* ed. Mohammad Moshiri (Tehran, 1348/1969), pp. 386-90.

material. This chapter also includes a history of Bushire prior to the 1730s. The study, finally, is concluded by two appendices that shed light on issues raised in the preceding chapters. The first appendix is a translation of a Dutch report dealing with a proposal to conquer Bahrain (1756) and the second appendix is the translation of a Dutch report about pearl fishing in the Gulf. Both have been published earlier in the journal *Persica*. I thank the editors of all five journals concerned as well as the *Société d'Histoire de l'Orient*, which publishes *Moyen-Orient et Océan Indien*, for their permission to publish these articles here.

In all chapters, emphasis is put on the political economy of the Persian Gulf and the main forces that were at work to shape the developments in the Gulf. There are four main developments that can be identified during the second half of the eighteenth century. First, there was a shift of commercial concentration from the lower to the upper Gulf, while at the same time there was a partial shift of trade from the Northern Persian coast to the Southern Arab coast. What this means is that Bandar 'Abbas totally disappeared as a port of international trade and that its role was taken over by Bushire on the Persian coast and Masqat and Zubara/Kuwait on the Arabian coast, while Basra after 1773 became a weak reflection of its earlier self. Also, after Bushire lost control over Bahrain trade relations between the two sides of the upper Gulf became insignificant. Second, the European Companies, but less so the European country traders, were very much on the defensive and in a reactive mode to developments in the Gulf. In fact, they were losing money and therefore the Companies first moved laterally within the Gulf and finally withdrew from the Gulf altogether—first the Dutch and then the English. Although the English kept a nominal presence in the Gulf this was not for commercial purposes, but rather to keep the lines of communications open between India and Europe. By the end of the eighteenth century most foreign (Indian, European) private merchants also had withdrawn from the Gulf. Third, local rulers, each in their part of the Gulf, dominated political developments, whether it was the Imam of Oman in Masqat, the Qavasem in the Straits of Hormuz, the Ka'b in the Shatt al-Arab, Sheikh Naser at Bushire and Bahrain, Mir Mohanna in Dashtestan and in the head of the Gulf, or the 'Otobis at Kuwait, Bahrain and Zubara. The only centralizing state that had a firm grip on its ports was Oman. The Zand regime in Persia was much less successful in controlling its ports and the coastal population, while the Ottoman government hardly had any control over Basra, and not at all over the roads (maritime and land) leading to it. Moreover, like the European Companies, they all were, except for Oman, in a reactive mode of action thus leaving the initiative to the coastal dwellers. Fourth, the inability of the Persian and Ottoman government to develop and implement a responsible policy for the Gulf ports only reinforced the tendency among the Gulf coast population to try and carve out a place for themselves independent of their nominal overlords. Fifth, the inability and/or lack of interest of both the Persian and Ottoman governments to establish security in the Gulf created a situation whereby increasingly the Bombay fleet of the EIC had to provide this, thus paving the way for the similar role played by the Royal Navy for the same reasons in the nineteenth century. Therefore, rather than European imperialism it was the need to protect the country trade of mainly Arab, Armenian, Persian and Indian merchants, who constituted the bulk of the Gulf traders, that was the driving force for the increased English presence in the Gulf after 1800. These five developments took place in a context of rebellions in Persia and Iraq leading to general insecurity, oppression and poverty of the population, and therefore significantly reduced economic output and purchasing power for these nations, which resulted in a decline of trade throughout the entire Gulf, a development further reinforced by political and commercial developments in the Levant, Europe and India (Bengal).

CHAPTER ONE
The Persian Navy in the Persian Gulf during the Eighteenth Century

In the eighteenth century, rather remarkably, Persia formed a navy. Up to that time the shahs of Persia had relied on other powers to maintain security in the Persian Gulf.[1] The dominant naval power in the Gulf during the sixteenth century was Portugal, while the Dutch, and to a lesser extent the English, were supreme during the seventeenth and the beginning of the eighteenth centuries. Oman also became a naval power in the Gulf of great importance after 1690, the more so, since neither the Dutch nor the English chose to exercise their naval strength in the Gulf at that time. Persia's southern borders were not safe and secure after the conquest of Hormuz in 1622, because the Portuguese attacked its ships and coastal settlements until 1631. Since it did not have a navy Persia relied for a time on the Dutch and the English to maintain security in the Gulf to the extent that these two powers were willing to provide such assistance, which they usually were not. Later in the seventeenth century, some naval support was provided by Portugal against the marauding of the Omanis.

PERSIAN RELIANCE ON FOREIGN NAVAL FORCE

English naval assistance in the conquest of Hormuz set the pattern for the next century. This reliance on other powers for maintenance of security in the Gulf proved to be a workable policy as long as there was no real threat to Persia's coastal areas. However, this policy put Persia in a dependent and vulnerable position vis-à-vis the Dutch and the English. The European powers had never formally entered into an agreement with Persia to protect Persian territory or ships in the Gulf, although discussions on this issue had taken place between the Dutch and Persia. The European naval powers were mainly, if not exclusively, interested in protecting their trade routes and their own ships. Therefore, attacks on the Persian coast that did not interfere with

1 I leave here aside an effort made under Shah 'Abbas to mobilize the vessels of the Arab inhabitants of Persian littoral and use them as to transport troops as well as to attack Portuguese merchantmen; see Floor, *Persian Gulf*, pp. 213, 215, 326.

their trading operations were not their affair. Neither the Dutch nor the English were interested in military operations in the Gulf. Their objective after all was to make money, not to make war.

When Persia needed naval power to defend itself against attacks from the Omani fleet this policy of relying on the Dutch and the English proved to be ineffective. The policy was also counterproductive when conflicts arose with these naval powers. For when such conflicts led to military action, as they did in 1645 and 1685 with the Dutch, Persia could not prevent a blockade of its southern ports. Not having any navy, moreover, inhibited Persian expansionist designs in the Gulf. All these considerations led to efforts to form a Persian navy in 1718 and again in 1734. Only the 1734 initiative produced results, although it was not a success.

After the conquest of Hormuz in 1622, which marked the end of Portuguese supremacy in the Gulf, the Persian government showed no further interest in extending its influence in that region, although the governor-general of Fars, Emamqoli Khan, still pursued the idea of ousting the Portuguese from Masqat. The *shahbandar* of Bandar 'Abbas intimated to the Dutch at the end of 1624 that the English would support such a Persian invasion plan with three ships. He asked the Dutch to supply naval assistance as well, which was refused. Huybert Visnich, the Dutch director of VOC trade in Persia, explained to the VOC directors that the Portuguese were still interfering with trade in the Gulf and that it would be better for the VOC than for Persia to do something about these Portuguese activities. However, he deferred any decision on this matter to the VOC directors.[2]

It may well have been that Emamqoli Khan sent out this feeler to gauge the willingness of the Dutch and English to be involved in military action in the Persian Gulf. At that time Persia was at war with the Ottoman Empire and Emamqoli Khan was engaged in military operations against Basra. Rumors had reached Amsterdam that Visnich had agreed to provide Dutch naval assistance against the Ottomans, which the VOC explicitly forbade.[3] European naval supremacy in the Gulf was clearly recognized by Shah Safi I (r. 1629-1642) when, at the end of 1629, he wrote to Prince Frederik Hendrik, Stadtholder of Holland, that the latter "would [continue] to keep the sea clear of the Portuguese, and that his subjects, none excepted, would open the road to all voyagers."[4] Towards the end of 1632, Emamqoli Khan once more suggested that the Dutch and English jointly undertake the conquest of Masqat. The Dutch believed that the English might agree to such naval assistance to ingratiate themselves with Emamqoli Khan and Shah Safi I, while the English believed that the Dutch had similar motives. The English finally agreed to provide naval assistance to the invasion plan, but the Dutch did not. Because Emamqoli Khan had granted the Portuguese the right to open a factory in Bandar-e Kong in 1631 the Dutch suspected his motives. The VOC director therefore was ordered to refer any decision on this matter to the governor-general in Batavia and to gather intelligence with regard to any promises made and privileges given by Emamqoli Khan to the English. However, the invasion plan was aborted by Emamqoli Khan's execution at the orders of Shah Safi I in early 1633.[5]

2 H. Dunlop, *Bronnen tot de geschiedenis der Oostindische Compagnie in Perzië* (The Hague: Martinus Nijhoff, 1930), p. 142.

3 Dunlop, *Bronnen*, pp. 157-59.

4 Dunlop, *Bronnen*, p. 315. This task was facilitated by the fact that the VOC and the EIC had formally concluded a joint naval pact against the Portuguese on 21 December, 1629. Ibid., p. 308ff. The two nations had already been cooperating and executing joint operations on an informal basis prior to that time.

5 Dunlop, *Bronnen*, pp. 389, 404-06. For a discussion of these plans to invade Masqat between 1622 and 1632 see Floor, *Persian Gulf*, pp. 326-35.

Persia continued to rely on Dutch protection of its southern ports. On April 5, 1639 the *shahbandar* of Bandar 'Abbas asked the Dutch to lend him a ship to catch a rebel. On 25 April the ship *de Santfoort* returned having achieved nothing. In early 1640 the *shahbandar* asked the Dutch to take action against the Portuguese, who were interfering with local shipping around Qeshm and Larak. However, before the Dutch could take action the Portuguese had left. It was therefore not an exaggeration when the VOC director in Persia, Wollebrandt Geleynsen, argued in 1641, that the Dutch were protecting Persia's southern borders against the Portuguese and that therefore the grand vizier, Mirza Taqi, should take this service into account in assessing the benefits of Persia's relationship with the Dutch.[6]

This lack of interest of the Safavid Shahs in the formation of a Persian navy was, to a great extent, due to the relative tranquility of their southern border as compared to their western, northern and eastern borders, which were beset with conflicts with the Ottomans, the Uzbeks and the Moguls respectively. Even the military conflict with the Dutch in 1645, who blockaded the Gulf and stopped Persian merchant vessels, did not lead to a change in this attitude. The Persian government realized that the Dutch were neither interested in territorial gain nor in a long conflict, which would hurt their trade and their profits.[7] During the subsequent negotiations the Dutch proposed, among other things, to protect Persian territory against naval attacks from any of Persia's enemies in exchange for a free and unhindered trade in Persia. However, the negotiations broke down in 1647 and this proposal was not raised in any of the subsequent discussions.[8] The new commercial treaty of 1652 did not refer to it either.[9]

In 1664 the *shahbandar* of Bandar 'Abbas again approached the Dutch, allegedly at the orders of Shah 'Abbas II (r. 1642-66) and asked for naval assistance to carry out an invasion of Masqat. Arab forces had expelled the Portuguese from the city in January 1650. Under the Ya'ariba dynasty Masqat prospered and became a strong naval power. Because of high customs tariffs at Bandar 'Abbas and unpleasant behavior by its customs officials many merchants preferred to take their business to Masqat where better terms were offered. The Persian government was worried about the drop in customs revenues from Bandar 'Abbas and wanted to correct this situation. Whether Shah 'Abbas II really wanted to undertake military action against Masqat is not known. However, by 1666 the situation had changed due to a rise in tariffs in Masqat, which may have been caused by the Persian threat. The Dutch, who were not pleased with the situation prevailing in Bandar 'Abbas at that time either, and who, moreover, had been invited by Imam Soltan b. Seyf to open a factory in Masqat, were in a quandary. The governor-general in Batavia wanted to keep the Masqat option open, while the VOC directors were not unwilling to give naval support to Persia. However, subsequent changes in Oman, the death of Shah 'Abbas II in 1666, and the outbreak of the Second Dutch-English War (1664-66) put an end to these deliberations.[10]

---

6 VOC 1149, Gamron to Batavia (28/04/1639), f. 1249; Ibid., 906/04/1639), f. 1283; VOC 1156, Gamron to Batavia (21/05/1640), f. 802; VOC 1160, Isfahan to Batavia (25/10/1641), f. 275. For a biographical assessment of Mirza Taqi see Willem Floor, "The rise and fall of Mirza Taqi, the eunuch grand vizier (1043-55/1634-45)," *Studia Iranica* 26 (1997), pp. 237-66.

7 On the causes, eruption and resolution of the 1645 conflict see Willem Floor and Mohammad Faghfoory, *The First Dutch-Persian Commercial Conflict* (Costa Mesa: Mazda, 2004).

8 VOC 1175, Petitie Verburch, f. 245.

9 A. Hotz ed., *Journaal der reis van ... Cunaeus naar Perzie in 1651-52* (Amsterdam, 1908); Floor and Faghfoory, *The First*, pp. 190-203.

10 Willem Floor, "First Contacts between the Netherlands and Masqat," *Zeitschrift der Deutschen Morgenlandischen Gesellschaft* 132 (1982), pp. 289-307; Ibid, *Persian Gulf*, pp. 378-83.

OMANI PRESSURE AND ATTACKS ON PERSIAN ISLANDS AND COASTAL SETTLEMENTS

Meanwhile, Oman's power increased considerably in the Persian Gulf, while Persia's hold on the Arabs on its side of the Gulf became less firm. For the time being, Persia experienced little trouble from the growing power of Oman, which focused mainly on fighting the Portuguese in the Gulf, in India and in Africa.[11] However, a new conflict with the Dutch in 1685, which led to the shelling and occupation of the island of Qeshm, again underscored Persian military weakness in the Gulf, and especially its lack of a navy.[12] In January 1695 the Omanis attacked Bandar-e Kong, pretending that their sole objective was to oust their arch-enemy, the Portuguese, from the Gulf. The Persian government was very disturbed about this violation of its territory and prepared an expeditionary force commanded by 'Ali Mardan Khan, which was to receive naval assistance from the Portuguese. However, the Persians were not ready (due to drought in Fars) and postponed the operation.[13]

Then the Dutch were asked to provide naval support, but they refused. Shah Soltan Hoseyn (r. 1694-1722) asked them to reconsider. In exchange for Dutch naval support he promised not only his favor and gratitude, but also free trade in Persia with exemption of all taxes and duties and an annual payment of 1,000 *tumans*. On June 14, 1697 the governor-general in Batavia decided to assist the Shah with six ships. These were to be employed only to ferry Persian troops to Masqat and to protect them en route. The Dutch admiral had strict orders not to use his ships to bombard Masqat's forts or Omani positions. Nor was he allowed to support the Persian invasion force with manpower. He was, however, permitted to supply the Persians with military hardware and with some military advisers to operate the cannons, if such assistance was requested. The fleet duly arrived, but it was unable to do anything, because the Persians had abandoned their plans to invade Masqat.[14]

During Shah Soltan Hoseyn's reign the attacks by the Omanis against Persian territory increased in number and vehemence. As long as the Omani attacks were incursions only the court in Isfahan did not worry too much about them. Nor did it pay much attention to the annual raids by the Baluchis in Southern Persia. Even the sack of Bandar-e Kong in 1714 hardly bestirred the lethargic court. Aroused by the event for one week it then slipped back into business as usual. However, loss of territory and the probability of losing more was something that no longer could be ignored. The first time Oman's Emam Soltan b. Seyf II tried to annex Persian territory occurred in May-September 1715 when he mounted a large scale attack on Bahrain.[15]

The attempt failed. Although Oman's fleet was active again in 1716 and tried in vain to occupy Bahrain, it was more successful in 1717 when it attacked and took possession of Bahrain. The conquest of Bahrain caused consternation in Isfahan. Shah Soltan Hoseyn asked the Dutch ambassador, Joan Josua Ketelaar, who happened to be at his court to discuss a new commercial treaty, for

11 Floor, *Persian Gulf*, pp. 407-08.

12 W. Ph. Coolhaas, J. van Goor, and J.E. Schooneveld-Oosterling eds., *Generale Missiven van Gouveneur-Generaal en Raden aan Heren XVII* 11 vols. (The Hague, 1960-1985), vol. 4 (1675-85), pp. 740-42, 826; Rudie Matthee, *The Politics of Trade in Safavid Iran* (Cambridge, 1999), pp. 183-92; Willem Floor, "Dutch Documents concerning the Attack on Qeshm Island (1684)," *Tarikh* 1/4 (2004/05), pp. 25-47.

13 Floor, *Persian Gulf*, pp. 409-13; Jean Aubin, ed. *L'Ambassade de Gregório Fidalgo à la cour du Châh Soltân-Hoseyn* (Lisbon, 1971).

14 Coolhaas, *Generale Missieven*, vol. 5 (1686-1697), pp. 743, 859-61.

15 VOC 1886, Gamron to Batavia (24/03/1716), f. 18; Floor, *Persian Gulf*, pp. 414-19.

Dutch naval support to retake Bahrain. Ketelaar refused the loan of Dutch ships, because he had no authority to grant such assistance. Ketelaar gave the same reply to a similar request by Fath 'Ali Khan, the grand vizier, to support his nephew, Lotf 'Ali Khan, who had been appointed governor-general of Fars and Azerbaijan and commander-in-chief of Persia and who was leading the operations against the Omanis on Bahrain.[16]

Although the Shah and his grand-vizier acquiesced in Ketelaar's refusal, Lotf 'Ali Khan did not. On his return to Bandar 'Abbas, Ketelaar was confronted by Ya'qub Soltan, one of Lotf 'Ali Khan's deputy-commanders, with the same demand. The demand was even more urgent, because the Omanis not only had taken Bahrain, they also had seized the islands of Larak and Qeshm and were laying siege to the fort of Hormuz. Both the Dutch and English rebuffed Ya'qub Soltan. In desperation he laid siege to their factories to force the loan of their ships. He eventually had to give in and Lotf 'Ali Khan punished him for his allegedly unauthorized action. However, Lotf 'Ali Khan made it clear that he still insisted on naval assistance. The Dutch replied that both Shah Soltan Hoseyn and the grand-vizier had accepted their reason for not providing support and asked why lesser officials were not content with that reply. The Dutch also pointed out that in February 1718 they had given passage to Goa to a Persian envoy named Tahmurath Beyg. The latter's mission was to ask the Portuguese for naval assistance.[17]

Loft 'Ali Khan had to content himself with that reply, which was made easier by his retaking of Bahrain. On 5 July, 1718 he had put 6,000 troops ashore using small vessels supplied by coastal Arabs, who acknowledged Persia's overlordship. The Omani forces responded by raising the siege of Hormuz and regrouping on Larak and Qeshm.[18] The Persian victory was of short duration, however. In November 1718 the Omanis retook Bahrain and almost completely annihilated the Persian relief force. Not only did Lotf 'Ali Khan lose many troops, he also lost many vessels. Because the promised Portuguese naval support had not yet arrived Lotf 'Ali Khan needed ships badly. He therefore wrote to the shah asking him to send money to buy ten well-armed grabs, "for without ships there is nothing much that we can do to oppose the Masqat Arabs." Writing to Jan Oets, the Dutch director in Bandar 'Abbas, Lotf 'Ali Khan regretted the fact that the Dutch had not shown friendship by helping him previously, but he hoped that they would prove their professed friendship by supplying him with at least five ships, for which he would pay in cash. Moreover, if they to procure 30 ships for him, these too would be welcome and paid for within four months' time.[19] Oets, who had just arrived from Batavia, replied that Ketelaar had discussed this issue with the shah and the grand-vizier. He further had brought with him the governor-general's reply to the shah's request, which Oets had given to the *shahbandar* to be forwarded to the shah. Oets therefore had to

16 Willem Floor, *The Commercial Conflict between Persia and the Netherlands, 1712-1718*, Durham University, Occasional Papers no. 37. (1988); Ibid., *Persian Gulf*, pp. 419-24. For a biography of Fath 'Ali Khan see Rudi Matthee, "Blinded by Power: the Rise and Fall of Fath 'Ali Khan Daghestani, Grand Vizier under Shah Soltan Hoseyn Safavi (1127/1715-1133/1720)," *Studia Iranica* 33/2 (2004), pp. 179-220.

17 VOC 1904, Gamron to Batavia (07/11/1718), f. 2363-65; Ibid., f. 2403-05.

18 VOC 1904, Gamron to Batavia (07/11/1718), f. 2363vs-64.

19 VOC 1928, Lotf 'Ali Khan to van Biesum (received 17/07/1718), f. 116; Ibid., Gamron to Isfahan (15/09/1718), f. 179; Ibid., idem to idem (01/10/1718), f. 181; Ibid., Lotf 'Ali Khan to van Biesum (received 18/09/1718), f. 118-22; Ibid., Isfahan to Gamron (13/08/1718), f. 17 (people are elated in Isfahan. The shah is said to have appointed Lotf 'Ali Khan as *tofangchi bashi* (commander of the artillery corps); Ibid., Isfahan to Gamron (12/10/1718), f. 80 (there were three days of bonfires in Isfahan to celebrate the reconquest of Bahrain).

act in accordance with the strictures of this reply; moreover, at that time there were no Dutch ships available to assist Lotf 'Ali Khan.[20]

Having not yet received the governor-general's letter Shah Soltan Hoseyn ordered the Dutch in October 1718 to send three ships that had just arrived from Batavia to assist Lotf 'Ali Khan and the Portuguese, who had promised five ships. If the Dutch refused to do so, they would be punished on account of disobedience. The grand-vizier wrote Oets to the same effect and added that Lotf 'Ali Khan had money to pay the Dutch for any expenses they would incur. Lotf 'Ali Khan wrote separately to the Dutch and asked them to execute the shah's orders so that he could retake Bahrain and punish the rebellious Arabs. He added that after the Portuguese ships would have arrived and Bahrain had been retaken it was his intention to execute another plan with the combined Dutch-Portuguese fleet. Although Lotf 'Ali Khan does not mention what this plan was, he probably intended to invade Masqat itself.[21]

Oets replied to the shah and the grand-vizier that the Dutch ships had already left. In his letter to the grand-vizier Oets added that since Fath 'Ali Khan had written that Bahrain and the other islands had been retaken, which at the time when Oets received the letter was no longer true, the support of the Dutch ships was not needed. Lotf 'Ali Khan received a similar reply.[22] It was only with the help of four Portuguese ships that Lotf 'Ali Khan was able to launch a counter-offensive against the Omani forces. After several inconclusive encounters between the two fleets the Portuguese were able to push the Omani fleet from Bahrain waters.[23]

As a result of these developments, along with the internal troubles in Oman, the two warring parties started negotiations, which in 1721 led to a peace agreement. Oman promised to return all conquered territories in exchange for commercial privileges at Bandar-e Kong and Persian support in case of Portuguese attacks on Masqat. But when Lotf 'Ali Khan sent some troops to Bahrain to reinstate Persian rule they were sent back. A dispute had arisen among the Omani leaders, some of whom refused to accept the terms of the peace treaty.[24] In April 1721 Omani forces still occupied Bahrain and it was unclear whether the peace treaty would be implemented.[25] However, at the end of 1722, because of dynastic problems, Oman proved to be unable to maintain its power in the Gulf. A nominal Persian subject, Sheikh Jabbareh of Taheri, one of the chiefs of the important Hula tribe, took possession of Bahrain on behalf of Shah Soltan Hoseyn.[26] But by that time Safavid rule had crumbled before the onslaught of the Afghan invaders who took Isfahan in October 1722 and forced Shah Soltan Hoseyn to abdicate.[27]

---

20 VOC 1928, Oets to Lotf 'Ali Khan (Gamron, 24/08/1718), f. 126-27.

21 VOC 1928, Shah to Oets (Dhu'l-Qa'deh 1130 – October 1718), f. 219-21.

22 VOC 1928, Oets to Shah, f. 221-24; Ibid., Oets to grand-vizier, f. 224-28; Ibid., Oets to Lotf 'Ali Khan, f. 232-35 all dated 3 January 1719.

23 VOC 1947, Oets to Batavia (21/09/1719), f. 82.

24 VOC 1964, Oets to Batavia (15/02/1721), f. 76.

25 VOC 1964, Oets to Batavia (05/04/1721), f. 767.

26 Slot has rightly pointed out that my reference for this statement (VOC 2009, Oets to Batavia (15/11/1722), f. 47) is incorrect. I have not been able to locate the proper reference among my notes, but, even after 25 years, I distinctly recall how pleasantly surprised I was at that time to find this reference to Sheikh Jabbareh. Nevertheless, my memory may play a trick on me and although I leave this statement here (also because he was confirmed in the same function in 1730; see below chapter seven) it may be incorrect. How Bahrain fared afterwards see chapter seven.

27 Willem Floor, *The Afghan Occupation of Safavid Persia 1721-1729* (Leuven, 1998), pp. 173-74.

CONTINUED RELIANCE ON FOREIGN NAVAL FORCE

With the temporary restoration of Safavid authority in 1730 the central government tried to reinstate its rule in the Persian Gulf and especially in the littoral. The costal Arabs had become independent in all but name, while those living in Larestan were in open revolt. The coastal Arabs not only offered the fleeing Afghans a safe haven, but they offered their vessels for hire to sail to safety. Consequently, Shah Tahmasp II's general, Tahmaspqoli Khan (the later Nader Shah), issued orders to the European Companies at Bandar 'Abbas not to assist the Afghans to escape by sea, but to prevent this with their ships.[28] This request for naval assistance by the new Safavid government heralds the 'era of the loan of ships" from the European Companies.

The period 1730-1734 was an unruly one for the Hot Country or the Garmsirat, because of a revolt by Sheikh Ahmad Madani as well as marauding activities by other coastal dwellers.[29] Persian expeditions sent to capture Sheikh Ahmad Madani were unsuccessful, because they had no naval force to complete the encirclement of his forces. The Persian commander, Mohammad 'Ali Khan, *beygler-beygi* of Fars asked for Dutch naval assistance several times.[30] When Tahmaspqoli Khan himself finally decided to deal with Sheikh Ahmad Madani in person, who had allied himself with another rebel, Mohammad Khan Baluch, he also had to ask for naval assistance to complete the job. In February 1734 his general, Tahmasp Beyg Jalayer, asked the Dutch and English Companies to patrol the Gulf and seize all rebels. The Companies gave a joint non-committal reply, hoping that Tahmasp Beyg Jalayer would not repeat his request. But on March 29 both Companies received a request to send ships to Bandar-e Charak to help capture Mohammad Khan Baluch and Sheikh Ahmad Madani. After some delay, the Dutch and English decided to send respectively one and two ships, to the island of Kish, where Sheikh Ahmad was alleged to have taken refuge. On May 14, 1734 Mohammad Latif Khan, Nader's "Admiral of the Gulph" as the English called him, arrived in Bandar 'Abbas "with orders to purchase Shipping of the Europeans of Gombroon. He, therefore, required our Compliance with the Caun's Desires in Sparing Two Ships for their Service which we should be paid for, and insisted on our Immediate Answer."[31] The Companies, after consulting one another, replied that they could not comply with this request, since they had no authority to sell ships, which, after all, they needed themselves for trading purposes. Latif Khan therefore had to satisfy himself with the ships that Companies had put at the shah's disposal at Kish and with those vessels supplied by Sheikh Jabbareh of Taheri and by Sheikh Rashed of Basidu. He informed Tahmasp Beyg that since the Europeans could not sell him ships and because building ships himself would take too long in view of the fact that timber would have to be ordered from elsewhere, he had asked the Companies' cooperation in acquiring the two ships, which were jointly owned by Sheikh Rashed of Basidu and "Sjeeg Mhamet Benalie."[32] Together with some other vessels that Latif Khan had acquired these formed the nucleus of the Persian navy.

The operation against Sheikh Ahmad Madani was completed by mid-June 1734 and the Companies were thanked for their cooperation. The Europeans hoped that they had heard the last

28 Willem Floor, "The Revolt of Shaikh Ahmad Madani in Laristan and the Garmsirat (1730-1733)," *Studia Iranica*, vol. 8 (1983), pp. 63-66; L. Lockhart, *Nadir Shah* (London, 1938), p. 44.

29 Floor, "The Revolt," pp. 63-98.

30 Floor, "The Revolt," pp. 67 (1731), 71-72 (1732).

31 L. Lockhart, "The Navy of Nadir Shah," *Proceedings of the Iran Society* vol. 1 (London, 1936), p. 6, n. 1; Ibid., *Nadir Shah*, pp. 78-79.

32 VOC 2357, f. 82, f. 455-57. Tahmasp Beyg wrote a reply to this letter on 20 Jomadi I, 1151 (15/10/1734) stating that Latif Khan had to prepare ships for the transportation of 3,000 foot and horse; how he would arrange this Tahmasp Khan left to his discretion. Ibid, f. 458.

of the sale of ships. They feared that the matter would not only create animosity among the Persian leadership, but if the actual sales would take place, it would also damage their own trading operations. They therefore suggested to Latif Khan that ships could be built and purchased at Surat. The English even offered to buy them there for the Persian government.[33] However, Tahmasp Beyg, writing both in reply to the European Companies and to Latif Khan, gave orders for the purchase of the Companies' ships.[34] The European Companies at first ignored these 'requests'. But Nader's grand plans for the Gulf demanded a response.

NADER SHAH DECIDES TO CREATE A ROYAL FLEET

Nader wanted to exert great control over the coastal Arabs. He also wanted to attack Basra, as part of his military strategy against the Ottomans, and he wanted to bring Bahrain back into the Persian orbit. Finally, he wanted to take action against Oman and the Moghul Empire. The European Companies were well aware of these intentions. Nader instructed Tahmasp Beyg in his army camp near Baghdad to form a navy as soon as possible. On his return from Baghdad to Isfahan on 26 November, 1734 Tahmasp Beyg told van Leypsigh, the VOC representative, and Geekie, the EIC representative, that they should inform their directors in Bandar 'Abbas to prepare some ships for use against the rebellious Arabs. If the directors refused, Nader would build a fleet himself. The number of ships he demanded was to be sufficient to transport 7,000 men. If the Companies could not comply with this request they were to inform Tahmasp Beyg immediately. He would then order timber to be felled in Mazandaran, which would be transported to the Gulf, where he would have a number of ships built. Van Leypsigh replied that he believed that there were no Dutch ships in Bandar 'Abbas at that moment. He pointed out, moreover, that Tahmasp Beyg would need 20 to 25 ships to transport 7,000 men. To bring together that many ships at least three years would be needed, for the Dutch would have to write to their directors in Amsterdam to get permission. If the directors would agree to such a sale, the ships still would have to be built, which also would take time. He added that Tahmasp Beyg would have to be more specific about the enemy, for he would never get any naval assistance from the Dutch if the ships were to be used against the Turks at Basra, the Omanis, or Hindustan (i.e. the Moghul Empire).[35]

The Dutch and the English in Isfahan sent a representative to Bandar 'Abbas to convey Tahmasp Beyg's request, which was officially raised by Latif Khan, who arrived in Bandar 'Abbas on 16 December 1734. Carel Koenad, the Dutch director, gave him the same reply that van Leypsigh had given to Tahmasp Beyg. He confirmed this in a letter to Tahmaspqoli Khan (Nader) on December 27.[36] Koenad also told Latif Khan that the Dutch would be more forthcoming were the Persian officials to show more respect for the Dutch and their rights. Latif Khan promised to do his best to improve matters and before he left for Bushire on 7 January 1735 he gave instructions to that effect to the local authorities.[37] Prior to his arrival in Bandar 'Abbas, Latif Khan had been able to buy a brigantine in Bushire called the *Patna* from a private English trader named Weddell. Weddell's example was followed by Cook, the master of the *Ruperall*, another brigantine. The EIC director at Bandar 'Abbas was much annoyed by this, but since they were not EIC-owned ships,

33 Lockhart, "Navy," pp. 6-7; Ibid., *Nadir Shah*, p. 97; Floor, "The Revolt," p. 90.

34 VOC 2357, f. 458; Floor, "The Revolt," p. 90.

35 VOC 2357, Isfahan to Gamron (05/11/1734), f. 1106-08, 1115-16; Lockart, "Navy," p. 6.

36 VOC 2357, f. 461-64; Ibid. Koenad to Tahmaspqoli Khan (27/12/1734), f. 463-64.

37 VOC 2357, f. 549.

there was little he could do about it. The EIC reacted by issuing instructions that owners of vessels sailing under its protection were forbidden to sell them to the Persians.[38]

In Bushire, meanwhile, Latif Khan was preparing a naval base and a fleet for the attack on Basra. On Nader's orders he repaired an old fort just outside Bushire, which was renamed Bandar-e Naderiyeh. To strengthen the fleet, the Persian government had asked the European Companies for ships on several occasions during the early 1735. On receiving the usual refusal and the referral to Surat, Latif Khan decided to indeed get ships from there in April 1735. He sent a vessel with a cargo of asafetida to Surat. With the proceeds of its sale the captain was to buy ships, masts, planks and other wooden necessaries required for the building of ships. Latif Khan asked the Dutch to allow his ship to sail in the company of a Dutch ship to Surat and to help its captain with the sale of its cargo and the purchase of the ships and other goods. Koenad replied that if the vessel could keep pace with the Dutch ships it could come along; but the Dutch could not take responsibility for the sale and purchase of goods in Surat.[39]

PERSIAN NAVAL ATTACK ON BASRA

Shortly thereafter, the Persian fleet had its first trial by fire during an operation against Basra in May 1735. The timing of the Persian attack on Basra may have been influenced by events in Basra itself. The new governor, Hoseyn Pasha, had entered the port on January 10, 1735 and his presence almost immediately resulted in the outbreak of hostilities. On February 12 the pasha had arrested the infamous Sheikh Annees, whom he ordered to be strangled and to be thrown like a dog on the square in front of his palace. This triggered an uprising of the Arab tribes who defeated the pasha's forces. The latter had to leave all their equipment on the battlefield, where both the commander of the pasha's janissaries as well as Mohammad Mane', the chief of the Montafeq were killed. To recuperate his losses Hoseyn Pasha's *motasallem*, 'Ali Beyg imposed a payment of 80,000 *qorush* (36,000 *mahmudis* or Dfl. 153,000) on the port city of which the Europeans had to pay 15,000 *qorush* (EIC 6,000, VOC 4,000, other Europeans the rest). This led to many protests, including by the English consul who left Basra for Baghdad. Also, the former governor, Mohammad Pasha, tried to fish in troubled waters by agitating in Istanbul against Hoseyn Pasha and to get himself reappointed. The Dutch hoped that he would be successful, because he was a very rich man and, although a difficult person, might behave less grasping than his successor.[40]

Strengthened by vessels of the Ka'b Arabs, who had once again fallen out with the Ottomans in Basra, Latif Khan's force of two *grabs*,[41] acting on Nader's orders, attacked Basra on 30 May, 1735. The Ottoman governor of Basra pressed two EIC ships into his service to defend the city together

38 Lockhart, "Navy," p. 7; Ibid., *Nadir Shah*, p. 93.

39 VOC 2357, f. 879-81 (received on 11/05/1735); Lockhart, *Nadir Shah*, p. 93. According to the Dutch, Mohammad Latif Khan was "an ingenious man, who has learnt too much about European customs at Istanbul, for he showed more curiosity than Mr. Waters, the English second-in-command, had credited him for, during their discussion about ship-building and navigation aboard an English vessel." VOC 2357, Gamron to Batavia (24/08/1735), f. 232.

40 VOC 2390, Basra to Batavia (16/11/1735), f. 137, 144; VOC 2390, Basra to Calkoen (Istanbul) (16/12/1735), f. 183r-vs.

41 For the term grab and other designations of the various types of vessels native to the Persian Gulf see A.H.J. Prins, "The Maritime Middle East: A century of Studies," *Middle East Journal* 27 (1973), pp. 207-220. For the role of the Banu Ka'b see Willem Floor, "The Rise and Fall of the Banu Ka'b – A Borderer State in Southern Khuzestan," 44 (2006) *IRAN*, pp. 277-315.

with 14 of his own galleys. After a three-day battle Latif Khan withdrew. He blamed the English for his defeat and promised them a taste of Nader's wrath. Fearing retaliation, the English director at Bandar 'Abbas, Cockell, wrote to Mohammad Taqi Khan Shirazi, *beygler-beygi* of Fars, that it was a case of *force majeure* and that if Latif Khan had warned him beforehand about the impending attack, he would have withdrawn the two English ships from Basra. To avoid Nader's fury the English withdrew part of their staff from Persia. Nader, who was indeed furious, dismissed Latif Khan and demanded an explanation from both the Dutch and English Companies. The former expressed their surprise and made it clear that they had nothing to do with the affair.[42] Having other, more pressing, problems to deal with, Nader did not take action against the English. He undoubtedly realized that he could not afford to antagonize the European Companies at that time since he needed their help to get ships.

CONTINUED BUILD-UP OF THE ROYAL FLEET

On 6 October 1735 Mohammad Taqi Khan's representative, the *qaputan-bashi* Mohammad Zaman Beyg, arrived in Bandar 'Abbas and behaved quite well towards the Europeans. Four days later he handed Koenad one letter from Nader and two from Mohammad Taqi Khan in which they asked both Companies to help Mohammad Zaman Beyg to buy ships or to sell him their own ships. Koenad told him that he had written one year earlier that without authorization from Batavia he was not allowed to sell ships. He also expressed his surprise that the letters were addressed jointly to the Dutch and the English instead of separately, as if there was no difference between them. Had Nader already forgotten, he wanted to know, that the Dutch had already three times put ships at his disposal? Mohammad Zaman Beyg assured Koenad that the Dutch services had been greatly appreciated.[43]

At Mohammad Taqi Khan's orders the *shahbandar* raised an extra 3,000 *tumans* from the population of Bandar 'Abbas to buy two ships and some pearls. The money was taken by force. The English contributed a considerable sum to smooth over the Basra affair and their various smuggling activities. On 22 November 1735 the *shahbandar* told the Dutch that he still lacked 1,000 *tumans* for the purchase of two ships. He asked them to pay half that amount; the other half would be paid by the English. Both Companies would be repaid later out of the customs revenues. He showed a letter from Mohammad Taqi Khan, which stated that if he did not have enough money he would have to ask the Dutch and English Companies to lend him the remainder, "for in these difficult times all subjects and friends of the Empire have to serve the Crown in accordance with their ability." The English had already paid, so the Dutch were asked to pay their share to avoid troubles. After an initial refusal Koenad finally gave 300 *tumans*.[44] On 5 December 1735 a Dutch vessel took the money to Sheikh Rashed at Basidu at the request of the *shahbandar*.[45]

---

42 Lockhart, "Navy," pp. 7-8; Ibid., *Nadir Shah*, pp. 93-94; VOC 2357, f. 917; Ibid., f. 1233 (received 27/07/1735; Mohammad Taqi Khan to European Companies). The Dutch in Basra believed that but for the support of the two English vessels the Persians would have taken Basra. VOC 2390, f. 184 vs.

43 VOC 2461, Resolution Gamron (23/10/1735), f. 526-29.

44 VOC 2416, Resolution Gamron (21/11/1735), f. 666-81.

45 VOC 2416, Resolution Gamron (22/12/1735), f. 736-39. Sheikh Rashed said that there was no need for the Dutch to give him a draft; a letter would have sufficed for the VOC had a very high credit rating, as far as he was concerned. He refused, however, to accept the English draft. Ibid., f. 365 mentions that the English captain Louis [Lewis?] had estimated the value of Sheikh Rashed's ship, the *Tavakkol*.

In March 1736 Nader crowned himself as Nader Shah and ended the nominal Safavid rule by deposing the infant-king 'Abbas III, whose father, Tahmasp II, he had deposed four years earlier.[46] Finally, his own master, Nader Shah embarked on further campaigns for territorial gain. The first item on his agenda was Bahrain, which he intended to retake that year. He informed the Dutch that Mohammad Taqi Khan, *beygler-beygi* of Fars and *qaputan-e savahel* (commander of the sea ports), had to retake Bahrain after his arrival in Bandar 'Abbas.[47] Whether in response to this development or to obtain Nader Shah's favor, or both, the English offered to buy ships for him. The Dutch were furious and taken aback. The English had already been giving presents to the authorities beyond what was customary, but this offer topped it. How could they now refuse the loan of ships and not lose the shah's favor, the Dutch commented.[48] The ships were not delivered immediately and Latif Khan, who had been reinstated as admiral and put in charge of the Bahrain expedition, forced the captain of an English vessel named the *Northumberland* to sell his ship at "a great price."[49]

According to the Dutch, as a result of this purchase the Persian navy in 1736 was composed of the following ships:[50]

Table 1.1: Composition and purchase price of the vessels of the Persian royal navy in 1736

Name or type of ship	White Money	Black Money
Fattie Sjahie, from the English	7,000	-
Capitaine, from the English	-	4,000
Fatta Mamoedie, from the English	400	-
Nastar Chanie, from the English	300	-
Toeckel, from Sjeeg Rasjet	3,000	-
Fattilhaije, from Sjeeg Rasjet	1,300	-
Fatta Rhamhanie, from the Arabs	400	-
Illhaiji, from Sjeeg Rasjet	400	-
Two trankis taken from Sjeeg Rasjet	?	-
Two galwets built by Latif Khan	?	-
Total	12,800	4,000

46 Lockhart, *Nadir Shah*, pp. 63, 96f.

47 VOC 2416 (dated Rabi' al-Avval 1148 – July 1735), f. 503-04; see also Ibid., f. 1036 (Nader Shah's decree of February 1736).

48 VOC 2416, f. 1014 and Ibid., Resolution Gamron (06/05/1736), f. 995; Lockhart, "Navy," p. 9.

49 VOC 2416, Resolution Gamron (05/04/1736), f. 337; Lockhart, "Navy," p. 9. Five years later the Dutch remarked that the English could spend so much money on the Persian officials, because they sold their ships to the Persian government with 200% profit. VOC 2548, f. 2592.

50 VOC 2417, Gamron to Batavia (04/05/1737), f. 3264. On the two trankis taken from Sheikh Rashed see Floor, "The revolt," p. 89. The term white money refers to good money, i.e., money that had not been debased. Black money refers to bad or debased money, which was exchanged at a discount of 50%. Thus, the total expenditure amounted to 12,800 *tumans* plus 50% agio or 19,200 + 4,000 *tumans* = 23,200 *tumans* of black money. Other expenditures brought the total to 23,600 *tumans*.

NAVAL ACTION AGAINST THE HULAS AT BAHRAIN

On 26 May 1736 an expeditionary force of some 4,000 troops boarded the ships, which then set sail to Bahrain. Sheikh Jabbareh was on pilgrimage to Mecca and without their leader the Hula garrison put up a feeble resistance. As a result of this move, many Hulas Arabs fled the coast of Persia to the islands offshore. Mohammad Taqi Khan asked the Dutch, who had not sent any ships to assist the Bahrain expedition, to delay sending their ships to Batavia in case the Hula Arabs, who were valuable to Persia as sailors, did not obey his orders to return to the mainland. If that happened he wanted to use the Dutch, and other, ships to force them to return.[51] However, the Hulas did not trust Mohammad Taqi Khan. During the summer of 1736 the Hulas and other coastal Arabs waylaid passing vessels and settled old scores among themselves. Sheikh Rahma Charaki, also known as Sheikh Rahma b. Fazl, acquired a fair amount of notoriety, but he informed the Dutch that he had not committed most of the piratical acts attributed to him.[52]

The situation became serious after the death of Sheikh Rashed of Basidu, probably in early October 1736. Local officials tried to arrest his widow to get hold of the Sheikh's property. A Persian force of some 40 men led by Mir Heydar was repulsed. Mohammad Taqi Khan, therefore, ordered the Persian fleet to attack Basidu, which it did, ransacking and plundering the town. Then Latif Khan decided to withdraw, because his force was not strong enough to hold the town. A force of Arabs in 200 vessels pursued him, but he outran them. Despite the fact that at that time the Persian fleet was reinforced the Hula Arabs continued their piracy. The reinforcement of the fleet consisted of two English 20-gun frigates, each of 400 tons and 145 feet long. One of them was named the *Cowan*. Their cost was 8,000 *tumans*. The Hulas attacked Qeshm and tried to stop supplies of water and firewood from reaching Bandar 'Abbas. They even went so far as to seize two Dutch and four English supply vessels carrying provisions. The Dutch, therefore, were willing to comply with a request from the authorities at Bandar 'Abbas to send a ship and suppress the piracy. They sent the ship *de Rithem* on October 19 to patrol the areas where supplies of water and firewood were obtained. The captain was authorized to act against the Hulas if he encountered them. However, if he found that these places were freely accessible the ship had to return to Bandar 'Abbas. After an uneventful patrol *de Rithem* returned on 8 November, 1736 to Bandar 'Abbas. Sheikh Rahma, perhaps alerted by the Dutch action, sent letters to the Dutch and English in November 1736. He assured the Dutch of his friendship and returned the goods taken from their vessels. The men who had committed this abominable act, he said, had been killed at his orders, and he expressed the hope that this event would not mar their good relations. Sheikh Rahma event sent a representative to the Dutch factory on 25 January 1737 to apologize once more.[53]

51 Lockhart, "Navy," p. 9; Ibid., *Nadir Shah*, pp. 108-09; VOC 2416, Koenad to Mohammad Taqi Khan (Safar 1149/June 1736), f. 1178-79.

52 VOC 2416, Resolution Gamron (13/10/1736), f. 1390-92; VOC 2417, Sjeeg Rhama bien Fassal Tjoerecki to Koenad (received 26/01/1737), f. 4095-97; see also Ibid., f. 4047 (Tjereckie).

53 VOC 2416, Resolutions Gamron (10/12/1736), f. 331-36 and (08/11/1736), f. 1506-08, and (08/11/1736), f. 1476-83. VOC 2417, Koenad to Mirza Esma'il (brother of Mirza Taqi Khan) (26/12/1736), f. 4013-18; Ibid., Koenad to Sjeeg Rama bien Fassal Tjerecckie), f. 4047; Ibid., Resolutions Gamron (12/02/1737), f. 3745-46 and (08/01/1737), f. 3677-78; Lockhart, "Navy," p. 9.

PERSIAN INVASION OF OMAN

On 24 February 1737 Mohammad Taqi Khan arrived in Bandar 'Abbas with a large force. Nader Shah had plans to add Oman to his empire. It is not clear who suggested that the English had promised to deliver Masqat into Persian hands.[54] On March 15 the Persian fleet, consisting of five ships, one grab, and some smaller vessels, commanded by Latif Khan and Captain Cook, his vice-admiral, arrived at Bandar 'Abbas. After embarking some 5,000 men and 1,500 horses, the fleet left for Khor Fukkan where a force was landed. The fleet then sailed to Jolfar where Latif Khan met with the Ya'ariba Imam of Oman, Seyf b. Soltan II. The latter had been unable to suppress a rebellion of his subjects and had appealed to Nader Shah for help; a coincidence that suited the latter's plans very well. The joint forces were very successful at Masqat, but then the Imam and Latif Khan quarreled with one another, the latter was forced to withdraw his troops to Jolfar. Already at the end of March 1737 Mohammad Taqi Khan had asked the Dutch to put a ship at his disposal for the transportation of troops. Because he had been instrumental in the renewal of Dutch trading privileges, the Dutch sent *de Anthonia* to Jolfar. Mohammad Taqi Khan also asked for mortars and gun-powder and in May he again asked for the assistance of a ship. Because he told the Dutch this would be the last time he would ask for a ship, they complied with his request and sent *tHuys Foreest*. Of their own accord, the English also had offered to transport troops and supplies to Jolfar. However, Mohammad Taqi Khan did not trust them, because they had just been caught in a smuggling affair, for which he had fined them 1,000 *tumans*.[55]

Despite his promise, Mohammad Taqi Khan continued to ask the Dutch for favors, especially for the supply of spare parts and other ships' supplies. Although it was annoying, the Dutch observed that he at least asked them politely, while the English just received orders to deliver certain supplies.[56] Nader Shah also sent them a letter in which he thanked the Dutch for their assistance. He added, however, that they should be ready to do more and keep their ships and grabs ready for action.[57]

Latif Khan despite his setback at Masqat still enjoyed Nader Shah's favor. There was even talk that he would succeed Mohammad Taqi Khan as *beygler-beygi* of Fars. After his return from Jolfar the sailors complained about insufficient food supplies and their lack of pay. Latif Khan was able to soothe the sailors, mostly Hula Arabs, by promising redress.[58] In view of his good standing with Nader Shah the Dutch reacted positively to Latif Khan's request for them to send three ships' carpenters to Bushire. Although they sent only one, he was well received and returned after one month.[59] Mohammad Taqi Khan, meanwhile, had returned to Bandar 'Abbas on 10 December 1737 accompanied by Sheikh Jabbareh. Nader Shah had rebuked him for not personally leading the expedition to Masqat and had given him orders to redress the situation there. Understandably, Mohammad Taqi Khan was not in good spirits. He immediately made preparations to embark a

---

54 VOC 2417, Resolution Gamron (09/03/1737), f. 3791; VOC 2416, Isfahan to Gamron (17/07/1737), f. 2490; Lockhart, "Navy," p. 9; Ibid., *Nadir Shah*, pp. 182-83.

55 VOC 2417, Resolutions Gamron (23/03/1737), f. 3822-24 and (30/03/1737), f. 3860-61; VOC 2448, Resolution Gamron (30/04/1737), f. 319-32; Lockhart, "Navy," p. 10.

56 VOC 2448, Resolution Gamron (13/06/1737), f. 419-22 (this may have been posturing by the council of Gamron to put an attractive face on something ugly to try and avoid criticism from Batavia and Amsterdam).

57 VOC 2448, Nader Shah to Koenad (Rabi' al-Avval 1150 – February 1737). The letter was written in Qandahar and was received on 19/07/1737.

58 VOC 2448, Resolution Gamron (30/11/1737), f. 822; Lockhart, "Navy," p. 10; Ibid., *Nadir Shah*, pp. 183-84.

59 VOC 2448, Resolutions Gamron (08/11/1737), f. 789-96 and (10/12/1737), f. 889.

large expeditionary force to reinforce the Persian garrison at Jolfar. Although the Dutch had promised him one ship, he became very angry when the ship was not yet ready when he wanted to leave. He accused the Dutch of ingratitude and told them that they could keep their ship. He did not care whether they left Persia or stayed, but if they stayed, he would punish them for their dastardly deed. The local authorities headed by Mohammad Taqi Khan's brother interceded on behalf of the Dutch, but Mohammad Taqi Khan remained angry. He indicated that it would take a present of 1,000 *tumans* to erase the shameful incident. The Dutch deliberated over what to do. If they left, everything would be lost; if they stayed and fought, they could not win. They therefore decided to pay and lodge a complaint with Nader Shah. Mohammad Taqi Khan told the Dutch, after the payment was made, that bygones were bygones and he acted very friendly towards them. Meanwhile, he commandeered all vessels in and around Bandar 'Abbas to supply Jolfar, including the small craft of the Dutch and the English. Needless to say, this had a negative impact on living conditions in Bandar 'Abbas.[60]

Seyf b. Soltan II, Imam of Oman, again welcomed the arrival of the Persian troops, for events had taken a bad turn for him. The combined forces defeated the rebel troops, seized several towns, and finally captured Masqat itself. When the Imam realized that the Persians wanted to occupy his land rather than just help him regain it, he switched sides and joined the rebels. The Persians were badly defeated and had to fall back on Jolfar. Their defeat may have been caused by Mohammad Taqi Khan's poisoning of Latif Khan. The fleet thus lost a capable commander; its deputy commander, the English vice-admiral Cook also died. The Omani fleet engaged the Persian fleet and defeated it. Mohammad Taqi Khan had to flee from Jolfar. The Omani fleet pursued him all the way to Bandar-e Kong. An English vessel, which had been assisting Mohammad Taqi Khan, had been unable to help him. He therefore blamed the Europeans for his defeat: the English by deserting him and the Dutch by not assisting him. The English gave him 1,200 *tumans*, while he asked the Dutch for a loan of 40,000 *tumans*, which they refused. The supply lines with Jolfar were cut and the remaining Persian garrison, commanded by *min-bashi* Assur Khan, was in dire straits. Because Mohammad Taqi Khan had treated the Arab crew of his fleet in a niggardly fashion they mutinied and deserted. The Omanis made use of the Persian defeat to attack the islands at the coastal settlements of the Garmsirat. They sacked Qeshm, Kong, and Bahrain and it was rumored that Sheikh Jabbareh wanted to seize Bahrain again for himself.[61]

In December 1737 a sea battle took place between the Omani and Persian fleet near Qasab. A heavy thunderstorm separated the two fleets and the Omanis lost one of their biggest ships, the

60 VOC 2448, Resolutions Gamron (10/12/1737), f. 858, 884-85, 888-89; (02/01/1738), f. 949-56; (28/01/1738), f. 957-75; (31/01/1738), f. 977-85; (03/03/1738), f. 1990-94; Ibid., Mohammad Taqi Khan to Koenad (23 Shavval 1150 – 13/02/1738), f. 1999; Ibid., Gamron to Batavia (30/04/1738), f. 1834, 1839-41.

61 VOC 2449, Resolution Gamron (06/05/1739), f. 2090-91; VOC 2416, Gamron to Batavia (25/02/1739), f. 87-91; Ibid., Resolutions Gamron (08/08/1738), f. 183-83; (12/08/1739), f. 190-91; (29/09/1739), f. 244-46; (03/10/1739), f. 255-56. On 17 July 1738/31 Rabi' al-Avval, Mohammad Taqi Khan had written to Koenad that the latter's lack of enthusiasm to lend him a ship was quite evident. However, he did not need his ships anymore, because he was almost finished there (Masqat). "If the Imam of Masqat, Seyf, wants to oppose me, I have 7 to 8 ships on the roadstead of Jolfar, one English Company ship, and about 100 small vessels of Arab and other subjects of the Shah. Seyf has only two rotten, decrepit ships and the royal fleet can handle those." VOC 2476, Mohammad Taqi Khan to Koenad (Kong, received 14/09/1738), f. 260-61; Ibid. Bushire to Gamron (17/08/1739), f. 1066; Ibid., idem to idem (16/09/1738), f. 1077; Ibid., idem to idem (12/11/1738), f. 1097; Ibid., idem to idem (12/01/1739), f. 1106; Ibid., Hoogeboom c.s. to Koenad (Qeshm, 23/07/1738), f. 1130; see also Ibid., f. 1140, 1146.

Malek, to a fire caused by its own crew.[62] In the meantime, the Persian troops in Jolfar received new supplies shipped on Dutch and other vessels. Sheikh Madhkur of Bushire supplied sailors to reinforce the crews of the Persian fleet. In February 1738 Abu al-'Arab attacked Jolfar with 20,000 men, but Assur Soltan and his troops were able to repulse him.[63] The supplies sent to Jolfar caused dearth and scarcity in Bandar 'Abbas to such an extent that in January 1739 the poor were forced to eat grass like animals. The streets were covered with dead bodies left unburied.[64]

Mohammad Taqi Khan returned to Bandar 'Abbas on March 16 with orders to persevere in the war with Oman. He promised the Dutch repayment, in installments, of Persia's debt to the VOC, which amounted to more than 70,000 *tumans*, if the Dutch would supply him with a fully equipped ship for which he would pay in cash. Moreover, the Dutch had to promise to deliver ships' supplies for the maintenance and repairs of the fleet. The Dutch told him they could not sell him a ship, but Mohammad Taqi Khan replied that his offer was not open to negotiation. At the same time, he gave them a list of ships' supplies that he needed. When the Dutch delayed their response he threatened to take these supplies by force. He gave them until March 28 to choose between war and peace. The Dutch decided that war was not in their interest. However, to give in would mean giving *carte blanche* to Mohammad Taqi Khan. They therefore decided to give what they could afford. If this proved to be unacceptable, they would resist and defend Dutch interests by force. Fortunately, Mohammad Taqi Khan accepted their offer. Probably to ingratiate themselves with Mohammad Taqi Khan (at least that it what the Dutch thought), the English gave him, unsolicited, a new 132-foot ship in addition to many presents. Satisfied with these results Mohammad Taqi Khan returned on 1 May, 1739 to Shiraz.[65]

The war in Oman, meanwhile, did not go well for the Persians. The garrison at Jolfar was under constant pressure and in great difficulty. In July 1739, the deputy-governor of Bandar 'Abbas literally begged the Dutch to send supplies to Jolfar. The Dutch refused because they had to repair their own ship. However, the Persian officials continued to pester them with increasing desperation until on August 5 the ship *tHof niet altijd Somer* left for Jolfar.[66] Meanwhile, the Persian authorities commandeered all local vessels in Bandar 'Abbas to send supplies to Jolfar, for it was a matter of life and death for the Persian troops there.[67]

Around the same time, peace talks began between the Imam and the Persians, which finally led to the end of the hostilities. The Persians probably took the initiative for these talks since Nader Shah needed his fleet for operations in Sind. In September 1739 Mohammad Taqi Khan was already making preparations for this campaign. When he arrived in Bandar 'Abbas on November 4, 1739 he asked the Dutch to transport troops and supplies to Divil.[68] The Dutch protested but then gave in to Mohammad Taqi Khan, who appeared to be even more powerful than before. He had an

62 VOC 2476, Gamron to Batavia (25/02/1739), f. 132-33.

63 VOC 2476, Bushire to Gamron (17/08/1738), f. 1067; Ibid., Hoogeboom c.s. to Koenad (Qeshm, 13/12/1738), f. 1193; Ibid., Gamron to Batavia (25/02/1739), f. 132-33.

64 VOC 2476, Resolution Gamron (20/01/1739), f. 470-71; (29/01/1739), f. 495-99; Ibid. Gamron to Isfahan (31/01/1739), f. 616.

65 VOC 2477, Gamron to Batavaia (20/03/1739), f. 84, 88. 109-11; Ibid., Resolutions Gamron (20/03/1739), f. 205-07, (28/03/1739), f. 235-39; Lockhart, "Navy," p. 11.

66 VOC 2510, resolutions Gamron (16/07/1739), f. 1370-73, (29/07/1793(, f. 252; Ibid., Mohammad Taqi Khan to Koenad, f. 1248-53.

67 VOC 2510, Resolution Gamron (29/08/1739), f. 278-79; Ibid., Gamron to Batavia (25/11/1739), f. 110-111.

68 VOC 2510, Resolution Gamron (10/11/1739), f. 411-16; Ibid. Gamron to Batavia (25/11/1739), f. 119-20; Lockhart, "Navy," p. 11. For a discussion of the location of the port of Divil see Monique Kervran, "Le port

army of about 25,000 infantry, seven big and small ships (both three- and two-masters), and about 100 smaller vessels. Supplies arrived as far away as and all vessels in the Gulf were pressed into service. On 17 December 1739 Mohammad Taqi Khan boarded the *tHof niet altijd Somer* and sailed to Makran, where he met with defeat.[69]

DUTCH VESSELS FORCED TO HELP SUPPRESS A MUTINY OF THE ROYAL FLEET

As a result of these developments Mohammad Taqi Khan was dismissed as *beygler-beygi* of Fars. Emamverdi Khan succeeded him. The admiral of the fleet, Mir 'Ali Khan Turkmen, was also dismissed and succeeded by Mohammad Taqi Khan Mashhadi. The fleet, which had returned to Bandar 'Abbas in April 1740, was in a bad shape. Mir 'Ali Khan was constantly asking the European Companies for ships' supplies to make repairs. The situation worsened when, as a result of a heavy storm in mid-August 1740, the royal fleet suffered heavy damage.[70] Not only were the ships in a bad shape, but the crews as well. Mohammad Taqi Khan Shirazi had treated them parsimoniously. As a result, the Arab sailors mutinied on 26 August 1740. They killed the admiral (*darya-beygi*) Mir 'Ali Soltan and a great many Persian soldiers. The leaders of the mutiny are named in Dutch sources as "Sjeeg Rama, Sjeeg Abdoel Sjeeg, and Sjeeg Abdoel Khoer." Each of them had fled with a few ships to a different part of the Persian Gulf.[71] Two Dutch ships helped bring the loyal part of the royal fleet safely back to Bandar 'Abbas. The new admiral, Mohammad Taqi Khan Mashhadi, demanded that the Dutch also assist him in punishing the mutineers and in bringing back their ships. Under pressure, the Dutch gave in. They put two ships at his disposal, which were joined by two brigantines flying English colors, which had been seized by the Dutch in August. Failing to trap Sheikh 'Abdol-Sheikh (Sjeeg Abdoel Sjeeg) the ships returned to Bandar 'Abbas at the end of September 1740.[72]

Emamverdi Khan, meanwhile, was gathering troops at Bushire where he also commandeered a Dutch vessel *de Valk*. He intended to attack the mutineers at Kish, where they had concentrated their forces. Since the English lent the Persians some soldiers and one small cannon, the Dutch had to something as well to remain on good terms with the Persian authorities. They, therefore, put two ships at their disposal, *de Middenrak* and *de Croonenburgh*. They sailed to Kish on 3 October 1740. On October 15, the Dutch-Persian squadron engaged the rebel fleet, which was much stronger and had a more determined crew. The small trankis of the mutineers were especially

multiple des bouches de l'Indus: Barbarké, Dēb, Daybul, Lahori Bandar, Diul Sinde," in Rika Gyselen ed. *Sites et monuments disparus d'après les témoignages de voyageurs*. Res Orientales VIII (1996), pp. 45-92.

69 VOC 2510, f. 114-116, 121; Lockhart, *Nadir Shah*, p. 184. On the disastrous campaign in Mekran see Willem Floor, "New Facts on Nader Shah's Indian Campaign," in: Kambiz Eslami ed. *Iran and Persian Studies. Essays in Honor of Iraj Afshar*. (Princeton: Zagros, 1998), pp. 198-219.

70 VOC 2511, Gamron to Batavia (31/04/1740), f. 157-58; VOC 2546, Gamron to Batavia (31/03/1740), f. 30-32.

71 Lockhart, "Navy," p. 11; Ibid., *Nadir Shah*, p. 212; VOC 2546, Gamron to Batavia (31/03/1740), f. 33ff; ("Sjeeg Rhama has left with the Fattisjahi, two smaller vessels, and most of the best other crafts to Kong, Abdoel Sjeeg has fled with two small ships and ten trankis and has hidden somewhere near Qeshm); VOC 2546, f. 1725 states that "Rhama son of Sjahin Naghiloehie has fled after the mutiny with some ships to Sjahi and Bandar Hoela."

72 VOC 2546, Gamron to Batavia (31/03/1740), f. 35-37; Ibid., Captain of *de Middenrak* to Koenad (10/09/1740), f. 1407; Ibid., idem to idem (18/09/740), f. 1408-10; Ibid., Dagregister *de Middenrak*, f. 1415; Ibid., Bushire to Gamron (11/10/1740), f. 1355.

effective, which was not the case with those accompanying the Persian ships. The fierce resistance put up by the mutineers made the admiral to disengage from the battle. Although he had not defeated the mutineers he was pleased with the outcome. Emamverdi Khan took a less positive view. He did not understand why the Dutch had not been able to defeat the Arabs. However, when he learnt how the battle had gone he changed his tune and thanked the Dutch for their support at the same time asking for additional naval assistance to transport troops and supplies to Kong and Jolfar. The Dutch refused, although by December 1740, with piracy increasing in the Persian Gulf and the situation of the Persian garrison in Jolfar growing more difficult, they decided to assist Emamverdi Khan. However, by that time Persian vessels could sail unprotected to Jolfar.[73]

In April 1741 the admiral again asked the Dutch for naval assistance. This time they refused in spite of the threat of incurring the shah's disfavor.[74] This was a month after negotiations between some of the rebels, who had quarreled amongst themselves and the Persian authorities failed to produce a settlement.[75] In June and August the admiral again asked for the Dutch ships; they again refused. The growing friction between the Dutch and the Persian authorities boded ill for the former. Therefore, when Emamverdi Khan arrived in Bandar 'Abbas in September 1741, they complied with his request for a short trip by one of their ships to Qeshm. They also took a force of 25 soldiers aboard. On their return, these 'passengers' refused to leave. As a result, it seemed for some time as if hostilities would break out. The Dutch put their forces on alert, while Emamverdi Khan trained his cannons on the Dutch factory. Then Emamverdi Khan gave in and withdrew his soldiers from *de Ketel*. He told the Dutch, however, that they would either have to lend him two ships to fight the Hulas or transport Mozaffar 'Ali Khan to Thatta. To defuse this potentially dangerous situation the Dutch agreed to make the trip to Thatta. Emamverdi Khan then changed his mind and asked them to help again against the Hulas. They refused and Emamverdi Khan again threatened to attack the Dutch factory. The Dutch council at Bandar 'Abbas was divided about which course to take. A minority was willing to fight, if need be, but the majority wanted to avoid such extreme measures. They finally decided to give in to Emamverdi Khan's request and allow Persian troops to embark. This led to difficulties with the Dutch crew; they refused to sail with that

73 The two Dutch ships were faced by two big ships, viz. the *Fattisjahi* and the *Capitaine*, as well as one two-master and 110 well-armed trankis, in addition to which more trankis were lying on the beach, which the rebels had as yet not put into action. Soon after the battle started the Persian trankis accompanying the Dutch ships had fled. It should be noted here that the ships of the Persian fleet were used for transportation, shelling of enemy positions and for fighting sea-battles. The European ships were superior in firepower, but as is clear from the various accounts, the smaller Gulf rowing vessels played an important part during these battles. For detailed information see VOC 2546, Dagregister (Diary on events near Keyts [Kish], Sjab [Abu Sho'eyb]), f. 1423-37, and Ibid., Resolution of the ship's council (01/10/1740), f. 403-14; Ibid., Emamverdi Khan to Schoonderwoerd (Bushire) (24/10/1740), f. 1153-54; Ibid., Emamverdi Khan to Koenad (received from Nakhilu on 28/10/1740), f. 1756-58, (30/10/1740), f. 1759-60, (11/11/1740), f. 1765; VOC 2546, Gamron to Batavia (31/03/1741), f. 38-46; Ibid., Koenad to Sjeeg Sjahin and Sjeeg Rhama at the long island (Qeshm) (20/04/1741), f. 1961-63; see also f. 1814-17; Ibid., f, 49-50 in January 1741 returned his vessels through the good offices of Mohammad Taqi Khan Mashhadi; Lockhart, *Nadir Shah*, p. 212.

74 VOC 2538, Darya-beygi to Koenad (04/04/1741), f. 187-88; Ibid., Emamverdi Khan to Mohammad Taqi Khan (received 03/04/1741), f. 182-85.

75 Lockhart, "Navy," p. 11 ("In March, 1741, however, the mutineers, as before, quarreled amongst themselves, and some of them opened negotiations with the Persian authorities. Strangely enough, these negotiations were conducted in English, as an English renegade acted as spokesman for the mutineers, while the Agent or one of his assistants interpreted for the Admiral. No settlement, however, was reached.")

many Persians, who were behaving very arrogantly, aboard. They refused to return if the Persians remained on board. Thereupon Koenad, the VOC director, charged them with mutiny.[76]

Emamverdi Khan decided to sail to Kish with the remaining Dutch skeleton crew, who were assisted by a few Arab sailors. On 25 October 1741 the two Dutch ships, the *Fata Sianga*, two gallivats and 40 other vessels engaged the Hulas at Kish. The Arabs put up a fierce resistance and Emamverdi Khan, to encourage his troops, himself loaded a cannon, but with too much powder. The cannon burst and killed him. The Dutch-Persian fleet continued to fight the Hulas, but disengaged at sunset. The next day the *darya-beygi* was appointed acting commander (*sardar*). Because the Dutch refused to continue the operation – having promised only assistance for a period of one month, which had long since past – and his own troops were discouraged the *darya-beygi* gave orders to return to Kong. He refused to allow the Dutch ships, as previously promised, to return to Bandar 'Abbas. Koenad planned a rescue operation, but the arrival of Hatem Khan made that unnecessary. He allowed the ships to return, but told Koenad that one of his ships had to make the journey to Thatta.[77] Since this was a direct order from Nader Shah, Koenad did not dare to refuse. He therefore put *de Ridderkerk* at the disposal of Mozaffar 'Ali Khan. It sailed to Thatta on 5 January 1742 and shipwrecked at Karachi on its return voyage in May 1742.[78]

NADER SHAH ORDERS SHIPBUILDING TO START AT BUSHIRE

In the second half of 1741 Nader Shah took measures to build his own ships and cast his own cannons in the Persian Gulf. A gun foundry at Bandar 'Abbas actually turned out two copper cannons and it was intended to cast another 300. The shipyard was at Rishar. Nader Shah asked the European Companies in December 1741 to send him carpenters and ship building materials. He had put four officials in charge of the project: Soleyman Beyg, Mohammad 'Ali Beyg, Hasan 'Ali Beyg and Mohammad Zaman Beyg. The latter two were stationed in Mazandaran to arrange for the transport of timber to Rishahr.[79] This royal decree was accompanied by a letter from Mohammad 'Ali Beyg in which he asked for three carpenters to build ships of at least 100 *gaz* (about 60 meters) length. He added that Nader Shah wanted to spend some 40,000 *tumans* on this project. The Dutch, therefore, were to send well-qualified people and not men who would waste the money.[80]

---

76 VOC 2583, Resolutions Gamron (15/08/1741), f. 395-99, (21/09/1741), f. 493-545, (07/10/1741), f. 558-96; VOC 2584, Gamron to Batavia (22/01/1742 - secret), f. 2495, 2504-15.

77 VOC 2584, Contract with Emamverdi Khan for the use of the Dutch ships (08/10/1741), f. 2117-19; Ibid., Emamverdi Khan to Koenad (14/10/1741), f. 2125-29; Ibid., Darya-beygi to Koenad (received 11/11/1741), f. 2134-35; Ibid., Ebrahim Sahid (VOC interpreter) to Koenad (received 18/11/1741), f. 2229-39; Ibid., Koenad to Zion and Deeldekaas (commanding officers of the two Dutch ships) (01 and 20/12/1741), f. 2664-70 (secret); Ibid., Zion to Koenad (11/11/1741), f. 2692-2701; Ibid., idem to idem (21/11/1741), f. 2712-17; Ibid., Hatem Khan to Koenad (received 06/12/1741), f. 2150; Ibid., idem to idem (received 17/12/1741), f. 2167-69; Ibid., idem to idem (received 25/12/1741), f. 2771-73 (all from Kong).

78 Koenad instructed his Isfahan office to obtain a royal order from Nader Shah "in which it is ordered that nobody can ask for our ships without showing a royal order." VOC 2584, f. 2546. Koenad also protested to Nader Shah about the high-handed behavior of Emamverdi Khan. Ibid., Koenad to Nader Shah (18/11/1741), f. 2559-2607. In a secret letter to Batavia, Koenad asked for permission "to have the Persian taste the sword for once, in case the oppression is too much." Ibid., f. 2501, which shows that the patience of the VOC council at Gamron had almost run out.

79 Lockhart, "Navy," p. 12; Ibid., *Nadir Shah*, pp. 213-14 for the possible reason for this scheme; VOC 2584 (decree) Nader Shah to Koenad (21 Rabi' al-Avval - 06/06/1741; received 17/12/1741), f. 2161-62.

80 VOC 2584, Mohammad 'Ali Beyg to Koenad (received 17/12/1741), not foliated, see also f. 2156. The intended length of the ship was wrong and not feasible, see Lockhart, *Nadir Shah*, p. 213.

Koenad's successor Clement wrote to Nader Shah that the Dutch had no carpenters, for these were only available in the Netherlands where all their ships were built. In a similar vein he replied to a second letter from Mohammad 'Ali Beyg in February 1742 asking again for carpenters and supplies.[81] After these negative reactions the matter was not raised anymore with the Dutch. Nader Shah had to make with the services of a Flemish gentleman named La Porterie, who was charged with the supervision of the construction of the ship. Although he protested that he was ignorant of shipbuilding, he was forced to go to Bushire. The climate undermined his health, but despite repeated requests he was not allowed to return to Isfahan. When he finally fell seriously ill he was allowed to depart, but he died before he had reached Shiraz.[82]

Although Nader Shah's shipbuilding plans failed to reach fruition he nevertheless was able to get a considerable fleet by purchase, gift and seizure. By mid-1742 his fleet consisted of four three-masters, three sloops, two gallivants, and a great many trankis, each with four to six cannons. Half of the four three-masters had been purchased by Mohammad Taqi Khan Shirazi for 7,000 *tumans* from the English in Bandar 'Abbas. Each ship had 22 cannons and was 110 feet long. The two other ships were at Bushire, where they had been bought from private English and French country traders, each one for 1,800 *tumans*. These were 16-cannon ships, 90-100 feet long. However, according to the Dutch, they were old, worn-out ships, from which the Persians would not get much satisfaction. The ships of the Persian fleet were mostly manned by Bengali sailors, who had deserted English and French ships calling at Persian ports. Neither Company could do anything about this, even when their sailors were pressed into Persian service in front of their own factories.[83] Moreover, Nader Shah expected another eight ships from Surat, bought by Nezam al-Molk, the Moghul governor of Hyderabad. The fleet, which was well stocked with supplies, was to grow even more during 1742. Gradually the Hula mutineers were reduced to obedience and their ships were recovered, thus reinforcing the royal fleet. Furthermore, the Imam of Oman gave Nader Shah two ships, one boasting of 64 cannons.[84]

81 VOC 2593, Gamron to Batavia (31/10/1742), f. 1778 vs; Ibid., Clement to Nader Shah (07/01/1742), f. 1780-81.

82 Lockhart, "Navy," p. 12; Ibid., *Nadir Shah*, pp. 220-21. La Porterie had come to Persia via Aleppo and Basra on 19 December 1731. He had been an engineer in French employ. On 20 December 1731 he left for Kerman (VOC 2254, f. 449). The fortune hunter, as the Dutch used to refer to him, arrived in Isfahan in February 1732, where he sought service with the Shah as an engineer, but he was not successful (VOC 2232, f. 363vs). One year later he was with Nader's army at Hamadan, who offered him too low a salary, reason why La Porterie returned to Isfahan, where he stayed with the English. (VOC 2323 (10/10/1733), f. 669). In May 1738 it is reported that La Porterie had entered into Persian service as a cannon caster (VOC 2476, f. 916) and that he would leave with the artillery to Kerman to fight against the Baluch of Makran. (VOC 2476, f. 936). According to the Dutch, La Porterie offered his services as a shipwright to Nader Shah. When he was not successful at this, he had to give up, and left in the company of a French captain, George Eustache, who had sold his ship, the *La Fortune*, to the Persian government for 1,800 *tumans* (VOC 2593, f. 1715 vs). His departure was a blow to the shipbuilding plans, despite the fact, according to Mohammad 'Ali Beyg, Nader Shah wanted to pursue this activity with diligence in Persia, in Surat and in other Indian ports. (VOC 2593, f. 1714vs-15r)

83 VOC 2593, f. 1807vs; see also f. 1715vs-1716r and f. 1842vs (*La Fortune, Robert Galley*). The EIC Agent commented (Lockhart, *Nadir Shah*, p. 215): "But what probability there is of such mighty Affairs being accomplished may in part be guessed at by the neabs they are obliged to use for procuring Timber Bringing it near Sixty Days, on Men's Shoulders from Mazenderoon, and They must come at every other materials with equal difficulty." At that time Nader Shah's navy consisted of 15 ships according to the English. Ibid., p. 216.

84 VOC 2593, f. 1801; Lockhart, *Nadir Shah*, pp. 215-16.

SECOND PERSIAN INVASION OF OMAN

In 1742 the Imam of Oman again appealed to Nader Shah for help. The shah willingly complied with this request. After defeating the Hulas at Khasab, Kalb 'Ali Khan, the new *sardar*, accompanied by Mohammad Taqi Khan Shirazi, arrive din Bandar 'Abbas on 2 June 1742. They made preparations for an Oman campaign, which they planned with the Imam himself, who was in their company. On June 18 they sailed to Oman with about 8,000 cavalry. This campaign initially was very successful for the Persians, for they were able to seize most towns and, by ruse, even the forts of Masqat. The Imam found out too late that he had been deceived by his allies. By July 1743 Mohammad Taqi Khan Shirazi held the greater part of Oman.[85]

In October 1743 Nader Shah sent a new *sardar* of the Garmsirat to Oman, Mohammad Hoseyn Khan. According to the Dutch, Mohammad Hoseyn Khan had orders to claim immediate restitution of the costs of the Oman campaign from Mohammad Taqi Khan Shirazi. Whether this is the true reason or not, but by November 1743 Mohammad Taqi Khan revolted against Nader Shah. He arrested Kalb 'Ali Khan and stopped all communications with Persia. Sardar Mohammad Hoseyn Khan escaped to Kong, however. On 1 December 1743 Mohammad Taqi Khan arrived at Bandar 'Abbas with the fleet. Mohammad Baqer Lari, the deputy-governor of Bandar 'Abbas, killed Kalb 'Ali Khan and some other military commanders. When Mozaffar 'Ali Khan arrived at Bandar 'Abbas from Sind with seven ships on 22 December 1743, Mohammad Taqi Khan asked the Dutch to lend him naval assistance to seize the seven ships. He had only three ships and two grabs of his own against Mozaffar 'Ali Khan's seven ships. The Dutch, however, decided to remain neutral in the conflict. During the night of 23 December 1743 Mozaffar 'Ali Khan seized two ships and two grabs from Mohammad Taqi Khan's fleet. The remainder fled. Mohammad Taqi Khan again asked the Dutch to attack Mozaffar 'Ali Khan. Again they refused. Mozaffar 'Ali Khan faced with water supply problems then sailed to Bushire. Mohammad Taqi Khan was furious at the Dutch and promised that as soon as his ships were back from Jolfar he would attack the Dutch factory, completely destroy it, and kill all Dutchmen. But he could not carry out his threat, for he left for Shiraz on 18 February 1744. Nader Shah meanwhile took measures to quell the revolt and asked the Dutch to prevent any rebels from escaping by sea, to look after his fleet, and to take care of Mohammad Taqi Khan's property.[86]

As a result of this revolt and the renewed war with the Ottoman Empire, the Persians were unable to maintain their positions in Oman and were driven back to Jolfar. This reduced the demands for ships from the European Companies. In fact, no more demands are reported. This circumstance may also have been due to the fact that Nader Shah had gathered quite a considerable fleet by the time. According to the English, Nader Shah had 30 ships and a large number of small craft. The English director also observed that "H.M. still seems to continue the Resolution of having a large Fleet for the support of which he has lately entered into a Scheme of Trade and has ordered two ships annually (which are now getting ready) with cargoes of the choicest Persian goods to the amount of 5,000 toman to be sent to Surat for purchasing stores and building of two other Ships."[87]

---

85 VOC 2593, f. 1797, 1803, 1806, 1808vs. Mohammad Taqi Khan also asked the Dutch to supply him with three ships, but they refused. Ibid., f. 1853-59; Lockhart, *Nadir Shah*, pp. 215-16.

86 Lockhart, *Nadir Shah*, p. 241ff; VOC 2680, de Poorter to Nader Shah (19/04/1744), not foliated; Ibid,. Resolution Gamron (20/01/1744), f. not foliated; Ibid., Gamron to Batavia (10/08/1745), f. 316-49.

87 Lockhart, *Nadir Shah*, p. 21; Ibid., "Navy," pp. 13-14. However, in January 1745 Mozaffar 'Ali Khan asked again for supplies. VOC 2880, f. 59. His successor as admiral of the Gulf fleet was Salim Khan. VOC 2860, not

THE ROYAL FLEET A FAILURE

Nader Shah had to neglect his navy during the last two years of his reign. The war with the Ottoman Empire and the increasing number on internal revolts in Persia required all his attention. By the time of his death in June 1747 several of his ships had been lost due to shipwreck. The remainder became objects of dispute among the commanders of the fleet. Molla 'Ali Shah, the vice-admiral, acquired a few, while Sheikh 'Abdol-Sheikh and Sheikh Naser of Bushire assumed control of most of the others.[88] However, they were unable to maintain the fleet. According to a Dutch report written in 1756, "of those ships which Nadier Scha had built at such large expense two still are left, which float above water. However, they are in such a bad condition that they cannot be repaired anymore. The ship that was lying at Bender Riek and which was also one of the best sank last year and is irreparable."[89]

Like Nader Shah's other schemes, the navy had been built and developed at great human and financial cost. Nader Shah failed to give his navy an institutional, political and financial basis, which would have ensured its continued existence after his death. His proud navy, like his kingdom, fell apart. The kingdom was finally restored after much internecine warfare, but it would take another 150 years before a new Persian navy came into being.

The picture of the Persian naval history would not be complete without mention of Nader's naval aims and achievements on the Caspian Sea. Lockhart has adequately treated this subject in his monograph on Nader Shah, but on one issue Lockhart's analysis has to be amended. He writes that "It does not appear to be on record when he [Nader] first thought of having a fleet on those waters, but there is no doubt that he did not do so until some time after he had begun to collect his flotilla on the Gulf."[90] It seems quite likely that Nader Shah had this idea about the time that he sought to create his navy in the Gulf, i.e. at the end of 1734. At that time Nader Shah was sorely pressed for supplies at Ganjeh, which he was besieging. The Russian commander at Darband helped him by sending ships with supplies.[91] Subsequent developments took Nader Shah's attention elsewhere, but from the fact that he appointed Mohammad Hoseyn Khan *qaputan-bashi* or admiral of the Caspian Sea in early 1738 we may conclude that Nader Shah was quite aware of the usefulness of having a fleet on the Caspian Sea.[92] The Dutch, who reported this appointment, did not mention whether this admiral had a fleet. However, it shows that Nader Shah had clear ideas about his maritime needs on the Caspian Sea prior to his decision of 1742 to build ships for the Persian Gulf.[93]

---

foliated; VOC 2705 (August 1745), f. 200. In 1746 Mohammad Reza Khan was admiral of the fleet sailing to Oman. VOC 2705 (March 1746), f. 426.

88 See chapters two, three and seven.

89 Lockhart, *Nadir Shah*, pp. 221-22; Floor, "A Description," pp. 66, 172-73 or chapter two.

90 Lockhart, "Navy," p. 14.

91 VOC 2357, Isfahan to Gamron (04/02/1735), F. 1145.

92 VOC 2474 (20/04/1738), f. 890.

93 Lockhart, *Nadir Shah*, pp. 204-05, 289; Ibid., "Navy," pp. 14-17.

CHAPTER TWO
A Description of the Persian Gulf and its Inhabitants in 1756

Although in 1752 the governor-general of the Dutch East Indies Company (VOC), Jacob Mossel, had proposed to abandon the VOC establishment in Persia altogether he, one year later, pushed through the Khark project as proposed by Tido von Kniphausen. The latter had run into great difficulties with the authorities in Basra where he had been in charge of the VOC factory, as is discussed in detail in chapter three. After he had been obliged to leave Basra von Kniphausen on his way from Basra to Batavia had been requested by the chief of Rig, Mir Naser Vaqa'i, to establish a factory on the island of Khark, a request which Mir Naser followed up with a written request to Mossel. Von Kniphausen was not only able to justify himself in Batavia against the accusations made by the authorities in Basra, but at the same time he was able to convince Mossel that to restore the VOC's position in the Persian Gulf the possession of the island of Khark would do just that. Although some members of the VOC's High Government in Batavia opposed the Khark proposal Mossel was able to convince the majority to approve it. In November 1753 von Kniphausen implemented the Khark project, which, incidentally, had not been approved by the VOC directors, when he arrived with the three ships at Khark to establish what should become the most profitable and secure factory in the Persian Gulf.[1]

The reason why the 'Description of the Persian Gulf' was written is not known to me, since it is not mentioned anywhere in the remaining correspondence of that period. In fact, the report, of which only one copy exists, bears neither date nor the name of its author. It was acquired by the Dutch National Archives at a public auction in 1889,[2] so it may never have formed a part of the VOC archives, which the Dutch State inherited in 1795, when the VOC went bankrupt. Nevertheless it has been possible to ascertain both the date and the authors of the 'Description' by relying on internal evidence.

The report, amongst other things, mentions several events which make it possible to give a precise date to it. In the first place it refers to the existence of the proposal for the conquest of Bahrain and in the second place it notes that the question of the chieftainship of Rig had not been settled yet. Since the former was written on November 1, 1754[3] and the latter was

1 For details about the genesis and development of the Khark project see chapter four of this publication.

2 The manuscript of this report may be found in the Dutch National Archives (NA) in The Hague under: *Aanwinsten* (Acquisitions) 1889, nr. 23 B.

3 VOC 2886, "Project aengaande het bemachtigen van 'tEijland Bahrehn" written by T.F. von Kniphausen and J. van der Hulst (Kareek, 01/11/17545), not foliated.

settled on June 6, 1756 with the murder of Mir Hoseyn by his brother Mir Mohanna, who then became the chief of Rig,[4] it seems that the report was written between these two dates. The report also mentions that the attack by Molla 'Ali Shah on Laft had taken place last year. Since this siege ended in October 1755[5] the report per force must have been written in 1756.

The report probably was written to set the High Government's mind at ease with regard to the consequences of the proposed conquest of Bahrain. Already in November 1754 von Kniphausen had reassured Mossel with the regard to the security of the Khark factory by pointing out that he had fostered friendly relations with the local chiefs and their people and that all chiefs in the Persian Gulf lived in disaccord with one another.[6] The opposition to the Bahrain proposal, which proposal was backed by Mossel, may have convinced von Kniphausen of the necessity to give the High Government a more comprehensive overview of the political and economic situation in the Persian Gulf to overcome its opposition. This is also indicated by letters that von Kniphausen wrote to the VOC directors in the Netherlands to ask for their support of the Bahrain project. One of these letters, written by Jan van der Hulst, von Kniphausen's deputy, to Jan Calkoen, burgomaster of Amsterdam and director of the VOC, mentions von Kniphausen's intention to provide additional information on the Bahrain project to show how attractive it would be to conquer the island. Van der Hulst would make a trip to Qatif, visiting en passant Bahrain, to collect this information.[7] Since in the Bahrain proposal information on the political and military situation in the Persian Gulf is limited to two short sentences and the fact that this report does not deal with Bahrain itself, but states that as to Bahrain "of which we have spoken on another occasion," which in my view is a reference to the Bahrain proposal, convinces me of the correctness of the above analysis. The above facts also have led me to the conclusion that the report has been written by Tido von Kniphausen and Jan van der Hulst in the first half of 1756.

Description of the littoral of the Persian Gulf and its inhabitants addressed,
To His Excellency His Honor and Widely Commanding Gentleman Mr. Jacob Mossel, General of the Infantry of the High Commanding Lords, the States-General of the United Netherlands as well as on their behalf and of the General Patented East Indies Company, Governor-General of the Dutch Indies.

Most noble, respected and widely commanding Lordship,
It is quite well known to everybody that the northern part of this Gulf is under the jurisdiction of the Persian kingdom and that the southern part is inhabited by the Arabs. However, because since ancient times the Persians did not have the least disposition or inclination towards navigation we find that all those places of the northern littoral, which, be it because of their natural situation, be it because of a brook or small river that runs into the sea, are capable of receiving vessels, are inhabited by Arab colonies. These live from navigation, pearl diving or fishing. All that they earn from this, which is not needed for their subsistence, these people spend on vessels, which are very expensive, because of the scarcity of wood in this Gulf.

A good broad-sword and shield, which they know how to handle very well and skillfully and a fuse match-lock, which they know how to shoot passably accurately at a short distance, are in

4 VOC 2885, Khark to Batavia (05/08/1756), f. 17 and chapter three in this publication.

5 Amin, *British Interests*, p. 29 and chapter three in this publication.

6 VOC Khark to Batavia (01/11/1754), f. 9.

7 VOC 2864, van der Hulst (Khark) to Jan Calkoen (Amsterdam) (08/01/1756), f. 4 (my numbering).

general all that they possess. For the rest they live poorly with tammer,[8] salt, and barley bread. Their settlements and houses are also miserable. They consider that the arid and infertile soil that they inhabit is not worth better [dwellings]. This is not a bad policy on their part, because having to loose nothing ashore they are able to leave their settlements as soon as the Persian nobles and officials are bothering them with [tax] quotas and other royal servitudes. They, accompanied only by their wives and children, get into their boats and go to the nearest islands until the time they think they may live in peace again in their previous settlements.[9]

Nadier Scha[10] who was the first among all of the Persian kings to have the courage to undertake to keep a fleet,[11] to which end he bought ships for large sums in Souratha[12] and Bombaij[13] and which were brought here by Moorish Indian sailors, had the intention to employ this [Arab] nation to serve in his fleet. However, because these differ from the Persian in particular in customs, nature and religion and even feel an innate hatred towards them he was never able to succeed. Te orders given to them were either badly executed or not at all and the confusion became at last such that the Arabs killed the nobleman who as Deria-Begie[14] or Admiral commanded the fleet, seized his ship and went with it to the Arabs on the opposite coast. Nadier Scha seeing that his hopes were deceived and that he would never be able to induce these peoples to complete obedience and loyal service to him at sea, decided on a project which nobody else but such a similar exceptional Prince, who liked all seemingly impossible exploits, would have dared to undertake, viz. to transplant all Arabs who lived on the Persian littoral and to bring them with wife and children to the shores of the Caspian Sea to serve there on a fleet against the Russians. On the other hand the people who lived on the Caspian Sea, who always preferred the Russians to the Persians, would be brought hither. Nadier Scha's death has foiled this plan, which may serve as a notion of his great spirit.[15]

As improbable as it is that Persia will be governed again by such a king for many centuries to come, as little hope there is also to see ever again a Persian fleet in this Gulf. Of those ships that Nadier Scha had built at such large expense two are still left, which float above water. However, they are in such bad condition that they cannot be repaired anymore. The ship that was lying at Bender Riek and which was also one of the best sank last year and is irreparable.[16]

Because we now live on an island here we have to deal mostly with the inhabitants of the littoral and have to associate with them daily I have considered it necessary to collect most precise information about them and hope to be able to give a complete idea about them.

---

8 *Thamr* or dates are meant.

9 Pedro Teixeira, *The Travels* (London, 1902), p. 190, reports that in medieval times the Hormuzis would thumb their nose at their enemies on the mainland, when fleeing to Hormuz Island, while singing: *del-e doshman bar man kebab ast – keh gerdagerd-e man ab ast*, meaning "the enemy is heart-broken [literally: barbecued] over me, for I'm surrounded by the sea," because the enemy on the mainland could not pursue them, having no boats.

10 Nader Shah (r. 1736-1747). For his life and activities see Lockhart, *Nadir Shah* and Axworthy, *The Sword of Persia*.

11 For a detailed discussion of this fleet-building effort see Floor, "Iranian Navy" or chapter one.

12 Surat, a port in Gujarat (India).

13 Bombay, a port in Gujarat (India), now called Mumbai.

14 *Darya-beygi* or admiral, a term introduced during Nader Shah's reign.

15 See also Lockhart, *Nadir Shah*, pp. 78-79, 221-22.

16 The authors of the report clearly only refer to that part of the royal fleet that was stationed in the head of the Persian Gulf and ignored that part which was stationed at Bandar 'Abbas (see chapter three).

The Persian Gulf begins at Cape Ras al Gatte[17] on the left and the shore of India on the other side. In order to speak with some order about it we will start at the said right hand side and then will go around the shores of the sea to end again with Cape Ras al Gatte, which the Arabs call Ras-el-Het.

Gouader[18] is considered to be the first sea town in the Gulf on the Northern coast, where the inhabitants are a caste of Arabs called Bloesch,[19] who are governed by a Sjeek Noer Mahomet.[20] He is, however, dependent on the Aguanen[21] in Calaat[22] and pays them tribute. This caste is very populous; they posses a fairly large number of vessels with which they sail to the coast of India as far as Mallebaar[23] and back again to Muscatte.[24] Each year 10 to 12 of their vessels come into the Gulf here and to Bassora[25] with rice and coarse Indian pound goods, while they return with wheat and tammer. They are a peaceful nation and carry broadswords, shields and lances and only a few match-locks or none at all.

The said Bloesch occupy an area as far as Tjalach,[26] called Cape Jasques[27] on our maps, behind which the Persian coast begins at Minauw.[28] Its inhabitants live from agriculture and not from navigation (having only a few flat-bottomed vessels). Moreover, as they are all Persian subjects one cannot count them among the navigators of this Gulf. Gamron or Bender-Abassi[29] as well as the islands of Lareek[30] and Ormus[31] we will pass by, since these have been known to us for many years as well as the small island of Zirri,[32] which is only inhabited by some able-bodied fishers and is known because of the tomb of a so-called Moslem holy man.[33] The Persian littoral reaches from Gamron

---

17 Ra's al-Hadd, which marks the entrance of the Gulf of Oman.

18 Gwadar, a port in Makran (Pakistan).

19 Baluch; in Arabic the name is Balush (plural) and Balushi (singular). In the Persian Gulf this term was used to designate those whose mother tongue was the Baluchi language.

20 Sheikh Nur Mohammad.

21 The Khans of Kalat, were Afghans (Aguanen), or rather Pathans, who were the leading clan of the Brahui Kambarani tribe.

22 Kalat or Qalat, located in the center of Baluchistan (Pakistan). In the mid-eighteenth century it was the capital of a state ruled by Brahui khans of the Ahmadzai dynasty, upon whom Nader Shah bestowed the title *beygler-beygi* (governor-general).

23 The Mallabar coast in West India is meant. Regular trade relations existed between Masqat and Mallabar, while Baluchis where used as sailors by the Omanis. See Willem Floor, "A Description of Masqat and Oman anno 1673/1084 H," *Moyen Orient & Océan Indien*, vol. 2 (1985), pp. 1-69 and Slot, *'Arab al-Khalij*, p. 358.

24 Masqat or Muscat, capital of Oman.

25 Basra.

26 I have been unable to identify this term. Probably Galaq, a location south-east of Jask is meant.

27 Cape Jask, 6 miles from the port of Jask in Makran (Iran), near the entrance of the Persian Gulf.

28 Minab or Minaw, a town nearly 50 miles east of Bandar 'Abbas.

29 Bandar 'Abbas (Gamron, Gombroon). For a history of this port see Floor, *The Persian Gulf*, pp. 237-322 (for the period until 1720); Ibid., *The Afghan Occupation*, pp. 63-80, 205-232, 307-72 (for the period between 1720 and 1730); Ibid., *Hokumat-e Nader Shah* (Tehran, 1368/1989), pp. 121-229 (for the period between 1730 and 1747).

30 Larak, an island 20 miles south by east from Bandar 'Abbas.

31 Hormuz, an island 11 miles east-south-east from Bandar 'Abbas. For its history see Willem Floor, "Hormuz", *Encyclopedia Iranica* and Ibid., *Persian Gulf*, pp. 7-88, 191-235.

32 Sirri, an island near the island of Kish.

33 I have been unable to find any other reference to this tomb, although a mosque "or white pagoda" was mentioned to be located on the island in the nineteenth century. James Horsburgh, *India Directory or Directions for*

and the island of Kismis[34] as far as Cape Verdistan.[35] All places that are fit for harboring vessels are inhabited by a caste of Arabs who are referred to by the general name of Houlas.[36] These are 400 big and small vessels strong, which are manned by 10 to 50 men. They are able to muster up to 6,000 sea-going men, of which one counts 3,000 to be armed with match-locks. The largest of their vessels carry 2 to 4 cannons of 2 to 3 pounds; the smaller ones are cannons of 1 to ½ pound of iron. They are fairly courageous and an enterprising people and would not yield to an equal number of Europeans with the broad-sword. However, with a gun they cannot do anything against us, [because] they can handle them very slowly.

This caste would be very powerful in the Gulf if two defects did not weaken them in particular. The first one is the disagreement about who governs them, and the second is the poverty of their chiefs or sjeeks,[37] who are never able to provide their people with food and ammunition for a long time. They also hardly ever are able to induce them to sea and if they have been able to do so they cannot keep them together. For as soon as something is lacking, which frequently happens, each of them leaves their sjeek to seek his livelihood with fishing, diving, or with the freight-trade.

The first place away from Gamron that is inhabited by the Houlas is Lenge[38] (near the of old famous, but now totally ruined Bender Lenge, which the Portuguese once possessed.[39] It is situated outside [the area referred to by] the general name of Houlas. The inhabitants of Lenge are called Mersousies.[40] They are 50 large and small vessels and 700 men strong, of which 350 are armed with match-locks. They are poor and live from [the sale of] firewood and charcoal, which is plentiful near them and which they transport throughout the Gulf. Their present chief is called Sjeek Saijd[41]; he keeps good friendship with us.

The islands of Troer,[42] Tombo[43] and Nabiau,[44] which are not inhabited belong to these Mersoekis and serve them as a refuge during bad times.

Following the coast from Lenge one comes to Tjarek,[45] which is inhabited by a caste of the often-mentioned Houlas, who one calls Ali.[46] They are also master of a pleasant fertile island that is lying thereabouts near the coast and on which still stand the outer walls of an old Portuguese

---

Sailing to and from the East Indies 4th edition (London, 1836), p. 340.

34 Qeshm or Kishm Island, 15 miles from Bandar 'Abbas. For detailed information on the island, including its history see Hoseyn Nurbakhsh, *Jazireh-ye Qeshm va Khalij-e Fars* (Tehran, 1369/1990).

35 Cape Bardistan.

36 Holi (singular) and Huwala or Hula (plural), a group of migrant Sunni Arabs in the Persian Gulf, who came from Oman and settled on the Persian littoral.

37 Sheikhs are meant.

38 Lengeh, a port about 96 miles west of Bandar 'Abbas. For a description of this port and its history see Nurbakhsh, *Bandar-e Lengeh*.

39 Here probably Bandar-e Kong is meant, which is situated at some four miles east of Lengeh. For its history see Floor, *The Persian Gulf*, chapter seven.

40 The Marzuqi Arabs are meant here, a branch of the Hula Arabs.

41 Sheikh Sa'id.

42 The island of Farur, situated at 20 miles south of Moghu.

43 Tonb Island, 17 miles south-east of Qeshm Island.

44 Nabiyu or Nabi Island or Little Tonb, 8 miles west of Tonb Island.

45 Charak, a small port situated at the bottom of the Bay of Charak.

46 A tribal group called Al 'Ali, see Sadid al-Saltaneh, *Bandar 'Abbas*, p. 617; Andrew S. Cook, *Survey of the Shores and islands of the Persian Gulf 1820-1829* 5 vols. (Gerrards Cross: Archive Editions, 1990), vol. 1, p. 190.

fortress.[47] This [island] is called on our maps Kesch and by the Arabs Geesch.[48] There are 60 vessels, both big and small, and 8 to 900 men strong, half of whom are at least armed with match-locks and broad-swords. This caste is considered to be the most courageous among the Houlas and they are almost always at war with one of the other [Houla groups]. Their chief is Sjeek Samra.[49] They live with us in very good friendship and they provide us throughout the year with firewood, which is to be found in plenty in Tjarek. Its transportation is almost their only livelihood. To this caste another one is subordinated, which has been very much weakened by wars. They are not more than 20 vessels and about 150 men strong. They live next to Tjarek in Mogo[50] on the island of Endrabo[51] and are governed by a certain Sjeek Achmet,[52] but they are completely dependent on the abovementioned [Charakis].

Continuing along the coast one finds Nechelon,[53] to which also belongs the island of Sjeek Schaib, on the maps Abou Schab[54] and the island of Sittuar.[55] Its inhabitants number more than 1,000 able-bodied men of whom more than half are armed and they are 60 vessels strong. They are governed by two sjeeks at the same time, [to wit] Mahometh Ebben Sent[56] and Racchma Eben Schain.[57] They live mostly from pearl diving, to which [and] we have taken 40 men into our service here as an experiment.

From the abovementioned place one arrives at Naband or Cape Nabon,[58] which includes an adjacent place Asselo[59] that is inhabited by the Harams.[60] For some time they have been the owners of the island of Babielm[61] until about three years ago, when Sjeek Nassier[62] of Boucheer[63] forced them to abandon it, which took place with great losses to both sides. Because of this these Harams are so weakened that they are estimated as not being stronger than 40 vessels and all in all 300 men. Of the two sjeeks who govern them, Mahometh Eben Maijd[64] and Abde Rachman[65] the first-mentioned has been treacherously murdered by the one of Thaarie,[66] which certainly will have

47 This fort has not been built by the Portuguese, see Floor, *The Persian Gulf*, p. 599.

48 Kish Island, near Charak.

49 Sheikh Shamra is probably meant here.

50 Moghu, a town 23 miles west of Lengeh. It is not situated on Henderabi Island.

51 Henderabi Island, 4 miles w.n.w. of Chiru.

52 Sheikh Ahmad.

53 Nakhilu, a town opposite Shatvar Island.

54 Sheikh Sho'eyb or Abu Sho'eyb Island at 10 miles from Nakhilu.

55 Shatvar island at one mile from Sho'eyb Island.

56 Mohammad b. Sand [?] is probably meant here.

57 Rahmah b. Shahin is probably meant here.

58 Ra's Naband at four miles south-west of 'Asalu. Naband town is situated at three to four miles from the Cape, on the north side of the bay.

59 'Asalu, a town nearly opposite to Cape Naband's low point at four miles' distance.

60 The Al Haram or Harami, a branch of the Hula Arabs.

61 Copyist's error for Bahrehn or the island of Bahrain. When the Al Haram controlled Bahrain there were some 300 trankis engaged in pearl fishing near the island. VOC 2705, Resolution Gamron, f. 340-42.

62 Sheikh Naser, for details about his career see chapter seven of this publication.

63 The port of Bushire, for its early history see chapter seven of this publication.

64 Mohammad b. Majid. ?

65 'Abdu'l-Rahman.

66 Taheri, the former famous port of Siraf, 20 miles south-east of Kangan. The sheikh of Taheri referred to is Sheikh Jabbareh.

possible consequences for the island of Bahrehn,[67] for (it is said) that the Sjeek of Sur[68] wants to revenge him.

Beyond Asselo further along the coast Tharie and Schielaw[69] are situated, which are inhabited by a caste of the Houlas called Nessour[70], who are reckoned to be 50 vessels and more than 900 men strong, of whom more than half are armed. Their chief, called Sjeek Chatum,[71] is the richest of all Houlas on this coast, which gives him some influence. However, he is hated by them because of his price and conceit. A Persian man-of-war that had run aground there has enabled him to build a gallivant, which is the cause of his power and influence as well as the fact that the chief of Bouchier pays him each year 14,000 rupees out of the revenues of Bahrehn in accordance with their agreement.

From here one arrives at Congon,[72] which is the last settlement of the Houlas. They are also called Nessour, although they are completely independent and apart from the abovementioned [Nessour]. They are reckoned to be 60 vessels and about 1,000 men strong as well as the most peaceful of the Houlas. Some Jews and Banyans[73] who live there come here to buy goods, do some business with upcountry [Persia] and start to make that place a bit flourishing to which end their chief Sjeeg Hutjer,[74] an old and peaceful man contributes his best [efforts].[75]

---

67 The island of Bahrain.

68 The Sheikh of the Qavasem is meant here, see below.

69 Shilaw, near Taheri. For its early role see Jean Aubin, "La survie de Shilau et la route du Khunj-o-Fal," *IRAN* 7 (1979), pp. 21-37.

70 The Nassuri clan, a branch of the Hula Arabs.

71 Sheikh Hatem is meant here; see for some of his activities chapter three in this publication.

72 Kangan, port at 20 miles north-west of Taheri. It had good anchorage (5-8 fathoms) and protection against north-westers.

73 Indian traders.

74 Sheikh Hajar. In 1756 a dispute had arisen with Sheikh Hajar about the salvage of the goods of two English ships, whose owners, being under EIC protection had complained to Bombay. "The owners of the *Pastorena* and the *Ali Rooka* had suffered considerably from the villainy of the Shaik at Congoone" Bombay concluded and ordered its Bandar 'Abbas factory to send the *Swallow* and the *Drake* to demand satisfaction from him. J. A. Saldanha, *The Persian Gulf Précis* 10 vols. (Gerards Cross: Archive Editions, 1986), vol. 1, p. 103 (Bombay, 17/07/1756). Francis Wood replied that the owners' complaint was not borne out by the facts, while militarily the operation did not look promising. "In regard to Shaik Haijar at Congoon, many of the freighters as well as the Commander and officers of the Pasterenia signed an agreement with him to share equally all that might be saved, so that what he has done bears in some degree an appearance of Justice, though I can't say that this is my Chiefest objection; but the village lies so straggling, and being extended along the Coast among date gardens as far in length as between Menelham's Point and Mallabar Hill, our cannonading it from the ships can give the inhabitants but very little annoyance it also ly's [sic] so near the mountains, that in case of landing, the Arabs can easily secure all their valuable Effects in less than half an hour's time, and after destroying a number of innocent People at the hazard of lossing [sic] many of our own, we should be obliged to return without any profitable satisfaction, leaving the Arabs so exasperated against us as to prove of very unhappy consequence to those of our nation who hereafter may chance to fall into their hands." Saldanha, *Précis*, vol. 1, p. 109 (in the Rig roads a/b the Swallow, 18/11/1756). Here the matter rested.

75 The people of Kangan still had a good reputation some 20 years later. In 1787, Plaisted went ashore at Kangan to visit the hot springs of Bardestan. Kangan "is a Village seated on the eastward of Cape Verdiston about four leagues: it is inhabited by Arabs, as most of the Villages are along this part of the Persian Coast. It was governed by a Sheik who seemed to be good sort of a Man, and treated us very politely: it appeared to have no Share in the common Calamities of the Country; for the Ground about it, though very stony, was every where sown with Wheat while the most fertile Soil in other Places lay barren and uncultivated. Here is likewise Plenty of Sheep. Congune stands on the South Side of a large River, and has a tolerable Trade, for most of the Pearl which is fished up at Bareen on the Arabian Side is brought hither to

Before I stop writing about the Houlas I will make some observations by which one may know them better.

These nations are Arabs, who are followers of the sect of Omar,[76] which makes that they feel a deadly hatred for the Persians, who are adherent of the sect of Ali.[77] Because they never mix with the Persians by marriage, but always marry within their caste, they always keep their own religion and customs. The most important thing to do to win their friendship is to treat them friendly and amiably. A sullen and proud face causes respect and awe among the Persians, but hatred and dislike among the Arabs.

The various chiefs of the Houlas are not only, as has been said above, independent from and always in disagreement with one another, but each chief is not at all [an] absolute and despotic [ruler] in his settlement and among his caste. They may not undertake anything without the cooperation and consent of the eldest and most prominent [men]. For the rest he does not collect any [tax] quota or contribution from his people, but lives from the profits of his vessels. The chief may even not demand toll on imports and exports in his settlement with the exception from foreigners. As soon as the caste is not satisfied with him, the chieftainship is conferred on another one of that family and he remains without any respect or authority.

Next to Congon, Cape Verdistan[78] protrudes into the sea. The beach there is inhabited by Persians, who live from agriculture and who own no vessels. They are a bad rapacious nation and therefore everybody is afraid to land there. On the other side of the Cape the situation is similar. Here two brooks, Choor Siarat[79] and Choor Chouer[80] and the bight of Helena[81] are inhabited by similar people, who live in the abovementioned manner and have no vessels at all.

At the end of the bight of Helena the fortress of Nadrie[82] is situated, which has been built by the Portuguese. After their retreat from the Gulf it has become dilapidated, but later on it has been occupied and repaired by the Persians. Thereafter it was abandoned again and because of the removal of the timber it has become a ruin now, so that nowadays nothing but the outer walls, which have been very well constructed, are still standing.

Boucheer is situated at 2 hours from the said fortress. It is also an Arab colony, not of the Houlas, but of a caste of Arabs who live above Mascatte and are called Abou Mehair.[83] The formation of a fleet by Nadir Scha and the residing of the admiral or Deria begi there (who was always a Persian duke[84]) has made this place flourishing. When after Nadier Scha's death the admiral did

be sold, and there are likewise many fine Horses exported from hence to be carried to India. You may anchor here at what Depth you may please, and it is four fathoms about a Quarter of a Mile distant from the Shore." Plaisted, *A Journal*, pp. 17-18.

76 Sunni Moslems are meant. Omar refers to 'Omar b. al-Khateb, the second caliph.

77 Shi'ite Moslems are meant. Ali refers to 'Ali b. Abu Taleb, the fourth caliph and the first Imam of the Shi'as, which is short for shi'at 'Ali or 'Ali's party.

78 Cape Bardestan was an alternative, be it an erroneous, name for a small projection forming the western rounding of Kangan Bay. The real Cape Bardestan is 8.5 leagues west of Kangan. For more information see Cook, *Survey*, vol. 1, pp. 182, 272.

79 Khur Ziyarat.

80 This probably is Khore Kwoire, a small creek, dry at the entrance at low water. Cook, *Survey*, vol. 1, pp. 179.

81 The bight of Halileh.

82 On this fort (Qal'eh-ye Naderiyeh), see chapter seven in this publication. It was not built by the Portuguese.

83 The Al Bu Moheyr tribe; for more information see chapter seven in this publication.

84 Europeans invariably referred to Persian officials with the title 'khan' as having the equivalent European title of 'duke,' because these khans mostly were provincial governors.

not receive [any] remittances for the pay and upkeep of the fleet he left Boucheer and the ships, gallivats and dingis remained lying there being abandoned by their captains and sailors. Sjeek Nassier[85] who has no less ambition than avarice thought first to profit from the remnants of its fleet to secure with them the island of Bahrehn. However, since he found that his own force was not sufficient, because at that time he could at the very maximum count not more than 400 armed men among his own people, he allied himself with Mier Nassier[86] who then at Bender Riek[87] could muster about 500 men armed men. Having manned 3 ships and 3 gallivats they then took the said island [of Bahrain] from the Harams with very small loss.

Mier Nassier succeeded to induce the chief of Boucheer with some pretexts first to return again to his town. Then, seeing that he (alone) was master of the island of Bahrehn he has never given the former anything from the revenues, not even willing to refund the cost that he had made for this exploit. This is one of the reasons for their deadly enmity.

In the meantime, Mier Nassier was obliged to keep the best and largest part of his people with him for the occupation of Bahrehn. The chief of Ghinova,[88] Kaijd Hedder[89] thought to make use of this [situation] to conquer Bender Riek. On receiving this information Mier Nassier was obliged to leave Bahrehn, arriving just in time to relieve his besieged town.

This made it possible for the Harams to take possession of Bahrehn again, in which [possession] they remained undisturbed for more than 2 years. Meanwhile, Sjeek Nassier was able to induce the Etoubies,[90] a caste of Arabs whom we shall mention hereunder, to assist him with the conquest of Bahrehn, having induced them to do so by having promised them that in such a case they would be allowed to dive on the [pearl] banks without having to pay the usual imposts. Because almost most of them are divers this was of no little importance to them.

Strengthened by this alliance Sjeek Nassier besieged the island of Bahrehn with 2 ships and 2 gallivats, but met with much more difficulties there than he had expected. For the Harams having been supported by some of the chiefs of the Houlas with men and by Molla Ali Schah[91] of Gamron with a gallivat defended themselves so well that they during an unexpected sortie from the castle surrounded 200 of Sjeek Nassier's men. These were massacred by them, although they had surrendered and put down their weapons.

After 6 months and the loss of ¾ of his force Sjeek Nassier not having been able to execute [his plan] was forced to promise to pay the chief of Tharie 14,000 rupees of the revenues of Bahrehn each year, with which he induced him to defect from the Harams and to support him. These seeing that they were weakened thereby surrendered to him and left the island. In this manner the chief of Boucheer became master of Bahrehn, where he has placed one of his brothers with 30 to 40 men, who receive a monthly pay from the islanders. For the rest, the island yields him less than one-quarter of the revenues that it yielded before that time. [For] the Etoubis did not pay the usual imposts for diving, in accordance with the agreement, while the Houlas also do not pay anything on account of the claim they pretend to have on the ownership of the entire island. Thus, only the people of Bahrain and Catieff remain from whom he collects these imposts.

85 Sheikh Naser of Bushire; for more information see chapter seven in this publication.

86 Mir Naser Vagha'i; for more information see chapter four in this publication.

87 Bandar-e Rig, a port 31 miles north-north-west of Bushire and situated opposite the island of Khark.

88 Ganaveh, a village 15 miles north of Rig.

89 Qa'ed Heydar; for more information see chapter four in this publication.

90 The 'Otobi or 'Otob Arabs; for more information see Hakimah, *History*.

91 Molla 'Ali Shah, governor of Bandar 'Abbas. For more information see chapter three in this publication.

What is more, the pearl divers both from the Etoubis and the Houlas, who dive during a 4-months' stay within the sight of the island, come ashore daily and ruin all the tamer bearing trees and gardens that stand near the beach so that their owners get nothing thereof and cannot pay their duties. They [therefore] abandon their land and flee to Catieff, Bassora or [somewhere] en route. Sjeek Nassier is unable to prevent this marauding, because they are partly done by his allies and partly by the Houlas, whom he has to respect. Moreover, he has no force or vessel there that strikes fear into [the heart of] these nations.

At Boucheer at present lie all remaining ships of the fleet, either sunk or capsized with the exception of one, which is bailed out every 2 to 3 days. Their pumps are not functioning anymore, while there is nobody capable to repair them. For the rest their state is so bad and they are so badly equipped that it has been impossible for them to put them ever to sea again. There is only one gallivat remaining that could be put to sea again as well as 2 dingis, which lack a deck, however. These can only be used for lading. Although almost 400 cannons, metal and iron, are [lying about] in Boucheer (half of which are lying under the sand) there, not even 10 of them, however, have a proper and sound carriage. The problem, however, of the lack of vessels and ammunition with them all is the least with Sjeek Nassier. He above all lacks people, for [because of] all of those of his caste who have died on Bahrehn, those who are dispersed here and there, and those who have gone to other places one cannot find even 12 vessels and 70 able-bodied seafaring men anymore. The town is passably well filled with Persian merchants, retailers and craftsmen, although not all of them are able-bodied and even less fit to be used at sea.

To obtain the favor of the Persian nobles who formerly were with the fleet that was at Boucheer the said Sjeek Nassier had then decided to become a follower of the sect of Alij or of the religion of the Persians. This has made him very much hated among the Arabs. For the rest Boucheer is one of the best ports in this Gulf. A ship drawing 12 to 13 feet of water can easily be brought completely as far as the houses at high tide.

Between Boucheer and Bender-Riek a small river runs into the sea (behind a tongue of low-land) called Schat Ebeni Temin,[92] on which the town of Bohilla[93] is situated, which Mier Nassier had made subject to him, but which is now again independent from Bender Riek. There at least 2 to 300 families, both Arabs and Persians, are living from agriculture, who do not own vessels. From there one reaches Bender Riek, which is also an Arab colony of a caste called Saabs,[94] who inhabit half an island that is situated at Cape Mousandan[95] and which is called the Red Island.[96] This town does not have such a good harbor as Boucheer. Ships have to remain lying in the roadstead, which is passably well. However, a small long island that is lying precisely in front of the town causes that one may only bring a few ships there, for on the banks that lie between the said island and the coast there is only 7 to 8 feet of water above them when there is high tide.

About 100 years ago there was a very large number of vessels and sea-faring people in Bender Riek. At about that time the inhabitants of Kareek who ever since the departure of the Portuguese

92 Shatt Bani Tamim, a creek called after Arabs who are living there and who claim to be Bani Tamin Arabs. The river itself is called Rud Hilleh.

93 Rud Hilleh, a district west of Bushire.

94 A clan of Arabs called Za'ab, Zu'abi. See Ernst Beer ed. *Das Tarikh-i Zendije des Ibn 'Abd al Kerim Ali Riza von Shiraz* (Leiden, 1888), p. xvii; Abu'l-Hasan Ghaffari Kashani, *Golshan-e Morad* ed. Gholamreza Tabataba'i (Tehran, 1369/1990), p. 275. According to Perry, "Mir Muhanna," p. 84, they were the Banu Sa'b.

95 Ra's Musandam, which the Arabs call Ru'us al-Jibal or 'Cluster of Peaks.'

96 Jazirat al-Hamrah, also called Jazirat al-Za'ab at 12 miles from Umm al-Quwayn.

have always been independent put themselves under the protection of Mier Hamad,[97] who ruled there and they promised him an annual sum of 240 rupees on the condition that he would accept them and would protect them against the marauding of the sea-faring Arabs. The first part of such an agreement the chiefs of Bender Riek have complied with only too well, but the other [part] very badly. The poor inhabitants have since then till our arrival here [in 1753] always been exposed to the outrages of the daily passing trankeys. They are now very happy to see that they have gotten rid of them. After the death of the said Mier Hamad Bender Riek has declined very much because of the murders and wards of those who had to succeed him and who [fought] each other. Until finally Mier Nassier came to power, when because of his good policy, strict authority over his caste, his friendliness and generosity towards all merchants and foreigners the town started flourishing again. Now, a short time after his death, Bender Riek has reverted to its old state again and it appears to go towards its total ruin.

The ship of the said Nadier Scha's fleet that was still lying at Bendier Riek and whose hull was still complete and in good condition two years ago has sunk during this winter. It remains lying there; the topmasts, yards, sails and ropes have all perished. There are still two gallivats in passable condition, but these will very soon become unusable due to neglect. Apart from that there are there about 30 both big and small vessels and about 300 sea-faring able-bodied men.

Mier Nassier's father had already become a follower of the religion of the Persians and as his descendant had married into the [families of] the Persian chiefs who live upcountry, one may not consider as belonging to the Arabs anymore.

Above Bender-Riek, Ghinova is situated in a bay at a stream that is not very fit to harbor vessels. It is inhabited by Persians who live from agriculture. They are a very unreliable and rapacious nation. Their chief is Kaijd Hedder who governs his people very despotically and he seeks tom profit from the decline of Bender-Riek by attracting the sea-faring people to his town. He and his nation are completely ignorant in these matters. He is also busy buying vessels and making the stream at which this town is situated more fitting to harbor vessels. He does everything in his power to attract native merchants to come to his town. Whether he will continue to do so and whether he will succeed time will have to tell. Among his people one counts 300 men, who, in the native manner, are very well equipped with match-locks, and are very much inclined to marauding and pillaging of which they have given proof enough on the coast thereabouts.

The bay of Ghinova ends with the protruding edge of Bang,[98] behind which one finds Bender-Delam,[99] which again is an Arab colony of a caste called Chaleijfat.[100] These continue to follow their old religion and customs. For the rest they are poor and live from navigation, pearl diving and fishing. Their town would not be so bad for trading since it is situated at only one day's journey from Beh-Bahn,[101] a fairly wealthy Persian town, from where the road to Isfahan is almost always passable. However, every merchant fears to come to Bender-Delam, because the common people there are much given to stealing from foreigners and molesting them, due to the fact that they are poor, while one will obtain no justice. In this town there are several chiefs, who are each independent from the others and are always living in disagreement and often are warring against

97 Mir Hamad, no particulars are known about him.

98 Kuh-e Bang of Cape Bang, near Ra's al-Tanb, which is about two leagues from Deylam.

99 Bandar Deylam, a port 85 miles west of Bushire. For details on the town and region of Deylam see 'Alireza Khalifehzadeh, *Bandar Deylam va haft shahr-e Liravi* (Bushire, 1382/2003).

100 The Al Khalifeh or Khalifat came to this area towards the end of the 17th century, see Floor, *The Persian Gulf*, p. 295, 585.

101 Behbahan, a town in Kuhgiluyeh province.

one another. At present there are three Sjeeks at Bender-Delam. The first one Ganum[102] is poor, although very popular among the population, because he allows everybody to be robbed and molested both merchants and foreigners, according to his pleasure. The second one is Sjeek Taan,[103] who is rich and a sensible man, who trades himself. He therefore tries to attract merchants by all ways and means and to prevent them from being treated badly, which makes him hated amongst the common people. The third one is Sjeek Hamet,[104] who is poor and has little influence in this town. At Delam 40 vessels, both small and large, are counted and more than 400 armed sea-faring men. This is the last town on this side of the Gulf where one finds navigation. Coming from Delam one arrives at Indian, where a fairly large but shallow river, which is overgrown with reed, runs into the sea.

Indian[105] is inhabited by a caste of bastard Arabs who are called Goragie[106] and who live from agriculture (however, for the greater part from cattle-raising). The land there begins to become very fertile. They are governed by Molla Ter Jalla,[107] who commands 50 horsemen and more than 200 footmen with matchlocks. For the rest they have neither vessels nor navigation.

From here, having passed Bender-Maskour[108] (where a few years ago robbers were staying who went marauding with small vessels up the river of Bassora, but who have now been completely exterminated), one reaches the river Dourat,[109] which runs into the sea very close to the river Euphrates. Although the former does not give way in depth, but only in width, there is no navigation there apart from 3 to 4 inferior vessels, which do not come farther than here or as far as Boucheer and which provide us with rice and butter that is to be found in abundance there. Dourak,[110] although governed by its own sjeek, depends on the government of Bassora and has to pay tribute to the latter.

Having arrived now at the mouth of the Euphrates we have to make mention of Bassora of whose navigation nothing very special may be told. The so-called galleys of the Porte do not dare to do anything and to come to the mouth of the Euphrates where it is a bit wide, for they then surely will fall apart because of the devil's water. They therefore serve no other purpose than nominally extorting taxes from the peasants in the river. Sometimes they are even incapable of doing that. From the mouth of the Euphrates as far as Bassora almost everywhere sea-faring people live, who transport tamer with their vessels throughout the Gulf as far as Mocha.[111] They are all, however, not able-bodied and have no match-locks, while they are also badly equipped with masts, yards, sails and rigging so that this serves as an indication by which one recognizes from afar a Bassora vessel. Leaving the Euphrates and keeping to the Arab coast one finds the island of Feltscha[112] and

102 Sheikh Ghannam.

103 I have been unable to identify this sheikh or his name.

104 Probably Sheikh Hamid is meant.

105 Hindiyan, a small port in Khuzestan. For a description see Floor, "The Rise and Fall," p. 304.

106 I have been unable to identify this clan of Arabs. Around the turn of the 20th century a small group of people called Gurgis were to be found at Hindiyan, who may have been the descendants of these Goragie.

107 I have been unable to identify this chief or his name; maybe Molla Yar Allah.

108 Bandar-e Mash'ur, a small port in Khuzestan.

109 The Khur Dowraq is a branch of the Khur Musa, an inlet of the sea east of the Shatt al-Arab and here probably the entrance to the river that leads to Dowraq.

110 Dowraq or Fallahiyeh was the capital of the Banu Ka'b. For a description of this town and a discussion of the Banu Ka'b see Floor, "The Rise and Fall," pp. 277-315.

111 Mokha, a port in Yemen, situated on the coast of the Red Sea.

112 Failak Island, from the local pronunciation, which is Failachah. It is situated on the north side of the entrance of Kuwait Bay.

opposite to it on the coast Grien.[113] Both are inhabited by a caste of Arabs called Etoubis of which we have spoken above. These are dependent on the Sjeek of the Desert[114] to whom they pay tribute, although very little. They possess about 300 vessels, most of which are small, which they only use for pearl-diving; this, apart from fishing in the bad monsoon, is their only means of livelihood. They are about 4,000 men strong, almost all of them are armed with broad-swords, shields, and lances, but hardly at all equipped with match-locks, which they do not even know how to handle.

This nation is almost always in dispute with the Houlas, who are their mortal enemies. Because of this reason as well as because of the small size of their vessels their navigation does not reach farther than to the pearl banks of Bahrehn on the one side and on the other side as far as Cape Verdistan.[115] Several different sjeeks govern them, who, however, live together in reasonable unity. The most important of them is Mobarek Eben Saback.[116] However, while he is poor and still young another one, Mahometh Eben Chalifa,[117] is rich and owns many vessels and is as such much respected by them.

Above Green one finds the ruins of a fortress which has been built by the Portuguese in former times, and further [one finds] no inhabited place until Catif.[118] The country is an arid desert. In the sea beyond sight from the shore 6 small uninhabited islands or shoals are situated, which are not shown on European maps.

Formerly Catif also was possessed by the Portuguese, of which the castle is still standing and rather well preserved. Nowadays it is only a well-constructed town, in the fashion of the natives, where the first purchase of the pearls takes place directly from the divers' hands. The merchants and the wealthiest inhabitants of Bahrehn have all gone there, which is 5 [German] miles[119] away, after the decline of the said island. Apart from the purchase of pearls there is also some trade in piece and pound goods in Catif, which are transported from there into the desert and to two towns that are situated in it, Neschde[120] and Lassa.[121]

The Sjeek of the Desert is the ruler of this town, who appoint one of the most prominent inhabitants as his deputy and allows him to live in the castle and who maintains a *vakil* or agent there for the collection of his duties and tolls. The inhabitants of Catif are like those of Bahrehn followers of the sect of Alij. They are also a defenseless and a timid people. Some of them are pearl divers, while the remainder lives from agriculture. The land around the town is very fertile. The town is a very unhealthy place, especially in spring and fall, when no foreigner who is not accustomed to the air will be free from fever. The sea-faring Arabs commit many outrages there. Apart from visiting at all occasions the tamer and fruit trees often one sjeek or another comes with 3 to 4 trankeys to blockade the stream at which Catif is situated on the basis of some frivolous pretext. There is no other remedy for these poor people than to settle the matter by payment of a few thousand rupees.

113 Qurain, the diminutive of *qarn* (a horn or hill), which is another name for Kuwait.

114 The chief of the Banu Khalid tribe is meant here, with whose permission the 'Otobis settled in Kuwait in the early 18th century.

115 This location most likely refers to Kangan (see above) and not the real Cape Bardestan.

116 Mobarak b. Sabah.

117 Mohammad b. Khalifeh.

118 Qatif, principle town of Qatif oasis, some 26 miles north-west of Bahrain. For its relationship with the Portuguese see Floor, *The Persian Gulf*, pp. 108, 159, 174-75, 550.

119 One German mile is equal to 7.4 km.

120 Nejd or Central Arabia is meant here.

121 Al-Hasa or al-Ahsa is meant here.

Passing Bahrehn of which we have spoken on another occasion we will only say that the pearl banks reach as far as Cape Moussand until Zur.[122] Between Catif and Zur there are situated on the shore Asseer,[123] Guhar,[124] and Scharge,[125] another three towns. Each of them consists only of some houses, where tamer and rice is brought from Bassora to be sold to the Arabs of the desert or to the pearl divers.

Sur is a rather well constructed town, in the native fashion, and it has some pieces of cannon. It is inhabited by [a group of people] whom the Houlas call the Guassum.[126] It has been dependent on the Imam of Mascatte in former times, but it does not acknowledge him anymore. The few campaigns mounted by the said Imam to subjugate the town again have all been in vain. [However,] he cannot do anything against the Sjeek of the Guassum, called Tschaid[127] or Rachma Eben Matter,[128] who is supported by several casts of Bedouins or Arabs from the desert.

A large piece of land, which protrudes into the sea near Zur and which becomes an island at high tide and therefore is called the Red Island by the Arabs is inhabited by a caste who carry the name of Saabs, who live from pearl diving. They are numerous and have many small vessels. They have to obey the Sjeek of the Guassums and have to pay him no small contribution. Last year the abovementioned Sjeek Rachma had with the assistance of the admiral of Gamron, Molla Ali Scha, to whom he is related by marriage, conquered Laft[129] and the island of Kismis. He expelled from there a caste of Houlas named Ebenu Temin,[130] who had been in possession thereof since the government of Nadier Scha. The siege of Laft, in which there were less then 250 men, lasted 6 months, despite the two ships of Molla Ali Scha[131] and all the might of Sjeek Rachma, who had brought a party of Bedouins with him to support his force. It possibly would not have surrendered, but for the accidental death of Abdij Sjeek[132] who governed there.

Coming from Sur and Cape Mousondon one enters the land of the Imam of Mascatta, who formerly was very wealthy and powerful. However, due to the bad conduct of his ancestor he has

---

122 This must be Jolfar, a town that is now known as Ra's al-Khaymah. Niebuhr's map shows at the location where Zur must have been a town called Seer.

123 Probably al-Sirr is meant here or al-Sirr of Oman as the Arabs call the coast.

124 I have been unable to identify this place, unless al-Ghuwar, a tract lying west of al-Hasa is meant.

125 Sharjah.

126 The Qavasem or Jawasem Arabs; see further chapter three and seven.

127 This name has caused some confusion as he seems to be the same person as Sheikh Rahma b. Matar. Slot has suggested that the name Tchaid (Chaueed) is a sobriquet, although he also points out that in 1729 the Dutch mention a Sheikh Saved son of Rahma, in which case the name might also be explained as Abu Tchaid (Saved), although, in my view, this is less likely. VOC 2152, f. 7707-vs.; Slot, *'Arab al-Khalij*, p. 323.

128 Rahmah b. Matar; see for more about him chapter three.

129 Laft is a small port-village on the island of Qeshm.

130 These seem to be the Bani Tamim Arabs, but, as is clear from chapter three in this publication, the term was also used to denote the Banu Ma'in. In English documents they are referred to as Benimine. Saldanha, *Précis*, vol. 1, p. 136 (Bombay, 15/04/1760) The Bani Tamim were also mentioned earlier as living in the Rud Hilleh district. However, this relationship is a spurious one, in my view, for one may not suggest that they came from that part of the Gulf, despite the fact that it is sometimes mentioned that the Banu Ma'in had originated from Carack (possibly referring to Khark), which is adjacent to that area, for Charak instead of Khark is meant here. Saldanha, *Précis*, vol. 1, pp. 139-40 (Bombay, 14/10/1760).

131 In 1758, Molla 'Ali Shah had "three ships of war lying at the former [Hormuz], but they are in no condition to put to sea." Ives, *Voyage*, p. 202.

132 'Abdol-Sheikh, chief of the Banu Ma'in, see chapter three in this publication for more information on this person and the siege.

been very much weakened. His excesses and bad government made his subjects rebel against him. Being besieged by them in Mascatte, he left 400 of his African slaves as a garrison of the castle there and with the remainder he went on the biggest of his ships to Gamron to enlist the Persian fleet's help against his subjects. The admiral Taki-Chan[133] availed himself of this opportunity so well that he destroyed the most important towns that belonged to the Imam and seized a lot of spoils from the country and remained in possession of Mascatte. In the meantime the Imam died of heart-ache and when a few years later Nadier Scha also died the Persian abandoned the said town again. The now reigning Imam[134] was during the lifetime of his predecessor his deputy at Zoar.[135] Due to his intelligence and good nature he has made himself so loved that he has acted in the place of the former Imam to the detriment of the sons of the latter who are still alive at present. He maintains himself throughout with a particular gentleness, but for the same reason he is obeyed badly and even less feared. In the meantime the whole of Amaan,[136] which extends from Cape Mousondon as far as Cape Ras al Gatte acknowledges him. Within it one counts a large number of villages that are all inhabited by fishermen and sea-faring people. Apart from Mascatte it has no towns worth mentioning with the exception of Soar, Mattra,[137] and Bertsch[138] where some wealthy people live.

Mascatte is rather well known to Europeans. It is located at the beginning of the Gulf and is very well situated for the sale of goods. The native vessels from this Gulf bring here tammer, wheat, liquorice, rosewater, raisins, almonds, tobacco and similar coarse goods, which are brought by native vessels from the opposite coast and [from] Mallabaar, to wit Kitscheri,[139] rice, coconuts, kapok-wool, bamboos, etc. The main trade of Mascatte is the sale of these goods. Into the country itself, which is inhabited by Bedouins or Arabs who live under tents almost no other goods are carried than the necessities of life, apart from a little lead, tin, iron and coarse, rough brown blue linen such as that from Devil.[140] In the meantime if the merchants, who are very well informed about the prices of goods in the Gulf, see a good profit they also buy all sorts of other goods and carry these into the Gulf up to Bassora. However, they will buy none other than those with which they see a chance to make a profit of 25 per cent.

The Imam of Mascatte still possesses the fortress on Bombassa on the African coast, which they conquered from the Portuguese in the past to which each year his ships carry tammer, wheat and coarse textiles and in return again with coconuts, hair,[141] elephant teeth, slaves and amber. Due to the abovementioned reason the deputy of Bombassa[142] only sends very little of his revenues and obeys him even less so,

The Imam's navy consists of two small ships nowadays, one of which is unusable. This he made good by the purchase of a beautiful new ship of 600 tons in Bombaij. In addition he has an-

133 Mohammad Taqi Khan Shirazi. On these events see Lockhart, *Nadir Shah*, pp. 182-83, 216-17.

134 Ahmad b. Sa'id, founder of the Al Bu Sa'id dynasty.

135 Sohar, port in Oman.

136 Oman.

137 Matrah, town at 2 miles west of Masqat.

138 Barkah, town 43 miles west of Masqat. The authors gave the local pronunciation of the town's name.

139 Kedgeree or Kitchery, a sort of rice and pulse mixed together.

140 Diul-Sind or Dewal, etc. was the name by which the major port of Sind was known. For a discussion of the name and the location of the port see Monique Kervran, "Le port multiple des bouches de l'Indus: Barbariké, Dēb, Daybul, Lāhore Bandar, Diul Sinde," in Rika Gyselen ed., *Sites et monuments disparus d'après les témoignages de voyageurs* (Paris, 1996), pp. 45-92.

141 With hair probably [coconut] coir is meant.

142 Mombassa in Kenya is meant here.

other two gallivats. Because the Imam's subjects have the reputation of being bad soldiers his army consists of nothing but Caffers[143] or African slaves from Bombassa, whose inhabitants are very capable at [waging] war. Formerly the Imams had 4,000 of them, but the present one has not been able to collect more than 500 of them, all of whom are equipped with matchlocks and straight swords, which they know to handle well and in this his whole might consists.

143 The Dutch referred to the Bantu tribes of Southern Africa as 'Caffers', a word derived from the Arabic word *kafir* or unbeliever.

CHAPTER THREE
The Decline of Bandar 'Abbas 1747-1763

The End of an Era

In this chapter I discuss the decline of Bandar 'Abbas as a major port of international trade and the political and other events that led to that situation, resulting in the departure of the Dutch in 1759 and of the English in 1763 as well as of the gradual departure of Asian merchants between 1755 and 1763. I describe the difficult national and local context in which both native and foreign merchants had to operate, a context that also highlights the increased activities of the Arab speaking inhabitants of the littoral. On the commercial side it is clear that the abandonment of Bandar 'Abbas was but a logical and long overdue step, the consequence of the changed political and economic situation in Persia and in the Persian Gulf. Politically, the mid-eighteenth century saw many changes in the Persian Gulf, not so much of a structural nature, but rather a shift in the relative importance of the various players and locations against the background of a worsening economic situation and growing insecurity in the countries adjacent to the Gulf. One of these locations was the port of Bandar 'Abbas, called Gamron in Dutch and Gombroon in English sources. It had been the major port for international trade on the Persian littoral since the 1620s. The English had settled there in 1622 and the Dutch in 1623. The relative stability of the political situation under the Safavids (although there had also been occasional problems with the local authorities) was transformed into one of total insecurity and no trade under the Afghan occupation (1722-1729), while Nader Shah's reign (r. 1736-1747) failed to re-establish conditions that would have allowed trade to return to its previous level. Instead, arbitrary rule and oppression increased resulting in a shrinking market due to high mortality among the population and a fall of purchasing power. There was a lot of military activity in the Bandar 'Abbas area due to the Masqat invasion of 1737, which resulted in troop, food, and ship movements and the pressing of European vessels into royal service. As a consequence, trade, at least for the European Companies, was a money-losing business, who, in the hope for better, still held on to their factory in Bandar 'Abbas. They finally left Bandar 'Abbas when the political and the commercial situation made it impossible for them to remain there thereby reducing Bandar 'Abbas to a minor port with a local distributive function.

The main events of this period, which are emblematic for other parts of the Persian Gulf as well, concern the conflict between two main protagonists, Molla 'Ali Shah, the deputy-governor of Bandar 'Abbas and admiral of the royal fleet and Nasir Khan, governor of Lar and Bandar 'Abbas. This and other similar conflicts in Fars and elsewhere in Persia was one of the main reasons why the country remained in an economic slump, which incited the various office holders to try and extract more from a dwindling resource base. For although this conflict was between persons, the fight was not personal, it was about power and money. After the death of Nader Shah many local and regional chiefs wanted to have a greater share of the economic pie and wanted to be independent. Nasir Khan of Lar, who clawed his way up to the governorship of Lar in 1748, was not willing to submit to Karim Khan, who was one of major contenders for the vacated throne. As long as Karim Khan's position continued to be challenged by other contenders for the throne Nasir Khan was able to carve out for himself a reasonably autonomous position. If he acted too independently Karim Khan had to intervene, despite his national concerns, because he could not allow Lar, which was in his backyard, to grow too independent. Molla 'Ali Shah, who formally was the subordinate of Nasir Khan, did not like this and wanted to keep him at more than arm's length. The success of his challenge oscillated as a function of Nasir Khan's preoccupation with Karim Khan and other local chiefs as well as the strength of the alliances that he could bring about. To that end Molla 'Ali Shah, first allied him with the Arabs of Charak (until 1751) and then with the Qavasem Arabs. To counter Molla 'Ali Shah's support base Nasir Khan sought an alliance with the Arabs from Charak as well as the Banu Ma'in from Bandar-e Kong, who were in search of a permanent home and who were the enemies of Molla 'Ali Shah. The ups-and-down of the encounters between these two main protagonists, supported by their respective allies is the main subject of this chapter. Occasionally Karim Khan intervened militarily, but never to make a permanent difference in the situation, while the staff of the Dutch and English Companies bemoaned these developments as trade grew less profitable due to the growing insecurity on the commercial routes and the growing oppression of the population and financial demands made on the Europeans by local and regional political leaders. When the conflict had finally resolved itself, more or less (both protagonists lost to third parties), the Europeans had abandoned Bandar 'Abbas that as of then sank to the level of an insignificant fishing port.

HOPE FOR REVIVAL OF TRADE DUE TO REGIME CHANGE

After Mohammad Taqi Khan's rebellion of 1743 and its aftermath Bandar 'Abbas once again became the scene of violence in 1747. As rebellions were breaking out all over the country the Persian troops in Oman also rebelled in March 1747. On April 13, 1747 some 40 *trankis* with about 4,000 men arrived in Gamron coming from Oman. These troops had rebelled and were commanded by Mir Mehr 'Ali. Qalij Khan (Galieds Chan), the commander of all these troops, followed with 3,000 men on April 27, 1747. Molla 'Ali Shah tried to stop the trankis coming from Oman to land, but he was unable to do anything effective. The rebel troops took Fazl 'Ali Soltan, the governor, prisoner when he wanted to resist them. Other government officials also were taken prisoner; the fort of Bandar 'Abbas was occupied. During the night a fierce battle took place, which turned into a sack of the town followed by pillage and arson. The population was killed to get their possessions. Those who were left fled to the Arab side of the Persian Gulf. Molla 'Ali Shah thereafter tried to stop any newcomers, but he was more worried about his wife and children who had been taken hostage during the rebellion of Arabs at Bushire than about the rebels coming ashore. Peace returned to the town when on June 8, 1747 Qalij Khan left

Gamron and marched to Bandar-e Kong.[1] These symptoms of the crumbling of Nader Shah's regime of were not good for trade, of course. On October 15, 1747 a shot fired from a cannon of the fort of Bandar 'Abbas officially announced the death of Nader Shah and thus confirmed the rumors of his death. The Dutch commented that "with the murder of Nader Shah there was renewed hope that the kingdom could find peace at last."[2]

The new power in the kingdom, Nader Shah's nephew, 'Aliqoli Khan was hailed as 'Adel Shah (the just king) and had money, a new *'abbasi*, struck in his name. The new Shah tried to do justice to his name and make a good impression on the mercantile community, for the Dutch and the English, initially, did not hear bad reports about him. In fact, rumor had it that he had lent merchants a great deal of money at 10% interest only, while the population was said to have been granted a three year tax exemption. The Dutch were less happy, however, about his request for the delivery of various goods to a value of 25,000 *tumans* (Dfl. 75,000). Jacob Schoonderwoerd, the VOC director in the Persian Gulf informed 'Adel Shah that he was unable to comply with his request.[3] 'Adel Shah apparently really wanted to encourage trade for apart from the measures referred to above he also wished to renew the friendly relations with the European trading companies in Persia as is demonstrated by his decree (*raqam*) to the Dutch in January 1748. This friendly overture was soon followed by a decree granting them the same privileges they had enjoyed previously.[4]

With the change in government there also was a change in officials. The quick turnover of these officials, many of whom did not even assume their function, is an indication of the instability of political power at the central government level. In July 1747, Mirza Musa, the rebel governor of Lar, informed the EIC that Molla 'Ali Shah was in charge of 'Essin, Bandar 'Abbas and the islands. Moreover, he also had to make the appointments of the lower-ranking officials there. Molla 'Ali Shah there appointed 'Abdol-Sheikh, chief of the Banu Ma'in and an ally as governor of Bandar 'Abbas.[5] However, this arrangement did not last long, because 'Abdol-Sheikh, one of the leaders of the 1741 naval mutiny, tried to take control of the royal fleet lying at Laft on Qeshm. He was joined in the rebellion by his brother and by the Al 'Ali of Bandar-e Charak, who also served as crews on the ships of the royal fleet. Molla 'Ali Shah was able to maintain control over the fleet, which resulted in great enmity between him and 'Abdol-Sheikh and his Banu Ma'in, a cleavage that would dominate politics in the area until 1763.[6]

---

1 Floor, *Hokumat*, pp. 228-29; Slot, *'Arab al-Khalij*, p. 311, referring to the Gombroon Diary entries between 30/03/1747 and 25/05/1747.

2 VOC 2705, Gamron to Batavia (28/02/1747), f. 538-39; VOC 2724, Gamron to Batavia (22/12/1747), f. 14; Nader Shah was killed on 21/06/1747.

3 VOC 2784, Gamron to Batavia (10/10/1748), f. 84; VOC 2724, f. 16; this happened on July 6, 1747, see Perry, *Karim Khan Zand*, p. 24.

4 For the text of the *raqam* see VOC 2748, f. 382-83. For a printed version see J.E. Heeres and F.W. Stapel, eds., *Corpus Diplomaticum Neerlando-Indicum* 6 vols. (The Hague, 1907-55), vol. 5. The English also received confirmation of their privileges. Amin, *British Interests*, p. 25.

5 Ricks, *Politics and Trade*, pp. 128-29, referring to Factory Records of Gombroon (02/07/1747) (henceforth cited as F.R. Gombroon). For a short history of the Banu Ma'in and the genealogy of their chiefs, who came from Bandar-e Kong, see Sadid al-Saltaneh, *Bandar 'Abbas*, pp. 610-16; Lorimer, *Gazetteer*, p. 1940. Molla 'Ali Shah had been governor of Qeshm from 1736 to 1747, while he also had been *vakil* of the royal fleet during that same period. VOC 2546, Koenad to Batavia (31/03/1740), f. 30-32; Ibid., Resolution Gamron (25/08/1740), f. 164-74. In 1748, the Dutch described 'Abdol-Sheikh "as a man belonging to an important family and with great influence among the Arabs and a former captain of the royal fleet, but a great enemy of Molla Alie Sjah." VOC 2788, Gamron to Batavia (10/10/1748), f. 90

6 Slot, *'Arab al-Khalij*, p. 325, referring to the Gombroon Diary entries on 08-09 and 08-10-1747.

Most of the officials were changed when shortly thereafter 'Adel Shah had assumed control of the state. In October 1748 he appointed Mir 'Ali Soltan as governor of Lar and Bandar 'Abbas and Sheikh Hatem of Taheri as *shahbandar.* The royal orders addressed to these officials also spelled out what royal policy they had to carry out, to wit: peasants had to be induced to return to their villages and tribes to their grazing grounds. Moreover, the new shah declared a three-year tax holiday for all his subjects. Molla 'Ali Shah was appointed admiral (*darya-beygi*) of the royal fleet, which was one step up from his previous position with the royal fleet as its *vakil.* It also gave him formal control of the remaining part of the royal fleet that was still in existence at Bandar 'Abbas and he was able to hold on to that function also in the future. He, moreover, skillfully translated this control over the fleet into political leverage to advance his career.[7] Saleh Khan Bayat, who had been appointed governor-general (*beygler-beygi*) of Fars in November 1747, brought some measure of security to the province. He opened the roads and implemented 'Adel Shah's declared commercial policy by making loans available to merchants from the treasury at a rate of interest of 10% per year. He appointed Hoseyn 'Ali Beyg instead of Mir 'Ali Soltan as governor and appointed Hajji Mohammad 'Ali Beyg as *shahbandar* of Bandar 'Abbas. A Mazandarani merchant who came to Bandar 'Abbas in December 1748 confirmed that there was indeed more security on the roads and thus an increase in trade, facilitated by the loans to merchants which had to be repaid in three years. As a result, the EIC Agent recommended to Bombay that shipments could be resumed to Bandar 'Abbas.[8]

That was good news, be it somewhat optimistic in nature, because trade in Bandar 'Abbas had been so bad since 1745 that it was only with humility that Jacob Schoonderwoerd, the VOC director, had dared to raise the subject of trade in his letter of October 10, 1748.[9] It was therefore not surprising that Batavia[10] on June 26, 1747 had decided to close down the VOC factory in Isfahan and to reduce the number of VOC staff in the Bandar 'Abbas factory. Henceforth, the staff of the Bandar 'Abbas factory would consist of one Resident (rank: merchant or junior-merchant), three or four assistants, one surgeon, one gunner and a garrison of 18 native Christian soldiers. The superfluous staff was recalled to Batavia.[11] Schoonderwoerd had no objections to these changes and commented that the new level of staff would be sufficient to continue trading on the same scale.[12] In fact, Schoonderwoerd would have had no objections to abandoning the Persian Gulf trade altogether, because trade had only been a loss for the VOC since the 1740s according to him.[13] A report drawn up in Batavia in 1756 confirmed the reduced commercial profitability of the Persian Gulf trade.[14]

---

7 Ricks, *Politics and Trade,* p. 130-31 referring to F. R. Gombroon VI (05/10/1747). In 1753, this fleet was described by the EIC Agent in Bandar 'Abbas as consisting of "only two old Rotten ships" and five six other vessels. Risso, *Oman & Muscat,* p. 54.

8 Ricks, *Politics and Trade,* p. 132-33 referring to F. R. Gombroon VI, (18, 25 and 26/12/1747); Amin, *British Interests,* p. 25; Hajj Mirza Hasan Hoseyni Fasa'i, *Farsnameh-ye Naseri,* 2 vols. Mansur Rastegar-e Fasa'i (Tehran, 1378/1999), vol. 1, p. 583.

9 VOC 2748, Gamron to Batavia (10/10/1748), f. 97.

10 Now Jakarta; the seat of the VOC's Asian headquarters managed by the governor-general and his council, which body was referred to as the High Government.

11 VOC 779, Batavia to Gamron (21/06/1747), f. 200. There was only a caretaker at the VOC factory in Isfahan, for the Dutch staff had already been withdrawn in 1745. VOC 2705, van der Welle to Batavia (31/07/1746), f. 101-03.

12 VOC 2748, Gamron to Batavia (10/10/1748), f. 172.

13 VOC 2710, Gamron to Batavia (15/06/1748), f. 1480-90; for a detailed discussion see Willem Floor, "Dutch Trade in Afsharid Iran (1730-1753)," *Studia Iranica* 34 (2005), pp. 43-93. This was not lost on the EIC either. "In 1748 the Dutch began talk of abandoning their Factory at Bandar 'Abbas, which no longer yielded much profit." Lorimer, *Gazetteer,* p. 128.

14 VOC 2762, chapter 15.

Table 3.1: Gross average annual profits of the Persia Directorate*

Years	**Amount (in Dutch guilders)**
1700-1709	402,859
1710-1719	363,728
1720-1729	185,856
1730-1739	72,587
1740-1749	73,912
1750-1754	137,131

* includes all Persian Gulf ports where the VOC had factories (Bandar 'Abbas, Basra, Bushire).

At the same time Batavia had decided to separate the VOC factories in Basra and Bushire from Bandar 'Abbas and thus constitute two separate, but equally important factories. Trade results at the end of 1747 had been so bad that Bandar 'Abbas had to take money out of a ship coming from Basra to get funds to pay its current expenditures, for the factory had only 76,161 *mahmudis* in cash.[15] The decision to separate the two main factories in the Persian Gulf had been based on the premise that so far Bandar 'Abbas had covered its losses with the profits of Basra and this constituted a disincentive for the Bandar 'Abbas staff to stand on their own feet and to see whether they would perform any better.

The directors of the VOC, the so-called *Heeren XVII*, who during the 1740s had been exasperated by the way in which Bandar 'Abbas had reported and acted, finally gave vent to their feeling in 1749. They welcomed the closure of the Isfahan factory, for they had been on the verge or ordering the withdrawal of the entire Persia Directorate. Trade results had gone from bad to worse, while there were no prospects for improvement. The separation of the Bandar 'Abbas and Basra factories might lead to better results, although the XVII doubted this very much, in fact, they did not believe it at all. Unless better profits were shown, they informed Batavia, they would order the immediate closure of the Bandar 'Abbas factory. The other Persian Gulf factories might be maintained through a caretaker to make sure that the VOC could return without any problems.[16]

It was not that the physical aspect of Bandar 'Abbas had suffered much, because its climate, its water supply, and its food situation had hardly changed at all in 100 years as is clear from a 1750 description of the town:[17]

> The best Houses are built with bricks dried in the Sun, made with a Composition of Clay, Sand, chopped Straw and Horse-dung mixed together. They stand close to each other and are flat on the Top, and have each a square Turret which rises considerably higher than the rest of the Structure, having Holes on each Side for the free Passage of the Wind and Air. Here those that stay in the Town sleep every Night during the Summer Season. The meaner Sort of People live in miserable Huts made with the Boughs of date or palm-trees and covered with their leaves.

15 VOC 2725, Gamron to Batavia (22/12/1747), f. 31.

16 VOC 331, XVII to Batavia (11/10/1749), section "Persien", not foliated.

17 Edward Ives, *A Voyage from England to India in the Year MDCCLIV ... also A Journey From Persia to England* (London, 1773), pp. 197-98 also made that observation. For a detailed description of Bandar 'Abbas in the 17th century see Floor, *The Persian Gulf*, pp. 247-72.

> The Streets are both narrow and short, with many Turnings; and the Houses almost join together at the Top, and yet sometimes when the Weather is hot one can hardly pass along them, they are so sultry/ The better Sort of People are clad after the Persian Mode, but those who are poor can scarce get any Cloths to their Backs, and many of them, both Men and Women, go quite naked, except for a Clout to cover what Decency requires them to hide.[18]

These signs of hope and optimism could not change the fact that the situation in and around Bandar 'Abbas, let alone upcountry, did not bear out such sentiments. In early 1747 the countryside had been the scene of rapine and plunder perpetrated by rebelling troops and the Dutch expected the same to happen again due to the change in power. They especially feared that the Baluch and Afghan elements in the area would start marauding. At the end of 1747, the VOC director therefore took 10 soldiers from the VOC ship *de Walcheren*, which was lying in the roads at that time, to reinforce the factory's garrison.[19] Moreover, the initial good reports about the new regime were not transformed into action. 'Adel Shah's brother, Ebrahim Mirza, who resided in Isfahan, behaved himself quite badly, and especially towards Europeans. The English, who had a Resident in Isfahan, were publicly offended by Ebrahim Mirza on several occasions. This behavior stood in contrast with the decree that he sent to the Dutch and the English in August 1748 in which he assured them of his favor and that they had been granted the same rights as they had enjoyed previously.[20] The newly appointed *beygler-beygi* of Fars and the Hot Countries (Garmsirat), Abu'l-Hasan Khan (Saleh Khan Bayat had become general or *sardar* of Fars), did not inspire any confidence amongst the Dutch and English either, for he was considered to be a cruel and evil person. After his arrival in Shiraz they received several reports about his bad behavior. Out of apprehension for his intentions towards the European Companies the Dutch concluded an agreement with their arch-rivals, the English that each party would not act upon requests from Abu'l-Hasan Khan without having consulted the other. In this way, i.e. through a united front, the European Companies hoped to withstand unreasonable demands from Shiraz.[21]

MOLLA 'ALI SHAH OPPOSES MIRZA ABU TALEB, THE NEW GOVERNOR

In March 1748 'Adel Shah appointed a new governor of Bandar 'Abbas, Mirza Abu Taleb, and it was hoped that his arrival would lead to an improvement in the political situation in the port and its hinterland. Mirza Abu Taleb made his entry into Bandar 'Abbas on March 26, 1748. He was welcomed by the EIC and VOC interpreters towards whom he behaved brusquely. The new gover-

18 Bartholomew Plaisted, *A Journal from Calcutta in Bengal, by Sea, to Bussera: from thence across the great Desart to Aleppo ... In the Year 1750* (London, 1757), pp. 6-7. Compare this description with my discussion of the port in the 17th century, see Floor, *Persian Gulf*, pp. 253-60.

19 On the fights that had broken out in the first part of 1747 in the Bandar 'Abbas area see Floor, *Hokumat-e Nader Shah*, pp. 228-29; VOC 2724, Gamron to Batavia (22/12/1747), f. 18; Ricks, *Politics and Trade*, pp. 125-29.

20 VOC 2784, Gamron to Batavia (10/10/1748), f. 85-86; VOC 2766, Ebrahim Soltan vice-roy of [Persian] Iraq [–e 'Ajam] to VOC director, dated Sha'ban 1146/August 1748, received 30/10/1748; Perry, *Karim Khan*, pp. 4, 27; Amin, *British Interests*, p. 25.

21 VOC 2748, Gamron to Batavia (10/10/1748), f. 85-86; Ricks, *Politics and Trade*, p. 133 referring to F. R. Gombroon VI (21/01/1748); Perry, *Karim Khan*, p. 27; Amin, *British Interests*, p. 26. The governor-general of the VOC approved of this agreement with the English to collaborate and he urged Schoonderwoerd to continue to live in harmony with them, because this might be useful to both sides. VOC 1003, Batavia to Gamron (22/08/1749), f. 549.

nor was not pleased with the lukewarm reception by the Dutch and English, despite the fact he was accompanied by six *yuz-bashis*. His troops consisted of about 300 robbers and thieves, according to the Dutch. Amongst his officers there was a certain *yuz-bashi* known as Hajji, who had acquired notoriety as a robber in the Bandar 'Abbas area only four month's earlier and who availed himself of the opportunity of this official visit to sell his ill-gotten goods right in Bandar 'Abbas. The Dutch, therefore, strengthened the guard at the gate of their factory. They also made an agreement with the English to act jointly, if need be. To present a united front they also jointly called upon Mirza Abu Taleb for a friendly visit. Meanwhile, they had recommended Molla 'Ali Shah, who was one of the few officials supporting the central government, to take refuge aboard his fleet.[22]

The new governor's arrival occurred right after an attack of the Arabs of Charak on Molla 'Ali Shah at Laft on Qeshm Island, which gave rise to a rumor that the governor of Lar was acting against the officials at Bandar 'Abbas with the help of the coastal Arabs. This seemed to be borne out by the warm welcome and support that 'Abdol-Sheikh governor of Hormuz, chief of the Banu Ma'in, who was the instigator of the attack and an arch-enemy of Molla 'Ali Shah, received from the new governor, while Molla 'Ali Shah, who not only was the principal government official in Bandar 'Abbas and who after all had been attacked and whom he allegedly had come to help against the Arab chiefs, was practically ignored. The same welcoming treatment was accorded to one of the captains of the Molla 'Ali Shah's fleet. Mirza Abu Taleb clearly hoped to engineer a mutiny among the officers of the fleet, who were Arabs and of doubtful loyalty to Molla 'Ali Shah. In fact, a few days later after the governor's arrival the Dutch learnt that he intended to arrest Molla 'Ali Shah and take charge of the fleet himself. This piece of information confirmed that Mirza Abu Taleb sought the cooperation of the coastal Arabs for his own plans. It was also believed that Mirza Abu Taleb wanted to use the royal fleet to attack the Dutch and English factories. This scheme did not work out as intended, because Molla 'Ali Shah had expected this possible move and therefore had sailed away to Laft, the main port on Qeshm Island. Although Mirza Abu Taleb's plot was aborted in this respect he did not remain inactive. Saleh Khan Bayat who had gotten wind of Mirza Abu Taleb's machinations against him ordered him to return to Shiraz. Mirza 'Abu Taleb did not do so; he engineered attacks on Molla 'Ali Shah's vessels and properties and on the EIC by the Charak Arabs. He further sent *yuz-bashi* Hajji to the Baluch chiefs to induce them to support him with troops. At the advice of the Dutch and English the Baluch chiefs did not send any troops to Mirza Abu Taleb, with the exception of a certain Ra'is Qanbar, who in person came to Bandar 'Abbas at the head of 200 men. In May 1748 Saleh Khan Bayat wrote that he would come in person to Bandar 'Abbas, but problems in Isfahan prevented him from doing so. Mirza Abu Taleb, however, soon realized that he could not get his way in Bandar 'Abbas and having quarreled with *yuz-bashi* Hajji he decided to leave for Lar, whither he departed on May 18, 1748. *Yuz-bashi* Hajji also left and like other brigands continued plundering caravans and travelers in the port's hinterland, while the *shahbandar* Ahmad Beyg had fled Bandar 'Abbas when he heard that Saleh Khan would come.[23]

'Abdol-Sheikh, the chief of the Banu Ma'in began peace talks with Molla 'Ali Shah and returned stolen goods to the EIC, thus pre-empting any possible action against him by Saleh Khan. By mid-May 1748 'Abdol-Sheikh had promised that Qeshm would belong to Molla 'Ali Shah, who, in return, would pay an annual compensation to the Banu Ma'in for the use of the port Laft. Molla 'Ali Shah probably

22 VOC 2748, Gamron to Batavia (10/10/1748), f. 87-88; VOC 2748, f. 307; Ricks, *Politics and Trade*, pp. 133-38 referring to F. R. Gombroon VI (21 and 26/01/1748 and 18/03/1748 and 19/03/1748); Fasa'i, *Farsnameh*, vol. 1, p. 584; Amin, *British Interests*, p. 27, n. 4.

23 Ricks, *Politics and Trade*, pp. 133-35 referring to F. R. Gombroon VI (21 and 26/01/1748 and 18/03/1748 and 19/03/1748); Fasa'i, *Farsnameh*, vol. 1, p. 586; VOC 2748, Gamron to Batavia (10/10/1748), f. 89-91; Amin, *British Interests*, p. 27, n. 4.

thought of starting his own 'enterprise' around Laft if he could not maintain his position at Bandar 'Abbas. However, Qeshm caused Molla 'Ali Shah more trouble than it yielded benefits. In July 1748, 'Abdol-Sheikh, who probably never had intended to yield the island, took his troops to Qeshm, which after a few days of fighting fell into his hands. He was supported by 20 *trankis* from the Arabs from Charak (Gareekse Arabieren) as well as by the lack of fighting spirit among Molla 'Ali Shah's men. The Dutch and English feared that further revolts would break out, and that 'Abdol-Sheikh would capture the entire royal fleet. If he succeeded to do so they feared that 'Abdol-Sheikh would start a career as a pirate, for the ships' crews had not received any pay for three years. 'Abdol-Sheikh had intimated that he would pay the crews their arrears, and that he moreover would attack any ship in the Persian Gulf to get the necessary money and supplies. This boded greater insecurity in the Persian Gulf and the first indications were that an English *grab* had been taken by the Arabs from Charak, while a Dutch private vessel had been attacked near Ra's al-Hadd. The VOC therefore had instructed their captains to be on guard for everybody, including Persian ships.[24]

CONTINUED INSECURITY IN THE BANDAR 'ABBAS AREA

Although 'Adel Shah's writ was not respected in the littoral, both the EIC and VOC considered it necessary to draw the attention of the nominal representatives of the Persian central government to the unsettled situation in the area, especially to the behavior of the various local chiefs. They in particular asked how they should react to these developments, and addressed this question to Molla 'Ali Shah and 'Abdol-Sheikh, two officials who still had some power and influence in the region. They also hoped that their action would bolster Molla 'Ali Shah's self-esteem and make him more sensitive to the European Companies' view point.[25]

How insecure, for example, the Dutch felt was demonstrated by the fact that the council of the Bandar 'Abbas factory dismissed its director, Abraham van der Welle, on May 6, 1748, an unheard of and unique action in VOC history. Van der Welle's authority had been eroded due to his bad management of the VOC affairs and what the council considered to be dereliction of duty. The council had first given him a warning and thereafter had exhorted him to change his behavior several times. When van der Welle had not responded to these warnings and allegedly had endangered the safety of the VOC factory during Mirza Abu Taleb's machinations against the EIC and VOC the council acted and took away his authority and deprived him of his office. Jacob Schoonderwoerd, his deputy, took over the management of VOC affairs.[26] Batavia was very upset about the council's high handed action. The governor-general was ready to

24 VOC 2748, Gamron to Batavia (10/10/1748), f. 89-93, 232-35 (after having been attacked near Ra's al-Hadd by a three-master ship and a *grab*, which attack was beaten off, the vessel *D'Kerseboom*, belonging to the deputy of the VOC factory in Bengal, Joan Karsseboom, under supercargo Mr. Jan Witte LeBlanc, was seized in the roads of Bandar 'Abbas by an English ship commanded by Philip Jodrell. Molla 'Ali Shah told him it was no French, but a Dutch ship and sent men aboard the vessel to stop all violence and disarm the English. Having realized his mistake and being outgunned Jodrell released the vessel. Schoonderwoerd had complained to his EIC colleague, who said that he could no do nothing as the captain had orders to inspect all vessels); Amin, *British Interests*, p. 27; Ricks, *Politics and Trade*, pp. 136-39 referring to F. R. Gombroon VI (17/05/1748).

25 VOC 2748, Gamron to Batavia (10/10/1748), f. 94.

26 VOC 2748, Gamron to Batavia (10/10/1748), f. 2-4. The council was not only strict with its director, but also with another council member Matthijs Krijgsman. The council had him arrested after he had been warned three times for disobedience, debauchery, and drunkenness. When the council had summoned him to appear before it he had ordered his servant to destroy all his furniture and had refused to come to the council to give an account of himself. Also, after his arrest he still refused to do so, despite the fact that an examination of his books had shown a shortage of Dfl. 114:6:8. After pressure he paid this amount on August 13. Although he asked the council twice

believe that van der Welle had been guilty of all the things he had been accused of, and, if he had not died en route to Batavia, these would have been thoroughly investigated by him, he informed Schoonderwoerd. However, that the council had taken upon itself the authority to dismiss van der Welle was without precedent. The governor-general agreed that the council had covered itself quite well with its arguments that had led to van der Welle's dismissal, but he did not like it at all. Batavia would not delve any further in the matter and preferred to let things be, because van der Welle had died. But, the governor-general assured the council, that if this had not been the case their behavior would have had very severe consequences for them. Schoonderwoerd was confirmed in his position as director, while the others, in conformity with the earlier decision of downgrading the Bandar 'Abbas factory, were ordered to return to Batavia.[27] The XVII did not comment on this event, and apparently agreed with Batavia *ex silencio*.

In May 1748 news reached Bandar 'Abbas that Ebrahim Mirza had rebelled against his older brother 'Adel Shah, whom he defeated, took prisoner and blinded in June 1748. The fraternal war led to all kinds of local uprisings throughout the country. As a result, the roads leading to Bandar 'Abbas were so insecure that the Dutch could not even send a messenger to Isfahan.[28] The Dutch and English were in a quandary after 'Adel Shah's fall. Ebrahim Mirza had sent them a robe of honor and promised them all kinds of privileges. At the same time there were rumors that Shahrokh Mirza had been hailed as Shah in Mashhad. The Dutch and English decided to send Ebrahim Mirza as well as to Saleh Khan Bayat, his governor in Shiraz, a non-committal letter, thanking him for his favor and friendly attitude, as well as sending him some presents.[29]

By September 1748 orders arrived from Ebrahim Shah appointing new or confirming old officials, such as Qasem Beyg the *shahryari* of Minab, Mirza Mozaffar or chief of Ahmadi and Molla 'Ali Shah, who remained *darya-beygi*. Ebrahim Shah also appointed various officials to the major functions of Fars and its dependencies such as Fath 'Ali Khan Arashlu Afshar, who replaced Taqi Khan Bogheyri as *beygler-beygi* of Fars and Karim Khan Afghan as *darya-beygi*, thus in fact the formal chief of Molla 'Ali Shah. At the same time Shahrokh Mirza, who had been hailed as Shah in Mashhad also appointed officials to the same functions in Fars and its dependencies, thus adding to the confusion of who was really in charge of the country. Trade continued, however, in particular on the road between Mashhad to the coast via Kerman, where by November 1748 caravans traveled "unmolested everyday." Moreover, these appointments had no impact on the reality on the ground, i.e. those officials who could use force against weaker rivals. This could lead to violence, such as in January 1749, when Mirza Abu Taleb the governor of Lar and Bandar 'Abbas was murdered in Lar by Hajji Khan Kali, brother of Nasir Khan Kali, the later governor of Lar. In February 1749 Sheikh Mohammad Sayyed took control of Lar, arrested the murderer of his predecessor and was confirmed as governor of Lar and Bandar 'Abbas in March 1749 by Saleh Khan Bayat *sardar*. The latter also confirmed Molla 'Ali Shah as *darya-beygi*, thus undoing Karim Khan Afghan's appointment. The *sardar* also wrote that Ebrahim Mirza wanted to build up the fleet again "and make the sea coasts of Arabia subservient to him" and that the necessary funds would be made available to him.[30]

---

for forgiveness it decided to deprive him of his function in view of his past behavior. Moreover, even during his arrest he drank and swilled with his guard and beat his poor wife in a cruel manner. He was returned to Batavia to face a court of justice. VOC 2748, Gamron to Batavia (10/10/1748), f. 210-12.

27 VOC 1003, Gamron to Batavia (22/08/1749), f. 452-53, 564-65.

28 VOC 2784, Gamron to Batavia (10/10/1748), f. 86-87; Perry, *Karim Khan*, p. 5.

29 VOC 2766, f. 94 and the VOC council's resolution on this matter is dated 08/11/1749, f. 95-97; VOC 2766, f. 162, letter from Mohammad Taqi Khan, *beygler-beygi* of Shiraz to VOC; Perry, *Karim Khan*, p. 28.

30 Ricks, *Politics and Trade*, pp. 138-42 referring to F. R. Gombroon VI (22/11/1748, 30/12/1748, 29/01/1749, and 13/03/1749); Kal is the name of a village on the road to Shiraz. The two brothers had been active in Lari politics trying to make a name for themselves. Fasa'i, *Farsnameh*, vol. 1, pp. 585-88; Perry, *Karim Khan*, p. 117.

On December 31, 1748 the Dutch and English received a decree from Shahrokh Shah in which he announced his accession to the throne and that he had money struck in his name. The Dutch and English decided to maintain a rather neutral position for the time being and only sent him a congratulation note. In reply Shahrokh Shah confirmed all privileges which the Dutch and English had previously enjoyed. Having secured this formal legitimization of their commercial operations the Dutch and English decided not to spend any money on presents, but to await further events. Even the information, in the beginning of July 1749, that Shahrokh Shah had defeated Ebrahim Mirza did not change their mind on this issue.[31] Shahrokh Shah also confirmed Molla 'Ali Shah in his functions of *darya-beygi* well as governor of Bandar 'Abbas and asked the Dutch to supply him with all his needs for the fleet. Because of the uncertain and above all insecure situation Schoonderwoerd decided to reinforce the Dutch factory. He took some cannons from a VOC ship that was in the roads and placed them at each of the points of the factory. Each point then had two 4-lbs cannons plus a seven-inch mortar, while behind the postern in the main gate there were two 2-lbs. guns.[32] The Dutch nevertheless welcomed Shahrokh Mirza's victory over Ebrahim Mirza, who had taken up residence in Tabriz and had acquired the reputation of behaving like Nader Shah, taking whatever he could to pay his troops. Shahrokh Mirza, however, was reported to rule benevolently, to encourage trade, and, moreover, to see to it that his troops were well paid and dressed. This caused an enormous demand for woolens and other kinds of textiles, commodities which had been hardly in demand since 1740. The Dutch, therefore, to cash in on this development, advised that a ship should be sent directly from Amsterdam to the Persian Gulf to get a piece of the broadcloth action, the more so, because the English wanted to oust the Dutch completely from the textile market. The English had told the Dutch that they would even be prepared to sell woolens at a profit of 7% only. Schoonderwoerd, exasperatedly, proposed that the VOC should be even prepared to sell woolens below cost.[33]

MOLLA 'ALI SHAH ALLIES HIMSELF WITH THOSE OF CHARAK

Molla 'Ali Shah meanwhile was busy bolstering his position by seeking an alliance with the coastal Arab chief who had attacked him only one year earlier. In January 1749, Sheikh 'Ali b. Khalfan of Bandar-e Charak came to pay him a visit, probably because he had fallen out with his ally 'Abdol-Sheikh of the Banu Ma'in. Together they went to see the chiefs of the two European Companies to discuss the troubles in Basra and the flight of merchants from that town due to the problems with Baghdad. They wanted to send a few gallivats to cruise the mouth of the Shatt al-Arab and stop trade altogether to punish the Turks for interfering with Persian Gulf trade, but the EIC discouraged them from doing so as it would interfere with its trade there.[34] This cooperation would soon fall apart, when both sides found more convenient allies, but for the time being it served the purpose of bolstering the postion of both parties.

In March 1749 a letter arrived in Bandar 'Abbas, reporting that Sheikh Mohammad had been appointed *beygler-beygi* of Lar and Bandar 'Abbas by Saleh Khan Bayat. The former would send the infamous *yuz-bashi* Hajji with a force to regulate the customs and revenues of Bandar 'Abbas and take over the

31 VOC 2766, f. 34, dated Shavval 1161/October 1748; VOC 2766, Resolution Gamron 17/01/1749, f. 104-09; VOC 2766, f. 163 letter conferring the privileges; via his E'temad al-Dowleh Mohammad Ja'far Khan, dated 18 Jomadi al-Thani 1161/6 June 1749; see also VOC 2766, f. 204, letter from Sardar Fath 'Ali Khan, received from Bushire on 30/06/1749; Ricks, *Politics and Trade*, pp. 138-42 referring to F. R. Gombroon VI (30/12/1748).

32 VOC 2766, Gamron to Batavia (25/12/1749), f. 30-31, 36-37.

33 VOC 3748, Gamron to Batavia (15/04/1749), f. 256-58; VOC 2483, Gamron to Batavia (01/10/1753), f. 12-15; Perry, *Karim Khan*, pp. 6-8.

34 Ricks, *Politics and Trade*, pp. 143 referring to F. R. Gombroon VI (25/01/1749).

management of the nearby sulfur mines. Traditionally the governor of Bandar 'Abbas received 1/3 of customs revenues (1/3 to governor of Lar; 1/3 to EIC) and with Molla 'Ali Shah's rise in importance he also had taken over control over the sulfur mines without which he could not 'subsist,' or so he claimed. Saleh Khan Bayat met with resistance when trying to collect taxes in Larestan due to the behavior of Sheikh Mohammad and *yuz-bashi* Hajji. The latter wrote to Molla 'Ali Shah asking to get him a 46- or 48-pounder cannon to oppose Saleh Khan, which shows that his appointment and that of Sheikh Mohammad had been the acknowledgement of the reality on the ground rather than Saleh Khan's exercise of political authority.[35] In the first half of 1749 there also was the rise of Ra'is Allahverdi a Baluch bandit plundering villages and attacking road transport the hinterland of Bandar'Abbas.[36] On May 22, 1749 he and his Baluchis came to Bandar 'Abbas threatening the port and its surrounding areas, while robbing cattle and grain. Although these Baluchi robbers eventually returned to their lands the 'local' bandits remained and continued to be a major problem for trade and life. One of them was called Gardu who blocked the road to Kerman at Tangzandan and there was also news about another unnamed robber. Molla 'Ali Shah wrote to Minab and other places to order its chiefs to take action against these bandits. Because Gardu was still there in May 1749 the EIC and VOC jointly wrote to Qasem Beyg, the *kalantar* of Minab to urge him to take action and keep the roads open. They also decided that if this did not work they would ask of all people the Baluch marauder Ra'is Allahverdi to take care of Gardu, the robber. The Minab chief did nothing, or at least he did not respond. The two chiefs therefore wrote again to Qasem Beyg in the first week of June 1749 reminding him that it was his task to secure the roads and if he did not do anything they would take steps themselves. Qasem Beyg then replied promising that Gardu would be taken care of. Danvers Graves, the EIC Agent shortly thereafter traveled the road and found it safe although there were reports of the plundering of villages in the hinterland.[37] In the fall of 1749 trade lived up again partly due to the fact that bandits had been cleared from the roads. The governor of Lar wrote that he intended "to settle that part of the country with orders for no suvamin [sevvomin] or 1/3 tax, or other taxes to be taken from the subjects."[38]

This situation did not last long, however, Shahrokh Mirza was deposed on December 30, 1749 and in his stead Sayyed Ahmad was hailed as Shah Soleyman III, whose reign only lasted till March 20, 1750 when Shahrokh Mirza was reinstated again. Meanwhile, the Persian littoral was in a total confused state. Not even the officials appointed by Shahrokh Shah, of whom Saleh Khan Bayat was the most important, obeyed him. The local officials acted as they saw fit, and behaved like persons who expected that their time would run out any moment. They took money where they could extort it, and Molla 'Ali Shah, who so far had tried to cooperate with the European Companies and promote trade, even bothered the EIC and VOC continuously with requests for presents and delivery of goods on credit. The Dutch therefore hoped that he would soon be out of office. Because the authorities feared the arrival of the newly appointed governor Nasir Soltan they put the town in state of defense. All inhabitants, including EIC and VOC servants, had to carry rocks and clay to repair the city wall and they allowed no exceptions to enforce compliance. The authorities (i.e. Molla 'Ali Shah) relented somewhat in their attitude towards the Dutch and English through the intercession of the *shahriyari* of Minab, because they realized that the hoped for discord between the two European Companies, which did not materialize. Both Shaw and Schoonderwoerd were

35 Ricks, *Politics and Trade*, pp. 144-46 referring to F. R. Gombroon VI (13and 21/03/1749).

36 Ricks, *Politics and Trade*, pp. 145 referring to F. R. Gombroon VI (29/04/1740).

37 Ricks, *Politics and Trade*, pp. 147-50 referring to F. R. Gombroon VI (19/04/1749; 29/04/1749; 30/04/1749; 19/05/1749; 24/05/1749; 28/05/1749 and 05/06/1749). The episodic incursions by Baluch marauders were an old pattern that had already started at the end of the 17th century, if not earlier. See, e.g., Floor, *Afghan Occupation*, pp. 25-27, 30, 63-79; Ibid, *Persian Gulf*, p. 275.

38 Ricks, *Politics and Trade*, p. 155 referring to F. R. Gombroon VI (30/07/1749).

then invited to a noon meal with Molla 'Ali Shah and the *shahriyari* to herald the new friendlier attitude towards the EIC and VOC. The *shahriyari* had to depart soon thereafter for Minab, because the Baluch had invaded his lands.[39]

DESPITE A TEMPORARY SURGE IN TRADE THE POLITICAL SITUATION DETERIORATES

Despite the political and military uncertainty of the moment the Dutch did not consider 1748-49 a bad year, because they had made more profit that in the previous year. This was due to the fact that the road to Kerman had been opened again, so that people had more money. Also the Dutch had less overhead due to their halved staff. However, structurally the commercial situation had not changed. This became clear in 1749-50 when the Dutch suffered a decline in profits. This was caused by a number of factors such as the impossibility to sell pepper, the higher cost of spices, the small selection of goods, a fact which in the previous year had been to their advantage.[40] The year 1750-51 continued to be bad, for only a few merchants had the courage to come to Bandar 'Abbas. It was not only out of fear for the greed of local officials and the insecurity on the roads, but also the very high transportation cost that bedeviled trade. This situation also had a negative impact on the supply of Persian export goods. This held especially for Kerman goat wool for which local entrepreneurs paid very high prices. This development was the result of the surge in demand for woolens, from which local producers profited.[41] The situation for the EIC was more positive, because between 1748 and 1751 it saw its export of English manufactured goods almost triple from £17,297 to £45,604, which represented about 30% of total EIC exports to Asia. Moreover, most of these exports to the Persian Gulf were sold not in Basra, but in Bandar 'Abbas. At the same time, the trade by English country traders also increased and so did the EIC revenues from consulage. As to the export of goat-wool the English experienced the same problems that the Dutch had.[42]

Meanwhile, the political situation was going from bad to worse. Shahrokh Mirza kept the Afghans at bay in Khorasan, but was running out of money and had money struck which was of bad alloy. Isfahan had been twice ransacked by the Bakhtyaris led by 'Ali Mardan Khan. The Bakhtiyaris had committed many excesses irrespective of rank or person. Even the English had suffered at their hands and had been beaten, robbed and left naked in the street. Their interpreter had part of his nose cut off and had been sold into slavery. Later an Armenian priest had purchased him back for 50 *tumans* or Dfl. 1,500 When the English had nothing left that could be extorted from them, they fled Isfahan to Bandar 'Abbas via Yazd. In the latter town they were held up for three months because their creditors had followed them and did not allow them to leave before they had paid off their debts. The Englishmen finally paid 90,000 rupees, some of it in Yazd and the rest in Bandar 'Abbas. One of the creditors went with the Englishmen to Bandar 'Abbas to be paid, so that the EIC Isfahan staff finally returned on February 2, 1751. The VOC factory in

39 VOC 2766, Gamron to Batavia (10/05/1750), f. 213-15, VOC 2766, Gamron to Batavia (25/12/1749), f. 38; Amin, *British Interests*, p. 27. In 1749, the Persian authorities of Bandar 'Abbas were (based on the list of New Year presents): (i) Molla 'Ali Shah; (ii) Mhamad Hadje Naib (castellan or *kutval*); (iii) Sjeeg Elisloem (Sheikh al-Islam); (iv) Kadie (qadi); (v) darroga (*darugheh*) or chief of the night watch; (vi) Hadje Abdul Hossein; (vii) deputy customs master; (viii) Hadje Ali Sjah. VOC 2766, f. 148-49; VOC 2748, f. 393.

40 VOC 2787, Gamron to Batavia (17/02/1751), f. 37.

41 VOC 2787, f. 26-27.

42 Amin, *British Interests*, pp. 40, 154-55; Floor, *Persian Textile Industry*, pp. 370-72.

Isfahan had been used by the Bakhtiyaris as a stable. All doors and windows had been used as firewood, so that the building had become a ruin.[43]

After the sack of Isfahan, 'Ali Mardan Khan proclaimed a descendent of Shah Soltan Hoseyn in the female line, a son of a certain Mirza Morteza, as Shah Esma'il III. However, 'Ali Mardan Khan was the real ruler, who continued to pillage and rob the population. The situation in Shiraz, Kerman, Lar and other towns was also one of violence and insecurity, where local notables were warring against one another. The local officials in Bandar 'Abbas only thought about enriching themselves and did not care in what way they had to achieve this. This also led to a deterioration of relations with the EIC and VOC, because the Persian officials did not respect any of the privileges granted to the Companies. The EIC therefore kept a ketch, the *Drake*, with a crew of 140 Europeans on the roadstead to protect their factory. The EIC and VOC continued to show a united front towards the local officials, which the latter did not like at all. They almost daily demanded goods on credit, which sometimes could be refused, but not always, for, despite the risk of a bad debt, it was in the interest of the Companies not to alienate the local officials too much.[44]

In the summer of 1750, Nasir Khan, the chief of the Sab'eh district, after the death of his older brother, who had been active in the Lar area since 1747 and was implicated in the murder of Mirza Abu Taleb, had consolidated his powers in Lar, meaning that he had eliminated all his competitors. It was rumored that he wanted to come to Bandar 'Abbas, formally to discipline Molla 'Ali Shah for harassing the Dutch and English as well as the country traders. In reality and more importantly, he wanted to come to collect taxes and customs duties. That it was more than a rumor became clear when Saleh Khan Bayat, *beygler-beygi* of Fars, sent an order to Molla 'Ali Shah "and the rest of the Governors of the Hot Countrys" instructing them to stop harassing the EIC and its servants.[45] However, given the feeble hold upcountry officials had over their jurisdictions, due to the unsettled state of the country, this order remained a piece of paper, although the *kalantar* of Hajjiabad wrote Molla 'Ali Shah that Saleh Khan Bayat and Nasir Khan had left Shiraz on September 1, 1750 to march to Bandar 'Abbas to call him to task and collect taxes.

The threat did not only come from upcountry, for in 1750 Molla 'Ali Shah also feared that the Omanis would attack Bandar 'Abbas to which end two ships and many *tranki*s had been prepared. 'Abdol-Sheikh of Qeshm was said to support the Omanis, thus the rift between him and Molla 'Ali Shah, which had been patched-up, became evident, and made the Companies' director even consider supporting Molla 'Ali Shah against what they judged to be a threat to trade. Molla 'Ali Shah felt greatly threatened in September 1750 and thus it was no surprise to the Dutch and English that he planned to attack their warehouses, supported by forces from Minab and Sheikh 'Ali b. Khalfan Charaki. He also continued his molestation of EIC and VOC Indian servants and even forced them to guard the town wall, clear houses for Arab troops and the like. At that time the news of 'Ali Mardan Khan having taken Shiraz only increased the confusion and insecurity at Bandar 'Abbas, with an outbreak of banditry in its hinterland.[46]

---

43 VOC 2787, Gamron to Batavia (17/02/1751), f. 21-22, 42, Saldanha, *Précis*, vol. 1, p. xxxviii (LVII); Lorimer, *Gazetteer*, p. 90; Perry, *Karim Khan*, p. 29.

44 VOC 2787, Gamron to Batavia (17/02/1751), f. 23-25; Perry, *Karim Khan*, p. 23; Amin, *British Interests*, p. 41.

45 Ricks, *Politics and Trade*, p. 195 referring to F. R. Gombroon VI (16/08/1750). His full name was Mohammad Nasir Khan, see VOC 3156, f. 51. Fasa'i, *Farsnameh*, vol. 2, p. 1350.

46 Ricks, *Politics and Trade*, pp. 196-97 referring to F. R. Gombroon VI (25/08/1750; 29/08/1750; 05/09/1750; 26/09/1750; 28 and 29/11/1750); VOC 2767, f. 50, 60-61.

MOLLA 'ALI SHAH, THE DUTCH AND THE ENGLISH DISCUSS MOVING TO THE ISLANDS

In November 1750 Shah Esma'il III appointed Nasir Khan *beygler-beygi* of Lar and the Garmsir and Molla 'Ali Shah *darya-beygi* of the fleet. The latter felt that this appointment gave him some level of protection against Nasir Khan's exactions and he discontinued his harassment of the Europeans. On November 9, 1750 the Dutch received information from Minab that the Baluch were marauding again in large numbers and intended to come to Bandar 'Abbas. The result of this news was that a great many people took refuge with their cattle under the walls and cannons of the Dutch and English factories. Another unnerving piece of information arrived about the same time, viz. that 'Ali Mardan Khan would come to Bushire to collect taxes and ships to attack Bandar 'Abbas. This was made worse by the news of (i) the sack of Shiraz, where his troops had behaved even worse than in Isfahan, (ii) the imprisonment of Nasir Khan and (iii) the demand by Saleh Khan of 50,000 *tumans* or three-years of taxes. Molla 'Ali Shah panicked and fled to his fleet.[47]

Because rumors had it that the Bakhtiyaris were extorting money and supplies from everybody and that possibly marauding Baluch would also attack, many peasants left their villages and came to the coast, many seeking protection under the walls of the Dutch and English factories, while those living on the coast prepared to leave for the islands. Such was the fear of the fury of the Bakhtiyaris that Molla 'Ali Shah changed his tune and wanted to come to an accommodation with the English. He approached the Dutch to mediate and as a result the conflict with the English was settled. Molla 'Ali Shah then proposed to 'Abdol-Sheikh of the Banu Ma'in, the EIC and the VOC to all move to Qeshm together with the merchandise and livestock, which location would permit the continuation of trade, he optimistically argued.[48] It was said that 'Ali Mardan Khan intended to take Bandar 'Abbas as well to pillage the Dutch and English factories. This caused more consternation among the local population and the Europeans than the news about the marauding Baluch. Molla 'Ali Shah and Savage, the EIC Agent, immediately asked Schoonderwoerd to keep *de Tilburg*, a large VOC ship, for another few days on the roadstead. Rumor had it that 'Ali Mardan Khan intended to demand five *lakh* of rupees from both the EIC and VOC. Shah Esma'il III had sent friendly letters to Molla 'Ali Shah, the EIC and VOC, but these letters were considered as means to put them off their guard. Molla 'Ali Shah, Savage and Schoonderwoerd discussed the situation and decided that it were best to put the most costly goods aboard *de Tilburg* as long as there was time, or on the ketch the *Drake*, or if their capacity did not suffice that then Molla 'Ali Shah would supply them with one of his ships, but crewed by European sailors.[49] On December 16, 1750 Molla 'Ali Shah and Sheikh 'Ali b. Khalfan Charaki met with the Dutch and English chiefs to discuss the move to Qeshm and the inclusion of Sheikh 'Ali in that move. Molla 'Ali Shah vouched for Sheikh 'Ali's character and called him his friend, but the EIC declined, because it did not want to be drawn in into the feuds and fights that Sheikh 'Ali was already involved in. On December 14, 1750 Molla 'Ali Shah received news that Nasir Khan and ten followers had escaped from Shiraz. The next day a *nakhoda* came from Bushire and made known that Sheikh Naser of Bushire and other coastal chiefs had refused to pay taxes to Esma'il III and were leaving to the islands.[50]

---

47 Ricks, *Politics and Trade*, pp. 196-98 referring to F. R. Gombroon VI (03/11/1750; 12 and 13/11/1750); Fasa'i, *Farsnameh*, vol. 1, p. 588.

48 VOC 2787, Gamron to Batavia (17/02/1751), f. 58; Ricks, *Politics and Trade*, p. 198 referring to F. R. Gombroon VI (28/11/1750).

49 VOC 2787, Gamron to Batavia (17/02/1751), f. 55-57; Saldanha, *Précis*, vol. 1, p. 73 (Bombay, 23/02/1751); Perry, *Karim Khan*, p. 28-29; Lorimer, *Gazetteer*, p. 98.

50 Ricks, *Politics and Trade*, pp. 198-99 referring to F. R. Gombroon VI (04/12/1750 and 04/01/1751).

On December 22, 1750 'Abdollah Khan, Esma'il III's tax-man, accompanied by six *mohassels* or tax collectors, arrived in Bandar 'Abbas, which put an end to the talks about the move to Qeshm. He had a decree which ordered Molla 'Ali Shah to pay 28,000 *tumans* (4,000 *tumans* in customs revenues and the population of Bandar 'Abbas to pay 24,000 *tumans* in taxes). It was also said that he had orders to demand a large amount of money from the EIC and VOC. When 'Abdollah Khan observed that Molla 'Ali Shah gave him a cool welcome, and that the Europeans were loading goods on their ships he did not produce his decree. In his discussion with Molla 'Ali Shah the latter said that the population was too poor to pay the amount demanded and they agreed on the payment of one year of tax revenues. Molla 'Ali wanted to assassinate 'Abdollah Khan, but the EIC refused to be a party to that. Nevertheless, the Europeans were now not so certain anymore about Molla 'Ali Shah's commitment to move the merchandise off-shore and the lending of one of his ships to that end. They decided to force the issue to know where he stood and if he denied them the ship they would await a ship coming either from Bombay or a large Dutch ship coming from Basra.[51]

News about troubles in Larestan and Karim Khan's march on Isfahan only increased people's anxiety. Esma'il III apparently left Shiraz for Lar by the end of December 1750, while security on the road to Kerman worsened. In mid-January 1751 the Dutch received news that the Bakhtiyaris had left Shiraz and were advancing towards Jahrom and Fasa under Nasir Khan and 'Ali Saleh Khan Bakhtiyari.[52] When it was confirmed that 'Ali Mardan Khan had taken Fasa, Jahrom and Darab and prepared himself for the assault on Lar the Dutch and English became very worried, for they had been unable to ship large volumes of their goods, because their vessels were already fully loaded. Moreover, they were uncertain about Molla 'Ali Shah's position; would he stick with them, or turn upon them? Savage and Schoonderwoerd held daily discussions and they finally decided that with the first arriving ship the remaining goods of both Companies would be loaded, and all remaining Europeans would leave with this ship. The Dutch had also intimated that they would leave Bandar 'Abbas altogether.

On January 24, 1751 news was received that Karim Khan Zand had ordered Nasir Khan to disobey 'Ali Mardan Khan and Esma'il III. Before he could be arrested Nasir Khan had fled from the Bakhtiyari camp. Meanwhile, 'Abu'l-Qasem Beyg, the *shahryari* of Minab, the chief of Rudan and the most important Baluch chief came to Bandar 'Abbas and persuaded Molla 'Ali Shah to declare for Shah Esma'il III, i.e. for 'Ali Mardan Khan. The Dutch and the English were quite taken aback by this change of heart, for instead of a friend they had an enemy on their doorstep, or so they felt. At that time news reached Bandar 'Abbas about Nasir Khan Lari's escape from his imprisonment by 'Ali Mardan Khan. Molla 'Ali Shah was mortified by his unwise chosing of political sides, because Nasir Khan's escape "encouraged all the Heads of the Tribes, on the Hot Countrys (Laristan and Fars) to assist Nasseer Caun with Soldiers who are now marching from all parts to meet him" to oppose 'Ali Mardan Khan.[53] This and another piece of news, viz. that a certain Karim Khan Zand had taken Isfahan and intended to expel 'Ali Mardan Khan, made Molla 'Ali Shah to change his mind and not declare for Shah Esma'il III.[54]

51 VOC 2787, Gamron to Batavia (17/02/1751), f. 59; Ricks, *Politics and Trade*, pp. 199-200; Saldanha, *Précis*, vol. 1, p. 73 (Bombay, 23/02/1751) (this letter states that 'Abdollah Khan had 10 men with him).

52 VOC 2787, Gamron to Batavia (17/02/1751), f. 60; Ricks, *Politics and Trade*, pp. 201-02 referring to F. R. Gombroon VI (08/01/1751; 23/08/1751).

53 Ricks, *Politics and Trade*, p. 202 referring to F. R. Gombroon VI (23/01/1751).

54 VOC 2787, (17/02/1751), f. 59-62; Saldanha, *Précis*, vol. 1, p. 73 (Bombay, 23/02/1751); Ricks, *Politics and Trade*, pp. 198-99 referring to F. R. Gombroon VI (13/01/1751 and 23/01/1751).

THE DUTCH TEMPORARILY DEPART FROM BANDAR 'ABBAS

On February 6, 1751 an EIC ship from Bombay arrived at Bandar 'Abbas heading for Europe. Savage contacted Schoonderwoerd and told him that whether it was 'Ali Mardan Khan or Karim Khan who won it did not make any difference. For the European Companies it would be impossible to carry on their trade peacefully and unhindered. He therefore intended not to unload the ship, but to put his goods, himself and his family aboard it and leave. The *Drake*, an EIC ketch, would remain on the roadstead for 10 days until the VOC ship *de Anna* would arrive from Basra and then it also would depart. The local merchants also started sending their goods to Hormuz and Masqat in February 1751. When *de Anna* arrived on February 22, 1751 there was not enough room for all VOC staff and goods. It was therefore decided to leave book-keeper Anthony van der Wall and assistant Alexander Diedriksz behind with some spices, pepper, and some other goods. Schoonderwoerd also believed that his departure would send a signal to the local officials that they needed to provide better incentives for the VOC in the future. He did not believe that the local officials would plunder the VOC factory, because there was not much of value in it and because they did not want to get a bad reputation. When Molla 'Ali Shah realized that the Dutch really were going to leave he personally visited Schoonderwoerd to ask him to stay. Schoonderwoerd said his decision was irrevocable, while he also accused Molla 'Ali Shah of duplicity, for he had been prepared to sacrifice the Europeans for his own safety. Molla 'Ali Shah apologized and promised to behave better in the future, but Schoonderwoerd did not believe him and told Molla 'Ali Shah that he would leave on March 8 and asked him to settle his debts with the VOC. Molla 'Ali Shah said that he had a cash flow problem, but he promised that he would pay as soon as possible to the staff who remained behind.[55]

Schoonderwoerd left on March 8, 1751. Savage had already left with the *Salisbury*, while the *Drake* remained on the roadstead. The EIC garrison had been reinforced with 48 soldiers from the *Salisbury*, while Graves remained in charge of the EIC factory. Their departure thus had been unnecessary, because 'Ali Mardan Khan did not come to Bandar 'Abbas. He was defeated in the narrow pass of Kotal-e dokhtar by local levies in early 1751. From there he went to the Kuhgilu area, where most of his troops, with the exception of his Bakhtiyaris, deserted him. This situation created a power vacuum in the Garmsirat, which nobody was able to fill in 1751.[56]

MOLLA 'ALI SHAH ALLIES HIMSELF WITH THE QAVASEM

With the decisive defeat of the Bakhtiyaris some measure of peace returned and so did trade inland, though not so much at Bandar 'Abbas. By mid-February 1751 Nasir Khan was back and in charge again of Lar and reconciled with his rival Sheikh Mohammad Sayyed. News also arrived that he was angry with Molla 'Ali Shah for having sided with the Bakhtiyaris and that he intended to visit Bandar 'Abbas. This news caused much consternation to Molla 'Ali Shah and his supporters as Nasir Khan had been appointed by Karim Khan as his general. But it was premature, for he did not come and Molla 'Ali Shah had other problems to worry about. All of a sudden a war had broken out among the Hulas about Sheikh 'Ali b. Khalfan's behavior and the control over shipping lanes. On one side were the Hulas of Jolfar (now Ra's al-Khaymah), Lengeh, Kangan, and Taheri and on the

55 VOC 2787, Gamron to Batavia (17/02/1751), f. 63-64; VOC 2787, Gamron to Batavia (08/03/1751), f. 63-73; Saldanha, *Précis*, vol. 1, p. xxxviii (LX).

56 VOC 2804, f. 84, Gamron to Batavia (01/10/1753), f. 20; VOC 2804, Gamron to Batavia (20/09/1752), f. 25-26; Perry, *Karim Khan*, pp. 30-34. Savage, who had gone to Basra, returned to Bandar 'Abbas on October 3, 1751.

other side those of Charak and Bandar 'Abbas. The stakes became even higher when Nasir Khan declared that he supported the Hulas against those of Bandar 'Abbas and Charak, while 'Abdol-Hasan Khan Shirazi, *beygler-beygi* of Fars supported Sheikh Naser of Bushire in his bid to take Bahrain from the Hulas.[57]

Molla 'Ali Shah learnt that the Charakis had taken seven *trankis* from the Hulas. The same report also said that the Hulas under Sheikh Hatem of Taheri and Sheikh Qa'ed of Jolfar had gathered a force of 100 *trankis* to move against Charak and then Bandar 'Abbas. This news greatly disconcerted Molla 'Ali Shah, the more since the Hulas had seized one of his gallivats that he had lent to the Charakis. On March 24, 1751 'Abdol-Sheikh of Qeshm joined the Hulas at Lingeh where they were preparing for the siege of Charak and the capture of the royal fleet. Molla 'Ali Shah asked the EIC for help, which uncharacteristically Savage promised, despite the EIC policy of non-interference in local affairs. He justified his decision by pointing out that the Hulas could disrupt trade with their ships, while given the advent of Karim Khan as the new king (which had led to a revival of trade inland) the EIC had to side with the Persians or leave Bandar 'Abbas.[58]

In the first week of April 1751 Molla 'Ali Shah and Sheikh Chaueed a.k.a. Rahma b. Matar of Jolfar[59] agreed to assist one another against their enemies. The reasons for this new and unexpected alliance are not very clear. Sheikh Rahma b. Matar had been chief of Jolfar since about the 1720s and this function Nader Shah had awarded to the sheikh as a hereditary position for his lineage. With the withdrawal of the Persian troops from Jolfar in 1747 Sheikh Rahma b. Matar seized power and considered himself to be an independent ruler of his territory, which stretched as far as Cape Mosandam. He refused to recognize the new power in Oman, Ahmad b. Sa'id, the founder of the new reigning Al Bu Sa'id dynasty, which in vain for the remainder of the eighteenth century and beyond tried to subdue the Jolfaris or Qavasem, as the tribal confederacy concentrated in the territory of Sir was known. Molla 'Ali Shah's control over the Persian royal fleet had a strong appeal for the Qavasem chief, as it was potentially a powerful instrument to be used in his struggle with Oman to maintain his independence. Moreover, an alliance with Molla 'Ali Shah made it possible to control the Straits of Hormuz, as both parties controlled the littoral and the sea in that part of the Persian Gulf.[60] The alliance was facilitated by the fact that the Jolfaris had no conflict with Molla 'Ali Shah, who just happened to be an ally of Sheikh 'Ali Charaki.

THE HULAS FLEX THEIR MUSCLES AND NASIR KHAN CONSOLIDATES HIS CONTROL OVER LARESTAN

After the conclusion of the alliance Sheikh Rahma left to join the Hulas to attack the Charaki Arabs. However, Molla 'Ali Shah's problems were not over, for he intercepted a letter sent by 'Abdol-Sheikh to the chiefs of Qeshm, Hormuz and Minab instructing them to disobey Molla 'Ali Shah. The latter also learnt on April 13, 1751 that the Hulas were cooperating with Nasir Khan and Sheikh Mohammad Sayyed of Lar. All this was disturbing news. On April 16 'Abdol-Sheikh wrote the EIC from Charak that 7,000 Hulas were ready to attack that port in a few days and that they then intended to attack Bandar 'Abbas to punish Molla 'Ali Shah and to seize the royal fleet. Also,

57 Ricks, *Politics and Trade*, pp. 202-03 referring to F. R. Gombroon VI (12/02/1751 and 05/03/1751). On the dispute about Bahrain see chapter seven and Appendix 1 in this publication. Nasir Khan was said to have an army of some 15,000 men, both cavalry and infantry. VOC 2804, Gamron to Batavia (15/02/1752), f. 7.

58 Ricks, *Politics and Trade*, p. 203 referring to F. R. Gombroon VI (05/03/1751).

59 This is the same person as Sheikh Rahma. See chapter two.

60 See chapter two; Risso, *Oman*, pp. 76-82.

that Sheikh Mohammad Sayyed's people had already seized his brimstone mines in Larestan. It thus would seem that between the Lar rock and the Hula hard place Molla 'Ali Shah had nowhere to go and would lose his fleet and thus his most effective instrument to display power and authority.[61]

Meanwhile, Nasir Khan was consolidating his hold over Larestan. On April 20, 1751 Molla 'Ali Shah received a letter from the *kalantar* of Hajjiabad in which he was informed that Nasir Khan had appointed Ra'is Qambar Baluch as *kalantar* of Rudan to whom he had vowed to subjugate Minab and Bandar 'Abbas. He also had dispatched Mohammad Beyg Safidbandi to prevent Molla 'Ali Shah's escape by land. The next day a traveler reported that Ra'is Allahverdi Baluch had been appointed governor of Minab and that his brother Ra'is Qambar had indeed been appointed as *kalantar* of Rudan by Karim Khan. Nasir Khan further had appointed Ra'is Masih as *shahbandar* of Bandar 'Abbas and Mohammad Beyg Safidbandi as governor of Bandar 'Abbas and deputy-governor of Lar.[62] This news was upsetting because Nasir Khan seemed to be carrying out Karim Khan's orders. As a result all his henchmen held important offices in Larestan, who, according to the EIC, were "common Balloches, Rogues who had been famous for some years past for plundering." It appeared as if Molla 'Ali Shah was done for.[63]

On May 2, 1751 it was learnt in Bandar 'Abbas that Charak had fallen and that Sheikh 'Ali had been taken prisoner by Sheikh Hatem of Taheri. The new chief of Charak was Sheikh Mohammad b. Salem, a member of the Al 'Ali more acceptable to the Hulas. It was further learnt that the Hulas had postponed their attack on Bandar 'Abbas, undoubtedly due to the influence of Sheikh Rahma of Jolfar. A few days later the EIC learnt that Nasir Khan had hurried back to Lar when he learnt that Saleh Khan Bayat was once again in Shiraz and that Sheikh Mohammad Sayyed was operating independently from him. This meant that for the moment, a year it would turn out to be, that Molla 'Ali Shah had nothing to fear from Nasir Khan. However, the Hulas were not done with him yet. In mid-May Sheikh Hatem of Taheri and Sheikh Chaueed of Jolfar let him know that they wanted to buy two of his ships. If he complied they would be good friends, if not they would just take them. On May 18 Sheikh Hatem came to Bandar 'Abbas and told Molla 'Ali Shah that the Hulas would return to their own lands. On May 28, Sheikh Chaueed came on behalf of all Hula chiefs to tell Molla 'Ali Shah of their wish for closer ties. This meant family ties and therefore 'Abdol Sheikh offered his daughter in marriage to his son, which Molla 'Ali Shah refused, referring to his agreement with Sheikh Chaueed of April 1751 and by approving his daughter's marriage with Sheikh Chaueed on June 8, 1751, promising "to stand by each other on all occasions."[64]

In July 1751 Sheikh 'Ali b. Khalfan escaped from his captors in Taheri and with five large *trankis* he landed near Kong, "cut off the whole village" and sought refuge with Molla 'Ali Shah. He also went to Hormuz with four gallivats and *trankis* that he had captured on raids against the Hulas near Hormuz. He then moved to Larek and sent Molla 'Ali Shah two merchants and some merchandise that he had seized from a tranki returning from Mokha and asked Molla 'Ali Shah permission to settle in Bandar 'Abbas or on one of the islands. Molla 'Ali Shah refused, because he did not need new trouble with the Hulas. Seven months later Sheikh 'Ali, who meanwhile had settled on Qeshm, begged forgiveness from Nasir Khan and permission to return to Charak, who acceded to his request.[65]

The people of Bandar 'Abbas took all the news of battles, victories and defeats that took place upcountry in stride; it was faraway and too much to deal with. On August 30, 1751 four couriers (*chapars*) from Shah Esma'il III arrived in Bandar Abbas with letters asking the EIC to re-establish a factory in

61 Ricks, *Politics and Trade*, pp. 204-06 referring to F. R. Gombroon VI (05/03/1751; 02/04/1751; 09/04/1751).

62 Ricks, *Politics and Trade*, p. 206 referring to F. R. Gombroon VI (09/04/1751 and 10/04/1751).

63 Ricks, *Politics and Trade*, pp. 206-07 referring to F. R. Gombroon VI (03/05/1751).

64 Amin, *British Interests*, p. 28; Ricks, *Politics and Trade*, pp. 207-08 referring to F. R. Gombroon VI (03/05/1751 and 28/05/1751).

65 Ricks, *Politics and Trade*, pp. 208-09 referring to F. R. Gombroon VI (26/06/1751 and 28/06/1751).

Isfahan and in another letter to ask the EIC to help the Shah by inducing Mohammad Beyg Shamlu, the royal *vakil*, to return from India with a ship that was part of the royal fleet. The EIC replied negatively to the first request and to the second the EIC promised to forward a letter from Esma'il III to Bombay. In fact, Savage recommended Bombay to confiscate his ship "in part satisfaction of the money loans they have sustained."[66]

In mid-September 1751 Molla 'Ali Shah learnt about the Hula victory over the allied forces of Bandar-e Rig and Bushire at Bahrain, another episode in the regular challenge to anyone who held the island so as to have access to its rich pearl grounds and its revenues. On September 26, 1751 Molla 'Ali Shah received Danvers Graves at Naband. He wanted to sound out the EIC as to the coming of the Hula chiefs to Bandar 'Abbas, who wanted Molla 'Ali Shah's support to win their war against Bandar-e Rig and Bushire, who the Hulas wanted to destroy because of their attack on Bahrain. Graves advised Molla 'Ali Shah to avoid the Arabs and side with the government of Persia. On September 30, a very large tranki arrived with Sheikh Hatem and Sheikh Qa'ed with whom Molla 'Ali Shah had a week-long discussion. During that time 12 more large trankis arrived with 3,000 Arabs.[67]

MOLLA 'ALI SHAH STRENGTHENS HIS TIES WITH THE HULAS

Molla 'Ali Shah called on Graves to tell him of the result of the discussions. He had married a second daughter to Sheikh Hatem and thus had assumed closer ties to the Hulas, which Graves did not like at all. Moreover, he had appointed Sheikh Qa'ed as his deputy at Bandar 'Abbas. Graves told him he was risking his authority, that merchants would not come to Bandar 'Abbas anymore, and that the central government in Shiraz and Lar would consider him a rebel and punish him severely. His task was to keep the roads open and maintain order in the district and port of Bandar 'Abbas, otherwise the EIC would depart if new troubles would occur. Molla 'Ali Shah listened and heard, for three days later he reached a compromise with the Hulas after a heated debate. The Hulas had wanted the use of the entire fleet and they finally left having borrowed one ship and two gallivats so that Molla 'Ali Shah had only one ship left at Bandar 'Abbas. Sheikh Hatem then left for Bushire with one gallivat and four months of provisions. Despite this setback Molla 'Ali Shah nevertheless behaved insolently towards the English, threatening to force money from people under their protection and to molest their servants.[68]

Naser Khan was concerned about these developments, because he wrote to Graves to that effect, while confirming that Lar was peaceful. He further announced that he would come to Bandar 'Abbas to install his own people, as Molla 'Ali Shah had appointed Arabs there. According to the English, the Hula Arabs wanted to have their own man in Bandar 'Abbas to be able to refit their trankis, obtain fresh water

66 Amin, *British Interests*, p. 30, n. 1; Ricks, *Politics and Trade*, pp. 209-11 referring to F. R. Gombroon VI (30/08/1751 and 28/05/1751). Already in 1750 Saleh Khan Bayat, *sardar* and *beygler-beygi* of Fars, had asked the Dutch and English to make Mohammad Beyg Shamlu, who was believed to be in Cochin, return to Persia. The Dutch replied that with the help of the English he had moved to Bombay. The *sardar* replied in a haughty manner and informed both the Dutch and English that if the Crown would loose because of this he would seek recompense from them. VOC 2787, Gamron to Batavia (17/02/1751), f. 50. Molla 'Ali Shah also had requested the EIC factory in Surat to help Mohammad Beyg in 1750, after the latter had complained about ill-treatment by the governor of Surat. The English replied that they done all they could. Saldanha, *Précis*, vol. 1, p. xxxviii (LVII and LVIII).

67 Ricks, *Politics and Trade*, pp. 211-12 referring to F. R. Gombroon VI (?/09/1751 and 15/09/1751); Saldanha, *Précis*, vol. 1, p. xxxviii (LXI).

68 Saldanha, *Précis*, vol. 1, p. 74 (Bombay, 17/02/1752); Ricks, *Politics and Trade*, pp. 212-13 referring to F. R. Gombroon VI (15/09/1751, pp. 27-28 and 25/09/1751, p. 30); Amin, *British Interests*, p. 30.

and firewood, and eventually capture the revenues and trade of the region. On October 18, 1751 Sheikh Rahma left for Bushire with one Persian ship, one gallivat and some trankis to assist in the Hula attack on Bushire. The Hula versus Bushire/Rig war lasted till December 1751 and ended in a victory for Bushire/Rig; as a result the Hulas retired to Bahrain. 'Abdol-Hasan Khan, *beygler-beygi* of Fars fell from power, due to excessive taxation and his role in supporting Bushire in its endeavor to conquer Bahrain.[69]

NASER KHAN CONTROLS LARESTAN AND SEIZES BANDAR 'ABBAS AND MOLLA 'ALI SHAH

Between October 1751 and February 1752, Nasir Khan and Molla 'Ali Shah exchanged a number of letters concerning revenue issues, the governor's responsibilities, and his relations with the Arabs and the EIC. On October 20, 1751 Esma'il III sent orders from Isfahan to the EIC assuring them that they would be treated on the old footing and would remain free from molestation and that Nasir Khan swore friendship to the EIC. At the same time letters arrived from Nasir Khan with a similar message and that he wanted to have half of Molla 'Ali Shah's revenues. The money, of course, was the real issue about which there was a conflict.[70]

In December 1751 it became known that Nasir Khan had killed Sheikh Mohammad his local rival in his bid for independence of and in Larestan. On December 22, 1751 the English received a letter from him in which he stated that he was averse to the Bakhtiyari-like methods used by 'Abdol-Hasan Khan and that he would bring security to the roads in Larestan. The next day the bearer of the letter, Ra'is Mohammad Saleh, *kalantar* of 'Essin, visited Graves. He told him that Nasir Khan wanted to visit to littoral, but not the port, because this would be too large a burden for the villagers. However, Nasir Khan insisted that Molla 'Ali Shah had to share the revenues and stop abusing Nasir Khan's name, while he furthermore maintained that Molla 'Ali Shah's behavior had driven off the Dutch, while his alliance with Baluchis and Arabs interfered with his governorship and that he (Nasir Khan) would not any longer obey the 'great people' in Isfahan, meaning Karim Khan and any of the other contenders for the throne.[71]

Nasir Khan Lari, the new power in Larestan between 1751 and 1765, was still too uncertain about Karim Khan's intentions to go beyond the confines of his own territory. However, towards the end of January 1752 he suddenly arrived at 'Essin, at a few hours distance from Bandar 'Abbas, informing Molla 'Ali Shah that he intended to come to Bandar 'Abbas. Molla 'Ali Shah wrote Nasir Khan that it would be better that he not come, because the people (meaning himself) feared him and wanted to flee to Hormuz and Qeshm. In early February 1752 news was received that Nasir Khan was at Fin, a few hours distance from Bandar 'Abbas. He intended to dismiss Molla 'Ali Shah and stop the Baluch incursion into the Minab districts. Molla 'Ali Shah immediately asked for EIC support, which was refused. Graves told him that the English would fight the Baluch, but not Nasir Khan, who was the governor of Larestan. The notables of Bandar 'Abbas also had no faith in resisting Nasir Khan as he had been appointed by the shah and, moreover, had a large army. Very late in the evening of February 5, 1752 Nasir Khan's staff bearer, Haqqverdi Beyg called on the EIC to assure them that his master wanted their friendship and advice regarding Molla 'Ali Shah. He asked that they sent a representative to his council at 'Essin. Graves replied the next day saying that the English were the only Europeans remaining at Bandar 'Abbas, which, without their presence would be a fishing village, and that he "was the judge how to manage" Molla 'Ali Shah. The

69 Ricks, *Politics and Trade*, p. 213 referring to F. R. Gombroon VI (28/09/1751 and 07/10/1751; 11/12/1751); Saldanha, *Précis*, vol. 1, p. xxxviii (LXI).

70 Ricks, *Politics and Trade*, p. 214 referring to F. R. Gombroon VI (09/10/1751).

71 Ricks, *Politics and Trade*, pp. 215-16 referring to F. R. Gombroon VI (11/12/1751 and 17/12/1751).

English clearly wanted to keep the devil they knew rather than have to deal with an unknown one. Later that same day Nasir Khan wrote to Molla 'Ali Shah asking for the revenues and customs of the last three years. Molla 'Ali Shah became so afraid that he threatened to plunder Bandar 'Abbas and to abandon the port the next day. Molla 'Ali Shah convened the leading merchants and the heads of the town quarters (*kadkhodas*) and ordered them to leave with him the next day to one of the islands near Bandar 'Abbas. Those who refused to accompany him would have their goods confiscated. However, Nasir Khan may have expected Molla 'Ali Shah's intended flight, for he took the town the next day at sunrise. In the afternoon of February 7, 1752 Nasir Khan himself marched into Bandar 'Abbas with about 2,000 men and Molla 'Ali surrendered to him without a fight. He met with the EIC and VOC representatives and assured them of his good intentions. He asked the VOC in particular to increase its trading activities. Nasir Khan also informed the population that Shah Esma'il III had appointed him *beygler-beygi* of the Banader (Gulf Ports), which meant that everybody, including the Europeans, had to give him presents.[72]

Nasir Khan stayed for five weeks in Bandar 'Abbas. During his stay Nasir Khan behaved correctly. He made it clear that he intended to make Bandar 'Abbas flourish again. He also arrested Molla 'Ali Shah and his fleet, confiscated all his property, both on land and on the ships, had the latter's family return from Hormuz and took possession of the fort. Nasir Khan, through his brother-in-law Masih Khan, asked the EIC for advice whom to appoint as governor of the port. Graves was taken aback by this and asked for time to make up his mind. After discussion he informed Nasir Khan that he would not recommend anyone and leave it entirely to his discretion. The English were afraid that their choice might offend others and if the choice did not turn out well they would be blamed. On February 15, 1752 during a visit to the EIC factory Nasir Khan told Graves that he would appoint Masih Khan, his wife's brother to govern Bandar 'Abbas, 'Essin, Shamil, Rudan, Minab and Qeshm. He would seek Graves's advice on matters concerning trade, while Nasir Khan himself would keep the roads secure. Nasir Khan then busied himself with collecting taxes and customs, appointing officials, and accepting presents. Molla 'Ali Shah had to pay three years of tax arrears or 60,000 Rs (3,000 *tumans*). 'Abdol-Sheikh came from Qeshm to confirm their friendship from whom Nasir Khan took also 3,000 *tumans*, which were paid in pearls and costly fabrics. Qasem Beyg, the *Shahriyari* of Minab and the chief of Shamil also came, who had to pay their arrears in taxes, amounting to 1,500 *tumans*, to which end they applied to the EIC for loans. The Imam of Masqat sent fine goods, sugar loaves and eight black slaves with the request to aid him with 1,000 men to put down a rebellion in Oman. On March 3, 1752 Sheikh 'Ali b. Khalfan came to plead his case and he was promised aid to recover Charak, with a view to establish 'Persian' control over the littoral. Ra'is Qambar, an important Baluch chief and *kalantar* of Rudan, came with several fine horses, oxen and sheep. Before he returned to Lar, Nasir Khan asked Graves what he wanted to which he said his protection of all caravans to and from Bandar 'Abbas, because now they were delayed and plundered by the road-guards (*rahdars*). On March 12, 1752 Nasir Khan left for Lar with Molla 'Ali and several other notables as prisoners, such as Sheikh 'Ali b. Khalfan's brother. Sheikh Ahmad was appointed as governor for Jask, Qasem Beyg *Shahriyari* as governor of Minab and 'Abdol-Sheikh as governor of Qeshm, all having been stripped bare. Nasir Khan left his brother-in-law, Masih Soltan, as his deputy-governor with 200 soldiers, who were stationed aboard the *Rahmani* to defend the port against attacks from Arabs or Baluchis. According to the Dutch, Masih Soltan behaved himself reasonably. In the absence of Molla 'Ali Shah, his arch-enemy, 'Abdol-Sheikh, reinforced his fort at Laft on Qeshm. He also took possession of Molla 'Ali Shah's ship the *Fatta Sultanie*, which had gone to Bombay for repairs on March 8, 1751. When the ship returned and its captain learnt about the changes that had taken place in Bandar 'Abbas he sailed to Laft to 'Abdol-Sheikh. Although it seemed that Nasir Khan had favored 'Abdol-Sheikh above Molla 'Ali Shah in the past nevertheless trouble

---

72 VOC 2804, Gamron to Batavia (15/02/1752) f. 7-8, 15-18; Perry, *Karim Khan*, pp. 30-34, 117-18; Ricks, *Politics and Trade*, pp. 216-17 referring to F. R. Gombroon VI (25/01/1752 and 26/01/1751).

arose between Nasir Khan and the chief of the Banu Ma'in about this ship. For when Masih Soltan asked for the ship several times, he was put off with fair words. Meanwhile, 'Abdol-Sheikh fortified his strongholds and mobilized his Arabs against Nasir Khan. He furthermore was inciting the Hulas to take action against Nasir Khan, who therefore wanted to come to the coast to punish the Hulas and take possession of Molla 'Ali Shah's ships. At that time, only the *Rahmanie* was lying in the roads of Bandar 'Abbas, but if the Arab crew would learn of Nasir Khan's intentions the Dutch were convinced that this ship also would disappear. Another of Molla 'Ali Shah's ships, the *Aganieta Maria*, which had gone to Jedda, had been detained in Masqat on its return. The *vali* of Masqat wrote to Masih Soltan that the ship had been in need of repairs and had therefore been drawn ashore, which meant that this ship also would not be returned soon, or so the Dutch believed. There were some other vessels that were lying on the beach of Hormuz, but these were all disabled.[73]

In July 1752 Nasir Khan invited two brothers of Sheikh 'Abdollah of Charak to Lar to settle the conflict with Sheikh 'Ali. He suggested that they made peace with one another, which they refused, because they, i.e. the Al Haram had been hurt so many times by Sheikh 'Ali that they would rather die than befriend him. When he brought Sheikh 'Ali into the council the two brothers became so infuriated that Nasir Khan imprisoned them. He sent Sheikh 'Ali with 300 men to plunder and burn the villages under Sheikh 'Abdollah. The force was defeated, Sheikh 'Ali was beheaded, and only 40 Lari soldiers escaped.[74]

Nasir Khan did reasonably well in Larestan, despite the fact that he received little cooperation from the Gulf Arabs. Moreover, Karim Khan, who had suffered significant setbacks in Northern Persia, was forced to seek support from the local political and economic powers in Fars and the Gulf coast. For the first time since 1747 Larestan was once again under a strong government. Nasir Khan informed Karim Khan that trade had suffered from extortion by local officials such as Molla 'Ali Shah and high customs duties (14-16%), which were more damaging than banditry on the roads and impeded trade. Raids by Baluchis were expected in April and May, while the Arabs were engaged in hostilities during May-July. In mid-May 1752 news arrived in Bandar 'Abbas about the attacks by those of Bandar-e Rig and Bushire along the coast as far as Taheri. Sheikh Naser claimed that Sheikh Hatem owed him 100,000 Rs (5,000 *tumans*) and with two ships, four gallivats and many trankis tried to recover the debt.[75]

THE EIC CONSIDERS ABANDONING BANDAR 'ABBAS

The English had experienced Nasir Khan's visit as most disconcerting, despite the fact that he had kept tight control over his troops. But he had taken Molla 'Ali Shah, his family, his valuables and his ship. Daily he had extorted money from all wealthy individuals by torture; one of them had died as a result. After having taken the fort Nasir Khan also had visited the English factory. They had given him a present of 100 *tumans*, the EIC Banyans 80 *tumans*, but the Dutch had given six times more, or so they claimed. They could not refuse to give unless it was decided to abandon Bandar 'Abbas, for which they believed there was ample justification. There was no central government, there only

73 VOC 2804, Gamron to Batavia (20/09/1752), f. 26-29; see however Amin, *British Interests*, p. 28, n. 4; Lorimer, *Gazetteer*, pp. 99-100; Ricks, *Politics and Trade*, pp. 217-20 referring to F. R. Gombroon VI (31/01/1752; 04/02/1752; 29/02/1752; 02/03/1752 and 03/03/1752); Perry, *Karim Khan*, pp. 118, 159.

74 Ricks, *Politics and Trade*, pp. 221-22 referring to F. R. Gombroon VI (16/07/1752).

75 Ricks, *Politics and Trade*, pp. 220-21 referring to F. R. Gombroon VI (04/04/1752 and 16/07/1752); see also chapter seven in this publication.

were warlords in each province and therefore the idea to move away from Bandar 'Abbas was raised once again.[76]

The EIC staff had been thinking about entirely relocating their factory away from Bandar 'Abbas to one of the islands in the Persian Gulf for the first time in 1750, when its hinterland had been ravaged by 'Ali Mardan Khan. These events and the threat of a direct attack of Bandar 'Abbas had been the reason why the Dutch had temporarily abandoned the port at that time. The EIC Agent, Savage had heard from a visiting Arab that Bahrain had a good fort, good water and that its revenues from taxes on date trees amounted to some 30,000 rupees or 1,500 *tumans* and another 50,000 rupees (2,500 *tumans*) in taxes from its subjects, which included 400 Hula Arabs. Savage liked this idea and proposed to London to move the EIC factory there, while he also proposed to seize Molla 'Ali Shah's fleet of three ships.[77] Bombay did not approve Savage's proposal, because it feared that the taking of the fleet would result in serious problems with whoever would take the Persian throne. It further gave orders that relocating the factory could only be done with the approval of London. The EIC directors supported Bombay's position with regards to the seizure of the Persian fleet, while it approved relocating the factory under certain conditions. The EIC staff was therefore instructed not to leave Bandar 'Abbas unless their life and the Company's merchandise was in danger and that the Company's goods had to be taken aboard in that case. "But should they find it impracticable to come to any agreement or to return to their Factory at least till the Government becomes settled under one head, and have any good encouragement to settle on any Island up the Gulph near Bunder, Bushire, or Bunder Rique where they are sure there is water and provisions & the inhabitants will permit them to land & join them for their mutual defence."[78] Furthermore, London had stressed the fact that the Company was engaged in the business of trade and not in real estate and it was the former that had to be expanded not the latter.[79]

Graves who had succeeded Savage, who had died in early 1752, did not like the Bahrain proposal, but after a trip to the islands close to Bandar 'Abbas he recommended moving to Qeshm or Henjam (Angar). The island of Qeshm was fertile and its chief, 'Abdol-Sheikh had agreed to cede the island to the EIC provided he and his family received a pension and English protection. Graves argued that merchants would come to live there in security, while the customs revenues would pay for the EIC's factory upkeep. To keep construction cost low, they could demolish the factory at Bandar 'Abbas and take all its timber with them, while adobe could be used as building material, for the great expense was to bring stones and mortar from Hormuz and Qeshm. To implement this plan would require two ships and 300 soldiers. To clinch the matter Graves argued that merchants had complained for years about the lack of civility at Bandar 'Abbas, "whereas now the shawbunders or customshouse Officers, without fixing any percentage on goods exacted frequently 16 or 17 per cent. that this Difference to Merchants would certainly establish the center of all Trade between Muscatt and Bussorah of that settlement." Bombay also disapproved of this idea, because the island was too large and would require a large and thus an expensive military force to defend it.[80] The new EIC Agent at Bandar 'Abbas, Francis Wood, who had gathered information concerning the situation on Henjam reported that it was totally unsuitable. Of Bahrain he knew only that

76 Saldanha, *Précis*, vol. 1, p. 76 (Bombay, 12/06/1752); Amin, *British Interests*, p. 32. The Dutch had given Nasir Khan a present of Dfl. 1677:7 or about 40 *tumans* thus 2.5 times less than the English. VOC 2804, Gamron to Batavia (15/02/1752), f. 17. The first time the English had raised the need to abandon Bandar 'Abbas had been in 1727. VOC 2088, f. 3413vs.

77 Amin, *British Interests*, pp. 30-31; Ricks, *Politics and Trade*, pp. 200-01 referring to F. R. Gombroon VI (17/12/1750).

78 Saldanha, *Précis*, vol. 1, p. 73 (Bombay, 26/02/1751); Amin, *British Interests*, p. 31.

79 Amin, *British Interests*, p. 31.

80 Saldanha, *Précis*, vol. 1, p. 76 (Bombay, 12/06/1752); Amin, *British Interests*, p. 32.

it had much water, which was as unwholesome as its air. He therefore also suggested to go to Qeshm, to the south-east point where there is "a good small Fortification ready built to our hands lying within Sight of Gombroon Factory, which might be defended 40 men and an Ensign against any Country Enemy, excellent Water in Plenty, and Prov$^{e.}$ very cheap."[81] However, later he had second thoughts and wrote that with a guard boat in the roads for protection and men and guns to defend the factory he saw no reason to depart from Bandar 'Abbas; also because if they went to an island the Dutch would "aggravate against us." This recommendation was accepted by Bombay, the more so since 1753 had been an excellent year for the export of woolens to Bandar 'Abbas. London therefore allowed the guard ship to stay at Bandar 'Abbas as long as required.[82]

THE VOC RETURNS TO BANDAR 'ABBAS

When Schoonderwoerd arrived in Batavia, the governor-general did not understand why he had abandoned the factory, while the English had remained in Bandar 'Abbas. Schoonderwoerd argued that he only had 17 men, most of them weakened, and defense against any hostile action would have been futile. The English had a factory only half the size of the VOC and, moreover, had a garrison of 80 people and the *Drake* on the roadstead. He therefore was only reprimanded, and the governor-general rather matter of fact proposed that until further notice no ships would be send to Bandar 'Abbas. However, the ship *de Wereld* coming directly from Europe had called on Bandar 'Abbas in 1752 and provided Batavia with information that Shah Esma'il III, Karim Khan's puppet king, had confirmed all VOC privileges and requested the Company to return to Bandar 'Abbas. The High Government therefore decided to comply with this request and to send Schoonderwoerd back. He was promoted to the rank of senior merchant, because of this previous good services and his knowledge of the Persian trade.[83] The XVII also expressed their surprise about Schoonderwoerd's departure. The more so, because this action was based on the flimsy notion that the local officials would not attack and sack the VOC factory. Later they wanted to have an explanation why the English had stayed behind, but not the VOC staff. They were totally surprised to find that Schoonderwoerd had been promoted and reappointed to direct the Bandar 'Abbas factory. Nevertheless, they acquiesced in this decision.[84]

The year 1751-52 was of course a lost and expensive year for the VOC. Not only was trade insignificant due to internal strife, greedy officials and scarcity of money, but also because of extra expenditures caused by the abandonment and subsequent reestablishment of the Bandar 'Abbas factory. A spell of quiet had encouraged merchants to come to Bandar 'Abbas in the spring of 1752, but the VOC was unable to

81 Saldanha, *Précis*, vol. 1, pp. 78-79 (Gombroon, 17/09/1752).

82 Saldanha, *Précis*, vol. 1, pp. 80-81 (Gombroon, 28/09/1752); Amin, *British Interests*, pp. 33-34 (of 2,700 bales sent to Asia 600 bales were sent to Bandar 'Abbas).

83 VOC 2863 (20/12/1754), f. 35; VOC 1006 (27/07/1752), f. 149; VOC 1005 (03/08/1751), f. 555. The English noted: "the 10th November last Mynheer Sconderwoert returned from Batavia upon a large European Ship & brought several Company's servants & guard of soldiers with him in order to establish the Dutch Factory again in its former footing." Saldanha, *Précis*, vol. 1, p. 81. Slot's observation (Slot, *'Arab al-Khalij*, p. 327, n. 28) that the English were impressed with the size of the military force that accompanied the returning director is misleading as this force was not meant for Bandar 'Abbas, but for Khark. For further details see chapter four.

84 VOC 332 (08/10/1753) and VOC 333 (10/10/1754), section 'Gamron', not foliated. On 27/09/1751 the XVII had written to "inform the Residents that in connection with the troubles in Persia, which appear to have no end, that if things are getting too hot there for the VOC goods, they must depart immediately from there." VOC 332 (27/09/1751), section 'Gamron', not foliated. Schoonderwoerd returned to Bandar 'Abbas in November 1752.

profit from this situation, because it had hardly any goods in the factory.[85] The year 1753 did not show much improvement either. Costs were higher due to late arrival of caravans from the North. The merchants, therefore, could not leave and thus were not very much inclined to trade. Towards the end of 1753 trade picked up again, but trade results remained disappointing. This also held for 1754, which was mainly caused by troubles in the interior, which led to a total standstill of trade with the littoral. Towards the end of 1754 it seemed as if merchants would come after all to Bandar 'Abbas, but unexpected troubles in Kerman and rumors that Karim Khan intended to come to Bandar 'Abbas made these merchants change their plans. As a result, the Dutch had Dfl. 415,000 of unsold goods in stock by the end of 1754.[86]

At the other end of the Persian Gulf, Tido von Kniphausen, the VOC Resident in Basra had fallen out with the local authorities, who arrested him and after having extorted 140,000 piasters allowed him to leave the country in 1752. Von Kniphausen was able to convince Batavia that it would be best to blockade Basra to get their money back, and establish a factory on the island of Khark where the VOC would not be exposed to unreasonable demands from local rulers. In June 1753, von Kniphausen initiated a blockade of the Shatt al-Arab, which had the desired result. The extorted money was paid back; the VOC withdrew their staff from Basra and established a new factory on Khark. The small factory in Bushire also was closed.[87] This surge in Dutch activities gave rise great concern to the English, who feared that the VOC intended to capture the bulk of trade in the Persian Gulf through a concerted effort of establishing a factory at Khark, re-opening its factory at Bandar 'Abbas, closing its factories in Basra and Bushire, and seizing Bahrain. When the VOC also started trade relations with Masqat in 1756 this only further confirmed English suspicion, the more so after their own Bandar-e Rig debacle, for which they blamed the Dutch.[88]

NASIR KHAN RETURNS TO BANDAR 'ABBAS AND REINSTATES MOLLA 'ALI SHAH

Nasir Khan returned to Bandar 'Abbas on November 24, 1752 with 2,000 Afghan and Persian soldiers to regulate the affairs of the petty chiefs as well as to reinstate Molla 'Ali as deputy-governor of Bandar 'Abbas and admiral of the royal fleet, because he had no other person who was capable to take care those functions or whom he could trust. He remained there till January 29, 1753 forced to do so to keep the Afghan soldiers in his employ from revolting at Hajjiabad by keeping strict discipline among them. He ran up a large debt with both Companies for the delivery of expensive fabrics. The English considered that Nasir Khan was the only person who kept order in the "Hot Countries" and in the case of his death there was no other person to control the petty chiefs and soldiers, who all believed that the European factories contained treasures and riches, and only the presence of a ship on the roads deterred them from attacking, or so the English believed. At that time, the regular garrison of the EIC factory at Bandar 'Abbas consisted of one ensign, one sergeant, one corporal, 24 Topass soldiers and 22 Bombay sepoys.[89]

---

85 VOC 2843 (01/10/1753), f. 35; VOC 2787 (08/03/1751), f. 76-77; VOC 2804 (10/02/1752), f. 9; VOC 2804 (01/05/1751), f. 20; VOC 2804 (20/09/1752), f. 31-32.

86 VOC 2443 (01/10/1753), f. 19, 24, 26; VOC 2443 (07/02/1754), f. 60; VOC 2863 (18/09/1754), f. 3; VOC 2863 (20/11/1754), f. 9; VOC 2863 (20/12/1754), f. 43; VOC 2863 (31/03/1755), f. 161-67.

87 VOC 1007 (21/07/53), f. 329-31; according to this instruction by the governor-general to von Kniphausen, the Resident of the new Khark factory, the factories at Basra and Bushire had to be closed down at the same time that the one at Khark would be established. The factory at Bandar 'Abbas would also be closed, but only when the one at Khark had attained a viable economic basis. For further details on the Khark factory see chapter four.

88 Amin, *British Interests*, pp. 34-35. For more information on the Khark operation see chapter four.

89 Saldanha, *Précis*, vol. 1, p. 83, 85-86 (Bombay, 25/07/1753); Ricks, *Politics and Trade*, p. 275.

The English maintained very friendly relations with Nasir Khan whom they gave continuously presents. Schoonderwoerd did not understand why they did that until he learnt that they hoped to obtain possession of the fort of Hormuz. Earlier they had promised Molla 'Ali Shah 2,000 *tumans* or Dfl. 60,000 and a similar amount to Nasir Khan. Molla 'Ali who held the island and had a garrison in its fort had apparently intimated that he was willing to transfer the island to the English, for the latter had given him already an advance on the transfer sum. Schoonderwoerd felt sidelined by these intrigues and wrote to Batavia if he would be allowed to pay Molla 'Ali Shah some money he would stand a better chance than the English to get possession of Hormuz. However, he did not see the advantage of doing so because of the high overhead (garrison) in addition to maintaining the factory in Bandar 'Abbas. Moreover, when there would be a new shah in charge of Persia Hormuz would have to be returned.[90]

Nasir Khan returned to Lar on January 29, 1753. Before his departure he reappointed Molla 'Ali Shah as deputy-governor of Bandar 'Abbas taking his sons as hostages to Lar. In November 1755 they were still there despite Molla 'Ali Shah's intrigues to obtain their release. From January to late summer 1753 Nasir Khan kept good order in Larestan and the coast. In October of that year, due to a conflict between Sheikh Hatem and Sheikh Mohammad b. Jaber Taheri concerning Bahrain and differences with Nasir Khan over the payment of tribute by the Banu Ma'in, Nasir Khan ordered Molla 'Ali Shah to sail with his two ships and six trankis to Qeshm to punish 'Abdol-Sheikh, the chief of the Banu Ma'in. Thereafter, he had to continue to Bahrain to support Sheikh Mohammad, the former governor of that island, against the claims made by Sheikh Hatem. Because of his family relationship with Sheikh Hatem Molla 'Ali Shah did not want to implement this order.[91] When he did not do so, Nasir Khan sent him strong reprimands foreboding a new conflict between Lar and the coastal population. By the winter of 1753 Nasir Khan was at war with almost the entire Arab coastal population.[92] According to the English, Nasir Khan had 12,000 men, which they considered were barely enough to keep the Arabs from usurping his government.[93] Nasir Khan also had his eyes on the remaining ships of the royal fleet. In June 1753, Nasir Khan asked Francis Wood, the EIC Agent, to prevent 'Abdol-Sheikh from selling the Persian ship that had come from Bombay in March 1752 to the Imam of Masqat as was rumored. He would come shortly and would resent it greatly if the ship would have been sold, because the previous Agent had engaged himself to protect the royal fleet against the Arabs or any other enemy. In fact, he argued, the EIC should not have allowed 'Abdol-Sheikh to take it to Laft. Wood fearing the consequences of a refusal sent the *Drake* and the *Ramauny* and 'Abdol-Sheikh delivered up the ship without any problem.[94]

---

90 VOC 2263, f. 15-16 (31/03/1755); VOC 2804, Gamron to Batavia (01/10/1753), f. 22-23; Lorimer, *Gazetteer*, p. 100.

91 Ricks, *Politics and Trade*, pp. 275-76 referring to F. R. Letters XVI, Gombroon (26/03/1753 and 27/10/1753); Perry, *Karim Khan*, p. 118.

92 Amin, *British Interests*, p. 28; Ricks, *Politics and Trade*, p. 224.

93 Saldanha, *Précis*, vol. 1, p. 88 (Bombay, 25/07/1753). According to Ives, *Voyage*, p. 201, in 1758 Nasir Khan "had not above five thousand troops in his pay, but that he possessed many strongholds and garrisons among mountains most inaccessible."

94 Saldanha, *Précis*, vol. 1, p. 82 (Bombay, 25/07/1753). The handing over of the ship was facilitated by the fact that 'Abdol-Sheikh had just seized most of the cargo of the grab the *Nancy*, which belonged to Dutch in Surat, which had shipwrecked and broken apart on the cliffs between Qeshm and the mainland, after it sailed away without a pilot in April 1752.

MOLLA 'ALI SHAH REASSERTS HIS INDEPENDENCE

Mollah 'Ali Shah acted totally independently from Nasir Khan, refused to support him against the Hulas, while he reinforced the citadel of Hormuz as a preventive measure against an eventual attack by Nasir Khan.[95] He also continued to keep one ship at Bandar 'Abbas and one at Hormuz, so as to embark on the former if Nasir Khan came. Nasir Khan also had problems with the people of the Garmsir, in particular the Hulas. He had executed a holy man from Bastak and the Arabs therefore hated him and caused him so many problems that he asked Karim Khan for the help of 4,000 veteran soldiers. By February 1754, without Zand troops which Karim Khan desperately needed himself, and after several defeats, Nasir Khan negotiated a peace agreement with the Arabs, except for Sheikh Mohammad Bastaki who continued to plunder the Bandar 'Abbas region. During the rest of 1754, Nasir Khan just waited for the outcome of the battle between the Zand and the Afghans culminating in the October battle at Khisht. This victory gave Karim Khan breathing space and the opportunity to give Nasir Khan and the Persian littoral his undivided attention. In January 1755 Karim Khan started making preparations to deal with Nasir Khan, weakening the latter's back by making promises to Molla 'Ali Shah and others. He also had made a "strict alliance with the Shaik of Bushire and the inhabitants of Dachtestown." As a result, Nasir Khan promised to pay tribute, despite the fact that Karim Khan had to postpone his intention to pay a visit to Lar.[96]

In February 1755 Karim Khan finally marched into Larestan to enforce the promises made to him. He sought revenues and soldiers in Fars and thus had to subjugate all autonomous chiefs in the coastal areas. Quite a few such as Sheikh Mohammad Bastaki, Molla 'Abdol-Karim Gallehdari, Hajji Mohammad Amin Asiri, Sheikh 'Ali b. Khalfan, and Sheikh Hatem pledged their allegiance. Nasir Khan was supposed to send 5,000 *tumans*, 500 soldiers and Masih Soltan as a hostage in exchange for being recognized as governor of Lar. Once that was done Molla 'Abdol-Karim Gallehdari, a staunch supporter of Karim Khan, would also come to Lar to serve as hostage for Karim Khan's end of the agreement. Molla 'Abdol-Karim refused, however, claiming that Nasir Khan would kill him just as he had killed his father. Karim Khan then stopped the negotiations and prepared for a siege of Lar. In April 1755 Molla 'Ali Shah and the EIC received letters from Karim Khan asking for 3,000 *mann* of gun-powder and lead, 350 "shot bombs" and orders to becalm the merchants who were daily leaving to Qeshm and Hormuz. On April 10, 1755 Nasir Khan was still defending Lar against a Zand army of 15,000, while the population of Lar's hinterland was fleeing fearing Karim Khan's taxes. However, Karim Khan and Nasir Khan reached an agreement at the end of April. On May 2, 1755 Nasir Khan wrote Graves that Karim Khan had returned to Shiraz with Masih Soltan as a hostage and 5,000 *tumans* in tribute. Molla 'Ali Shah felt bolstered in his behavior towards Nasir Khan by the latter's defeat at the hands of Karim Khan Zand. Having made peace with Karim Khan, Nasir Khan could then give his undivided attention to the coastal areas. In June 1755 he began preparing for a campaign against Molla 'Abdol-Karim, Sheikh Hatem and other Arabs who actively had supported the Zands. However, after the departure of the Zand army Nasir Khan first attacked some of Karim Khan's possessions to seek compensation for his financial loss. For as soon as Karim Khan had returned to Shiraz, Nasir Khan behaved as if he were still an independent ruler and attacked Gallehdar, which was Karim Khan's territory, to get compensation for his loss. However, he was again defeated in June 1755 by local forces loyal to Karim Khan, consisting of those led by 'Ali Khan Shahsevan, one of Karim Khan's commanders, Sheikh Hatem and Molla 'Abdol-Karim, which signaled the end of

95 VOC 2885, f. 7-8 (Memorandum by Schoonderwoerd; 28/12/55); Lorimer, *Gazetteer*, pp. 91-92; Amin, *British Interests*, p. 28.

96 Saldanha, *Précis*, vol. 1, p. 90 (Bombay, 17/10/1754); Ricks, *Politics and Trade*, pp. 276-77 referring to F. R. Letters, Gombroon XVI (27/10/1753 and 07/02/1754); Ibid, (F.R. Gombroon VII (01/02/1755); Mehdi Roschan-Zamir, *Zand-Dynastie* (Hamburg, 1970), pp. 32-33; Perry, *Karim Khan*, pp. 58-59, 118.

the April agreement. Nasir Khan had to flee for his life abandoning his entire army camp. As a result, it was expected that Karim Khan would infest the lower lands and also come to Bandar 'Abbas, which was bad for trade and everybody concerned. Indeed, in July 1755 the authorities in Bandar 'Abbas learnt that Karim Khan had ordered Sheikh Mohammad Bastaki and 'Ali Soltan to collect the taxes of Bandar 'Abbas.[97] 'Ali Khan Shahsevan remained in the Lar area and sent a certain Soltan Mohammad Amin with 25 horsemen to Bandar 'Abbas to collect the annual revenue and *pishkesh*. However, he was given the cold shoulder by the local chiefs and sent back empty handed.[98] Karim Khan meanwhile recalled 'Ali Khan Shahsevan, because he needed his troops to oppose Azad Khan, the powerful Afghan contender for the throne. 'Ali Khan before withdrawing from Larestan to join Karim Khan at Isfahan ravaged the area around Lar. Out of fear for a possible visit to Bandar 'Abbas Molla 'Ali Shah and the leading merchants fled to Hormuz. The Dutch and the English reinforced their garrison by hiring local Arab riflemen and kept a sharp watch.[99]

'Ali Khan Shahsavan returned to the Hot Countries after Karim Khan had regrouped his forces at Shiraz. He then had defeated Nasir Khan several times and was about besiege Lar again. At the beginning of October 1755 'Ali Khan Shahsavan was at Datchou [?]. On October 2, 1755 he sent two couriers to Bandar 'Abbas with orders to collect two years of taxes from Bandar 'Abbas and 'Essin. The couriers then went to Minab, but the *shahriyari* sent them back without paying one *shahi*. They then returned and were awaiting orders. 'Ali Khan Shahsevan also had demanded a list of sundries from Molla 'Ali Shah to the value of 4,000 rupees for Karim Khan; he also sent letters to the EIC and VOC indicating that large presents were also expected from them.[100]

Meanwhile, Karim Khan ordered Nadr Khan Zand, who remained in Shiraz, to send Turab Khan to Kangan to recruit 2,000 cavalry from Sheikh Hatem, Molla 'Abdol-Karim, Sheikh Mohammad and others to attack Lar for the third time that year. At Isfahan Karim Khan was joined later by the Dashtestan and Tangestan levies and others to oppose Azad Khan the Afghan contender. The Dashestani riflemen were not happy with their living conditions and complained about their barracks and the bitter cold of Isfahan. At the battle of Golnabad in March 1756 the coastal Arabs deserted, which was an indication how bad their relationship had become with Karim Khan. The latter had to flee to Shiraz and as soon as he was there made preparations to invade Dashtestan to revenge himself for the treachery of Golnabad.[101]

The English kept Karim Khan abreast of developments at Bandar 'Abbas in secret, because they wanted to get rid of Molla 'Ali Shah and cause problems for the VOC, or so the Dutch believed. Schoonderwoerd even claimed that the English had conspired with Nasir Khan that during the latter's

97 The term used to refer to Bandar 'Abbas on this occasion was Jarun (Jarroun), which was an obsolete name by that time. In the past the governor of that port was also referred to as governor of Bandar 'Abbas and Jarun, which is the old name for the island and town of Hormuz. See Floor, *Persian Gulf*, pp. 9-10, 281.

98 Ricks, *Politics and Trade*, pp. 257 referring to F. R. Gombroon VIII (30/07/1755); Perry *Karim Khan*, pp. 118-19; Mirza Mohammad Sadeq Musavi Nami, *Tarikh-e Giti-gosha* ed. Sa'id Nafisi (Tehran, 1363/1984), p. 50; Fasa'i, *Farsnameh*, vol. 1, p. 597

99 Ricks, *Politics and Trade*, pp. 254-57 referring to F. R. Gombroon VII (03/04/1755; 15/04/1755; 16/05/1755; 10/05/1755 and 02/08/1755); VOC 2885, Memorandum by Schoonderwoerd for his successor Gerrit Aansorgh (Gamron; 28/11/1755), f. 7- 8 (the Dutch recorded the payment of tribute as being Dfl. 300,000 or 7,500 *tumans*); Perry, *Karim Khan*, pp. 120-21.

100 Saldanha, *Précis*, vol. 1, p. 93 (Gombroon, 11/10/1755); Nami, *Tarikh*, p. 50; Fasa'i, *Farsnameh*, vol. 1, p. 597; Anonymous, *A chronicle of the Carmelites in Persia and the Papal mission of the seventeenth and eighteenth centuries*, 2 vols. (London, 1939), vol. 1, p. 661.

101 Ricks, *Politics and Trade*, pp. 258-61 referring to F. R. Gombroon VIII (13/01/1756); Perry, *Karim Khan*, p. 65; Fasa'i, *Farsnameh*, vol. 1, 597; Nami, *Tarikh*, p. 50. See also chapter four.

planned visit, which was aborted due to the siege of Lar by Karim Khan, he would take the Dutch staff prisoner and close down the VOC factory. He would then seal the VOC merchandise and neither release the VOC staff nor their merchandise, unless the VOC would withdraw from Khark. Although it was clear that Nasir Khan neither had the power to take Bushire nor Bandar-e Rig, Schoonderwoerd reported that Sheikh Naser of Bushire and the English had induced Nasir Khan to follow this strategm. He therefore advised his successor, Gerrit Aansorgh, not to go and meet with Nasir Khan during his next visit, but to send his deputy. Schoonderwoerd further advised Aansorgh to maintain friendly relations with Sheikh Sayyed Mohammad Bastaki (Sjeeg Syjd Mhamed Bastagie), whom he described as a respected and wealthy man, who governed Ghamir and the sulfur mines of Jahangari (Jongerie) and an area as far as the Kahurestan river (Gabristan). The same held for the Banu Ma'in chief of Qeshm as the VOC bought its water, firewood and other provisions there as well as with Mir 'Alidad (Mier Alidaad), chief of Ahmadi (Achmeddie), who controlled part of the route to Kerman.[102]

From April 1754 Molla 'Ali Shah had bothered the European Companies to exert themselves and bring about that the royal ship that had been taken to India for repairs be returned to him. He furthermore strengthened his position by having made an alliance with Qasem Beyg of Minab, while he even had made overtures to 'Abdol-Sheikh to patch up their differences. These activities clearly were aimed to strengthen his position *vis à vis* Nasir Khan. He abandoned these efforts when the danger of an attack by Nasir Khan seemed less likely by the spring of 1755. Lar was under siege by a Zand army and Karim Khan had written to the coastal chiefs to abandon Nasir Khan's cause and join him in the siege of Lar. Given these circumstances, Molla 'Ali Shah and the Qavasem chief Sheikh Rahmah believed that the timing was perfect for a joint operation against the Banu Ma'in and invade Qeshm to take over control over the island. In May 1755 Molla 'Ali Shah boarded the *Fayz Rabbani* and sailed to Laft to attack and blockade Abdol-Sheikh of the Banu Ma'in with the help of Sheikh Rahmah. This was in retaliation for the attack on the fort of Qeshm by 'Abdollah, a nephew of 'Abdol-Sheikh. The allies captured a tranki belonging to the Banu Ma'in and laid siege to Laft. The sudden death of the eighty-year old 'Abdol-Sheikh in mid-October 1755 ended the five-month siege, and Qavasem and Bandar 'Abbas troops occupied the island. According to Ives, Molla 'Ali Shah "caused the head of the brave, deceased governor, to be cut off, and returned in triumph with it to *Bandarabbassi*, and *Ormus*." The Banu Ma'in had to depart from Laft and took up residence elsewhere on Qeshm. On his return to Bandar 'Abbas, Molla 'Ali Shah taxed the Moltani and Banksally merchants (1,500 rupees for each group) to pay the Qavasem troops, thus further contributing to the economic downturn of the port. Soon thereafter he took the revenues of Taziyan-'Essin and of several sulfur mines, which were part of Larestan and thus belonged to Nasir Khan, giving the latter sufficient grief and cause for a new attack on the port.[103]

When Karim Khan's plans to come to Bandar 'Abbas did not materialize, due to his agreement with Nasir Khan in April 1755, trade had picked up and the Dutch had been able to sell most of their unsold goods. Nevertheless, 1755 was a bad year, for the Dutch still had many unsold goods left. Some of the new goods that had been brought by a ship from Batavia were not even unloaded and had been forwarded to Khark for sale. The year 1756 was not so much different from 1755. The VOC could have sold more goods if its staff had been allowed to barter goods, in particular to accept cut diamonds in payment. The

102 VOC 2885, Memorandum by Schoonderwoerd for his successor Gerrit Aansorgh (Gamron; 28/11/1755), f. 11-12.

103 Saldanha, *Précis*, vol. 1, p. 95 (Gombroon, 02/12/1755); Ricks, *Politics and Trade*, pp. 325-27 referring to F. R. Gombroon VIII (13/05/1757; 05/11/1755 and 26/06/1757); Ives, *Voyage*, p. 202; Amin, *British Interests*, p. 29. The enmity between the Banu Ma'in and the Qavasem had been heightened by the fact that the latter had expelled the former from Kong and since that time the Banu Ma'in had been looking for a permanent place to settle. Sadid al-Saltaneh, *Bandar 'Abbas*, p. 612.

bad trade prospects persisted thereafter. Fewer merchants were coming to Bandar 'Abbas due to the bad treatment accorded to them by Molla 'Ali Shah.[104]

KARIM KHAN IMPOSES HIS WILL AND TAXES ON THE PERSIAN LITTORAL

In early October 1756 Karim Khan marched to Kazerun and sent couriers to the chiefs in Larestan and Bandar 'Abbas to gather at Qir Karzin. Nasir Khan wrote to the EIC on November 2, 1756 that he was on good terms with the Dashtestani Arabs who had sent him their principal men to force an alliance against Karim Khan. The latter had written to Sheikh Hatem and other Hula chiefs to join him in the Dashtestan campaign. Nasir Khan was to join with Sheikh Rahma of Jolfar to attack these pro-Zand Hula Arabs, although that alliance did not last long. Sheikh Rahma with a force consisting of the *Fath Rabbani* and some smaller vessels attacked Sheikh Hatem of Taheri. An additional reason for Sheikh Rahma's attack may have been Sheikh Hatem's involvement in the murder of Sheikh Mohammad b. Majd one of the al Haram sheikhs in 1754. What followed was not war, but peace between Sheikh Rahma and Sheikh Hatem as well as between the Dashtestanis and Karim Khan, after they had been defeated by 'Ali Khan Shahsevan. The Dashestani chiefs then had promised to pay 3,000 *tumans* and supply 2,000 soldiers, according to their assessment. And they did, for the crew of shipwrecked *Phoenix* met Sayyed Mansur, brother of Ra'is Ahmad, chief of the Tangestanis, who was collecting taxes for Karim Khan at Halla on the Dashestan coast. Nasir Khan thus was on his own again.[105]

In May 1757 Nasir Khan had resolved one of his problems in Larestan by having at long last subjugated Sheikh Mohammad of Jahangiri and Molla 'Abdol-Karim of Gallehdar, who paid 100 *tumans* in tribute each, sent their brothers as hostage and pledged obedience to Nasir Khan. The latter immediately thereafter wrote to Molla 'Ali Shah that he had to give an accounting of his revenues and the illegal seizure of the sulfur mines as well as to pay the back taxes from 'Essin-Taziyan and the 100 *tumans* annual tax on Bandar 'Abbas. Nasir Khan did not ask for the total of 7-8,000 *tumans*, but only 2,000 in exchange for returning Molla 'Ali Shah's children he held at Lar. Another positive development was that in June 1757 Karim Khan had sent Mirza Nur al-Din Mohammad to Lar to conclude the agreement with Nasir Khan, who was appointed governor of Lar, from Bushire to Jarroun (i.e. Jarun; meaning Bandar 'Abbas). On July 30, 1757 Molla Hoseyn, one of Nasir Khan's tax collectors, with 200 horsemen was at 'Essin to collect the arrear taxes and the levy of troops owed.[106]

From the autumn of 1755 until mid-June 1757 Molla 'Ali Shah had full control over Bandar 'Abbas, Hormuz and Qeshm. He continued to support the Qavasem in their expansion against Taheri and other Hula sheikhs. In mid-June 1757 Molla 'Ali Shah began to flex his muscles again towards the Europeans. He imprisoned an EIC broker on Hormuz, claiming that he was more important than Mir Mohanna and therefore he could do what he liked and expel them from Bandar 'Abbas as the former had done at Bandar-e Rig. Molla 'Ali Shah changed his tone when Nasir Khan's army approached in September 1757. Several meetings took place between EIC, Sheikh Rahma and Molla 'Ali Shah about the nature of his apology to the EIC and how to behave towards Nasir Khan.[107]

---

104 VOC 2863, f. 70-71; VOC 2885, f. 5 (08/09/1756), f. 5-6.

105 Ricks, *Politics and Trade*, pp. 261-63 referring to F. R. Gombroon IX (02/11/1756 and 20/11/1756); Perry, *Karim Khan*, pp. 119-20; chapter one. See chapter seven in this publication on what other chiefs had to pay.

106 Ricks, *Politics and Trade*, pp. 266, 284 referring to F. R. Gombroon IX (29/06/1757 and 21/06/1757). Ra'is Mohammad Saleh the *kalantar* of 'Essin had been appointed deputy governor of Bandar 'Abbas by Sheikh Mohammad.

107 Amin, *British Interests*, p. 42; Ricks, *Politics and Trade*, pp. 328-29 referring to F. R. Gombroon X (02/09/1757).

On August 1, 1757 Molla Hoseyn, one of Nasir Khan's tax collectors, ordered Ra'is Mohammad Saleh to return to 'Essin from Bandar 'Abbas; he then occupied the fort at 'Essin. Molla Hoseyn wrote several letters to Molla 'Ali Shah trying to reach an agreement with him regarding the back taxes without result. He then ordered the surrounding villages not to send any supplies to Bandar 'Abbas on which the port depended for much of its daily food and water. He also sent Ra'is Mohammad Saleh a copy of a letter from Nasir Khan to several officials ordering them to supply Molla Hoseyn with food and grains and to assist him in his task of tax collection at Taziyan and Shamil. Molla Hoseyn also demanded Ra'is Mohammad Saleh to pay 50 *tumans* or else suffer the consequences. On August 7, Sheikh Mohammad Hoseyn arrived in Bandar 'Abbas en route to Qeshm to finalize the negotiations between Molla 'Ali Shah and Molla Hoseyn regarding the 2,000 *tumans* in taxes due. On that same day Molla Hoseyn's troops plundered the villages of Takht, Namordi, Giru, Qal'eh Qasi and Chahistan thus dispelling any doubts about Nasir Khan's intentions about those who refused to pay their taxes. On August 11 Sheikh Mohammad Hoseyn returned from Qeshm with a pledge of 100 *tumans* on the Shamil and 50 *tumans* on Taziyan-'Essin account. Five days later Molla Hoseyn came to Bandar 'Abbas; he stayed for two days and then went to Laft to meet with Molla 'Ali Shah. Nasir Khan was not satisfied with Molla Hoseyn's agreement, however, for he sent Mahmud Sharif Beyg with 100 horse and 300 foot to settle Molla 'Ali Shah's affairs.[108]

The people of Bandar 'Abbas were not reassured by assurances given by Nasir Khan to the chiefs of the European Companies, for according to rumors, Nasir Khan's soldiers were said to be plundering Shamil and its surrounding villages. Molla 'Ali Shah and Sheikh Rahma of Jolfar visited the EIC to seek advice and support; the former swore to fight Nasir Khan. Shaw, the EIC Agent, said that Nasir Khan's position was different from that in 1753-54 and Sheikh Rahma agreed, but Molla 'Ali Shah was not convinced. The next day (4 September) Sheikh Rahma assured Shaw that Molla 'Ali Shah would change his mind. Although both had often promised to give Nasir Khan 1,000 *tumans* and two brass cannons soon they had not done so, nor had they any intention of ever doing so. It was feared that Nasir Khan was so furious about this that if he would get hold of Molla 'Ali Shah he would treat him and the inhabitants very badly, because they had left despite assurances given that he would treat them well. Molla 'Ali Shah and his son-in-law went to Hormuz and forced the principal inhabitants to go to the islands where they still were at the end of 1757. Molla 'Ali Shah did not intend to pay 1,000 *tumans* from his own pocket to get his children back, but by levying it from the Minab area. Sheikh Rahma marched there and returned on September 28, 1757 with empty hands because Qasem Beyg, Shah Savar Beyg and Mir Musa 'Ali refused to pay the annual tax. They were willing to pay 3,000 rupees, i.e. the balance due of what they already had paid, but not one penny more, in which case they would fight if need be.[109]

In October 1757 Nasir Khan was in the Bandar 'Abbas area and exacted tribute from Mir 'Ali Da'ud of Ahmadi and marched on Shamil demanding five years of arrears and apologies for failing to support him against the Zands. By mid-November he had received 1,200 *tumans* in annual tribute from Minab. He then returned to Shamil where he appointed a kinsman as governor and marched back to Shiraz, when it was rumored that Karim Khan intended to attack Lar. Molla 'Ali Shah was still at Hormuz on January 11 and his affairs with Nasir Khan were the same, i.e. unresolved.[110]

---

108 Molla 'Ali Shah was emboldened to take a tough position due to the presence of Sheikh Rahma at Bandar 'Abbas at that time. Ricks, *Politics and Trade*, pp. 285-86 referring to F. R. Gombroon X (13/08/1757 and 02/09/1757).

109 Ricks, *Politics and Trade*, pp. 286-87 referring to F. R. Gombroon X (03/09/1757 and 04/09/1757). Molla 'Ali Shah appears to have paid after all, because Nasir Khan had released his children by the end of 1757 (Ibid. 26/10/1757 and 23/02/1758).

110 Saldanha, *Précis*, vol. 1, p. 114 (Bombay, 13/12/1757); Ibid., vol. 1, p. 124 (Bombay, 30/01/758); VOC 2986, Gamron to Batavia (01/05/1759), f. 13-14; Ricks, *Politics and Trade*, pp. 288 referring to F. R. Gombroon X (23/11/1757 and 26/11/1757).

Although Karim Khan had been able to defeat his main contenders for power, the situation in the Garmsirat remained as unsettled as before. The population had been imposed upon to such an extent that those who still possessed something and did not want to fall prey to whatever person who was in power were forced to flee to Khark or Basra, two places that were still relatively flourishing. Those who fled announced that they only would return when peace and security had been established. As a result there was a lack of porters to load and unload ships and caravans. To be able to sell goods the Dutch had to extend special credit arrangements to the few remaining merchants, but even that did not result in better trade results. Schoonderwoerd, who returned to Batavia in September 1755, therefore en route made a trial visit to Masqat to test the market there.[111] This was followed by a larger trial voyage in 1756 and 1757 organized by the governor-general. However, the Masqat option was abandoned when the Khark factory complained that its sales suffered from the sales in Masqat.[112]

Naser Khan was at Toutioun [?] and had fought with Karim Khan who claimed victory. During that time Mir Mast 'Ali (Meir Mastally) had taken Shamil Fort in the night, which worried Nasir Khan as his garrison there had served as a check on the towns of Shamil and Minab. Molla 'Ali Shah on hearing that news had the guns fired by way of rejoicing and gave presents to the messengers. It was also reported that he had asked the Qavasem sheikhs of Jolfar and Lengeh to assist the people of Minab. This is quite possible, for Molla 'Ali Shah crowed at any inconvenience or setback for Nasir Khan and slighted him whenever he could, and would cause him trouble as he was wont to tell the Arab crew of his ships. Meanwhile, the EIC had decided to take offense action if Molla 'Ali Shah would behave towards it like he had done in 1757. During February-June 1758 there was a conflict in the Shamil, 'Essin and Minab area due to interference by Mohammad Reza Khan of Sirjan with caravans coming to and fro Kerman. The EIC and VOC urged Nasir Khan to take action. He immediately sent Zeynal Khan with Lari horse and foot, who in March-April fought with Mohammad Reza Khan finally defeating him in May 1758 near 'Essin, "a fort with a garrison of three to four hundred men". Zeynal Khan then left to Hajjiabad. Nasir Khan's kinsman at Shamil returned to Lar, because he had been driven out by Mir Mast 'Ali, the rebellious *kalantar* and ally of Mohammad Reza Khan of Sirjan. On June 18, 1758 Molla 'Ali Shah attacked 'Essin Fort and totally unexpected ousted Nasir Khan's *kalantar*, Ra'is Abdol-Qasem; once again there was public rejoicing. He also had sent the Persian ships from Hormuz to help his son-in-law Sheikh Rahma who was at war with the Imam of Masqat. However, the English commented if that really was Molla 'Ali Shah's intention then "he would be more expeditious in getting them away as he knew the Immaum's fleet left Muscat last month [June 1758] for Dubba [Dobbah]."[113] Molla 'Ali Shah's taking of 'Essin and the change of power at Shamil were considered significant setbacks for Nasir Khan and forced him to take military action, which led to the 1760-63 war about Bandar 'Abbas and Qeshm.

As a result of this and other similar events the Dutch doubted whether the situation in Persia ever would return to normal again. Nasir Khan, the main power in the area, moreover did not contribute to a secure situation either. He quarreled with Karim Khan, the ruler of Shiraz and main contender for the throne of Persia as well as with Shahrokh Khan, the governor of Kerman, both of whom had defeated him. In addition, he was at odds with most of the local rulers of the Garmsirat. When it looked as if Karim

111 VOC 2986, Gamron to Batavia (01/05/1759), f. 12.

112 See chapter seven.

113 Saldanha, *Précis*, vol. 1, pp. 125-26 (Bombay, 26/07/1758), the English also were worried about the fact that the captain of an English ketch from Bombay had "let out his vessel to the Imaum of Muscat to assist in his Present War," which was prohibited. Ricks, *Politics and Trade*, pp. 301, 329 referring to F. R. Gombroon VIII (15/05/1758); Ives, *Voyage*, p. 201 (after their victory Nasir Khan's troops went on a rampage and one of the marauding groups was attacked by "their lately defeated enemy, the chief officer of the Khan was killed on the spot, with four or five others of inferior rank, and the surgeon of the English factory at Gombroon was called on to assist those who were wounded.")

Khan would loose his fight against Mohammad Hasan Khan Qajar in 1758, Nasir Khan, who supported the latter, had used that opportunity to threaten the *shahryari* of Minab and Molla 'Ali Shah and to demand tax arrears from them. Fortunately for them he had to hurry back to Lar when Mohammad Hasan Khan Qajar fled when part of his army defected. He reinforced his defenses, but warned the *shahriyari* of Minab and Molla 'Ali Shah that he had still unfinished business with them.[114]

ZAND TROOPS INFEST THE PERSIAN LITTORAL AND THREATEN BANDAR 'ABBAS

When Karim Khan proved to be victorious over his main contender Mohammad Hasan Khan Qajar in 1758, Karim Khan sent a victory letter to all coastal chiefs, who were each ordered to pay a certain sum. The chiefs of Minab and Shamil encouraged by Karim Khan's success invited him to send troops to assist them against Nasir Khan, who had supported the Qajar chief. Karim Khan responded favorably and sent one of his generals, Vali Khan at the head of 4,000 troops.[115] Molla 'Ali Shah retreated to Hormuz and it was reported that the *shahryari* had imposed a tax of 30,000 rupees on the inhabitants of Minab as a present for Mohammad Vali Khan and his principal officers, who had been raiding in the Kerman roads. In October 1758, Nasir Khan had sent a group of soldiers to guard some passes at Hajjiabad (Hodjeland), who clashed with Mohammad Vali Khan's troops, who killed Nasir Khan's commanding officer. Since then Nasir Khan had not moved having his hands full. The Dutch meanwhile intended to abandon Bandar 'Abbas and were expecting a ship from Khark any day.[116]

Mohammad Vali Khan was clearly not well received by the local chiefs and he had to force their cooperation. Vali Khan therefore arrested the local chiefs and forced them to keep their word. Mohammad Vali Khan demanded 2,000 *tumans* and 100 soldiers from the *shahryari* and he also made demands on Mir Mast 'Ali (Meer Mastally) and Mir 'Ali Da'ud (Meer Ally Doud). Moreover, as long as he stayed in the neighborhood no trade was possible. The result was that most people fled to the islands, Oman and Baluchistan, to which end Molla 'Ali Shah had sent boats to transport them and their effects, so that in an area of 10 hour's travel one did not find anybody anymore. When Mohammad Vali Khan was at six days' journey from Bandar 'Abbas at the beginning of January 1759 there were hardly any people left in Bandar 'Abbas. Only a few porters were left, who had been induced to stay because Aansorgh had paid them to do so and had promised them Dutch protection. They left town, however, when the Dutch withdrew from Bandar 'Abbas. It was not only the various military operations that interfered with people's life and trade, but also the behavior of local officials such as Molla 'Ali Shah who in a variety of ways had pressed the commercial community in Bandar 'Abbas to pay more than was usual. As a result most of them had left by the end of 1758 to Masqat via Minab. There they also could obtain what they needed much easier in exchange for sugar, although occasionally they still would call on Bandar 'Abbas. The English, who had maintained good relations with Nasir Khan throughout this period feared Vali Khan's action, the more so, since he had plundered an EIC copper caravan. The English were loading their most valuable goods in the two ships that were lying in front of their factory, which were as close as possible to the beach to enable

114 VOC 2986, Gamron to Batavia (01/05/1759), f. 14-18. Trade had been very bad in 1758, and the English even sent back their ship the *Admiral Watson* with a cargo of woolens to Bombay after it had been in the roads for two months. Ibid., f. 24.; Fasa'i, *Farsnameh*, vol. 1, p. 598; Perry, *Karim Khan*, pp. 65, 71-62, 119-20.

115 VOC 2986 (01/05/1759), f. 14-16; Perry, *Karim Khan*, pp. 119-20.

116 Saldanha, *Précis*, vol. 1, p. 127 (Bombay, 23/12/1758).

a rapid and timely flight, despite the fact that the English had a garrison of almost 100 European soldiers in addition to locally hired ones.[117]

Mohammad Vali Khan stayed 15 days at Minab, which as a result was destroyed. He departed on January 28 and two days later arrived within 10 leagues of Bandar 'Abbas. If he did not come to Bandar 'Abbas the English expected him to take the road to 'Essin (Asseen), because the shorter mountain roads were well guarded by Nasir Khan.[118] When Mohammad Vali Khan was at Naband the EIC sent its interpreter to him, who was nicely received and received a robe of honor. The general said he was going to attack Lar and that until that had happened he fully realized that the area would remain unsettled. He was much dissatisfied with Molla 'Ali Shah, who was very much mistaken if he thought he could escape him. When he attacked Bandar 'Abbas he expected the EIC to help with vessels and if the English refused he would act as Mirza Taqi had done in 1738. Molla 'Ali Shah was still at Hormuz, but came occasionally to Bandar 'Abbas to collect taxes when it was safe to do so and then behaved with the greatest arrogance; he asked Agent for a loan of 4,000 rupees and was very displeased when this was refused. All inhabitants of Bandar 'Abbas save for EIC servants were in the islands. Some of Molla 'Ali Shah's Arab allies took advantage of this situation and also plundered houses belonging to EIC staff. "The Arabs had broke [sic] open their houses and carried away doors, timber, &c., of which complaint was made by the Agent to the deputy Governour." The EIC staff caught some Arabs at their houses and when these drew their swords the deputy-governor sent for help from the fort, but the Arabs cut several of the governor's servants. No redress could be obtained as they were members of Sheikh Rahma's Qavasem, who had joined with the Charak Arabs. They had fitted out armed trankis, and under the pretense of cruising on Sheikh Hatem and Mir Mohanna, and like the latter they took every vessel they could lay their hands on, and the EIC staff feared that "the Gulph would soon be full of Petty Robbers."[119]

THE VOC ABANDONS BANDAR 'ABBAS

Because of the mistrust that the Dutch bore Mohammad Vali Khan's intentions towards the European Companies they abandoned Bandar 'Abbas on February 3, 1759.[120] Although Vali Khan had sent letters promising friendship the Dutch decided not to wait any longer, because they valued his letters as much as his words, viz. not at all. The Dutch decision was not a sudden one, because already in 1757 Aansorgh had proposed to withdraw from Bandar 'Abbas. Aansorgh, the new VOC Resident, faced with no prospects for an increase in sales and profits had suggested to Batavia to abandon trade in Bandar 'Abbas and leave the factory in the hands of two caretakers. Their task would be to buy goat-wool and brimstone, two commodities that still yielded a profit. For the Khark factory was too far away to organize the purchase of these two goods, although it would be Khark that would be financing the transactions. In addition to the reduced trade prospects, Aansorgh also had little hope for an improvement of the security in Bandar 'Abbas. The town was continuous harassed by all kinds of hostile elements. He ascribed their unwanted visits to Molla 'Ali Shah's intrigues, who constantly changed his allegiance to one or the other contender. Whenever his opponents showed themselves in Bandar 'Abbas Molla 'Ali Shah fled to Hormuz leaving the town at their mercy. A case in point was the visit by Molla Hoseyn, a self-styled Lari *sardar*, who headed a

117 VOC 2986, Gamron to Batavia (01/05/1759), f. 14-18, 24.; Saldanha, *Précis*, vol. 1, p. 128 (Bombay, 23/01/1759); Amin, *British Interests*, p. 43; Perry, *Karim Khan*, p. 120.

118 Saldanha, *Précis*, vol. 1, pp. 129-30 (Bombay, 11/03/1759).

119 Saldanha, *Précis*, vol. 1, pp. 130-31 (Bombay, 17/04/1759); Amin, *British Interests*, p. 43.

120 Saldanha, *Précis*, vol. 1, pp. 129-30 (Bombay, 11/03/759).

group of marauding bandits, and had plundered the town, exacted a contribution and finally had to be paid to make him leave.[121] As a result of one decade of unrest, revolt, plunder, oppression Bandar 'Abbas did not look very appealing to a chance visitor like Ives, who described the port in 1758 as follows:

> At present it is a place of no kind of consequence, except what it receives from the English and Dutch Factories, beside whom no other European nation has any settlement here. The two factory houses are the only buildings remaining of any importance; the whole city besides, is almost one entire scene of ruins, which served to convince us of its once flourishing state.[122]

Von Kniphausen, the Khark chief, independently agreed with Aansorg's analysis. He submitted that Bandar 'Abbas was lying outside the normal trade route at that time. Towns such as Isfahan, Shiraz and Yazd could be as easily reached via Bushire, a port that was the gateway to Persia for the Khark factory. Those merchants who still called upon Bandar 'Abbas only did so, because the English sold lead, iron and low-priced English woollens. If the EIC would not sell these goods at Bandar 'Abbas anymore the merchants would not bother to come to Bandar 'Abbas, according to von Kniphausen. In addition, merchants were exposed to extortion and loans and other forms of harassment. Also, von Kniphausen pointed out that it would not do when he refused to give presents to Persian rulers that the latter were able to 'obtain' these form the Dutch at Bandar 'Abbas. He therefore urged Batavia to abandon the Bandar 'Abbas factory. Although von Kniphausen had ulterior motives, viz. he wanted to increase the profitability of the Khark factory, he basically was right. As we will see his prediction that merchants would abandon Bandar 'Abbas proved to be right.[123]

The High Government in Batavia having received these two negative recommendations with regard to Bandar 'Abbas decided to approve the closure of the factory in that port. The factory had been loosing money for quite a number of years, the rich merchants had left, and VOC interests could be maintained by one or two caretakers in Bandar 'Abbas. As in the case of von Kniphausen, they also hoped that this would result in higher profits for the Khark factory. Because Batavia had decided to follow Aansorgh's recommendation to abandon Bandar 'Abbas, the VOC staff did not wait for Vali Khan to arrive. When the vanguard of his troops entered Bandar 'Abbas the VOC staff boarded *de Tilburg* and sailed away.[124] Von Kniphausen who had been ordered to assist Aansorgh with regard to unsold goods and other matters relating to the closure of the factory in Bandar 'Abbas did nothing of the kind. He claimed that he only had learnt about the imminent closure of the factory on September 25, 1759 through a private letter from Buffkens, the interpreter of the Bandar 'Abbas factory. Aansorgh had sought no contact with him and neither had he; apparently no love was lost between the two gentlemen. Von Kniphausen proposed that Buffkens be kept on as caretaker of the Bandar 'Abbas factory, but that he himself would see to the purchase of Kerman goat wool (*kork*) and brimstone.[125]

---

121 VOC 2937, Khark to Batavia (29/10/1757), f. 19-20; VOC 2937, Gamron to Batavia, (24/09/1757), f. 7. Aansorgh arrived in Bandar 'Abbas on 25/09/1755. On the situation in the Persian Gulf in general at that time see chapter two.

122 Ives, *Journey*, p. 198.

123 VOC 2968, f. 8-10 (25/04/1758).

124 VOC 1012 (25/04/1758), f. 125-27; VOC 2986 (01/05/1759), f. 14-18; Amin, p. 43; Lorimer, *Gazetteer*, pp. 100-101.

125 VOC 2968 (25/11/1758), f. 9; VOC 2968 (26/12/1758), f. 2-4.

THE FRENCH ATTACK AND SEIZE THE EIC FACTORY AT BANDAR 'ABBAS

Meanwhile, in Europe the so-called Seven-Year-War (1756-1763) had broken out among the major European powers, with England and France on opposing sides, while the Netherlands were neutral. London therefore had informed Bombay about the war and had sent instructions about what measures had to be taken, while Bombay was warned from Masqat in February 18, 1758 about the presence of a large French warship at the mouth of the Persian Gulf.[126] Although they were on the lookout for French ships the English at Bandar 'Abbas nevertheless were taken by surprise. On October 12, 1759 the EIC had received information that a French fleet was coming.[127] Lt. Bembou was ordered to take the *Speedwell* to Laft, but before he could sail the French had already arrived and they seized the vessel. They came in the evening of the 12th sailing under Dutch colors; the *Condé* a vessel with 64 guns, another one with 22 guns, the *Mary* taken from a certain Cheleby and the *Mamoody* taken from Mahomet Soffy. The former, belonging to an inhabitant of Bombay, the French had seized at Ra's al-Hadd, while the latter they had taken in the roads of Masqat while under fire of the guns of the two forts. The French landed their troops on the 13th west of the factory with two mortars and four cannons and started to batter the English factory. Few of the *topasses* and *sepoys*[128] had the nerve to stand at the guns. At high water at 11 o'clock the 22-gun ship came to within one quarter of a mile from the factory and then the French started to play on the English factory both from land and sea. At 15.00 hours the French summoned the English defenders. Talks ensued and council was taken and the result was that the English surrendered, because they could not hold out against this superior force. The French had 450 Europeans and 150 Africans ashore with bamboos and had made scaling ladders for an assault on the 14th. The French unloaded the *Mamoodie* which had a cargo of dates and gave them to Molla 'Ali Shah, who helped them in every way. On the 12th Molla 'Ali Shah had come to see the EIC Agent and promised to do his utmost to prevent the French from landing. When he was warned the next day that the French were going to land he did not move and remained in his fort. At 10 o'clock the EIC Agent had asked for some men to help him, but nobody came. Molla 'Ali Shah clearly was afraid of the French and of what they might do to his ship that was in the roads. After the French had landed Molla 'Ali Shah cooperated with them and sent them fresh vegetables and fruits. The French let the sepoys go, but the Europeans and *topasses* were taken aboard as hostages. They had promised to give the English factory to Molla 'Ali Shah, but privately they told the English that they would blow it up because the English had destroyed their fort at Chandernagore. The Dutch estimated the combined value of the booty from the English factory at Dfl. 600,000.[129]

---

126 Saldanha, *Précis*, vol. 1, pp. 116-19, 121 (London, 11/02/1756; London 25/03/1757; London, 29/03/1758); Ibid., vol. 1, p. 124 (Bombay, 28/02/1758). The French ship was the *Bristol*, with a crew of 140, of which 85 Europeans, and 30 guns, which was at Basra at the end of March 1758, see Ives, *Voyage*, p. 206; Amin, *British Interests*, p. 44.

127 This may have been occasioned by the event reported in a letter from an unnamed Banyan in Masqat to Batavia dated Rabi' al-Akhar 1173 (November-December 1759), f. 2-3, that on 13 Safar 1172 (06/10/1759) a French and English ship had arrived at Masqat, respectively commanded by captains "Marmarasi" and "Fariyet", who fought one another and in which battle the French were victorious. They took the English crew to Bandar 'Abbas and set fire to their ship there. The French, four ships strong, then departed. The "English" ship mentioned here was the *Mary* that belonged to a merchant named Chelebi, which was en route to Jedda. VOC 2996, Khark to Batavia (06/12/1759), f. 18.

128 The term *topass* or *topaz* was used in eighteenth century India to refer to Christians, dark-skinned claimants of Portuguese descent, generally to soldiers of that class. Sepoy is an Anglo-India word to refer to a native soldier, disciplined and dressed in the European style.

129 Saldanha, *Précis*, vol. 1, pp. 132-33 (Gombroon, 22/10/1759), 134-35 (articles of capitulation October 14, 1759); Amin, *British Interests*, p. 45. According to Ives, *Voyage*, p. 202, note*, "It is believed, that he [Molla 'Ali Shah] secretly

The French left Bandar 'Abbas on November 2, 1759. They had boarded their ships on the 30th after having set fire to the factory wherein they had dug mines and placed combustibles. As a result the factory was very much destroyed. According to the English, had it not been for the villainy of Molla 'Ali Shah the factory might have been saved. The French had left the factory unscathed, but when they had left Molla 'Ali Shah had set fire to it to get the iron work therein. The French also had left 30,000 *mann* of copper and other goods, but instead of guarding it as Molla 'Ali Shah had been asked he had made it a free for all and later admitted that there was nobody in town who did not have a share in the plunder. Molla 'Ali Shah may have gained this way 60,000 rupees in all, exclusive of the guns left to him and his Arab friends by the French. The latter clearly did not want to encumber themselves with unnecessary goods, because rather than taking or selling it as a prize they burnt the *Speedwell*. Molla 'Ali Shah also had entered into a defensive and offensive alliance with the French, which had no real meaning, of course, because the French had no presence in the Persian Gulf and he had no real military force. Had it not been for d'Estaing, des Essars who hated all Englishmen would have behaved even worse than he already did, according to the English.[130]

ANARCHY TAKES HOLD OF THE BANDAR 'ABBAS AREA

After the departure of the French, the English took up temporary residence in the Dutch factory. Meanwhile, the security situation in and around Bandar 'Abbas was deteriorating. Molla 'Ali Shah had promised to lend his ships to Sheikh Rahma, his son-in-law, to be used in an operation against Masqat. This collaboration came under severe pressure when Molla 'Ali Shah married a daughter of Molla Hoseyn, one of Nasir Khan's generals, in November 1759, which marriage was opposed by Sheikh Rahma. Through this marriage, Molla 'Ali Shah would get control over the revenues of Qeshm, but Sheikh Rahma nevertheless opposed it. In January 1760 he occupied the forts of Hormuz and Bandar 'Abbas. After holding both forts for 14 days he left taking all of Molla 'Ali Shah's goods with him including the ship the *Fath Rahmani* and sailed to Laft. This falling out meant a significant weakening of Molla 'Ali Shah's position at a time when he needed friends, although it was only a temporary rift.[131] These events (the war that had broken out between the Imam of Masqat, the Hulas of Charak and the Banu Ma'in on the one hand against Molla 'Ali Shah and the Qavasem on the other hand) had upset the inhabitants of Bandar 'Abbas very much. On February 15, 1760 some sixty Hormuzi soldiers and villagers revolted against Molla 'Ali Shah and took the town and the fort of Bandar 'Abbas, which signaled the start of the three-year war. They "obliged his deputies and tribe of Conjees to fly the islands," who indeed went to Qeshm to seek aid from the Qavasem and the Al Haram Arabs, who had been settled on the island by Sheikh Rahma. That same day Molla 'Ali Shah was arrested and imprisoned in the fort of Hormuz. The rebels also seized the ship the *Fayz Rabbani*. They did not keep the fort of Bandar 'Abbas for very long, because

---

assisted the *French* Count *de Estaing* in his attack and conquest of our factory house at *Gombroon*, in the year 1759." VOC 2996, Khark to Batavia (06/12/1759), f. 18; Chandernagore a town in W. Bengal, now a suburb of Calcutta, was a permanent French settlement since 1688. In 1757 it was bombarded by an English fleet under Admiral Watson, who took the town and totally destroyed it. See also R. Crowhurst. "D'Estaing's cruise in the Indian Ocean, a landmark in privateering voyages," *Studia* 35 (1972), pp. 53-66; A. Auzoux, "La France et Mascate aux XVIIe et XVIIIe siecles," *Revue d'histoire diplomatique* 23-24 (1909-10), pp. 518-40 and 234-65

130 Saldanha, *Précis*, vol. 1, pp. 135-36 (Bombay, 26/12/1759); Amin, *British Interests*, pp. 45-46. The vessel take in the roads of Masqat was returned by the French after a formal Omani protest. Auzoux, "La France," pp. 524-25.

131 Ricks, *Politics and Trade*, p. 330 referring to F. R. Gombroon XI (18/01/1760); Saldanha, *Précis*, vol. 1, p. 134 (Gombroon, 22/10/1759).

Ja'far Khan, the brother of Nasir Khan of Lar, had arrived at 'Essin to occupy Bandar 'Abbas; he had taken the fort of 'Essin with 200 men. On February 16, 1760 Ja'far Khan entered Bandar 'Abbas, took possession of the citadel and the government. It remained quiet until February 18-20 when the Qavasem and Al Haram unsuccessfully attacked Hormuz to free Molla 'Ali Shah, but they were repulsed. They were back on Qeshm on February 29 with the *Fath Rahmani*. The Banu Ma'in had given the *Fayz Rabbani* (Furzarabioony) to the Charak Arabs, who delivered it to Nasir Khan's brother when they both arrived in Bandar 'Abbas to support Ja'far Khan. The latter took the side of the opponents of Molla 'Ali Shah. This local conflict as a consequence disrupted the entire surrounding area.[132]

The Banu Ma'in (Benimine) Arabs were concerned about their families on Qeshm, who were in danger of being plundered. On March 11, 1760 they therefore went to Qeshm joined by 100 men of Nasir Khan and wanted to lay siege to Laft. When they were at six miles from the port the Qavasem Arabs there wrote threatening letters to Nasir Khan to prevent his interference. Because the *Fath Rahmaniyeh* (Roumania) was not in his hands gave him unease and he therefore asked the EIC to help contain Laft. The attackers were beaten off by the more numerous Qavasem, who received daily reinforcements from Jolfar. They then withdrew with the *Feyz Rabbani* to Charak. Molla 'Ali Shah was kept in the fort of Hormuz and the population did not want to hand him over even though Nasir Khan had promised them half of his goods. However, they did not want to be enslaved by him; moreover it gave them leverage *vis à vis* Nasir Khan. By the end of February 1760 Ja'far Khan had failed to quell the Hormuz rebellion or to get satisfaction from Molla 'Ali Shah. From February to August 1760 Ja'far Khan in vain tried to bring about a peaceful government and could only look on, while the fighting between the two sides, Banu Ma'in/Charak Arabs versus Molla 'Ali Shah/Qavasem, intensified. Molla 'Ali Shah was considerably weakened. He had only 200 men at his command and had no ties with chiefs on the mainland, until November 1759 when he had married his daughter to Molla Ma'sum (Moolah masson) who could raise about 400 men. His chief supporter was the chief of Jolfar, who always made him pay for his assistance. Molla 'Ali Shah had two ships, one large gallivat and one armed tranki. When they went to sea the soldiers were partly Jolfaris. Ja'far Khan had only 250 men in Bandar 'Abbas although Nasir Khan had promised to send more men to conquer Qeshm Island. However, the soldiers were not very willing to go to Qeshm, "where they would have no back door to fly to."[133] The situation became even tenser, when in May 1760 Molla 'Ali Shah managed to escape from Hormuz and fled to Qeshm.[134]

Nasir Khan therefore tried to intervene in the Qeshm dispute. In April 1760 he sent his kinsman, Zaynal Soltan, *kalantar-zabet* of Hajjiabad with 300 men to negotiate with Sheikh Rashed of Jolfar; not only did he fail, Ja'far Khan did not want him in Bandar 'Abbas. On receiving news that the Qavasem Arabs were making preparations to attack Bandar 'Abbas, Ja'far Khan "had begun to make an inner wall to it to the old one being too large to defend with the Troops he had, that the new wall joining to the House they dwelt in Jaffer Chan insisted on their defending that part of the Town in case the Arabs came." The wall was as high as the house; the EIC thus had to keep its soldiers under arms, but also to make the wall of the house higher in case Ja'far Khan might attack them. The latter also asked for two guns to defend the Dutch factory; the EIC chief said he had only enough for his own house, because he did not want to offend the Arabs.[135]

---

132 VOC 3027 (30/11/1760), f. 19; Saldanha, *Précis*, vol. 1, pp. 136-37 (Bombay, 15/04/1760); Amin, *British Interests*, p. 46; Ricks, *Politics and Trade*, pp. 331-32. His full name was Mohammad Ja'far Khan. VOC 3156, f. 51.

133 VOC 3027 (30/11/1760), f. 19; Saldanha, *Précis*, vol. 1, p. 137 (Bombay, 15/04/1760); Amin, *British Interests*, p. 46; Ricks, *Politics and Trade*, pp. 332.

134 VOC 3027 (30/11/1760), f. 19; Amin, *British Interests*, p. 46.

135 Saldanha, *Précis*, vol. 1, p. 146 (Bombay, 18/09/1761); Ricks, *Politics and Trade*, p. 290.

On June 24, 1760 Molla 'Ali Shah and Sheikh Rashed with 1,000 Jolfar Arabs landed at Bandar 'Abbas, which they took that same evening. They continued firing at Nasir Khan's men in the fort until the 28th. The Qavasem Arabs then embarked again and returned to Qeshm. Both they and Nasir Khan's people had plundered the population of Bandar 'Abbas.[136] The attack on Bandar 'Abbas was a direct challenge to Nasir Khan's autority and thus he had no choice but to come in person to the coast to resolve the conflict. He also took steps to reinforce the relations with his allies as well as to secure strategic locations. Nasir Khan therefore had sent the Banu Ma'in and the Charak Arabs to Hormuz to prevent the *shahriyari* of Minab to take possession of it. The *Fath Rabbani* (Fuzeraboony) and a vessel of the Imam of Masqat, an enemy of the Qavasem, also had come to Hormuz to assist Nasir Khan and the Banu Ma'in and other Arabs against the Jolfaris.[137]

In mid-July 1760, after having declined a peace offer by Jolfar, Nasir Khan left Lar and via Charak, where he strengthened his ties with Sheikh 'Ali b. Khalfan, he in vain besieged Lengeh, a Qavasem stronghold, from August-October 1760, but it was better prepared than he had thought. He then moved his camp to Khamir, from where in August he tried to plunder Jolfar, "but finding it too well prepared he proceeded to Kishme and laid waste and plundered every where he came to."[138] Ja'far Khan's oppressions prevented merchants from coming to Bandar 'Abbas, but as his brother Nasir Khan was there they did not want to let it come to a rupture with him. They approached Nasir Khan and asked whether his brother's behavior met with his approval. Then it became clear to Nasir Khan that Ja'far Khan had told him many falsehoods and he promised to set things aright when he came to Bandar 'Abbas. He asked that the *Drake* transport the Banu Ma'in from Hormuz to Bandar 'Abbas and intimated that he would be very displeased if the EIC refused. The English had no force to oppose Nasir Khan's force of 2,500 men and thus the English ship sailed away on September 11 to perform that service; the English also gave him a loan of 1,000 *tumans*. Nasir Khan was willing to have the EIC get the island of Hormuz, but he categorically refused to surrender the fort to the English even when money was offered. The English did not consider it feasible to take the fort without Nasir Khan's cooperation with their available force. Meanwhile, the Banu Ma'in and the people of Hormuz had agreed to live together. According to the English, the former's stated desire to go to Bandar 'Abbas was but a subterfuge "to get away from Carack."[139]

Nasir Khan reprimanded his brother and proposed to put one of his officers in Bandar 'Abbas as a check on him. While he still was in Khamir, he learnt that Karim Khan would accept an arrangement whereby he would pay annually 4,000 *tumans* in tribute and deliver 200 Laris soldiers. To finalize this agreement forced him to make a speedy return to Lar and thus he tried to conclude a quick peace with Molla 'Ali Shah. The *shahryari* had tried to have Molla 'Ali Shah's family released, but without success. Nasir Khan proposed that: (i) Ja'far Khan marry one of Molla 'Ali's daughters; (ii) Molla 'Ali Shah and Ja'far Khan govern Bandar 'Abbas jointly, keeping half the revenue and paying the other half to Nasir Khan, and (iii) Sheikh 'Abdollah of the Banu Ma'in would govern Qeshm and Laft jointly with one of Nasir Khan's officers, paying Nasir Khan 50% of the revenues. Without waiting for the acceptance of his proposal Nasir Khan returned to Lar without having made peace with Molla 'Ali Shah and thus leaving everything in great confusion. The more so, since according to rumors Sheikh 'Abdollah was peeved by this. He had better luck in Lar, for in January 1761 an agreement was quickly reached between Karim Khan and Nasir Khan, stipulating that (i) Karim Khan will cede some land west of Lar (Deh Pish); (ii) Nasir Khan is recognized as governor of Lar and Bandar 'Abbas on payment of an annual tribute of 2,000

---

136 Saldanha, *Précis*, vol. 1, p. 139 (Bombay, 14/10/1760); Ricks, *Politics and Trade*, pp. 290 referring to I.O. Letters from Bombay, 451, 'Gombroon' (05/08/1760), 332.

137 Saldanha, *Précis*, vol. 1, p. 141 (Bombay, 17/10/1760).

138 Saldanha, *Précis*, vol. 1, p. 139 (Bombay, 14/10/1760), p. 141 (Bombay, 17/10/1760).

139 Saldanha, *Précis*, vol. 1, pp. 139-40 (Bombay, 14/10/1760).

tumans and the permanent stationing of 200 Lari musketeers in Shiraz, and (iii) that a relative of Karim would reside in Lar and Ja'far Khan, brother of Nasir Khan, would reside in Shiraz as guarantee of the agreement. This treaty meant that Nasir Khan could devote his attention entirely to the coast.[140]

The conflict at Bandar 'Abbas-Qeshm continued unabated. During October-December 1760 there had been some skirmishes at sea, in which the Omani fleet participated helping the Banu Ma'in. Meanwhile, the situation of Bandar 'Abbas got worse with declining trade and the harsh rule by Ja'far Khan.[141] The combined Omani-Banu Ma'in fleet reinforced by the Hulas of Charak that had earlier delodged Molla 'Ali Shah from Hormuz now besieged his supporters the Jolfar Arabs in the fort of Laft at Qeshm.[142] Eyken, the captain of *de Slot van Capelle*, who had arrived at Bandar 'Abbas to take in salt rock, brimstone and iron oxide on October 8, 1760 reported that the town had been besieged by the Qavasem from Jolfar, who had taken away all vessels, including fishing boats. This meant that loading and unloading of ships was not possible anymore. The Persians, moreover, had taken possession of the VOC factory at the orders of the new governor of Bandar 'Abbas, Ja'far Khan, brother of Nasir Khan Lari. Although Buffkens had refused them entrance, the Persians had forcibly taken the keys of the factory. All rooms had been broken into and had been occupied by soldiers, traders, and whole families with their cattle and other possessions. Moreover, the factory had become an unsanitary and unhygienic place. The VOC warehouses had been partly demolished and salt rock was to be found all over the factory in small heaps. This was a memento of the siege of the Qavasem, who had been repelled by *inter alia* showers of salt rock. The brimstone had been left alone in a closed dilapidated warehouse. However, it had not been packed in bags as was customary. The Dutch captain called upon Ja'far Khan to inquire why he had taken possession of the VOC factory and had not returned it to its caretaker. The captain asked him to remove the current occupants and to assist him with porters and two lighters to bring the brimstone aboard. Ja'far Khan replied that he had been forced to take possession of the VOC factory, because else his enemies would have done so. He promised, however, that when peace would have been restored in the area he would repair and return the factory. He also promised to help the captain get his goods aboard with the two small vessels that he had, if there was no hostile activity. Eyken tried to find bags to transport the brimstone, but was able to find 70 bags only. Moreover, at the slightest rumor about enemy activity Ja'far Khan recalled his porters so that loading the ship would take a long time. Eyken, therefore, in view of increased activity of Arab pirates decided to leave Bandar 'Abbas on October 14, 1760. He sent a letter to Khark requesting the director there to fetch the remaining goods.[143]

Skirmishes and peace missions between the warring sides continued during 1761 and 1762, while the question whether Ja'far Khan was going to be dismissed or not was a major issue. Because the remaining brimstone in the former Dutch factory still had to be fetched, and because Buffkens' activities had to be investigated (he was suspected of fraud), Khark sent a vessel to Bandar 'Abbas in June 1761. On June 30, 1761, Messrs. Nicolai and Christant arrived in Bandar 'Abbas where they arrested Buffkens and sequestered his property. Ja'far Khan sent for Nicolai, complained about the Dutch action and asked that Buffkens be allowed to stay ashore to settle his debts. Nicolai refused, but promised to pay all small debts. Those with large claims had to write to Khark, a solution that was agreeable to Ja'far Khan. Nicolai also

---

140 VOC 3027, f. 19 (30/11/1760); Amin, *British Interests*, p. 46; Saldanha, *Précis*, vol. 1, p. 141 (Bombay, 17/10/1760); Ricks, *Politics and Trade*, pp. 290-91 referring to F. R. Gombroon XII (03/10/1760, pp. 3-4, 6); Perry, *Karim Khan*, p. 120. When the agreement was implemented not Ja'far Khan, but Masih Khan went as hostage to Shiraz.

141 Ricks, *Politics and Trade*, pp. 332-33. Christant also mentioned that a fleet had come from Masqat and he hoped that it would win the war so that finally peace would return to the area. VOC 3027, f. 6-7 (14/10/1760).

142 VOC 3027, Khark to Batavia (30/11/1760), f. 19.

143 VOC 3027, Gamron to Batavia, f. 6-7 (14/10/1760); VOC 3064, Khark to Batavia, f. 40-41 (01/10/1761); Lorimer, *Gazetteer*, pp. 1-2, 107.

contacted Molla 'Ali Shah, who asked for a respite, because he was unable to pay his debts due to his loss of Bandar 'Abbas and Hormuz. Before leaving Bandar 'Abbas on July 28, 1761 Nicolai urged Ja'far Khan to look properly after the VOC factory.[144] Batavia agreed with the way Khark had handled the Bandar 'Abbas affair so far, but made it clear that Ja'far Khan should be held to his word with regard to the repair of the VOC factory. Moreover, the next time a VOC ship would call on Bandar 'Abbas it would have to claim rock salt from Molla 'Ali Shah in lieu of payment of his debt.[145] Christant was left behind to look after the VOC factory in Bandar 'Abbas. Batavia allowed him to remain there and approved that he keep sufficient funds to buy brimstone. Buschman, the new Khark director, did not want to risk that kind of capital in Bandar 'Abbas, however, and arranged for the brimstone to be transported by native vessels to Khark.[146]

GOVERNMENT OFFICIALS SUPPORT AND ARE ENGAGED IN PIRACY

The worsening economic situation of Larestan and its littoral as well as the continued fighting meant that all parties were short of money. In June 1761 two tax collectors arrived in Bandar 'Abbas (Afghan Shah Beyg and 'Abdol Ja'far Beyg) to collect the taxes of Minab. The past basis for the tax burden of 600 *tumans* in cash and 12,000 *mann* of grain from the several governors of the Bandar 'Abbas region was no longer considered to be appropriate. Nasir Khan proposed that henceforth each governor pay an annual tax of 1,500 *tumans* in cash and 12,000 *mann* of grain or that the total of the Bandar 'Abbas taxes be fixed at the former system of 3,700 *tumans* and that:

> Such Places as are not in their Possession he deducted in their Proportion as also deductions for such Lands as are deserted by their Proprietors and lay uncultivated the places which are deemed belong to Jairoun [Bandar 'Abbas] and not in Possession of the Governours and Chiefs are Gombroon, the Islands of Kishme, Ormuse, etc.[147]

This revision was a reflection of Nasir Khan's own increased tax burden, the price of his peace agreement with Karim Khan. Furthermore, Nasir Khan intended to control the roads and revive trade and come to Bandar 'Abbas to settle issues with Ja'far Khan and his deputy Aqa Kamal. Nasir Khan was aware of a shift of maritime trade from Bandar 'Abbas to Minab and other ports.[148] However, he did not do anything to improve the situation, on the contrary. The new higher tax assessment was partly the reason that Ja'far Khan started to look for money where he thought he could find it. According the English, his

144 VOC 3027, f. 3-4 (22/06/1761) (the VOC wool buyer Ouwannees Katschik Crouse also accused Buffkens of having used violence against him, which the EIC Agent Douglas confirmed. There also was somebody at Bandar 'Abbas who said he was a Roman Catholic priest named Ferdinand, a name given to him by the priest at Khark named Angelo); VOC 3027, f. 8-10 (28/07/1761); VOC 3064, f. 22-23 (30/09/1761). Assistant Nicolai was also sent to Masqat to collect a claim on Mir Hassen Beek, chief of the sayyeds of the Mamenys family of Hydarabad. Many of these Mamenys were merchants in Masqat, Surat and elsewhere and the VOC usually had accepted the bills of exchange made out to the chief, to whom his adherents sent each year large sums of money. However, in recent years too many bills had been drawn on him so that the VOC had decided not to accept them anymore. However, Ouwannees still had one of 8,168 rupees and hence the trip to Masqat, which was in vain. VOC 3062, Khark to Batavia (01/10/1761), f. 30-31.

145 VOC 1015, f. 72-74 (31/03/1761).

146 VOC 3092, Khark to Batavia, f. 37-38 (19/10/1762).

147 Ricks, *Politics and Trade*, p. 292 referring to F. R. Gombroon XII (21/06/1761).

148 Ricks, *Politics and Trade*, pp. 291-93 referring to F. R. Gombroon XII (07/01/1761 and 21/06/1761).

oppressions were even worse than those by Molla 'Ali Shah. He harassed the EIC staff and continuously demanded presents and loans. He even went so far to pressure the EIC by "forbidding the Inhabitants to serve us, stopping our water camels, and placing parties of men in the houses round the place where we reside."[149] However, that was not enough to satisfy his needs and greed. Because of his lack of money and interest the Dutch factory was becoming more dilapidated, while Ja'far Khan's behavior towards the population became more oppressive. His demands for money, also from the Europeans, made trade impossible. The situation grew even worse when Ja'far Khan and other chiefs in the area were forced to piracy, because the local inhabitants had been picked bare. Ja'far Khan became a partner in banditry with his allies the Banu Ma'in. They were forced to robbery and piracy due to want, having neither land nor trade to support themselves, to prey on the population at large and the few merchants still coming to Bandar 'Abbas. In particular those coming from Kerman became their target, because they felt as if they were licensed privateers, arguing that the governor of Kerman was at war with Nasir Khan and thus vessels carrying goods belonging to merchants from Kerman were free game at Bandar 'Abbas. They gave Ja'far Khan a share of the spoils, who therefore encouraged them to continue with their marauding. This short-sighted policy led, of course, to a complete standstill of trade at Bandar 'Abbas and thus to a drying up of his main source of revenue.[150] Molla 'Ali Shah and his allies, the Qavasem, also had recourse to piracy, and were likewise forced to this way of life by their lack of income. They had been fully engaged in hostilities since 1760 and thus had not been engaged in trade, while Molla 'Ali Shah moreover had been cut off from Bandar 'Abbas, his major source of income. His men seized a boat with rice and araq coming from Masqat belonging local merchants and Mr. Lyster, a member of the EIC council at Bandar 'Abbas. The araq was found on Qeshm. Molla 'Ali Shah had used the rice for his own use, although he claimed he had no knowledge of the affair and that the goods should be returned.[151] In February 1762 there was no trade, while the war for Qeshm still raged on.[152] In the summer of 1762 Douglas reported that compared with 1759 Bandar 'Abbas had lost two-third of its population.[153]

The Banu Ma'in had for some time tried to have Ja'far Khan removed so that they might bring their families from Hormuz, where they could not live due to lack of water. Rather than to be removed Ja'far Khan wrote to his brother to be allowed to see his family in Lar, which was granted and he was temporarily replaced by a certain "Hodgee Ally Morviagin." Ja'far Khan left for Lar with money and rich presents, which he had extorted from the inhabitants and the EIC brokers just prior to his departure to convince his brother to allow him to keep his governorship. He frequently wrote that he would come back, but Nasir Khan did not let him return. The population of Bandar 'Abbas was pleased with the interim governor, because his behavior was the opposite of that of his predecessor. When Ja'far Khan left, Nasir Khan strengthened his ties with Banu Ma'in. Sheikh 'Abdollah married a woman from Nasir Khan's family, thus solidifying his relationship with the governor of Lar, who also gave Sheikh 'Abdollah Khan full control over Hormuz. Sheikh 'Abdollah also pursued the war with greater vigor. During 1762 and early part of 1763 he raided and plundered the villages and his former date groves on Qeshm. Because of their agreement with Nasir Khan the Bani Ma'in had brought their families to Bandar 'Abbas. They all had become impoverished due to the war with the Jolfaris. They therefore were constantly on the look out to plunder something, if not for Hajji 'Ali, the governor who watched them. Molla 'Ali Shah had gone to Jolfar to get Arab support to recover Hormuz, as his family was still held hostage in Lar. With the help of

149 Amin, *British Interests*, p. 47 referring to F. R. Gombroon XII (22/12/1760).

150 VOC 3092, f. 37-38 (10/10/1762); Amin, *British Interests*, p. 47.

151 Saldanha, *Précis*, vol. 1, pp. 147-49 (Bombay, 27/12/1761); Amin, *British Interests*, p. 47.

152 Ricks, *Politics and Trade*, pp. 293-94.

153 Amin, *British Interests*, p. 47.

the Jolfar Arabs he then made an attack on Hormuz, but after some skirmishes he was forced to retreat; the Jolfaris then made a second attack but again were forced to withdraw.[154]

On February 3, 1762 Ja'far Khan unexpectedly came to Bandar 'Abbas as the new governor, although Nasir Khan had sworn that he would not allow him to return if the Banu Ma'in would take their families to Bandar 'Abbas, which some of the chiefs then had done and who now were very much taken aback. The Jolfar Arabs were massing a large body of men at Laft and therefore Nasir Khan had sent Ja'far Khan to Bandar 'Abbas where he intended to come himself as well. Under the previous governor, Hajji 'Ali, many people had returned to Bandar 'Abbas hoping that the place would flourish again and they now noted that Nasir Khan could not be relied upon.[155] For Ja'far Khan had resumed his oppressions, in particular of those persons who traded with the EIC, and the few remaining Multanis who still had something bore the brunt. It was impossible for any person with some credit to remain in Bandar 'Abbas. The English believed that Nasir Khan was quite aware of his brother's doings. The EIC Agent had tried everything to remove these oppressions, but it was too much. For Ja'far Khan would continue to oppress the population for as long as he had the power and until he "had reduced the town to a few Cajan Huts."[156] After he had tried many times to avoid it Ja'far Khan finally was obliged to go to Lar on January 10, 1763. He was replaced by his father-in-law, who was known as an avaricious man. In January 1763 the Banu Ma'in made a surprise attack on Kustak, which belonged to the *shahryari* of Minab, an ally of Molla 'Ali Shah. They immediately wrote to Ja'far Khan to send some soldiers as they had taken it for his brother. They had done this to show their loyalty to Nasir Khan in the hope that he would give them the governorship of Bandar 'Abbas. It was said that Nasir Khan instead would give them an annual payment "on condition they carry on no trade but only cruise in the Gulph and act according to his orders which, if true, they will soon become freebooters." It was also said to reinforce their ties that Nasir Khan would marry a daughter of the late 'Abdol-Sheikh.[157]

In early 1763 Molla 'Ali Shah and the Jolfaris made peace with the Banu Ma'in, who were to keep Hormuz, get the Laft fort as well as all their lands at Basidu, while the revenues of the islands were to be divided among the three parties. The Qavasem Sheikh of Jolfar would keep the *Fath Rahmaniyeh*. The Qavasem also reached a peace agreement with the Imam of Masqat and his Hula allies. The Dutch took a deep interest in the developments in the power structure in the Bandar 'Abbas area, because Molla 'Ali Shah owed them money and they were worried that he would not be able to pay them due to his heavy losses. In fact, Molla 'Ali Shah had lost all his ships and vessels in this conflict and thus it was expected that he would have few means to pay his debt to the VOC. The *shahriyari* of Minab also had reportedly lost all his vessels and the Dutch also reminded him to pay his debt. Sheikh 'Abdollah was recognized as governor of Hormuz and Qeshm by Nasir Khan, while his Banu Ma'in would serve Nasir Khan as sailors. In short, those who benefited most were the Qavasem and the Banu Ma'in, while Molla 'Ali Shah lost, for his role in the Bandar 'Abbas area was over.[158]

154 Saldanha, *Précis*, vol. 1, pp. 147-49 (Bombay, 27/12/1761); Amin, *British Interests*, p. 47.

155 Saldanha, *Précis*, vol. 1, p. 154 (Bombay, 05/05/1763).

156 Saldanha, *Précis*, vol. 1, pp. xliv (Gombroon 09/05/172; 25-26/09/1762 – CXIX), 156 (Bombay, 02/09/1763).

157 Saldanha, *Précis*, vol. 1, p. 158 (Gombroon, 09/02/1763).

158 VOC 3027, Khark to Batavia (22/06/1761), f. 4; Saldanha, *Précis*, vol. 1, p. 158 (Gombroon, 09/02/1763); Ricks, *Politics and Trade*, pp. 332-33. According to Niebuhr, Molla 'Ali Shah had regained control again over Hormuz in 1764, but his statement must refer to an earlier situation as all other data say otherwise. He further reports that Basidu belonged to the Banu Ma'in, while Laft was held jointly by Molla 'Ali Shah and the Qavasem. Carsten Niebuhr, *Beschreibung von Arabien, aus eigenen beobachtungen und in lande selbst gesammleten nachrichten abgefasset nachrichten* (Kopenhagen: N. Möller, 1772), p. 329. In 1760 the governor-general had written to van der Hulst to seize the vessels that belonged to the *shahriyari* of Minab and his subjects, who were going to Basra and to hold them until the debt to the VOC had been

THE EIC ABANDONS BANDAR 'ABBAS

This untenable situation of increasing oppression, insecurity and hardly any trade made the English finally decide to abandon Bandar 'Abbas. Bombay had discussed the proposal by Douglas to move from Bandar 'Abbas to another location. The latter had argued that the high defense overhead could not be reduced "as they lived amongst People who only regarded the present and has neither honour nor honesty, who kept troops at the expense of the industrious and who paid no regard to the fair trade."[159] The Agent's choice was to move the factory to Hormuz, the more since in March 1760, the English at Bandar 'Abbas had received information that the Dutch intended seizing Bahrain, which information was entirely erroneous. Because Bombay was considering the proposal from its Bandar 'Abbas factory to relocate this operation to another location in the Persian Gulf it instructed its Agent to try to get possession of the fort of Hormuz and the nearby islands in concert with Nasir Khan or any other fit person.[160] However, Douglas reported that Hormuz was not a good place to establish a factory. Nothing grew on the island and there was only one water well on the entire island at two leagues' distance from the fort.

> However there were several Reservoir for water but [they] were out of repair, and in it they were told were two Tanks capable of holding a twelve months' water, for two hundred men. That the parapets of the Fort were much out of repair and the buildings in a ruinous condition and the Agent was told it would cost 80,000 Rupees to put it in proper order. That there was on the Island about 300 people, 100 of which were soldiers for its defence.[161]

Bombay had not been enthusiastic about the suggestion to relocate to Hormuz and in January 1761, after this negative assessment of the island's prospects, it instructed Douglas to move to the most appropriate spot in the Persian Gulf. It considered that it might be desirable to keep a house and one servant in Bandar 'Abbas to receive wool from Kerman, an arrangement not unlike the Dutch had.[162] In November 1761 Bombay finally had approved the proposal to move the English from Bandar 'Abbas to an island in the Persian Gulf.[163] To that end Douglas made an exploratory voyage into the Persian Gulf and on his return in November 1761 he reported to Bombay that the only viable alternative Persian port was Bushire. He also added "that was the Government of Gombroon in proper hands, it would be the best port in the Gulph for the inland trade, its situation being proper for the supplying many places with Woollens."[164] However, he did not propose to relocate to Bushire, because the English did not trust Persian officials anymore and did not want to risk a repeat-situation of Bandar 'Abbas in Bushire. London therefore instructed in April 1762 that the Bandar 'Abbas factory operation had to move in its entirety to Basra, where a stable and friendly government offered objective favorable conditions for the expansion of

---

paid. This clearly had not happened otherwise the Dutch would not have reminded the chief of Minab to pay his debt. VOC 1013, Batavia to Khark (10/06/1760), f. 192.

159 Saldanha, *Précis*, vol. 1, p. 145 (Bombay, 01/05/1761); Amin, *British Interests*, p. 47.

160 Saldanha, *Précis*, vol. 1, p. 138 (Bombay, 21/04/1760).

161 Saldanha, *Précis*, vol. 1, p. 140 (Bombay, 14/10/1760).

162 Saldanha, *Précis*, vol. 1, p. 142 (Bombay, 29/01/1761).

163 Saldanha, *Précis*, vol. 1, p. 150 (Bombay, 03/11/1761).

164 Saldanha, *Précis*, vol. 1, p. 152 (Bombay, 30/01/1762).

trade. To carry out this order Bombay sent several vessels, an artillery battery and about 100 men, which arrived on February 26, 1763 at Bandar 'Abbas.[165]

Douglas had sent part of the Company's goods to Basra with two ketches on February 16, 1763 under convoy of the *Drake*. Because the deputy-governor (*na'eb*) had let him know that he would prevent the English to leave Bandar 'Abbas by all available means, Douglas therefore had intimated that the EIC would not discontinue its activities in the port. Meanwhile, he took further steps for the EIC's departure, including how not to leave with empty hands. The deputy-governor and all government officials had stored their valuables in the Dutch factory, which had become Government House since 1760 and which also housed the Persian garrison. It was therefore decided to attack the Dutch factory on March 4, 1763, get hold of these valuables as compensation for the oppressions the EIC had suffered and secure a safe retreat for the EIC staff. During the attack the EIC force only gained entry to the factory after a firefight that lasted one and half hour during which time the Persian defenders had spirited away most of their effects, while the deputy-governor's family also escaped. The *Prince of Wales* that was lying in the roads could not come close enough to bear its guns on the factory, but the *Drake* and the *Swallow* were able to come to anchor at about three-quarter's of mile and bombarded the factory until the morning of the 5th, when the Persians abandoned the factory. The Persian force then retired to Suru (Serou) a village at one and a half mile distance from Bandar 'Abbas. The English force then also took that location, but found little of any value. The English side suffered eight Europeans and five sepoys as casualties. On the arrival of the *Prince of Wales* and the *Drake* the deputy-governor had realized that trouble was in the air and he had immediately sent an express messenger to Lar to inform Nasir Khan that the English were up to no good. He asked that Nasir Khan come immediately with a sufficient force. He also sent a similar message to Zeynal Khan at Hajiabad (Hodjeaab). The English reported that it was only on the morning of the 7th that some 250 horsemen had arrived and Douglas gave orders that all personnel and goods had to be on aboard that same evening. Because they could not load the cannons from the English factory within that timeframe it was decided to spike them and burn their carriages, "which was no great loss most of them being honeycombed." It was only because of lack of explosives that prevented them from blowing up the walls as well. Because little of value had been taken in Bandar 'Abbas Douglas decided to sail past Laft where he believed Molla 'Ali Shah's ship the *Fath Rahmaniyeh* to be which he intended to seize as compensation. He also believed that nothing would be gained by attacking his fort on Qeshm, because their main piece of artillery, the mortar had become unserviceable. "The Drake and Swallow's Cannon we found at Gombroon did little or no execution against the walls, the weight of metal they carry not being of a sufficient bore for battering." However, having arrived near Laft the naval commanders considered the operation too risky to carry out (because of the shoals and the size of their ships) and it was decided to proceed to Basra.[166]

Batavia was understandably very much annoyed about the English attack of the Dutch factory and the destruction brought about, the more so since Buschman had not even bothered to report it

165 Amin, *British Interests*, pp. 49-50; Saldanha, *Précis*, vol. 1, pp. xliii (CVI) (Bombay, 28/01/1761) ("If Gombroon is abandoned, a servant should be left there to keep communication with Carmenia [Kerman]), xliv (CXVIII) (London, 26/04/1762) ("The Gombroon Agency to be withdrawn and only a linguist to be left there to keep up the British flag.")

166 Saldanha, *Précis*, vol. 1, pp. 159-61 (Gombroon Road a/b Prince of Wales, 10/03/1763); VOC 3092, f. 37-38 (10/10/1762); VOC 1018, f. 111 (25/04/1764). During the sack of the Dutch factory the English also robbed Christant, the Dutch caretaker, as well as destroyed all doors and windows in the factory. VOC 3123, Khark to Batavia (08/05/1763), f. 9-10. Christant, who had lost all his property due to the English attack, had fled to Khark out of fear for his life. At the end of April or beginning of May 1763 letters arrived from Nasir Khan, governor of Lar and Ja'far Khan, the governor of Bandar 'Abbas requesting the Dutch to return to the port and offering the VOC the moiety of the customs revenues. Christant returned to Bandar 'Abbas to politely explain why he would remain only as a caretaker and not as a factor.

or to protest to the English and demand an indemnification.[167] Having been reprimanded by Batavia, Buschman sent an official protest to his EIC colleague in Basra, who forwarded it to Bombay, commenting without blushing that the English had neither caused damage to the Dutch factory nor had they stolen any of Christant's goods and there the matter seems to have rested.[168]

BANDAR 'ABBAS BECOMES A FISHING VILLAGE

Having lost all attraction for merchants, Ja'far Khan found himself in charge of an unimportant fishing village instead of an international trade emporium. He therefore sent a letter to Batavia in 1763 inviting the Dutch to return to Bandar 'Abbas, arguing that merchants had always come to Bandar 'Abbas to buy goods from the Dutch, and now, because of their absence, the merchants did not come anymore.[169] However, neither Batavia nor Buschman even contemplated such a return. Khark received once a year the goods that Bandar 'Abbas had to offer, viz. brimstone, which was transported by local vessels to Khark. Batavia, therefore, informed Ja'far Khan that as long as it was difficult to sell the cargos of two ships in Bandar 'Abbas it did not want to restore trading activities in Bandar 'Abbas. Once peace would be restored in Persia the matter would be looked into again.[170] The subsequent deaths of Molla 'Ali (who had been replaced by Sheikh 'Abdollah of the Banu Ma'in) and of Nasir Khan (replaced by Masih Khan) in 1765 was a kind of an end to an era. Masih Khan, a cousin of Nasir Khan, had betrayed him during the siege of Lar in 1765 by allowing Zand soldiers into the fort. He was then appointed *beygler-beygi* of Larestan and Bandar 'Abbas, with Aqa Mohammad Marbini Esfahani as his deputy and governor of Bandar 'Abbas.[171]

In the beginning of 1765 Christant was recalled to Khark. Buffkens, who had been allowed to return to Bandar 'Abbas after he had settled his affairs, would look after the factory. Ja'far Khan used that occasion to write again to Batavia. He wrote that if the VOC did not repair the factory it would become a ruin within one year. Ja'far Khan therefore invited the VOC to send an Agent to Bandar 'Abbas

167 VOC 1018, f. 110-13 (25/04/1764). This unpleasant news was quickly overshadowed by the news of the shipwreck of the ship *de Amstelveen* en route to Khark on the coast of Oman on August 5, 1763 at 18' 15" latitude near Cape Mataraqa (Materace) and Kuria Muria with total loss of its cargo and of the 105 men European crew 75 drowned. On September 11, eight men of the survivors finally reached Masqat after a journey of 31 days. VOC 3123, Khark to Batavia (05/10/1763), f. 16-18; Ibid., Cornelis Eijks, mate of *de Amstelveen* from Masqat to Khark (11/09/1763), f. 20-21.

168 Saldanha, *Précis*, vol. 1, pp. 178-79 (Buschman's protest is dated 29/08/1763). Buschman had been instructed to demand indemnification and to submit a detailed and costed loss and damage report, but he did not submit a claim for a certain sum of money. VOC 31-3, Protestation contre etc.(29/08/1764), f. 2760r-vs. He excused himself writing that the EIC Agent in Basra, Douglas, had returned to Bombay before he was aware of the sack of the Dutch factory and his departure. The protest, written in French, had been sent to the English consul Rens, who had forwarded it to Bombay writing that he had neither knowledge of the affair nor the authority to give satisfaction. VOC 3156, f. 40-41.

169 VOC 3092, f. 55-57 (01/03/1763); VOC 1018, f. 110-13 (25/04/1764); VOC 3156, f. 51-53 (17 Rabi' al-Akhar 1178 – 15/10/1764; received 08/01/1765); VOC 3156, f. 48-50 (received 08/01/1765); Lorimer, *Gazetteer*, p. 92. Trade had moved to Masqat and trend that had already started at the end of the 1750s. Risso, *Oman & Muscat*, p. 83; Abbé G.T.F. Raynal, *A Philosophical and Political History of the Settlements and Trade of the Europeans in the East and West Indies* 4 vols. (Dublin, 1779), vol. 1, p. 310.

170 VOC 1018, f. 122-23 (18/05/1764).

171 Ricks, *Politics and Trade*, pp. 293-94, 364; Fasa'i, *Farsnameh*, vol. 1, p. 609 (his son and their descendants would later also become governor of Lar and control that function until 1858; see Ibid, vol. 1, p. 638); Roschanzamir, *Zand-Dynastie*, pp. 60-61. In June 1762 a force of Zand troops or Dashestani irregulars had almost taken Lar killing many of Nasir Khan's troops and capturing some of his cannons. Perry, *Karim Khan*, p. 120.

to resume trading activities. Although all merchants had left for Masqat these would return if the Dutch would settle again in Bandar 'Abbas, or so he argued. This request was supported by Sheikh 'Abdollah Mohammad, the chief of Hormuz. He wrote that if the VOC did not want to return to Bandar 'Abbas it could come to Hormuz, Henjam or Qeshm, which were Dutch property anyway! The Dutch, he wrote, would be allowed to build a factory wherever they wanted. The Persians had no authority over the islands and therefore could not interfere with the Dutch.[172] Batavia, of course, replied negatively to both letters and repeated that as soon as peace would be restored in Persia trade relations would be renewed with Bandar 'Abbas.[173]

Ja'far Khan's letter was the penultimate contact the VOC would have with Bandar 'Abbas; the last contact took place in January 1766 when the Dutch twice called on Bandar 'Abbas after the fall of the Khark factory. The VOC as a result of these events decided to abandon the Persian Gulf trade, which was only resumed in the 1770s by private Dutch traders, but who went no farther than Masqat.[174] Although the English had abandoned their Bandar 'Abbas factory they later would be involved in a dispute with among others Sheikh 'Abdollah of Hormuz about the murder of an English captain-owner of an EIC protected ship in 1765, which events are dealt with in chapter seven.

As no Dutch ships came to the Persian Gulf anymore there is no information available from that source about Bandar 'Abbas. English ships occasionally called on the port after 1763, so that there are some snippets of information available of events in Bandar 'Abbas for later years. In 1773, for example, an English ship called on the port and reported that "Shaikh Mahmud", the governor of Bandar 'Abbas was in Shiraz. However, his son received the English well and offered them the Dutch factory if they chose to settle in Bandar 'Abbas. "The town appears in a most ruinous condition-the Dutch factory seems to be the only tolerable habitation, and most of the inhabitants left the place through fear of Tachey Caun [Zaki Khan Zand] who with a large body of troops is said to be very near." Thus, conditions had not changed very much in Bandar 'Abbas, for apart from the threat from land there also was such peril from the sea when two ships were burnt on its roadstead due to the Persian-Oman conflict (see chapter seven).[175]

A Persian source mentions that the Qavasem made three times an attack on Qeshm and occupied the island and other Persian lands. The governor of Bandar 'Abbas, Sheikh Mohammad Khan Bastaki, with Arab and other troops gathered on the mainland each time was able to expel them. After the third attack the Qavasem supported by Arab Bedouins and the Al Marzuq furthermore seized Kong, Lengeh, Bastaneh and Moghu. The levies mobilized by the governor of Bandar 'Abbas defeated the Arabs and the Al Marzuq surrendered. The Qavasem continued fighting, but again were defeated. Through intercession of the Sheikh of the Marzuq and other Sheikhs the Qavasem agreed to withdraw and to desist from new attacks and pay tribute. After this third attack Sheikh Mohammad Khan Bastaki moreover was able to make peace between the Sheikhs of the Qavasem and the Banu Ma'in and allowed the Qavasem to settle in Lengeh and Lashtan, although his own soldiers continued to hold the forts of Lashtan and Kong for some time to ensure that the peace held. Sheikh Saqr b. Rashed of the Qavasem nevertheless was later engaged in untoward activities and was expelled by the levies mobilized by the Persian government in an unspecified year. He first fled to the fort of Kong and then, when he was besieged there, he fled to Jolfar.[176] The dates given by this source for the attacks, however, (in 1750s) cannot be right, because Sheikh

172 VOC 3184, f. 75-76 (14/10/1765); VOC 3156, f. 51-53 (17 Rabi' al-Akhar 1178 = 15/10/1764, received 08/01/1765); VOC 3165, f. 48-50 (received 08/01/1765); Lorimer, *Gazetteer*, p. 92.

173 VOC 1019, f. 267-69 (19/02/1765).

174 See chapters six and seven.

175 Saldanha, *Précis*, vol. 1, pp. 279-80 (Masqat, 01/12/1773). Sheikh Mahmud probably is Sheikh Mohammad Bastaki.

176 Nurbakhsh, *Jazireh-ye Qeshm*, pp. 167-69.

Mohammad Khan Bastaki became the governor of Bandar 'Abbas only in 1769. Thus, these attacks, with the exception of the first attack, must have taken place after that date, most likely in 1773-1774 and 1777-78. The first attack took place in 1765 when the governor of Bandar 'Abbas, Hormuz and Minab, probably Sheikh 'Abdollah Banu Ma'in, asked the help of the Qavasem to resist the "unjust levy of tribute on the part of the Persian Government" and they then took "possession of the town of Kishm, Luft, Lingah and Shinas (on the Persian Coast)." The second attack most likely took place in 1773-74, when Sheikh Rashed was involved in an operation against a Zand army at Lengeh and the attack on Qeshm may have been part of this operation, while the third attack must have taken place before the two sides made peace. This conclusion is borne out by the marriage of Sheikh Saqr b. Rashed after his father's death (who died in 1777) with a daughter of Sheikh 'Abdollah of the Banu Ma'in, which settled all differences between them.[177] Thereafter the Qavasem did not attack Qeshm or Persian territory anymore and those living in Lengeh and became productive members of society.

The relative peace, that returned to Bandar 'Abbas thereafter, did not do anything to improve its commercial prospects. By 1790 its exports were "confined to a small quantity of dried and wet Fruits and Tobacco to the Port of Muscat; from whence it imports Rice, Coffee, coarse and Bengal and Surat Goods sufficient for the consumption of the Town itself, and of the Inhabitants of the country within a few Miles of its Neighbourhood.[178] Bandar 'Abbas came to the attention of the EIC again when in 1798, Mehdi 'Ali Khan, the EIC resident at Bushire, en route to his post, reported that he had learnt in Masqat that through a Banyan broker the Dutch and French allegedly had requested the Imam of Masqat "to let them have factories in the Port of Gombroon on the former footing, offering in such case, to make good to the Imaum what he had to pay as Revenue on that account to the Sovereign of Persia." He further reported that the Dutch factory at Bandar 'Abbas required an expenditure of 10,000 rupees in repairs, "whilst the English, and French factories there, are altogether in ruins, nor is there any likelihood of advantage derivable for these two or three years, to come, in the re-establishment of our factory there, but should a lac of Rupees be expended there in a good fortification, mounting thirty, or forty Guns and with three of four Companies of Sepoys, and 8 or 10 English Gentlemen the first advantage certainly resulting would be that all fear of the French or Dutch making any settlement in Persia, would be done away with."[179] Clearly it was the French threat[180] rather than the attractive trade prospects at Bandar 'Abbas that caused that this matter was even raised and as the former was not considered a very likely threat the subject of Bandar 'Abbas was

177 Sarlashkar Moqtader, *Kelid-e Khalij-e Fars* (Tehran, 1333/1954), pp. 733-34; Government of Bombay, *Selections from the records of the Bombay Government* No. XXIV- New Series (Bombay, 1856), pp. 129, 301; Risso, *Oman & Muscat*, p. 83; see also chapter seven (section on the Persian-Omani conflict).

178 Saldanha, *Précis*, vol. 1, p. 422 (Report on the Commerce of Arabia and Persia by Samuel Manesty and Harford Jones, 1790). In 1762 van der Hulst wrote that his long experience in the Gulf had taught him that bales of Mokha coffee were always mixed with coffee shells and dust. It was so common that nobody opened a coffee bale prior to weighing or sale. VOC 3092, Khark to Batavia (19/10/1762), f. 32.

179 Saldanha, *Précis*, vol. 1, pp. 346-47 (received at Bombay 14/10/1798). I have not found any mention of such a plan in Dutch sources, which also seem quite unlikely given the state of Dutch affairs at that time. The French, who sailed from Mauritius to Masqat, may have raised this matter, if only to give the English something to worry about. The French continued to be active in the Indian Ocean and even seized a vessel belonging to the EIC Resident in Basra in the Bay of Masqat in 1799. Ibid., vol. 1, pp. 364-67, 383-85. The Imam of Masqat also employed several Frenchmen in his service to the great consternation of the English. Ibid., vol. 1, p. 378. The Imam had leased Bandar 'Abbas from the Shah for 6,000 *tumans* per year as of 1794, an arrangement that would last until 1869. S.B. Miles, *The Countries and Tribes of the Persian Gulf* (London, 1969), p. 287.

180 For details on the activities of the French rivals and how the English dealt with it, see Risso, *Oman & Muscat*, pp. 139-57.

shelved. Bandar 'Abbas therefore remained a fishing village and a minor port, such as many of other similar villages on the Persian littoral.

TRADE, ITS UPS AND DOWNS

The situation at Bandar 'Abbas was dominated by the conflict between the governor of the Garmsirat or Hot Countries, i.e. Lar and Bandar 'Abbas, Nasir Khan and the deputy-governor of Bandar 'Abbas and admiral of the fleet, Molla 'Ali Shah. The latter wanted to remain autonomous, while the former wanted full control over the port and its revenues. To oppose Nasir Khan, Molla 'Ali Shah allied himself first with the Arabs of Charak, and when its chief offended the Hulas and was defeated, Molla 'Ali Shah came to an agreement with the Hulas. He supported the latter in their conflict with Bushire (about Bahrain), but soon (in 1752) Molla 'Ali Shah in particular allied himself with the chief of the Qavasem Arabs of Jolfar, who married one of his daughters. Although not free from the occasional dispute this alliance held during the entire period under discussion. Nasir Khan to find maritime allies in his conflict with Molla 'Ali Shah, first allied himself with the Arabs of Charak, but later in particular with the most immediate enemies of Molla 'Ali Shah, the Banu Ma'in. These Arabs who hailed from Bandar-e Kong, whence they had been driven by the Qavasem, alternated their place of residence between Qeshm and Hormuz, depending on how their conflict with Molla 'Ali Shah developed, although they finally were able to secure both. To bolster their position the Banu Ma'in not only had good relations with Nasir Khan and his agents, but also with the Hulas, and in particular with the Imam of Masqat, who was the enemy of the Qavasem, the ally of Molla 'Ali Shah.

Molla 'Ali Shah was reasonably successful in maintaining an autonomous situation, despite the fact that in 1752 Nasir Khan had taken him as a prisoner to Lar. However, after a few months he not only released Molla 'Ali Shah, but he also reinstated him as deputy-governor of Bandar 'Abbas and admiral of the fleet, because there was nobody else whom he could rely on to assume and execute these functions. Molla 'Ali Shah soon reasserted his autonomy enabled by Nasir Khan's pre-occupation to hold Karim Khan at bay. Molla 'Ali Shah therefore sought the latter's cooperation, which brought him a stay of execution from Nasir Khan's wrath. When the latter finally had reached an agreement with Karim Khan in 1758 he was able to focus his attention on the situation at Bandar 'Abbas. The next year Molla 'Ali Shah withdrew to the islands and as a result the entire region became immersed in hostilities. This had a negative impact on trade, because neither of the warring sides could make money in trade and therefore had to have resource to piracy. These developments caused the Dutch to abandon Bandar 'Abbas in 1759 and due to the deteriorating political and commercial situation the English followed their example in 1763.

The Dutch and English decision to abandon Bandar 'Abbas was based on both political and commercial grounds and the same holds for Asian traders, who had started to move to Masqat and elsewhere already since the mid-1750s. The political ones were that neither security nor stability existed in Persia, which had led to an erratic and reduced level of trading activities, to extortions and 'loans', to flight of capital and people, lack of porters and pack animals and thus higher transportation costs, as well as to a reduced state of productivity and purchasing power. The inability of the local, regional or national rulers to restore law and order made the Dutch lose hope for a speedy recovery of Persia's previous level of economic activity and wealth. Commercially speaking Persia had become a loosing proposition for the VOC.[181] Not only had sales gone down, but also profits as is shown in Tables 3.2 and 3.3. The apparent positive profit

181 Unfortunately no statistical data are available on the trade by Asian merchants and thus I cannot discuss their problems, although these must have been similar to those of the Dutch and English.

figures are misleading, because they only have been corrected for local overhead and not for cost of shipping, insurance, loss of interest on unsold goods, loss on exports and the Batavian overhead, and loss due to long periods of credit. Schoonderwoerd made this clear in a simple example to his successor Aansorgh and reminded him that all expenses had to be paid for out of the profits. He wrote that if Aansorgh had Dfl. 80,000 in goods which he could sell for Dfl. 100,000, he would thus think to have made a handsome profit. However, the cost of an average ship that was sent from Batavia and which was 10-12 months en route amounted to Dfl. 45,000. If the annual cost of the factory of Bandar 'Abbas was added, which amounted to Dfl. 25,000, then only Dfl. 35,000 remained, which meant a low profit of only 43% not taking into account all other cost elements.[182]

Table 3.2: Profits and losses of the VOC's Bandar 'Abbas factory (in Dutch guilders)

Year	Gross profit	Local overhead	Loss	Profit
1747-48	28,098	49,426	20,428	-
1748-49	140,250	26,286	-	113,014
1749-50	97,061	21,509	-	75,551
1750-51	n.a.	n.a.	n.a.	n.a.
1751-52	4,735	584	-	4,149
1752-53	84,049	24,226	-	59,782
1753-54	93,771	24,824	-	68,947
1754-55	88,416	29,837	-	58,579
1755-56	116,857	26,965	-	89,692
1756-57	108,395	24,647	-	83,748
1757-58	52,831	24,796	-	28,034

Source: VOC 2766, f. 65; VOC 2787, f. 37; VOC 2843, f. 38; VOC 2863, f. 54; VOC 2968, f. 22; VOC 2885, f. 37; VOC 2937, f. 24.

There were various issues which negatively influenced VOC turnover and profits. First, of course, there was the fact that the purchasing power of the population of Persia had decreased. How much it decreased we do not know, but if the drop in VOC sales (50%) is any measure it must have been substantial. Also, overall annual profit rates consistently dropped. Sales could have been boosted, if the VOC staff had been allowed to carry on barter trade. For money was becoming a scarce item in the Persian Gulf trade, especially after 1754. Merchants increasingly offered barter deals, or jewelry at what the VOC considered inflated prices. Such trading deals were highly risky, due to the uncertainty about the value of the offered goods. In Persia they had a scarcity value, which elsewhere was not the case. In 1754, the VOC therefore was forced by circumstances to accept payment in copper and asafetida, despite Batavia's prohibition to do so. Batavia therefore forbade barter, because the VOC lost money on these deals and henceforth it only allowed payments in copper as an alternative to cash. Schoonderwoerd had argued that even in this case he had to be allowed to accept copper at a conversion rate of Dfl. 85 per 100 lbs. or else trade would be impossible. He alleged that the EIC was able to sell copper at Dfl. 100 per 100 lbs. in India.

182 VOC 2885, Memorandum by Schoonderwoerd for his successor Gerrit Aansorgh (Gamron; 28/11/1755), f. 16.

Table 3.3: Profit rates on main VOC commodity groups in Bandar 'Abbas (in %)

Commodity group	1747-48	1748-49	1749-50	1750-51	1752-53	1753-54	1754-55
Spices	1653	1974	1068	1316	1211	1099	1182
Pound goods	123	166	191	157	135	100	98
Piece goods	45	48	51	59	31	42	33
Woolens	38	-	-	-	27	20	30
Total sales	140	137	143	187	160	117	92

Source: VOC 2748, f. 121; VOC 2766, f. 47; VOC 2787, f. 31; VOC 2761, f. 216; VOC 2843, f. 27; VOC 2863, f. 45; VOC 2885, f. 36; VOC 2937, f. 14; VOC 2968, f. 18.

Schoonderwoerd therefore blamed the VOC factory in Surat (India) for any losses incurred on exports from Persia. He also adduced evidence that the EIC was able to sell Persian goods with a profit in India, while the VOC factories were not. The Bandar 'Abbas factory, therefore, in 1755 again accepted goods in barter. However, Batavia put an immediate stop to that. Schoonderwoerd reacted in 1756 that in this way he had been forced to forgo a barter deal involving one lakh of rupees in diamonds, one of which weighed 55 carats. He urged Batavia to allow barter trade, because he had hardly any money to meet the daily expenditures of the Bandar 'Abbas and Kerman operations.[183]

The problem with barter trade was that not only did Persia produce very little that was exportable, but even those goods that qualified as such, were either difficult to obtain and/or very expensive. For some time the export of raw silk had been considered by Batavia, but Schoonderwoerd strongly advised against it. He argued that the price of silk was Dfl. 6 per 1 lb. at Isfahan. If exported to Batavia the silk would have to pass not less than 40 road-guard (*rahdar*) stations. This would mean that 1 lb. of silk would cost Dfl. 10 in Bandar 'Abbas or 65% more, which was much higher than the cost of silk exported via Russia.[184]

The main VOC export items prior to 1721 had been specie and goat-wool (*kork*) in addition to some madder (*runas*), wine, and dried fruit. These last three products were hard to obtain and thus, with the exception of an occasional shipment of madder, were not exported anymore. Goat-wool continued to be an important export commodity to which end the VOC like the EIC kept a separate trading station in Kerman or sent a wool buyer. However, it was very difficult to obtain goat-wool, for the Kerman area had become a very insecure place. But, as soon as Nader Shah had died, both the Dutch and the English had sent a goat wool buyer to Kerman.

Table 3.4: VOC exports of goat-wool from Bandar 'Abbas 1749-1758 (in lbs)

1749	1,098
1750	n.a.
1753	5,767
1754	9,111
1755	17,844

183 VOC 2885, f. 5 (08/09/1756).

184 VOC 2784, f. 101 (10/10/1748). On the *rahdar* system see John Emerson and Willem Floor, "Rahdars and their tolls in Safavid and Afsharid Iran," *Journal of the Economic and Social History of the Orient* 30 (1987), pp. 318-27.

1756	1,595
1757	21,828
1758	13,621

Source: VOC 2968, f. 4 (26/12/1758); VOC 2863, f. 61 (20/12/1754); VOC 2863, f. 19 (24/11/1754); VOC 2863, f. 73 (24/07/1755); VOC 2766, f. 87 (30/12/1749); VOC 2843, f. 45 (01/10/1753); VOC 2885, f. 2 (08/09/1756); VOC 2885, f. 29 (28/12/1755); VOC 2937, f. 27 (24/09/1757).

Due to a sudden long suppressed demand for woolens in 1748-49 Persian weavers competed in the wool market to a greater extent than before. As a result the price of wool rose to 80 *stuivers* per 1 lb. in 1750 in Kerman. The VOC and EIC goat-wool buyers were not able to buy any goat wool and returned to Bandar 'Abbas. After consultation between the two Companies, who coordinated their goat-wool buying efforts since 1734, it was decided to send the goat wool buyers back with instructions to buy goat wool directly from the tribal herders. The EIC and VOC Residents had agreed to equally divide the quantities of wool that their staff would be able to buy in this way. The goat wool buyers were instructed not to pay more than 25 *stuivers* per lb.[185]

This scheme, however, did not work, for even uncleaned goat wool was bought by local Persian merchants at 60 *mahmudis* or 18 *stuivers* per lb. The Dutch goat wool buyer, therefore, returned empty handed in August 1750. He was sent back on September 12, 1750 with a small caravan with some spices and ordered to stay in Kerman until the next goat-wool buying season.[186] It is unknown whether he was withdrawn during the abandonment of the VOC factory in 1752, but the VOC goat wool buyer was back in Kerman in 1753. By September that year he had bought 5,767 lbs. and he expected to be able to buy another 5,000 lbs. in barter for spices. Meanwhile, the agreement of joint purchase of goat-wool with the EIC had fallen through. The EIC agent, allegedly, had incited the shawl weavers in Kerman to complain to the governor that the Dutch had bought all available goat-wool and they as a consequence would find it difficult to make a living. It is unknown whether the EIC really was behind this protest. The Dutch had concluded this from the fact that the protesting shawl weavers said nothing about EIC goat-wool purchases. At first, the weavers had no success, but when they persisted in their protests the governor confiscated the kork the VOC had bought, undoubtedly in exchange for a financial inducement. After the Dutch paid him Dfl. 500 he returned the goat-wool to them.

Whoever of the two parties was to blame for the break-up of the joint goat wool buying agreement is not known, but a fierce competition started between the EIC and VOC. The VOC goat wool buyer was ordered to offer 2 *stuivers* per 1 lb more than his EIC counterpart and to pay whatever price was demanded. He also was allowed to draw drafts on Bandar 'Abbas without agio to further hurt EIC purchases, which did not amount to more than 3,000 lbs, according to the Dutch.[187] Despite these efforts the Dutch got less than they had hoped, for instead of the additional 5,000 lbs. they only were able top buy 2,890 lbs and 24 goats. However, during the 1754 season the VOC was able to buy more than 6,000 lbs of goat wool.[188] In 1755 less goat wool was exported, despite the fact that good relations existed with the local authorities in Kerman. The Dutch had given presents to the governor of Kerman and to various chiefs in the goat wool producing areas such as Mier Sekaal Alewerdie and to Resa Chan. The cleaning of goat wool had become a problem due to lack of labor in Kerman. Nevertheless, by mid-1755 some 10,000 lbs had been purchased and the Dutch hoped for more. However, due to lack of cash, especially silver *saheb qeranis*, the only coin

185 VOC 2766, f. 219 (10/05/1750). One *stuiver* is five cents.

186 VOC 2787, f. 26-27 (17/02/1751).

187 VOC 2843, f. 31-32 (01/10/1753).

188 VOC 2843, f. 60 (07/02/1754); VOC 2683, f. 3 (18/09/1754); VOC 2863, f. 9 (20/11/1754).

the peasants accepted these high hoped foundered. In Kerman itself no silver was to be obtained, even at a 10% agio. Silver therefore had to be sent from Bandar 'Abbas, which made goat-wool more expensive, also because the EIC was doing the same.[189]

In 1756, some 1,596 lbs of goat wool was exported and some 21,000 lbs in 1757. Despite orders to send cleaned wool only and to select it properly, goat wool arrived in the same sorry state as before due to lack of labor in Kerman. Goat wool, moreover, remained expensive and could not be had below 50 *stuivers* per lb. In 1758 more goat wool than ever before since 1750 was bought, but due to the high risk nature of the goat wool trade, Hovannes, the VOC goat wool buyer went bankrupt. The Dutch asked Shahrokh Khan, the governor of Kerman, to help Hovannes in collecting outstanding debts. Hovannes was ordered to return to Bandar 'Abbas, but he remained in Kerman. The Dutch suspected that he had made a deal with Shahrokh Khan to defraud the VOC, for he owed the Company Dfl. 17,262.[190]

Goat wool had been urgently requested by Amsterdam in 1752, but where the quantity, quality and price were concerned the VOC found the shipments disappointing. The sale of goat wool invariably resulted in losses reason why as of 1761 the VOC stopped trading in this commodity altogether.[191] The EIC continued trading in this commodity until 1763.

Table 3.5: VOC export of specie and copper from Bandar 'Abbas (1747-1754)

Category	1747	1748	1749	1750	1752	1753	1754
Piasters	29	-	-	-	-	-	-
Copper	47,338	45,161	687	4,341	-	-	74,646
Copper cakes	7,065	4,839	-	-	-	-	1,673
Bullion	-	30,546	-	136,348	-	-	-
Silver riyals	-	-	140,000	-	32,000	92,000	-
Surat riyals	-	-	1,320	-			
Persian silver riyals	-	-	11,369	-			
Gold riyals	-	-	-	-	-	208	-
Ducats, Turkish	-	-	-	-	-	1,700	-
Shahbumis	-	-	-	-	-	2,300	-
Ducats, Venetian	-	-	-	-	-	1,872	1,077
Gold riyals	-	-	-	-	-	116	1,211

Source: VOC 2968, f. 5 (26/12/1758); VOC 2863, f. 61 (20/12/1754); VOC 2863, f. 73 (13/04/1755); VOC 2766, f. 225 (10/05/1750); VOC 2766, f. 87 (30/12/1749); VOC 2748, f. 240 (10/10/1748); VOC 2843, f. 45 (10/10/1753); VOC 2863, f. 11 (24/11/1754); VOC 2804, f. 13 (15/02/1752); VOC 2724, f. 33 (22/12/1747). Copper and copper cakes are in lbs.; the coins indicate their number, while bullion is in Dutch guilders.

Apart from goat wool the other major export commodity was specie. It gradually decreased in importance, however, due to its growing scarcity and the growing role of copper in exports. The VOC

189 VOC 2863, f. 40 (20/12/1754); VOC 2863, f. 71 (24/07/1755); VOC 2885, f. 30 (28/12/1755); VOC 2885, f. 11 (28/11/1755).

190 VOC 2885, f. 2 (08/09/1756); VOC 2937, f. 7 (24/09/1757); VOC 2968, f. 10, 20 (01/05/1759).

191 VOC 1007, f. 309 (21/07/1753); Floor, "The Dutch on Khark island."

lost money on both commodities, whether it was specie or copper, because the conversion rates at Bandar 'Abbas were higher than at the other VOC factories in Asia.[192]

In addition to goat-wool, specie and copper only brimstone and red oxide, partly as ballast, were exported as well as some occasional agricultural products. However, these goods constituted negligible products in the VOC trade, both in value and quantity.

Table 3.6: Other VOC exports from Bandar 'Abbas, 1747-1758 (in lbs.)

Item/ Year	1747	1748	1750	1752	1753	1754	1755	1758
Dates	61,143	-	-	-	-	-	-	-
Brimstone	-	18,375	-	-	93,627	750	-	-
Rex oxide	-	-	1,557	167,837	-	-	-	10,500
Runas	-	-	-	-	-	5,254	3,600	-
Asafetida	-	-	-	-	-	9,300	1,584	-

Source: Source: VOC 2968, f. 5 (26/12/1758); VOC 2863, f. 61 (20/12/1754); VOC 2863, f. 73 (13/04/1755); VOC 2766, f. 225 (10/05/1750); VOC 2766, f. 87 (30/12/1749); VOC 2748, f. 240 (10/10/1748); VOC 2843, f. 45 (10/10/1753); VOC 2863, f. 11 (24/11/1754); VOC 2804, f. 13 (15/02/1752); VOC 2724, f. 33 (22/12/1747).

The situation was not that much different for the English, although until 1758 they had been able to do a reasonable amount of business. This was due to the fact that the EIC sold about 25-30% of all its English woolens exported to Asia in the Persian Gulf, most of which were marketed in Bandar 'Abbas. In 1759, there were still 1,089 bales of woolens exported to the Persian Gulf (3,657 bales in total to Asia), but the next year the number of bales exported to the Gulf dropped to 660 and in the next two years that number hovered at that level. This meant that instead of 30% the Gulf absorbed only about 13% of total English exports of this commodity.[193] Likewise, income from consulage also had dropped significantly, viz. from 419,339 *shahis* in 1754 to 103,435 *shahis* in 1758 and trend that persisted.[194] These indications of worsening trade conditions were also reflected in goat-wool, the only significant and profitable export good, apart from specie and copper, which yielded a loss in India.

Table 3.7: EIC Export of Kerman goat wool from Bandar 'Abbas , 1747-1763

Year	Quantity (in lbs.)
1747	19,887
1748	16,281
1749	16,281
1750	2,375
1751	-,-
1752	2,500
1753	16,906
1754	22,525
1755	37,437

192 VOC 3064, f. 10-12 (30/09/1761); VOC 2710, f. 1480-90 (15/06/1748); VOC 2885, f. 10 (28/12/1755).

193 Amin, *British Interests*, p. 151.

194 Amin, *British Interests*, p. 154.

1756	56,250
1757	86,250
1758	75,375
1759	-.-
1760	30,000
1761	11,250
1762	1,250
1763	28,125

Source: Thomas Ricks, *Politics and Trade in Southern Iran and the Gulf,* 1745-1765 (unpubl. thesis, Indiana University, 1974), appendix H, p. 418. The EIC data have been converted from *man-e Tabriz* (=6.25 lb) into pounds.

However, after 1758, despite the disappearance of Dutch demand for goat wool, the supply of this commodity became increasingly difficult due to the war between the governors of Kerman and Lar and the attacks on the caravan routes to Kerman.[195] As a result, by 1762 "British Commerce in Persia had declined so much, that setting aside extortions which the factory at Gombroon was constantly experiencing, from Persian Governors, neither prudence nor interest could justify or induce the Hon'ble Company, to support, so expensive an establishment.[196]

CONCLUSION

The departure of the Dutch (1759) and the English (1763) signaled the end of Bandar 'Abbas's role as an international port as well as of its reduction to a minor port for local trade. For not only the Europeans left, but so did the Asian traders. The port had experienced other crises and downturns during its heyday as that of the major gateway to the Persian market, but it had been able to overcome these hurdles.[197] However, this time in the absence of an effective central government the port fell victim to the inability of the local and regional authorities to work together and provide stability and security to the inhabitants living in and the merchants calling on Bandar 'Abbas as well as to the caravans roads connecting the port with the markets in the interior of Persia.

For the Dutch the year 1759 was the end of a long history of their presence in Bandar 'Abbas which had begun in 1623. During that period this port had been the VOC's most important factory [trading station] in the Persian Gulf, both commercially and administratively. Until 1747 it had been the seat of the chief of the so-called 'Persian Directorate' which included the following factories: Isfahan, Kerman, Bushire and Basra. Sales in Bandar 'Abbas had always been considerable and its proceeds formed an important input into the so-called Indies Fund, a kind of revolving fond used by the VOC to finance its Asian trade. This important role of Bandar 'Abbas decreased after 1721, when trade was reduced consider-

195 Willem Floor, *The Persian Textile Industry in historical perspective 1500-1925* (Paris: L'Harmattan, 1999), pp.372-73; Ricks, *Politics and Trade*, pp. 309-12.

196 Saldanha, *Précis*, vol. 1, p. 419 (Report on the Commerce of Arabia and Persia by Samuel Manesty and Harford Jones, 1790).

197 On the early history of Bandar 'Abbas and its rise and development as Safavid Persia's major port, see Floor, *The Persian Gulf*, chapter five.

ably, due to the Afghan occupation of Safavid Persia. Thereafter Basra acquired an increasingly important role. The unsettled conditions prevailing in Persia after 1730, especially during Nader Shah's reign (1737-47), changed Bandar 'Abbas's position negatively for trade with Persia did not reach its pre-1721 level.[198] Moreover, the VOC and its competitor the EIC were increasingly exposed to all kinds of vexations, demand for ship loans, demands for money loans, demands for presents, and other forms of obnoxious behavior. Formerly, such behavior had been incidental, and had been set off by good profits, but after 1721 this additional burden coincided with decreasing profits and finally with losses.[199]It was hoped that after Nader Shah's death stability would return and trade would increase. This did not happen, because of the succession war that broke out between numerous contenders for the throne, a process that would only end in 1763. The succession war was complicated by the outbreak of local conflicts such as that between the governor of Lar and his nominal subordinate, the deputy-governor of Bandar 'Abbas. The latter's position was furthermore challenged by the Banu Ma'in, who were supported by the Imam of Masqat, while the deputy governor of Bandar 'Abbas received support from the Qavasem of Jolfar and Lengeh and even the Hulas. Apart from the breakdown of political stability in Persia concomitantly insecurity in the Persian Gulf increased adding to the burden of the European Companies in military expenditure. The continuous state of war also led to a fall in purchasing power of the population of Persia and hence to less sales. Moreover, cash became scarcer and more expensive relative to the price of bullion elsewhere in Asia due to these same wars. Consequently, the European Companies lost considerably on the export of bullion due to the inflated value of the Persian currency. Finally, the internal situation in Persia also had led to a downfall in production and hence less opportunity to export Persian commodities.

The VOC, EIC as well as Asian traders tried to offset this trend by increasing their sales in Basra and elsewhere in the Persian Gulf. The EIC appears to have made a more concerted effort of expanding its trade with Persia due to the fact that its main import, woolen cloth, could only be sold there, while the VOC could sell its spices and sugar anywhere. Moreover, the VOC had a lot of troubles elsewhere in Asia as well, which handicapped its maneuverability, although its establishment of a factory on Khark aimed to revive its commercial fortune in the Gulf. The EIC, moreover, was considerably helped, through the levying of consulage, by the increase in importance of the so-called country trade, which in fact was more important than its own trade. However, these country traders (Asian and European) increasingly also suffered from the same insecurity and economic downturn that the Europeans suffered from and thus also sought other venues and port where better conditions prevailed and in fact abandoned Bndar 'Abbas earlier than the VOC and EIC. The VOC had no direct navigation anymore between India and the Gulf and thus lost its edge *vis à vis* the EIC. Nevertheless, the difference between the two rival companies was one of degree rather than of nature, because both, for the same reasons, abandoned their Bandar 'Abbas factory and moved to other ports in the Persian Gulf.

198 Floor, "Dutch Trade;" Lorimer, *Gazetteer*, pp. 116-18.

199 Floor, *Hokumat*; Lorimer, *Gazetteer*, pp. 88-89.

CHAPTER FOUR
The Rise and Fall of Khark Island 1748-1770

Bandar-e Rig was a small port on the Persian coast that was not much different from many other similar ports on the same coast. The population was mainly engaged in fishing, pearling, and some regional trade. After Nader Shah's death in 1747, its chief Mir Naser Vagha'i tried to transform the small port into a bigger one by trying to attract more ships induced by low customs rates and a pleasant reception. He also tried to become richer by joining his chief rival in this commercial endeavor, Sheikh Naser of Bushire, in the attempt to seize Bahrain and its pearl banks. His greatest success was to convince the VOC to establish its principal factory in the upper Gulf on his island of Khark that was situated just opposite Bandar-e Rig. However, the greed of his power-lusting youngest son, Mir Mohanna, undid all his achievements. Mir Mohanna killed his father, mother, brother, sisters and many other relatives to become the uncontested chief of Bandar-e Rig. After initial success, he was expelled and imprisoned, and later he and his oldest brother were reconciled. Shortly thereafter Mir Mohanna killed his brother and not being interested in the slow process of gaining wealth through honest trade he started a career as a highwayman and pirate. He became the scourge of the Gulf and Dashtestan and at times totally paralyzed the caravan trade. Karim Khan had no choice but to try and eliminate Mir Mohanna as his activities impacted negatively on the revenues of the latter's neighbors and thus on their ability to pay taxes to Karim Khan. As the latter had no fleet the Dutch and English Companies were drawn into this local conflict against their will and reluctantly were forced to provide naval assistance. This led to a direct conflict between the Dutch and Mir Mohanna, who in 1766 seized their fort and expelled them. The English also got involved in the conflict (1765, 1768) and were defeated, while Mir Mohanna even captured some of their ships. His infamous career finally came to an end when his own followers could not stomach his cruel behavior anymore and tried to kill him. He fled to Basra where he was executed. With Mir Mohanna's death the role of Khark as a pirate's nest was soon over and both Bandar-e Rig and Khark fell back to their age-old way of life of fishing, pearling and a little trade as if nothing had happened between 1753 and 1770.

DUTCH PROBLEMS AT BASRA

The VOC had operated a factory in Basra since 1724, which was subordinate to the VOC director in Bandar 'Abbas. When in 1747 the VOC decided to close down its factories inside Persia and only to maintain the coastal factories in Bandar 'Abbas and Bushire, it was also decided that Basra would henceforth be an independent factory.[1] The VOC resident at that time had mismanaged the Company's affairs and was replaced by Tido Baron von Kniphausen in 1749. Jan van der Hulst was appointed as his deputy. It was their task to restore the VOC's commercial position in that part of the Persian Gulf.[2] Von Kniphausen arrived in Basra on January 3, 1750 and immediately received a taste of the unruliness that prevailed in that city. The new governor of Basra, Kaisariyyali Ahmad or Ilchi Ahmad had appointed the *qaputan-basha* as his *vakil* in Basra.[3] However, he was soon thereafter appointed to replace the new governor of Baghdad (Hajji Ahmad Pasha) due to financial problems and an uprising among the military and the Arab tribes, which the latter had been unable to resolve. Istanbul then appointed Hajji Hoseyn Jalili Pasha of Mosul as the new governor of Basra, but neither he nor Ilchi Ahmad Pasha was able to maintain order in the province. Soleyman Pasha, the great Ahmad Pasha's deputy (*kahya*), who after the death of his master had been appointed governor of Adanah, but had continued to intrigue to be appointed governor of Basra, like his former chief, incited the Arabs to rebel to prevent Hoseyn Pasha from assuming his new function. He wanted to show Istanbul that he was the only person who could govern the Arabs and guarantee peace. By promising to pay Ahmad Pasha's debts and to finance himself the troops needed to establish peace Istanbul annulled Hoseyn Pasha's appointment and confirmed Soleyman Pasha in his stead. Meanwhile Ilchi Ahmad, who had proved to be totally ineffective, had been replaced in Baghdad by Tiryaki Mohammad Pasha. Soleyman Pasha's appointment caused much fear among the Banu Ka'b ("the Gabaanse Arabieren"), while the Turks at Basra were encouraged by this news. He immediately sent a new *motasallem*, 'Omar Agha to Basra.[4]

Soleyman Pasha marched to Basra, which resulted in scarcity and high prices of food necessities. Wheat rose from 8 to 60 and barley from 7 to 40 *mahmudis*, because he confiscated all grains that he could lay his hands on en route. He also imposed a contribution of 700 purses on Basra, of which the Armenians had to pay 300 purses. His arrival was opposed by the Arabs who had taken possession of the date groves around Basra. In reaction the governor sent war galleys to the villages, which led to the flight of the villagers. The result was that the city was filled with women and children. On 26 July 1748 Soleyman Pasha demanded a cash payment of 100 purses from both the Dutch and English. In August 1749 the pasha went to Hillah, while he also ordered houses in Basra to be vacated for his own use in preparation for his arrival. As a result many left the town, such as the Armenians who left for Bandar-e Rig. On 12 November 1749 the janissaries plundered the bazaar of Basra during a 10-day period. Soleyman Pasha then ordered the troops to camp outside the city, but this brought no improvement. He imposed himself on the business community, clapped many merchants in irons and confiscated their grains. Soleyman Pasha also occupied the VOC fac-

---

1 VOC 779, Batavia to Gamron (26/06/1747), f. 200. For pre-1724 VOC activities in Basra see Floor, *The Persian Gulf*, ch. 8.

2 On von Kniphausen see M.A.P. Meilink-Roelofsz, "Een Nederlandse Vestiging in de Perzische Golf," *Spiegel Historiael* (1967), pp. 481, 487; W. Wijnandts van Resandt, *De Gezaghebbers der Oost-Indische Compagnie* (Amsterdam, 1944) and annex 1 to this chapter. Von Kniphausen after his return to the Netherlands in October 1760 led a rather licentious life in Paris, where he died a poor man. Jan van der Hulst arrived as a junior merchant in Batavia. In September 1749 he was appointed Second of the factory in Basra. In 1755 he returned to Batavia and remained there as an unemployed junior-merchant. In 1758 he was sent as commander to the Malacca Straits. In 1759 he was appointed Agent at Khark with the rank of merchant. After his recall to Batavia in 1762 he deserted from VOC service (see below).

3 VOC 2724, Basra to Batavia (15/01/1748), f. 46. He was called Ilchi Ahmad, because he had been once sent as ambassador to Persia. S.H. Longrigg, *Four centuries of modern Iraq* (Oxford, 1925), p. 166.

4 VOC 2724, Basra to Batavia (15/01/1748). Longrigg, *Four Centuries*, pp. 166-67.

tory and forced the Dutch to pay him Dfl. 61,363, while the English had to pay a similar sum. On 4 February 1749 the pasha left Basra to attack the Marsh Arabs. There was a shortage of food in the city, which was not improved when the pasha plundered the city before his departure. The English wanted to close down their factory and abandon Basra, but were prevented by the local authorities from doing so, although the EIC chief Finly was able to flee to Bushire. He was afraid that more demands of money would be made after he had once again been forced to pay 40,000 sjalottes. Meanwhile the situation with the Marsh Arabs seemed hopeful. Sheikh Bandar (Sjeeg Bendher), who had withdrawn to the desert since 1748, had sent his younger brother to Basra promising that he would keep the tribesmen under control. However, this was subject to the *a'yan* or olama to make an agreement with him. However, the latter refused to do so, because they neither trusted Sheikh Bandar nor the Montafeq. The Sheikh then left Basra for the Montafeq as he was faced with the threat of armed opposition from the town's people and returned with 7,000 armed and horsed tribesmen. Faced with this threat the *a'yan* came to him to make peace, but he then all arrested them. The Montafeq now demanded the arrest of the *kahya*, *shahbandar* and Ebrahim Aqa. If this would be agreed to they would come with a new *motasallem*, who had been appointed by Soleyman Pasha. This resulted in even less support for Soleyman Pasha in Basra and increased support for Mostafa Pasha, the *qaputan-basha*, who had been the de-facto governor of Basra since 1748.[5]

Because Soleyman Pasha had to return to Baghdad, where he had assumed control of its government, he had to leave Basra to the *qaputan-basha*, although the latter did not oppose the installation of the new *motasallem* or deputy-governor of Basra, Hasan Aqa in early 1750. Towards the end of the year, the *qaputan-basha* rebelled against the government and closed the river on 10 November 1750 with his vessels. Hasan Aqa's forces were not able to take the city, due to popular support for the *qaputan-basha* and thus there was constant fighting and shooting, which made it impossible, for example, for the Dutch to unload their ship *de Anna*. The deputy-governor's forces waited for troops to arrive from Baghdad, of which finally some 5,000 arrived on 15 December 1750, both foot and horse. The *qaputan-basha* tried to flee with all his vessels, but the *motasallem* or governor of Basra, Hasan Aqa, requested VOC naval assistance to prevent the *qaputan bashi* from fleeing via the river. Because the Ottoman government and the *qaputan-bashi* owed the VOC money von Kniphausen considered this a good opportunity to agree to this request hoping that the Company would get its money back. At von Kniphausen's orders *de Anna*, without firing one shot, stopped the 17 galleys commanded by the *qaputan bashi* and forced them to return to Basra and surrender. Although the *qaputan bashi* was able to flee to Persia with two gallivats, the Dutch thus gained credit with the *motasallem*. He extorted money from the Basra population to pay the troops from Baghdad, including money from the EIC, which had to pay 15,000 *qorush*. The Dutch, however, did not have to pay anything and also were exempted from paying Dfl. 32,413, their arrears in customs duties.[6] Trade had suffered, of course, because of the *qaputan-basha*'s rebellion, while the rebellion of the Banu Ka'b (the Arabs of Durak and Affar), who had effectively closed the Shatt al-Arab, due to their marauding activities, even plundering a VOC vessel, had not improved trade

5 VOC 2766, Basra to Batavia (30/06/1749), f. 46-61. The use of the term *a'yan* by the Dutch, a word meaning the notables or men of influence in general, not just the olama, is interesting. Abdullah, *Merchants*, p. 32.

6 VOC 2766, Basra to Batavia (30/03/1750), f. 88, 94; VOC 2787, Basra to Batavia (07/02/1751), f. 18-23. Von Kniphausen referred to the Banu Ka'b as the "Arabs of Durak and Affar. [Dowraq and Haffar]" On these events see Longrigg, *Four centuries*, pp. 170-71.

prospects either.[7] On 27 January 1750 the Ottoman troops returned to Baghdad and thus peace returned to Basra, for these troops had behaved like a group of brigands.[8]

In the letters which describe the course of events from this successful moment for the Dutch in Basra until von Kniphausen's arrest in 1753 there is no reference to be found at all to the events, disputes, ruptures, which may explain this arrest as a natural consequence thereof.[9] His early political success due to his support of the government of Basra, followed by commercial success, may have made von Kniphausen too self-confident. This appears to be borne out by the Carmelites who report that "in the year after his arrival he won the kindly regard and esteem of everybody; but with fortune favouring him and becoming anon too much puffed up with the breath of applause he thought he could turn everything upside down to get his own way, and ruin and trample underfoot others."[10] It would appear that von Kniphausen's opponents were three of a kind. In the first place there was the *motasallem*, Hasan Aqa, who after the initial honeymoon in vain tried to 'borrow' and extort money from von Kniphausen.[11] He later wrote that he had not reported these difficulties to the High Government, because they seemed to be of small significance. Moreover, Batavia had given orders that reports should be succinct and to the point.[12] Nevertheless, in 1751 von Kniphausen had contacted the Dutch ambassador at to the Porte, Baron Elbert de Hochepied, "in connection with the collection of outstanding debts and to remain unencumbered from new extortions."[13] De Hochepied had responded favorably to von Kniphausen's questions and had suggested that he should obtain a copy of the Dutch-Ottoman Treaty of Friendship. At the same time, he had also written a letter of recommendation to the *motasellem* of Basra.[14] Von Kniphausen had only asked for a consular *barat*, which would give him more or less diplomatic immunity. To this end he had sent 2,000 piasters to de Hochepied, for he had found out that the French had obtained such a *barat* for a similar sum. Although de Hochepied promised von Kniphausen to get him a consular *barat*, he pointed out that 2,000 piasters would not be enough, while it also would take longer than von Kniphausen believed. Von Kniphausen replied that if getting the consular *barat* would take a long time then he did not need it, the more so if the price would be much higher. In that case the cost and trouble would not outweigh the advantages in view of the disregard Soleyman Pasha, the governor of Baghdad and Basra, had for orders from the central government.[15] Nevertheless, knowing that

---

7 VOC 2766, Basra to Batavia (30/03/1751), f. 92-97.

8 VOC 2787, Basra to Batavia (10/08/1750), f. 18-21.

9 For example, von Kniphausen makes no mention at all of any difficulties in his last letter just prior to his arrest. VOC 2824, Basra to Batavia (11/01/1753). The letter was pre-dated January 11, because that was the fixed date of the departure of the ship *'t Fortuyn*.

10 Anonymous, *A Chronicle of the Carmelites in Persia*. 2 vols. (London, 1939), vol. 1, p. 689.

11 VOC 2824, Vertoog van den tegenwoordigen staat der regeering en negotie te Bassora and Boucheer by von Kniphausen a/b 't Fortuyn (15/02/1753), f. 57-59.

12 VOC 2804, Basra to Batavia (11/01/1751), f. 19.

13 NA, Legatie archief Turkije, nr. 168, de Hochepied to von Kniphausen (02/09/1752), f. 2; Ibid., nr. 420, letter from the Capigilar Chiaja of the Sadik Aga, agent of the Pasha of Babylonia [Baghdad] in Constantinople [Istanbul] to the Sultan, undated (probably 1751).

14 De Hochepied "was one of the few ambassadors who did try to 'recoup himself' for all extra expenses involved in the Turkish embassy, amongst other things by means of sale of Dutch consular and interpreters' berats." G.H. Bosscha Erdbrink, *At the Threshold of felicity. Ottoman-Dutch relations during the embassy of Cornelis Calkoen at the Sublime Porte, 1726-1744* (Ankara, 1975), p. 266.

15 VOC 2893, Replicq van den opperkoopman Tido Frederik von Kniphausen op de klagten van H.H.M. Ambassadeur de Hochepied, undated (1757), f. 1504-06. For de Hochepied's view see NA, Collectie de Hochepied 108, de Hochepied to Heeren Zeventien (XVII) (17/05/1761). This last letter also contains an interesting discus-

he was covered by the treaty against possible action by the local deputy-governor von Kniphausen "haughtily" resisted all attempts to extort money from him.[16] Nevertheless, he appears to have taken "so much offense at this gentleman's behaviour that he had him dismissed from the governorship of Basra by giving presents to Sulaiman Basha."[17]

The second group of opponents consisted of the merchants of Basra and several notables. Von Kniphausen seems to have quarreled with them as well as taken unjustly money from them, according to English sources.[18] Since von Kniphausen corresponded with de Hochepied about means to facilitate "the collection of outstanding debts" this statement may be based in fact.[19] Although we do not whether von Kniphausen had these debts unjustly taken from the merchants, he certainly may have done it in a rather ruthless manner. Nevertheless these misgivings about von Kniphausen cannot have been universal since in August 1752 he reported that the Basra merchants preferred to ship their goods with Dutch rather than with English ships, so not all merchants bore him ill-will, for those who did undoubtedly would not have given him their business.[20]

The third group was formed by the English, who considered the increased and successful activities of the Dutch, especially in the vital sector of trade for the EIC such as woolen goods, disadvantageous to their commercial activities. The EIC had been ordered to undersell the Dutch and to wreck their trade in Basra. Because of the fierce competition between the two Companies there was a strong animosity between its personnel as well. Von Kniphausen held no communication with the English, whom he even accused of wishing to poison him.[21]

Von Kniphausen's haughty and independent behavior alienated him even more from those people who already hated him, both among the Europeans and the locals. Among the former, Mr. Ellis, the EIC resident was prominent, whilst among the Turks there was the dismissed Hasan Aqa. All these persons, for unknown reasons, complained about von Kniphausen's behavior to Soleyman

sion concerning the *barats*. The importance of being recognized as consul had been driven home to the Dutch already in 1734, when the EIC chief Martin French had been allowed special privileges such as that of hoisting a flag on the English factory. As a result, the Ottoman authorities treated the EIC chief as if he was the consul (*balyus*) of all Europeans in Basra, and the Dutch felt that they were not treated with the same respect as before. Only with French's consent could caravans and vessels with European-owned goods depart for respectively Aleppo and Baghdad. The Dutch chief at Basra protested and even proposed to send all VOC goods directly to Aleppo and Baghdad and open a factory in Istanbul. Ahmad Pasha of Baghdad therefore wanted the Dutch enjoy the same privileges as the English, but only if they would give him considerable presents. This finally happened and as of 1741 the Dutch were allowed to hoist a flag and received a reduction of 1% in customs duties. VOC 2390, Basra to Batavia (28/10/1735), f. 84-85, 127; VOC 2390, Basra to Calkoen (Istanbul), (16/12/1735), f. 176; Coolhaas/van Goor, *Generale Missieven*, vol. 10, p. 339 (05/12/1742). These were not treaty privileges, but those granted by the governor of Baghdad and they lost their validity on his demise. In 1764, therefore, the English ambassador had obtained a consular *barat* for the EIC Agent in Basra from the Porte, although the governor of Baghdad-Basra refused to allow the levying of duties by the consul. Saldanha, *Precis*, vol. 1, pp. 180-82 (Constantinople, 09/1764).

16 VOC 2824, Vertoog, f. 57-59.

17 Anonymous, *Chronicle*, vol. 1, p. 689.

18 A.A. Amin, *British Interests in the Persian Gulf* (Leiden, 1967), p. 143.

19 VOC 2804, von Kniphausen to de Hochepied (11/01/1752), f. 19.

20 VOC 2804, Basra to Batavia (24/07/1752), f. 37.

21 NA, Legatie Archief Turkije, nr. 168, de Hochepied to von Kniphausen (02/09/1752)- this was a reply to a letter by von Kniphausen in which he discussed the jealousy of the English with regards to Dutch commercial activities in Basra; Roelofsz, *Vestiging*, p. 482 (I have not been able to trace her source for this remark concerning the poisoning); VOC 2824, Rapport der enorme behandelingen en geweldenarijen van 't Turks gouvernement (Basra, 24/01/1753), f. 21.

Pasha in 1752. Hasan Aqa appears to have made much about the customs duties that the Dutch did not pay as a result of an agreement that he himself had made with von Kniphausen in 1751, for the English report that von Kniphausen was accused of withholding and deceiving the pasha on the matter of customs duties.[22] Soleyman Pasha gave in to these complaints and instructed the *motasallem* at Basra, 'Ali Aqa, that "should the English Resident agree, he should knock on the head of Baron Kniphausen's too great freedom of speech and ways of living."[23] 'Ali Aqa appears to have received this order in early January 1753.[24] At that time, von Kniphausen was preparing the departure of the VOC ship *'t Fortuyn* on January 11. On January 10, 1753 he was summoned by the *motasallem*. Suspecting nothing, von Kniphausen accompanied by his usual suite of the Company interpreter and janissaries went to the governor's residence. After having been kindly received by some officials in the audience room he was kindly asked to come into another room, where he and those with him were arrested. Von Kniphausen was then put into a small dark prison, where he and the interpreter were manacled at their feet. He remained there for 24 hours. According to the Carmelites, the *motasallem* then called a meeting of the leading Europeans and notables of Basra to inform them about his action. He explained to them that von Kniphausen's case was a bad one and that execution was inevitable. He even went so far as to send an executioner into the prison to intimidate von Kniphausen.[25] According to an anonymous English source, von Kniphausen had indeed caused the problems with the Basran authorities himself.

> The truth is this: the Baron was a great schemer and thought very high of his abilities to please the fair sex. He often boasted of favours which he never had enjoyed. For a European in a public function like von Kniphausen it was not very easy to begin a relationship with Muslim ladies. The law forbids it, even with those belonging to the lower classes. However, von Kniphausen's ambitions made him look for the confidence of duchesses and married ladies and the go-betweens of Basra like their kind allover the world promise Junos but pay with clouds. One of them made him believe that the young wife of an old rich Turkish merchant longed for his embraces. Hidden passage-ways, valve-doors, and all kinds of ingenious preparations were made in the Dutch factory. Money to keep people silent was showered like a

---

22 Amin, *British Interests*, p. 134; Anonymous, *Chronicle*, vol. 1, p. 689. Von Kniphausen expressed himself in the following manner about his English colleague: [an Irishman looked down upon by the English who come here as often as country merchants] "un Irlandois meprisé des Anglois qui viennet ici autant que des Marchans du pais," see NA, Stadhouderlijke Secretarie, nr. 1.19.5 9, annex 8), von Kniphausen to de Hochepied (a/b 't Fortuyn, 30/01/1753), not-foliated.

23 Anonymous, *Chronicle*, vol. 1, p. 690.

24 The description of the events from January 10 until 24, 1753 is based on, unless otherwise indicated, VOC 2824, Rapport der enorme behandelingen, f. 19-32; Ibid., Verklaring der pennisten en chirurgijn, f. 35-39; Ibid., Verklaring van Oostrum, first mate of 'tFortuyn, f. 40-42; Ibid., Verklaring Carmeliters, f. 45-46; Verklaring Mogenie, f. 42. Mogenie, a European merchant, declared that the action against von Kniphausen had been caused by greed. The merchants and leading citizens of Basra had been forced to denounce von Kniphausen. Only the mufti (the leading Moslem religious dignitary) publicly had dared to state that the governor's actions were contrary to religious and customary law. Mogenie further declared that he had heard that the governor had promised 1,000 *zelottes* to the *tofangchi-bashi* (commander of the guard), if he could introduce a Moslem woman into the houses of Europeans. It is interesting to note that von Kniphausen makes no mention at all in any of his letters of the accusation that he had relations with Moslem women, although one would have expected him to react to such an accusation in particular.

25 Anonymous, *Chronicle*, vol. 1, p. 690.

golden rain. A goddess raised in a public whore-house was led with great circumspection into the Baron's arms. The training of the pleasurable lady, her elegant clothes paid for by the Baron's liberality, added to her ignorance of the Turkish and Arabic language enabled the go-between to deceive him for some time. However, his arrogance caused his fall. He boasted of his fortune so publicly that the qadi's officer heard about it. The factory was surrounded and the couple was arrested. The Baron was put into prison, the lady was led in shame through the city and the go-between lost his nose and ears.[26]

Nothing about these alleged amorous events is found in Dutch sources. According to von Kniphausen, the only person who was allowed to visit him was the French consul and Agent of the French East India Company, M. Litout de la Berteché. The latter reports that, to his great astonishment, he had heard about von Kniphausen's arrest at 11 o'clock AM. At 12.30 he was sent for by the *motasallem*. In the latter's residence he met Ellis, the EIC Agent, whom he tried to persuade to jointly protest against the disregard for treaty obligations. Ellis, however, refused to cooperate, saying that everybody had to fend for himself. The *motasallem* told Litout that the French had nothing to fear and would remain unmolested; he only wanted to get rid of the Dutch. He further explained that he had imprisoned von Kniphausen because he had intercourse with Moslem women and had interfered in internal government affairs. For the first accusation the *motasallem* offered no proof other than his words. For the second accusation he showed Litout a letter in French, which von Kniphausen allegedly had written to the French bishop in Baghdad in which he complained about Hasan Aqa, the former *motasallem*. Litout took his leave and returned home. He then sent a request to the *motasallem* asking him whether he might visit von Kniphausen in prison. After having repeated the same request a few times, and each time it had been refused, Litout was finally allowed to see von Kniphausen. On that occasion the *motasallem* once again assured Litout that he did not want the Dutch to remain in Basra anymore, possibly to get the support of this European representative by dangling before him the likelihood of being able to get rid of an important competitor in exchange for his silence. Litout told von Kniphausen what the *motasallem* had told him. They then agreed that Litout would propose the *motasallem* to offer bail for von Kniphausen, who would leave Basra after three days. The *motasallem*, however, refused to receive Litout and threatened him with force if he continued to interfere in this matter.[27]

Jan van der Hulst, von Kniphausen's deputy was aboard *'tFortuyn* when his chief was arrested. On hearing this news he refused to come ashore. However, after repeated assurances by the *motasallem* he went ashore on January 11. The governor told him that von Kniphausen had been arrested for having relations with Moslem women and for interfering with government affairs, although he did not tell him that he wanted to get rid of the Dutch. The governor did not tell him either what the contents of the letter was that von Kniphausen allegedly had written nor did he show it to him. The *motasallem* told van der Hulst that he had nothing against him and suggested that to solve the conflict van der Hulst had better contact Ellis, the EIC Agent. The latter told van der Hulst that von Kniphausen had given the *motasallem* every good reason to act as he had done by having written the famous letter to the French bishop in Baghdad. He admitted that he did not

26 This is a summary of NA, Collectie Alting, nr. 68, Vijf brieven van een vrij koopman in Bengalen aan Warren Hastings, f. 53-54.

27 VOC 2824, Verklaring Litout de la Berteché (Basra, 22/01/1753), f. 40-42; for a French version see NA Collectie de Hochepied, nr. 108.20. See also Ives, *Voyage*, pp. 209-10 with von Kniphausen's version of the events, which do not disagree with what he wrote to Batavia.

know its contents, however, since he did not know French. Ellis further told him that he could continue trading in von Kniphausen's place, but that he would have to pay a substantial sum to the *motasallem*. The Carmelites state that both Ellis and van der Hulst went through the motions of trying to get von Kniphausen's release, but that both in fact rejoiced at his predicament.[28] This, however, is not borne out by Dutch sources although Ives reports that von Kniphausen told him in 1758 that he "was informed of some underhand dealings of Mynheer *********** his second, which made him resolve immediately to compromise matters with the Turkish government."[29]

Litout had written that same day to Ellis asking him to act jointly and lodge a formal protest. Ellis refused and replied that the governor had forbidden him to interfere in the matter. Van der Hulst went to see von Kniphausen in prison after his discussion with Ellis. Together they decided to propose Batavia to blockade the Shatt al-Arab like the English had done in 1727 to get their money back and have the Ottomans taste the power of the VOC. Van der Hulst therefore paid that night 75,000 *qorush* to Pogus, the EIC interpreter. For the Dutch this was another proof of English involvement in the entire affair. The *motasallem* stopped talking about capital punishment and von Kniphausen and his interpreter were set free the next day "to the feigned prayers and promises of the Europeans."[30] Von Kniphausen was then told he had to go to the EIC factory, which he refused, for he would only go to the Dutch factory or to th ship *'tFortuyn*. Because it was already late von Kniphausen was allowed to spend the night in the *motasallem*'s residence.

In the afternoon of the following day, January 12, 1753 Pogus the EIC interpreter came to see van der Hulst in the Dutch factory. He told van der Hulst that the *motasallem* had decided to send von Kniphausen directly to the ship *'t Fortuyn*. Van der Hulst was informed that he could stay as VOC Agent, if he paid an additional 50,000 *qorush*. Van der Hulst then went to see Ellis to ask him what the purpose of this new extortion was. Ellis agreed that this was something that could not be countenanced and he promised to talk to the *motasallem* about it immediately. However, after he had spoken with Pogus in another room he told van der Hulst, who was completely taken aback, that he had no other advice for him than to pay otherwise van der Hulst would run the risk of bad treatment and being subjected to all kinds of offenses. Van der Hulst then went to the *motasallem*'s residence to discuss this new development with von Kniphausen. According to the Carmelites, von Kniphausen himself had suggested this additional demand for money as a means of paying back his deputy, who had betrayed him and who had already started to concoct letters to be sent to Batavia in praise of himself, warning the High Government about von Kniphausen's manner of living."[31]

Van der Hulst paid the money, also for the VOC broker and money changer from whom the *motasallem* also had demanded money, after he had consulted with von Kniphausen. The latter two were immediately set free after payment of 30,000 *qorush* and for himself van der Hulst paid 25,000 *qorush*. Since von Kniphausen still refused to go to the EIC factory he was taken to *'tFortuyn*. On that same day of January 12 the *motasallem* sent for Ellis and van der Hulst. He appointed

28 Anonymous, *Chronicle*, vol. 1, p. 690. The Mr. Oust mentioned by the Carmelites is van der Hulst; see also NA, Collectie Alting, nr. 68, Vijf brieven (third letter), f. 54, according to which, Ellis intervened with the *motasallem* to prevent that von Kniphausen would be whipped. Although Dutch sources do not mention any underhand dealings by van der Hulst, this may indeed have been the case, because von Kniphausen apparently held that opinion later, although there is nothing found of that nature in the official correspondence by either von Kniphausen or van der Hulst. Ives, *Voyage*, p. 210.

29 Ives, *Voyage*, p. 210.

30 Anonymous, *Chronicle*, vol. 1, p. 690; Ives, *Voyage*, p. 211.

31 Anonymous, *Chronicle*, vol. 1, p. 690. This is not borne out by Dutch sources nor the other statements by the Carmelites that von Kniphausen and van der Hulst were at odds with one another. For another reason for this payment, viz. the recognition of van der Hulst as the chief of the Dutch factory at Basra see Ives, *Voyage*, p. 211.

the latter in von Kniphausen's place and gave him a robe of honor. Ellis even received a costlier robe, which normally was never given to Europeans, which was another fact that convinced the Dutch even more of English involvement in this intrigue, the more so since the *motasallem* called it a payment for services rendered. On January 14, a Moslem merchant came to see von Kniphausen aboard *'tFortuyn*. He showed von Kniphausen a copy of the formal accusation, which the *motasallem* had drawn up against him. This document was to be validated by the seals of all leading merchants of Basra. He therefore thought that it would be unwise for von Kniphausen to return to Batavia. He had better go somewhere else to which end he offered him a vessel that was ready to depart. Von Kniphausen thanked him for having shown him the accusation and said that he would take it in person to Batavia. The merchant then changed his tune and asked him whether it would not be better to present the *motasallem* with more money, for he would then allow von Kniphausen to return and destroy the accusation. Von Kniphausen who realized that the merchant had been sent by the *motasallem* told him that he had paid when he was a prisoner, but now that he was on board a VOC ship he would not even pay one penny. The same proposal was repeated by others, but von Kniphausen refused to go along with it. In the evening of January 14, 1753 the *motasallem* sent the complaint, which was written in Turkish, to the VOC factory with orders to van der Hulst to put the VOC seal under it, which he did out of fear for his safety.[32]

Von Kniphausen and van der Hulst sent a complaint to the Porte. Van der Hulst joined him aboard *'t Fortuyn* on January 20, 1753 which left the next day, because he feared that the *motasallem* would take action against him once he had heard that he had complained about him. According to the Carmelites, the entire VOC staff boarded the ship, but this is not borne out by Dutch sources.[33] Unfortunately the ship got stuck in the mud at Minawi just in from of the house of the *qaputan-*

32 The summarized contents of this complaint are as follows: Von Kniphausen's behavior had been unruly and improper; he had done all kinds of foolish things. Von Kniphausen had set one man against the other; he had behaved outrageously and had tried to overthrow the government of Basra. Moreover, von Kniphausen had taken persons into his service whose task it was to harm Moslems. When the signatories had asked von Kniphausen to mend his ways it had been to no avail. On the contrary his behavior became worse. Gradually all merchants had become hostile to him. The latter also had sought the company of Moslem women, thereby showing disrespect for Islam. On those occasions von Kniphausen had worn frivolous clothes. He had engaged in these activities for such a long time that they were common knowledge. People from all religions took offense at this and at long last the offended persons convened a meeting to draw up a request to the Pasha of Baghdad to execute von Kniphausen. The Pasha had replied that he had to be chased out of the country so that people would know peace again. Van der Hulst who is a man of great intelligence had to be put in von Kniphausen's place. The signatories expressed the hope that the governor-general would punish von Kniphausen and appoint van der Hulst in his place. VOC 2843, Dutch translation of a declaration in Arabic of 33 persons to the governor-general, undated, f. 46-48. Both the Pasha of Baghdad and the *motasallem* of Basra had added a short note to this complaint stating that they had always shown friendship to von Kniphausen, who had repaid this kindness with improper behavior. They asked the governor-general to punish von Kniphausen and appoint van der Hulst in his place, whom they would show their friendship, for he was a good man and appreciated by everybody. VOC 2843, translation of the letter by the Pasha of Baghdad to the governor-general, n.p., n.d., f. 49-50; Ibid, letter from the moesalim [sic] to the governor-general, n.p., n.d., f. 51-52. On April 28, 1753 Schoonderwoerd reported that van der Hulst had sent him three letters for the governor-general, VOC 2824, f. 42. Batavia returned the letters because nobody in Batavia could translate them. VOC 1007, f. 316. According to von Kniphausen, the *mufti* of Basra had refused to sign this document and also was upset by the irregular procedures followed, which were contrary to just law. The complaint was also sent to Batavia via Bandar 'Abbas. At the latter port von Kniphausen boarded the very ship in which the document was sent and thus came prepared "to reply to every article of complaint that was exhibited against him." Ives, *Voyage*, p. 210, 212.

33 Unless other sources are quoted the description of the events from January 20 until February 11, 1753 is based on VOC 2428, Vervolg van het voorgevallene naar het opstellen van het neevens leggende rapport by von

bashi. At 8 o'clock in the morning of January 22 Litout also came aboard *'tFortuyn*. He wanted to go to Bandar-e Rig, because he feared extortion by the *motasallem*, who had been incited by the English to do so. Litout had left all his possessions behind, at least that is what von Kniphausen reported, so it looked like he really wanted to flee. The *motasallem* who had been informed about the flight ordered van der Hulst and Litout to come ashore. Von Kniphausen informed the *motasallem* that the ship's cable had broken and Messrs. Litout and van der Hulst happened to be aboard to settle some affairs and thus they had no intention to flee. The *motasallem* did not believe this story and had some cannon readied at the *qaputan-bashi*'s house and aimed at the ship which was in range. He further had seven gallivats readied and told von Kniphausen that if Litout and van der Hulst did not come ashore he would attack the ship. Because *'t Fortuyn* was unable to get adrift the two gentlemen went ashore. The *motasallem* told them that he had been afraid that they had been detained by von Kniphausen and ordered them not to go aboard the ship again. Any business that still had to be settled had to be done by one of his clerks, while *'tFortuyn* had to leave within two days to which van der Hulst agreed. The latter then sent word to von Kniphausen to inform him about this discussion as well as that he would send assistant Croes or surgeon Filch to carry out the necessary steps that had to be taken.[34]

On January 22 and 23 the tide was too low to get the ship afloat again. During that time the *qaputan-bashi* came aboard and offered von Kniphausen his intercession to come to an understanding with the *motasallem*. He also asked how much von Kniphausen had paid for his release. Von Kniphausen told him that he could not tell him, because the *motasallem* had ordered him to keep this information secret to avoid that he would take action against the Dutch staff. Because the *motasallem* had heard about this conversation and feared that von Kniphausen had divulged the payment information he ordered von Kniphausen on January 24 get the ship afloat and leave or else depart per tranki. After van der Hulst had protested he allowed von Kniphausen to depart in his own boat with a European crew. Von Kniphausen was not allowed to stop en route and had to sail directly to Bushire where he had to await the arrival of *'tFortuyn*. He offered, if the Dutch were willing, to send as many vessels and men as necessary to Moccan[35] to get the ship afloat, which indicates how much he wanted to get rid of von Kniphausen.[36] Meanwhile, the latter had agreed with van der Hulst to flee together to Batavia and to leave the factory in charge of assistant Benjamin Croes. They were certain that the *motasallem* would take retaliatory action against them once he would have found out that they had lodged a formal complaint about him to the Porte. It was agreed that von Kniphausen would go to Khark and wait there for van der Hulst. From Khark they would send their complaint to Istanbul. In the evening of January 24, van der Hulst sent a letter to von Kniphausen assuring him that he would abide by the plan and to wait for him up to 30 days after receipt of the letter.[37]

Kniphausen and Jan van Oostrum (a/b 't Fortuyn near Gareek (Khark), 14/02/1753), f. 29-32; Anonymous, *Chronicle*, vol. 1, p. 691.

34 VOC 2824, van der Hulst to von Kniphausen a/b Fortuyn (n.d., [22/01/1753]), f. 33. Von Kniphausen later told Ives, *Voyage*, pp. 211-12 that the *motasallem* had invited him to come back again, with assurances of protection.

35 Moccan probably is Maqam, or in full Maqam 'Ali, a quarter of Basra, opposite Minawi (see figure 4.1??).

36 VOC 2824, van der Hulst to von Kniphausen a/b Fortuyn (n.d., [24/01/1753]), f. 33-35.

37 VOC 2824, van der Hulst to von Kniphausen a/b Fortuyn (n.d., [24/01/1753]), f. 34-35.

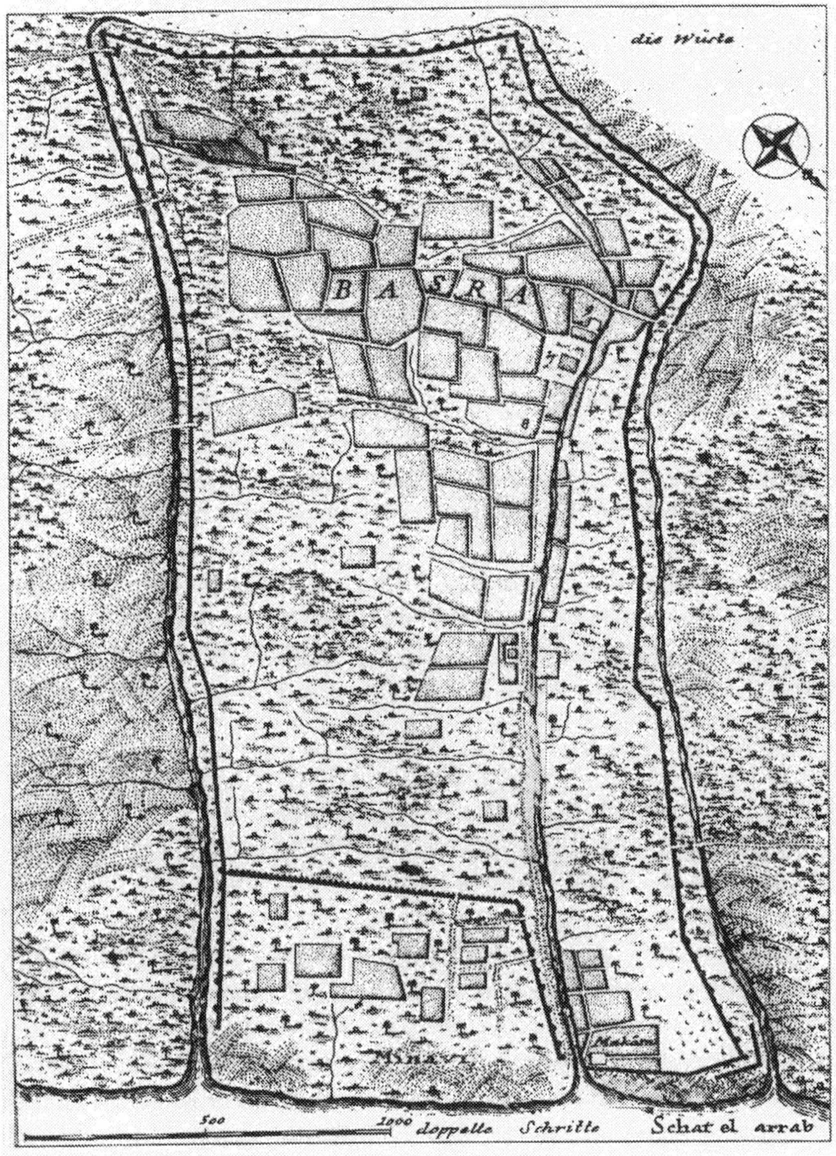

Fig. 4.1 Plan of Basra by Niebuhr

Von Kniphausen left that same night in a small boat and at the mouth of the Shatt al-Arab waited for *'t Fortuyn* to pick him up. This happened on January 30, because the ship got stuck once again a few times in the mud. By that time von Kniphausen received another letter from van der Hulst in which he asked him to send the boat back as soon as possible, because it was his only means of escape.[38] The ship sailed to Khark where it arrived on February 11, 1753. From here von Kniphausen sent his interpreter, Philip Catafago, to Istanbul to lodge a complaint. In the accompanying letter to the Dutch ambassador, Elbert de Hochepied, von Kniphausen and van der Hulst gave a summary of the events that had led to their departure and wrote that they were considering blockading the Shatt al-Arab on their return from Batavia, just as the English had done in 1727.

38 VOC 2824, van der Hulst to von Kniphausen a/b Fortuyn (n.d., [26/01/1753]), f. 35.

They also asked the ambassador not to write to the Netherlands about this incident, because bad news about the Company in Asia would have negative effects on the Company in Europe.[39]

PROPOSAL FOR THE KHARK PROJECT

During his stay at Khark von Kniphausen held discussions with Mir Naser Vagha'i, the chief of Bandar-e Rig and Khark Island. This led to the latter's request to the VOC to build a factory in his territory.[40] Mir Naser was of the Vagha'i lineage of the Zo'abi tribe that originated from Oman, which had held the function of *kalantar* (chief) and *zabet* (tax administrator) of Bandar-e Rig since about the mid-seventeenth century.[41] Around 1640 Philippe de Trinité described it as a rather large village, with many palm trees and very few houses built from stone, because most were made from mud and palm wood and branches. Raphael du Mans some 20 years later observed that only some small vessels from Basra called on Bandar-e Rig, which came from Arabia to Persia.[42] Bandar-e Rig was indeed a small port in the 17th century, which acquired some role in international trade after the mid-1650s, when merchantmen from India started to call on it attracted by the lower customs rates and better treatment than at Bandar 'Abbas. However, in 1666 the central government appointed a *shahbandar* at Bandar-e Rig, who, as of 1668, was subordinate to the farmer of the customs of all Persian ports, who was based in Bandar 'Abbas. This new arrangement made Bandar-e Rig a less attractive port, because the customs regime had become uniform along the Persian coast. Nevertheless, some private traders continued to call on Bandar-e Rig, where some Banyans had up taken permanent residence to facilitate trade with foreign ships.[43]

Bandar-e Rig was not the most attractive port on the Persian coast, because ships had to come at anchor quite far (some three leagues) from shore due to two sandy banks, which could only be crossed at high tide and which fronted a small creek, which, at high tide, provided an inner roadstead for vessels drawing less than one fathom of water. In 1672, Carré met some Banyans there, who were "brokers to the Franks" as well as the Persian *shahbandar* and the port's Arab sheikh, whose name he unfortunately does not report.[44] According to the Dutch, writing in 1756:

> About 100 years ago there was a very large number of vessels and sea-faring people in Bender Riek. At about that time the inhabitants of Kareek [Khark] who ever since the departure of the Portuguese have always been independent put them-

39 VOC 2824, von Kniphausen and van der Hulst to de Hochepied (Basra, 24/01/1753), f. 47-49; NA, Collectie de Hochepied, nr. 108, von Kniphausen to de Hochepied (30/01/1753); Ives, *Voyage*, p. 212. According to G.J. Lorimer, *Gazetteer of the Persian Gulf* 2 vols. (Calcutta, 1915), p. 1196, the English only retired to their ship the *Britannia* in 1727, but did not really blockade the Shatt al-Arab.

40 Ives, *Voyage*, p. 212. On Mir Naser Vaqa'i see J. Perry, "Mir Muhanna and the Dutch. Patterns of Piracy in the Persian Gulf," *Studia Iranica* 2 (1973), p. 84 and Floor, "A Description," pp. 170, 173.

41 Abu'l-Hasan Ghaffari Kashani, *Golshan-e Morad* ed. 'Allameh Tabataba'i-Majd (Tehran, 1369/1990), pp. 274-75; Mirza Mohammad Sadeq Musavi Nami, *Tarikh-e Giti-gosha* ed. Sa'id Nafisi (Tehran, 1363/1984), pp. 161-68; Abu'l-Hasan b. Mohammad Amin Golestaneh, *Mojmal al-Tavarikh* ed. Modarres Razavi (Tehran, 2536/1977), p. 458; Perry, "Mir Mohanna," p. 79; Floor, "Description," p. 173 or chapter one.

42 Philippe de S. Trinité, *Voyage d'Orient du R.P. Philippe de la tres-saincte Trinité* (Lyon, 1669), p. 43; Raphael du Mans, *Estat de la Perse en 1660* ed. Charles Schefer (Paris, 1890), p. 9.

43 Floor, *The Persian Gulf*, pp. 242-43, 291-92.

44 Abbé Carré, *The travels of Abbé Carré in India and the Near East (1672-74)*, 3 vols. (London: Hakluyt, 1947), vol. 3, pp. 835-36, 838.

> selves under the protection of Mier Hamad, who ruled there and they promised him an annual sum of 240 rupees on the condition that he would accept them and would protect them against the marauding of the sea-faring Arabs. The first part of such an agreement the chiefs of Bender Riek have complied with only too well, but the other [part] very badly. The poor inhabitants have since then till our arrival here [in 1753] always been exposed to the outrages of the daily passing trankis.[45]

This lack of protection that had been promised was probably due to the fact that the chiefs of Bandar-e Rig were unable to do so. As a result of the intra-Arab rivalry Bandar-e Rig had been destroyed in 1678, probably by the Hula Arabs, who were reported to be their mortal enemies, due to a falling out over access to the pearl grounds at Bahrain. Bandar-e Rig had usually cooperated with Bushire in opposing the challenge by the Hula Arabs about who controlled the pearl banks. In 1684, the Dutch reported that Bandar-e Rig had been almost totally ravaged and plundered by marauding Arabs so that for a long time nobody dared to live there nor ships to call on it. Instead of going via Bandar-e Rig, as had been usual, vessels now went via Rishar (Bushire) to Basra.[46] The attackers probably were the Arabs of 'Asalu and Kangan and other places inhabited by Hula Arabs, for Carré reported that they and the people Bandar-e Rig were mortal enemies.[47]

It took some time before the port regained its former status but in the eighteenth century it functioned again as one of the other typical small Persian Gulf ports, being engaged in (pearl) fishing, some trade – mainly exporting wheat- and, via its satellite (the island of Khark) providing pilots for vessels going to Basra.[48] In 1705, the Dutch even sent a ship to Bandar-e Rig to test the market, which was not considered to be large enough and thus no Dutch ships called on Rig anymore thereafter.[49] By 1720 it had a "pretty good inland Trade, by reason of its Vicinity to Shyrash."[50] When Nader Shah died in 1747 it had become a reasonably thriving community, although less so than Bushire, due to Mir Naser's "friendliness and generosity with regard to all merchants and foreigners."[51] Around 1750 Bandar-e Rig once again allied itself with Bushire in Sheikh Naser's bid to seize Bahrain. Although the first expedition failed in 1751, the second one in 1752 was successful. Mir Naser felt that he had it almost made, but he wanted more. He therefore invited the EIC to come and establish a factory in his lands, where he aimed to promote English shipping. According to Brabazon Ellis, the EIC resident at Basra, most ships called on Bandar-e Rig at that time, because "Karavans every months of the year go to and from thence [Bandar-e Rig] to Schiraz and Cozaroon."[52] In 1753 Mir Naser tricked his partner Sheikh Naser to leave him in charge of the Bahrain and then refused to give him his share of the revenues or even to recompense him for his cost in mounting the expedition. Unfortunately for Mir Naser his neighbor Qa'ed Heydar of Ganaveh observing that most of Bandar-e Rig's forces were at Bahrain attacked the town hoping to sack and plunder it to fill his empty coffers. Mir Naser had to hurry back to relieve his town in which he was

---

45 Willem Floor, "A Description," p. 173 or chapter one.

46 VOC 1406, van de Heuvel to Batavia (28/02/1684), f. 1161 vs; Carré, *The Travels*, vol. 3, pp. 836-37.

47 Carré, *The Travels*, vol. 3, pp. 828-29.

48 Providing pilots had been the function of Khark for centuries, see Floor, *The Persian Gulf*, pp. 242-43.

49 Coolhaas, *Generale Missieven*, vol. 6, p. 378 (30/11/1705).

50 Alexander Hamilton, *A New Account of the East Indies*. 2 vols. in one. (London, 1930 [Amsterdam 1970]), vol. 1, p. 59; Floor, *The Persian Gulf*, pp. 242-43.

51 Floor, "Description," p. 173 or chapter one.

52 Ricks. *Politics and Trade*, p. 346, note 117.

successful, but he lost Bahrain and thus was off the worse for it. He was therefore very pleased that the Dutch were willing to settle in his lands, for the English had not bothered to reply.[53]

Von Kniphausen then continued his journey to Batavia via Bandar 'Abbas, where he arrived on February 22, 1753. From there Schoonderwoerd, the VOC chief of Bandar 'Abbas, sent orders to van der Hulst that he had been appointed VOC resident in Bushire. This news was a godsend for van der Hulst, because 'Ali Aqa, the *motasallem*, did not allow him to leave and had him closely watched. Van der Hulst had sent news about this to Khark, but by the time his letter arrived von Kniphausen had already left. Now 'Ali Aqa had to give in to his departure, although initially he had been unwilling to. Van der Hulst accompanied by assistant Jan Jacob Catusse arrived in Bushire on March 19, 1753. He had left assistant Croes and others behind to look after the VOC factory, sell the remaining merchandise and collect outstanding debts.[54] The VOC ship *de Anna* meanwhile had arrived at Bushire on March 17, 1753, but did not continue to Basra, about which the *motasallem* was very angry when he learnt that it had returned to Bandar 'Abbas. Frustrated he claimed payment of customs duties, but Schoonderwoerd did not believe that he really meant to collect them. If only the staff at Basra would not loose their head each time the *motasallem* claimed something unreasonable. The latter, for example, forced the staff to present him with the keys of the Dutch factory.[55]

After van der Hulst's departure the *motasallem*'s thirst for money had not slaked, for shortly thereafter one of the VOC assistants "was caught at night in a garden near the town with a Turkish woman and taken before the governor; and, as in those critical days Europeans were being held in the greatest contempt, he only got out with difficulty for the sum of 50,000 *isolatas* and then went off to Bushire: the rest of the staff of the Dutch Company after the lapse of some months secretly and unexpectedly escaped from Basra."[56] In fact, the only one who remained behind was the interpreter Ebrahim Sa'id (Sahid), who only functioned as a kind of post-office.[57]

When von Kniphausen arrived in Batavia in June 1753 he had his case prepared at Khark. During his stay there von Kniphausen had prepared a lengthy report on the present state of government and trade of Basra and Bushire. He also had written a report on the trade prospects in the Persian Gulf; both reports served to convince the High Government of the soundness of his proposal, viz. the establishment of a factory on Khark.[58] In the first report von Kniphausen pointed

---

53 Floor, "Description," p. 173.

54 VOC 2824, Cornelis Bijleveld and Jan van der Hulst (Bushire) to Batavia (25/03/1753), f. 71-73; VOC 2824, van der Hulst (Bushire) to Batavia (25/03/1753), f. 74-77. On the difficulties caused by the *motasallem* after von Kniphausen's departure see Anonymous, *Chronicle*, vol. 1, p. 691. The Mr. Chus mentioned by the Carmelites is Benjamin Croes, first assistant at Basra. VOC 2824, Bushire to Batavia (25/03/1753), f. 70-71.

55 VOC 2824, Gamron to Batavia (30/04/1753), f. 44-45.

56 Anonymous, *Chronicle*, vol. 1, p. 692; VOC 2843, Gamron to Batavia (01/10/1753), f. 40 (the amount was 4,000 *zelottes*, *isolatas*, or *zolotta*, a word derived from the Polish coin *zloty*, which circulated widely in the Ottoman Empire having been introduced via the Crimea).

57 NA, Collectie de Hochepied nr. 108, Coets to de Hochepied (Bushire, 11/09/1753). Coets reported that he fled Basra in the company of the VOC surgeon in mid-July; Ibid., nr. 108, Sahid (VOC interpreter) to de Hochepied (Basra, 07/09/1753). Sa'id wrote that Coets fled 50 days ago and that there were no Dutchmen in Basra anymore. He was the only one in charge of the factory and would pass on letters in secret. Later he was accused of not having looked well after the factory and especially the archives. VOC 3064, van der Hulst (Khark) to Batavia (30/09/1761), f. 16. Members of the Sa'id (Sahed) family had acted as interpreters for the VOC in Persia since about 1650. Often more members of the Sa'id family had been employed in this capacity in the factories of Isfahan and Bandar 'Abbas

58 VOC 2824, Vertoog van den tegenwoordigen staat der regeering en negotie te Bassora en Boucheer (a/b 'tFortuyn, 15/02/1753), f. 50-68. The report is dated 15/02/1753 when von Kniphausen was still at Khark. The

out that the central Ottoman government was unable to take action against governors of the outlying provinces, such as Baghdad. This implied that VOC operations were subject to the wiles of these local governors. Von Kniphausen 'proved' his case by analyzing the career of Soleyman Pasha of Baghdad and what this had meant for the province of Baghdad and the merchants living there. Because Soleyman Pasha had paid so much to the Porte to get his way he also needed a lot of money to keep what he had by continuing to pay the Porte substantial sums of money. Moreover, he had to run an expensive establishment all of which had led to increasing extortion and oppression of the population and the merchants in particular. Now Soleyman Pasha had not hesitated to lay his hands on Europeans (i.e. von Kniphausen), who were protected by Treaty.

Von Kniphausen further pointed out that he had been subjected to all kinds of demands for loans, grants of credit and petty extortion from the very beginning of his arrival in Basra. He further had withheld payment of customs duties to reduce the Ottoman government's debt to the VOC, which had not made him very popular with the government. The more so, since the English accommodated the Ottoman officials in this respect because they had the means to do so. Four to five English ships called on Basra each year, paying a substantial amount in customs duties, while the English also were able to make money from the customs arrangements. For the Armenian merchants who shipped their goods with English ships and who normally paid 7% customs duties imported their goods under the name of the EIC and then only paid 3%, a practice known as the 'coloring' of merchandise.

Nevertheless, many Armenian merchants had already left Basra and had gone to Bandar-e Rig out of fear of the increasing extortion by the Ottoman authorities. The Europeans so far had believed that they were protected by their Treaties, but due to English envy and the Pasha's lack of intelligence this had proved to be untrue, or so argued von Kniphausen. The Pasha had allowed himself to be persuaded by the English that if he extorted money from the Dutch, the VOC would not take retaliatory action. The worst he might expect would be the closing of their Basra factory, which he would not mind very much, because the extorted sum of money exceeded 10-year customs revenues on Dutch imports. Therefore, the *motasallem* had to be forced to repay the extorted money, also to prevent that the local governors in Bandar 'Abbas and Bushire, where the situation was not much different from that in Basra, would be encouraged to follow the Basra example. Schoonderwoerd, the VOC director at Bandar 'Abbas, concurred with his analysis.

Military action would be necessary once de Hochepied had obtained a *farman*, which would order Soleyman Pasha to repay the extorted money, for the latter would first claim that he did not know anything about the matter, because his *motasallem* was to be blamed for this terrible deed. He would then promise to punish him and force him to repay the money. However, such action would never get beyond the verbal stage and therefore it was necessary to force the Pasha by other means. Von Kniphausen, therefore, proposed that the VOC sent two ships drawing 10-12 fathoms of water to blockade the Shatt al-Arab in August-September. During that period Basran trade was at its busiest with ships laden with coffee, slaves, and other goods heading for Basra, while exporting the country's only produce, dates. The government's revenues very much depended on this trade and stopping it would give the VOC leverage to get its money back. Soleyman Pasha would not protest much, because the ones who would have to pay were the merchants and notables of Basra. In this way, the VOC would not only get its extorted money back, but also all outstanding debts. Von Kniphausen further felt that it would not be a good idea to continue to trade at Basra or at Bushire as before, because

---

following is a brief discussion of the contents of the report unless otherwise indicated. The contents of the second report is analyzed in Floor, "Khark: A Commercial Mishap", see chapter five.

(i) The governments of Basra and Bushire had committed all kinds of extortion and violence against merchants;
(ii) The market of Basra alone was too small for the volume of Dutch imports; and
(iii) The port of Basra was inadequate for receiving and handling ships.

Concerning point (i), von Kniphausen pointed out that apart from the above, as far as Basra was concerned, native merchants received an even worse treatment than he had. He emphasized that the wealth of the VOC depended on the capability of native merchants to buy and transport VOC merchandise. As far as the information in Bushire was concerned, von Kniphausen pointed out that the native merchants there were as badly off as those at Basra. For in Bushire there was no merchant who was allowed to buy merchandise with a value of more than 100 rupees without the permission of Sheikh Naser. As soon as goods were imported into Bushire the Sheikh did not allow merchants to buy these or even to let them come to the Dutch factory before he himself or his agent had inspected the merchandise. He then would offer a price for the goods above which nobody else dared to bid. The merchants therefore were forced to make a deal with Sheikh Naser. The latter would allow Moslem and Armenian merchants to buy between one-third and one-fourth of the goods at the price that he had bought them, while for the remainder they had to pay prices that were 20-30% higher. Finally, Sheikh Naser never paid for the goods that he had 'bought' before he had received payment himself for the same goods that he had resold. Thus, the Sheikh in effect invested not even one penny, but only acted as an undesirable intermediary, appropriating part of the profit himself. This practice was not exceptional in the Gulf and was not restricted to Bushire only.

As to item (ii), the consumption of VOC goods at Basra and Bushire was insignificant. From Basra about 50% of the goods were exported to Persia, 25% to Turkey and 25% to the Arabian Peninsula. Transit trade from Basra inland was difficult, because Soleyman Pasha forced merchants to use the Euphrates route via Baghdad. This journey lasted at least three months, during which time he had ample time to levy many and heavy imposts. The alternative route via Kuwait and Aleppo through the desert was not only shorter, viz. 25 days, but it was also cheaper, because no duties were levied.[59] It was because of this reason that Soleyman Pasha saw to it that this route was not used.

Persian merchants coming to Basra from Bandar-e Rig came with cash and those from Shushtar and Dezful with old copper. At Basra they paid 7% duties on the capital that they imported and on leaving Basra they had to pay another 7% on exports. In this way Persian merchants lost 14% of their capital, apart from being exposed to extortion and bad treatment by Ottoman officials. The same held true for Arab merchants, all of whom would gladly forgo a journey to Basra, if they were able to get merchandise elsewhere and not too far away.

With regards to item (iii), ships drawing 14-15 feet of water could only navigate the Shatt al-Arab with great difficulty. When they reached the port of Basra their cargos had to be unloaded into smaller vessels, which often also got stuck in the mud and thus sometimes up to 15 days were wasted. In short, just by entering and leaving the river one might lose one entire month. Having arrived at Basra's roadstead one again lost at least one month with unloading, because there were only

59 Later von Kniphausen would use this route for regular trade in collaboration with the al-Sabah sheikh of the 'Otobis of Green (Kuwait). As Slot has pointed out this route was already in use prior to von Kniphausen's arrival in Basra. In fact, Frans Canter the VOC director of Basra, who had deserted in 1749, took this route to make his escape and made it clear that it was a route that was in regular use. Slot, *'Arab al-Khalij*, pp. 343-44.

five lighters in Basra. There were, of course, more vessels at Basra, but the unloading of the ships was the prerogative of the *shahbandar* and therefore it was impossible to hire other vessels. Moreover, the *shahbandar*'s vessels could each only hold 15 canisters of sugar at most. Because the VOC ships often arrived during the rainy season the situation was even worse. For then unloading was stopped altogether, as the canals were then packed with other vessels. In this way the merchandise was soaked before it got ashore. Another problem was the obtaining of ballast. You could not get sand or stones in Basra, for only clay was available, which could only be loaded during dry days and then only with the five lighters of the *shahbandar*. The cargo of *'tFortuyn* had required 78 cargos of these five vessels, even though the ship had been only half laden and not really well ballasted, and in this way one month had been lost. Finally, although the VOC only paid 3% customs duties in Basra, in reality this amounted to 5%, because each ship had to give presents to the various officials.

Basing himself on the above arguments von Kniphausen concluded that neither Basra nor Bushire was a good transit port for the VOC. The Company's interests required that one could trade in freedom, with good security without being exposed to the whims of local government. Von Kniphausen therefore drew the High Government's attention to Mir Naser's invitation to build a factory on his lands wherever it wanted, which would be to the advantage of both parties.[60]

Von Kniphausen proposed that this factory be built on Khark, which was a small barren island where only a few fishermen lived. It was, however, excellently situated *vis à vis* the Shatt al-Arab, Bushire and Bandar-e Rig. There was a good anchorage for ships between Khark and its smaller companion, Kharqu, while its climate was good. The island had fresh water, plenty of firewood and its soil was fertile, so that even the fishermen were able to reap an abundant harvest. Von Kniphausen did not forget to point out that the Portuguese had made big profits on the island in the past, partly due to pearl fishing around the island.[61] He assured the High Government that there was no doubt that Khark was the best place to establish a factory in Persian Gulf, whence Persian, Arab and Ottoman merchants might be supplied. If the VOC could settle Europeans on the island it might even become the most important establishment and staple for the entire Persian Gulf within a short period. To take away any doubts that he might just have had a brainstorm as a result of his troubles in Basra and had not given the matter serious reflection von Kniphausen stressed the fact that already in 1751 Armenian merchants had urged him to propose this plan to Batavia. However, he had not responded to this suggestion, because the Armenian merchants had been thinking only of their own private interests.[62] Moreover, Schoonderwoerd, with whom von Kniphausen had discussed the project, was very much in favor of it, since he had toyed with the same idea when he

---

60 VOC 2824, Mier Nassier to Mossel, undated, f. 68-71. This is a Dutch translation of a letter written in Armenian. The same letter also had been written in Arabic and Persian, only the Dutch translation has survived.

61 The first Dutch contacts with Khark and Kharqu date from July 14, 1645 when the first Dutch voyage was made to Basra. A pilot from Khark was taken on board to continue to Basra. A. Hotz ed. "Cornelisz. Roobacker's scheepsjournaal, Gamron-Basra (1645)," *Tijdschrift v.h. Koninklijk Aardrijkskundig Genootschap* 20 (1879), p. 362. During their first visit the Dutch noted that some 150 small vessels were lying between Khark and Kharqu and were fishing for pearls. About von Kniphausen's pearling activities see Willem Floor, "A report on pearl-fishing in the Persian Gulf in 1757," *Persica* 10 (1981-82), pp. 209-22; see also Saldanha, *Précis*, vol. 1, p. 99. The reference to the Portuguese was a red herring to make the Khark project more attractive, for the Portuguese had never been involved with the island, see Willem Floor, *The Persian Gulf. A political economy of five port cities 1500-1730* (Washington DC, 2006). In 1720 or thereabouts Kharqu was uninhabited, but for some deer and antelopes, while Khark had some 200-300 fishermen as inhabitants, who also served as pilots for Basra voyagers. "It affords good Mutton and Fish, and Potatoes and Onions, with good Water. The Anchoring-place is at the North End of the inhabited Island, in 12 Fathoms Water." Hamilton, *A New Account*, vol. 1, p. 59.

62 VOC 2824, Vertoog, f. 66.

was resident of the factory in Bushire.[63] In fact, he apparently had considered this option when he was director in Bandar 'Abbas, because the English reported that "at the beginning of 1751 it was ascertained by the British Agent that they [the Dutch] had thought of seizing Kharg and removing their Bandar 'Abbas Factory to that island."[64] Von Kniphausen therefore came to the point and proposed that the VOC close down its factory in Bushire, where no profits had been during the last three years. The Bushire staff could be placed in Basra, once the situation had become normal again. The Basra staff could be reallocated at Khark, where the VOC could build a small defensible fort. Although on Kniphausen did not bother the High Government with a detailed account of the advantages of this project he pointed out that the effective customs rate of 5% at Basra amounted to Dfl. 25-30,000 per year. The construction of the fort did not have to cost much, so he asserted. Because rocks and lime were to be had in plenty on Khark itself. The only thing needed from outside would be timber and iron and the wages for the masons, which would not amount to much in that area. The operational cost of the factory would be equal to that of Basra in addition to the cost of 12-16 soldiers. These, added to the European and native servants would amount to a staff of about 60 men, which von Kniphausen considered to be sufficient to defend the fort.[65]

From this proposal it is quite clear that the idea of beginning a new factory on Khark had not come suddenly to von Kniphausen. Not only had Armenian merchants already suggested it in 1751, but he also had discussed it with his colleague Schoonderwoerd, who had entertained the same idea. Also, he wrote the proposal while on Khark on February 15, arriving on February 22 at Bandar 'Abbas, thus within a rather short period, which suggests prior deliberation. Moreover, von Kniphausen instead of going to Bushire where he was expected to have gone he went straight to Khark. Finally, Mir Naser had already invited both the Dutch and English to settle in his lands prior to 1752, since Ellis mentions such a proposal in a letter dated May 28, 1752.[66]

APPROVAL OF THE KHARK PROJECT

Although not unanimously, the High Government agreed to von Kniphausen's proposal on June 29, 1753. It ordered him to build a small fortress on the island of Khark, which the chief of Khark had offered to the VOC "without any condition, not only with regard to its possession, but also to its ownership."[67] In the absence of Mir Naser's original letter it is difficult to determine whether he relinquished his rights to Khark. In the Dutch translation no mention of this is made at all, for he only invited the Dutch to use Bandar-e Rig as a port, as if it was theirs or to build a factory anywhere else in his lands. No mention at is made of Khark or a cession of ownership of Khark.[68] The Governor-General's, Jacob Mossel, letter to Mir Naser does not mention the cession of ownership either. He only refers to Mir Naser's request to come and trade and build a factory in his lands. Nor

63 VOC 2824, Vertoog, f. 66-67. This is confirmed by VOC 2824, Schoonderwoerd/von Kniphausen to Batavia (Gamron, 26/05/1753), f. 30.

64 Lorimer, *Gazetteer*, p. 128. Saldanha, *Précis*, vol. 1, p. 72 (Bombay, 23/02/1751) reports "The Dutch ... have thoughts of seizing upon the Island of Carrack near Bouchier."

65 The construction cost and those of the staff were very high as discussed in what follows. The EIC Agent Wood, who visited Khark in 1754 commented: "The scale on which the factory had been established seemed to show a total disregard of expense." Saldanha, *Précis*, vol. 1, p. 100; Lorimer, *Gazetteer*, p. 130.

66 Amin, *British Interests*, p. 35, note 2.

67 VOC 1007, Instruction to von Kniphausen and van der Hulst (Batavia, 21/07/1753), f. 327.

68 VOC 2824, Mier Nassier to Mossel, undated, f. 68-71.

is any mention made of a payment for the possession and use of Khark or of a present with the same purpose.[69]

It is possible that Mir Naser made a verbal agreement with von Kniphausen, but this has not been reported in the available documents. Nevertheless, the fact remains that the High Government was convinced that Mir Naser had offered the ownership of Khark to the VOC. The Carmelites also report that Mir Naser had granted "cession of the island or Kharg without payment ... and that the Dutch Company would grant him asylum there, and he might flee there when troubled by internecine strife in Persia."[70] It is of course possible that Mir Naser in exchange for the right to continue to use Khark as an asylum ceded the island to attract Dutch trade to Bandar-e Rig to turn that place into the most important emporium in the Persian Gulf. Whatever may be the truth of the matter, some people in the region (in particular Sheykh Naser of Bushire) expressed their surprise that Mir Naser allowed infidels to settle on Khark, which also boasted the reputed tomb of Imam Mohammad b. al-Hanafiyeh. The English expressed their surprise for the same reason, although in the following years this issue proved to be of no importance at all.[71]

Von Kniphausen was ordered to keep Schoonderwoerd at Bandar 'Abbas informed of his activities. The first thing he had to do was to construct a new factory and unload the merchandise in a safe place. The High Government, i.e. those in favor of the plan, had high hopes of the Khark factory, for they believed that all rich and leading Greek, Georgian, Armenian and Moslem merchants would be obliged to flee to Khark, because of the tyranny in the countries of the littoral.[72] For on Khark, under Dutch protection, they might carry on their trade in complete freedom. These were some of the prospects that von Kniphausen had referred to in his proposal and which were supposed to be borne out by the petition of five Armenian merchants living in Bandar-e Rig asking Batavia to

---

69 VOC 1007, Mossel to regent Bender Riek (Batavia, 21/07/1753), f. 313-14. Niebuhr's first German edition (Niebuhr, *Beschreibung*, p. 322) as well as its English translation entitled *Travels through Arabia, and other countries in the East* 2 vols. (Edinburgh, 1792), vol. 2, p. 155 mention that Mir Naser allowed the Dutch to settle and build their fort on Khark in exchange for the payment of an annual rent. However, this is not mentioned at all in the later German version. Carsten Niebuhr, *Reisebeschreibung nach Arabien und andern umliegenden Ländern* 3 vols. in one with continuous pagination (Zürich, 1992), p. 570. Sheikh 'Abdollah made a similar offer with regards to Hormuz in 1764 stating that the island was a Dutch possession (see chapter three), when it clearly was not, and Mir Naser may have used a similar hyperbole.

70 Anonymous, *Chronicle*, vol. 1, p. 691. As late as 1758, von Kniphausen told Ives, *Voyage*, p. 212, that Mir Naser had offered to "surrender up to them his right of sovereignty." According to an anonymous source, Mir Mohanna had ceded the sovereignty of Khark to the Dutch in exchange for their support. "Le nouveau Cheh de Bendrik non seulement a confirmé la convention passé entre feu son père avec la Comp. de Hollande mais il a encore cédé à Msr. Le baron de Kniphaus. l'entierre domination des Isles de Karek ou son père setoit pourtent reserve une certaine souvereneté sur les Arabes. NA, Stadhouderlijke Secretarie, nr. 1.19.5 (annex 13), Extrait d'une letter de Bassora du 20 Aout 1854 (non-foliated). Ives, *Voyage*, p. 203 mentions "Karec, an island belonging to the Dutch." Although other contemporary sources also mention that Mir Mohanna had good relations with von Kniphausen they do not mention that he relinquished his right to Khark. NA, Collectie Alting, nr. 68, Vijf brieven (third letter), f. 55. This source also states that Mir Mohanna's father had come to power in 1747 and was named 'Abdollah, which is clearly wrong; maybe his grandfather is meant here.

71 Perry, "Mir Muhanna," pp. 84-85. According to Ives, von Kniphausen's "opinion, and which was confirmed by the most sensible of the *Arabs* and *Persians*, is, that this monument was only erected in remembrance and honour of that sage, and that neither his, nor the bones of any other person were deposited under it." Ives, *Voyage*, p. 208.

72 VOC 1007, Instruction (21/07/1753), f. 327-32.

be allowed to trade under its protection.[73] Because the VOC had three factories in the Persian Gulf, the High Government decided to close down the ones in Basra, Bushire and Bandar 'Abbas, but the latter only once Khark had acquired a solid commercial base.[74] For the moment Khark would formally be under the jurisdiction of the Bandar 'Abbas factory, although it would operate independently from it.[75]

With regard to the conflict with the Basra government von Kniphausen was ordered to take offensive action against Basra as soon as possible after his arrival. But before doing so he had to ascertain whether Soleyman Pasha was still in power. If he was not, von Kniphausen was ordered to settle the dispute by peaceful means based on the treaty that existed between the Netherlands and Turkey.[76] To carry out the Khark project and the blockade of Basra four ships were sent from Batavia with merchandise and building materials, to wit: *'tFortuyn, Getrouwigheid, Kerkdijk*, and the barque *Jacatra*. The first and the last vessel had to carry out the blockade.[77]

The Khark project was less enthusiastically welcomed by the XVII, the VOC directors. They pointed out that there was nothing new in this situation; money had been extorted from VOC staff before, both in Persia and the Ottoman Empire. In fact, when comparing profits with losses most, if not all profits had been consumed in this way. Therefore, was it advisable to have a factory in those countries or to establish a new one? The advantages of the new factory did not convince them at all, it was all based on make-belief. They further wrote: "You have not given enough thought to it, for these advantageous propositions have only been made to entice the Company hither, and, when it shall have established itself after a lot of expense, will the said chief or his successor not change his mind then?" Was Khark in such an event capable of defending itself? But even if these problems did not arise, the XVII were not convinced of the soundness of the proposal. For, as they understood it, Khark would only be a warehouse where merchants would come and buy goods to take these elsewhere. In that case the Persian and Turkish governments would do everything to thwart the new factory, for these governments would be losing the revenues that Dutch trade had provided them with prior to the creation of the Khark factory. The XVII had many other objections, but awaiting further information from Batavia they deferred their decision on the Khark factory.[78] As we will see later, it would seem that the XVII had a clearer view of the situation in the Persian Gulf than the High Government, for they were right on almost every point of objection raised by them.

On July 27, 1753 von Kniphausen sailed from Batavia, but in the Sunda Straits the foremast of *de Jacatra* broke. Although the mast was repaired the ships continued to have problems and *de Getrouwigheid* lost sight of it and continued alone, assuming it would have returned to Batavia. He arrived October 6, 1753 at Bandar 'Abbas, where since June three other VOC ships were lying, viz. *de Hartekamp, 'tFortuyn* and *de Batavier*. Schoonderwoerd and von Kniphausen then decided to use *de Batavier* instead *de Jacatra* against Basra. Four days later von Kniphausen set sail to Bushire to gather information about Basra and the situation in that part of the Persian Gulf. When he ar-

73 VOC 2824, letter by Aga Mal, Sarfras, Sarquis Nichuales, Babtista Pirataam, Errapiet Vanos, Sadier Kaluts to Batavia (Bandar-e Rig, 20/02/1753), f. 78-80.

74 VOC 1007, Instruction (21/07/1753), f. 329.

75 VOC 1007, Instruction (21/07/1753), f. 308, 332. Schoonderwoerd was not allowed to interfere with Khark unless instructed to do so by Batavia. In case von Kniphausen died, Schoonderwoerd and not van der Hulst would succeed him.

76 VOC 1007, Instruction (21/07/1753), f. 330-31.

77 VOC 1007, Instruction (21/07/1753), f. 327. Von Kniphausen finally left with three ships only, because *de Kerkdijk* remained at Batavia.

78 VOC 333, XVII to Batavia (13/10/1753), section Bassora, not-foliated.

rived there on November 4, 1753 he found his interpreter Philip Catafago who had carried his official protest to Istanbul and had just returned. The latter carried an order from the Porte ordering Soleyman Pasha to return the extorted money to von Kniphausen.[79]

DUTCH ACTION AGAINST BASRA

On Khark von Kniphausen was welcomed by Mir Mohanna, the youngest son of Mir Naser, who was ill.[80] Von Kniphausen therefore went to visit Mir Naser in Bandar-e Rig to give him the letter and presents sent by Jacob Mossel, the governor-general. Mir Naser reaffirmed that he would stick to the agreement made with von Kniphausen with regard to the ownership of the island and assured him "that from now on the Hon. Company was the full owner and master of the island of Ghareek and he offered his help for the collection of the money that had been extorted in Bassora, of the outstanding debts and the merchandise that was still lying there."[81] Von Kniphausen welcomed this offer, because Mir Naser had four gallivats, which could be used against small local vessels.

Together with Mir Naser the Dutch planned the strategy against Basra. Because of the time of the year navigation was hazardous in the Persian Gulf. At the suggestion of Mir Naser it was therefore decided to first try and obtain the money by peaceful means and to send one of Mir Naser's men with a copy of the Porte's order to Soleyman Pasha. This messenger had to make it clear that if Soleyman Pasha refused to implement the imperial *farman* that Mir Naser would support any Dutch action against Basra. Soleyman Pasha did not take Mir Naser's threat seriously, because Sheikh Naser of Bushire had created doubt about Mir Naser's preparedness to support the Dutch. The reason for Sheikh Naser's behavior was that he was Mir Naser's enemy after their falling out over Bahrain and because he feared that a Dutch factory on Khark would be detrimental to the revenues of Bushire. Moreover, he feared that once the Dutch had settled on Khark that they would cast covetous eyes at Bahrain, the island that he now governed jointly with a Hula chief (see chapter two).

Meanwhile *'tFortuyn* arrived on November 23 after a luckless voyage. It had lost three anchors between Bandar 'Abbas and Khark, and had suffered 9 dead and many ill people among its crew. This also held for *de Getrouwigheid*, while 12 of the soldiers had died. The crew of *de Batavier* was reduced to 58 due to death and desertion, so that von Kniphausen considered it too dangerous an undertaking to have these ships cruise between the dangerous shoals. The more since some were heavily laden, and there was a shortage of anchors and ropes which could not be obtained locally. Therefore quickly a large wooden shed was erected to store the goods that were unloaded from the ships.

In March 1754, Soleyman Pasha sent a defiant reply. He accused Mir Naser of "helping the infidels and giving them room in his lands. He threatened him that if he would allow us to continue

---

79 VOC 2843, Gamron to Batavia (10/10/1763), f. 53-56; VOC 2853, Gamron to Batavia (10/10/1753), f. 7; VOC 2864, Khark to Batavia (01/11/1754), f. 4; VOC 2864, de Hochepied, Tharappia to von Kniphausen (18/08/1753), g. 29-31; see also Saldanha, *Précis*, vol. 1, p. 87 (the English thought that he either would undertake hostile action Basra or Bahrain. "If it should be against Bahreen their success at this time is hardly to be doubted, the Hooly Arabs being unable to make any considerable Resistance as they are already engaged in a War with Nasseir Caun [of Lar]; and in Discord also among themselves."

80 VOC 2864, Khark to Batavia (01/11/1754), f. 3-28, which describes the events from von Kniphausen's arrival on Khark until November 1754.

81 VOC 2864, Khark to Batavia (01/11/1754), f. 5.

to stay on Ghareek, or would assist us in any way, he would not fail to attack him over land."[82] To the Dutch Soleyman Pasha made it clear that he would not pay them anything. He was willing to allow a Dutch Agent to return to Basra on condition that this would not be von Kniphausen and that such a person would not be imposed by force. These sentiments appear to have been inspired by the petition sent by the principal notables of Basra who strongly objected to von Kniphausen's return. They expressed their readiness to pay whatever sum the government wanted to refund him, but that they all would leave the city if he returned.[83] In consultation with Mir Naser the Dutch decided to attack Basra when the date harvest began, when local manpower and vessels were most in demand. When the Dutch learnt that about the secret actions undertaken against them by Sheikh Naser of Bushire they closed down their factory in Bushire. According to the English, the Dutch resident there "destroyed his house and garden at that port before leaving it, but his action seems to have been due to a difference with Shaikh Nasir." The merchandise and other goods were taken aboard *de Getrouwigheid* and *de Batavier* without any trouble from Sheikh Naser. In fact, he denied all allegations made by von Kniphausen and asked the Dutch to remain in Bushire. However, von Kniphausen refused because of the ill-will that Sheikh Naser bore the VOC, leaving aside the fact that he had orders to close the Bushire factory. Von Kniphausen justified his decision by reporting that Sheikh Naser was trying to incite other local chiefs against the Dutch telling them that the Dutch were unbelievers, which was true and already known, of course. He further stated that once the Dutch had a fixed station on Khark they would soon control the entire Persian Gulf just like the Portuguese had done in the past. Sheikh Naser's warnings fell on dear ears, however, partly because the Dutch were fostering friendly relations with local chiefs and their people and partly because of the distrust and discord that existed between the local chiefs. For the peace of mind of Batavia von Kniphausen added that there were not two chiefs, who had more than 300 men at their back-and-call or who would agree with a fellow chief or live in peace with him.[84]

Sheikh Naser's and Wood's suspicion that the Dutch wanted to take Bahrain was not unfounded, for at the time that von Kniphausen and van der Hulst reproached him for voicing these fears they ironically proposed Batavia to carry out part of the things that Sheikh Naser had accused them of. On November 1, 1754 von Kniphausen and van der Hulst in a private letter to Mossel, the governor-general, proposed that the VOC should seize the island of Bahrain. This proposal, however, was immediately shot down by the High Government as well as by the XVII.[85]

During the winter of 1753-54 the Dutch had proceeded with the construction of the fortress on Khark, which was called Mosselsteijn, in honor of Jacob Mossel, the governor-general of the VOC. Soleyman Pasha in spite of the negative and defiant reply to Mir Naser twice sent emissaries to Bandar-e Rig and Khark to have the Dutch accept half of the extorted money or to assign them the customs revenues of Basra until they would have been repaid completely to settle the dispute.[86]

82 VOC 2864, Khark to Batavia (01/11/1754), f. 8.

83 Amin, *British Interests*, p. 144, n. 3; Lorimer, *Gazetteer*, p. 1207; Saldanha, *Précis*, vol. 1, p. 91.

84 Niebuhr, *Travels*, vol. 2, pp. 144, 153; Ibid., *Beschreibung*, pp. 314, 332; Amin, *British Interests*, p. 145; Lorimer, *Gazetteer*, p. 1207.

85 Willem Floor, "The Bahrein Project of 1754," *Persica*, vol. 11 (1984), pp. 129-148 or Annex I.

86 Meanwhile, Soleyman Pasha tried to have the *farman* revoked by the Soltan. To that end he obtained a statement from the leading citizens of Basra alleging that von Kniphausen had been involved with Moslem women. Further that he constructed the Dutch factory so high that it dominated the city of Basra and offered a view of the seraglio of the *motasallem*. De Hochepied drew up an aide-memoire, after having been informed about this statement, in which he refuted these accusations as being totally ridiculous and spurious. As a result of his intervention the Porte once again sent orders to Soleyman Pasha to implement the *farman* forthwith. Shortly thereafter

The Dutch refused and as the favorable monsoon approached three ships (*de Getrouwigheid*, *'tFortuyn* and *de Batavier*) sailed to blockade the Shatt al-Arab on July 3, 1754 under the command of van der Hulst. Mir Naser had already sent two of his gallivats to Khark and he would join them on July 5 to depart for Basra as well. However, on July 6 the Dutch learnt that the aged and blind Mir Naser had been murdered by Mir Mohanna, his youngest son, on the previous day. Mir Hoseyn, his eldest son, had been on the gallivats at Bandar-e Rig preparing for the expedition against Basra. Because he was unarmed and had only a few people with him Mir Hoseyn fled to Khark in a small vessel, on learning about his father's murder. Mir Mohanna by giving presents and the use of force had been able to persuade the people of Bandar-e Rig to accept him as the new chief. The two gallivats at Khark left during the night of July 7, attracted by these presents, to join Mir Mohanna. It is unclear why Mir Mohanna murdered his father. According to the English, it was because Mir Naser had given one of Mir Mohanna's favorite Georgian women to von Kniphausen, which seems highly unlikely. It is more likely that Mir Mohanna wanted to take over control of Bandar-e Rig from his ailing, old and blind father as a pre-emptive strike to prevent his oldest brother take over the rule of Bandar-e Rig. It is, of course, possible that he disagreed with his father with regards to the Dutch settlement of Khark, as some have claimed, but there is nothing in his behavior in the first years after the parricide that confirms this.[87]

Notwithstanding this set-back the Dutch detained to vessels belonging to the Turkish merchant Saleh Chelebi.[88] The vessels had a Dutch pass from Surat, but von Kniphausen made it clear to Chelebi that his vessels would remain sequestered at Khark until Soleyman Pasha would have paid. Despite this early success von Kniphausen felt insecure at Khark. He only had one undermanned ship on the roadstead, which had to guard the two Chelebi vessels, and only 21 Europeans on the island. Since he feared an attack from Mir Mohanna, von Kniphausen ordered the ships to return to Khark where they arrived on July 27, 1754. The ships had stopped navigation to and from Basra completely and had raided a village, which belonged to a prominent notable of Basra, where they had taken a herd of 300 sheep and cattle. This news caused panic and consternation in Basra. The *motasallem* discussed the problem with his council (*divan*), which decided to send two emissaries to Khark, one of whom was a European named Simon d'Amandan.[89] On behalf of the Ottoman government, they invited von Kniphausen back to Basra. Both the *motasallem* and the *qaputan-bashi* guaranteed that he and the Dutch in general would be given a most honorable welcome and that they would do their utmost to see to it that the Dutch would be indemnified completely.

---

it was rumored in Istanbul that von Kniphausen had arrived with three ships before Basra and that another seven were to follow. This news caused consternation at the Soltan's court. The Porte demanded an explanation from de Hochepied, who claimed that he knew nothing about such a hostile action. He therefore demanded von Kniphausen that he sent him particulars about his operation and intentions as soon as possible, because de Hochepied expected that otherwise the political situation would explode in the Levant. NA, Legatie Archief Turkije, nr. 168, de Hochepied to von Kniphausen (Therappia, 06/12/1744), f. 75 (in French).

87 VOC 2864, Khark to Batavia (01/11/1754); Perry, "Mir Muhanna," p. 86; Niebuhr, *Beschreibung*, pp. 316-18 for a graphic description of the murder. It certainly had nothing to do with the settlement of infidels on Khark, because Mir Mohanna later proposed the Dutch to stay on condition that they paid him an annual rent (see below). Another reason may have been that Soleyman Pasha had allegedly offered financial and other inducements to the 19-20 year old Mir Mohanna if he killed his father so that the planned joint action against Basra would be, if not torpedoed, at least weakened. Ya Hoseyni, *Mir Mohanna*, pp. 50-51.

88 See also Anonymous, *Chronicle*, vol. 1, p. 692; Ives, *Voyage*, p. 213.

89 According to Schoonderwoerd, these emissaries were merchants sent by Chelebi. VOC 2863, Gamron to Batavia (18/09/1754), f. 2. According to Ives, *Voyage*, p. 214 the governor of Basra wanted to repay the extorted money immediately, which is a later embellishment.

Von Kniphausen replied that disrespect had been shown to the European nations, in particular the Dutch, and that the open wounds were of too a recent date to allow them to return to Basra. Moreover, even if he personally would be ready to trust the fine promises of the *motasallem* he could not return, because Batavia had decided to close the Basra factory, which in fact had to be sold. With regards to the indemnification von Kniphausen told the emissaries that it was his intention to send the owner of the two ships with the necessary instructions to Basra to obtain the restitution of the extorted money and the outstanding debts. On August 2, 1754 the emissaries concluded an agreement with von Kniphausen of the following nature:[90] The extorted money would be paid back, as much as possible in cash. The outstanding Dutch debts would be collected by the Basran government. All merchandise and furniture in the Dutch factory and private property of VOC staff would be returned. The money would be turned over "where the river joins the sea (i.e. the 'bar' of the Shatt al-Arab)." After implementation of these terms all hostilities would cease and the Dutch would release the two Chelebi vessels.

On August 7, 1754 the emissaries returned to Basra where they arrived on August 11. Saleh Chelebi put pressure on the *motasallem* to convene the council (*divan*) and decide on the draft agreement. Chelebi who attended the council meeting declared that he had orders to go to Soleyman Pasha in Baghdad, when some notables expressed doubt about the possibility of collecting such a huge amount of money. The fact also that Chelebi mentioned that he at the same time would present Soleyman Pasha with letters that incriminated various council members clinched the issue. He divan immediately decided in what manner and by who payment would be made, viz. half the amount due would be paid by the notables in dates at harvest time. Chelebi was appointed to act as security for this payment. The other half would have to be paid by levying extra high imposts on goods produced in the region as well as on imports. The customs rate was raised from the usual 7% to 10.5%. The *motasallem* also ordered that all outstanding debts to the Dutch had to be collected within a period of three days. Willy-nilly he also had to agree to the closure of the Dutch factory, also the *motasallem* said that he did not want the Dutch to leave. However, in view of von Kniphausen's determination and the fact that the latter had already sold his country-house the *motasallem* also gave in on this point. On September 7, 1754 the emissaries returned to Khark with the agreement signed by the *motasallem*. On September 21, 1754 von Kniphausen and van der Hulst received 80,000 *qorush* in Turkish gold specie, the remainder was promised to follow soon and to be paid in dates, for which Shaw, the EIC Agent, stood security. By the end of 1754 the agreement had been fulfilled. Von Kniphausen had decided to agree to the settlement, because he considered that it would be unwise to go to extremes. Moreover, it would have taken more time to obtain better terms and to collect the money, while possible problems might have totally derailed the settlement. Therefore, he had accepted partial payment in dates to enable the Basran government to pay the remainder in cash. He knew that it would have been impossible to get payment in cash to the full amount, because there was not that much cash money around. The 70,000 *qorush* had been collected by force from the merchants and shopkeepers. As a result money had become so scarce that the English ships coming from Surat and Bengal had been unable to sell anything that year in Basra, according to von Kniphausen. The Dutch sold the dates, while the Turkish coins were changed into rupees, which were more in demand by the VOC. The VOC goods and the private possessions of VOC staff were sent to Khark in a vessel belonging to Shaw, the EIC Agent.[91]

---

90 Von Kniphausen's demand for indemnity of maintaining three ships at Khark was thus not met, see Perry, "Mir Muhanna," p. 85.

91 Von Kniphausen gave a receipt in exchange. For a copy see NA, Collectie de Hochepied, nr. 108. When the *chavus* (messenger) arrived with receipt in Istanbul towards the end of November 1754 the situation there became

Both the XVII and the High Government were very satisfied with the result of the expedition against Basra. The XVII sourly added that their satisfaction was conditional, in so far that they assumed that von Kniphausen and van der Hulst had not been the cause of the difficulties with the Ottoman government.[92] The High Government took the practical view; they had their money back and respect for the VOC had been restored. It therefore also approved the construction of fort Mosselsteijn,[93] while the XVII commented that the High Government had been a bit too hasty with its approval. But such a reaction was to be expected, because the XVII were not at all convinced of the wisdom of establishing a new factory in the Persian Gulf as we have seen.

DUTCH RELATIONS WITH MIR HOSEYN AND KARIM KHAN

Meanwhile, Mir Hoseyn had been able to recapture Bandar-e Rig with the help of some local chiefs and some Dutch funds. Mir Hoseyn landed with his force near Bandar-e Rig on July 25, 1754. He arrived at Bandar-e Rig on August 6. Most of its inhabitants joined Mir Hoseyn as a result of which Mir Mohanna fled. On August 10, 1754 Mir Hoseyn formally was installed as chief of Bandar-e Rig and its dependencies.[94] Shortly thereafter the chiefs of the littoral joined forces with Karim Khan to stop the latter's opponent, Azad Khan, progress towards the Persian Gulf. The Dutch doubted whether the motley crowd of 10,000 badly armed peasants could defeat Azad Khan's 15,000 battle-hardened soldiers, who had been part of Nader Shah's victorious armies. In the narrow Kamaraj pass, where 10 men armed only with rocks might stop a force of 1,000, the local Persian Gulf forces with 4,000 match-lock men defeated Azad Khan in October 1754. Towards the end of November 1754 Mir Hoseyn and Sheikh Naser of Bushire returned home due to lack of food and pay and so one by one did many of their 'soldiers'.[95] Despite their victory many people in the littoral believed that Azad Khan would take another route to the coast and subjugate them. Therefore the inhabitants of Bandar-e Rig and Bushire fled with their valuables to Khark when Shiraz was taken. The Armenians in both towns had all come to Khark and formed a community of more than 100 souls, who had their own priest. Among them were 10 wealthy merchants who traded with Surat, Bengal, and Coromandel. Moslem and Banyan merchants also came to Khark, despite the fact that building materials were not available due to the construction of the Dutch fort.[96]

Because of the late arrival of *de Kerkwijk* and *de Jacatra* von Kniphausen had not sent the three VOC ships back. Moreover, *de Batavier* had a crew of only 58 men and *'tFortuyn* only of 57 and between them only three anchors and four heavy cables, which made the return voyage risky. Von Kniphausen therefore decided after the settlement of the Basra affair to lay up *'tFortuyn* so as to enable the two other ships (*de Getrouwigheid* and *de Batavier*) to make the return journey with an adequate crew and proper equipment. The two ships left on November 1, 1754 and von Kniphausen therefore was very happy to welcome the arrival of *Pasgeld* on November 22. He kept the ship at

---

normal again. De Hochepied wrote to von Kniphausen to congratulate him with this success. Legatie Archief Turkije, nr. 168 (06/12/1754), f. 75; see also NA, Stadhouderlijke Secretarie, nr. 1.29.5, Extrait d'une letter de Bassora (20/08/1754); Saldanha, *Précis*, vol. 1, p. 93 (Bombay, 19/02/1755); Ives, *Voyage*, pp. 213-14.

92 VOC 334, XVII to Batavia (02/10/1757), section Karreek.

93 VOC 1009, Batavia to Khark (22/04/1755), f. 71-72.

94 VOC 2864, Khark to Batavia (01/11/1754), f. 15.

95 Roschan-Zamir, *Zand-Dynastie*, pp. 32-33; Perry, *Karim Khan*, pp. 58-59; VOC 2864, Khark to Batavia (01/11/1754), f. 17-18.

96 VOC 2864, Khark to Batavia (01/11/1754), f. 17-18; Perry, *Karim Khan*, p. 154.

Kharck during the winter claiming that it could not return due to the contrary monsoon. As he knew very well that Batavia insisted on fast turn-around time of its ships, von Kniphausen must have kept *Pasgeld* because of security considerations.[97]

This is a reasonable assumption given the high level of insecurity in the Persian Gulf and the Khark area in particular. At that time Mir Mohanna used the political confusion to try and retake Bandar-e Rig. On December 7, 1754 supported by Qa'ed Heydar of Ganaveh, who was related to him via his mother, and 300 men he had surrounded Mir Hoseyn. After 30 of Mir Hoseyn's men had died his house was stormed. The latter was wounded and taken prisoner. All local chiefs were taken aback by this deed with the exception of Sheikh Naser of Bushire, who promised his support to Mir Mohanna. According to the Dutch, he supported Mir Mohanna in the belief that this would be detrimental to the Dutch position on Khark and he even said so publicly. The Dutch felt threatened by this development and urged those chiefs supporting Mir Hoseyn to oust Mir Mohanna. On January 15, 1755 Mir Hoseyn's allies counter-attacked with 6,000 men. Mir Hoseyn had escaped his prison on January 16, and his allies retook Bandar-e Rig on January 20. The Dutch had supplied the allied force with two 3-pounders, gun-powder and balls. Mir Mohanna was taken prisoner and handed over for imprisonment to the chief of Tangesir, an enemy of Sheikh Naser.[98]

The High Government[99] approved von Kniphausen's support of Mir Hoseyn, nevertheless it hoped that henceforth he would not interfere anymore in local affairs. He was ordered to maintain a policy of strict neutrality and to let the local chiefs "drift on their own wings." The XVII were of a different mind, because they were totally opposed to interference in local affairs.[100] The trouble with the sons of Mir Naser was exactly what they had warned about and thus the events confirmed them in their negative opinion about the Khark factory. Von Kniphausen promised to remain neutral regarding local disputes. However, he pointed out that the Company would lose influence that way. The support to Mir Hoseyn had produced no negative effect; on the contrary, it only had earned the Company respect and had put the fear into Sheikh Naser's heart who had abandoned his designs on Khark, although he was trying to have von Kniphausen killed.[101]

At the beginning of February 1755 Mir Hoseyn visited Khark to thank von Kniphausen for his support. He transferred a gallivat to the VOC as part payment of his father's debt incurred in 1753. This debt amounted to Dfl. 30,024, incurred just prior to Mir Naser's death. He had wanted to encourage trade via Bandar-e Rig and therefore had asked von Kniphausen to supply him with merchandise to form a caravan that he would send to Shiraz. Out of friendship and because he believed that it was in the VOC's commercial interest von Kniphausen had supplied the goods. Because the customs duties paid in Bandar-e Rig were collected by the VOC broker von Kniphausen also had some kind of guarantee as to repayment. Mir Naser's murder and the subsequent rivalry between

97 VOC 2864, Khark to Batavia (01/11/1754), f. 20; Ibid, idem to idem (27/02/1755), f. 33, 37. Although Batavia agreed to the sale of *'tFortuyn* (VOC 1009, Batavia to Khark [22/04/1755]) the XVII were very surprised and furious about this acquiescence. The XVII argued that von Kniphausen had given no good reason for selling *'tFortuyn* and that he even had admitted that the ship could have made the return voyage to Batavia. They ordered Batavia to instruct von Kniphausen that he should not arrogate decision-making authority, which he did not have. VOC 333, XVII to Batavia (02/10/1755), section Karreek, not foliated.

98 VOC 2864, Khark to Batavia (27/02/1755), f. 33-34. Qa'ed Heydar was described as someone who "keeps himself alive with robbing and plundering of caravans." See also Floor, "A Description," pp. 171, 174 or chapter one.

99 VOC 1009, Batavia to Khark (28/07/1755), f. 257.

100 VOC 334, XVII to Batavia (0/11/1757), section Karreek, not-foliated.

101 VOC 2885, Khark to Batavia (09/12/1758), f. 8-10.

his two sons had delayed repayment of the debt. By the end of May 1755 most of it had been paid in one way or another, including Mir Hoseyn's transfer of 20 iron and one metal cannon and one 7-pounder, which were valued at Dfl. 9,370. Von Kniphausen put a good face on this payment by writing that it was not a bad investment, since he needed these canons anyway, while they always could be resold for a good price. He did not put a value on the gallivat, however, while he intended to collect the remainder of the debt overtime.[102] Von Kniphausen completely overhauled and armed the gallivat with eight guns and used it to protect the sea lanes around Khark. Now he felt safe on the island, claiming to have the fastest gallivat in the Persian Gulf and the respect of most local chiefs and therefore allowed a VOC ship that he had held over to return to Batavia. He further noted that Sheikh Naser had planned an attack on Khark a few times, but each time he had to abandon his plans due to contrary winds.[103] The XVII believed that von Kniphausen concocted the stories about local respect and insecurity to enhance his own reputation. Batavia, however, believed them and advised von Kniphausen to get the support of local chiefs and Karim Khan. In particular, he had to request the later to induce Sheikh Naser to lower the high customs duties on VOC merchandise at Bushire, which otherwise might negatively impact the success of the Khark factory.[104]

THE REINFORCEMENT OF KHARK AND ITS POPULATION

By November 1, 1754 fort Mosselsteijn was almost completed, with the exception of one bastion of which the breastworks were lacking. The three other bastions of the square fort were in state of defense. Although all VOC personnel could be housed during the winter, quarters were still a bit cramped. Von Kniphausen had high hopes for 1755, for then the construction of the first storey would begin, so that the problem of space would be satisfactorily resolved. The main problem of finishing its construction was the lack of timber. The progress made so far had been possible, because the grange that had been built in November 1753 had been taken down as well as some pre-existing buildings on Khark, which had supplied enough timber to construct the fort's ceiling and strong enough to withstand the precipitation of the coming winter.[105] The fort had been built at the only place on Khark where one could land at low tide. Von Kniphausen therefore intended to make the fort impregnable by constructing a crescent-shaped man-high breastwork in front of the gate; it

102 VOC 2864, Khark to Batavia (27/02/1755), f. 34-36; Ibid, idem to idem (31/05/1755), f. 51-52.

103 VOC 2864, Khark to Batavia (31/05/1755), f. 43-44. The gallivat had a crew of one second mate, one quarter-master, four gunners and 12 native soldiers.

104 VOC 1010, Batavia to Khark (08/07/1756), f. 192; VOC 334, XVII to Batavia (10/10/1759), section Karreek, not foliated.

105 VOC 2864, Khark to Batavia (18/09/1754), f. 19; VOC 2863, Gamron to Batavia (18/08/1754), f. 2 reported that "the so-called fort has been provisionally built with clay and stones; so far only the outer wall is ready." For further information on the fort see VOC 2864, Khark to Batavia (27/02/1755), f. 38; Ibid., idem to idem (31/05/1755), f. 46-48; VOC 2885, f. 8-9 (29/05/1755); VOC 797, f. 1112-17; VOC 1010, f. 193. See also Saldanha, *Précis*, vol. 1, p. 91 ("a regular fort of four bastions, each mounting ten guns."); Ibid., vol. 1, p. 93 (19/02/1755) ("it would prove to be a very beneficial Settlement in a few years."). According to Ives, *Voyage*, p. 212 the fort was built with the help of "workmen from Persia and Arabia." The rains could be destructive like those in the winter of 1757 when many houses of the inhabitants of Khark were much damaged by the rains and the lower part of the island was totally inundated. The fort and the warehouses sustained the water onslaught, except for one warehouse of which the roof had not yet been completed. VOC 2968, Khark to Batavia (05/12/1757), f. 26-27. For the location of the fort see A on figure 4.3.

9 minuten
10
11
12
13
14
15
16
'T Eyland Groot Carreek
De Rheede

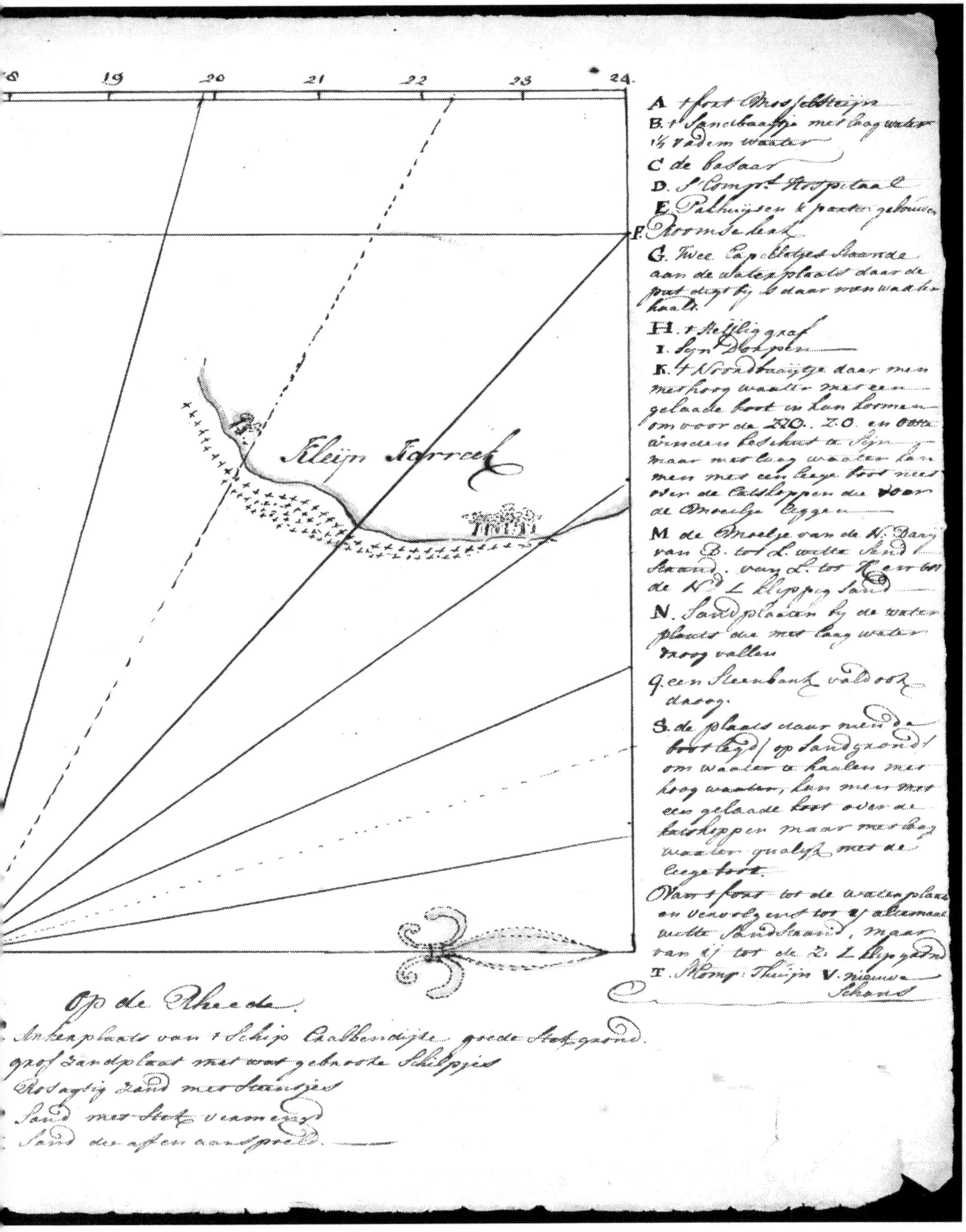

Fig. 4.2 Map of Khark Accompanying Von Kniphausen's Report

needed six heavy 24-pouders. He needed timber to finish it and to strengthen the ceiling and urged Batavia to send him that which he had ordered.[106]

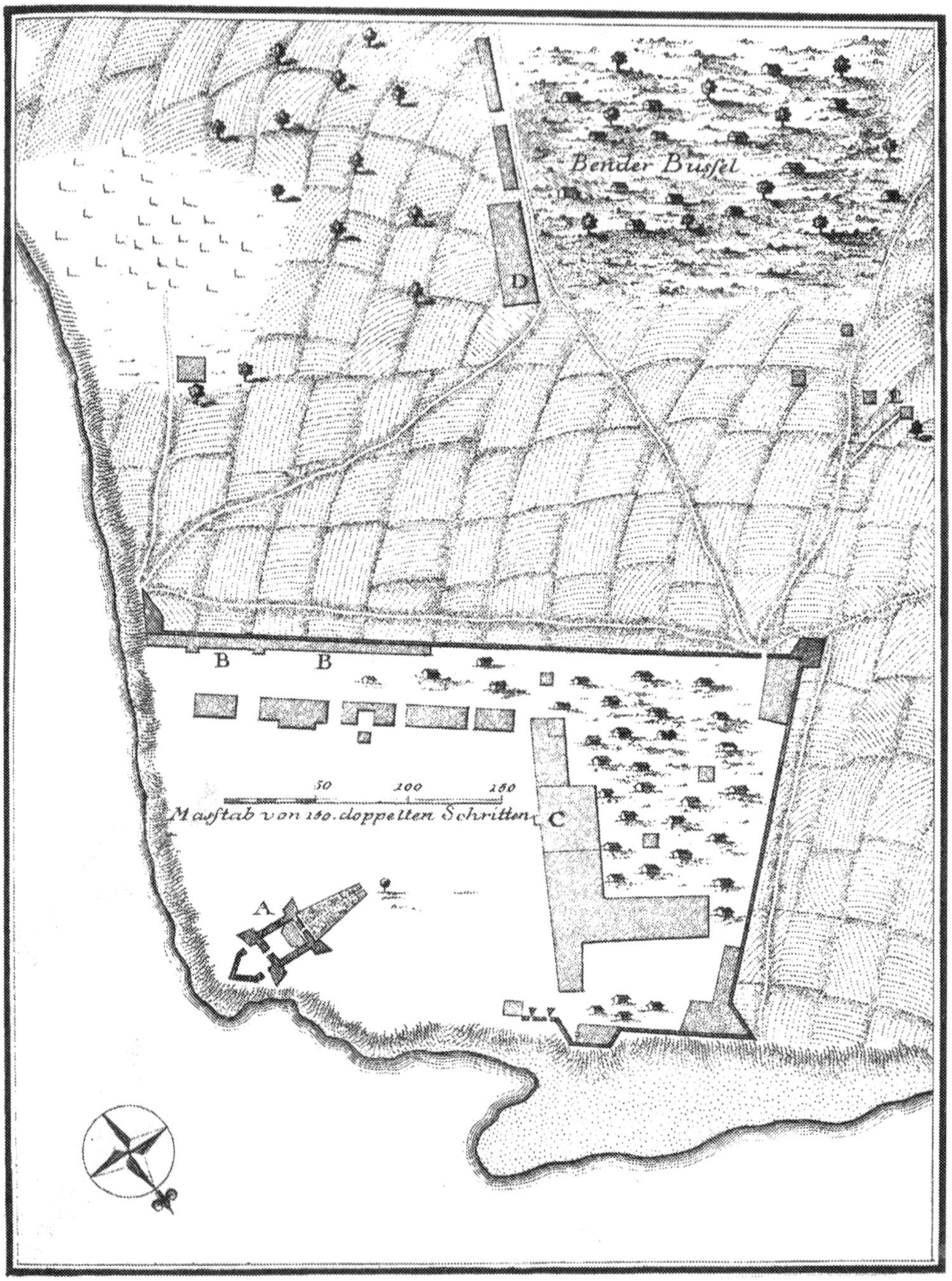

Fig. 4.3 Plan of Khark by Niebuhr

Von Kniphausen wanted to make the fort even more formidable by separating it from the island by way of a wide canal. During winter al native vessels would be secure in that canal, which

106 VOC 2864, Khark to Batavia (27/02/1755), f. 38. The lower lying area of the island sometimes was inundated when Khark experienced heavy rains such as in Novermber 1757, when also much damage was inflicted on the houses of Khark's inhabitants. VOC 2968, Khark to Bataavia (05/12/1757), f. 26.

otherwise was impossible due to the hard S.E. winds. This would allow the easy and uninterrupted loading and unloading of the ships. The safety offered would increase trade, while the cost of construction might be recovered by an impost levied from the vessels using this canal, in accordance with their size. The soil was very well suited for this plan, because rocky soil had been found at 2-2.5 fathoms. Von Kniphausen further suggested that one might erect walls on both sides of the canal. He one on the inner side of the fort would have to be of a man's height and could serve as a breastwork. If cannon were mounted on this wall the fort would be completely secure on the landside. Von Kiphausen estimated the cost of construction at Dfl. 30,000 with a pay-back time of six years, based on the number of vessels that came to Khark for drinking water and the construction time at five months. Batavia did not approve of this proposal, unless the merchants who would benefit from this construction would pay for it.[107]

During 1755 the construction of the fort made good progress. The redoubt in front of the gate at the seaside was completed during that summer, while spacious barracks for the soldiers had been completed as well. The lack of timber was still great and the danger of severe damage by rain was still great, if additional timber did not arrive on time. This also was the reason that there was as yet not enough storage space for merchandise, reason why von Kniphausen decided to keep the goods on board the ships to keep them dry.[108] In 1758 Ives visited the island and fort of Khark and described the latter as follows:

> The fort is a square, built of stone, with four bastions, each of which has eight guns mounted upon it; six of these were in the two faces, and the others were so contrived as to flank the two curtains. Before the gate, facing the sea, was battery of ravelin, with twelve guns mounted, from six to eighteen pounders. There were also thirty of forty more of various sizes lying upon the ground, for want of carriages. This irregularity in the weight of cannon, was owing to the baron's being obliged to get them as he could from different ships, and at several times. An esplanade also extended itself about 200 yards, beyond which, they had just finished some houses for Europeans to dwell in, and a wall, which joined those houses. This wall, it was designed, should hereafter be continued from sea to sea, as a security to the fort and the inhabitants within. It ran nearly north-west and south-east. The fort was garrisoned with an hundred European soldiers. There also was a triangular bastion at the north-west of the island, mounted with six guns; two of these pointed towards the sea, two to the shore, and the other two were to flank the intended curtain-wall of the town. About mid-way between this north west point and the fort, there was a small pier-head of stone-work, designed to protect a little haven, wither all the Trankeys, Gallivats, and Feluccas run, when the south wind blows hard, and where they lay in perfect security. In this haven we saw three armed Gallivats, with six or

107 VOC 2864, Khark to Batavia (31/05/1755), f. 46-48; VOC 1010, Batavia to Khark (08/07/176), f. 193; Ives, *Voyage*, p. 214.

108 VOC 2885, Khark to Batavia (29/05/1755), f. 8-9. When the fort was completed it not only boasted of impressive living quarters for the Agent, but it also had separate quarters for the officers and administrative staff in addition to barracks for the soldiers, sailors and African slaves. There was further a hospital, houses for artisans and five warehouses for sugar. VOC 797, f. 1113-17. For a description of the buildings and how the Dutch lived see Niebuhr, *Beschreibung*, p. 316f. According to Wood, the Dutch also constructed "Hummums, Houses, and Carravanseroys." Saldanha, *Précis*, vol. 1, p. 98 (Bandar-e Rig, 03/05/1756). For the location of the warehouses see B on figure 4.3.

> eight carriage guns, which is superior to any force the Turks or their neighbours have in these seas.[109]

The Dutch establishment on Khark did not fail to make an impression on the English who reported that the fort held

> about sixty Europeans including seven to eight petty officers and they are all neat handsome fellows, kept under the strickest [sic] discipline, besides these Mynheer Kniphausen has above one hundred Coffree [i.e., black] Slaves well armed according to the Country manner with swords and Targets, who from his manner of treating them, are likely to remain faithful and contented under their Bondage, he takes care to supply them with plenty of dates, Fish and Bread, gives them decent Cloathing, cools the natural Fervour of their Constitution, by allowing a Considerable number of Coffree women to live among them, in Common, and never Controls, or even advises them in regard to Religion, but when they commit a fault, he punishes them very severely, and whenever he has occasion to drab any of the Arabs or Country people he orders two or three of the Slaves to take him in hand, which service seems to be peculiarly adopted to their Capacity and in my life I never saw people acquit themselves in a duty of this kind with greater dexterity and Judgement.[110]

The English also reported that von Kniphausen encouraged Christians to settle on Khark by promising them 10 *tumans* and a house,[111] but this is not borne out by Dutch sources and seems unlikely, because Batavia would never have approved such an expenditure. Nevertheless, it would fit von Kniphausen's plan to create a thriving 'European' community on Khark. He also proposed to Batavia to send him Chinese workers, whom he would use for agricultural, construction and artisinal activities.[112] According to Francis Wood, the English Resident at Bandar-e Rig, he was shown "the particular Lands that were allotted for the Chinese, to Cultivate, and Confirmed what I had before heard of their intending to settle eighty Families of them upon barrack [sic; Khark] when the Arab Inhabitants are all to be sent off."[113] The latter assertion is not borne out by Dutch sources and it would have run counter to Dutch commercial interests as well as official VOC policy to maintain good relations with the local population. Therefore, this statement must be ascribed to English rumor mongering as part of 'friendly' rivalry that traditionally existed between the two countries.

---

109 Ives, *Voyage*, p. 214. Some members of the European staff, such as the deputy Buschman and his wife, had a pleasant garden near their house. Ibid., p. 224. One of the gallivats, which von Kniphausen had bought in 1758, had a keel length of 57 feet; on top it was 18.5 feet wide. VOC 2968, Khark to Batvia (15/11/1758), f. 20. In 1760 van der Hulst had a heavy wall built in front of the ravelin at the eastside of the fort to prevent the crumbling away of the beach there and provide protection against storms and high tide. He reported that since the completion of the wall the beach had increased by 60 feet; furthermore that the fort itself needed repairs and he asked for timber from Batavia. VOC 3027, Khark to Batavia (30/11/1760), f. 17-18.

110 Saldanha, *Précis*, vol. 1, p. 99 (Bandar-e Rig, 03/05/756); also Ives, *Voyage*, p. 214.

111 Amin, *British Interests*, p. 148; Lorimer, *Gazetteer*, p. 131.

112 VOC 2864, Khark to Batavia (31/05/1755), f. 53. As far as I know, only one Chinese man ever came to Khark, VOC 1013 (11/05/1659), f. 12 which states that "the Chinaman Thee Theeke is sent herewith," without any further explanation.

113 Saldanha, *Précis*, vol. 1, p. 99; Lorimer, *Gazetteer*, p. 131; Amin, *British Interests*, p. 148..

There must have been nevertheless a considerable permanent population on Khark (Arabs, Persians, Banyans, Armenians, Africans and Europeans), in addition to a transient part, consisting of merchants, sailors and fishermen. First, there was a need for men to support the trading and shipping activities, i.e. to load and unload ships, to carry goods to and from the caravanserais and other related activities. Second, there must have been craftsmen to provide both repair and production facilities as well as retail trade. In fact, Niebuhr explicitly mentions the "Persian and Arab shopkeepers, fishermen, craftsmen and the like, who lived here behind these [stone] buildings in inferior huts covered with mats and here was also the bazaar or the market streets." Third, there was and had always been cultivation on the island, which also required field laborers. When Ives visited the south end of the island in 1758 he "passed through some agreeable fields of corn, and some gardens, where we saw cole-worts, beans, and peas in perfection."[114] The supposition of the presence of a considerable population on the island is further borne out by Niebuhr's description of the theatrical performance of a Shi'ite religious passion-play (*ta'ziyeh-khvani*) on Khark in 1764, which suggests that quite a large number participated in this festival. Because of the noise they made, Buschman only allowed its performance in the 'town' of Khark on the last or tenth of the festival, during the preceding nine days the activities took place outside the 'town'. There was complete freedom of religion on the island. In addition to Shi'ites, there were also Sunnis on the island and both groups, which had about the same number, prayed at the tomb of Mohammad b. Hanafiyeh.[115]

In view of the growing Christian population on the island von Kniphausen reported in 1757 that he had given the Roman Catholic Arabs and Georgians as well as Greek Catholic Armenians permission to each build a church on Khark, for which he hoped that Batavia would give its approval. On May 1, 1757 Von Kniphausen and Buschman reported that "At the request of Roman [Catholic] Arab, Georgian and Armenian Christians we have given permission without any objection to the request for the construction of a church in the hope that you would approve of this, on condition that only Italian and German priests may serve there, following Bombay's example. We have given the same permission to the Armenians of the Greek-Orthodox church. Both churches have already a roof and the Armenian arch-bishop who formerly resided in Isfahan wants to take up residence here."[116] By September 1757 the construction of both churches had almost been completed, while the arch-bishop, who formerly resided in Isfahan, intended to take up residence on Khark. Although von Kniphausen welcomed such an influx of Christians, which also might increase trade, he realized that his Protestant masters would look askance at too granting that much public freedom to Catholics. Von Kniphausen, whom the Carmelites described as a "follower of no religion," had regular contacts with the Carmelite missionaries. Already as early as March 1754 Fr. Angel Felix had "spent Easter with the Christians there [i.e. Khark]." In 1755 the Carmelite Vicar Provincial, Fr. Cornelius of St. Joseph went to Khark. In that year the Carmelites obtained permission from von Kniphausen to "build there a Residence for two of our Religious, with a church open to the public, ... but he also granted me permission to add to its quarters for the Bishop of Isfahan,

114 Ives, *Voyage*, p. 207. For the location of the caravanserai and other stone buildings to house VOC staff, Indians and Armenians see C on figure 4.3. Adjacent to it was the bazaar and the settlement of the local population. For the cultivation of the island prior to the presence of the Dutch see Floor, *The Persian Gulf*, p. 243. Europeans also wanted to settle on Khark. In August 1756 von Kniphausen forwarded a request by a sailor and soldier to be allowed to remain on Khark. They were already making money by distilling alcohol and wanted to settle on Khark as free citizens after the expiration of their contract and continue their business. VOC 2885, Khark to Batavia (05/08/1756), f. 30-31.

115 Niebuhr, *Reisebeschreibung*, pp. 573-78.

116 VOC 2937, Khark to Batavia (29/10/1757), f. 26. For the same information as well as on the implementation of the construction plans see Anonymous, *Chronicle*, vol.1, pp. 693-94 ("our tolerably large House"), 710, 840, 1090-92; VOC 3156, Khark to Batavia (30/09/1764), f. 32-34.

realizing that residence of that prelate on the island would attract many Christians from Persia to establish themselves there, to the advantage of the Company." Although building materials were already sent that same year the construction plans had to be postponed due to the death of Mgr. Sebastian in Basra and the departure of the Vicar Provincial. Since von Kniphausen did not mention any of this in his letters to Batavia, it is clear that when in 1757 another opportunity offered itself he immediately grasped it. Caring little about religion he saw, as the Carmelites rightly observed, the advantages of creating a strong Christian population on the island. He therefore wanted to confront the High Government with a *fait accompli*, implying that disapproval would have a negative impact on VOC trade. He even went so far as to supply the Carmelites with ironwork and beams at low prices, which materials he may have ordered from Batavia under the pretext that he needed these to repair the fort.[117]

Von Kniphausen had counted on the High Government not objecting too strongly against the construction of the churches and indeed Batavia gave its approval. The directors of the VOC, however, were furious and they wrote that

> We are very surprised about your silence concerning the permission to build Roman Catholic churches without awaiting our agreement. We would have never thought that our subaltern staff would be so bold as to take such a decision that is only ours to take. We withhold our permission to start building the churches and those persons who have given permission to do so have to indemnify the people out of their own pocket, for the churches have to be demolished. We are not only displeased with von Kniphausen's irresponsible behavior, but we also do not approve of you having permitted it. You have to immediately instruct von Kniphausen to make an inventory of the number of Armenian Christians residing there (Roman Catholic or Greek Orthodox rite), who their priests are and whether, apart from the reason to increase the number of inhabitants of Khark and thereby as it were its trade, there were some other reasons to grant the public performance of the Roman Catholic religion.[118]

Due to the long lines of communications Batavia only received answers to these questions by the beginning of 1761. According to van der Hulst and Buschman, there were 25-30 Roman Catholics on Khark in 1762, and that their number fluctuated with the number of people coming from and going to Basra and Persia. They had built a small church with surplus funds from the Basra congregation and voluntary gifts. They were served by an Italian Carmelite monk would come occasionally from Bushire for the Catholics. The Roman Catholic church probably was too grand a word to describe the locale, for Niebuhr stated that both Catholics and Protestants had the use of a room in the 'town' to hold church services and did not mention the Roman Catholic church at all. The 115-120 Armenians on Khark in 1762 had also raised money to construct a small church outside the 'town' that even had a church bell, which was very unusual in the Persian Gulf as this is not allowed in Moslem countries. They were served by two secular Armenian priests (*kahana*), who were supervised by the VOC interpreter Auweek di Oannes (Aweteek di Hovannes).[119] From Dutch

117 *Chronicle*, vol.1, pp. 693-94 ("our tolerably large House"), 710, 840, 1090-92; VOC 3156, Khark to Batavia (30/09/1764), f. 32-34.

118 VOC 334, XVII to Batavia (30/09/1760), section Karreek, not foliated.

119 VOC 3092, Khark to Batavia (19/10/1762), f. 36-37; Niebuhr, *Reisebeschreibung*, pp. 573-78. For the location of the Armenian church see D on figure 4.3.

sources it is not clear whether the churches were demolished and if so whether the Christians were indemnified. Since the Carmelite do not report on this issue anything either we may assume that Buschman, who, despite being the son of a Protestant minister, bore the Catholics no ill-will, for practical reasons just ignored the order. Although Buschman became less forthcoming towards the Carmelites he could not very well antagonize the Christian community on Khark. When the bishop of Isfahan, however, wanted to reside on Khark Buschman refused him permission to stay there any longer "on the pretext that though, true, his Company did allow a missionary Father to dwell there, they would not permit the fixed residence of a bishop."[120]

The African slaves also were allowed to practice their own ancestral religion which they mostly continued to adhere to. To that end they had built a small temple in honor of their great holy man, whom they called Sheikh Faraj (Shech Feradsch), while their religious ritual consisted mainly in dancing accompanied by music. Reference is also made to a small number of Jewish merchants on Khark, but their number is not known, and it is likely that they did not live permanently on the island.[121]

ENGLISH REACTION TO DUTCH SETTLEMENT ON KHARK

Mir Naser also had invited the EIC to come to settle in his lands, but the English were slower in reacting than the Dutch. By the time that London had decided that it would be worth their while to look into this option the Dutch were already firmly established in their fort Mosselsteijn on Khark. This fact and suspicion about a Dutch grand design for the Persian Gulf propelled Bombay to immediately order the execution of this option. The English were quite apprehensive about their position in the Persian Gulf. The EIC feared Dutch supremacy would be total if the VOC would seize Bahrain.[122] The EIC council in Bombay therefore sent a letter to Mir Naser reminding him that he also had invited the EIC to come and trade in his lands. The EIC, therefore, intended to send him a Resident, who would establish a factory in Bandar-e Rig; this letter was brought by the *Neptune Galley* in March 1754. Because of Mir Naser's death no reply was given. Because Francis Wood had just been replaced as Agent of Bandar 'Abbas by Douglas, and thus was thoroughly familiar with affairs in the Persian Gulf, he was charged with the execution of this project. Even the knowledge that Mir Naser had been killed and that the political situation at Bandar-e Rig was tense did not deter them. According to Wood's instruction the sole purpose of the Bandar-e Rig factory was to try and sell above all English woolens and to hinder the sale of all other woolens, in particular by "the Aleppo adventurers." He further was not allowed to give loans, had to try to collect duties on all imports and exports from those that were under EIC protection, if the chief of Bandar-e Rig would

120 Anonymous, *Chronicle*, vol.1, pp. 693-94 ("our tolerably large House"), 710, 840, 1090-92.

121 VOC 3092, Khark to Batavia (19/10/1762), f. 36-37; Niebuhr, *Reisebeschreibung*, pp. 573-78.

122 Ricks, *Politics and Trade*, p. 346, note 117 referring to Mir Naser's invation letter to Ellis dated 22/05/1752 inviting the EIC to establish a factory in his country. Francis Wood reported "I have done all in my power to learn whether the Dutch really intend to take Possession of Bahreen or not, but can get no intelligence to be depended upon, if they have any such scheme in their heads they are very secret, and will not put it in execution I believe, till the Chinese are well settled at barrack [sic; Khark]." Saldanha, *Précis*, vol. 1, p. 100. The secret was indeed well kept, because von Kniphausen proposed to conquer Bahrain, which Batavia immediately forbade, see Willem Floor, "The Bahrain Project of 1754," *Persica* 11 (1084), pp. 129-48 and Appendix 1. The English also had considered seizing Bahrain at various times after 1749.

allow it, and to avoid any problem with the government or the Dutch by being open and transparent about his mission.[123]

Von Kniphausen, who had not taken the English show of interest in establishing a factory at Bandar-e Rig seriously, was very much surprised when Francis Wood arrived in the Persian Gulf in February 1755 to establish a factory in Bandar-e Rig. Schoonderwoerd reported from Bandar 'Abbas that Wood had told him that the English were very jealous of the Khark factory and that he was going to build a fort "just like ours" in Bandar-e Rig.[124] Wood had intimated that a ship with building materials would follow shortly, but when he left Bandar 'Abbas on March 6, 1755 this ship had as yet not arrived.[125] Because Wood had no merchandise with him and was only accompanied by one native clerk and two servants the Dutch mistrusted his intentions, which they believed were to stir up trouble for the Khark factory, for which von Kniphausen, according to Schoonderwoerd, had supplied an excellent excuse by having militarily supported Mir Hoseyn. This negative impression of English intentions was reinforced by other information intercepted and gathered by the Dutch as well as by Wood's visit to Bushire instead of Bandar-e Rig. The Dutch did not believe that Wood wanted to establish a factory at Bushire, because Sheikh Naser did not allow any private English ship to leave Bushire without having extorted money from it. Wood, therefore, only had come to fish in troubled waters and stir up trouble for the Dutch at Khark. This impression was further reinforced by some careless remarks made by English captains who passed through Khark, by letters written by Shaw, the EIC Agent in Basra, to Mir Mohanna and Sheikh Naser, but above all by Dutch suspicion of the English and the latter's open envy of the Dutch factory at Khark. According to von Kniphausen, the English were continuously warning everybody that the Dutch would soon control the entire Gulf and he feared that they also were encouraging the enemies of Dutch to take action against them. For that reason von Kniphausen decided that the VOC ship *Pasgeld* should not depart before he was sure there was no trouble brewing, because he had only 1,800 lbs. of gun-powder.[126]

Although ordered to go to straight to Bandar-e Rig, Wood went to Bushire because of the ouster of Mir Mohanna in early 1755 by his brother, Mir Hoseyn. Shortly before Wood's arrival in Bushire on March 22, 1755, Mir Mohanna had been released by the chief of Tangesir after intercession by other local chiefs on his behalf. After his release Mir Mohanna went to Bushire, where he together with Sheikh Naser and Wood held secret talks. During his stay in Bushire Wood had come to the conclusion that it offered better commercial opportunities than Bandar-e Rig and he informed Douglas about his conclusion. In May 1754 Francis Wood had discussed with Sheikh

123 Saldanha, *Précis*, vol. 1, p. 91-92 (Bombay, 18/10/1754); Amin, *British Interests*, pp. 35-36; VOC 2864, Khark to Batavia (27/02/1755), f. 35-36.

124 VOC 2864, Khark to Batavia (31/05/1755), f. 41-43; Ibid., Gamron to Batavia (31/05/1755), f. 15-16 (Wood had arrived at Bandar 'Abbas in February 1755); Amin, *British Interests*, pp. 36-39; Lorimer, *Gazetteer*, p. 130; Saldanha, *Précis*, vol. 1, p. 100 reports "Inclosed is a plan of barrack [sic; Khark] Fort, which I had the leisure and opportunity of taking to the greatest exactness, as I lodged in it the whole time I stay'd upon the Island, they do not intend to have any wall round the Town, but instead of it a Deep Toss, with draw Bridges, capable of receiving and proving a safe harbour for the Gallivats and Trankeys."

125 VOC 2909, List of ships calling on Khark, f. 2 lists on January 20, 1756 "an unknown English brig foundered at Cape Bardistan. It came from Bombay with cannons, ammunition and 30 soldiers for their factory" in Bandar-e Rig, which, in addition to subsequent events, showed that Wood was not boasting at all.

126 VOC 2864, Khark to Batavia (27/02/1755), f. 41-43; VOC 2864, Gamron to Batavia (31/03/1755), f. 16; Amin, *British Interests*, pp. 36-39. Ironically, the Dutch were able to replenish their stock of gun-powder by the arrival of the private English vessel the *Ganges Valley* from which they also bought a few hundred six-pound balls. VOC 2864, Khark to Batavia (31/05/1755), f. 43.

Naser the possible establishment of an EIC factory in Bushire with exemption from payment of customs duties. The obstacle was Wood's demand that the EIC levy customs duties which the Sheikh believed would make merchants go elsewhere. This additional English levy probably referred to the consulage that the EIC collected from English private vessels and those under English protection, which is an issue that also occurs in later negotiations.[127] The Dutch did not believe that Wood really wanted to establish a factory at Bushire, because Sheikh Naser did not allow any English ship to leave Bushire without having extorted money from it.[128] There was also the fact that according to his instructions Wood had to establish a factory at Bandar-e Rig and not at Bushire and he greatly surprised the EIC factory at Bandar 'Abbas of having gone there, which reprimanded him and gave instructions to carry out his orders. It argued that only if he had found it impractical to establish a factory at Bandar-e Rig he might have gone to Bushire.[129]

At the beginning of April 1755, following his discussions with Mir Mohanna and Wood, Sheikh Naser assisted by some other chiefs from Dashtestan marched on Bandar-e Rig with about 500 men to install Mir Mohanna. However, having arrived at one day's journey from Bandar-e Rig his allies abandoned him induced to do so by presents from Mir Hoseyn. Sheikh Naser and Mir Mohanna hastily withdrew to Bushire. Wood, who had just received orders from Douglas to go to Bandar-e Rig, was at first unable to leave, because Sheikh Naser forbade all native vessels to give him passage. Wood then departed from Bushire and arrived at the end of May 1755 in Bandar-e Rig, which he found "destitute of Marchants." He just arrived in time to speak with Mir Hoseyn, who was about to depart for Shiraz, but stayed three days longer. Unknown to the Dutch, Mir Hoseyn gave Wood permission to build a factory of Bandar-e Rig, but asked him to remain in Bandar-e Rig until his return, because he feared that Wood might leave because of the bad and destitute condition of Bandar-e Rig. He assured Wood that "the credit of the English would very soon draw all the merchants back again to Bunderick and restore the place to its former flourishing condition." After Mir Hoseyn's departure the population of Bandar-e Rig was hostile and insolent towards Wood, who then via Basra (where he stayed until July) returned to Bushire from where he was able to get a decree from Karim Khan confirming the EIC's rights to build a factory at Bandar-e Rig. Because of Sheikh Naser's no longer friendly attitude, but rather one of continued and insufferable hostility he left. Wood characterized Sheikh Naser as a man "who regards nobody but for the sake of what he can defraud them of." Wood returned to Bandar-e Rig on September 9, 1755 where Mir 'Ali, Mir Hoseyn's deputy, once again assured him that he was allowed to build his factory. The population now behaved friendly towards him and Wood therefore sent for goods (in particular woolens) from England and started to construct his factory.[130]

After his first discussion with Wood, Mir Hoseyn had left for Shiraz in June 1755 to complain about Sheikh Naser's past and continued support of Mir Mohanna. As a result Karim Khan wrote the Dutch informing them that he had appointed Mir Hoseyn as chief of Bandar-e Rig and asking them to assist Mir Hoseyn against his enemies. Von Kniphausen sent a neutral reply and promised nothing. In September 1755 Karim Khan sent an express messenger to Khark with the

---

127 Grummond, *The Rise*, 83, n. 39 believes that Wood insisted on a division of the normal customs duties, thus copying a situation that existed at Bandar 'Abbas.

128 VOC 2864, Khark to Batavia (27/02/1755), f. 41-43; VOC 2864, Gamron to Batavia (31/03/1755), f. 16.

129 Saldanha, *Précis*, vol. 1, p. 91-92 (Bombay, 18/10/1754); Ibid. vol. 1, p. 95 (Gombroon, 02/12/1755).

130 VOC 2864, Khark to Batavia (31/05/1755), f. 41-43; Saldanha, *Précis*, vol. 1, p. 95-96 (Gombroon, 02/12/1755), 97 (Bombay, 09/03/1756) (the soldiers for Bandar-e Rig were sent per the *Ali Rooka Grab*); Amin, *British Interests*, pp. 37-39; Lorimer, *Gazetteer*, p. 112. Mir Hoseyn's willingness makes it hardly likely that the latter had anything to do with Mir Mohanna's action in April 1755 as von Kniphausen has it.

request to send him a physician to heal a certain Sheikh 'Ali. Von Kniphausen sent senior-surgeon Filch, who at the same time was charged to complain to Karim Khan about Sheikh Naser's hostile activities. Karim Khan replied that if he was unable to call Sheikh Naser to order he permitted the Dutch to do so. This reply shows that Karim Khan's hold over the littoral was still very shaky. Von Kniphausen was very annoyed about this answer, because he was very vexed by Sheikh Naser's decision to levy 10% customs duties on all goods coming from Khark. Sheikh Naser had made it clear that the sole purpose of this measure was to induce merchants not to buy anything on Khark. In Bandar-e Rig, Ganaveh and Deylam the local chiefs only levied 3% or less on imports. Although these towns were better situated than Bushire as far as transportation to Shiraz was concerned, Bushire boasted of the presence of a few Persian merchants. These had a large share in caravans coming from upcountry and therefore other Persian merchants were wont to stick to them to get their share of trade as well.[131]

FINAL VOC WITHDRAWAL FROM BASRA

In 1754, von Kniphausen had sold the Dutch factory in Basra to Shaw, the EIC Agent, for 13,500 *qorush*. Both the XVII and Batavia were furious about this, because they had never given von Kniphausen orders to do so, because this was the exclusive prerogative of the XVII. Although the latter protested that he thought that his instruction authorized him to sell the factory, Batavia wrote that the entire cost would be charged to his personal account. Von Kniphausen seems to have been in the right here, because his orders stated that he could abandon the factories at Basra and Bushire at his own discretion.[132] Soleyman Pasha was equally upset by the departure of the Dutch, for his revenues had diminished. He "left no stone unturned to get the Dutch to transfer themselves to Basra, proposing so many opportunities, so many favours: and when it proved to no avail, became so obsequious as to send an Aga from his court at Baghdad with a robe of honour to Kharg."[133] On February 25, 1755 this emissary, named Mohammad 'Ali Beyg, arrived on Khark with the robe of honor and other presents. He asked the Dutch to return to Basra and to give assurances that the Dutch would undertake no actions against Turkish territory. Because he had been instructed not to antagonize the Pasha, and it was in Khark's interest to have good relations with Basra, Mohammad 'Ali Beyg was sent back with Dfl. 3,000 in presents and a friendly letter assuring Soleyman Pasha of Dutch friendship. However, without permission from the XVII the Dutch could not return to Basra, von Kniphausen wrote.[134]

---

131 VOC 2885, Khark to Batavia (27/09/1755), f. 5-7. The XVII, of course, pointed out that they were proven right once again about what would happen in Khark. VOC 335, XVII to Batavia (10/10/1759), section Karreek, not foliated. The sick person concerned probably was Sheikh 'Ali Zand, Karim Khan's brother.

132 VOC 2864, Khark to Batavia (01/11/1754), f. 15 (the VOC lost 1,858 *qorush* on this sale compared with the original purchase price of 15,358 *qorush*, which difference von Kniphausen had to pay); VOC 1009, Batavia to Khark (22/04/1755), f. 73; VOC 334, XVII to Batavia (10/10/1758), section Karreek, not foliated; VOC 2885, Khark to Batavia (09/12/1755), f. 8.

133 Anonymous, *Chronicle*, vol. 1, p. 692.

134 VOC 2864, Khark to Batavia (27/02/1755), f. 37. Soleyman Pasha had written to Istanbul that the Khark factory was disadvantageous to the Ottoman Empire and other nations (meaning the English and French). De Hochepied wrote von Kniphausen that thanks to his influential friends at court Soleyman Pasha's attacks had no effect. His main problem was the reduced customs revenue at Basra about which he continued to complain to the Porte. De Hochepied had promised information to the Porrte showing that Soleyman Pasha was wrong. For further information see also NA, Legatie Archief Turkije, no. 168, de Hochepied to von Kniphausen (01/06/1756),

Von Kniphausen had no intention whatsoever to re-establish the VOC factory in Basra, because he feared that this would hurt sales of the Khark factory. Schoonderwoerd, the VOC director at Bandar 'Abbas, however, argued that it would boost VOC sales. He therefore suggested that the VOC should send one or two persons to Basra, who could order goods from Khark, which would function as a kind of warehouse. They should order small lots and send the proceeds of the sale immediately to Khark, after which they could order new merchandise. To facilitate this option a small VOC barque should ply between Basra and Khark, which also could be used for trips to Masqat, where trade was flourishing and where one might sell goods at higher prices than at Bandar 'Abbas. Schoonderwoerd did this for his own reasons, being envious of von Kniphausen's success. Although he was formally von Kniphausen's superior in reality he had no say at all over Khark. Moreover, trade in Bandar 'Abbas got worse, so that Schoonderwoerd looked for other possibilities to boost his image. As a result there was petty friction between the two Dutch factories and there was hardly any communication between them. Bandar 'Abbas sometimes took goods destined for Khark from the ships coming from Batavia, while also sending invendible goods to Khark. These were normal practices, but in this context, where Bandar 'Abbas also tried to increase sales that hurt Khark, was resented by von Kniphausen, because Batavia had decided that all efforts should be made to increase sales at Khark. After a few years the factory at Bandar 'Abbas was to be abandoned, but Schoonderwoerd was acting as if he had been ordered to put the trade at Bandar 'Abbas at its former footing.[135]

Unaware of the budding friction between the Khark and Bandar 'Abbas factories Batavia accepted Schoonderwoerd's proposal, instructed von Kniphausen to use his gallivat for the Basra trade and promised to send him two additional assistants.[136] The XVII were completely baffled by this decision. They reminded Batavia that the rationale for Khark had been to avoid extortion, trouble with local chiefs, heavy customs duties and the unattractive port facilities at Basra. By agreeing to Schoonderwoerd's proposal Batavia was acting against the raison d'être of the Khark factory. By opening a sales office at Basra there was no incentive for merchants to come to Khark, why then should the VOC maintain this factory. Out of which profits would this Basra operation be financed, and what guarantee was there that the VOC would have to face the same difficulties as in 1753? If Khark was only to be a warehouse then this was to the detriment of VOC commercial interests, for merchants would prefer to go directly to Basra, where the VOC only could show some samples or at best a small range of goods only. It was further absurd to think that the VOC could transport merchandise cheaper from Khark to Basra than native merchants, apart from the fact however cheap these cost might be that they were additional cost. This would have to be paid for by higher prices,

---

f. 229-30. Perry, "Mir Muhanna," p. 86 summarizes the gist of the letters exchanged between von Kniphausen and Soleyman Pasha. According to de Hochepied, Soleyman Pasha, through his envoy, presented von Kniphausen with a well-accoutered horse, saber and a furred robe of honor. He also offered to dismiss and punish the *motasallem* of Basra and appoint a new one who was acceptable to von Kniphausen as part of the incentives to induce the Dutch back to Basra. NA, Staaten-Generaal, Lias Turkije, nr. 7005, de Hochepied to Fagel (02/05/1755). Notwithstanding the good relations between Khark and Basra the Porte still did not know in which way its *farman* had been implemented by Soleyman Pasha. The Porte therefore asked de Hochepied to find out how matters stood, because Soleyman Pasha, the French and English were all saying that Khark was a threat to Ottoman interests in case of war with Persia at the same time insinuating that the Dutch had other ambitions than just carrying out trade in the Persian Gulf. NA, Staaten-Generaal, nr. 7005, Lias Turkije, de Hochepied to Fagel (17/05/1755); see also NA, Stadhouderlijk Secretarie, nr. 1.29.5.

135 VOC 2863, Schoonderwoerd to Batavia (31/03/1755), f. 18; VOC 2885, Khark to Batavia (09/12/1755), f. 4-7.

136 VOC 1009, Batavia to Khark (28/07/1755), f. 258-59.

but was there a guarantee that the VOC could obtain these at Basra and higher than before Khark had been established? Moreover, Batavia itself had written that trade at Basra at the prices obtaining in the past was of little interest to the VOC, so how would the expected advantages materialize? With these parting words the VOC directors made it clear what they thought about the past decision to establish Khark as well as it future prospects.[137]

Von Kniphausen as expected reacted negatively to the proposal. He replied that he, of course, would comply with the order, and he also would try to get the factory back because Shaw had not paid yet. However, his experience so far as well as information that he regularly received from native merchants taught him that the Company's interests were better served at Khark, which was more profitable and secure. A trial batch of goods that he had sent to Basra had met with little success, thus reinforcing his opinion. Moreover, the *motasallem*'s current behavior was not very conducive to the development trade, because he pressed native merchants not to do any trade with European merchants. The *motasallem* wanted to become the sole importer of goods imported by European merchants, which he then wanted to sell to native merchants with a profit. According to von Kniphausen, the English had sold their goods only to the *motasallem* during the last two years, a practice which the VOC always had opposed. He therefore also had contacted Aleppo merchants in Basra who were interested in fine, white Bengal fabrics, which were only marketed in Turkey. They had bought a lot of these fabrics and had sent them via Kuwait (Green) to Aleppo. Von Kniphausen wanted to stimulate this trade via Kuwait, because this allowed merchants to circumvent payment of heavy customs duties at Basra and he hoped that they would respond by coming directly to Khark.[138]

Although von Kniphausen admitted that prices for VOC goods at Basra were higher than at Khark, he pointed out that this was due to the longer credit terms (four months) that had to be granted. He strongly advised against such practices as it would expose the Company to bankruptcies by merchants buying on those terms. Although prices indeed seemed higher, this was mainly because of the 12% difference in conversion rates used between Basra and the VOC. On January 30, 1756 van der Hulst[139] and assistant Nicolai arrived in Basra with the barque *'tLoo* with a cargo of Bengal textiles with a value of Dfl. 106,000, where they stayed for one month. Nicolai would make an evaluation of the market of Basra taking into account the difference in prices and of the cost of living. The VOC team had to act as if they were there to finalize the sale of the factory and if buyers were found they should not unload the goods, but only show samples as much as possible. On their arrival they found Basra in total uproar; the English and French Agents had fled to Baghdad, because of a conflict with the *motasallem*. After one month they returned having spent 25,000 rupees in presents and having received little satisfaction. Trade was bad; no goods could be sold for cash, only at 3-6 months credit, which was against Batavia's orders to meet these higher cost. Also, the cost of living was much higher than expected and van der Hulst sent Nicolai back to Khark, because his pay did not suffice. Despite a very friendly reception by and presents from the *motasallem*, van der Hulst advised against any further trade with Basra. He pointed that even Armenian merchants, the sharpest traders in the Persian Gulf, had been forced to sell their Bengal textiles at 9-months'

---

137 VOC 334, XVII to Batavia (10/10/1759), section Karreek, not foliated.

138 VOC 2885, Khark to Batavia (09/12/1755), f. 11-16; VOC 2864, Khark to Batavia (31/05/1755), f. 49-50; Amin, *British Interests*, p. 135.

139 This was van der Hulst's last voyage to Basra, before he would return to Batavia. His successor, Wilhelmus Buschman had arrived at Khark on December 21, 1755 with *'tHuys ten Duyn*. For a brief biography of Buschman see Resandt, *Gezaghebbers*, p. 258; see also Niebuhr, *Beschreibung*, p. 318. The English believed that "the Dutch had re-established their Factory" at Basra. Saldanha, *Précis*, vol. 1, p. 97 (Bombay, 09/03/1756).

credit to merchants from Diyarbekr. This situation had been brought about by the English and the French who had imported large quantities of the same commodity. The English and French, who sold these goods at low prices, therefore accepted precious stones, copper, wheat and various drugs in lieu of cash payment. If the VOC would do the same it would have to sell spices only, he commented. Because of the barter nature of trade van der Hulst was not able to give an indication of prices of goods in cash sales. Batavia went along with the recommendation to discontinue the Basra office. The XVII bitingly remarked that they had not been surprised by the result of the trade mission. What else could have been expected, because Batavia's orders were directed at the very justification of the Khark factory.[140]

MIR HOSEYN'S MURDER

The abundant imports combined with the fact that transit trade via Persia had been abandoned since mid-1755 had caused a complete standstill of trade in the upper part of the Persian Gulf. The Dutch did not expect this situation to change soon, because anarchy continued to prevail in Persia. According to von Kniphausen, anyone who had the command over a few hundred of men and a reasonable amount of courage was able to secure a province for himself and might even participate in the contest for the throne. He cited Karim Khan as an example, who had subjugated the littoral with only 600 horsemen. In October 1755, he had even forced them to accompany him to Isfahan. Depending on their importance they each had to supply Karim Khan with 200-300 men, so that the latter commanded an army of 10,000. With this army he had taken Isfahan, where Azad Khan had only a small garrison. Karim Khan had imposed a contribution on the population of Isfahan and had ruled there until December 1755, when he had been attacked by Mohammad Hasan Khan Qajar. The coastal chiefs, against their will, had been drawn into the power struggle between Karim Khan and the other contenders for the throne. In March 1756, the Dashtestan and other levies from the littoral had refused to fight as a result of which Karim Khan was forced to flee to Shiraz by Mohammad Hasan Khan Qajar. The latter disarmed, stripped and plundered the Dashtestan troops and let them return home. However, he kept three of their most important chiefs in prison, amongst whom Sheikh Naser of Bushire, who had to give "an account of the Kings Ships and paying also 5,000 Tomaunds for the last three years' revenues of Bahreen". Among those who returned, in a miserable state, were Mir Hoseyn and Mir Mohanna, "in consideration of their known poverty," who had been held in custody in Shiraz for almost one year.[141] On April 20, 1756 they, accompanied by Qa'ed Heydar of Ganaveh, arrived at Bandar-e Rig having made the journey of foot. Wood found them "quite bare of provisions, clothes and money" and therefore had been unavoidably obliged to give them clothes and money as well as a present, "Consisting chiefly of Rice and piece goods to the amount of near three hundred and sixty (360) Rupees."[142]

During Mir Hoseyn's absence Wood had started to build a fort on an elevated place in the center of Bandar-e Rig. The fort, a copy of Mosselsteijn, was almost completed when Mir Hoseyn returned. Their deprivations had made them forget their former enmity and discord and the two

140 VOC 2885, Khark to Batavia (05/08/1756), f. 5-8. Saldanha, *Précis*, vol. 1, p. 105 mentions that the fact the *motasallem* was turned out also played a role in this negative advice; see also Ibid., vol. 1, p. 99 (Bandar-e Rig, 03/05/756). Lorimer, *Gazetteer*, p. 1209 on the difficulties of the French and English. VOC 334, XVII to Batavia (10/10/1759), section Karreek, not foliated.

141 VOC 2885, Khark to Batavia (05/08/1756), f. 8-11; Perry, *Karim Khan*, p. 69-70; Roschan-Zamir, *Zand-Dynastie*, pp. 35-36; Saldanha, *Précis*, vol. 1, p. 100 (Bandar-e Rig, 03/05/756).

142 Lorimer, *Gazetteer*, p. 112; Saldanha, *Précis*, vol. 1, p. 100.

apparently reconciled brothers had decided to govern together and Wood promised them that Bandar-e Rig would flourish as a result of the presence of the EIC factory. However, this required that the Dutch factory did not prosper. The three of them deliberated what their strategy should be. Wood argued that open hostility would be counterproductive as Dutch naval power was too strong for the Bandar-e Rig gallivats. A night attack with three small native vessels would be more successful. The attacking force should land on some isolated spots and from there would have to pillage and set fire to the many dispersed houses made of mats and reeds. The attackers would have to retreat by day-break. These attacks had to be repeated a few times after which the inhabitants might be induced to leave Khark so that the Dutch would be left alone in their fort.[143]

Because von Kniphausen had been informed about this plan he and Buschman discussed how to prevent it. They agreed that they did not have enough military to prevent night attacks on the island. Moreover, any preventive military measures on land might create fear among the rich inhabitants who then would flee. They finally decided to put a naval screen between Khark and Bandar-e Rig consisting of the gallivat, the barque *'tLoo* and the ship *de Crabbendijke* and block both arms of the river at Bandar-e Rig. However, Batavia might consider such an action too hasty and therefore it was decided that it would be their contingency plan. To have an excuse to break with the Dutch, so von Kniphausen alleged, the two brothers had to look for one. On their return from Isfahan von Kniphausen had given them presents and had sold them goods on credit. It was finally Wood, according to von Kniphausen, who suggested that they sent a letter to him in which they claimed 900 *tumans* per year rent for Khark, which the Dutch had promised to pay, according to reliable witnesses. Von Kniphausen replied that such an agreement had never been concluded, but if they would submit written evidence he would pay, of course. This reply was hand carried by the VOC interpreter, who had orders to talk to the brothers in private, and try to convince them of the error of their ways and to sow doubt in their hearts about the English fort. He had to tell them that the fort was not a trading station, being right in the center of Bandar-e Rig, but rather served as an English instrument to subdue them. This worked out well, in so far that Mir Mohanna gave a letter to the VOC interpreter in which he claimed that Mir Hoseyn and not he was the cause of the current dispute with the Dutch. He did not approve of it and also intended to resolve that issue shortly. Von Kniphausen must have had an idea of, if not a hand in, what was going to happen. For on May 28, 1756 Wood received a letter from him in which von Kniphausen warned him "to be aware of the impending danger, for that he himself had at last come to a Resolution of Chastising the Meer and I might expect Bunderick to be involved in troubles very suddenly."[144] However, von Kniphausen does not mention ever to have written such a warning note to Wood. In fact, he reported that Wood had grown so confident about the imminent rupture between the Dutch and Mirs Hoseyn and Mohanna that he felt safe enough to make a short trip to Basra to buy construction materials. Wood, however, reported that he feared for his own life, given the fact the Mir Mohanna's men "are more abjects than slaves," because his men had no arms and he needed timber to complete the factory, which "I was very anxious to have in a posture of defence before the Dutch party in favor of Shaik Ally Mossom and Meer Manna might come to a head sufficient to dispossess Meer Hassain of the Government. He therefore left to Basra for a few days to back come when the storm was over, but without warning Mir Hoseyn, who was killed on June 6, 1756 together with a number of men, whom Wood called "my friends." Mir Mohanna gave out that his brother had tried to kill him with the support of a neighboring chief. A few days later Mir Mohanna sent his half-brother Mir 'Ali to

143 This alleged scheme is not confirmed by published English sources. VOC 2885, Khark to Batavia (05/07/1756), f. 11-17.

144 Saldanha, *Précis*, vol. 1, p. 101; Perry, "Mir Muhanna," p. 88; Lorimer, *Gazetteer*, pp. 115-16.

von Kniphausen to assure him of his good intentions towards the Dutch. Von Kniphausen, who considered Mir 'Ali the only one of the Vaqa'i family to have sense and good judgment, suggested that as proof of such good intentions the demolition of the English fort would do nicely. On June 20, shortly after Mir 'Ali's return to Bandar-e Rig the demolition of the English fort was begun, which was completely razed. Wood returned from Basra on June 22, 1756 and decided to stay on Khark for the time being, although he had brought arms with him to defend his house. He collected more information and then sold his construction materials on Khark. He went to Bandar-e Rig on June 27, where Mir Mohanna explained that he could not possibly permit the construction of a fort in the center of Bandar-e Rig. Wood was free to build one on the beach, in which case he would receive all the assistance that he required.[145] The EIC Agent at Bandar 'Abbas was furious and scoffed at Wood's claim that he had left Bandar-e Rig, because he had feared for his life. If that were the case why were none of his people subjected to any violence during the takeover, he asked? If he really had been so worried why did not he warn Mir Hoseyn about the designs that the Dutch and Mir Mohanna had against him? Because he had no arms and timber he should have stayed rather than have left. Douglas urged him to do his utmost to convince Mir Mohanna of the advantages of having the EIC settlement at Bandar-e Rig.[146] Batavia was very pleased with the turn of events and assured von Kniphausen that "the prevention of this action does not leave us disinterested." The XVII were not taken in by these events. Experience had taught them that such events were usually reported by those who had ulterior motives, viz. to get a promotion or make a reputation for themselves. If it were true, then von Kniphausen had behaved irresponsibly by allowing Wood to stay at Khark for such a long time.[147]

Wood stayed in Bandar-e Rig, but he was unable to rebuild his factory. In fact, until the day he left and despite his protests, Mir Mohanna used many laborers to carry away the building materials of the destroyed EIC fort to build a wall around his town, with which he was still busy when Wood left Bandar-e Rig. Mir Mohanna also did not allow Wood "Collecting Dutys from merchants trading under the English Protection, unless I would agree to pay him two thousand Rupees a year." Mir Mohanna was not interested to listen to Wood's arguments that the presence of an EIC factory would be beneficial to Bandar-e Rig's welfare and his own revenues. He described Mir Mohanna as "a young indiscreet young man wholly given up to the most destructive vices, and so extremely Revengefull that it's dangerous to give him even the slightest occasion of offence [...] his intemperance in point of Drinking at frequent, nay almost daily visits." Wood advised against the use of two EIC ships (the *Drake* and the *Swallow*) to demand satisfaction, because he agreed with its commanders that their force was not strong enough. They could not land more than 70 men, while the EIC gallivats could not come closer to Bandar-e Rig that at two miles distance. Mir Mohanna had more than 500 armed men within one hour's warning, "who are tolerably good Soldiers when stationed in houses or behind Walls according to their manner of fighting." Moreover, Mir Mohanna was "miserably poor," while the inhabitants of Bandar-e Rig only had salt fish and dates, so unless

145 VOC 2885, Khark to Batavia (05/08/1756), f. 17-20; Saldanha, *Précis*, vol. 1, pp. 101-02 (according to Wood, to raze the EIC factory "it is currently reported that the Dutch gave Meer Manna two thousand Rupees and Shaikh Ally Mossoom having also received twelve hundred Rupees and four Sharols from them.")

146 Saldanha, *Précis*, vol. 1, pp. 103-04. In Basra, Wood had told the EIC staff that he feared that Bandar-e Rig would meet with little success and "the preference that shou'd in his opinion be given to a settlement at Bushire which was absolutely contrary to what Mr. Wood had wrote to Gombroon a few days after." Ibid., vol. 1, p. 105 (Bombay, 16/09/1756).

147 VOC 1011, Batavia to Khark (06/04/1657), f. 83; VOC 334, XVII to Batavia (10/10/1758), section Kareek, not foliated.

the EIC force could seize a few trankis and the gallivats belonging to Mir Mohanna there would be no gain. He counseled therefore to remain on a friendly footing with Bandar-e Rig. It was to no avail, however. Wood was suddenly ordered to leave with all other Europeans at 10 o'clock P.M. on November 6, 1756 within half an hour, because Mir Mohanna suspected the English to be his enemies. Wood pleaded with "Shaik Channon" who had been sent to carry out the expulsion. He even refused 40 rupees if he would allow Wood to talk to "Hodjee Hossain Saffary the Meambassy of the Tribe a sedate and well disposed man." However, Sheikh Channon was afraid of Mir Mohanna's displeasure and told his men, who had their matches burning, to expel the English staff. Wood and his men then left with nothing but the clothes on their back and boarded the *Dragon*. During that night the Indian EIC guards, who had remained behind, were disarmed, after which money, merchandise and provisions were carried away. The next day Mir Mohanna sent Aqa Mahmud and invited Wood to come ashore again. Wood, however, did not trust either Mir Mohanna or his officers, who had accused him of all kinds of things. He took Aqa Mahmud prisoner and informed Mir Mohanna that he would release him once he would have received his money and goods. He also sent him two barrels of gun powder as a friendly gesture. As a result Wood received his goods within the course of ten days, except for those that had been stolen during the first night. In exchange for those goods Mir Mohanna offered the lives of the two men who had been entrusted with the guarding of Wood's house. Wood refused this and because he also knew that Mir Mohanna would rather let Aqa Mahmud live in slavery than return the money and goods he released him and sailed away. Wood was reprimanded by his superiors about the way he had handled the Bandar-e Rig affair, including that he had misrepresented the trade prospects of a factory at Bandar-e Rig.[148]

Douglas left it to Wood what to do. "If you thought that you could Establish a factory either there [Bandar-e Rig] or at any other port in the Gulph you might wait for a more favourable opportunity but if that was not practicable you might return."[149] Wood replied that in his opinion the only eligible place for a factory was Bandar-e Rig, for there the sale of English cloth could be greatly increased. Also, the EIC's Indian settlements could be supplied from there with grain and wine. Furthermore, the Dutch would be prevented from settling there, to engross the whole trade of Bandar-e Rig, as they would now certainly do,

> both on account of Trade and the Convenience of getting provision, as in winter season they have no certain supply from any other Port, they find also that the Persian Merchants are very averse to risking their Goods over thither in Boats, (as in case of a southerly wind) without which they cannot go from Busshier; it's an even chance they are dashed to pieces on the Rocks; and if we were able to supply them with Goods upon the Continent not a man of them would ever purchase of the Dutch; and their schemes of that island must of course be totally translated.

Wood emphasized that the EIC did not have the force (a ship like the *Swallow* and 200 soldiers and a couple of gallivats to lie in the river) to establish such a factory, because that would be required, because one could not rely on whatever Mir Mohanna said, who, moreover, would create all kind of obstacles instigated by the Dutch. However, with the necessary force available Mir Mohanna would become cooperative and help with labor and materials to build the factory.[150] It

148 Saldanha, *Précis*, vol. 1, p. 108-12 (in the Bandar-e Rig roads a/b the Swallow, 18/11/1756); Amin, *British Interests*, p. 38; Lorimer, *Gazetteer*, p. 115.

149 Saldanha, *Précis*, vol. 1, p. 111 (Gombroon, 05/12/756).

150 Saldanha, *Précis*, vol. 1, pp. 111-12 (Gombroon, 05/12/756).

was clear that Wood had learnt nothing from his experience and had to have recourse to the Dutch bogeyman to try and incite the EIC into action, which it wisely declined to do.

After these events Bandar-e Rig declined in importance, "and it appears to go towards its total ruin."[151] All Armenian, Banyan and Moslem merchants left as did its inhabitants who had some wealth. Von Kniphausen expected that within one year Bandar-e Rig would have become an unimportant fishing village once again. Mir Mohanna was drunk every day and surrounded himself with a group of licentious people, who had killed his father and brother. Caravans henceforth avoided Bandar-e Rig. In a similar fashion Bushire also suffered because all merchants abandoned the town when the news of Sheikh Naser's imprisonment was received. The merchants feared that they would have to pay his ransom and therefore left, some of whom settled on Khark with their families. One of them was a very wealthy merchant, Aqa Ebrahim, who was reputed to possess five lakh of rupees. As a result the ports of Deylam and Ganaveh prospered; its chiefs tried to attract caravans and foster good relations with the Dutch.[152] This was exactly the opposite what Mir Naser had in mind when he had asked the Dutch to settle on Khark. An English market assessment of 1790 saw this relationship as follows:

> To this Establishment of the Dutch Factory at Carrack, the little Port of Bundereeg situated on the Persian shore nearly opposite the Island of Carrack, became endebted for many Advantages. The Ports of Bushire and Bundereeg though situated at much the same distance, by Water from the Island of Carrack, differed very materially in respect to their situation to Scherauze, the Market for which the greatest parts of the Dutch Imports were designed. A Cofla [sic; from Arabic *qafila* or caravan] departing from the former of these Ports, for Scherauze, generally performed its Journey in twelve to fourteen days, whilst those who proceeded from the latter, required no more than Seven to Eight days on the Road. This difference in Time of performing, necessarily created a difference in the Expence of the Journey, and the Dutch Commpany or on Account of private Merchants, uniformly preferred to land them at Bundereeg rather than at Bushire; fortunately however for the Port of Bushire, the Governor of Bundereeg was a character but little entitled to the confidence of the Merchants, the greatest part of whom, residing at Bushire, made frequent Commercial Trips from thence to Carrack and concluded large Purchases there of Spices and Sugars, which on their return to Bushire were dispatched from thence to Schrauze. The Port of Bundereeg depending entirely upon the settlement at Carrack for its Commercial Importance, relapsed naturally, into its former obscurity.[153]

DUTCH RELATIONS WITH KARIM KHAN

At the end of 1756, Karim Khan marched with 15,000 men towards the Dashtestan to collect taxes from its chiefs and by January he had imposed his will on them. Qa'ed Heydar of Ganaveh

151 Floor, "Description," p. 173.

152 VOC 2885, Khark to Batavia (05/08/1756), f. 20-21.

153 Saldanha, *Précis*, vol. 1, p. 430 (Report on the Commerce of Arabia and Persia by Samuel Manesty and Harford Jones, 1790). This quote ends with the line "on the Dutch withdrawing themselves from that Island," which shows that the author's of the report did not know the detailed history of the Khark factory.

had refused to submit to Karim Khan, who then laid siege to Ganaveh. Karim Khan received naval assistance from Mir Mohanna with three gallivats during the siege. When Mir Mohanna sighted a gallivat with merchandise coming from Basra he abandoned the blockade and took the vessel, with its goods and merchants, which belonged to von Kniphausen. Karim Khan was furious about this act of piracy and laid siege to Bandar-e Rig as well. He had the inhabitants know that if Mir Mohanna did not surrender within three days the town would be plundered and razed. To ingratiate himself with Karim Khan and to take revenge for his seized gallivat, von Kniphausen wanted to contain Mir Mohanna from the seaside, but contrary winds made that impossible during those three days. Nevertheless, it forced Mir Mohanna to surrender to Karim Khan and he therefore lusted for revenge.[154] He in vain tried to induce Karim Khan to launch an attack on Khark to plunder its alleged riches. Von Kniphausen sent his interpreter to Karim Khan with presents and assured him that the Dutch were only there to carry on trade. He expressed the hope that Karim Khan would become the sole ruler over a peaceful Persia, which would be good for trade. Karim Khan gave a friendly reply, a robe of honor and returned the gallivat seized by Mir Mohanna to von Kniphausen. Unfortunately, most of the goods in that gallivat had been lost for which compensation was promised. Despite this promise, von Kniphausen, knowing human nature, seized all goods on Khark belonging to inhabitants of Khark as security. Mir Mohanna made an effort to convince Karim Khan that the Dutch had not honored the agreement made with his father of paying an annual fee for the use of Khark. In fact, they even denied the existence of such an agreement. Karim Khan preferred to have friendly relations with the Dutch and told Mir Mohanna that he as overlord made Khark a present to the Dutch and that he did not want to discuss the matter anymore. Karim Khan appointed Mir 'Ali, Mir Mohanna's cousin, the chief of Bandar-e Rig, because he was well-disposed towards the Dutch and von Kniphausen welcomed the appointment as Mir 'Ali was the only man in the family from whom one might expect something positive. Karim Khan continued to plunder and subjugate the coastal area during the winter of 1757 and laid siege to Behbahan in October 1757, where he obtained booty of six lakh of rupees in cash, gold and silverware and much copperware. He then returned to Shiraz taking the chiefs of the littoral or their children as hostages with him.[155]

Towards the end of 1757 the cost of life necessities became very high, due to a bad date harvest and the destruction of the agricultural fields by Karim Khan's troops earlier that year. Von Kniphausen therefore ordered rice from Batavia. Although the expected downfall of Karim Khan did not happen it was expected any time. Von Kniphausen believed that by mid-1758 Mohammad Hasan Khan would have eliminated his rivals and he wrote to Batavia that once Persia had an uncontested ruler again thus would be good for trade. However, things turned out different and the Dutch were not happy, because chaos and anarchy still held Persia in their grip. Exasperatedly von Kniphausen commented that Persia was where it had been in 1756.[156] Encouraged by his success against Mohammad Hasan Khan Qajar, Karim Khan sent a victory note to all coastal chiefs, who

154 VOC 2885, Khark to Batavia (16/01/1757), f. 34-35; VOC 2937, Khark to Batavia (29/10/1757), f. 5-7.

155 VOC 2937, Khark to Batavia (29/10/1757), f. 7-11; VOC 2885, Khark to Batavia (16/01/1757), f. 35-36. According to Ricks, *Politics and Trade*, p. 264 referring to F. R. Gombroon IX (04/04/1757) Mir Mohanna's replacement was a certain Mir Mohammad. As far as the Companies were concerned they only cared that any strong ruler would take charge of the country, who "undoubtedly appoint proper persons to reduced [sic] these petty Shaiks to his obedience and give encouragement to all merchants." Saldanha, *Précis*, vol. 1, p. 104. Despite his overtures to Karim Khan, von Kniphausen was convinced that the man who would win the throne of Persia would be Mohammad Hasan Khan Qajar.

156 VOC 2968, Khark to Batavia (18/05/1758), f. 23-24; Perry, *Karim Khan*, pp. 71ff.

were ordered to pay a certain sum. Sheikh Naser of Bushire had to pay 60,000 rupees. Karim Khan also talked about attacking Bushire and other coastal towns to punish them for some infraction, but instead he went to Yazd. Mir Mohanna remained under arrest from which he was released in July 1758 at the intercession of one of his influential officers, Mohammad Beyg, the chief of Khormuj, who had married Mir Mohanna's sister. On the promise of the payment of a sum of money Mir Mohanna was released and also reinstated as chief of Bandar-e Rig. On his return Mir Mohanna killed his half-brother, Mir 'Ali and two cousins. He also made friendly overtures to the Dutch, who also remained friendly towards him.[157]

THE RISE OF MIR MOHANNA THE PIRATE

Because Karim Khan was too busy consolidating his power in Persia Mir Mohanna started on his road towards notoriety by bringing navigation in the Persian Gulf to a complete standstill for some time. Despite his dissolute lifestyle he had not been idle. In the first half of 1756 the Dutch had described the situation at Bandar-e Rig as down-hill and its naval capacity in similar terms.

> The ship of the said Nadier Scha's fleet which was still lying at Bender Riek and whose hull was still complete and in good condition two years ago has sunk during this winter. It remains lying there, the topmasts, yards, sails and ropes have all perished. There are still two gallivats in a passable condition, but these will very soon become unusable because of neglect. Apart from that there are about 30 both big and small vessels and about 300 sea-faring able-bodied men.[158]

However, three years later the situation had changed significantly. In early November 1759, he attacked the Soerse Arabs[159] who lived near Basra. He sent his three gallivats into the Shat al-Arab claiming that he only wanted to collect what was due to him. However, there were no debts, only a pretext for piracy. The Soerse Arabs united their forces and Mir Mohanna withdrew. He took a number of native vessels intending to live off the proceeds of his piracy. The division of the plunder attracted all kinds of criminal elements to his home-base at Bandar-e Rig. Every 20 or 30 days one of Mir Mohanna's gallivats went to sea for four days and then returned dragging a tranki behind it. Mir Mohanna's piracy worried von Kniphausen, because it endangered traffic to and from Khark, while the pirates had become vain and proud of their success. The Dutch had written to Mir Mohanna asking him to return the goods seized by him that belonged to inhabitants of Khark. As Mir Mohanna did not bother to reply the Dutch felt that they were justified in taking measures against him, the more so, since he took trankis in the sight of Khark, one of which belonged to Qa'ed Heydar. His vessels were no longer given access to Khark and were chased away if they came too close to the island. However, this was ineffective, because Mir Mohanna's vessels had large crews

157 VOC 2968, Khark to Batavia (15/11/1758), f. 16-18 (von Kniphausen sent a present to Karim Khan with a value of Dfl. 1,745); Perry, "Mir Muhanna," p. 89; Nami, *Tarikh*, p. 161. Mohammad Beyg, son of Mirza 'Ali Beyg Khormuji Dashtestani, was a strong supporter of Karim Khan and had played an important role at the battle of Khesht against Azad Khan, hence his influence. Fasa'i, *Farsnameh*, vol. 1, pp. 609-10.

158 Floor, "Description," p. 173.

159 The Soerse Arabs probably are the Arabs from Sir (Ra's al-Khaymah), otherwise known as the Qavasem, who once dwelled on the northern littoral of the Gulf, but being harassed by their neighbors had moved to the Arabian coast. They were one of the Arab tribes mainly employed in transporting coffee by sea. Niebuhr, *Travels*, vol. 2, pp. 123-24; see also J.B. Kelly, *Britain and the Persian Gulf, 1795-1880* (Oxford, 1968), p. 18.

with many oars and they always escaped. Things got a turn for the better on April 4, 1759 when Dutch gallivats seized one and chased another of Mir Mohanna's vessels when they were trying to seize a tranki. The Bandar-e Rig vessel fled over the banks, but the Basra tranki could not pass because it drew too much water and the pirates left it there. The commander of the Dutch gallivat *de Draak* did not know the shoals too well there and decided not to give chase but to stay with the Basra tranki, for there was only four feet of water. The Bandar-e Rig pirates believed that the Dutch gallivat had some problem with its rigging, and because the other Dutch gallivat *de Tijger* was still about 3 km away they believed they could take *de Draak*. The pirates therefore hurried back from the safety behind the banks to the Dutch gallivat which allowed them to approach until they were within shooting distance of their muskets. The crew of *de Draak* then welcomed the pirates by firing every arm that they had, which caused panic among the pirates who jumped overboard and tried to haul their vessel across the banks. *De Draak* weighed anchor and prevented this and thus took the best of Mir Mohanna's gallivats. However, the other gallivat got away before *de Tijger* had arrived. This incident led to a temporary halt in Mir Mohanna's piracy activities, although his marauding activities on land continued looking for wheat and cattle. Von Kniphausen received accolades from the mercantile and shipping community in the Persian Gulf and from Batavia, but not from the XVII, who did not see VOC trade increase because of this and they did not care about the satisfaction of the natives at their expense.[160]

Although the Dutch had scored a victory over Mir Mohanna they also had created a problem for themselves. Until that time they had relied for food supplies on procurement mainly via Bandar-e Rig. Von Kniphausen therefore looked for alternative sources of supply and decided to maintain closer ties with Qa'ed Heydar of Ganaveh. Although he considered Qa'ed Heydar quite an unsavory character, but a relationship with him had two advantages. First, Qa'ed Heydar was a thorn in Mir Mohanna's side as the two were sworn enemies. Second, in this way the Dutch acquired access to abundant food supplies at Ganaveh. The friendship was concluded with a present costing Dfl. 713.[161] Batavia was less happy about the new relationship and admonished von Kniphausen reminding that presents were to be given only when unavoidable. The XVII also frowned on the giving of the present and the friendship, but they agreed that the rupture with Mir Mohanna had been necessary.[162]

In December 1759 von Kniphausen was relieved by Jan van der Hulst, his former deputy at Basra. That was not the only change in the area, for Mir Mohanna attacked Ganaveh on December 29, 1759. Qa'ed Heydar who supplied Khark with life necessities therefore received assistance from the Dutch. Their gallivats fired at the besiegers who withdrew of January 15, 1760 to Bandar-e Rig. Mir Mohanna then started to raid the countryside, thus making many enemies. In August 1760, Sheikh Naser of Bushire and the various chiefs of Dashtestan joined their forces to attack Mir Mohanna. However, through dissension the allied force broke up, even before it had arrived before Bandar-e Rig, after Mir Mohanna who had taken the field against them had defeated a small group

160 VOC 2996, Khark to Batavia (30/11/1759), f. 7-11; VOC 2968, Khark to Batavia (15/11/1758), f. 18; VOC 1013, Batavia to Khark (10/06.1760), f. 187; VOC 335, XVII to Batavia (25/10/1762), section Karreek, not foliated. In 1756, the Dutch naval force consisted of "T Loo Sloop of ten Carriage and six Swivel Guns, the Dragon Gallivat mounting six three pounders and four swivels, with three new trankey's are all the marine Force that properly belongs to the Island." Saldanha, *Précis*, vol. 1, p. 100.

161 VOC 2996, Khark to Batavia (30/11/1759), f. 12-13.

162 VOC 1013, Batavia to Khark (10/06/1760), f. 187; VOC 335, XVII to Batavia (25/10/1662), section Karreek, not foliated.

of their horsemen. Mir Mohanna, who was now in trouble with all his neighbors, remained close to Bandar-e Rig.[163]

After their failed attack Mir Mohanna's enemies complained to Karim Khan about his plunder campaigns. The latter having consolidated his power in Central Persia sent an army under Vali Khan against Bandar-e Rig to bring peace to the littoral.[164] Supported by the chiefs of Dashtestan this army laid siege to Bandar-e Rig. An envoy from Karim Khan asked the Dutch to contain Bandar-e Rig from the seaside, which van der Hulst promised to do, for which he was reprimanded by Batavia. Although Vali Khan was killed on January 25, 1760 the army under Baqer Khan continued the siege. Mir Mohanna was able to defeat this army during a night attack, but fresh troops under Sam Khan returned on March 18, 1760, which were supported by Ra'is Mosaddar the most important of the Dashtestan chiefs. Mir Mohanna was able to make peace with Ra'is Mosaddar, which forced Sam Khan to raise the siege of Bandar-e Rig on May 21, 1760. Sam Khan retreated to Kazerun awaiting further orders. Everybody expected Karim Khan to lay siege again to Bandar-e Rig and to punish Ra'is Mosaddar to enforce respect for his authority in the littoral, the more so since he was not engaged militarily elsewhere. Moreover, Mir Mohanna had lost many men and thus was an easier target for the Zand troops. Mir Mohanna therefore immediately began repairing his defenses as well as his marauding to strengthen his position and capabilities. He recovered so quickly that he even was able to drive Qa'ed Heydar from Ganaveh. The latter's people had not been able to cultivate their fields for three years, so that many people had already left. Qa'ed Heydar had therefore weakened and was unable to muster enough forces to withstand the continuous harassment and skirmishes by Mir Mohanna's forces. Finally Qa'ed Heydar fled and established himself and his family on Khark, which the Dutch could not refuse as he had been a good friend.[165]

The Persian Gulf in 1760-61 offered a confused spectacle, for Bandar-e Rig was not the only place of war. In the lower part the Imam of Masqat supported by the Hula Arabs of Charak had chased Molla 'Ali Shah and his Qavasem allies of Jolfar from the island of Hormuz.[166] On the other side of the Persian Gulf war had broken out between Sheikh Salman of the Bani Ka'b and Sheikh Sa'dun of Bushire. The Bani Ka'b with four gallivats had in vain tried to take Bahrain in February 1761; apart from some vessels they returned empty-handed. Sheikh Sa'dun of Bushire, who governed Bahrain, with the help of his allies the 'Otobis of Kuwait, attacked Bani Ka'b territory with one ship, three gallivats and 30 other vessels. While this force was blockading the Shatt al-Arab four of Sheikh Salman's gallivats left the estuary via another passageway and attacked Bushire. They set fire to two ships that were lying in the roadstead and seized a few others. They then returned to their home base without encountering any opposition. Thus Sheikh Salman was able to bring the war to a stalemate, so that 'Ali Aqa, the *motasallem* of Basra, wanted to make peace between the warring parties. Sheikh Salman sent back a haughty reply, which angered the *motasallem* to such an extent that he declared himself for Sheikh Sa'dun. He started to attack the Bani Ka'b overland and finally besieged Sheikh Salman in his fort by the end of July 1761. 'Ali Aqa had been able to convince the English to support him with the *Swallow*, while he also appeared to have called on troops from Baghdad and Bedouin tribal levies. The conflict developed further when the Hula Arabs split over the question which side to support, and each faction assisted one of the opposing parties. This involvement of so many groups in the conflict brought trade in this part of the Persian

163 VOC 3027, Khark to Batavia (01/10/1760), f. 3-4.

164 VOC 3027, Khark to Batavia (30/11/1760), f. 18; Perry, *Karim Khan*, p. 27; Roshan-Zamir, p. 44.

165 VOC 3027, Khark to Batavia (22/06/1761), f. 5-6, 16 (Van der Hulst had also sent Karim Khan a present costing Dfl. 1,137 during the siege of Bandar-e Rig); VOC 1015, Batavia to Khark (24/11/1761), f. 142-43.

166 VOC 3027, Khark to Batavia (22/06/1761), f. 4; Amin, *British Interests*, p. 47.

Gulf to a complete standstill. Van der Hulst was proud to report that only Dutch ships and vessels could pass unmolested, while he maintained a position of strict neutrality. The combined force that had contained Sheikh Salman in his stronghold was unable to avoid a stalemate. Despite the fact that rumors had it the Soleyman Pasha insisted on the total destruction of Sheikh Salman, the Dutch to their great astonishment learnt on September 30, 1761 that 'Ali Aqa and Sheikh Salman had concluded a peace, which led to the end of the siege, but not of the hostilities.[167]

This war also had consequences for other parts of the Persian Gulf. Mir Mohanna had begun his maraudings after Sam Khan had lifted the siege of Bandar-e Rig on May 21, 1761. Since that time he had not only forced Qa'ed Heydar from Ganaveh, but he also had plundered two rich caravans on the Bushire-Shiraz route, which carried merchandise with a value of 20,000 rupees. As a result of this success Mir Mohanna had become a rich man and he could reinforce himself. His marauding increased in frequency and went further away so that during the summer of 1761 no caravans plied between Bushire and Shiraz. This would have a negative impact on trade if this was allowed to continue. Sheiks Sa'dun of Bushire was unable to protect the roads to Bushire alone, because of his war with the Banu Ka'b. The leading chiefs of Dashtestan did not interfere and allowed Mir Mohanna to continue with his marauding unimpeded. Karim Khan did not act either, despite rumors that he would send an army, Mir Mohanna took heart. Although so far he had kept his gallivats at Bandar-e Rig, he now tried to see how far he could go. In September 1761 he sent a few of his smaller vessels out on the sea, which took two unarmed ships from Bushire. Another of Mir Mohanna's successes was his defeat of the chief of Deylam, who for some time at the request of Sheikh Salman of the Banu Ka'b had sought refuge on Khark.[168]

MIR MOHANNA ATTACKS KHARK

Emboldened by his success and seeing that nobody would stop him Mir Mohanna unexpectedly carried out a night attack against Khark on March 29, 1762.[169] The guards were misled because they believed that the approaching vessels were the supply boats from Bushire as the attackers had fowls aboard.[170] They killed 16 Dutch sailors and seized two gallivats (*de Draak* and *de Tijger*). Because the Dutch had only one gallivat (*de Fervisch*) left they could not prevent Mir Mohanna from attacking Khark with his entire force, including the two captured gallivats, on the next day.[171] Mir Mohanna landed a force of 200 men, which was repulsed by a Dutch force consisting of 31 soldiers, 31 African slaves supported by two cannons. On April 5, 1762 Mir Mohanna withdrew from Khark and returned to Bandar-e Rig having suffered a few dead and wounded. Mir Mohanna had tried to seize the caravanserai and the VOC warehouse outside the fort. However, van der Hulst had mounted a cannon there one year earlier, which now had served its purpose. The Dutch had too small a force to

167 VOC 3027, Khark to Batavia (22/06/1761), f. 4-5; VOC 3064, Khark to Batavia (30/09/1761), f. 25-26.

168 VOC 3064, Khark to Batavia (30/09/1761), f. 26-28.

169 VOC 3093, Khark to Batavia (21/08/1762), f. 59.

170 Niebuhr, *Beschreibung*, p. 318.

171 The Dutch immediately had a new gallivat constructed with a keel of 63.5 feet and its total cost fully equipped was 6,365 rupees. In comparison the gallivat *de Tijger* with a keel of 58 feet, built in 1758, had cost 7,160 rupees. They were built with timber that had been imported from Indonesia. Khark, for example, ordered timber for Sheikh Salman of the Banu Ka'b with an indication of their current market prices. *Moerbalken* (long supportive beams) 20 rupees; *sassemse balken* [? beams] 25-30x7-8 feet and 7-8 inches square; *moleplanken* (sail-arms?) 4.5 rupees of 3 inches; and *moleplanken* 4 rupees of 2 inches. VOC 3092, Khark to Batavia (19/10/1762), f. 28-30; VOC 3156, Khark to Batavia (30/09/1764), f. 18.

pursue Mir Mohanna's force and drive them off the island, while they could not prevent him to land men on the island wherever he wanted due to lack of a naval force. As a result Mir Mohana stayed for another five days on the island, but he did not come within range on the Dutch guns during the day-time. At night his men sometimes would appear before the fort, but they were repulsed with losses each time. On April 5, 1762 Mir Mohanna and his men boarded their vessels and returned to Bandar-e Rig. The only damage that he had been able to do was plundering the inhabitants of Khark. The Dutch had sent for help on March 30 to Basra to order the Dutch private vessel de *Cornelia* to come immediately to his assistance. During the attack there also was an English ship on the roadstead of Khark going to Surat to whom van der Hulst gave a letter for the VOC factory in that port asking his colleague for one gallivat or enough timber to build a new one. As soon as Sheikh Sa'dun had learnt about Mir Mohanna's attack on Khark he had ordered his fleet to sail for Khark, which arrived on April 6 under Sheikh Gheyth, brother of Sheikh Sa'dun of Bushire, with two gallivats, one dingi and seven armed vessels and 350 men. Qa'ed Heydar of Ganaveh with 100 men and Sheikh 'Ali b. Hoseyn of Charak with 50 sailors, both enemies of Mir Mohanna, accompanied the relief force, which later was joined by Sheikh Sa'dun himself in a well-accoutered ship to give the final blow to Mir Mohanna together with the Dutch. On April 7, the Dutch vessel de *Cornelia* together with the English vessel the *Monmouth*, commanded and owned by Captain Price, arrived at Khark. Price had left his goods at Basra and offered van der Hulst his assistance, which he accepted until such time as the new gallivat that the Dutch were already building would be ready. Because the *Cornelia* was a poor sailing ship and under-crewed van der Hulst allowed it to return on April 15 to Basra. Although by April 6 the Dutch had enough sea and manpower and felt quite secure Mir Mohanna did not oblige them by coming out to meet this force, although he had six gallivats under his command at that time.

Because the Dutch had suffered 17 dead and many wounded van der Hulst hired local troops to defend the fort and the hurriedly dug trenches, because he also had to put his own people on *de Cornelia*, the *Monmouth* and *de Fervisch*. Because Qa'ed Heydar's men were already on the island and sworn enemies of Mir Mohanna he decided to hire them. However, Mir Mohanna seeing the forces arrayed against him did not give them a chance to defeat him. Van der Hulst therefore thanked his allies for their assistance and gave presents to Sheikh Sa'dun, Qa'ed Heydar and Sheikh 'Ali b. Hoseyn to the value of Dfl. 2,628. The Bushire force left in May 1762, and the Monmouth on July 30, while the last local 40 soldiers under Qa'ed Heydar left on October 10, 1762, although an unspecified number was kept on until February 28, 1763 when they returned to Bushire. This assistance had cost the Dutch some Dfl. 45,000 (Dfl. 37,733 for the Bushire force and Dfl. 4,590 for the Monmouth). Van der Hulst had a new gallivat of 63.5 feet built and reinforced the defenses of Mosselsteijn. The bastion in front of the gate only partially protected the caravanserai and warehouse, where not only goods were stored, but where during the attack also many inhabitants of Khark had sought refuge. Without better protection Mir Mohanna or any attacking force might be able to cut off that entire area from the fort, if he was able to take them. Van der Hulst felt therefore obliged to protect this area by building two semi-bastions with gun-powder rooms, quarters for gunners and soldiers, and an interconnecting wall with parapets of 1,488 feet in length, six feet wide and 12 feet high at the cost of Dfl. 7,846. In 1759 that area was still unprotected, where also the VOC warehouses were located. Up till then their only protection had been an open room that served the soldiers as guard-house. This situation made that the soldiers were vulnerable to a sudden night raid and thus also endangered the warehouses. Van der Hulst had already out of his own pocket financed the construction of a point one year earlier, which he had reinforced with one cannon. This had been a good move, so he reported, for when the island had been attacked the cannon had prevented the attackers from seizing the warehouses. However, if the caravanserai had been taken by the attackers, it would have meant that the defenders of the fort could not have protected the warehouses. Because the new defenses were also for their protection, for they now could seek refuge behind the wall, the local population had to contribute to the cost of the new construction by receiving only 50% of the cost of the materials and of their wages. Van der Hulst had not wanted to demand more as the population, who lived from fishing, also had to make a living at the same time. Captain-engineer van Luipken had concluded that the tri-angular batteries at the north-side of the forts were useless and therefore they had been demolished. Their cannons and gunners had been placed inside the fort.[172] Batavia was very displeased with van der Hulst and his deputy, Buschman, and bemoaned the fact that not only had the VOC suffered a material loss, but also a loss of respect, because of their fumbling. Buschman, who was to replace van der Hulst, was ordered to take measures to prevent such an event from happening again and to punish severely any one who shirked his duty. The new defensive measures were approved, while Buschman was ordered to officially thank Sheikh Sa'dun for his assistance.[173]

The XVII in both 1759 and 1760 had pointed out to Batavia that Khark was a money losing affair and that the High Government's promises about its profitability were empty ones. Because the main promoter of the Khark factory, Jabob Mossel had died on May 11, 1761 more members of the High Government became critical of Khark. As a result on March 11, 1762 Batavia decided to close down the Khark factory. However, one month later the High Government had second thoughts and decided to slim down Khark and make an effort to make it finally profitable. Van der Hulst was recalled, because Batavia "considered him guilty of suspect, if not disloyal activities in the sale of goods and other matters."[174] On opening the new orders van der Hulst was immediately relieved of his function and Buschman had to replace him immediately. No deputy was appointed and Buschman had to designate a successor pro-tem in case of illness of death. Also, private trading had to be brought under control, if that did not happen Batavia would replace the entire staff of Khark. Buschman was ordered, *inter alia*, to cut his staff by 50%, which left him with still 94 men, which was considered to be ample. Moreover twice a year there would be a VOC ship on the roadstead, while two gallivats were allowed to be maintained at Khark. The third one (*de Fervisch*) had to be sent to Batavia.

---

172 VOC 3093, Khark to Batavia (21/08/1762), f. 59-64; VOC 3092, Khark to Batavia (19/10/1762), f. 14-25. The new fortifications were designed by a French engineer, Noirsosse, who passed through Khark on his way from Pondicherry to Europe. The map of Khark as shown by Niebuhr is most likely the one drawn by Noirsosse. The normal cost of materials at Khark was: stones 1.5 rupees, clay 1 rupee. Ibid., f. 21.

173 VOC 1017, Batavia to Khark (15.06/1763), f. 134. Buschman was ordered with the implementation of the orders as van der Hulst had been relieved of his function.

174 VOC 3003, Besoigne over Karreek (Batavia, 11/03/1762), f. 1843-55; VOC 1016, Batavia to Khark (27/05/1762), f. 99. Van der Hulst had transferred his authority to Buschman on August 24, 1762 and left Khark on October 20, 1762. Instead of returning to Batavia, however, he deserted to the English. When his ship called on Bandar 'Abbas van der Hulst took advantage of the fact that an English ship heading for Bombay was lying in the roads. He wrote the governor-general that he had done so for reasons of health and that once returned to Europe he would give an account of himself to the XVII, if necessary. VOC 3092, van der Hulst to van der Parra (Gamron, 04/11/1762), f. 65-66; see also annex four. Although he had been ordered to deposit security in Khark van der Hulst had not done so. On March 9, 1763 the High Government decided to start legal action against him (VOC 3129, f. 2102r-vs) and to sequester his property. On August 31, 1765 van der Hulst was sentenced by a court in Batavia to banishment from all VOC possessions on pain of severe punishment, sequestration of all his property and salaries due to him. VOC 3129, Sententie van der Hulst, f. 2103-04.

Table 4.1: Staff of the VOC factory at Khark in 1762 and proposed reduced staff

Occupation	Present staff	Future staff
Resident	2	1
Assistants	6	4
Senior surgeon	1	0
Carpenters	3	2
Sergeants	3	2
Corporals	7	4
Drummers	2	1
Soldiers	100	50
Junior mate	1	0
Boatswain	1	0
Quartermasters	2	1
Gunners	19	8
Sailors	18	8
Boys	-	-
Native servants	31	3
Total	186	94

He also had to cut other recurrent cost such as operational and maintenance expenditures and for each cost category a maximum allowable target was set, with a total annual operational budget of Dfl. 34,800. Buschman received these orders one month after Mir Mohanna's attack. He therefore replied that he would implement these orders, except that he could not reduce his staff. Khark had lost 44 men during 1761-62. Buschman therefore took 27 soldiers from the VOC ship de *Rebecca Jacoba* and had hired 60 native soldiers. Not only was the fort big, but he also kept 24 soldiers with 2 corporals at the two gallivats at night.[175] Batavia was not convinced, however. Mir Mohanna was inactive and therefore the staff at Khark had to be halved and the native soldiers dismissed.[176]

DUTCH RELATIONS WITH THE BANU KA'B

The situation in and around Basra, meanwhile, was also in a turmoil. Soleyman Pasha had died in May 1762, which led to anarchy in Baghdad and Basra. In Basra the shops were closed, trade came to a standstill and Esma'il Aqa, the *motasallem*, lost control over the city. The janissaries had split into two groups that fought one another daily. The roads to Basra were blocked by Arab tribes. Houses of European and other merchants were plundered. This situation lasted until August 1762,

175 VOC 116, Batavia to Khark (27/05/1762), f. 97-117 (Buschman also had to send the three horses that were at the factory to Batavia); VOC 3092, Khark to Batavia (19/10/1762), f. 48; VOC 792, Nadere bedenkingen (06/04/1762), f. 265-82.

176 VOC 1017, Batavia to Khark (15/06/1763), f. 135-37.

when 'Ali Aqa, the former *motasallem* of Basra became Pasha of Baghdad and Basra and vizier of three tails. He restored order and security in the city and roads by beheading some leading *aqas* of the janissaries on his arrival in Baghad and re-appointed Esma'il Aqa as *motasallem* of Basra. In May 1762 Sheikh Salman had taken advantage of the situation in Basra by blockading the Shatt al-Arab under the pretext that he wanted to protect the merchants who wanted to go to Basra. In reality, he wanted to become independent and to draw the Basra trade to Qobban and Dowraq, in his own territory. He therefore asked the Dutch to send him somebody to conclude (i) an offensive and defensive treaty with him. He also offered (ii) to buy all Dutch imports and asked the Dutch (iii) to intercede with Sheikh Sa'dun to make peace wit him. Because of Sheikh Salman's influence, the Dutch sent senior assistant Tam to Qobban. He had orders to politely decline items (i) and (ii), but he was allowed to make peace between the two Sheikhs. Tam was able to bring this about and also went to Bushire to finalize the peace negotiations between the two parties. Trade resumed again, because until then no Bushiri vessels had dared to go to Basra. Sheikh Salman still had not submitted his allegiance to 'Ali Pasha, and by the end of 1762 he still had not recalled his vessels in the Shatt al-Arab nor did he obey orders from Basra, although in 1763 he came to an understanding with him.[177] In early spring 1763 the country above Basra was in revolt against 'Ali Pasha. Sheikh 'Abdollah, the chief of the Arab (Montafeq) tribe who held the area between Qorna and Basra had cut communications between Basra and Baghdad completely. This disrupted navigation in the Persian Gulf, the more so, because Masqat was also in revolt. 'Ali Pasha was able to quell the revolt, but on his return to Baghdad he was killed by Turkish *aqas*. During the short interregnum the *motasallem* of Basra had extorted money from the population. He was, however, taken prisoner by the newly appointed 'Omar Pasha, who reappointed Esma'il Aqa the former *motasallem*.[178] A grateful Sheikh Salman sent a gallivat as a present to the Dutch in October 1763 with a view to strengthen their ties. Buschman was in quandary; if he refused the present he would offend a powerful local chief, if he accepted the gift he would have to give a present in return, which Batavia would criticize. Because there still was no peace with Mir Mohanna, Buschman decided to accept the gallivat, which had been built at Khark a few years earlier.[179]

RAPPROCHEMENT WITH MIR MOHANNA

Those who hoped that during the winter of 1762-63 Karim Khan would destroy Mir Mohanna were disappointed. Since his attack of Khark his gallivats had not been out into the Gulf and people hoped that an army would be sent to eliminate him and indeed an army had come down to Kazerun. However, the Dutch had little faith in its effectiveness. Buschman remarked, "we already write for many years that Mir Mohanna is about to be eradicated, but due the poor condition of the besiegers and the discord between the generals this has never happened." Mir Mohanna indeed had defeated that army and as a result Mir Mohanna was able to control the whole of Dashtestan with the exception of Bushire and Khark. He pressed Bushire daily in January 1763; all access road were closed, so that Sheikh Sa'dun feared loosing his town. This caused also inconvenience for the Dutch who

177 VOC 3092, Khark to Batavia (19/10/1762), f. 38-54; John Perry, "The Banu Ka'b an amphibious state in Khuzistan," *Le Monde iranien et l'Islam* 1 (1971), pp. 131-52; Lorimer, *Gazetteer*, pp. 1217-18; see also chapter seven.

178 VOC 3123, Khark to Batavia (08/05/1763), f. 8-9; Lorimer, *Gazetteer*, pp. 1211-12.

179 VOC 3123, Khark to Batavia (30/09/1764), f. 16-17. Batavia approved his action, although it wanted to know what Buschman had given in return, to which he did not reply. VOC 1019, Batavia to Khark (27/03/1765), f. 252.

received their supplies from Bushire. Meanwhile, Karim Khan had a serious rebellion of Fath 'Ali Khan to deal with, who caused him much problems and who surrendered only on February 20, 1763. This made that there was no help from Shiraz, although after the latter date rumors circulated about the coming of another army to deal with the situation in Dashtestan[180]

Mir Mohanna had ever since Buschman had become Agent at Khark in August 1762 indicated that he wanted peace with the Dutch. He also indicated that he would return the two captured Dutch gallivats. Because of Mir Mohanna's control of the littoral and the supply situation of Khark Buschman responded favorably to this overture. Mir Mohanna then sent two envoys to discuss peace, who also brought a letter from Mir Mohanna. In this letter, to show how sincere his wish for peace was, Mir Mohanna formally relinquished his claim to Khark and to all agreement his father had made with the Dutch. He also reiterated his decision to return the gallivats. To emphasize his good intentions Mir Mohanna allowed normal traffic to resume with Khark. Although the Dutch had decided to make the trade it did not happen, because there was some difference of opinion about the arms and accouterment of the vessels to be exchanged. Meanwhile, some vessels from Khark went to Bandar-e Rig to fetch sheep and other supplies. Mir Mohanna also had seized a vessel with more than 9,000 lbs of dates belonging to the inhabitants of Khark, which he returned of his own accord as well as five other vessels that he had taken some years prior to that. Mir Mohanna also repaid 700 rupees that belonged to the VOC broker, which he had taken from a Bushire vessel. It was obvious that Mir Mohanna wanted peace to ensure his escape route via the sea in case Karim Khan would attack him. Armenian and Moslem merchants went to and fro Khark and Bandar-e Rig to buy and sell goods. For the time being, however, only vessels from Khark did the shipping between the two locations. Because of this traffic the Dutch had good information what was happening at Bandar-e Rig, to have warning in case of a sudden attack. On February 13, 1763 Mir Mohanna totally unexpected returned one of the gallivats (*de Tijger*), which was in very bad repair, to the Dutch and promised to send the other shortly thereafter. He left it to Buschman whether the latter wanted to give in return the gallivat (*de Fervisch*) that the Dutch had seized from Mir Mohanna. Buschman was still undecided, although he wanted the exchange, because *de Draak* was larger and stronger than *de Fervisch*, which was leaking and required continuous repairs.[181]

Because of these peaceful overtures Batavia insisted on the implementation of its cost-cutting decision and wrote Buschman to send one gallivat, for he was allowed to keep two vessels only. The staff had to be decreased in spite of the size of the fort. As the fortifications had been build to protect the people of Khark these also had to take up arms when Khark was attacked. Batavia further suggested that Buschman reduce the naval protection given to merchants coming to and fro Khark so that he could manage with the lower number of soldiers.[182] Buschman disagreed with his instructions. In March 1763 he reported that he had been unable to reduce the number of soldiers and sailors in view of the continuing dangerous situation in the Persian Gulf. Moreover, with less than 150 men he would be unable to hold the fort, for with the additional fortifications he needed 100 men, given the incidence of illness. For the same reason he could not send the gallivat to Batavia. After the High Government had suggested in vain that he should put a native crew aboard

180 VOC 3092, Khark to Batavia (16/02/1763), f. 9-10; Perry, *Karim Khan*, p. 86.

181 VOC 3092, Khark to Batavia (16/02/1763), f. 10-12; VOC 3132, Khark to Batavia (08/05/1763), f. 4-5; Perry, *Karim Khan*, pp. 102-09; Niebuhr, *Beschreibung*, p. 318 gives a colorful description of the arrival and reception of Mir Mohanna's envoys on Khark.

182 VOC 1018, Batavia to Khark (24/05/1764), f. 114.

it, Batavia then sent a second-mate with 12 sailors to Khark in 1765, but by then it was no longer necessary.[183]

Batavia approved of the exchange of gallivats negotiated with Mir Mohanna in January 1763,[184] which did not place, however, because shortly thereafter Mir Mohanna took the field against Bushire, which he attacked three times during February-March 1763. Ironically Batavia had advised Buschman to maintain good relations with Sheikh Sa'dun, because he was an enemy of Mir Mohanna, and such friendships might benefit the VOC. The High Government forgot that such expectations worked both ways and might endanger the newly established peace with Mir Mohanna. Buschman realized this and therefore kept strict neutrality *vis à vis* the warring parties during this period. As a result Dutch vessels could navigate the Persian Gulf without being hindered by anybody, while Khark continued to be supplied by Bandar-e Rig. The expected military intervention by Karim Khan did not come, because he had his hands full with his brother's (Zaki Khan) rebellion. Mir Mohanna felt encouraged by this and felt that he finally would be able to take the last remaining stronghold in Dashtestan, viz. Bushire. However, his attacks failed to achieve his objective, because the English denied him his victory.[185]

KARIM KHAN'S CAMPAIGN AGAINST THE BANU KA'B AND MIR MOHANNA

In 1764 Karim Khan sent two envoys to Khark with letters expressing his friendship and an order for the delivery of merchandise to the value of 15,000 rupees. The Dutch were happy with his order and gave him a present of Dfl. 435. The English likewise sent a present while at the same time pointing out that the Dutch did not have the goods he had asked for, but they did. At that time, Karim Khan was at the summit of his power. Most of Persia was under his control, while trade flourished. The roads between Shiraz and the Russian border, for example, were heavy with commercial traffic that year. On the littoral of the Persian Gulf, however, Mir Mohanna remained a nuisance, although he had not attacked any caravans for several months at that time. In September 1674 rumor had it that an army was approaching Bandar-e Rig.[186] Mir Mohanna immediately took precautions; he laid in supplies and evicted those from Bandar-e Rig who did not have the necessary supplies to last them one year. Although they were at peace with Mir Mohanna the Dutch hoped that Karim Khan would destroy him. Relations with other chiefs in the littoral also were good and the Dutch benefited in particular from Sheikh Sa'dun's conflict with the EIC in early 1764. Merchants from Bandar-e Rig and Bushire regularly came to Khark, the latter at the insistence of Sheikh Sa'dun to thwart the English and increase his own revenues. For while EIC imports were exempt from customs duties, VOC goods were not, or so Buschman wrongly believed because the EIC paid 3% duty. Batavia commenting on events in the Persian Gulf reiterated that Buschman should stay out of local conflicts and remain neutral.[187]

---

183 VOC 3123, Khark to Batavia (08/05/1763), f. 12-13; VOC 1019, Batavia to Khark (24/05/1765), f. 262.

184 VOC 1018, Batavia to Khark (24/05/1764), f. 114.

185 VOC 3123, Khark to Batavia (08/05/1763), f. 4-5; Perry, *Karim Khan*, p. 102-09, Amin, *British Interests*, p. 70. Karim Khan had made a formal demand for payment of tribute in 1762, which Mir Mohanna had rejected with contempt, causing the beard of the messenger to be shaven. Lorimer, *Gazetteer*, p. 1815.

186 VOC 3123, Khark to Batavia (08/05/1763), f. 6-10; VOC 3156, Khark to Batavia (30/09/1764), f. 24-27, 37; Amin, *British Interests*, p. 70.

187 VOC 3156, Khark to Batavia (30/09/1764), f. 37; Amin, *British Interests*, p. 73; VOC 1018, Batavia to Khark (24/05/1764), f. 113; VOC 3156, Khark to Batavia (03/12/1764), f. 66; Roschan-Zamir, *Zand-Dynastie*, pp. 56-60.

Peace with Mir Mohanna was still uneasy and in fact had still not been formally concluded. The gallivats had just not been exchanged between the two parties. Because *de Draak* had become unseaworthy due to neglect Buschman did not press the issue and waited for Mir Mohanna's proposals. The expected action by Karim Khan did not happen, because he concentrated on the pacification of Kerman and Lar. When he had completed his task there Karim Khan's troops marched into Dashtestan. Towards the end of November 1764 they were at only six days' distance from Bandar-e Rig. Mir Mohanna appeared unconcerned by these troop movements because he had resumed attacking caravans. Karim Khan's troops had business with Sheikh Salman and not with Mir Mohanna with whom Karim Khan tried to make peace. He sent an envoy to Bushire, who from there ordered the Armenians of Khark to try and make peace with Mir Mohanna. This did not happen as a result of which the situation in that part of the Persian Gulf remained very unsettled.[188]

When Karim Khan granted the EIC new privileges in 1763 he also made it clear that he wanted to eliminate Mir Mohanna and asked for English naval assistance to make this happen.[189] Having made his preparation during the winter Karim Khan marched against the Banu Ka'b in March 1765. This operation was the result of 1764 agreement between Karim Khan and 'Omar Pasha of Baghdad. The intention was to grab Sheikh Salman with a pincer movement executed simultaneously by Persian and Turkish troops. The Banu Ka'b, however, withdrew into their marshlands where they were difficult to find. Moreover, the Turkish troops did not arrive, whether delayed and stalled is unclear. Karim Khan wrote a few angry letters to 'Omar Pasha, the final one informing him that he was withdrawing his troops. At that time the *motasallem* was embarking his troops to launch his side of the campaign, to which end he also had chartered the private English vessel the *Fanny*. Karim Khan destroyed an important irrigation dam thus ruining large tracts of agricultural lands this forced Sheikh Salman to make peace with him in July 1765. The Ottoman forces belatedly decided to attack Sheikh Salman. Although they had the larger force it was unable to take effective action against the Banu Ka'b. In fact the latter made a fool of the Ottoman force by continuing their piratical activities. After three weeks the *motasallem* preferred to make peace with Sheikh Salman, who promised to pay a small tribute. This did not mean that Sheikh Salman had also made peace with the English against whom he delivered a heavy blow in the night of July 18, 1765 by seizing three English ships.[190]

During Karim Khan's campaign against the Banu Ka'b the provinces of Fars and Dashtestan were infested by roving troops that plundered the countryside between Bushire, Shiraz and Kangan. Merchants did not dare to travel anymore, or if they did they did not take bulk goods with them, which especially hurt VOC trade. Trade therefore came to a standstill, for apart from some spices nothing else was sold. The situation on the littoral had become so unsafe that people living there stayed on their boats at night and returned ashore in the morning when it seemed to be safe to do so. Mir Mohanna was also active and plundered the few caravans that still dared to travel. At the of May 1765, Karim Khan therefore sent Emir Guneh Khan Afshar with 1,100 horse and 500 foot to Khormuj to pacify the littoral between Bushire and Kangan, and in particular to attack Mir

188 VOC 3156, Khark to Batavia (03/12/1764), f. 66; Roschan-Zamir, *Zand-Dynastie*, pp. 56-60.

189 Amin, *British Interests*, p. 72 greatly exaggerates when he writes that Karim Khan was "impressed by the rising power of the British in India." I doubt whether he had any inkling of this and the fact that he was making the same noises to the Dutch only indicates that he was looking for a partner with naval power to deal with Mir Mohanna. The problem with the Ka'b was less of an issue for him than Amin suggests, which Karim Khan therefore did not mention in his letter, and which he took care of, more or less, with his own land forces.

190 Perry, Banu Ka'b," pp. 132-42; VOC 3148, Khark to Batavia (01/05/1766), f. 8-9.

Mohanna.[191] Although Khormuj was a district that was obedient to Karim Khan's rule, the chief's brother, Ja'far Khan had blinded his uncle, who was the care-taker chief, and had committed other atrocities. He tried to oppose Emir Guneh Khan's troops, but he was too weak to do so. The Emir punished him and the town that he totally sacked and destroyed, except for the mosque and cemetery. He also cut many palm trees that he used to reinforce an adobe wall of five feet high that he built around his army camp, next to the destroyed fort of Khormuj, which also had a moat.[192]

Emir Guneh Khan needed naval assistance to cut off Mir Mohanna's lines of retreat. All local chiefs were Mir Mohanna's men[193] and thus Emir Guneh Khan had to look for support among his enemies and foreigners. Therefore, Sarkis, the *kalantar* of the Armenians in Persia and *beyglerbeygi* of Kuhgiluyeh, was sent as an envoy to Khark in March 1765 to ask for Dutch assistance. He had a letter from Karim Khan asking for a joint naval blockade of Bandar-e Rig with Sheikh Sa'dun. Sarkis further told Buschman that all Armenians would have to leave the island and that the VOC had to pay 5% duties on all goods brought to Khark retroactively as of 1753. Buschman got the impression that Sarkis really believed that he would comply with "these impertinent proposals." Sarkis even went so far as to order merchandise that was to be paid out of the customs duties that the Dutch would have to pay. Buschman did not show Sarkis how exasperated he was, but instead he wrote a letter to Karim Khan in which he explained that he could not help with the war effort. He lacked both men and equipment to do so and suggested that this might be done when the regular VOC ships would call on Khark later that year. With regards to the Armenians Buschman raised by Sarkis, which did not figure in Karim Khan's letter, he wrote that the Armenians were free to stay or leave, but the Dutch would not expel them. When Sarkis tried to force Armenian merchants to give him money to buy goods Buschman told him to stop his interference right away, unless he showed him Karim Khan's orders to such effect. As to the payment of 5% customs duties, Buschman replied that customs duties were paid on all Dutch goods when they were imported into the Persian mainland. If Karim Khan wanted that money he had to address himself to those who collected the customs duties. Khark was Dutch territory, which Karim Khan himself had acknowledged and confirmed in 1756. Furthermore, the VOC had always enjoyed exemption from customs duties, granted by past shahs, while the kingdom of Persia still owed the VOC a huge debt. Buschman promised that he would report these demands to Batavia, but he assured Sarkis that if Karim Khan would insist on them the VOC would abandon the trade with Persia altogether. Sarkis remained two months on Khark during which time he did not refer to the various demands at all, saying that he awaited further orders. When these finally came they were just a simple demand for naval assistance.[194]

The fleet of Bushire was too small, the Dutch had refused, but fortunately the English, who also had been asked by Karim Khan for assistance, were willing to help. Jervis thought this was an occasion such as allowed by Bombay in 1764 and asked the Agent at Basra that the *Tartar* might be

191 VOC 3148, Khark to Batavia (01/05/1766), f. 9. The roving troops probably were the Liravi, a sub-section of the Luri Jaki tribe. Perry, Mir Muhanna," p. 91; Roschan-Zamir, *Zand-Dynastie*, p. 60. According to Niebuhr, *Reisebeschreibung*, p. 514 the army consisted of 4,000 horse and 2,000 infantry, but a Georgian confided in him that of the cavalry only 1,100 and of the foot only 500 were regular trained soldiers. The cavalry had carbines and pistols and the infantry flint guns with fuses.

192 Niebuhr, *Reisebeschreibung*, pp. 512-13.

193 The people of Kangan, for example, refused to assist the Zand army with vessels and threatened to defend themselves if attacked. As a precautionary measure they slept on board their vessels at night rather than on land. Lorimer, *Gazetteer*, p. 1824.

194 VOC 3148, Buschman to Batavia (01/05/1766), f. 9-17. The daily cost of defraying Sarkis and his suite amounted to Dfl. 405 excluding wine, which was another reason Buschman found him an annoying presence.

used for this purpose. Wrench was not pleased by this request, because it had not been addressed to him nor had Jervis included the original text of Karim Khan's request, and out of pique raised all kinds of objections (the *Tartar* was not fit for such an operation; it might miss its return voyage to India, it was not convenient to the Company, success was unlikely, and even that Mir Mohanna was bound to take revenge and attack Basra as well as all English vessels sailing in the Gulf). Finally, Basra gave in and on May 25, 1765 instructions were drawn up for Jervis for the use of the *Tartar* against Mir Mohanna and for the *Islamabad* affair. A few days later the *Tartar* left for Bushire.[195]

On May 22, 1765 Emir Guneh Khan attacked Bandar-e Rig supported by troops arrived from Karim Khan's army at Qobban. Mir Mohanna first aimed to defend Rig to which end he had laid in large stores. Initially, he may have felt encouraged that a mortar that was launched by the Zand troops at Rig exploded among those who launched it killing several persons. However, Mir Mohanna soon abandoned the idea of a long siege as desertion among his ranks began. He had asked Buschman whether he might seek refuge on Khark, which Buschman friendly refused saying that there were not enough provisions and that he wanted to avoid problems with Karim Khan. Mir Mohanna then decided to move to Kharqu with all his people and property on 17 vessels, of which 6 gallivats, on June 1. Before his departure he slaughtered all cattle that he could not take with him. Because there was no naval blockade by the Bushire and English vessels as promised most of Mir Mohanna's troops were able to escape. Mir Mohanna left on June 2 to Kharqu Island, a waterless, sandy place without shade or fodder, but he had come well-prepared. Here he entrenched himself at the North Bay, which was protected by crags and low water, and where he also built gabions. According to the English, the Dutch did not deny his men access to Khark to graze their sheep, but the Dutch report that they had turned them away (see below). Nevertheless conditions were difficult on Kharqu and a well-planned and executed operation might have meant the end of Mir Mohanna. He himself was already blind at one eye and the other was so inflamed that he had to leave the defense to his subordinates, some of whom had lost their ears due to disobedience to or drunken ire of Mir Mohanna. Also, some of his men died of the heat. It was only on June 4, 1765 that the Bushire-English fleet arrived consisting of three gallivats, two *batils* and one English three-master.

Because there was no naval blockade by the Bushire and English vessels as promised most of Mir Mohanna's troops were able to escape. The English factory in Basra had approved to use the *Tartar* against Mir Mohanna, but had stipulated that she could not stay too long. It further suggested that Mir Mohanna might have had bought his peace even before the *Tartar* would get there, which probably was a face-saving device *vis à vis* Bombay, in case it disapproved the use of the ship in this manner. Therefore, the Agent at Basra furthermore pressed upon Jervis, the EIC resident at Bushire that the *Tartar* alone was not enough to attack Khark even if Sheikh Sa'dun would join it with his vessels. Nevertheless, he emphasized that feinting to attack would not be good for the Company's reputation either. The best therefore for the EIC was to destroy Mir Mohanna entirely, "and if we do not he will be the more incensed against us and declare war on the Comp. When the army withdraws he probably then will attack Bushire to seize the Comp.'s property and wil attack English passing ships. We leave it up to you how to best use the vessel."[196]

Mir Mohanna left on June 2 to Kharqu Island, two days before the arrival of the Bushire-English fleet consisting of three gallivats, two *batils* and one English three-master. According to the Dutch, they skirmished a bit with Mir Mohanna's vessels, but not seriously. In fact, Mir Mohanna continued his acts of piracy at sea without any hindrance. Captain Price commanded the *Tartar*, Mr.

195 Lorimer, *Gazetteer*, p. 1784.

196 Saldanha, *Précis*, vol. 1, p. 188-89 (Basra, 31/05/1765); VOC 3148, Khark to Batavia (01/05/1766), f. 10-11.

Natter the clerk of the EIC factory at Bushire commanded the largest Bushiri gallivat, the others were commanded by Bushire captains, one of whom was Sheikh Sa'dun's son. During the night of June 4 Mir Mohanna had sent out five gallivats and a *batil* that had been drawn ashore out to sea. The next morning the Anglo-Persian fleet saw them and tried in vain to hit them with gun fire and had to let them go. Mir Mohanna's vessels were back again on June 6, and had stationed themselves between Khark and Kharqu. The Anglo-Persian fleet was dispersed and Sheikh Sa'dun's son had returned to Bushire for unknown reasons. Unsupported by the remaining large Bushiri gallivat, Price and Natter frontally attacked Mir Mohanna's vessels, who received them so warmly, supported by the guns mounted at Kharqu that they had to withdraw. No action was undertaken for a few days. Mir Mohanna had the freedom of the sea and three of his gallivats and one *batil* sailed away on June 15; it was surmised to meet the returning gallivat of Sheik Sa'dun who was expected back. The expected engagement indeed would have taken place with three Bushire vessels if the unexpected appearance of a large English ship from Madras that in all ignorance of the situation headed straight for them had not forced the two opposing parties to separate. On June 19 Sheikh Sa'dun's son returned, who tried in vain to obtain Dutch support. On June 20, Sheikh Sa'dun's son learning that two fishing boats belonging to Mir Mohanna's people were at Khark decided to seize them. He succeeded in doing so killed one of the fishermen. However, the Dutch intervened and did not allow the boats to be taken and when the Bushiri captors opposed them the Dutch opened fire on them. One of the boats was able to get away; the other was taken ashore where the Bushiris were arrested, where they stayed until the other fishing boat had been returned. Price, the captain of the English vessel was so fed up with the situation that he asked Emir Guneh Khan to land troops on Kharqu. The latter replied that this was impossible because of the advent of Moharram (on June 20, 1765). He would have to wait until Moharram (June 29) and thereafter 5,000 men would be made available. Mir Mohanna did not sit still. His men were diligent because he paid one rupee per canon ball retrieved and had built redoubts of sand to protect his people, who were repairing his vessels at the same time, against the desultory bombardment from the ships. He also was building new batteries at the most exposed points of Kharqu, while at the same time celebrating *'Ashura*.

As a result nothing happened until June 29, when several days later three gallivats and one *batil* of Mir Mohanna showed up with a gallivat seized between Bahrain and Bushire with a cargo of specie and pearls. The *batils* that had been with this seized gallivat had run ahead and alerted the Bushire vessels at Khark of its capture. When Mir Mohanna's vessels showed up with the gallivat the smaller Bushire vessels, which were numerically superior in strength and were right in the pirates' path, made way for them who went straight to Kharqu. Price immediately ordered an attack of Mir Mohanna's position and vessels at Kharqu. Price commanded the *Tartar* and Natter the large Bushire gallivat, but they were not supported by the other Bushire vessels that were sailing to and fro at a safe distance. Price and Natter were fed up with Sheikh Sa'dun's son, who refused to take orders from Price or to adhere to the system of signals that Price had arranged. On June 30 therefore Mr. Natter and some European gunners who had been distributed over the Bushire vessels all returned to the *Tartar* and to a small yaught that belonged to the EIC agent of Basra. On July 2, Mir Mohanna's men took a small Bushire vessel and on July 9 the Basra agent's yacht together with a large English ship from Bengal, the *Fort William* that had called on Khark left for Basra. On June 10 Mir Mohanna's fleet joined that of Sheikh Salman of the Ka'b within sight of Khark. Price departed on July 12, 1765 because he was exasperated by this lack of action by the Bushire vessels and the incompetence of Sheikh Sa'dun's son who commanded them. The Sheikh's son, who had run out of money and supplies, also decided to depart and thus the entire operation blew over. It was reported that Karim Khan was furious with the English and blamed them for the failure of the operation, although according to Lorimer, Mir Mohanna "would inevitably have been defeated altogether, if only Captain Price and Mr. Natter had not been deserted in such a cowardly manner by the Bushire Arabs." During these actions Sarkis had asked Buschman to assist Emir Guneh Khan, who, despite being threatened by Sarkis, refused to do so.[197]

Prior to his flight to Kharqu, Mir Mohanna had asked for refuge on Khark. Buschman had refused politely but firmly, saying that he did not want any trouble with Karim Khan and that there were not enough supplies on Khark. However, both during and after the hostilities many of Mir Mohanna's men visited Khark. Because Buschman did not trust them he ordered them to leave. If he allowed them to stay he would not only have an enemy for neighbor, but also one at his doorstep. He also wrote to Mir Mohanna explaining his eviction order. Later some reproached Buschman for even having allowed Mir Mohanna to stay on Kharqu, for this was also considered to be Dutch territory. In 1757, von Kniphausen had erected two pillars with the VOC seal on the islet, thus claiming it for the Company.[198] However, this was not fair to Buschman since as far as can be ascertained now the VOC never had considered Kharqu to be one of its possessions.

THE VOC DECIDES TO ABANDON KHARK

In January 1765 the High Government in Batavia discussed the future of the Khark factory. Although the XVII leaned towards closing down the Persian Gulf factory, Batavia, based on Buschman's positive letters about trade prospects and lower overhead, decided to continue the Khark factory. Batavia would send two ships with mainly sugar each year and re-assess the situation each year. A further element that played a role was the increased EIC activity. If the VOC would abandon the Persian Gulf it would leave the field to the English who then would become so entrenched in vacated Dutch positions that it would be so much more difficult later, if it were decided to come back in view of better trade prospects, to achieve the trade objectives. The High Government also decided on April 6, 1765 to replace Buschman with Pieter Houting. In June 1765 orders arrived in Batavia from the XVII ordering the High Government to close down the Khark factory. On August 20, 1765 the High Government decided to abandon the Khark factory. Houting was ordered to sell the fort and other buildings to Mir Mohanna at a reasonable price. If he did not want them Houting was ordered to sell the buildings to any other local chief. If no buyer was found Houting had to cede the island to a local chief free of charge on condition that the latter would restore them to the VOC when the Company would return to the Persian Gulf. Moreover, the caretaker had to promise not to allow any other European nation access to the island and to guarantee freedom of religion and property of the island's inhabitants. Houting also had to inform the population of Khark about the intended sale so that they could take their own appropriate steps. Houting had to sell all military equipment at 100% profit and if there were no takers he had to take it back to Batavia. The merchandise he was allowed to sell at somewhat lower prices and the unsold goods he had to take to Malabar, although he had to try and sell them en route at Bandar 'Abbas and Masqat. The entire operation had to be completed by September 1766. Batavia decided to keep the decision a secret, because two ships had already left with a substantial cargo and had therefore decided to send a ship from Surat

---

197 VOC 3184, Buschman to Batavia (01/05/1766), f. 15-18; VOC 3184, Khark to Batavia (14/10/1765), f. 69-73; Perry, "Mir Muhanna," p. 92; Ibid, *Karim Khan*, p. 156; Lorimer, *Gazetteer*, p. 139, 1784-88; Roschan-Zamir, *Zand-Dynastie*, pp. 61-63; Ghaffari Kashani, *Golshan-e Morad*, p. 275.

198 VOC 3148, Buschman to Batavia (01/05/1766), f. 18-19; Lorimer, *Gazetteer*, pp. 1786-87; VOC 3250, Verklaring J.J. Christant (Batavia, 02/09/1769), f. 407vs-408. Emir Guneh Khan destroyed the fort of Bandar-e Rig. VOC 3184, Khark to Batavia (14/10/1765), f. 67

to take the Khark staff back to Batavia. To keep an eye of the development of trade prospects in the Persian Gulf the High Government also decided to have somebody from the Surat factory, joined by a staff member from Khark, to remain in Masqat and serve there as the Company's eyes and ears. The Surat council decided to send assistant Dubordieux to Masqat in the guise of a private merchant. By the time this letter was sent to Houting Khark had fallen into Mir Mohanna's hands.[199]

THE DUTCH ATTACK MIR MOHANNA

After the departure of the Bushire fleet Mir Mohanna revived his claim on Khark and made all kinds of outrageous requests. He also brought trade almost to a standstill both on land and at sea. Only those vessels escorted by Dutch gallivats dared to navigate that part of the Persian Gulf, while Sheikh Sa'dun prevented merchants from Bushire to go to Khark to put pressure on the Dutch. However, the Dutch did not have sufficient resources to protect all shipping. The arrival of *de Walcheren* on July 21, 1765 brought some relief. Buschman transferred his authority to Houting on August 19. *De Kronenburg* arrived on August 31, 1765. Houting was immediately confronted with a difficult situation. On the one hand there was the threat of an attack by Mir Mohanna as soon as the Dutch ships would have left in September. On the other hand, Karim Khan and Sheikh Sa'dun continuously pestered him with demands to join forces and make a pre-emptive strike against Mir Mohanna, while they also prevented merchants from coming to Khark. Trade, the reason why the VOC was there, had come to complete standstill. On September 17, 1765 letters arrived from Karim Khan and Sheikh Sa'dun asking a categorical answer from Houting whether he would join forces with them or not. In case of a negative reply Karim Khan stated that he would forbid all Dutch goods to be imported into Persia and would consider the Dutch his enemies. Being caught between a rock and a hard place Houting decided to join what he believed to be the strongest side. Houting had asked Buschman for advice as to the feasibility of an attack on Kharqu. Buschman said that he might do it, but then he needed a very good justification for it, although he thought that Dutch forces were not strong enough for this task. Later Buschman reported that that Houting had felt the operation necessary notwithstanding his advice.[200]

On September 19, 1765 Houting sent assistant Christant to Bushire to discuss the invasion plan with Sheikh Sa'dun. Christant had been on Kharqu several times, under the pretext of buying horses, to spy on Mir Mohanna's strength and he thus knew the lay of the land. He returned to Khark on September 24 having reached an agreement with Sheikh Sa'dun.[201] Houting appointed Captain Cornelisz. of *de Walcheren* the commander of the invasion force.[202] The Dutch naval force consisted of *de Walcheren, de Kronenburg* and three gallivats, which were joined by three gallivats

199 VOC 795, Besoigne over Karreek (20/01/1765), f. 103-08; VOC 795, Resolution High Government (20/06/1765), f. 521-41; VOC 3365, XVII to Batavia (04/10/1765), section Karreek, not foliated. On the commercial considerations to close down the Khark factory see chapter five.

200 VOC 3148, Buschman to Batavia (01/05/1766), f. 20-25; VOC 3250, Extract Memorandum, undated f. 420vs. (It is a pity that the full text of this memorandum has not been preserved, for its table of contents promises much interesting data on Khark, its population and the Persian Gulf). Mir Mohanna insisted that Houting should suspend trade with Bushire. Lorimer, *Gazetteer*, p. 1817.

201 VOC 3148, Buschman to Batavia (01/05/1766), f. 25-26; VOC 3250, Verklaring J.J. Christant (Batavia, 02/09/1769), f. 408vs; Nami, *Tarikh*, pp. 162-68. The Dutch had no faith at all in the warlike qualities of the Bushire troops, who "had no experience at all and would fly at the merest sign of danger." VOC 3184, Khark to Batavia (14/10/1765), f. 67.

202 VOC 3148, Instruction for Corneliszen (Khark, 02/10/1765), f. 58-59.

and smaller vessels commanded by Sheikh Sa'dun. The allied fleet left Khark on October 9, 1765. The fleet arrived the same day at Kharqu at 15.00 hours where it shelled the gabions, trenches and wooden platforms with some cannons made by Mir Mohanna as well as at his gallivats that were still lying on the beach. One of them burnt and the others were riddled with balls. The shelling continued until October 13. Meanwhile, Kharqu was put under a naval blockade to prevent anybody and in particular Mir Mohanna from escaping. On October 13, at 9.00 hours A.M. 60 European soldiers and some 500 Bushire soldiers supported by nine gunners with three swivel guns landed on Kharqu. The Dutch force was commanded by Sergeant Jan Jurgen Noder, also called Nodorp, who had lived on Khark for a long time and knew Arabic as well as local warfare techniques. The landing party proceeded without meeting any opposition. The troops then started to plunder the abandoned houses, and from an organized force it had become a disorganized rablle. Seeing the landing force disorganized Mir Mohanna's cavalry all of a sudden frontally attacked it and his infantry on its flanks. The Bushire force having suffered 150 casualties was routed and fled the field. The Dutch force, whose commanders had died during the first attack, withdrew, whilst continuing to fight, to the beach where most of them died, because the landing boats manned by Khark inhabitants had fled. Only five of the Dutch force survived and the entire action was over by 9.30 AM. Houting blamed the disaster on the Bushire naval force that had not mounted an effective blockade thus allowing Mir Mohanna to reinforce his troops that had consisted of only 200 men on October 10. According to Christant, Mir Mohanna confirmed this as a fact after the capture of Mosselsteijn.[203]

After this disaster Mir Mohanna's cannons started shelling the fleet without doing any damage. Seeing that it could not do anything anymore, the fleet withdrew to Khark where it arrived at 13.00 hours. Houting was exasperated and maintained that if the ships had continued bombarding Mir Mohanna's positions at Kharqu things would not have turned out so bad. The captains of the ships disagreed and refused saying that they needed their ammunition for the long journey back. The Bushire vessels also wanted to leave and asked for payment which Houting refused.[204] Houting was in despair. He wrote to Karim Khan asking for help, which, though promised did not materialize. Houting also wrote to the Dutch factory in Malabar for the help of 100 men. *De Walcheren* and *de Kronenburg* were ordered to stay until Karim Khan's promised relief force would arrive.[205]

FALL OF KHARK

The Dutch waited in anxious anticipation of events to happen. It was decided that *de Walcheren* would depart mid-December. On December 12, 1765 the Dutch suffered another setback when they lost two gallivats with 40 European and 18 local sailors to Mir Mohanna's fleet. A vessel had

203 VOC 3148, Corneliszen to van der Parra (Batavia, n.d. [probably 16/06/1766), f. 50-52; VOC 3148, Corneliszen to van der Parra (a/b Poppiensburg) (31/08/1766), f. 77; VOC 3184, Houting to Corneliszen (Khark, n.d. [probably 10/10/1766]), f. 78-79 and 79-80 (same letter to du Pree the captain of *de Kronenburg* who had taken over command due to illness of Corneliszen); VOC 3148, Buschman to Batavia (01/05/1766), f. 36; VOC 3250, Verantwoording Houting (Batavia, 13/10/1769), f. 398vs-99; VOC 3250, Verklaring J.Z. Engelhardt (Batavia, 05/09/1769), f. 416vs-17; VOC 3250, Verklaring Christant (Batavia, 02/09/1769), f. 408vs-09; VOC 3148, Corneliszen to van der Parra (Batavia, n.d. [probably 16/06/1766), f. 52-53; Perry, "Mir Muhanna," pp. 92-93; Ghaffari Kashani, *Golshan-e Morad*, pp. 276-77; Lorimer, *Gazetteer*, p. 1817.

204 VOC 3148, Corneliszen to van der Parra (Batavia, n.d. [probably 16/06/1766), f. 52-54; VOC 3184, Buschman/Houting to Batavia (14/10/1765), f. 72-73; VOC 3250, Verklaring Christant (Batavia, 02/09/1769), f. 409 vs.

205 VOC 3184, Buschman/Houting to Batavia (14/10/1765), f. 73-74.

been sighted coming from Basra and Houting sent two gallivats as a convoy. When the two Dutch vessels were close to the Basra ship they saw that Mir Mohanna was lying in wait with four gallivats and five *batils*. Due to contrary south-eastern winds the Dutch vessels had been forced to go to Bandar-e Rig where they faced a superior force to which they surrendered. This caused much consternation, which did not abate, because Mir Mohanna's *batils* cruised all around Khark. Houting thus having lost his naval shield asked Sheikh Sa'dun for help. The latter replied that he would send help only if his vessels would be escorted by the two Dutch ships. Houting did not dare to do this fearing that Mir Mohanna would immediately attack Khark. Buschman meanwhile (who was on board one of the ships) urged Houting to abandon Khark and put the VOC staff and merchandise abroad the two ships. Houting refused, because that would have been cowardly. He also feared problems from the local population when realizing that they were being abandoned to their fate. They had already threatened to refuse to serve the Dutch any longer if they would observe that cash, merchandise and valuables were taken from the fort to the ships.[206]

Houting therefore tried to make peace with Mir Mohanna and get the gallivats back. He sent Cristant to Kharqu where Mir Mohanna agreed to a peace agreement on condition that the Dutch paid him 1,000 *tumans* per year retro-actively as rent for Khark. This was refused. Three days later Mir Mohanna came to Khark, where a large part of his troops had already been arriving since December 17 in their *batils*. He came ashore at the North side, near the Armenian quarter, which was situated outside the walls. Mir Mohanna's men started to dig trenches and from behind the walls of the Armenian houses and the trenches they started sniping at the Dutch defenders. The latter found out that their cannons caused little damage to the enemy, due to the thick walls and good retrenchments. The crews of the two Dutch ships observed the guns of the fort firing during the night of December 21, while during the following days small arms fire was also heard. On December 22, 1765 Mir Mohanna attacked Mosselsteijn; first the houses outside the fort, and then he started to dig trenches and commenced sniping at the Dutch defenders. The latter were unable to dislodge Mir Mohanna's troops given the small size of the garrison; 80 Europeans and 120 natives. Houting did not totally trust the latter, who were a mixture of all sorts, and therefore they were only armed when necessary. To pressure Mir Mohanna, Houting sent a vessel with two pilots to instruct the captains of the two Dutch ships to take up position between Khark and Kharqu to force Mir Mohanna to withdraw his men out of fear for the fate their families on Kharqu. The captains refused because they did not trust the pilots Houting had sent as well as because of the changing winds.[207]

On December 30, 1765 Mir Mohanna carried out a night attack with 700 men and was able to seize the outer defenses of Mosselsteijn, which were held by the native soldiers and two Europeans. The Arab attackers scaled the wall with ladders and cut down anyone they encountered. The outer bastions were defended until 07.00 hours, but then the defenders were forced to withdraw into the fort, because they were being attacked from all sides. As soon as the Arabs had taken

206 VOC 3250, f. 399vs-401; VOC 3159, f. 711vs-712; VOC 3184, f. 27-28; VOC 3148, f. 54-55. Meilink, p. 488 has suggested that the captains Corneliszen and Dupree knew about Batavia's decision to close the Khark factory. She also asserts that Mir Mohanna had intercepted the letter from the High Government ordering the closure of the Khark factory. This is impossible, because no such letter was ever sent. The captains had left Batavia on May 24, 1764 thus well before the closure decision was taken on June 20, 1765. It was only on August 20, 1765 that Batavia decided to order the VOC Surat factory to send a ship to Khark to carry out the High Government's decision. This ship left Surat after Khark had fallen.

207 VOC 3184, f. 29; VOC 3250, f. 400, 409vs-410, 413, 418; VOC 3148, f. 54; VOC 3159, (Winkler-Brandt) Masqat to Batavia (17/03/1766), f. 618r-vs; VOC 3159, (Houting) Bushire to Batavia (06/02/1766), f. 711-13; Ghaffari Kashani, *Golshan-e Morad*, p. 276; Lorimer, *Gazetteer*, p. 1818.

the bastions they also occupied the bazaar and the neighboring houses, from where they sniped at the defenders. After the fall of the bastions all native soldiers left the Dutch, who were discouraged by the defeat and Mir Mohanna's quick success; moreover, they were dog-tired due to constant guard-duty during the previous 12 days. Houting therefore decided to open negotiations with Mir Mohanna. The drinking water was also almost finished in the fort and he expected no more outside help. He was about to send an envoy to Kharqu when Mir Mohanna in a *batil* displaying a large flag came to Khark, and although the two Dutch ships saw this as well they did not take any action. The two ships received the news of the disaster unfolding at Khark from a small vessel that had escaped from the island with 36 refugees amongst whom Sheikh 'Ali, the chief of the Khark Arabs. The refugees told the ship's council that nobody could leave the island anymore. They also intimated that Mir Mohanna felt confident enough to attack the two Dutch ships, because he had some 60 vessels under his command. In the evening the fort did not fire the sign-gun as usual, which did not bode well. Houting flew the white flag and under it the Dutch flag upside-down signaling that he still was in possession of the fort. Negotiations started on December 31. Mir Mohanna gave Houting three choices:

(i) The Dutch could remain on Khark provided they paid a lump sum of 300,000 rupees and an annual payment of 20,000 rupees;
(ii) The Dutch could leave Khark unhindered, if they left all their possessions in the fort; or
(iii) Houting had to come outside the fort to conclude in person a peace agreement with Mir Mohanna. In that case Mir Mohanna would restitute everything that he had taken from the Dutch.[208]

Houting had asked the two Dutch ships to come closer to the fort to evacuate the Europeans, but they refused to do so. This was not out of cowardice, they claimed, but due to contrary winds and the fact that half of their crews consisted of native sailors, whom they did not entirely trust to stay and fight if battle ensued with Mir Mohanna, whose many *batils* posed a threat. *De Walcheren*, for example, had a crew of 60 European and 55 local sailors and of the latter only three had been on a ship before. The captains even offered the refugees from Khark 100 rupees to deliver a message to Houting, but they all refused, being afraid to lose their live.[209]

On the morning of January 1, 1766 the captains of the two Dutch ships observed that many people were going in and out of the fort and that the barrier in the gate was down. They did not see any European soldiers on the battlements of Mosselsteijn and that the fort did not reply to their signal. The captains concluded that Mosselsteijn had fallen, because it also failed to respond to a second signal and many *batils* had beached under the guns of the fort. The ships' council then decided to depart for there was not anything that they could do anymore. They once again fired a signal, but again there was not any response. At 15.00 hours both ships set sail to Bandar 'Abbas.[210]

208 VOC 3159, (Houting) Bushire to Batavia (06/02/1766), f. 713-14vs; VOC 3148, f. 54-56; VOC 3250, f. 402-03, 414, 418vs-419, 437vs; VOC 3184, Houting to Corneliszen/duPree (31/12/1765), f. 81 (this letter was brought by Sheikh 'Ali); VOC 3184, Resolution taken aboard *de Walcheren* (01/01/1766), f. 61-63.

209 VOC 3250, f. 414, 419, 437vs; VOC 3184, f. 61-63.

210 VOC 3148, f. 56-57; VOC 3148, f. 60, 64; VOC 3250, f. 403vs, 435vs; 438vs. Houting countered that the captains could not have seen what was going on as they were one German mile (ca. 7 km) away. Moreover, he could not fire the signal as this would have created misunderstanding among Mir Mohanna's men as negotiations were ongoing.

When the captains decided to depart Houting was negotiating with Mir Mohanna, whom he had decided to see himself. Mir Mohanna received him well and it was he who drew Houting's attention to the fact that the ships were leaving. It was then decided that Mir Mohanna would take council with his advisers and Houting left to return to the fort. On his way back he and the two clerks with him were taken prisoner, however, and he was told to write a letter to the commander of the garrison to surrender. Seeing no way out Houting complied and that same evening Mir Mohanna took possession of Mosselsteijn at sunset. Refusal would have been futile anyway, because the garrison had mutinied that same afternoon and refused to obey its commander any longer or to fight. Houting ascribed the defeat to Mir Mohanna's superior force, treason and deceit. He was unable to save anything for the VOC, because he was not even allowed to take the archives with him. Mir Mohanna, however, allowed the Europeans to carry a sword on leaving the fort, after which they were imprisoned.[211]

THE DUTCH LEAVE KHARK

On January 4, 1766 Mir Mohanna released all VOC staff and gave them two vessels. At first the Dutch wanted to head for Kangan, but Houting later decided to sail to Bushire, due to the rapacious reputation of the population of Kangan. The other boat was too far away to hail and continued to Kangan, where they were not molested and whence its crew continued to Masqat. Houting and his group arrived in Bushire on January 5, from where he sent second mate Meyer overland to Bandar 'Abbas.[212] The latter was able to catch up with the two Dutch ships that had put the Khark refugees ashore there on January 11. The captains refused, however, to send one of the ships back to fetch Houting and his men, because of the winds and lack of supplies, which were not available at Bandar 'Abbas. It was decided to send Meyer back to Bushire on January 15, 1766 with a letter explaining their refusal. The ships would wait until February 15 at Bandar 'Abbas enabling Houting to catch up with them. Houting on receiving this news on February 4 decided against sending his men to Bandar 'Abbas in view of the weather and the shortness of time. In Bushire the Dutch had been well received by Sheikh Sa'dun and the English Agent. With the sheikh's help Houting began collecting outstanding debts. Houting also informed Karim Khan about his defeat, which he added was due to Karim Khan not sending any help. In reply Karim Khan immediately sent 400 horsemen to Bandar-e Rig to hold it for him, awaiting a larger force that would have to destroy Mir Mohanna. He also sent Qa'ed Heydar as his envoy to Houting and assured him that he would revenge the Dutch and that their loss would be compensated.[213]

---

211 VOC 3250, f. 402-03; VOC 3159, f. 714-16. To save Dutch honor treachery by Houting's Moslem clerk was also submitted as an explanation for this disaster in a contemporary Dutch source, although this is not borne out by Houting's own account. This clerk allegedly had convinced Houting to meet Mir Mohanna outside the fort to conclude an agreement. During the night of December 31 the gate was opened, much to the surprise of the guard and Mir Mohanna followed by his officers entered. When he was in the fort instead of negotiating Mir Mohanna ordered Houting's hands to be tied behind his back. He then dismissed all VOC personnel that did not take service with him and gave them some bread and dates, see NA, Legatie Archief Turkije, nr. 671, Relaas van een onpartijdige (report by an independent party); see also Anonymous, *Chronicle*, vol. 1, p. 667, n. 1 and Lorimer, *Gazetteer*, p. 1818 (Houting and party also had about 50 soldiers with him when he arrived in Bushire).

212 VOC 3159, f. 716; VOC 3184, f. 33. See chapter two for a different appreciation of the people of Kangan

213 VOC 3184, f. 31-35 (Bushman had written to Houting that he assumed that he had no money and that he therefore would leave some merchandise at Bandar 'Abbas and Masqat for him. Houting sent assistants Win-

On February 1, 1766 the VOC council at Surat learnt that Mosselsteijn was under siege and that the two Dutch ships were unable to so something about this situation. The council, therefore, concluded that the fort probably could not hold out very long. It decided to send *de Welvaren* to the Persian Gulf to carry out the High Government's decision with regards to Khark. Captain Wellemsz left on February 7; his first stop was to be Masqat where he had to disembark Dubordieux and collect information with regards to Khark. If the Dutch still held out he had to hasten immediately to their assistance and give Houting the letter with Batavia's decision to close the factory, but if Mosselsteijn had been taken he had to return.[214]

De Welvaren arrived on March 16, 1766 in Masqat where Wellemsz found 17 VOC staff, amongst whom Meyer. They told Wellemsz how matters stood, that some of the lower ratings had taken service with the English, and that Houting could get passage on an English ship. The Imam of Masqat offered Wellemsz his three ships and one gallivat with assault troops to take revenge on Mir Mohanna. Wellemsz thanked the Imam politely, but left Masqat on March 22 for Bandar 'Abbas. From there Wellemsz sent a message to Houting telling him that he would wait for him until May 1, but Houting replied that Wellemsz had to come and fetch him in Bushire. Wellemsz set course for Bushire where he arrived on May 20, 1766.[215]

Houting waited in vain for Karim Khan's assistance. The latter's troops only took Ganaveh, infested the countryside, and then returned to Shiraz. Houting then asked the English for assistance, who he had learnt were expecting a fleet to take punitive action against Sheikh Salman. The English, however, refused. Houting had hoped that jointly with *de Welvaren* the fleet could have retaken Khark. Having lost all hope Houting left Bushire on July 12 with *de Welvaren*. Via Surat he finally arrived in Galle (Ceylon), where he fell ill and could not continue to Batavia to face the music, or so his physicians claimed.[216]

REACTION IN AMSTERDAM AND BATAVIA

Only six months after the fall of Khark the XVII learnt about this disaster via Aleppo. They did not doubt the information, although Batavia had not yet confirmed it. Because they never had

---

kler and Brandt to fetch the goods, but when they arrived there were no goods); VOC 3159, Houting to Batavia (06/02/1766), f. 716vs-717.

214 VOC 3179, Extract translaat Norrotemdas (Masqat, 01/01/1766), f. 405-06; VOC 3179, Resolution policy council Surat (07/02/1766), f. 407-08; VOC 3170, Instruction for *de Welvaren* (Surat, 07/02/1766), f. 409-10.

215 VOC 3159, Winkler, Brandt (Masqat) to Senff (Surat) (17/03/1766), f. 618-19. Surat learnt about the fall of Mosselsteijn on March 3, 1766 through a letter sent from Masqat. VOC 3179, f. 413, 418-21. The Imam's offer was not without self-interest, see Lorimer, *Gazetteer*, p. 411 ("In 1765 the coffee annually exported from Masqat to Basrah was loaded, for the sake of security against the Ka'b, who were marauding in the Shatt al-Arab, on one of the Imam's men-of-war; but this ship, not venturing to proceed beyond Kharag, halted there towards the end of the year to warehouse her cargo in the Dutch settlement, and was taken along with the island on the 1st of January 1766, by Mir Muhanna"). In a letter to the EIC Agent at Basra, Mir Mohanna denied that this coffee had been found on Khark. Slot, *'Arab al-Khalij*, p. 358. The *motasallem* of Basra wanted to take retaliatory action against Mir Mohanna by confiscating cargo from his vessels that called on Basra. The EIC Agent Moore asked him not do so. However, when Mir Mohanna had attacked vessels under English protection in 1768 he advised the *motasallem* to go ahead with his plan. The authorities at Basra then seized 8 vessels belonging to Mir Mohanna, confiscated 130 bales of 50 bales were given to Moore in reduction of the Pasha of Baghda's debt owed to the EIC. Risso, *Oman & Muscat*, p. 79.

216 VOC 3159, Houting (Galle) to Batavia (?/09/1766), f. 719-21; VOC 3179, Toosie Norratemdas Ramtjender, broker in Masqat to Senff (Surat (08/08/1766), f. 422-vs; Perry, "Mir Muhanna," p. 94; Ibid., "Banu Ka'b," p. 143ff.

agreed to the Khark factory this outcome was the more unpalatable. If only the High Government had executed their orders to discontinue the Khark factory earlier the XVII complained.[217] The information that the XVII finally received in 1768 was considered to be incomplete. It had become more difficult to investigate the matter by that time, because important witnesses had died such as Buschman and the captains of the two ships. The XVII therefore concentrated on Houting about whose decisions they had many questions. They were surprised that the High Government had already acquitted Houting from any wrongdoing in 1767. According to the XVII, the landing on Kharqu had been rashly undertaken and sloppily executed and they therefore asked for more information.[218]

The High Government was clearly in a quandary as is indicated by the selected information it provided the XVII with, by the slowness of supplying that information and by the fact that it more or less absolved all the important officials involved in the disaster. One may point out that Buschmann had been very ill for a long time and then died. But the two captains were available, who gave testimony that conflicted with that given by Houting. The High Government was embarrassed by the events. It had decided to continue the Khark operation against the wishes of the XVII. Also, Houting's letter written in Bushire and Galle (Ceylon) in 1766 arrived in Batavia only in 1770! They used this delay to explain why they were unable to take a decision, despite the fact that Houting had been in Batavia since 1768. Since Buschman, Corneliszen and Du Pree had conveniently died in 1767 the High Government decided on July 24, 1771 that it could not find fault with Houting's decisions. It therefore decided to write off the loss and the XVII could not do nothing but acquiesce, because they could not find a culprit either.[219] Some people had tried to implicitly put the blame for the disaster on Buschman. In their statements Christant, Keller and Engelhardt all declared that Buschman was a chronic alcoholic, who more often than not was completely drunk. In that state Buschman did all kinds of foolish and untoward things, which he could not remember the following day. Everybody was on his guard for him, because, when drunk, Buschman was totally unpredictable and dangerous. Keller even declared that Buschman when drunk had once threatened to kill himself and shoot out his brains; he also slept with a loaded pistol under his pillow. According to Christant, Buschman had been unable to manage the VOC affairs, because of his alcohol problem.[220] However, everybody wanted to move on and forget about this defeat, which was so embarrassing to Dutch *amour propre*, and thus the matter was laid to rest and soon forgotten, as the VOC faced more serious problems at that time.

---

217 VOC 336, XVII to Batavia (06/10/1766), section Karreek, not foliated. Ironically the XVII wrote to Batavia at that time that the Dutch were humiliated at Kharqu that "undoubtedly you have carried out our orders to close down Khark." VOC 335, XVII to Batavia (04/10/1765), section Karreek, not foliated.

218 VOC 336, XVII to Batavia (28/09/1768), section Karreek, not foliated; VOC 797, Besogne over Karreek, f. 1113-17 with a detailed list of the goods lost on Khark. The total loss for the VOC amounted to Dfl. 29,396 in goods and arms exclusive of Dfl. 194,044 invested in the fort and buildings.

219 VOC 335, XVII to Batavia (05/10/1767), section Karreek, not foliated; VOC 336, XVII to Batavia (28/09/1768), section Karreek, not foliated; VOC 797, Besoigne over Karreek (Batavia, 24/07/17661), f. 1105 (the total loss of the VOC amounted to Dfl. 29,396 in merchandise, supplies and arms exclusive of fl. 194,044 invested in the fort, buildings and some merchandise). For a detailed list of the goods lost on Khark see VOC 797, f. 1112-17. Due to his family connections Houting experienced no further trouble for his handling of the Khark affair. VOC 832 (q.v. Houting) for further details on his VOC career.

220 VOC 3250, f. 410vs-411, 414, 419. About Buschman's personality and drinking problem see Niebuhr, *Reisebeschreibung*, p. 572 (he believed a soothsayer's prophecy that he would die when he would reach the age of 40 and therefore he drank).

THE DEATH OF MIR MOHANNA

After his conquest of Khark on January 1, 1766 it was generally believed that Mir Mohanna would move either against Bushire or Bahrain. But Mir Mohanna had remained mostly very quiet since his capture of Khark, although he continued raiding, be it on a much lower level. Karim Khan had written Sheikh Naser that he would send him a large force, but none came, although a large force under Sadeq Khan operated at Lar against Naser Khan.[221] Mir Mohanna, meanwhile, enjoyed his buccaneer's dream in peace: a very rich booty and the strongest fort in the Persian Gulf were his. Because he feared a Dutch attack Mir Mohanna laid in large stocks of supplies and put Khark in a state of defense. To that end he had additional fields tilled and new fortifications made. He also tried to introduce European style discipline among his troops. Despite these activities the French consul in Basra, Pyrault, was not much impressed. He wrote to the Dutch consul in Aleppo that one big man-of-war and a bombardment of six hours would reduce Mir Mohanna's stature and would lead to the recapture of Khark.[222]

Jervis preferred to take action against the pirate and destroy him, because that would be better for trade. Moreover, it could be done with two bomb vessels, he added optimistically.[223] However, Bombay instructed them not to get involved either with Mir Mohanna's "dispute with the Dutch or country Government."[224] Jervis was allowed to discuss with Sheikh Naser naval support against the Banu Ka'b, but he was not allowed to make any promises regarding operations against Mir Mohanna, with whom they had to maintain friendly relations unless his behavior towards EIC compelled it to change this position. So far he had behaved friendly, when the *Berkshire* and the *Four Friends* called on Khark for pilots to Basra. Sheikh Naser complained about that. Wrench, the agent at Basra, wrote that it would also be inadvisable to join forces with Bushire against the pirate because if our vessels would leave the Ka'b "would immediately Embrace the Opportunity of getting out with his Galivats & sending them away his most valuable, Effects &c.," apart from the fact that Mir Mohanna has reinforced the fortifications of Khark and taken defensive measure and has 3,000 men on the island, which the EIC captain saw when Mir Mohanna reviewed them in his presence, "many of which are Good Horsemen, well Train'ed all in Coats of Mail" so that current EIC force was inadequate.[225]

After Karim Khan's general, his cousin Zaki Khan, had invaded Bandar-e Rig and Ganaveh in 1766 he had tried to induce the EIC to provide his troops with naval assistance. The negotiations between Karim Khan and the EIC dragged on due to the differences of opinion amongst the English. For not only had they demanded the possession of the island of Khark, but also Karim Khan's assistance in getting compensation from Sheikh Salman of the Banu Ka'b, with whom the English were at war. Although an agreement in principle had been reached, the EIC Agent in Basra rejected it for his own personal reasons.[226] However, it was clear that sooner or later the EIC had to come to terms with Karim Khan, for the EIC needed Karim Khan's assistance in settling their dispute with Sheikh Salman, while Karim Khan needed English naval assistance to make an end to Mir Mohanna's interference with trade in the Persian Gulf. For Mir Mohanna had become the

221 Saldanha, *Précis*, vol. 1, p. 198 (Bombay, 21/07/1766).

222 NA, Legatie Archief Turkije, nr. 671, Pyrault to van Maseyk (04/02/1767). Pyrault was very much mistaken in this assessment as the English would find out in 1768, when they did more than what Pyrault had suggested and nevertheless failed to take Khark. Saldanha, *Précis*, vol. 1, pp. 240-43.

223 Saldanha, *Précis*, vol. 1, p. 197 (Bombay, 25/02/1766).

224 Saldanha, *Précis*, vol. 1, p. 197 (Bombay, 01/03/1766).

225 Saldanha, *Précis*, vol. 1, pp. 199-200 (Basra, 29/05/1766).

226 Lorimer, *Gazetteer*, pp. 141-42; Perry, "Mir Muhanna," p. 94. See on this issue chapter seven.

scourge of the Persian Gulf in 1767 from which especially Basra and Bushire suffered. He controlled all navigation in that part of the Persian Gulf and levied toll from passing ships. In 1767 he even appropriated in this way the greater part of the coffee imports of Basra. Mir Mohanna 'bought' the coffee by fixing a low piece and paid with sugar for which he fixed a high price. The result of this action was that coffee became scarce in Basra, where its price increased by 100%. In addition, Mir Mohanna had collected high customs duties from the unfortunate merchants. In Basra it was feared that in 1768 the coffee fleet, at least the smaller vessels, would not return out of fear of Mir Mohanna's depredations. Despite these acts of piracy the Ottoman authorities continued to supply Mir Mohanna with life necessities, for it did not dare to take action against him.[227]

The EIC negotiator, Skipp, had received new orders from Bombay allowing him to make a new agreement with Karim Khan similar to the one that had been agreed upon in 1767. The result was that Skipp obtained an agreement "under which, in consideration of the British reducing or making a serious effort to reduce Mir Muhanna, Karim Khan was to obtain compensation for them on account of the outrages committed by the Ka'b, if it were taken in the operations."[228] As a result of the agreement reached with Karim Khan the EIC fleet moved against Khark. However, Moore the EIC Agent at Basra sabotaged the agreement before it even had been implemented by instructing the EIC fleet to attack Khark before the Persian troops had arrived, which at that time were being prepared.[229] On May 19, 1768 the EIC squadron consisting of the *Revenge*, the *Fancy*, the *Wolf*, the *Storeship*, the *Eagle*, the *Albion* and the *Bombay Grab* arrived at Khark and started to bombard the Dutch fort for three hours with little success. The ships were farther away than had been planned due to a change in the wind. The grab caught fire, the wind increased and the signal was given to disengage. The *Revenge* and *Bombay Grab* "had suffered a good deal in their masts and rigging, and a number of shots in their Hulls, the enemy directing their shot very well, and stood to their Guns, much better than could be expected." The *Revenge* had three wounded and the *Bombay Grab* 10, some of them mortally; the *Dolphin* schooner had one man killed. In the evening it was decided to attack again in the morning, weather permitting. It was also decided to defer another attack until it was clear that Karim Khan would really send troops to assist, which would be needed to make sure of victory which otherwise was uncertain. Also, even if victorious the EIC force was too small to hold the fort and therefore Persian troops were needed to hold the island. However, given Moore's instructions not to wait for Persian troops the naval operation was a disaster.[230]

A few days later the EIC fleet tried to burn three of Mir Mohanna's gallivats in the morning between 3-4 o'clock, but they were too far ashore. Meanwhile, the *Eagle*, the *Wolf* and the *Storeship* needed water and on May 27 they went to Kharqu (Corgo). Its commander was instructed not to land if he saw any people there. For the protection of those casking water one soubadar[231] and 50 sepoys were also sent. The area was reconnoitered and nobody was seen. Unfortunately, the English

227 NA, Legatie Archief Turkeije, nr. 671, Pyrault to van Maseyk (20/10/1767). However, regional chiefs sought to put an end to Mir Mohanna's depradations. Khalifa, the sheikh of Kuwait (probably not a member of the al-Sabah family, but of the Al Khalifa, one of the three major clans ruling Kuwait) sent an emissary to Sheikh Naser of Bushire with a proposal to jointly attack Mir Mohanna in retaliation for his interference with pearl fishing, which activity hurt the 'Otobis (as pearl fishers) and Sheikh Naser, as ruler of Bahrain. Slot, *'Arab al-Khalij*, p. 363.

228 Lorimer, *Gazetteer*, pp. 141-42; Perry, "Mir Muhanna," p. 94. For more details see chapter seven.

229 Amin, *British Interests*, p. 99.

230 Saldanha, *Précis*, vol. 1, pp. 240-41 (a/b the Revenge, 21/05/1768).

231 A *soubadar* was, amongst other things, the title of the chief native officer of a company of *sepoys*. The latter Anglo-Indian term was used in India to denote a native soldier, disciplined and dressed in the European style.

had not learnt from the Dutch mistake in December 1765. "But it seems in the night the Meer had sent over forty or fifty men in small boats who hid themselves in trenches in the sand; they this morning suffered the waterers, and the guard of sepoys to land, and about and hour and half afterwards the Enemy all at once rushed out from their place of concealment." Mir Mohanna's ruse worked once again with the same results as in 1765 against the Dutch. The sepoys panicked, threw their arms away and ran into the sea; those that stood were all cut to pieces (12 and 6 wounded), two Europeans were killed and two captured. From the sea the *Eagle* and the *Wolf* kept a fire on the enemy while the *Revenge* and the *Bombay Grab* sent soldiers in boats. The enemy fled in the small boats with which they had come and neither the *Bombay Grab* nor the *Fancy Signal* could do anything, because there was hardly any wind. The wounded were taken aboard. "We also received letter from Skip to-day telling that the Khan will find some new excuse for not sending his troops. The water at Corgu is bad, the Mir not to be trusted" and thus they were forced to send the *Fancy*, the *Wolf*, and the *Storeship* to Bushire to fetch water, firewood and send the wounded. The *Eagle* and the *Albion* were sent to Basra for water and to return, unless different orders were given.[232] Moore then ordered the fleet to return to India, although he kept a few ships to maintain the blockade against the Ka'b, while Karim Khan's troops marched on Ganaveh, where they were supposed to join forces with the EIC fleet. Moore, the Basra Agent, who did not trust Karim Khan at all, defended his action by arguing that, "we are sure no man will ever leave land and the march is only to deceive us and blame us for the failure of the negotiations.[233]

London also disagreed with an attack on Mir Mohanna or taking possession of Khark or even residing on it, supposing that Mir Mohanna would allow it. It even gave explicit orders not to quarrel with Mir Mohanna, "judging it very improper that our effects and servants should be under the protection of a Man who is a publick Robber, his present situation at the entrance of Bussorah river makes it necessary for us to keep on good terms with him, as otherwise many of the small vessels trading from the different settlements in India belonging to our servants and Inhabitants might be molested by him, and we now positively order that you do not attack him unless he begins."[234]

Bombay was very displeased with the turn of events in the Persian Gulf. It berated the staff at Basra to have returned the EIC flotilla to India, because a few days after its departure Zand troops had arrived at Ganaveh and thus the joint operation could have been executed and benefits might have accrued. Furthermore, Bombay wanted to know why Basra had not sent the remaining ships to ferry Persian troops across so that EIC could have received the promised 15,000 *tumans*. After all, why would Karim Khan go to such great expense of sending a large force to Ganaveh and then not use it? Bombay was also baffled by Moore's orders to attempt to stop communications between Khark and the mainland, and to begin negotiations with the islanders and then to stipulate the demolition of the fort and the delivery of ordinance, which of course exasperated them and resulted in a negative reply. Bombay argued that the negotiations should have been with Zaki Khan, who, if there had been difficulties in getting the island, would have granted the EIC good terms or would have paid compensation for the losses incurred. Now it was difficult to say what to do given the mess that had been created. Although Bombay was not exactly sure how to proceed, it knew what it wanted, to wit: (i) the EIC's expenses have to be reimbursed; (ii) EIC losses have to be made good, and (iii) EIC trade has to be established on a firm footing. If that could be achieved then this would be an excellent result, whether such an agreement would have been reached with Karim

232 Saldanha, *Précis*, vol. 1, p. 242 (a/b the Revenge, 29/05/1768); Ibid., vol. 1, p. 243 (a/b the Revenge, 29/05/1768) (Total result: 24 killed, 5 wounded, 1 missing).

233 Saldanha, *Précis*, vol. 1, pp. 247-48 (Basra, 30/10/1768).

234 Saldanha, *Précis*, vol. 1, p. 246 (London, 02/03/1768).

Khan or the islanders. However, Moore was ordered not to keep the ships there longer than necessary, except the ships needed for the blockade of the Banu Ka'b. Bombay also had concluded that the attack on Khark in May had been done improperly and therefore it wanted an inquiry.[235]

While the English and Persians were bickering (Skipp was still negotiating in Shiraz), Mir Mohanna meanwhile continued his piratical activities unchallenged and now also considered English vessels a target. He seized the *Speedwell Snow* on August 17, 1768. The EIC at Basra, who had wanted to make an alliance with Mir Mohanna against Karim Khan, immediately sent a letter to Muscat for all commanders to warn them about the danger of being the prey of Mir Mohanna's gallivats. It was further decided that EIC protected vessels would leave Basra in convoy all the way to Bushire. If Mir Mohanna's gallivats were not at Khark then the convoy would continue till Verdistan. Moroever, the squadron was split into two and moved constantly between Verdistan and Basra.[236]

To the great surprise and joy of all in the region internal dissent among Mir Mohanna's followers put an end to the pirate's carreer. After the disaster of the naval attack of May 1768 the EIC Agent at Basra, Moore, dismissed the fleet and thus once again sabotaged the recent agreement concluded with Karim Khan. The latter had sent an army to the littoral to make a joint landing with the EIC fleet. But when the Persian army appeared in August 1768 the only naval assistance consisted of the Bushire fleet. The Persians were determined to bring an end to Mir Mohanna's terror and throughout the winter contained him on Khark by maintaining a blockade. The hardship from which Mir Mohanna's men suffered as well as his continuing brutality led to a revolt against him by some of his kinsmen.

> The Meer having confined one Durbass, a person of the greatest note in his service, and treated him with the utmost severity for some trivial offence, the heads of the most considerable tribes of Arabs on the island were so much alarmed at this proceeding as to apprehend themselves in a very dangerous situation from the Meer's cruel disposition and therefore entered into a conspiracy to destroy him.

The conspirators seized the so-called small fort on Khark on January 26, 1769 before Mir Mohanna knew what was happening and then surrounded him to take him prisoner. Mir Mohanna and his bodyguard were set upon by a hostile mob in the bazaar. However, some of his henchmen gave him time to escape to one of the bastions of the large fort, where he hoped to make a defense awaiting reinforcements. These did not come and at long last he fled "in a small boat, with about 20 men who still adhered to him."[237] Mir Mohanna after a three weeks' journey landed in a creek near Basra on February 17, 1769, "with the intention of entering the services of some Shaikks of the Arabs in the desert; but the Mutasallim (of Basra) being forewarned of this immediately got to horse with his guards and cut off the escape of Mir Muhanna, whom nolens volens he took off to his palace and kept in the inner ward, where he was treated with much respect and kindness until the Pasha of Baghdad prepared for him a halter worthy of him, in which he had his reward this night."[238] His plea for asylum was rejected by the *motasallem* of Basra. At midnight of March 24, 1769 Mir Mohanna with one attendant was strangled and thereafter beheaded at the direct orders of the Pasha of Baghdad. The English considered this to be a dishonorable deed. "How great so ever might

235 Saldanha, *Précis*, vol. 1, pp. 254-56 (Bombay, 24/04/1769)

236 Saldanha, *Précis*, vol. 1, pp. 248-49 (Basra, 30/10/1768).

237 Saldanha, *Précis*, vol. 1, pp. 249-50 (Bushire, 04/02/1769).

238 Anonymous, *Chronicle*, vol. 1, p. 670.

have been the Meer's crimes he was not a Turkish subject, and his being powerless and a prisoner ought surely to have entitled him to their humanity and protection. If not that they ought to have given him up to the Caun, and not have stained their honour with his blood."[239] His head was sent to the Pasha of Baghdad and his body was thrown to the dogs. Thus ended the career of the one-eyed scourge of the Persian Gulf, who also was infamous for having "murdered Father, Mother, Brother and about twenty other relations."[240] Although Mir Mohanna indeed had killed many of his close relatives and could be cruel, he in general seems to have reacted with restraint and not have killed the crews of the vessels that he pirated. He behaved graciously towards the English when he ousted them from Rig as he did towards the Dutch whom he took prisoner after the conquest of Khark and even gave them two small boats so that they might reach a safe haven. Although he still appeals to the imagination of many as one local chief who stood up against the Europeans, his actual contribution to his people was negative as he had not created anything (institutionally, commercially, politically) on which they could build something of a more lasting nature, for Khark's role soon was reduced to one of insignificance .

Moore believed that Mir Mohanna had amassed great wealth on Khark and therefore hoped that by blockading the island he could get a share of that wealth as compensation for the EIC's losses from his successors of Karim Khan, who he just had snubbed. However, things worked out differently than Moore had thought. The EIC flotilla had demanded that Mir Hoseyn destroy his fortifications and surrender his cannons was met with a blunt refusal by the new chief. By April 1769 when it became clear that the blockade was ineffective and that Karim Khan was mobilizing a fleet Moore withdrew the EIC flotilla. Its commander nevertheless was ordered "not to act offensively against the Caun, Chaub, or Meer, unless a favourable opportunity offers, whereby if he thinks he can get possession or destroy the Gallivats of both or either of the latter powers, if he can, he is by all means to attempt it."[241]

The new governors of Khark, Durbass and Hassan Sagadeen, invited Zaki Khan (Zaiky), the governor of Fars, to send two persons to take inventory of the goods remaining on the island. Hasan Soltan then had gone to Shiraz to give an inventory of Mir Mohanna's possession. Karim Khan came to an agreement with the leaders of the revolt. Hasan Soltan, who in exchange for acknowledging Karim Khan's rule and accepting a Zand garrison was appointed chief of Bandar-e Rig and given the title of Khan, with orders to look after the fort of Khark and, like the Dutch, make the island an inhabited and thriving place. Karim Khan furthermore returned one-third of Mir Mohanna's goods to Hasan Soltan (and his men) thereby creating a material basis for the latter's

239 Saldanha, *Précis*, vol. 1, p. 253 (Basra, 02/04/1769). This source does not mention the foreknowledge that the *motasallem* was supposed to have had. Mir Mohanna was simply recognized in the streets and then immediately arrested.

240 Saldanha, *Précis*, vol. 1, pp. 197, 249-50, 253; Nami, *Tarikh*, pp. 162, 169-70; Ghaffari Kashani, *Golshan-e Morad*, pp. 277-78. He also was accused of having ordered "two of his own sisters to be drowned in the sea [in August 1765], apparently because the Ka'b Sheikh, whom he disliked, had demanded one of them in marriage for a son and he considered this the most convenient way of evading the request." He also was said to have killed "his own first-born child by causing it to be exposed to the sun upon the sea beach, his only reason for doing so being that it was a daughter and not a son." Niebuhr, *Beschreibung*, p. 318; Ibid., *Travels*, vol. 2, p. 147; Lorimer, *Gazetteer*, p. 1815. If this is true then it would have been in direct contravention of a Koranic prohibition (Sura 6, al-An'am, 136, 140, 151).

241 Lorimer, *Gazetteer*, p. 1802.

loyalty.[242] After having pledged allegiance to Shiraz he had second thoughts about it, however, believing that maybe elsewhere he might get a better offer.

> Meer Hussain Sultan, the Sheikh of the island, seems to be wavering between his fear of the Caun [i.e. Karim Khan] and his desire of keeping possession of carrack and its riches. Some reports say that his people are much disaffected to His Government and are daily leaving the Island, that he intends delivering the effects to the Caun and that they are to be equally divided between the Meer and the Caun and the Persian Army; others that he is very desirous of our setting on the Island where he would give us a Factory, but not the fort as he first proposed and others again say that the Meer has wrote to the Imaum of Muscat requesting his friendship, and promising to deliver over the effects and gallivats of the island if he will grant him his protection and admit of his and his followers living unmolestedly at Muscat.

Karim Khan was aware of the wavering loyalty of the new chief of Rig and Khark and therefore to enforce his adherence to their agreement as well as his control over Khark he ordered the Ka'b to send their fleet to Ganaveh and to join there with the Bushire fleet there. It was reported that the Ka'b fleet consisted of 10 gallivats and two boats with about 250 men in one and 70 to 80 in the rest. The Bushire fleet consisted of one small ship, 4 gallivats and about 30 armed boats, and the Banu Ka'b fleet allegedly was met last Monday by a boat from Bushire. However, the EIC Agent doubted this news, for he was convinced that the Ka'b would never go as far as Ganaveh. He believed that some Ka'b vessels might show up near Bushire in a show of obedience, but that these then would return to Dowraq. He added that if he were wrong in his assessment and the Ka'b really would obey Karim Khan's summons he would withdraw the EIC's small fleet from Khark. Because apart from the fact that the weather was dangerous, the EIC vessels were not in a good condition, the combined Ka'b and Bushire fleet and the Zand land army was too big a force to oppose, while messages between the island and land could not be stopped, all of which would make it a dangerous situation for the EIC fleet. Moreover, if the EIC flotilla were to attack the Ka'b fleet, with whom they still were officially at war, it would have grave political consequences, even if the EIC would be victorious which he considered very uncertain. Therefore he had ordered the EIC flotilla to return to Basra, not to give offense, and to detain gallivats only where it could be done without too much trouble.[243]

There would be another attack on an English ship by Khark gallivats in June 1770, which was the result of the unresolved conflict between the EIC and Karim Khan. Despite this hostile act, Hoseyn Khan the chief of Bandar-e Rig and Khark, wrote to Moore, the EIC Agent, offering friendship and assistance to EIC ships as well as the right to build a factory at Bandar-e Rig. Moore sent a polite reply that at that time the EIC was not able to settle at Bandar-e Rig.[244] How the capture of this ship was resolved is discussed in chapter seven.

242 Ghaffari Kashani, *Golshan-e Morad*, p. 277; Saldanha, *Précis*, vol. 1, p. 250 (Bushire, 04/02/1769). Hassan Sagadeen and Durbass were the new governors of Bandar-e Rig and Khark, although Hasan governed alone later. The name Durbass perhaps is from the term *dur-bash* ('begone'), an official in a notable's retinue to announce his master's imminent arrival and to warn the people in the street or passage-way to be gone, to get out of the way. Sagadeen may be a bastardization of the name Shoja' al-Din. Amin, *British Interests*, p. 137.

243 Saldanha, *Précis*, vol. 1, pp. 252-53 (Basra, 02/04/1769).

244 Saldanha, *Précis*, vol. 1, pp. 267-68 (Basra, 15/10/1770).

A KNIPHAUSENESQUE END

Here the Khark matter did not rest, for in 1769 William Eaton was appointed vice-consul for the Netherlands in Basra. Eaton had been in Aleppo before that time and worked for the British firm of David Hays & Co. in that city. He knew the Dutch consul van Maseyk there, who in fact appointed him when the previous Dutch consul in Basra, the Frenchman Pyrault was about to leave Basra. Eaton continued to serve as agent of Hays & Co in Basra, which firm could only exist there because of its protected status with the Dutch, otherwise the EIC would have turned it out.[245]

Although the Dutch ambassador to the Porte had agreed to Eaton's appointment he later wanted to know why Eaton had been appointed instead of Pyrault, who was still in Basra. Van Maseyk informed the ambassador that Pyrault was waiting for the settlement of some affairs and would leave shortly.[246] Eaton's task as consul was only to forward letters in transit. Van Maseyk had written to his friends in Surat that he did not want to be engaged in the East Indies trade in Basra. If the VOC wanted to trade it would have to send its own staff.[247]

Meanwhile Eaton had taken the initiative to write to van der Parra, the governor-general of the VOC in Batavia. He proposed that the VOC restarted its trade with the Persian Gulf and Basra. To facilitate such a decision Eaton had made a list of what kind of goods a VOC ship should bring to Basra. The High Government, however, more or less numbed by the Khark disaster, decided against such an action. The navigation to the Persian Gulf area was considered to be too dangerous. Nevertheless, the High Government authorized Eaton to try and get back the VOC monies which Sheikh Sa'dun of Bushire still held for the VOC. Eaton similarly was authorized to get back the VOC goods and monies that it had lost at Khark, either in the form of merchandise, cash or drafts. If successful, Eaton would be entitled to 10% of the amount recuperated.[248]

One year after his arrival in Basra, Eaton got into trouble with the local authorities, possibly incited by the English and Jews, as he himself asserted.[249] In view of the fact that he was barely tolerated by the English, being under Dutch protection, and that he intended to re-establish VOC trade there, this may lend credence to his accusation. Anyway, the opportunity was provided by Eaton himself when he dismissed his Jewish banker (*sarraf*) on November 8, 1771 and imprisoned his Jewish interpreter on November 13. On November 14, Eaton was informed that his newly appointed *sarraf*, the Banyan Munseram, had been arrested by the *motasallem* and that his house and effects had been sealed. The *motasallem* then had sent for Eaton's Turkish clerk and asked him whether Munseram was really Eaton's *sarraf*. Eaton meanwhile asked the commander of the guard to intervene and bring about Munseram's release. The commander agreed to do so and accompanied

245 The enmity the EIC Agent apparently bore Mr. Eaton probably was caused by the fact that he wanted to extend trade of Hays & Co., although Amin, *British Interests*, p. 137 is wrong in stating that Eaton came to Basra "early in 1770."

246 NA, Legatie Archief Turkije, nr. 691, de Weiler to van Maseyk (27/02/1771) and letters from the same dated 14/08/1771 and 14/12/1771. The reason for Pyrault's continued presence had to do with Khark. For "at the same time Pyrault, the agent of the Compagnie des Indes at Basra, was intriguing through friends at the Persian court to gain Kharg for the French in a package trade agreement, and indeed in September [1769] obtained Karim Khan's consent; but for various reasons this was never put into effect." Perry, "Mir Muhanna," p. 95.

247 NA, Legatie Archief Turkije, nr. 721, van Maseyk to de Weiler (25/11/1771).

248 VOC 801, Decision High Government (Batavia, 25/05/1771), f. 117-19.

249 NA, Legatie Archief Turkije, nr. 721, Eaton to de Weiler (16/01/1772) enclosed in van Maseyk to de Weiler (17/03/1772); D. Sestini, *Viaggio da Constatinopoli a Bassora* (n.p., 1786), p. 260

Eaton's clerk to the *motasallem*. Eaton also had given his clerk a message demanding that Munseram should be given a coat of honor as recompense for the affront done to the Dutch nation.

The *motasallem* was surprised at Eaton's interference. Munseram owed Mir Muhanna 10,000 *tumans* and that very morning orders had arrived from the Pasha of Baghdad to have Munseram arrested. The commander of the guard informed Eaton accordingly. Eaton reacted that if it were true that Munseram owed Mir Mohanna money then "it belonged to my nation whose money he had taken when he took Carick [Khark] & not that of the Basha, who must have been misinformed." Eaton therefore suggested that he would keep Munseran in his house and wait for the Pasha's response. If he did not come he would go in person to Baghdad to complain to the Pasha, for the *motasallem* was acting contrary to the articles of the Dutch-Ottoman Treaty. On the evening of November 14, 1771 Eaton sent for an important Jewish leader, Jacob Haaron,[250] whom he informed likewise. That same night the *motasallem* sent for Eaton's clerk and threatened to cut off his head, "if the Balius [consul] sent again to demand the seraf [*sarraf*]."

Early the following morning Eaton's clerk was sent again for by the *motasallem*, who again uttered threats against him. The *motasallem* further told the clerk that he did not acknowledge Eaton as consul, for he had never paid him an official visit. The clerk said that Eaton had made preparations to do so when the Munseram problem started and "had sent to Cogie Jacob [Khvajeh Ya'qub] to settle the manner of my reception of the honours to be paid to me; that I had not was because the French & English had been put three or four days before, & I had been sick at 7ber [September] whence I only returned three days before." The *motasallem* then asked where the Dutch ships were and why Eaton had not hoisted the Dutch flag on his house? Moreover, he wanted to know why Eaton had taken a piece of land from a Moslem in settlement of a debt? This piece of land was *vaqf* property and could not be alienated by anybody. The clerk countered that the debt had been paid and that Eaton had not taken any piece of land at all.

The *motasallem* then asked a few Christian merchants, who were present, whether they had heard that Munseram was Eaton's *sarraf*, which they denied. Eaton then obtained declarations from a number of Englishmen, who stated that Eaton had told them so on November 13, 1771. Pyrault, the French consul, who still had not left Basra, urged the *motasallem* to settle the mater amiably. Eaton also tried to engage EIC support, but the Agent declined. Because the interpreter's arrest was not contrary to the Dutch-Ottoman Treaty the *motasallem* informed Eaton that he dropped this grievance against him, the more so, because the man had not asked for his intercession. However, on November 16, 1771 Eaton's clerk was arrested, but when the soldiers passed the Dutch consulate he was set free by Eaton's servants. Eaton then sent his second interpreter to lodge a complaint with the *motasallem* who "abused him in a very scandalous manner & forbid him coming there again." The following day Eaton set free the interpreter, whereupon the *motasallem* released Munseram, but not before he had taken 6,000 sarmebous from him.[251]

Eaton then asked for help from van Maseyk, the Dutch consul at Aleppo. He wanted a decree from the Porte allowing him to get the money back from the *motasallem*. In case of the latter's refusal Eaton would have to be allowed to charge the amount to the Jewish servants of the Basra government. Because Eaton apparently was still harassed in Basra he decided to retire to Persia and await the outcome of his request for support. He also suggested to van Maseyk that like von

---

250 Eaton, in his diary, writes about this person: "no material step is taken without his approbation on acco[un]t of his connexion w[i]th the Seraf bashee of Baghdad or in more adequate terms the acting Basha." Eaton's diary is enclosed in van Maseyk to de Weiler (17/03/1772), see NA, Legatie Archief Turkije, nr. 721.

251 All English quotations are from Eaton's diary. On his release Munseram was threatened with death if he dared to return to Eaton's service. NA, Legatie Archief Turkije, nr. 721, Eaton to de Weiler (16/01/1772).

Kniphausen he might blockade the Shatt al-Arab. To this end Eaton enlisted the assistance of a certain Hasan Khan, commander of the gallivats in Persia, who had promised to help him with this project, if asked to do so. Van Maseyk supported Eaton's request as did his principal, David Hays. Van Maseyk at the same time wrote to Surat to inform the Dutch there of the events and urged them not to send any Dutch goods or Dutch ships to Basra for the time being, because of these problems.[252]

The Dutch ambassador in Istanbul admonished Eaton by writing that he might have behaved more sensibly by first having presented himself to Soleyman Aqa as Dutch vice-consul and by displaying the Dutch flag, before arresting his interpreter and dismissing his *sarraf*. The ambassador nevertheless understood Eaton's difficult position. For neither the Pasha nor the *motasallem* would investigate whether Munseram's money was Eaton's or Mir Mohanna's. Nonetheless, the ambassador pointed out that the *motasallem* had the impression that Munseram had only joined Eaton's service to flee his creditors. If this was true then it was Eaton's own fault that he was in trouble. However, the ambassador believed Eaton's side of the events and had asked and had obtained a strongly worded *farman* addressed to the Pasha of Baghdad and his deputy. The Porte expressed its displeasure about what had happened and ordered the *motasallem* to repay the money. Because Eaton had left for Persia van Maseyk was charged to have the decree implemented. It had been impossible to obtain a payment order on the government of Basra and, in case of refusal, permission to blockade Basra, the ambassador added.[253] In an accompanying letter to van Maseyk, the ambassador gave his opinion that Eaton probably had gotten into trouble, because of other people's affairs. He also agreed that Surat should not send any Dutch goods to Basra for the time being.[254] Van Maseyk promised to do his best. He pointed out that in his view the entire affair was Eaton's own fault. It would not have happened if Pyrault had still been Dutch vice-consul. The latter who was still in Basra, therefore was appointed again in that function.[255] At the beginning of 1773, van Maseyk informed the Dutch ambassador that he had received a letter from Batavia in which he was informed that the VOC was not interested in carrying on trade in the Persian Gulf. The Gulf route would only be used for letter and parcel post. To that end the VOC factory in Surat had already engaged the services of a Turkish merchant in Basra in 1772.[256]

Although Dutch sources do not mention the outcome of van Maseyk's endeavors it is unlikely that Munseram's money was ever returned.[257] Eaton meanwhile had gone to Karim Khan's court where he appears to have been well received. As a result of his visit Karim Khan allegedly granted him the cession of Khark and promised to return Dutch goods when the VOC had settled again on Khark. However, as we have seen, the VOC did not want to trade in the Persian Gulf anymore. To start again as a result of another Kniphausenque scheme would have put off the VOC anyway. Sestini, therefore, is wrong to ascribe the VOC's negative attitude to the ensuing Persian-Ottoman war. The same holds true for his statement that the Dutch thereafter did not trade in the Persian Gulf anymore.[258] The last vestige of their 133 year presence in the Gulf was fort Mosselsteijn, which

252 NA, Legatie Archief Turkije, nr. 721, van Maseyk to de Weiler (17/03/1772).

253 NA, Legatie Archief Turkije, nr. 691, draft letter from de Weiler to Eaton (23/05/1772).

254 NA, Legatie Archief Turkije, nr. 691, de Weiler to van Maseyk (02/04/1772).

255 NA, Legatie Archief Turkije, nr. 721, van Maseyk to de Weiler (17/07/1772); nr. 691, de Weiler to van Maseyk (23/12/1772) (draft).

256 NA, Legatie Archief Turkije, nr. 721, van Maseyk to de Weiler (02/02/1773).

257 Sestini, *Viaggio*, p. 260.

258 Sestini, *Viaggio*, p. 260; Willem Floor, "Dutch Trade with Masqat the second half of the 18th century" or chapter six.

continued to serve those who had control over Khark. It was finally used "as a quarry for building material which was exported, both to the mainland at Ganaweh and to Basra and Abadan, between 1914 and 1924" and thus no trace of its remains anymore.[259]

CONCLUSION

The decision to establish a factory at Khark was part of a companywide reform policy aimed at turning the tide of diminishing returns, and not a whim of a few individuals, as Amin has suggested.[260] The High Government or chief executive body of the VOC in Asia, based in Batavia (now Djakarta, Indonesia) hoped to sell large quantities of Java sugar to the Persian and Turkish market via Khark. This was especially important for the well-being of Batavia, the headquarters of the VOC in Asia, which had trouble selling its ever-growing sugar production. Its other main commodities, spices and pepper, the VOC could sell anywhere.

Although the new establishment on the island of Khark proved to be a failure, its creation did not fail to make an impression on the competition and the local powers in the Gulf. In fact, the EIC staff was convinced that the establishment of the Khark factory and other VOC plans and initiatives (the conquest of Bahrain, trade with Masqat and Sind, the abandonment of Bushire) formed part of a Dutch master plan for the domination of the Gulf. Amin likewise and mistakenly also believed this, and he is therefore wrong to assert that the Dutch had failed in expanding their authority to any part of the Persian Gulf, for it had never been the intention of the VOC to do so, and therefore its policy could not fail in that respect. There never was a Dutch master plan to dominate the Persian Gulf militarily and politically. On the surface Dutch intentions may have looked that way. The blockade of the Shatt al-Arab in 1753 was followed by the establishment of the fort on Khark in that same year. Also, the fears about Dutch intentions with regards to Bahrain (1754-56), the destruction of the EIC fort in Bandar-e Rig (1756) and the beginning of trade relations with Masqat (1756) all looked like elements of some master strategist's plan. The Bahrain plan, although it was proposed by von Kniphausen, was flatly turned down by Batavia and thus never materialized. The Dutch had nothing directly to do with the Bandar-e Rig disaster of the English, and the plan to establish a factory in Masqat or even to start trading there was immediately and successfully opposed by the chief of the Khark factory. Also, the VOC closed down its Bushire factory in 1753 and its Bandar 'Abbas factory in 1759. Thus, there remains no basis at all for Amin's assertion.

Dutch failure was not caused either by an uncompromising spirit with local inhabitants that turned them into enemies rather than friends, as suggested by Amin. For the subsequent VOC Agents had all good relations with the local chiefs, with the exception of Mir Mohanna, and in that case only after 1762. Even with their erstwhile 'enemies', the Ottoman governor in Basra and the Sheikh of Bushire excellent and friendly relations existed. Von Kniphausen had his own gallivat to ply between Khark and Basra without meeting with any problem in Basra. The Sheikh of Bushire supported the Dutch after 1757 and succored them after the fall of Khark. This did not prevent the Dutch from having good relations with Bushire's enemies such as the Banu Ka'b of Dowraq. Similar

---

259 J.W. Winchester, "Note on the Island of Karrack in the Gulf of Persia," *Transactions of the Bombay Geographical Society* 2 (1838), pp. 35-39; A. W. Stiffe, "Persian Gulf Notes-Kharag Island," *Geographical Journal* 12 (1898), p. 179-82; Anonymous, "The Island of Kharak of Charack," *Asiatic Journal* 27 (1838), pp. 23-24; Wilson, *Persian Gulf*, p. 182.

260 Amin, *British Interests*, p. 149.

good relations existed with other local chiefs such as the Mirs of Ganaveh and Charak and not to forget the Imam of Masqat. This was the result of traditional VOC policy in the Persian Gulf to try and keep good relations with all local chiefs in the interest of trade. The VOC's motto was "make trade not war," although it also made war at times, especially elsewhere in Asia. True, it was Dutch involvement in a local conflict which led to their downfall, but this conflict was not of their own making. The Dutch would have preferred not to interfere, because they had reached a *modus vivendi* with Mir Mohanna. They were forced into this conflict by Karim Khan and handled it badly led by a young inexperienced resident, which led to the fall of Khark and the withdrawal of the VOC from the Persian Gulf altogether.

SHORT BIOGRAPHY OF VON KNIPHAUSEN

Tido Frederik von Inn und Kniphausen was a scion of a well-known East Frisian family, of which also a Dutch branch existed. He was born in 1718 in Gödens and became at an early age, after his father's death, an officer in the Prussian army. His father, Friedrich Ernst von Kniphausen, had been Prussian ambassador at the French court and his brother Prussian ambassador at the English court. According to an anonymous English source, von Kniphausen told his life story as follows. During the war with Austria in 1742-43 the king of Prussia fled during the battle. Von Kniphausen was so angry about this flight, which had been unnecessary because Prussia won the battle, that he wrote a satire about the king. The latter took offense and had von Kniphausen put in prison. Von Kniphausen was able to induce one of his guards to escape with him to the Netherlands. Through the support of the governor-general of the VOC, baron van Imhoff, who was a friend of the von Kniphausen family, both Tido von Kniphausen and his fellow-escapee the guard were offered posts with the VOC. According to Meilink, von Kniphausen was offered a post through the good offices of a cousin of the Dutch branch of the von Kniphausen's. The same English source adds that von Kniphausen openly bragged about his misdeeds by which he tried to show how clever he was. The anonymous Englishman, who clearly disapproved of von Kniphausen and his way of life, also added that "he was totally free from the fetters by which people are restricted such as virtue, Christian religion and morality."[261] In 1746 von Kniphausen arrived in Batavia and in May 1747 he was appointed junior merchant in China. In 1748 he was promoted to supervisor of maritime and commercial affairs (*commisaris van zee- en commerciezaken*). In 1749 von Kniphausen was promoted to the rank of merchant and appointed as Agent of the Basra factory. The rest of his career is described in this study.

261 NA, Collectie Alting nr. 68, Vijf brieven van een vrij koopman (third letter), f. 51-52; see also Ives, *Voyage*, p. 208 (he left "Prussian service from some disgust and then served as a lieutenant in a regiment of French dragoons and then went to the East Indies.")

DISPUTE ABOUT THE INTERVENTION AT THE PORTE

A long and bitter dispute was the result of the *farman* that ambassador Elbert de Hochepied had obtained, or rather concerning the (alleged) expenditures paid for obtaining it. De Hochepied has sent a few letters to von Kniphausen in reply to his request for help. De Hochepied had expressed the opinion that if von Kniphausen would have had a consular *barat* all this would not have happened. He also agreed that the English were behind the Basra events. After having tried a few times in vain to get the Ottoman authorities interested in the matter de Hochepied finally obtained a *farman* after having intimated that he would be unable to prevent ant retaliatory action in the absence of an adequate resolution of the problem. He wrote that such a *farman* was only granted in extraordinary cases and it had to be complied with immediately. The *farman* was treated as if it were a secret project, so that most of the leading officials of the Porte did not even know about it, for the Soltan did not want to consult them about it. Nevertheless, de Hochepied considered it necessary to show the text to some officials, who expressed their surprise at the tone of the *farman* and wondered who would be selected to deliver it to Soleyman Pasha. De Hochepied also informed von Kniphausen that the cost for obtaining the *farman* amounted to 30,000 piasters.[262] When von Kniphausen refused to pay these costs de Hochepied wrote to the States-General, who referred the matter to the XVII, the directors of the VOC. The latter asked for information from Batavia, who in their turn ordered von Kniphausen to provide that information to the XVII.[263]

Von Kniphausen replied that since his experience with de Hochepied concerning consular *barats* he had taken the precaution of limiting the possibility of the ambassador to drawn on VOC financial resources. Especially important is a letter written by von Kniphausen to de Hochepied, which the latter used as an argument in favor of his own case. In this letter, however, it would seem von Kniphausen indeed had indicated that de Hochepied could not unlimitedly call on VOC funds as far as expenses were concerned. Von Kniphausen began to point out to de Hochepied that Batavia had not agreed to the payment of 2,000 piasters to obtain a consular *barat* and that von Kniphausen would have to pay those out of his own pocket. He added that he therefore did not dare to spend more money on the matter, since without prior approval from Batavia such expenses would be charged to his personal account. After this introduction von Kniphausen gave a brief outline what had happened to him in Basra and he asked the ambassador's assistance to recover the extorted money.

262 VOC 2893, de Hochepied to von Kniphausen (09/07/1753), f. 1524; Ibid., idem to idem (18/08/1753), f. 1526-27.

263 VOC 2893, Replicq van den opperkoopman von Kniphausen, undated (1757), f, 1503; NA, Collectie de Hochepied, nr. 108, XVII to de Hochepied (15/10/1756).

> C'est apresent a la prudence reconnu de Vôtre Excell. A saisir les moyens qu'elle jugera les plus propres pour optenir justice de cette avanie." [Later returning to the same subject von Kniphausen wrote:] "Comme a la Porte aucune affaire ne peut reussir sans qu'on debute prelablement par quelque depence ou present Votre Excell. Pourra prendre des nommes Pogus et Mikkertar ce qu'elle jugera necessaire et leurs donner de letter de changes sur nôtre Comptoir, qui seront acquittés quand on les presentera a ceux qui nous laissons ici.

Moreover, von Kniphausen made it clear that he did not attach great importance to a *farman* from the Porte, for in that case he still had to see by what ways and means Soleyman Pasha might be induced to repay the extorted money. To put de Hochepied's mind at ease on this score von Kniphausen wrote him that this would be easy for the VOC for he would return with a few ships to blockade the Shatt al-Arab.[264]

Because he understood that de Hochepied had to give presents to obtain a *farman* from the Porte he had written him that he could draw money from two Armenian merchants in Istanbul. Von Kiphausen had instructed these two merchants not to pay more than 2,000 rupees to de Hochepied and if he claimed more they were to pay nothing at all until his return from Batavia. Philippe Catafago had hardly arrived in Istanbul when de Hochepied had already asked for 30,000 piasters, which was refused.[265]

De Hochepied denied all these allegations and tried to prove that von Kniphausen had intimated that he expected much from his actions as well as his credit at the Porte, and that the two Armenian merchants had not even be prepared to give him 1,000 piasters. After consultation with Catafago, who had told de Hochepied that the VOC would repay him immediately and would be eternally grateful de Hochepied borrowed money on his own credit. After von Kniphausen had refused to pay de Hochepied had sent his bill with expenditures to Batavia, but he had heard nothing from the High Government.[266] Von Kniphausen commented that this bill was incomplete, for de Hochepied had not specified the costs and had only listed the presents that he had given. According to von Kniphausen, these presents had been in the possession of de Hochepied prior to the Basra affair and had been destined for the Soltan himself. However, before the sale of the jewels concerned was concluded the *qizlar aghasi* (chief of the harem), who acted as broker in this matter was executed. As a result, de Hochepied was left with costly presents to the value of 20,000 piasters which he wanted to sell as soon as possible. The baroness de Hochepied had written to von Kniphausen to ask him whether he could sell them to the Shah of Persia, the Great Moghul or to one of the Javanese princes. Von Kniphausen clearly implied that de Hochepieds were out to cheat the VOC. He also made the point that the ambassador conveniently had not submitted his report to Batavia about the outcome of the entire affair, while von Kniphausen also expressed his surprise about the extravagant claim made by de Hochepied. Von Kniphausen had written to him that if de Hochepied would

---

264 The French quotes are in the original orthography without the accents where they should be etc. It was quite common for noblemen to correspond with one another in French rather than in Dutch to show that they were really a class apart. NA, Stadhouderlijke Secretarie, nr. 1.29.5 (annex 8), von Kniphausen to de Hochepied (Bassora dans la Riviere a Bord du Vaisseau la Fortune, 30/01/1753), not foliated.

265 VOC 2893, Replicq van den opperkoopman von Kniphausen, undated (1757), f, 1503-09.

266 NA, Collectie de Hochepied nr. 108, de Hochepied to XVII (17/05/1761); VOC 2893, Replicq van den opperkoopman von Kniphausen, undated (1757), f, 1503-09; VOC 2893, Statement by Philippo Catafago (Khark, 15/09/1757), f. 1528; VOC 2893, Baronesse de Hochepied to von Kniphausen (09/1753), f. 1529-30. For the nature of the present see NA, Stadhouderlijke Secretarie nr. 1.19.5, de Hochepied to Steyn (05/1755).

submit to him a reasonable amount of expenditures he would be willing to try and get payment for it.

From the evidence we have it is impossible to decide who was right in this matter. Von Kniphausen's papers, in my view, show a stronger case than the documents produced by de Hochepied. Both noblemen were not "unacquainted with the vicissitudes of the world" and not averse to making money in a dishonest manner, they were noblemen after all.[267] The XVII who were quite out of their depth in this matter, having insufficient data, felt sympathetic towards de Hochepied. They finally decided, however, that it was not their problem- it was rather a dispute between de Hochepied and von Kniphausen. They, in view of the real service which de Hochepied had rendered to the VOC in handling the Basra affair by obtaining the imperial *farman*, offered his heirs a lump sum payment of 1,000 gold ducats. In exchange his heirs had to relinquish any claims they might have in the VOC. The ambassador's son agreed to this offer and there the matter ended.[268]

267 Before de Hochepied was appointed ambassador to the Porte he was so much in debt that his friends had sought desperately to find him an appointment and had urged him to apply for this function. Bosscha Erdbrink, *At The Threshold of Felicity*, pp. 265-66. For example, to make some money for himself, de Hochepied had already suggested to von Kniphausen's predecessor to acquire a consular *barat*. NA, Legatie Archief Turkije, nr. 596, Canter to de Hochepied (Basra, 21/09/1749).

268 NA, Collectie de Hochepied, nr. 108, extract resolutie van de Kamer van Amsterdam (26/09/1771) as well as the receipt signed by Elbert de Hochepied's son, Gerrit Jan de Hochepied.

RECRUITMENT OF NATIVE SOLDIERS AND SAILORS

The Dutch had recruited natives from the Persian Gulf area for military service in Batavia since 1755.[269] The factories in Bandar 'Abbas and Khark had been ordered to recruit as many Arabs, Turks or Persians as possible for military service. Their pay was five *rijksdaalders* (1 *rijksdaalder* =2.5 guilders or 5 makes 12.5 guilders) per month. They had to be sent to Batavia in groups of 50 men under an ensign. The ensign received a pay of 15 *rijksdaalders*. Over each group of 24 men a sergeant was put at 10 *rijksdaalders* and one corporal per 12 men at 6.5 *rijksdaalders*.[270] It seems that only at Khark recruitment had taken place, since no information is met in the letters from Bandar 'Abbas regarding this subject. Von Kniphausen at first had some difficulties in signing up enough men, but in May 1755 he was able to send 40 men to Batavia.[271] Prior to their departure to Batavia the soldiers had served at Khark, where a partisan of Sheikh Naser of Bushire even had tried to foment a mutiny among them. This failed, however, and the man was banished to Cochin. The soldiers do not seem to have been happy with their lot as is indicated by the fact that a few of the first group tried to desert when their ship stopped at Masqat, but the local authorities returned them to the Dutch.[272] In August 1756 von Kniphausen even sent 100 soldiers to Batavia. At the same time he stopped recruitment awaiting further orders from Batavia about the quality of the men sent so far.[273] The governor-general had the same idea, because one month earlier he had written to Khark that the soldiers did not live up to expectations and that therefore recruitment had to be discontinued.[274] The following year the soldiers were returned to Khark after having served their term. They were dismissed from VOC service on arrival at Khark. Two had been employed at Batavia as interpreter. Von Kniphausen was allowed to rehire a number of them as sailors, because in that field "the janitsares" performed well Batavia reported.[275] The governor-general thus approved von Kniphausen's

---

269 This was different from the occasional recruitment of a number of sailors when the crew of a ship had become so undermanned due to illness and death that it could not continue the journey in the Persian Gulf itself. See, e.g., VOC 2748, Gamron to Batavia 910/101/1748), f. 65 (6 sailors hired in Bushire to sail to Bandar 'Abbas at Dfl. 9 per month). Already decades earlier it had been usual to hire local soldiers to help defend the factory in case of a Baluch incursion.

270 VOC 1008, Batavia to Gamron (30/07/1754), f. 426.

271 VOC 2864, Khark to Batavia (031/05/1755), f. 52-53. Schoonderwoerd reported that nobody in the Bandar 'Abbas area was interested to be away from their family for such a long period. However, if they were allowed to bring their wife and children with them then he would be able to recruit people. However, since he did not dare to do so without authorization from Batavia he did not hire anybody. VOC 2863, Gamron to Batavia (20/12/1754), f. 31.

272 VOC 2885, Khark to Batavia (27/09/1755), f. 7, 12.

273 VOC 2885, Khark to Batavia (05/08/1756), f. 28-29.

274 VOC 1010, Batavia to Khark (08/07/1756), f. 197.

275 VOC 1012, Batavia to Khark (09/05/1758), f. 4.

decision of October 1757 to hire 25 Moorish sailors, because there were then many ill cases among the European crew of the VOC ships.[276] Thereafter the hiring of native sailors in the Persian Gulf became customary. Each year Batavia invariably asked for native sailors to be sent in two groups of 25 men. Children and handicapped persons were not allowed to be sent, however.[277] This practice explains why almost 50% of the crews of VOC ships on the Persian Gulf run, such as *de Walcheren,* consisted of local sailors. The practice was not without its risks as the murderous incident on the English vessel the *Islamabad* in 1765 shows (see chapter seven).

276 VOC 2937, Khark to Batavia (29/10/1757), f. 25. Von Kniphausen also hired 30 sailors for each of two VOC ships in November 1758, because due to death and sickness their crews had not enough strength to make the return journey. VOC 2968, Khark to Batavia (15/11/1758), f. 7.

277 VOC 3064, Khark to Batavia (30/09/1761), f. 13; VOC 1016, Batavia to Khark (26/05/1762), f. 640; VOC 1018, Batavia to Khark (26/05/1764), f. 121.

SOME ASPECTS OF EUROPEAN LIFE IN THE PERSIAN GULF

When Jan van der Hulst decided not to return to Batavia to give an account of himself, but instead went via Bombay to London, he wrote a letter to a friend, which contains interesting information on certain aspects of life of Europeans stationed in the Gulf.

Source: VOC 3092, Jan van der Hulst to my friend Mr. Pieter Vogelsang, captain of the ship *de Vrouwe Rebecca Jacoba*. Gamron (03/11/1762), f. 67-71.

Mr. Douglas, the English Agent at Bandar 'Abbas, will give you a letter which I beg you to remit to the governor-general. I will return via Bombay and London to Amsterdam with an English ship. Captain Nesbitt is ready any day now to depart. Everything that is on board that belongs to me you may have, to wit: all foodstuffs, the cattle (cows, sheep, goats, billlys, hens, ducks), honey, rusks, wine, barley, dried apples, butter, dried fish, porcelain and copper cooking utensils on condition that you transfer to Mr. Douglas whatever else is on board that belongs to me, to wit: chests with books, clothes for me and my child, and some other stuff that are all known to Gerrit and Blom. There is nothing of value in it. Mr. Douglas has the keys and you may open them (all valuables I have already stored long ago). If you do not agree, then please hand everything to my attorney in Batavia, whom I will send a list. I also will complain and demand satisfaction in Europe. Messrs. Nesbitt and Douglas will also complain in Bombay and demand satisfaction on behalf of the king. You surely do not want to cause a conflict between two nations? Concerning my nine slaves: Abdoel the cook, Slamat the cook's mate, both Malays, Jacob from Abyssinia, five kaffirs, viz. Raye Solemin the big one, Salomin the small one, Songor and two maid-servants, viz. Cenecasserin and Hadie and one Persian named Malaty, if you give me 900 rupees for them, i.e., 100 rupees for each one, you may have them; they are worth twice as much. If you agree, hand this money to Mr. Douglas and they are yours. If you do not want them please send them to me via Mr. Douglas. The latter also will pay you whatever I owe you for hams, rumpsteaks, cheese, etc.

BREAKDOWN OF THE OPERATIONAL COST OF THE VOC FACTORY AT KHARK

Regulation voor Khark, in stead of or as ampliation and alteration of that which has been found to have been reported in the Memorandum concerning the condition and interest of the Hon. Company at its respective factories. Dated 19 May 1755.[278]

Wages vary, not only as to the nominal amount, but also after they have been paid. In general it amounts to, as is usually the case, 9,600 rupees or Dfl. 14,400 and with two *stuivers* premium per rupee, or Dfl. 960, the total amounts to Dfl. 15,360.

Although the monthly wages are taxed with 40 *stuivers* per rupee in the book of wages when paid out, or altogether, because of the above [amount], Dfl. 19,200.

This is about equal to three-quarters of the wages of the staff that has been allowed there, to wit:

1	Merchant	Dfl. 60 to 80 per month
1	Junior merchant	40
4	Clerks	96
1	Visitor of the sick	24
1	Surgeon	36
1	Junior surgeon	20
1	Ensign	40
2	Sergeants	48
4	Corporals	56
1	Bombardier	20
2	Gunners	28
2	Boatswain or 1 mate and 1 boatswain	50
2	Quartermasters	28
40	Helpers (*handlangers*) and sailors	440
1	Smith	20
1	Mate	20
1	Cooper	20
	Per month	2,166
146	Men / per year	25,992

Board-monies en rations

Chief				
	Board-money	Dfl. 24:19	299: 8	

278 VOC 2942, f. 470-73.

12.5 jugs	wine	At 5 *stuivers*	112:10	
12.5 lbs	Butter	At 10 *stuivers*	75:00	
1 jug	Oil	At 20 *stuivers*	12:00	
2 jugs	Vinegar	At 6 *stuivers*	7:00	
1 lb.	Spices		4:00	
120 lbs.	Rice		36:00	
				545:18
Junior merchant				
	Board-money	At Dfl. 11:10	138:00	
4 jugs	Wine	At 15 *stuivers*	36:00	
60 lbs.	Rice		18:00	
				192:00
4 clerks				
	Board-money	At Dfl. 9:15	117:00	
40 lbs	Rice		12:00	
				516:00
Chief surgeon				
	Board-money	At 11.10		
4 jugs	wine			
60 lbs.	Rice			192:00
Visitor of the sick				192:00
Ensign				192:00
Junior surgeon 1				129:0o
Sergeants 2				258:00
Corporals 4				
	Board-money	At 7:10 /year		
40 lbs.	Rice	Year		408:00
Soldiers 80				
	Board-money	At 4:10/year		
40 lbs.	Rice			5,280:00
Bombardier 1				129:00
Gunners 2				204:00
Boatswains 2				258:00
Quartermasters 2				204:00
Sailors 40				2,640:00
Artisans 3				387:00
Total				11,726:18

Care has to be taken that the factory has these supplies in store, because the rice etc. does not exceed two lbs. per person, which then causes an increase of Dfl. 1,560.

The common expenditures are fixed as follows:

Chief			
15 jugs	Lamp oil from Batavia	100 *stuivers*/month	90
15 lbs.	Wax candles	At 20 *stuivers*	180
	Firewood		200
Junior merchant 1			
5 lbs.	Candles	Dfl. 48	
6 jugs	Lamp oil	Dfl. 36	
	Firewood	Dfl. 80	164
Clerks 4/junior surgeon 1			
1 lb.	Candles	Dfl. 12	
1.5 jug	Lamp oil	Dfl. 9	
	Firewood	Dfl. 20	205
Visitor of the sick and surgeon 1			
3lbs.	Candles	Dfl. 36	
4 jugs	Lamp oil	Dfl. 24	
	Firewood	Dfl. 40 /100 each	200
Ensign			164
Garrison/stables/artillery			
12 jugs	lamp oil		72
6 guinea fabrics	for flags		71
1-2,000 lbs	gunpowder	From Batavia	400 (maximum)
Writing implements	Ink		120
50 *man*	of firewood	for the guard, etc.	400
Overhead for horses			500
Tinning	of pots and pans		100
Cotton yarn, support	for firehose	All general overhead	3,066
Carpentry	and repairs	Estimated at	3,000
Small common presents	for reception	of local chiefs	1,000

[Expenditures of vessels]

Overhead of vessels			
4.5 jugs	Araq/month	For the 2 boatswains and 4 quartermasters	60
3 jugs	Araq/month	For the sailors	400

1.5 lbs	Meat	For the officers	
1 lb.	Meat	For the common soldiers/every other day at 1.5 *stuivers*	1,035
3 lbs.	Fish	Monthly at 1.5 *stuivers*	119
120 lbs.	Pepper	Dfl. 17	
240 lbs.	Salt	Dfl. 5	
3 jugs	Oil	Dfl. 1:8	
360 *man*	Firewood	Dfl. 96	136
6 guinea fabrics	For flags		71
	Anchors, etc.	Estimated	200
Hemp, tar, coir, sailing cloth, linseed oil, pint		Estimated	400
Expenditures of vessels			2,421

Monthly expenditures of native servants are too ample and should not exceed Dfl. 2,400.

Hospital expenditures

12 guinea fabrics	For making plasters etc. Dfl. 142	
60 jugs of araq	as a medicine/ Dfl. 17	
Medicines	from Batavia/ Dfl. 200	
3 jugs of lampoil	per month/ DFl. 18	
10 *man* of firewood	Dfl. 80	
Small items in cash	Dfl. 100	
Total		557

The other hospital expenditures are covered by the rations and else will be charged to account of the sick at a fixed rate, which will be little and only a small part of their pay. Thus total expenditures add up to about Dfl. 41,000.

Expenditures of the ships; 20 vessels are allowed to be charged for the transportation of ballast. For one ship of 100 *last* at Dfl. 12 [the cost are] Dfl. 240. Together with the cost for 100 mats at 12 *stuivers* or Dfl. 60, it amounts to Dfl. 300.

CHAPTER FIVE
The Dutch on Khark Island 1753-1766

A Commercial Mishap

THE REASONS FOR CREATING THE KHARK FACTORY

In 1752, Governor-General Jacob Mossel proposed to the VOC directors that they close down all VOC factories in the Persian Gulf. In view of this it is strange that less than a year later he can be found promoting the establishment of the Khark factory. In a detailed and long proposal written in November 1752, Mossel outlined a reform policy for the VOC that would lead to greater profits performance. He argued that, if his measures were not taken soon, the Company would go bankrupt.[1] With regard to the state of the factories in the Persian Gulf he remarked that

> Persia is a profitable place in flourishing periods, because one may sell there at least 30,000 lbs of cloves, 10,000 lbs of nutmegs, one million lbs of sugar, 100,000 lbs of tin and other goods, amongst which piece-goods. The weight goods yield [Dfl.] 200,000, so piece-goods are only a feasible commodity for one voyage, before [the market] is flooded with. For else the Company cannot compete with those who import them directly from Coromandel and Bengal. For freight, one should deduct [Dfl. 100,000, thus only [Dfl.] 100,000 remains.[2]

Because the capital used for the Persia trade amounted to Dfl. 400,000, which only yielded Dfl. 100,000 gross profit, while the fixed cost amounted to Dfl. 50,000, Mossel concluded that

1 For the text of Mossel's proposal, see VOC 11.154.

2 VOC 11.154, art. 75.

> One may sell quite a quantity of sugar, species, etc. in Persia, but if we would abandon that trade, these same goods would be bought from us in Bengal or Surat, and so we would not loose much by ceding [this trade] to the English. The same holds for the factory of Basra, whose situation is exactly the same. The textiles which are now selling well in Bandar 'Abbas, Bushire and Basra will be shortly in plentiful, because of the direct navigation of our competitors from Bengal and Coromandel against which our way of doing business cannot compete. We usually come with the same goods, when the market is already glutted with them.[3]

Mossel, however, did a complete turnabout when von Kniphausen arrived in Batavia with his proposal for a new, streamlined, efficient, low-cost trade policy, which promised higher sales and profits in the Persian Gulf area. Persia had yielded considerable profits in the past, and under von Kniphausen's management the Basra factory appeared to have received a new impetus. Although profits had declined (see Table 3.1), the average gross profits per year looked more encouraging than they had in previous decades.

The new factory promised to increase sales, especially of sugar and manufactured goods, while overhead would be cut. For the Khark factory would free the VOC of the obnoxious 'borrowing' practices by local rulers to which the VOC had been exposed in recent years. The factory's garrison would be small, and the construction costs would be low. Moreover, the factories in Basra and Bushire would be closed down, and Khark would eventually become the only VOC factory in the Persian Gulf. Once the new factory had begun to perform well enough, the Bandar 'Abbas factory would also be closed down.

All these arguments did not convince the *Heeren XVII*, the VOC directors. They preferred to close down all factories in the Persian Gulf and go along with Mossel's original proposal. However, in the subsequent discussion between the XVII and Mossel, the Persian Gulf trade hardly played a role. This in itself was quite understandable, for this trade amounted to only 1 percent of the VOC's total turnover. Nevertheless, Mossel took the view that the Persian Gulf trade could only be continued if higher profits could be made. Von Kniphausen's proposal held out promise for such higher profits and thus fitted nicely in Mossel's plans.[4]

PROFIT OR LOSS?

Some years ago, Meilink and Perry took the view that, despite the high costs of maintaining the Khark factory, its garrison, the ships calling there, and the payments of 'presents', the factory showed "a satisfactory net annual profit from 1753 to 1760."[5] If they were correct then it would seem that the XVII were wrong and Mossel was right. Indeed, the figures available for the entire Khark period show both the historians and Mossel to be right: throughout the period 1753-65 the factory made profits (Table 2). Only in the year 1754-55 did it lose money. The profit rates for each year also appeared to be satisfactory (Table 5), in view of the fact that the VOC had to make a net profit of 50 percent to make Khark a sustainable commercial enterprise.

---

3 VOC 11.154, art. 127.

4 VOC 11.154, arts. 14, 30.

5 Meilink-Roelofsz, "Vestiging," p. 486; John R. Perry, "Mir Muhanna and the Dutch: Patterns of Piracy in the Persian Gulf," *Studia Iranica* 2 (1973), p. 93.

These figures are very misleading, however, because of the peculiar book-keeping system that was used by the VOC, for 'general expenses' only refer to the cost of the Khark factory itself and not the cost of the ships carrying the goods to and from Khark, nor the loss of interest on invested capital, nor the loss on exports from Khark. Thus, the figures in Table 4.2 present a distorted picture of the 'real' cost of maintaining the Khark factory. The XVII were very quick to point this out to the High Government of the Indies. They argued that the Khark factory showed a loss if its performance was calculated according to merchant's reckoning *(koopmansrekening)*. This meant that the loss of interest on unsold merchandise, loss on exported specie, write-offs on the ships, and the cost of sea insurance had to be deducted from the so-called net profits. As we will see, the XVII were right.

Unfortunately, we do not have data on all of these costs. However, the cost of unsold stock could be considerable, as the XVII pointed out. The XVII made a very important point, for unsold merchandise represented a value of Dfl. 1.2 million per year between 1753 and 1756. Von Kniphausen himself had reported that the cost of the competitors in the Persian Gulf increased by 20 percent if merchandise had to lie over for another year.[6] The relevant figures for the VOC certainly were not lower.

Table 5.2: Profit-and-loss account of the Khark factory, 1753-1765 (in Dutch guilders)

Year	Gross profits	General Expenditures	Net Profit/Loss
1753-54	98,213	33,230	64,319
1754-55	56,682	183,001	(126,319)
1755-56	144,244	95,473	18,771
1756-57	115,414	69,469	45,944
1757-58	192,504	91,055	101,449
1758-59	243,719	77,910	165,808
1759-60	226,260	80,040	146,220
1760-61	249,660	67,785	213,282
1761-62	168,618	62,566	106,141
1762-63	225,535	65,474	160,060
1763-64	106,567	49,767	56,799
1764-65	105,739	n.a.	n.a.

Source: VOC 3003, Besogne over Karreek (Batavia; 11/03/1762), f. 1844-45 (1759-62); VOC 3156, f. 6-7 91762-63); Ibid., f. 18-19 (1763-64); VOC 3148, f. 38-39 (1764-65)

The High Government persisted in its optimistic view of the state of affairs at Khark. A calculation made in August 1761 by its accountant-general showed that Khark had made a profit of Dfl. 416,858 during the period 1753-60, or Dfl. 59,555 per year.[7] The XVII were again quick to point out that this profit and loss statement was completely misleading, for they themselves had concluded from the statement that the VOC had suffered a loss of Dfl. 194,520 or an annual

6 NA, Hooge Regering Batavia, nr. 789, app., not foliated.

7 VOC 2998, f. 522-23.

average of Dfl. 21,162 by using the merchant's reckoning method. Batavia had used the antiquated method of comparing sales revenues with the local costs of Khark, and not taking into account expenditures such as cost of ships and loss of interest. The XVII further made it clear that they wanted to close down Khark, even if the Batavia profit-and-loss statement had shown a real profit. For their objections that they had made clear from the very outset still held true.[8]

Taking this criticism to heart the High Government had its new accountant-general draw up an improved profit-and-loss statement.[9] This statement indeed showed a loss of Dfl. 194, 520. The new calculation had not only taken into account expenses incurred on Khark, but also the loss on the export of specie and the recurrent cost of the visiting ships.[10]

During the period 1753-62 a total of thirteen ships had made the voyage to Khark. The long time that ships were kept at Khark, especially in the beginning, had exasperated the High Government, and it had urged the agent at Khark not to allow ships to stay any longer than was necessary. When admonition did not help, a strict order was issued that after unloading and loading, ships should depart forthwith. This helped for two years (1755-56), but then, for various reasons, the length of the voyages began again to increase. The High Government did not find the reasons given very convincing, and in 1761 ordered a separate log to be kept for the unloading-loading period, so that it would become clear who was to be blamed for the long delays.[11] This had a positive effect, for the average length of the voyages until that time had been twelve months; between 1762 and 1765 it was reduced to eleven months.

REASONS FOR FAILURE

Although the Khark factory was a commercial failure and never really got off the ground, it cannot be argued that this failure could have been anticipated from the very outset. True, the XVII had taken that position, but they in fact did not move to discontinue the Khark factory until ten years had passed, so despite their strong convictions even they had apparently been ready to give the project the benefit of the doubt. From a commercial point of view this may have been a sound policy, the more so since interested insiders took a very positive view of the new Dutch factory. The EIC, for example, was very apprehensive about the Khark factory from the beginning. If one's most important competitor is not only worried about a new step, but even tries to copy it, one may assume that there was something to say in its favor. The EIC resident in Bandar-e Rig commented that "if the situation in Persia were to become settled, Kharag might become a populous and flourishing place."[12]

In addition to all these opinions, the hard facts also verify that von Kniphausen had not just been engaged in wishful thinking when he had succeeded in convincing the High Government in Batavia. The level of prices for the best-selling goods that he had established as the condition for the success of Khark had been achieved (see Table 4.3). In fact, the prices realized during the Khark period were generally even higher than the ones von Kniphausen considered to be minimally acceptable. Where von Kniphausen was proved wrong, however, was in the volume of sales as well as in the pattern of trade required to make the Khark factory a profitable one. But this was not entirely his fault.

8 VOC 335, XVII to governor-general, 29 September 1763, section Karreek, not foliated.

9 VOC 3003, f. 1843-55.

10 VOC 3003, f. 1846vs.

11 VOC 1015, Batavia to Khark (31/03/1761, f. 68-70.

12 Lorimer, *Gazetteer*, p. 130; Amin, *British* Interests, pp. 145-48.

Table 5.3: Estimated and real prices for selected commodities, 1759-1765 (in Dutch guilders)

Commodity	Projected prices	1759-60	1760-61	1761-62	1762-63	1763-54	1764-65
Cloves	5:5	5:5	5:5	5:5	5:5	5:5	5:5
Nutmegs	3:0	3:13	3:0	3:0	3:0	3:0	3:0
Sugar (crystal)	16-18	15:10	16:10	22:10	23:0	21:0	20:0
Sugar (candy)	25	-	21:0	-	32:0	29:0	29:0
Tin	45	50:0	50:0	50:0	50:0	45:0	50:0
Lead	15	18:0	18:0	18:0	-	-	-
Iron	16	17:10	18:0	18:0	-	-	-
Zinc	35	26:0	26:0	26:0	-	-	-
Steel	25	30:10	30:10	-	30:10	-	-
Pepper	36-40	43:0	42:0	44:0	44:0	-	-
Benzoin	65	-	45:0	45:0	45:0	45:0	45:0
Curcuma	15	18:0	-	18:0	18:0	18:0	18:0

Source: VOC 3027, f. 10-11 91759-60); VOC 3064, f. 6-7 (1760-61); VOC 3092, f. 8-9 (1761-62); VOC 3156, f. 6-7 (1762-63); Ibid., f. 18-19 (1763-64); VOC 3184, f. 38-39 (1764-65).

What, then, went wrong? What turned Khark into a failure? I believe we can distinguish two kinds of causes: those endogenous to the VOC itself, and those peculiar to the Persian Gulf area at that time.

Table 5.4: Total sales per financial year, 1759-1765 (in Dutch guilders)

Year	Sales
1759-60	566,000
1760-61	499,881
1761-62	284,098
1762-63	358,438
1763-64	181,254
1764-65	176,370

Source: Source: VOC 3027, f. 10-11 91759-60); VOC 3064, f. 6-7 (1760-61); VOC 3092, f. 8-9 (1761-62); VOC 3156, f. 6-7 (1762-63); ibid., f. 18-19 (1763-64); VOC 3184, f. 38-39 (1764-65).

Around 1750, the VOC had arrived at a critical point. Both the XVII and the High Government were painfully aware of the fact that all was not well with the Company. From the beginning of the 18th century, the XVII had been criticizing the weak points in the Company's management and trade policy. This criticism and the persistence of its causes gave rise to a number of proposals for redress and reform after the 1750s, of which the one by Mossel was only an example.[13]

In its competition with the other contenders for the Asian markets, the VOC was handicapped by its weakening financial position, its antiquated bookkeeping system, its management structure, and the changing patterns of trade. Especially this last, together with ever-rising costs, kept the VOC from acting vigorously. The growing burden of debt did not improve the situation either.

Although the VOC held the spice monopoly, this did not mean that the company had an easy task. For spices were only one part-and a diminishing one at that of its sales. With regard to other goods, it had to deal with the EIC and with new companies and the country traders. The XVII and the High Government were quite aware of this trend and took several measures to set things right. "The high fixed expenses for forts, military forces, patrol ships, etc., were felt to be hampering. Various factories were at intervals sentenced to being closed, but few of them actually did so. The sailing time was the object of great interest. Then there was the abuse of office in connection with private trade."[14] This overall picture of the VOC perfectly fits the case of the Khark factory. It is against this background, therefore, that we have to place and to understand its creation and continuation.

The weakening position of the VOC, combined with the conditions prevailing in the Persian Gulf area, handicapped the development of VOC trade, especially in a few sensitive commodities. The anarchy that prevailed in Persia, and sometimes in Iraq, made trade routes insecure, which especially hurt Dutch trade, for an increasing part of VOC trade consisted of weight goods. These were more difficult to sell and transport than piece goods, when pack-animals were scarce and roads insecure. The general instability of the area also decreased the production capacity of the population, leading to a lower standard of living and less demand for imported goods (see Table 4.5). Although the Persian Gulf area hardly ever had produced commodities for export, this lack acquired a special significance at that time. For apart from the fact that it is bad economics to export cash, the VOC lost considerably on the exported specie. Finally, the VOC was obliged to maintain an expensive establishment on Khark. Because of the insecurity of the area and the prevailing piracy, its costs absorbed a considerable part of the profits.

Although the conditions prevailing in the Persian Gulf also held for the VOC's competitors, they appear to have been less hurt by them, probably because the EIC was in a better financial and management position and its pattern of trade more suited to Persian Gulf conditions.

This was especially true in the piece goods and European manufactured goods markets where the VOC failed to hold its market position. The energetic trade policy implemented by von Kniphausen had allowed the VOC to attract its fair share of the Basra textile market: "So successful were the Dutch at Basra at least until 1752 that the British found it difficult to compete with them even in the sale of woolen goods."[15] This policy was continued by von Kniphausen on Khark and his sales show an upward trend until 1759. Wood, an agent of the EIC, when visiting Khark in 1756, remarked about the Dutch textiles that "some medleys of which the patterns-he was sorry to say-seemed to be exceedingly well chosen."[16]

The Dutch were handicapped in this trade because their orders for textiles arrived too late: by the time they got there the market was already saturated or the design, quality, and color

13 VOC 2998, f. 322-23.

14 Kristof Glamann, *Dutch-Asiatic Trade* (The Hague, 1958), p. 31.

15 Amin, *British Interests*, p. 142.

16 Saldanha, *Précis*, vol. 1, p. 99 (Bunderick, 03/05/1756); Lorimer, *Gazetteer*, p. 130.

were either out of fashion or unsuitable. If sales increased, especially later on, this was thanks to the scarcity of textiles in the market rather than to an enterprising VOC commercial policy.

Table 5.5: Gross revenues of selected commodities per financial year 1759-1765 (in Dutch guilders)

Commodity	1759-60	1760-61	1761-62	1762-63	1763-64	1764-65
Cloves	116,618	100,343	75,966	107,073	37,513	62,426
Nutmegs	18,745	10,479	8,592	9,840	4,503	13,365
Sugar (crystal)	142,358	127,215	124,987	192,829	112,949	38,940
Sugar (candy)	10,703	132,001	-	11,563	6,496	22,206
Tin	24,470	15,359	15,582	14,344	5,714	23,904
Lead	11,823	10,580	5,533	-	-	-
Iron	8,131	2,499	8,223	-	-	-
Zinc	134	4,857	424	-	-	-
Steel	510	116	-	72	-	-
Sappanwood	1,531	6,143	1,427	2,425	-	-
Pepper	20,427	46,460	30,488	1,625	-	-
Benzoin	-	1,401	553	4,177	2,239	117
Curcuma	-	894	-	2,754	1,899	-

Source: Source: VOC 3027, f. 10-11 91759-60); VOC 3064, f. 6-7 (1760-61); VOC 3092, f. 8-9 (1761-62); VOC 3156, f. 6-7 (1762-63); ibid., f. 18-19 (1763-64); VOC 3184, f. 38-39 (1764-65).

These handicaps were inherent in the decision not to have any direct VOC navigation between the textile-producing areas and the Persian Gulf. All orders from Khark had to be relayed via Batavia to, say, Coromandel and the same held for deliveries. This definitely put the Dutch in a more vulnerable and less competitive position and finally led to the marginal role of piece goods in their pattern of trade. In 1760, Batavia decided to cut down the export of Coromandel textiles because profit rates and sale were too low.

It seems quite likely that the low profit rates were the result of VOC policy rather than a function of market conditions. Von Kniphausen, for example, also complained about the cost price of textiles sent from India, which, according to him, were 25 percent higher than those imported by the English and Armenians.[17] In view of the fact that an export commodity had to yield at least 50 percent profit, if the VOC wanted to stay with such goods, it is clear that the factors mentioned earlier hardly made such an objective attainable.

The situation with European manufactured goods was not much different. Like the EIC directors, the XVII set much store by the sale of Dutch products. The fact that the English were able to sell their woolens in the Persian Gulf - which trade amounted to 33 percent of their total export of that commodity[18]- was a major reason for them to continue to trade there. Moreover, the desire to create outlets for Dutch industry equally played a role. Schoonderwoerd, the VOC Resident in Bandar 'Abbas, wrote to the XVII that support of the Dutch export industry could

17 VOC 2968, Khark to Batavia (15/11/1758), f. 14-15.

18 Amin, *British Interests*, p. 120.

be the only possible incentive for the VOC to sell European woolens in Persia, for only some 30 percent profit could be made on them. If this export incentive had no relevance for the VOC, he strongly advised against including woolens in the VOC list of export commodities.[19]

Another factor detrimental to the VOC position was the decreasing consumption of sugar in the Persian Gulf area. Formerly Persia had bought about 35 percent of Batavia's sugar production.[20] Since the VOC was having trouble with the sale of sugar in the Persian Gulf, and in other parts of Asia as well, the High Government ordered its staff to try and increase sugar sales. To this end it was even decided to make 'sugar voyages' to Masqat and Sind.[21]

In addition to the high cost of operating the Khark factory was the reality that competition for the dwindling market had grown stronger. The VOC had maneuvered itself into a vulnerable position because it did not allow its staff to make barter agreements or to grant long-term credit. The EIC not only took all kinds of local produce in exchange for its imports, but also was ready to pay better prices for copper, which had become the Persian Gulf's most important currency after 1750. The EIC, moreover, also facilitated trade by granting relatively long-term credit, while the VOC staff had to demand cash. This led to a situation where the VOC could only compete with the EIC in those markets where it had a quasi-monopoly, namely, spices and sugar.[22]

Table 5.6: Profits (in %) per financial year per commodity group, 1749-1765

Year	Spices	Weight goods	Piece goods	Manufactured goods	Total
1749-50	**1193**	**139**	**43**	-	**131**
1750-51	1150	99	43	-	148
1751-52	1210	86	34	-	67
1759-60	1209	79	79	18	91
1760-61	1209	66	66	2	101
1761-62	1203	104	104	-	167
1762-63	1203	99	99	-	169
1763-64	1195	103	103	-	142
1764-65	1220	97	97	-	149

Source: Source: VOC 3027, f. 10-11 91759-60); VOC 3064, f. 6-7 (1760-61); VOC 3092, f. 8-9 (1761-62); VOC 3156, f. 6-7 (1762-63); ibid., f. 18-19 (1763-64); VOC 3184, f. 38-39 (1764-65).

The XVII also rightly suspected that its employees were undercutting the VOC's position in the market for piece goods. Although information is fragmentary, it seems, for example, that von Kniphausen was able to return to Europe with a well-lined pocket. It is known that he

19 VOC 2843, Gamron to Batavia (10/10/1753), f. 14.

20 On the problems of the sugar production of Batavia, see J. J. Reese, *De suikerhandel van Amsterdam van het begin der 17e eeuw tot 1813* (Haarlem, 1908), pp. 178-84.

21 Floor, "The Dutch East India Company Trade with Sind in the 17th and the 18th Centuries," *Le Moyen Orient et l'Ocean Indien*, 3 (1986): 111-44. See also chapter six in this publication.

22 See, for example, the complaints by von Kniphausen, VOC 2885, Khark to Batavia (12/12/1755), f.17; Ibid., (05/08/1755), f. 8.

owned his own vessel and dealt in piece goods as far away as Aleppo. The same holds true for his deputy and successor van der Hulst. The latter fled because he feared an investigation of his activities on Khark and apparently was able to travel and live in style. Of the third director of the Khark factory, Buschman, it is said that when he left Khark he had amassed a fortune of three lakhs of rupees![23]

These private trading activities by VOC staff fitted well into the system of the very important so-called country trade in Asia. Von Kniphausen had drawn Batavia's attention to this trade. In his view "the navigation by the competitors of the Dutch was only profitable because of the lively freight trade in which these [competitors] had a large share." In fact, according to von Kniphausen, the other European nations trading in the Persian Gulf were essentially carriers. Only profits from freight enabled them to trade in the Persian Gulf at all. Without the freight trade their navigation was burdened by overheads that amounted to 40 percent of their annual turnover. If during their short stay they did not sell their goods, the cost might even reach 60 percent. Von Kniphausen therefore proposed that the VOC also engage in carrying freight in view of the considerable profits that could be made in it.[24]

VOC IMPORTS INTO THE PERSIAN GULF

Detailed information on value, volume, and composition for the import trade of Khark is only available for fiscal years 1759-66. Before then information is available only on the value of the import trade; for exports we have much less information. The reason for this unevenness of data is that almost nothing was exported. One reason for the lack of information is that until 1760 the financial accounts of Khark were presented to the High Government separately from the routine correspondence, and they seem not to have been preserved. Only in 1760, after von Kniphausen's departure and after repeated and urgent demands by the XVII, were the financial accounts finally included in the regular correspondence.[25] The exasperation the XVII felt with regard to this matter made von Kniphausen highly unpopular with them.

Spices

Among imports to the Persian Gulf area, by far the most profitable were high-quality spices, especially cloves and nutmegs (Table 6). Profits were high and remained quite stable throughout the Khark period because the VOC had a monopoly on these commodities. In their share of total sales spices were quite important, too, taking second place only to sugar (Tables 7 and 8).

23 NA, Legatie Archief Turkije, nr. 671, Relaas van een onpartijdige, not foliated; see also Meilink, "Vestiging," pp. 481, 487.

24 NA, Hooge Regering Batavia, nr. 789, app., not foliated.

25 VOC 334, XVII to Batavia (10/09/1758), section Karreek, not foliated.

Table 5.7: Profits (in %) per financial year per selected commodity, 1749-1765

Year	Sugar (crystal)	Sugar (candy)	Tin	Lead	Iron	Pepper	Benzoin
1749-50	189	147	58	358	133	133	-
1750-51	154	106	48			129	-
1751-52	128	93	48	152	107	263	-
1759-60	93	47	50	69	47	194	-
1760-61	88	44	50	76	47	195	7
1761-62	105		50	74	47	194	7
1762-63	112	52	50	-	-	214	46
1763-64	118	51	50	-	-	-	17
1764-65	106	44	35	-	-	-	15

Source: VOC 3027, f. 10-11 91759-60); VOC 3064, f. 6-7 (1760-61); VOC 3092, f. 8-9 (1761-62); VOC 3156, f. 6-7 (1762-63); ibid., f. 18-19 (1763-64); VOC 3184, f. 38-39 (1764-65).

Table 5.8: Projected and real sales per selected commodities, 1759-1765 (in lbs.)

Commodity	Projected Sales	1759-60	1760-61	1761-62	1762-63	1763-64	1764-65
Cloves	20,000	22,213	19,113	11,469	20,395	7,145	11,890
Nutmeg	40,000	6,248	3,493	2,864	3,160	1,501	5,455
Sugar	1,200,000	918,444	771,000	694,375	1,035,507	667,666	243,380
Sugar (lump)	300,000	196,540	615,027	-	45,171	28,000	95,717
Tin	100,000	48,941	30,719	31,165	28,688	12,698	53,121
Lead	150,000	65,737	58,782	30,850	-	-	-
Iron	300,000	7,823	13,886	15,685	-	-	-
Zinc	15,000	516	18,681	1,631	-	-	-
Steel	30,000	1,674	381	-	237	-	-
Pepper	300,000	47,505	110,620	69,292	3,695	-	-
Benzoin	40,000	-	3,115	1,230	11,603	6,499	2,202
Curcuma	15,000	-	4,969	16,316	15,302	10,555	-

Source: VOC 3027, f. 10-11 (1759-60); VOC 3064, f. 6-7 (1760-61); VOC 3092, f. 8-9 (1761-62); VOC 3156, f. 6-7 (1762-63); ibid., f. 18-19 (1763-64); VOC 3184, f. 38-39 (1764-65).

Von Kniphausen had estimated that the VOC could sell 20,000 pounds of cloves annually at the usual fixed VOC price. He believed that once the Khark factory was established, the VOC could serve the entire Turkish market from there. Correspondence with Aleppo had convinced him that this would be a profitable undertaking.[26] Mossel had written that in normal times the VOC could sell 30,000 pounds of cloves. But the 1750s in the Gulf were not normal times, and one wonders how von Kniphausen arrived at his estimate. In 1751-52, he had only sold 4,200 pounds of cloves in Basra, and even if the 4,200 pounds of sales to Bandar Abbas[27] are added, the sum does not even come close to his estimate. As is clear from Table 4.8 these estimated sales were hardly ever realized. Average annual sales in the 1750s probably amounted to about 10,000 pounds only. After an increase in annual sales in 1759-62, reflecting a general rise in the volume of sales of all commodities, the level of both total sales and of cloves dropped off again. This up-and-down trend must be ascribed to the politico-economic situation in the Persian Gulf and had nothing to do with cloves as such, which remained a best-selling commodity in the Persian Gulf after the Dutch had left the area. Because of the VOC's monopoly, prices for cloves, of course, remained stable.

The same was true of nutmegs, of which von Kniphausen had estimated that 40,000 pounds per year could be sold. This was not only considerably higher than the 3,600 pounds he had sold in 1751-52 in Basra, but was also more than the 10,000 pounds per year Batavia considered to be average for normal times. Not surprisingly, these estimated sales were never realized, even after the Dutch had abandoned their factory in Bandar 'Abbas.

Two other fine spices, mace and cinnamon, were hardly sold at all. According to von Kniphausen mace was not much used in Turkey and Persia. In his view only one sockel[28] (154 pounds) per year would suffice to fill the demand. Only Indian cinnnamon could be sold in the Persian Gulf, but the Turks and Arabs did not know the difference between Ceylonese and Malabar cinnamon, as the Persians did, and would buy, he estimated, some 6,000 pounds a year. Even here von Kniphausen's estimate was overly optimistic, for in 1751-52 he had only sold 119 pounds in the Basra market. Even if sales in Bandar 'Abbas (1,300 lbs.) were added, the actual level of sales fell far short of von Kniphausen's estimate. In 1757, he therefore had to send back both mace and cinnamon, for at the prices fixed by the VOC he could only sell 200 pounds of cinnamon. He maintained, however, that at the old price of Dfl. 3 per pound, he would have been able to sell 8,000 pounds.[29]

Weight Goods

Of the next group of commodities, weight goods, the most important was powdered sugar, followed by lump sugar. Von Kniphausen estimated that the VOC could sell between 1 and 1.2 million pounds of powdered sugar per year. To make it unattractive for the English to dabble in this line of trade, he thought it would suffice to lower the price a little. This measure worked effectively indeed. Some 300,000 pounds of lump sugar could be sold, despite the Persian preference for Chinese over Javanese sugar, which was the only kind the VOC imported, but the estimated levels were never realized. Nevertheless, sugar sales from Khark showed an improvement over the 1751-52 sales, even when the Bandar 'Abbas sales are added to those of Basra.

26 NA, Hooge Regering Batavia, nr. 789, app., not foliated.

27 VOC 2863, f. 44-45.

28 A sockel is a small bale made of leaves or reeds, and was used to transport mace. One sockel of mace weighed 154 pounds.

29 VOC 2937, Khark to Batavia (29/10/1757), f. 22-23, "Persians prefer the false Malabar cinnamon, which is imported in a very fresh and smelling state here."

Sugar sales increased slowly, but they did increase, which must have pleased the High Government in Batavia. The sale of sugar was of enormous importance to the welfare of the city of Batavia, which produced an increasing surplus of sugar. During the 1750s, an average of 600,000 pounds of powdered sugar and some 200,000 pounds of lump sugar were sold by Khark.[30] The increased sales during the early 1760s gave the High Government unrealistic expectations about the absorption capacity of the Persian Gulf market. It was the obsession with sugar sales that delayed the decision to close down the Khark factory.

Although sugar prices were in general higher than they were in the Basra period, Batavia nevertheless complained that these were still too low as compared with, for example, those in Surat. Profits, however, increased, which, together with the growing burden of the Batavia sugar surplus, led to the 'sugar voyages' to Masqat and Sind in 1757-58. These were discontinued after protests from Khark, for these sales had an adverse effect on the Khark sales.[31]

Pepper

Another important commodity, profitable and in great demand, was black pepper. Von Kniphausen estimated that some 300,000 pounds could be sold in the Persian Gulf, another estimate that was much higher than the quantities sold in normal times. Pepper, however, was a best-selling commodity all around the world, and thus Khark received only what Batavia could spare from its supplies for other factories. This explains the rather spasmodic behavior of pepper sales, which stopped altogether in 1764, not because demand was lacking in the Persian Gulf, but because pepper was scarce and Batavia preferred to reserve the available supply for its more important markets.[32]

Base Metals

A last important group of commodities were base metals, particularly iron. According to von Kniphausen, the VOC could sell some 30,000 pounds per year, and a similar quantity of steel in small bars. The corresponding estimates for lead, tin, and zinc were, respectively, 150,000, 100,000, and 15,000 pounds. Von Kniphausen expected to make good profits on lead in particular, which was in great demand because of the continuous warfare. Although, with the exception of zinc, his estimated prices were realized, the level of sales fell far short of the estimates. After 1762, of the base metals, only tin was still being shipped to Khark; profits were too low on the rest. Iron, for example, had to yield at least 75 percent, but in reality it yielded only 47 percent in the 1760s. Tin remained on the import list until the end; demand for it remained rather stable, and so did its profit rate.[33]

30 VOC 792, f. 277.

31 See chapter six in this publication and Floor, "The Dutch East India Company Trade with Sind in the 17th and the 18th Centuries," *Le Moyen Orient et l'Ocean Indien*, 3 (1986), pp. 111-44.

32 Glamann, *Dutch Trade*, pp. 83-84.

33 NA, Hooge Regering Batavia, nr. 789, app., not foliated; VOC 1017, Batavia to Khark (15/06/1763), f. 142.

Miscellaneous Goods

Of the other commodities sold by the VOC at Khark, only benzoin and curcuma continued to play a role, though a minor one. According to von Kniphausen, the common wild benzoin was quite in demand by the Arabs, and the Istanbul market consumed about 10,000 pounds of it. In both annual turnover and profit rates benzoin was not important. The same was true for curcuma, for which von Kniphausen had estimated a potential sale of 15,000 pounds per year.

For textiles von Kniphausen suggested that orders should be sent directly from Khark to the manufacturing centers in India rather than through Batavia. If this procedure had been followed, orders would have taken three years for delivery, by which time the market situation might have completely changed. Von Kniphausen reported that the Coromandel textiles were the ones most in demand. Total demand for textiles he estimated at 15,000 to 20,000 pieces. Sales were reasonably good until 1760, when they dropped so much that Batavia decided to stop sending Coromandel textiles to the Persian Gulf. Although the VOC continued to offer a selection of various Indian textiles, profits on them continued to be low.[34] Woolens were and remained a minor item, in which the Dutch could not compete with the English. At the end of 1758, von Kniphausen reported that the English had delivered 1,000 bales of woolens to Bandar 'Abbas and Basra, which they sold just above cost, causing much damage to the position of Dutch woolens. Moreover, by that time English perpets had become of better quality than the Dutch ones. This situation was also undesirable for another reason, because unsold woolens could not be preserved well in the Gulf climate due to the dust and excessive humid heat. As a result of the disappointing sales, as of 1761 the VOC discontinued the import of woolens into the Persian Gulf.[35]

VOC EXPORTS FROM THE PERSIAN GULF

As von Kniphausen had already pointed out, possibilities for exporting Persian goods were negligible; the only exportable items available were cash and Kerman wool. Cash had in fact been the most important export commodity of the VOC since the 1640s. This lack of exportable commodities had not been a drawback when Persia had a stable, wealthy economy, but when anarchy and chaos prevailed after Nader Shah's death, trading with Persia became less advantageous and profitable.

The insecure and chaotic internal situation impaired the country's ability to produce; even the few exportable commodities were no longer to be had. This at first had no significant impact on the investment and buying capacity of the population, because of the great amount of money circulating in the country as a result of Nader Shah's campaigns. However, after a few years this source of money dwindled, while Persia itself did not produce sufficient goods to make up for the loss. The ensuing structural poverty had a depressing effect on exports, and buying capacity was

34 VOC 2937, Khark to Batavia (29/10/ 1757), f. 22; VOC 2968 (15/11/ 1758), f. 13; VOC 2996 (30/11/ 1759), f. 6; VOC 3027 (30/11/1760), f. 18 (the *botidar chits* with large flowers were invendible); VOC 1017, Batavia to Khark (15/06/1763), f. 141-44. The VOC also sometimes imported rice. In 1760 Khark reported that the market price for rice was low, because that year's harvest of wheat, barley and dates had been good. Moreover, people preferred Persian and Bengal rice to Java rice. VOC 3027, Khark to Batavia (15/10/1760), f. 8.

35 VOC 2968, Khark to Batavia (15/11/1758), f. 13. The Dutch competitiveness was also hampered by the fact that Batavia had instructed Khark to sell woolens at fixed prices leaving no room for flexibility. Moreover, some varieties, such as *kroonrassen*, which Khark was allowed to sell at cost, were not liked by the market, because these came in two unwanted colors (blue and green) and thus remained unsold. VOC 2996, Khark to Batavia (30/11/1759), f. 6-7; see also VOC 3027, Khark to Batavia (01/10/1760), f. 3; VOC 3027 (30/11/1760), f. 18; VOC 3027, Khark to Batavia (22/06/1761), f. 2.

even further impaired as Persia's coinage became less and less acceptable in international trade. Its substitutes (old copper, precious stones) were risky assets for merchants.[36] The absorption capacity of the internal market was even further reduced as communications in the country were poor and roads dangerous, making trade a very hazardous affair.

Specie and Copper

Exports to Batavia were made up mainly of cash. Payments were in principle accepted in all kinds of currencies at fixed rates, but in practice these were restricted to only a few. The main currencies were the gold Indian rupee, the silver Persian rupee, and the silver *naderis*. By 1755 Venetian golden ducats became common in the Gulf, which von Kniphausen preferred at a five percent agio to silver.[37] Nevertheless, silver payments were more important than gold, as gold became less and less available. Old copper was not a negligible quantity either, but we do not know how much the VOC exported from Khark.[38] However, Batavia considered old copper undesirable, because it could only be disposed of in India with very little profit, and it was subject to underweight because it was delivered mostly in small chips. The High Government therefore ordered von Kniphausen in April 1755 to stop accepting old copper in payment and to accept golden rupees only at the rate of exchange of 27 *stuivers* to the rupee. Although von Kniphausen would gladly have rid himself of copper payments-copper was cumbersome to collect, and it took merchants months to accumulate sufficient quantities-he advised strongly against this directive, fearing that the measure would result in a complete standstill of trade. For after increasing its prices, the VOC would not be competitive with the British and others. These competitors were not only lowering their prices, but accepted both copperware and drugs in payments for their merchandise. The VOC was about to price itself out of the market, all the more because the VOC was mainly an importer of spices.[39]

As the loss bullion export from Khark grew too high Batavia stipulated the following conversion rates for Khark in 1761:

Gold bullion per *methqal* (19 carats)	Dfl. 7
Gold bullion per *methqal* (18 carats)	Dfl. 6.5
Gold rupees normal weight	Dfl. 19:10
Portuguese doubloons	Dfl. 22:10
Silver Persian rupees	Dfl. 1:8
Silver *naderis* (large)	Dfl. 1:8
Silver *naderis* (small)	Dfl. 16:12

(1 Dfl. = 20 stuivers = 12 penningen)

The High Government was not prepared to pay more for these currencies. This policy was maintained by the VOC until the demise of the Khark factory and quite understandable in view of the considerable losses that Khark suffered on the export of specie. In 1762, the VOC had cal-

36 Amin, *British Interests*, p. 134.

37 VOC 2864, Khark to Batavia (31/05/1755), f. 51.

38 VOC 1009, Batavia to Khark (27/06/1755), f. 213.

39 VOC 2885, Khark to Batavia (27/09/1755), f. 17, 44.

culated that from 1753-54 to 1761-62 the company had lost Dfl. 251,227:3:12, which represented 31 percent of the total loss incurred by the operation of the Khark factory.[40]

In addition to cash, Persia still offered some other export goods, but they were negligible and von Kniphausen never claimed he could organize a profitable export trade from the Gulf area apart from specie and copper. Desirable export products such as Kerman goat hair and asafetida were hard to obtain and, if available, had often to be purchased at very high prices. Merchants, moreover, preferred to take pearls and precious stones with them rather than weight goods, for this made them more mobile in case they had to evade the many marauders in Persia.[41] Although some Kerman goat hair and asafetida were exported, this was the exception. The XVII finally dropped Kerman got hair from the order list in 1762, because it only yielded a loss in the Netherlands.[42]

Sulfur dioxide, rock salt, and iron oxide-which were obtained at Bandar 'Abbas and did not cost much-were other options. The VOC regularly exported these minerals, both as ballast and for use in Batavia. However, profits on them were insignificant.[43] According to von Kniphausen, the only commodity that would yield acceptable profits (50%) were pearls. However, the VOC took no active interest in this commodity, apart from one trial in 1757, which proved von Kniphausen wrong.[44]

THE COMMERCIAL MANAGEMENT OF KHARK

The VOC had invested capital in a money-losing business, and it would have been better for the company if it had closed down its Persian Gulf factories in 1753 or earlier. One reason for its failure was the high cost of maintaining the operation. Although profits increased, the 'real' cost of Khark increased too. It is therefore interesting to find out how the principal actors-namely, the resident of the Khark factory, the High Government in Batavia, and the XVII in Amsterdam-reacted and interacted while the Khark factory was being developed.

From the year-to-year discussions of the Khark operation, it becomes clear that the XVII did not contribute much to the improvement of its performance. They only continued to repeat their old complaint that Khark was operating at a loss. It is difficult to say why it took so long for them to order Batavia to abandon the Persian Gulf trade altogether. They probably hoped that the situation might improve and a loss could be turned into a profit. But when after ten years of hope that did not materialize the XVII finally ordered the closure of the Khark factory.

40 VOC 1015, Batavia to Khark (31/03/1761), f. 75-76; ibid., (24/11/1761), f. 144; VOC 3003, f. 1844vs-1845vs.

41 NA, Hooge Regering Batavia, nr. 789, app., not foliated; see on Kerman goat hair, Willem Floor, *The Textile Industry in historical perspective 1500-1925* (Paris, 1999), pp. 357-73.

42 VOC 335, XVII to Batavia (25/10/1762), section Karreek, not foliated; VOC 1017, Batavia to Khark (15/06/1763), f. 150.

43 Iron oxide, sulfur oxide (brimstone), and rock salt were exported by the VOC factory in Bandar 'Abbas and mined near Shamil and on Hormuz. After the factory closed, some of these minerals continued to be exported by the VOC. Khark once, in 1759, exported brimstone to Batavia, which was mined at Kuwait, but it proved to be unsaleable (VOC 1013, f. 5). The later exports all were obtained from Bandar 'Abbas (1763: 75,000 lbs. of brimstone; 1764: 172,000 lbs.). Because the 1763 shipment consisted of 30 percent rock, Batavia gave orders to stop buying this mineral (VOC 1018, f. 107).

44 Willem Floor, "Pearl-Fishing in the Persian Gulf in 1757," *Persica* 10 (1982), pp. 209-22 or Appendix II in this publication.

The High Government was mainly concerned with finding ways and means to cut expenses, shorten the time of voyages and stopovers in Khark, and increase the sale of sugar. The resident of Khark finally had to make the best of a difficult situation, though in the end he had very little to show for it. He could not do much about the political situation in Persia, the depreciation of the currency, the impoverishment of the area, or the changing patterns of trade. One may nevertheless wonder whether the invariable optimism of the subsequent residents about future developments in Persia did not have more to do with the prospects for their own private trading than with Khark's potential for success. Von Kniphausen believed that once the internal chaos had ended and law and order had been reestablished over the littoral, trade would pick up again. The High Government therefore took the view that the new factory had to be given a chance to prove itself. In fact, in 1755 Batavia remarked that profits looked acceptable so far.[45]

On 11 March 1762, the High Government finally decided to discontinue its activities in the Persian Gulf. It had already closed down the Bandar 'Abbas factory in 1758.[46] Governor-General van der Parra had second thoughts about this decision, however. On 6 April 1762, he proposed that an effort be made to show that Khark really could make a profit, by cutting overhead and increasing sales and profit margins, on condition that the XVII would agree to the continuation of the Khark operation.[47] The available sources do not shed light on the reason for this sudden change of heart, but the most likely one is that Batavia needed to sell its sugar surplus. The High Government agreed to the governor-general's proposal and ordered Buschman to act accordingly.[48] On learning about this proposal, the XVII immediately ordered the Khark factory to be closed down.

Trade results for 1764-65 were no better than in the previous year, while the volume of unsold goods was considerable. The High Government's "reform" policy clearly had failed and once again the XVII were right. They had not bothered to comment on Khark trade matters since 1763, because things did not change for the better there and because they assumed that Batavia had carried out its orders to close down the Khark factory.[49] Meanwhile, as discussed in the first part of this chapter, two VOC ships could not prevent Mir Mohanna, the ruler of Bandar-e Rig, from taking the Dutch factory on January 1, 1766. Mir Mohanna allowed the VOC staff to depart, but they had to leave all their possessions behind.

CONCLUSION

Thus ended the Dutch presence in the Persian Gulf that had lasted for 133 years. Business had been poor for the VOC in Persia since the 1720s, when the VOC staff had been exposed to extortion and 'requests for loans,' and those inconveniences were no longer offset by good trade returns. Not surprisingly the VOC's directors considered abandoning the Persian Gulf trade altogether by the end of the 1740s. Von Kniphausen's Khark scheme must had held out hope for improvement, however, for it is impossible to explain the acquiescence of the VOC directors in any other way. Against their

45 VOC 1009, Batavia to Khark (22/04/1755), f. 74; VOC 334, XVII to Batavia (30/09/1758), section Karreek, not foliated; VOC 1009, Batavia to Khark (22/04/1755), f. 74.

46 See chapter three.

47 VOC 792, Nadere bedenkingen (Batavia; 06/04/1762), f. 265-82. The sugar surplus problem of Java played an important role in van der Parra's change of mind.

48 VOC 1016, Batavia to Khark (26/05/1762), f. 97f.

49 VOC 335, XVII to Batavia (05/10/1765), section Karreek, not foliated.

better judgment they gave in to the superficial and flimsy arguments from the High Government and agreed to the Khark scheme. For if there is one lesson to be drawn from this episode in VOC history, it is how well informed the XVII were about even marginal trade activities such as the Persian Gulf trade.

Another striking aspect was the High Government's lackadaisical, possibly self-interested attitude towards the Khark project. There appears to have been a kind of special understanding between governor-general Jacob Mossel and von Kniphausen, but no tangible evidence for actual collusion. The Khark residents certainly had a personal interest in this venture, but their private trading activities were no exception to normal VOC practice.

Although commercially Khark proved to be a failure, this was not because, as Amin has it, the Khark policy was pursued by only some individuals. There is no evidence that private commercial interests were pursued by members of the High Government, and Batavia supported the Khark project fully. Even the VOC directors, who could have nipped the Khark factory in the bud, decided to give it a chance for a ten-year period. If we assume that it was the Mossel-von Kniphausen axis that was instrumental in the creation of the Khark project and its continuation, it still does not support Amin's assertion. It is true that the High Government had only agreed to the Khark project by majority, not unanimously. Nevertheless, Mossel's successor, van der Parra - a one-time opponent of the Khark project- in 1762 suspended his own decision to close the Khark factory and even devised his own new trade policy to get Khark to show a profit. The decision to cut their losses and leave Khark was not taken by the High Government, but by the XVII. If the whole operation really had been artificial, it could not have lasted twelve years. The XVII put an immediate end to the Masqat voyages begun in 1756, which had been a real desperate bid to sell Batavia's surplus sugar. The XVII could have ordered Khark discontinued at the same time, but they did not. The only explanation is that the High Government, in its need for a better outlet for Batavia sugar, still had hopes for the Persian Gulf market.

The Khark project was a failure. Although trade had substantially increased, the absorption capacity of the Persian Gulf market was too limited to make good the substantial overhead in staff, ships, and factory. The EIC could only sell its woolens there.[50] The VOC could sell its merchandise in Surat as well. However, it preferred to stay with the Gulf market. If the situation in Persia had stabilized, things might have taken a turn for the better, a promise constantly held out by the Khark residents. However, it never happened.

Apart from market forces, the VOC's internal situation was most to blame for Khark's downfall. Notwithstanding all kinds of proposals for internal reform, the differences of opinion between the XVII and the High Government were not resolved. The VOC had gradually lost the initiative, and in this atmosphere of general stagnation, Batavia was attracted by von Kniphausen. He was an entrepreneur, a fresh wind blowing through dead wood, which held out promise for new life. However, no plant can grow in barren soil. This lack of innovative management finished Khark more than anything else. The Dutch Company had lost the ability to initiate new projects, to adapt, to make things happen, unlike its main competitor, the EIC. The English company stimulated the country trade by English and other traders with English goods. The consulage levied by the EIC on this trade was sufficient to bear the cost of its establishments in the Persian Gulf. Freight taken from India to the Persian Gulf also improved the overall profitability of the EIC. Finally, the EIC had a stake in the Persian Gulf, for this was one of the few places where it could sell British woolens, a major export commodity. The sale of these fabrics was in the interest

50 In particular in Basra after 1758, which port continued to be more attractive for merchants than Khark. In 1762 van der Hulst reported that few of the passing ships unloaded or bought goods at Khark, because the captains of these vessels only sold their private merchandise there. VOC, Khark to Batavia (19/10/1762), f. 36

of English industry, for 75 percent of all sales in the East were made in Persia. By contrast, apart from incidental remarks about national industrial interests, the VOC only talked and wrote new proposals for the redress of old complaints. No decisions were taken with regard to the sale of Dutch woolens in Persia. The EIC sold large quantities at low profits; the VOC insisted on at least a 50 percent rate of profit and priced itself out of the market. Thus ended the Khark factory and with it the VOC chapter on relations with Persia.

CHAPTER SIX
Dutch Trade with Masqat 1755-1796

Trade with Masqat was not something new for the VOC and it even contemplated to start trading with Masqat again in 1756 and 1757. However, because these sales negatively impacted sales of its Khark factory the VOC abandoned Masqat as a possible outlet for its merchandise. When the VOC abandoned the Persian Gulf trade altogether after it had been ousted from Khark in 1766 the Dutch nevertheless resumed trade with the area one decade later with direct voyages from Batavia to Masqat to sell sugar and some spices. However, these voyages were made by private Dutch merchants who bought their merchandise from the VOC. This chapter relates the development and demise of the commercial contacts between the Dutch and Masqat in the second half of the eighteenth century.[1]

INTRODUCTION

When the VOC extended its trade to Masqat in 1756 the event greatly disturbed the EIC Council in Bombay and their superiors in London. The English Company servants believed that the Dutch sought no less than complete control of the Persian Gulf. The English and some of the local chiefs such as Sheikh Naser of Bushire took this view because the Dutch had first taken military action against the governor of Basra to force him to refund the money he had extorted from the VOC servants. This successful action had been followed by the establishment of a factory, or rather a fortress on the island of Khark, while at the same time the Dutch factories in Basra and Bushire were abandoned. The English, chagrined at the Dutch success, believed that the latter would continue with their forceful policy and seize Bahrain. Such an operation was indeed proposed by von Kniphausen, the VOC Resident of the Khark factory. However, both the High Government at Batavia and the Company directors in the Netherlands had rejected the proposal.[2] In response to these Dutch activities the English established a factory in Rig, but it was destroyed less than one year later by the chief of Rig, Mir Mohanna. The English were convinced that the Dutch at Khark had been involved in this as well, and probably were even the instigators.[3] A punitive expedition against Rig also failed and that same year the Dutch arrived with two large ships at Masqat.

1 For Dutch trade with Masqat prior to 1756 see Floor, *Persian Gulf*, pp. 370, 386-95, 398-506, 424.

2 See Floor, "Bahrain Project," in Annex I.

3 See chapter four in this publication.

The English were understandably apprehensive about Dutch encroachment on their position in the Persian Gulf, particularly as they had been ordered by the Court of Directors in London to advise it on "what new may be opened" to expand their trade.[4] The fact that the Dutch had been able to settle in "one of the most important trade centres in the Gulf whose rulers had hitherto refused to allow any European to open a factory on their territories" must undoubtedly have alarmed the EIC directors.[5]

The English did not know, however, that there was no grand design for Dutch control of the Persian Gulf. Some VOC servants like von Kniphausen may have harbored such thoughts, but these were not shared by their superiors either in Batavia or Amsterdam. What appeared to have been a consistent Dutch commercial expansion policy was in fact merely a succession of uncoordinated and chance incidents that were in search of a policy. While it is true that Dutch activities at Basra, Khark, Bahrain, Bushire and Rig were all engineered by von Kniphausen, not all of his actions had the approval of his superiors. Moreover, his activities had nothing to do with the events in Masqat, which he actually opposed.

PROPOSAL FOR ANNUAL MASQAT VOYAGES

The idea of extending Dutch trade to Masqat originated with Jacob Schoonderwoerd, the VOC Resident in Bandar 'Abbas. On March 31, 1755 he suggested to the High Government in Batavia that the VOC accept the invitation of the pasha of Baghdad to resume trade in Basra. He proposed that the Dutch remain on Khark and sent two assistants to Basra, who would order more goods from Khark once they had sold their existing stock. To enable them to do so Schoonderwoerd further suggested that one small bark be put at the disposal of the VOC staff in the Persian Gulf. This vessel might also be used to send goods from Bandar 'Abbas to Masqat at times when certain merchandise fetched higher prices there.[6]

Schoonderwoerd's suggestion was approved by Batavia and von Kniphausen was ordered to appraise the feasibility of the idea; the proposal to extend trade to Masqat was made conditional on his approval. This condition was of a formal nature rather than one of policy, for Schoonderwoerd, who until then had been the highest ranking VOC servant in the Persian Gulf, was to return to Batavia. Since he was succeeded by a lower ranking colleague, the High Government had decided to make the Khark factory the Residency of Dutch activities in the Persian Gulf. If von Kniphausen agreed to send surplus goods from Bandar 'Abbas to be sold in Masqat instead of Khark, Schoonderwoerd would be authorized to make the voyage to Masqat.[7] Seeing that the reply from von Kniphausen was not forthcoming, Schoonderwoerd decided nevertheless to leave Bandar 'Abbas for Masqat on December 299, 1755.[8]

He arrived in Masqat on January 7, 1756 on board *de Vlietlust*. On arrival he was informed that the Imam of Masqat, Ahmad b. Sa'id (1744-1783) had come to the city a few days before from the royal residence at Rustaq. Schoonderwoerd went to pay his respects to the Imam, who received him warmly. He told Schoonderwoerd that it would please him if the VOC established a factory in

4 Amin, *British Interests*, p. 146.

5 Amin, *British Interests*, p. 145.

6 VOC 2803, Gamron to Batavia (31/03/1755), f. 18-19; see also chapter four in this publication regarding the resumption of trade at Basra.

7 VOC 1009, Batavia to Gamron (18/07/1755), f. 249.

8 VOC 2885, Gamron to Batavia (28/12/1755), f. 21.

Masqat. He also inquired whether the Dutch might be able to supply him with a ship identical to *de Vlietlust* at cost price. Schoonderwoerd made it clear that he had no authority to commit the VOC on these matters. Moreover, he had to react cautiously, as the Imam might not agree to the price that the High Government would ask. Therefore, Schoonderwoerd offered his opinion that payment would have to be in advance of delivery for Batavia to agree to such a transaction. The Imam assured Schoonderwoerd that the Dutch need not worry about payment or price, on which they would surely reach agreement. To that end he suggested that the Dutch send an official with power of attorney to deal with these matters. The Imam indicated his sincerity by giving Schoonderwoerd a letter to Jacob Mossel, governor-general of the VOC in Batavia, in which the Imam formally proposed the establishment of a Dutch factory and ordered the delivery of one ship of *de Vlietlust* class.[9] As evidence of his friendly intentions and his wish to promote amicable relations with the Dutch, the Imam gave Schoonderwoerd two stallions and fodder as a present for Mossel. In return Schoonderwoerd gave the Imam a gift worth Dfl. 605:3.

Although Schoonderwoerd's voyage to Masqat was a diplomatic success, his commercial activities were not. Immediately on arrival Schoonderwoerd had inquired about the state of the market. It became clear that trade prospects were not bright; a few days before an English sloop, the *Kedrie*, had arrived from Bengal with a cargo including zinc and iron. Schoonderwoerd could only get an offer for zinc at cost price and for iron at the VOC's fixed price. He therefore sold part (24,200 lbs.) of his iron at Dfl. 17 per 100 lbs. and 300 canisters (100,121 lbs.) of powered sugar at Dfl. 16 per 100 lbs. Schoonderwoerd was unable to sell more for ready cash, but he believed that if he could have stayed for another three months the entire cargo might have been sold.[10]

Although he sold little, Schoonderwoerd believed that profitable business might be done in Masqat. For this it would be necessary to send a medium-sized ship for three or four months. The merchants would have to be granted a short period of credit, which at the same time would have an inflationary effect on prices. The best time for trading in Masqat, Schoonderwoerd believed, would be at the beginning of October when the so-called Mokha monsoon began.[11] At that time coffee could be purchased at six *stuivers* or slightly more per lb.; high quality aloe from Socotra and other kinds of gums were also procurable. Finally, the cash situation in Masqat was most favorable then, and as the Dutch had orders to sell for cash this was an important factor. Schoonderwoerd also reported that he had again been asked by a representative of the king of Sind to come and trade. Although he had little knowledge of that country or its trade, he believed that the proposal was worth further investigation.[12]

9 VOC 2885, Achmed Bein Sijjd to Mossel (Masqat, 24/01/1756), f. 57-59 (Dutch translation only).

10 The cost price of iron was Dfl. 2,902:15 (including 2 per cent costs in Batavia). The proceeds were Dfl. 4.117:8 at a net profit of Dfl. 1,214;13 or 41 per cent. The cost price of sugar was Dfl. 8,638:13 (including 2 per cent cost in Batavia). The proceeds were Dfl. 16,019:7 at a net profit of Dfl. 7,380:14 or 85 per cent. Total costs were Dfl. 11,541:8, while total proceeds were Dfl. 20,136:15 or a net profit of Dfl. 8,595:7 or 75 per cent. VOC 2885, Schoonderwoerd (Masqat) to Batavia (24/01/1756), f. 53.

11 The Mokha monsoon refers to the coffee traders who traveled from Mokha (Yemen) to Basra in July to sell their coffee and buy dates and other goods. On their return to the Red Sea many stopped at Masqat in the hope of benefiting from lower prices.

12 VOC 2885, Schoonderwoerd (Masqat) to Batavia (24/01/1756), f. 52-56.

THE FIST MASQAT VOYAGE

Meanwhile the High Government had decided to send *de Marienbosch* with a cargo of various goods, but mainly sugar, to Masqat instead of Khark, to be followed later by a second ship. When Schoonderwoerd finally arrived in Batavia towards the end of May 1756, the High Government accepted his proposal with minor changes. On June 8, 1756 the council thus decided that the second ship, *'tPasgeld*, would travel to Diewil-Sind if trade prospects in Masqat were unfavorable.[13]

On July 9, 1756 Captain de Nijsz of *de Marienbosch* and Captain Brahé of *'tPasgeld* received their orders for the voyage to Masqat.[14] The ships were to sail together to Masqat and to try and sell their goods there. Only if it proved impossible to sell the cargoes of both ships was Brahé to set course for Sind. Because the greater part of the cargoes consisted of sugar, de Nijsz and his colleague were allowed to follow the market trend. They nevertheless were to seek the highest possible prices. The High Government had fixed the prices for the other goods that they carried.[15] Both captains were instructed to deliver the goods only after payment had been made aboard their ships, if possible. If cash was scarce, they were permitted to make a deal with the Imam of Masqat for the sale of goods at four months' credit. This was a practical measure, since *de Marienbosch* had to stay in Masqat for that period anyway.

Because of the fluctuating exchange rates owing to scarcity of cash and the changing intrinsic value of coins, the High Government charged the captain to employ only trustworthy money changers. They also were authorized to accept the various currencies only at the following fixed rates:

Keyzerdaalders	60 *stuivers*
Rupees	26 *stuivers*
Golden rupees	Dfl. 18:18
Venetian ducats	Dfl. 6:12
Copperware	Dfl. 80:00 per 100 lbs.

On arrival in Masqat the captains were to contact the VOC factories in Bandar 'Abbas and Khark. They would provide them and Batavia with information about trade and other matter and perhaps with letters for Batavia. The captains were also instructed to proceed to these factories if sales in Masqat proved to be unsuccessful.

The vessels left Batavia on July 19, 1756, but en route *de Marienbosch* proved to be faster so that it arrived in Masqat on August 27, 1756.[16] De Nijsz and his deputy Gotsche went ashore the next day and were well received by the governor (*vakil*) of Masqat, Khalfan b. Mohammad. They told him that they had a letter and presents from the governor-general for the Imam.[17] The governor immediately sent runners to the Imam, who was staying at Rustaq at that time. Pleased at the arrival of the Dutch ship, the Imam invited de Nijsz to visit him. The captain and Gotsche left Masqat on September 3, 1756 by native craft for Bocca,[18] which they reached the following day. They learnt

13 VOC 786, year 1756. See the resolutions of March 30, April 20 and 30, June 8 and July 5, 1756.

14 VOC 1010, Instructions from the High Government for Captains de Nijsz and Brahé (Batavia, 05/07/1756), f. 213-15.

15 Prices per 100 lbs. after deduction of expenses were as follows (in Dfl.): iron 18; tin 40; zinc 22:10; pepper 35; mace 640; nutmegs 280; cloves 500; and cinnamon 600.

16 The following is based VOC 2909, De Nijsz to Batavia (06/05/1757), f. 6-15, unless otherwise indicated.

17 For the Dutch text of this letter see VOC 1001 (06/07/1756), f. 216-19.

18 I have been unable to identify Bocca. Dikkah is probably meant here, which is almost a suburb of Matrah.

that the Imam had arrived there the night before. De Nijsz therefore had his presence announced by a Banyan.[19] The Imam sent a group of military to welcome de Nijsz and escort him to the palace. An hour later the Dutch party arrived to be greeted by a guard of honor; they were then taken to the Imam, who received them warmly. After the usual compliments he requested that de Nijsz read the governor-general's letter aloud in Dutch and have the Banyan translate it into Arabic.

In this letter the governor-general gladly accepted the Imam's offer of friendship with the Netherlands. To indicate Dutch goodwill he announced the arrival of *de Marienbosch* to initiate Dutch trade in Masqat and requested the Imam's assistance in promoting it and his subordinates' activities. As for the sale of a Dutch ship to the Imam, the governor-general regretted that no such vessel was available at that moment. If the Imam was prepared to wait, however, he would see to it that a ship would be sent as soon as the opportunity arose. The governor-general also mentioned that a ship would cost some Dfl. 150,000. Finally, he thanked the Imam for the gifts that he graciously sent to Batavia, a gesture that the governor-general reciprocated.[20]

After the official audience was over de Nijsz requested the Imam's protection and assistance in furthering Dutch trade in Masqat, which the latter promised to do. He added that he would grant the Dutch more privileges than any other nation and he invited the Dutch delegation to stay at Rustaq with him during the holidays.[21] De Nijsz politely declined the invitation pointing out that his absence would delay trading activities too much. De Nijsz then took his leave accompanied by two of the Imam's secretaries.

On September 6, 1756 the Dutch returned to Masqat where the governor, accompanied by some merchants, visited them at their residence on September 9. The governor told de Nijsz that he had received a letter from the Imam granting the Dutch the right to build a house in Masqat wherever they desired.[22] De Nijsz thanked the governor for this privilege, but told him that for the time being the rented house sufficed. He nevertheless would convey notice of this favor to the High Government and let them decide on the matter.

They then discussed trade. De Nijsz asked the governor what duties the Dutch would have to pay. The latter stated that the English and French had to pay seven per cent,[23] to which de Nijsz replied that the Dutch were not in the habit of imitating their competitors, false though this claim was. He therefore asked for total exemption from customs duties for Dutch goods. Replying that the Dutch were to pay less than other nations, as ordered by the Imam, the governor therefore proposed a duty of three per cent. De Nijsz, however, continued to insist on complete exemption. The governor finally promised to inform the Imam about this demand. Since the matter was not

19 The Dutch used the term Banyan to refer to Hindu merchants from India, especially those from Gujarat.

20 For a list of the gifts see VOC 1001 (06/07/1756), f. 216-19.

21 The holidays referred to are *'id al-adha*, on 10 Dhu'l-Hijja and *'id al-kabir* on 18 Dhu'l-Hijja. In 1756 the corresponding CE dates were September 6 and 14 respectively.

22 Amin mistakenly states that the Dutch requested permission to build a factory and hoist the Dutch colors. This also holds for the Imam's alleged reply to this request, viz., "The Imam agreed that the Dutch land their cargo, hire a suitable house, and leave proper persons to carry out the business, but he refused to permit them to build a factory or hoist their colors." Amin, *British Interests*, p. 145, n. 5.

23 According to Dutch sources, the English and French paid a customs rate of 7 per cent; see VOC 1011, instruction for Rood, Karsseboom, Verschuur (Batavia, 25/07/1757), f. 204. According to English sources, however, the customs rate in 1756 was as follows: "Import duty in those days was determined by national or religious status of the merchants; it was 5 per cent. ad valorem for Europeans, 6½ per cent. for Muhammadans, and 9 per cent. for Hindus and Jews." J.G. Lorimer, *Gazetteer of the Persian Gulf, 'Oman, and Central Arabia* (Calcutta, 1915), p. 416.

raised again either by the Imam or the governor during the Nijsz's stay in Masqat, the Dutch paid no customs duties on the goods that they sold.

On September 19, 1756 *'tPasgeld* arrived in Masqat. In view of the dim prospects of selling a second cargo of merchandise, it was decided that the ship would set course for Sind in accordance with their orders. *'tPasgeld* therefore left Masqat on October 26, 1756.[24] Trade in Masqat was slack so that only by February 15, 1757 all goods were sold, with the exception of one bale of Ceylonese cinnamon and five cases of manufactures. Gotsche did not live to see this result, for he died on January 29, 1757.[25]

THE SECOND MASQAT VOYAGE

The profit realized by de Nijsz was not encouraging, for only Dfl. 85,134:18 net was made, while both prices and the rate of exchange in specie had been disappointing. Mossel and his High Government decided nevertheless to send another ship, *de Barbara Theodora*, to Masqat in the hope of better results. Not only did the council wish to get rid of surplus stocks of sugar, but the mere eight-month voyage to and from Masqat was considered promising. The captain of *de Barbara Theodora*, Simon Rood or Root, was therefore ordered to sail directly from Batavia to Masqat and to sell sugar at the highest possible price, since the High Government believed prices had risen in Masqat. To give Rood an indication of what was expected of him the council informed him that the 1756 prices for powdered sugar and candy sugar had been Rupees 15 and 13.5 respectively (both yielding a 50 per cent profit), but these had been insufficient.

Although given a free had where sugar was concerned, Rood was required to stick the prices fixed by the council for the other commodities, which were the same as in 1756. The same held for the rates of exchange where specie was concerned as well as the period of credit Rood was allowed to extend to trustworthy merchants.

Rood was furthermore instructed to inform the Imam that the VOC did not wish to construct a factory in Masqat as it already had a sufficient number of factories in the Persian Gulf. The VOC did, however, wish to extend its commercial operations to friends and neighbors, which was why the Dutch had come to Masqat. Captain Rood was to communicate this only if asked why Batavia had not responded to the Imam's offer.[26]

De Barbara Theodora left Batavia on July 27, 1757 and arrived in Masqat on September 21, 1757.[27] Rood had his presence announced to the governor of Masqat, Sheikh Khalfan b. Mohammad, through the VOC broker, the Banyan Narrotam.[28] Rood inquired whether the Dutch would again be allowed free trade in Masqat and whether they would enjoy the same privileges they had had in 1756. He pointed out that this was the reason why the High Government had again decided to send

---

24 See Willem Floor, "Dutch East India Company's Trade with Sind in the 17th and 18th centuries," *Moyen-Orient & Ocean Indien*, vol. 3 (1986), pp. 111-144. This study was re-published by the Institute of Central & West Asian Studies (University of Karachi, 1993-94) enriched with comments from Pakistani scholars.

25 Here ends the information based on VOC 2909, De Nijsz to Batavia (06/05/1757), f. 6-15.

26 VOC 1011, Instructions for Rood, Karsseboom, Verschuur (Batavia, 25/07/1757), f. 198-205.

27 Unless otherwise indicated the following is based on VOC 2937, Rood to Batavia (08/03/1758), f. 77-104.

28 The broker was Narrotam (or Noerotoem) Anak Rama Djiendil Djoezie, see VOC 2937, f. 107-09, which includes a letter from him to Mossel. The broker received separate appointments for each voyage. He sent presents to Mossel, who reappointed him for the second voyage, exhorting him to sell the VOC goods at higher prices. VOC 1011, Mossel to VOC broker (Batavia, 25/07/1757), f. 209-11.

a ship to Masqat. Rood then presented the governor with the governor-general's letter[29] to the Imam and mentioned that he had brought gifts for the Imam as well. The governor received the governor-general's letter with bows and kisses and gave Rood and his men a friendly welcome. He told Rood that he had been looking forward to the return of the Dutch and that he was certain that the Imam would grant them free trade this year as well. At Rood's request the governor advised him to wait few days in Masqat before presenting the Imam, who was due to arrive in Masqat shortly, with the gifts from the governor-general.

On September 23, 1757 the governor suggested Rood that trade negotiations could begin, for a number of merchants were on the point of leaving for the upper part of the Persian Gulf. However, the prices these merchants were willing to pay were too low. They bid only 13-14 Rupees per *picol* for powdered sugar and 19 Rupees of candy sugar and asked for five months' credit. The only attractive part of the offer was that they were willing to buy the entire stock of sugar. However, Rood did not accept their offer.

No trade was done until September 25, when the merchants returned. After much haggling they offered 15 Rupees per *picol* for 800-1,000 canisters of sugar at five months' credit and payment in monies current in Masqat. Rood finally accepted this offer, fearing that with the departure of these merchants he would have less chance of selling his cargo. He reduced the period of credit, however, to three months and required that both the governor of Masqat and the VOC broker guarantee the time of payment and the currencies used. These conditions were accepted by both the governor and the broker.

Table 6.1 List of all goods offered for sale in Masqat in 1757 and the prices usually obtained

Name	Price (Rupees)	Price (Rupees)
Old copperware per *man* of 8 lbs. at 5 ½ -5 1/4 Rs per 100 lbs.	68 ¾	68 5/8
Asafetida per *picol* of 125 lbs.	110	105
Hing Herati, fine, per *picol* of 125 lbs.	225	250
Hing Troesie or Toercesa [?] per *picol* of 125 lbs.	126	125
Gum Arabica per *picol* of 125 lbs.	13	12
Gum myrrh per *picol* of 125 lbs.	44	42 ½
Gum olibanum per *picol* of 125 lbs.	8 ½	8
Socotra aloe per *picol* of 125 lbs.	56	55
Persian *runas* [madder] per picol of 125 lbs.	40	35
Dry dates per *bar* of 200 *man* of 1,600 lbs.	60	65
Wet Masqat dates per *bar* of 1,600 lbs.	50	52
Wet Basra dates per bale of 144-145 lbs.	5	6
Persian rosewater per case of 50 bottles	23	20
Moorish coffeebeans per *man* of 8 lbs. Rs 3-2 ½ or *per* picol of 125 lbs.	46 7/8	39 1/16
Sulfur soil per *picol* of 125 lbs.	11	10

29 For the Dutch text see VOC 1011 (Batavia, 25/07/1757), f. 205-08.

Kapok per bale of 20 *man* of 460 lbs. at Rs 160-150 or per 125 lbs.	43 ½	41
Elephants teeth from Bombassa [sic] per *picol* of 125 lbs.	150	140

Source: VOC 2937, f. 11 (Mascate, 07/12/1757).

The Imam finally came to Masqat, accompanied by his youngest son Mohammad and three mollahs, in November 1757. At the advice of the governor, Rood and his officers welcomed them at Matrah, according to the country's custom. The Imam had come from Rustaq to send off two small ships, two grabs,[30] and two to three gallivats[31] to Mombassa[32] with military supplies to punish rebels, who challenged his rule.

On November 3, 1757 Rood, accompanied by 26 European and Buginese[33] soldiers and the VOC broker, marched to the Imam's palace to offer him the governor-general's gifts. During the presentation the VOC soldiers offered three salutes with their matchlocks, while *de Marienbosch*, the Imam's admiral's ship and the Masqat forts fired their guns. The reception of Rood and his party was very friendly. The Imam expressed the hope that the Dutch would continue their annual visits, for they were, so to speak, like brothers to him and were as free in his country as in their own home. He then invited Rood and his officers to his residence in Rustaq, but the captain politely declined this honor, since time was pressing. Accepting this reason, the Imam nevertheless insisted that Rood and his party visit the largest fort of Masqat at the east side of the bay.[34]

On November 7, 1757 Rood and his officers were given a tour by the Imam and saluted by gunfire from all forts and ships in the bay. The Imam took the opportunity to show Rood how many of the guns and gun carriages had deteriorated with age. He asked that Rood report this to Batavia and he also ordered ten new pieces. He further mentioned to Rood that never before had any nation been honored by him with even one salute. Rood obliged him by thanking the Imam for this unique honor as well as inviting him to visit his ship *de Barbara Theodora*. After the Imam had accepted this invitation they returned to his palace. The Dutch continued to be saluted until their arrival there. Later that day the Imam sent fruit and sweetmeats to Rood.

On November 10, 1757 the Imam, his sons, the governor of Masqat and a party of officials were given a stately reception aboard *de Barbara Theodora*. The Imam visited al parts of the ship and compared it with his 130-feet admiral's ship, which had been built in Bombay and bought at 90,000 Rupees from the English in 1757. According to Rood, the Dutch ship was considered a better vessel by the Imam, but then he could hardly have said anything else.

On November 18, 1757 the Imam returned to Rustaq and Rood took his leave of him. The Imam presented him with two Arab stallions for the governor-general and instructed Khalfan b. Mohammad to write a letter to the governor-general.[35] He then asked when Rood would return to Batavia. Rood replied that he would leave as soon as possible he had collected his money. To that end he had seized the opportunity to take up the main problem in this respect, viz. the high price of exchange for golden rupees and ducats. Rood requested that the Imam fix the rate of gold coins at their intrinsic value or at a minimum at 5 Rupees. The Imam replied that he was unable to do so

30 A common type of small sailing vessel at that time, popular with country traders.

31 A kind of war boat with oars and sails, of small draft of water.

32 Zanzibar, Mombasa and some other parts of the East African coast were part of the Imam's dominions.

33 Inhabitants of the Indonesian island of Bugi (Central Sulawesi).

34 This probably is the Jalali fort, see Lorimer, *Gazetteer*, pp. 1180-81.

35 For the text of this letter (Dutch translation only) see VOC 2937, f. 105-06.

in view of the scarcity of specie in his country, which was the real cause of the high rates. He would, however, order the governor to see to it that the merchants honor payment of their debts speedily. Rood had to be satisfied with that reply and thanked the Imam for all the honors shown to the VOC. The Imam then wished Rood a safe voyage and left for Matrah, where the official farewell took place. There, mounted on camels, the Imam and his entourage continued their journey.

Having no other official duties to perform and wishing to return as soon as possible, Rood sold his remaining stock, which no merchant had expressed an interest in buying, to the VOC broker on November 29. Barring these few items, Rood was very pleased with trade results. Not only had he sold his entire cargo, in spite of the fact that that three VOC ships had preceded him to Khark and Bandar 'Abbas, but most of his transactions had been in cash and he had been able to make a profit of 101 per cent, or 30 per cent more than in 1756. This was mainly due to the sale of greater quantities of sugar and a lower price than in 1756 (see Table 5.2).

On December, 1757 Rood left Masqat. A few days prior to his departure the Imam had sent him a letter for the governor-general requesting that two of his servants be allowed to make the voyage to Cochin. The servants had been charged to settle an affair with the king of Calicut. Because *de Barbara Theodora* was scheduled to call on Cochin to take in water and firewood, Rood could not refuse. After an uneventful voyage he returned to Batavia on March 8, 1758.[36]

Table 6.2: Profit and Loss Account of *de Marienbosch* (in Dutch guilders)

Imports according to the Batavian invoice			113,605: 2: 8
Ship's supplies in Batavia			15,292: 8: 0
Profit after deduction of brokerage and commission	107,338: 4: 0		
Less underweight of benzoin	274: 0: 0		
Gross profit		107,612: 4: 0	
Deduction of the cost of 2.5 month's stay in Masqat			
Supplies and domestic needs	656:19: 3		
Ship's expenses and cost of voyage	1,636: 4: 0		
Fodder for horses 160:13 Rupees			
Two grooms at 6 Rupees/month at two month's advance 32:8			
	193: 1: 0		
Cost dispatched documents to Khark and Gamron	16:17: 8		
Payment for letter received	6:15: 0		
Supplied to ship in Batavia	15,292: 8: 0		
Supplied in addition to the cargoes	141: 6: 8		
Various presents	1,993: 9: 8		
Commission for the ship's officers	2,319: 0: 0		

36 Here ends the information based on VOC 1011, Instructions for Rood, Karsseboom, Verschuur (Batavia, 25/07/1757), f. 198-205.

		22,255: 1: 0	
Net profit on cost price 1,059,42:11. 8 = 80.6%			85,357: 3: 0
Total			214,254:13: 8

Source: VOC 2937, f. 89-91.

VOC DECIDES TO DISCONTINUE MASQAT VOYAGES

Although the High Government was extremely pleased with the trade results of *de Barbara Theodora* and its quick journey, it nevertheless decided to discontinue all voyages to Masqat. The chief of the Khark factory, Tido von Kniphausen, had complained that Masqat's profit was Khark's loss. In view of inter-Gulf trade relations that which was sold in Masqat could not be sold at Khark, as the Persian Gulf merchants frequently called on all ports in that region. As far as the High Government was concerned Java sugar could just as well be sold in Khark, which already had a VOC factory and therefore had to show a profit. The High Government stressed the need to sell all the sugar they sent, so that they finally could be rid of it. Von Kniphausen was instructed to inform the Imam of Masqat that no VOC ships would call in 1758 due to a delay, which made it impossible to undertake the voyage. Company ships would return to Masqat at a later date, if possible. This fabrication was intended to save face, for the council felt embarrassed about the turn of events. It also wished to maintain friendly relations with the Imam.[37]

In view of the delicate commercial situation of Khark the High Government's decision was completely justified.[38] Rood's argument for continued voyages to Masqat was too weak and uncertain a basis to rely on. He pointed out that much rice had always been carried from Bengal and Malabar to Masqat. In 1757, five small private English grabs had come from Malabar with rice, pepper, sandalwood and cardamom. They had bartered these goods for dry and wet dates and other items. Because the trade carried on by the English country traders was not as important as before Rood proposed that one ship from Batavia (carrying spices, sugar, and base metals) and two from Bengal (carrying rice and textiles) be sent to Masqat each year. However, in that case the second ship from Bengal would have to depart three months after the first one. This schedule also would allow the return of such a ship as soon as possible. These goods were to be bartered for pearls, copperware, rosewater, dates, various gums, brimstone, rock salt and drugs in addition to gold ducats. In this way, Rood argued, the VOC could take away business from English country traders, see what prices the VOC might obtain for its goods from Batavia, and make short swift voyages.

Table 6.3 Proposed cargos for continued voyages to Masqat

Commodity	Quantity	Price
From Batavia		
powdered Java sugar	2,000 canisters	
candy sugar	100 canisters	
iron bars	800 *picol*	

37 VOC 1012, Batavia to Khark (25/04/1758), f. 123-24, 131.

38 See chapters four and five in this study.

lead	200 *picol*	
tin	200 *picol*	
steel	100 *picol*	
sappanwood, thick, long, straight	400 *picol*	
curcuma from Java	250 *picol*	
curcuma from Malabar, new variety	250 *picol*	
cloves, not mixed with nutmegs	40 chests	
cochineal	5 *picol*	
camphor, Chinese or Japanese	100 *picol*	
benzoin, zinc, mace	on account of abundance little trade	
From Bengal		
fine and coarse Bengal rice in gunny bags of 150 lbs. each	Two cargos	6 ½-7 Rs per bag fine kind 5 ½-6 Rs per bag for coarse kind
new dried ginger	250 gunny bags	12 ½-15 Rs per picol of 125 lbs.
curcuma from Bengal	250 gunny bags	9 -10 Rs per bag
Bengal gum-lac on sticks in bags of 70-80 lbs.	250 gunny bags	30 -32 Rs per 125 lbs.
unbleached *baftas*; 150 per bale; each piece 24 long, 2 cubids wide	25 bales	78 -88 Rs per corgie of 20
soesjes with red-yellow stripes in 3 varieties; each bales with 200; each piece long 40, wide 2 cubids; 2nd variety long 50, wide 1 ½ cubid, and 3rd variety long 40, wide 1 ½ cubid	25 bales	12 -13 Rs/piece variety one 12 -13 Rs/piece variety two 7 - 8 Rs/piece variety three
sjeklassen; 150 per bale; each piece long 40, wide 2 cubid	2 bales	11 -12 Rs per piece
various textiles of all kinds	2 pieces of each kind	sample as a try-out

Source: VOC 2937, Root-Karseboom to Batavia (08/03/1758), f. 101.

Rood clearly had no idea the position the VOC found itself in at that time. Even Khark had no means of direct navigation with Bengal, although von Kniphausen had pointed out that this meant the VOC's loss of the textile market in the Persian Gulf. Moreover, the Masqat voyages were but a gamble by the High Government to rid itself of large stocks of Java sugar; there was no future in the continuation of these trade relations with Masqat, because this would negatively impact on the financial performance of the Khark factory.[39] The total commercial failure of the voyage of *'tPasgeld* may have contributed to the High Government's decision to discontinue the Masqat voyages.[40]

The decision met the total approval of the VOC's directors, the *Heeren XVII*. In 1759 they expressed their surprise at the Masqat voyages. Whereas Schoonderwoerd had proposed that a medium-sized ship be employed, the High Government had sent one of its largest ships, one of 140

39 VOC 2937, Rood to Mossel (Batavia, 08/03/1758), f. 87 (should be f. 101).

40 See Floor, "Dutch East India Company."

feet length, to Masqat in 1756. In view of the slack market one had to expect low profits, for what else could Batavia expect of two fully laden ships? The XVII bitingly observed that the so-called profit made by de Nijsz in 1756 amounted to little. Moreover, *'tPasgeld* had not yet returned from its voyage to Sind. Notwithstanding these hard facts the High Government had decided to send *de Barbara Theodora*. This decision had only been taken to get rid of sugar and not so much with a view to the profitability of the Masqat trade, the directors commented. Since the voyages to Masqat and Sind were considered disadvantageous for the VOC factories in Khark and Surat, the directors insisted that Batavia discontinue all voyages to Masqat as soon as it had disposed of its sugar stocks.[41]

Upon hearing of the outcome of trade on *de Barbara Theodora*, the XVII could not help but point out that its results only justified its earlier position. The net profit was hardly enough to cover the ship's expense, the loss on the rate of exchange and other costs, so that in fact little profit remained. Moreover, sales at Masqat had resulted in lower profitability of the Khark factory. The directors were therefore pleased with the High Government's decision to discontinue the Masqat voyages.[42]

The decision did not, however, signal the end of relations between the VOC and Masqat. In reply to a request of the former VOC broker, the High Government had written in 1761 that the Company would not resume trade. The XVII commented that even were the Imam to ask himself the answer had to remain negative.[43] Nevertheless, friendly relations were maintained. The Khark factory communicated with Masqat in connection with trade matters, ship wrecking, and private trading by VOC servants.[44] The Dutch were still very much in the favor of the Imam of Masqat. When survivors of the Khark debacle arrived in Masqat, they were warmly welcomed; and when a Dutch ship sent from Surat came to see what could be salvaged in 1766, the Imam even offered naval and military assistance to help the Dutch retake Khark.[45] This ship carried a VOC servant to Masqat, who was to remain behind and serve as the Company's eyes and eras in the Persian Gulf. He was soon withdrawn, however, when the Surat factory received notice that the VOC had decided to cease all activities in the Persian Gulf.[46]

---

41 VOC 334, XVII to Batavia (12/10/1759), section Masquetta, not foliated.

42 VOC 334, XVII to Batavia (30/09/1760), section Persien, not foliated.

43 VOC 335, XVII to Batavia (25/10/1762), section Masquetta, not foliated.

44 See chapter four in this publication.

45 See chapter four in this publication; Lorimer, *Gazetteer*, p. 411.

46 VOC 795, Resolution of the High Government (Batavia; 20/06/1765), f. 521ff.; see also chapter four in this publication.

RESUMPTION OF ANNUAL MASQAT VOYAGES

The eclipse of the VOC in the Persian Gulf did not preclude the sailing of Dutch ships to the area, as has been asserted by Amin, for instance.[47] The VOC factory at Surat continued to maintain contact with Basra for the purpose of the forwarding of letters, but shipping from Batavia to Masqat and the Persian Gulf was resumed only in 1777. On July 15, 1777 the High Government allowed merchant Willem van Hogendorp to buy 1,500 canisters of sugar from the VOC stocks at 5 *rijksdaalders* per *picol* plus 30 *stuivers* per *picol* as tax, on the condition that he also purchase and export 150 leaguers of arak and transport these with his own private ship to Masqat.[48] Van Hogendorp's initiative set an example and soon was followed by other private Dutch merchants, who likewise requested permission to send ships with sugar and arak to Masqat.[49] By 1780 two ships per year were sailing to Masqat (see Table 5.4), causing the High Government to reconsider the feasibility of direct VOC trade in the Persian Gulf. The private merchants van Hogendorp and Wiegerman were therefore instructed to examine the quantities in which and prices for which cloves, nutmegs and mace could be sold. Both merchants reported in 1781 that nutmeg and mace were not much in demand in Masqat, but predicted a sale of 28 *picols* of cloves as the price and demand were good. They were unaware of trading possibilities in the rest of the Persian Gulf area, as they had been unable to penetrate into the Persian Gulf any further during their voyage.[50]

---

47 Amin, *British Interests*, p. 132.

48 VOC 807, Resolution High Government (Batavia; 15/07/1777), f. 759. One *rijksdaalder* equals 2.5 guilders and one *stuiver* equals five cents.

49 For example, Mr. Boesjes, owner of the grab *de Snelheid*. VOC 809, f. 251 (23/11/1779) (left with 300 canisters of sugar, 100 leaguers of arak and some macis); VOC 810, f. 622 (30/06/1780) (left with a cargo of 400 canisters of sugar). See also VOC 809, f. 380vs (17/12/1779) (*Concordia*); VOC 810, f. 1307 (12/09/1781) permission granted to Jan Hendrik Wiegerman, president of the council of aldermen of Batavia to make voyages to Masqat with details of the cargo; see also VOC 811, f. 287-88 (07/12/1781).

50 NA, COC 811, Resolution of the High Government (Batavia; 07/12/1781), f. 287ff; VOC 810, f. 1308-09 (12/09/1781).

Table 6.4: Dutch ships sailing to Masqat, 1777-1793

Year	Name ship	Source
1777	Unknown	VOC 807, f. 759
1778	*De Snelheid*	VOC 809, f. 251
1779	*De Snelheid; Concordia; Hercules*	VOC 809, f. 251, 380vs; VOC 810, f. 1308
1780	*Nepthunus; de Snelheid*	VOC810, f. 662, 1308
1782	*Hoorn;*[†]	VOC 813, f. 232
1783	*Hoorn*	VOC 813, f. 232
1784	*Battavier*	VOC 814, not foliated
1785	*Nepthunus, Hercules;*[††]	VOC 815, f. 284, 287
1786	*De Nagel,*[†††] *Nepthunus, Hercules,*[††††] *Java's Welvaren*	VOC 815, f. 284, 395, 555-56
1787	*Hercules, Nepthunus, Java's Welvaren*	VOC 819, f. 469; VOC 818, f. 868, 1292; VOC 820, f. 1243
1788	*Nepthunus, Java's Welvaren*[†††††]	VOC 820, f. 102, 972, 1243
1789	*Hercules*	VOC 821, f. 1046
1790	*Nepthunus, Java's Welvaren*	VOC 825, f. 268-69
1791	*Java's Welvaren, Hercules*	NA, Hooge Regering Batavia, not foliated; see index on resolutions (04/01/1791)
1792	*Java's Welvaren*	VOC 827, f. 3559
1793	*Maria Catherina*[§]	NA, Archief Oost-Indisch Comité, nr. 78, Dagregister Batavia 1793/94, f. 195

† VOC 811, f. 287 (07/12/1781) also mentions a voyage by *de Jonge Hugo* with, among other things, 300 lbs. of spices.

†† The alderman Alexander Agerbeek financed the voyage of both *de Nepthunus* and *Herculus;* both carried sugar and spices as well as 30 *picol* of macis for the account of the VOC. VOC 815, f. 284-87 (22/11/1785); seel also VOC 815, f. 228 (11/11/1785).

††† *De Nagel* was a ship that had just been built in Batavia. It was commanded by captain Hermannus Folkers. VOC 815, f. 396 (16/12/1785). It left with 38 *picol* of macis.

†††† Alexander Agerbeek asked for permission to repair *de Hercules* in the VOC yard to make another voyage to Masqat. This was approved, but on condition that he would invest half of the cash with which he would return from Masqat in VOC letters of credit (*credietbrieven*), amounting to 50,000 *rijksdaalders.* In addition the VOC would earn 7,415 *rijksdaalders,* the proceeds of its 30 *picol* of macis that had been part of the ship's cargo. VOC 817, f. 555-56 (28/11/1786). In 1787 the macis yielded 6,846 *rijksdaalders.* VOC 819, f. 470 (18/12/1787). In 1788, it yielded 6,890 *rijksdaalders.* VOC 820, f. 972 (15/07/1788). *Java's Welvaren* returned with half of its proceeds in gold and half in *keijzerdaalders.* The sale of VOC macis had yielded 6,650 *rijksdaalders.* VOC 820, f. 1243 (1788).

††††† Francklin, *Observations,* p. 38 noted that in January 1787 there "was a Dutch ship lying in the harbour [of Masqat], commanded by Captain Stewart."

§ *De Maria Catherina* may have been a Portuguese ship, as stated in the index of the *Dagregister,* but the text itself refers only to "a private (*particulier*) ship." The cargo of these ships invariably consisted of powdered and candy sugar (generally 1,200 canisters of the former and 300 of the latter) and 38 *picols* of cloves.

The profits made by private merchants, together with the sales prospects for cloves, caused the High Government to promote such voyages. It allowed the VOC to sell 30 *picols* of cloves per year, enabling the Company to acquire much needed cash for its commercial operations. The High Government thereforee also decided that private merchants could continue their voyages to Masqat provided they sold 30 *picols* of cloves for the account of the VOC and invest half of the proceeds of the voyages in VOC letters of credit.[51]

To sustain the pattern of Masqat voyages the High Government assisted the private merchants in various ways. When in October 1779 Wiegerman's ship, *de Nepthunus*, suffered heavy damage near Bantam (Indonesia) and had to return to Batavia, the High Government permitted Wiegerman to hire a VOC ship of 140 feet length. It realized that repairs would take some time, forcing Wiegerman to store his cargo of sugar and so lose a great deal of money. It further agreed to this request, because the export of sugar was in the interest of the economy of Batavia, and ships were lying idle due to lack of crews, and charged Dfl. 16,000 for the ship's lease.[52] The High Government also permitted Wiegerman to export tin, believing his voyage would set a good example for other private merchants.[53] In addition, it permitted repairs to be made in the VOC shipyards and encouraged the import of *aureum pigmentum* and brimstone.[54] Even when stocks of sugar were low, the High Government allowed some export to Masqat, because of the advantages this afforded the VOC. It also held hopes of reestablishing trade relations with Persia via these voyages.[55]

To the best of my knowledge, voyages to Masqat continued until 1793.[56] The available Dutch documents do not yield further information on departing ships. The Batavia Diary (*Dagregister*) for 1793 mentions one ship returning from and another en route to Masqat, but the 1794 diary does not mention any ship bound for that destination.[57] The documents do not offer any clues either as

51 See, for example, VOC 815, f. 284-87, 395; VOC 817, f. 555, VOC 818, f. 1321 (24/07/1787); VOC 820, f. 1243 (1788).

52 VOC 810, f. 210-13 (24/10/1780). *De Nepthunus* carried 2,000 canisters of powdered sugar, 60 canisters of candy sugar and 20 leaguers of arak. VOC 810, f. 622 (30/06/1780). The High Government also agreed to the request by J.H. Wiegerman in 1784 to be allowed to repair the cutter *de Battavier* to make a voyage to Masqat with abput 400 canisters of sugar. VOC 814, not foliated (02/03/1784).

53 VOC 810, f. 1308-09.

54 VOC 814, not foliated; VOC 717, f. 555. The reason was that the factory owner Cornelis de Keyser and the manager of the plumber's manufactory Godfried Welke liked the *aureum pigmentum* that had just arrived with *de Hoorn* coming from Masqat, which product was better than the so-called royal yellow. The High Government therefore ordered the captain of *de Hoorn*, Gerrit Bruijn, to buy 100 lbs. of *aureum pigmentum* on his next voyage, which he was about to start. VOC 813, f. 232 (02/05/1783). Batavia's 4-year reserves of brimstone amounted to 350,000 lbs. The High Government needed 50,000 lbs. per year for the production of gun powder and in addition for other users (ships, etc.) it required 87,500 lbs/year of that ore. It therefore ordered to buy 350,000 lbs. at Masqat. VOC 818, f. 1615 (21/08/1787).

55 VOC 825, f. 268; VOC 815, f. 228, 285; but it did not allow the export of additional quantities of sugar in times of scarcity. VOC 820, f. 102 (21/01/1788). The Omanis also sent their own ships to Batavia. Risso, *Oman & Muscat*, p. 101. Captain Johannes Florens of *de Hercules* was fined Dfl. 500 because he had called on Poeloe Pinang, an English port to buy 300 bags of saltpeter. He was, however, allowed to ship them to the Gulf for sale to Persia. VOC 821, f. 1046-47 (13/12/1788). The Netherlands was at war with England at that time, hence the fine.

56 The voyage of *Java's Welvaren* in 1791 had been disappointing due to low sugar price and long voyage. The return cargo consisted of gold and silver specie plus gum Arabica. The VOC mace, 60 *picol*, had not been sold and they were returned to the Company at the fixed price of 90 *stuivers* per lb. VOC 827, f. 3559 (19/12/1791).

57 NA, Archief Oost-Indisch Comité, nr. 78, Dagregister Batavia 1793/94, f. 57 (return of *Java's Welvaren* on March 30) and f. 195 (departure of *de Maria Catherina* on November 7). The likely reason for the discontinuation of these voyages is the closure of the Dutch factory in Cochin in 1793. Ashin Das Gupta, *Malabar in Asian Trade 1740-1800* (Cambridge, 1967), p. 122

to why these voyages seem to have been discontinued.[58] Perhaps profits had diminished; although this seems unlikely considering that a proposal was made in 1796 to send a VOC ship to Masqat financed by private merchants. Moreover, two private merchants asked permission to send ships there in the same year.[59] It would therefore seem that these voyages were indeed made, be it that the Dutch ships sailed under foreign flag, because of the war between France and England.[60] The so-called East Indies Committee that had replaced the High Government took a rather negative view of these voyages in light of the difficulties involved. It was for this reason that the Committee had decided to refuse the invitation of the pasha of Baghdad to reestablish VOC trade in 1793.[61] Thus ended Dutch trade relations with Masqat in the eighteenth century.

CONCLUSION

The pattern of Dutch relations with Masqat reflects that of trade with the Persian Gulf area in general. We observe a decrease (and in the VOC case a complete abandonment) of trade by European Companies and an enormous increase in the so-called country trade.[62] The Dutch flirtation with Masqat had no real economic basis, and only served to rid Batavia of its surplus stocks of Java sugar. The speedy abandonment of Masqat by the VOC bears this out. That it took ten years before Dutch country traders returned to Masqat was probably the result of impact of the sack of Khark. Merchants in Batavia undoubtedly were informed as to the profitability of trade with Masqat through their contacts with the VOC factories in Surat and Malabar, which had regular contacts with Masqat. When these country traders finally reestablished contact an annual trade pattern came into being,[63] which were temporarily disrupted by the Napoleonic wars, the occupation of Java by the English and the build-up of Dutch rule in the east-Indies thereafter. That this trade pattern of annual voyages remerged at the beginning of the nineteenth century is a sign of its tenacity and financial attraction.[64]

---

58 Most of the information on ship movements was obtained from the resolutions of the High Government, which do not exist for 1793 and thereafter. The Batavia Diary continues only to 1794 and does not mention any ships leaving for Masqat. Other sources do not yield information either.

59 NA, Hooge Regering Batavia, nr. 873; see index on resolutions in 1796 under "Persien in 'talgemeen" and "Musquette in Persien." The texts imply that the ships may have left, for the committee did not oppose the voyages (see also next footnote).

60 As the Netherlands had been conquered by France in 1795 and the newly constituted Batavian Republic therefore supported the revolutionary French state the Bombay Council instructed its broker in Masqat to oppose "by every means in your power to prevent these Nations' [i.e. French and Dutch] ships sailing to and from Muscat under Arab and particularly the Imam's color." Saldanha, *Précis*, vol. 1, p. 336 (Bombay; 25/03/1797). Apparently two Dutch ships flying Arab colors had been to Masqat in 1796. Ibid., vol. 1, p. 337 (Bombay; 25/03/1797) and one in October 1797, a dinghy, called the *Latokinu* commanded by Captain Crouch. Ibid., vol. 1, p. 338 (Masqat, 27/12/1797).

61 NA, Archief Oost-Indisch Comité, nr. 71, f. 575 (08/11/1793). Contacts with the Persian Gulf continued to be maintained; in 1798 a letter was received in Batavia from the Dutch ambassador in Istanbul requesting Dutch ships to call on Basra. NA, Archief Oost-Indisch Comité, nr. 10, f. 78 (21/06/1798). Earlier requests from the governor of Basra had been made in 1771 and 1780. VOC 791, Resolutions High Government (27/05/1771) and NA, Legatie Archief Turkije nr. 784.

62 Amin, *British Interests*, pp. 127ff.

63 "The Sugar, Sugar Candy, Metals and Prices imported at Bushire, by Boats, from Muscat, is commonly brought to the latter on Dutch and French Vessels." Saldanha, *Précis*, vol. 1, p. 423 (Report on the Commerce of Arabia and Persia by Samuel Manesty and Harford Jones, 1790).

64 For the resumption of these voyages in the 19th century see Willem Floor, *Traditional Crafts in Qajar Iran* (Costa Mesa, 2003), pp. 332-33.

CHAPTER SEVEN
The Rise of Bushire (1734-1792)

We have now come to the last important port on the Persian littoral, the one that would remain the most important international Persian port in the nineteenth and the beginning of the twentieth century. There are other Persian ports in the head of the Persian Gulf, but they never posed a serious threat to the rise of Bushire and they therefore, like Basra the only major Ottoman port in the Gulf, will only be discussed, when this is relevant to Bushire's situation.

Because there is no good history of Bushire I have decided to begin this chapter with an introduction to its little known early history. For centuries Bushire like many other similar ports on the Persian coast played a minor role in regional trade; its population being mainly engaged in fishing and pearling. This did not mean that Bushire did not want to pay a bigger role. In fact, it tried to do so both in the sixteenth and the seventeenth century, but central government policy as well as objective commercial market conditions did not allow it to become a major contender for Hormuz (until 1622) and Bandar 'Abbas (after 1622). Bushire's chance came when Nader Shah established his ship building yard at that port as well as located part of hs royal fleet there. Bushiris served as sailors on the fleet, while the Sheikh of Bushire held the function of vice-admiral of the fleet. Although Bushire grew in importance, from a commercial point of view it still remained a minor port despite the fact that the VOC opened a trading station there in 1737. However, with the death of Nader Shah central government control collapsed and Sheikh Naser of Bushire by default became the de-facto governor of Bushire and 'owner' of part of the royal fleet. He used his new found situation to strengthen his influence among his neighbors and with the help of Mir Naser of Rig he seized Bahrain in 1752. He stumbled when he was drawn into the succession war, was imprisoned, which cost him money, but not influence. Other coastal chiefs had been in the same situation and thus Sheikh Naser quickly tried to build up his sphere of influence. He was peeved when the Dutch left Bushire and settled on Khark. Initially, he supported Mir Mohanna, who soon became his principal enemy. Due to the dwindling commercial role of Bandar 'Abbas, Bushire gained in importance as it offered a stable market with merchants and a safe caravan route up-country. In 1763 Sheikh Naser was able to induce the EIC to settle in Bushire thus securing more trade for the port. However, Karim Khan's desire to destroy Mir Mohanna and the EIC's objective to destroy the Banu Ka'b brought them at loggerheads, which led to the departure of the EIC from Bushire in 1768 and increased insecurity. This also meant that the conflict between the EIC and the Banu Ka'b became part of the history of Bushire, because it was the major stumbling block that constrained relations between Karim Khan and the English at the expense of Bushire. Sheikh

Naser tried to make the best of the situation to offer his help as go-between. The fact that he also had a growing fleet meant that he gained influence at the Zand court and in 1774 Karim Khan even appointed Sheikh Naser as chief negotiator to resolve the conflict with the Imam of Masqat, while he also tried to bring Karim Khan and the EIC together. He was able to be helpful in bringing this about in 1775 when the EIC returned to Bushire. In that year he further commanded the Persian fleet that supported the siege and conquest of Basra, but instead of benefiting from the fall of that port, Bushire came under pressure from Zubara where many Basrene merchants had gone as well as from Masqat and Kuwait. Moreover, in 1783 the 'Otobis seized Bahrain and Bushire was unable to get it back. Despite this setback, Bushire was a player in the region, actively competing with its commercial rivals, while Sheikh Naser even played king-maker in 1789. However, he abandoned the Zands in 1792 and supported the Qajars. Sheikh Naser got more than he bargained for, because although the Zand dynasty was destroyed the new Qajar regime was a much stronger power than he had counted on and one that would exercise tighter control over Bushire and thus the Sheikhly family saw its role diminished in the years ahead, although that is not the subject of this study. The EIC who after the VOC had abandoned trade with the Persian Gulf in 1765 seemed to be the only main remaining commercial player. However, it got involved in local conflicts, was defeated several times, and almost abandoned the Gulf altogether in 1777, but decided to keep a presence in Bushire and Basra to ensure communications between Europe and India.

THE EARLY HISTORY OF BUSHIRE

According to Curzon, "Bushire is a town without history."[1] He was not the only one who thought so, for Mirza Hasan Khan E'temad al-Saltaneh (1840-1896), the Minister of Information of Naser al-Din Shah (r. 1848-1896) and author of many historical works wrote in 1877 that Bushire had only "recently been established, viz. by Naser, the Arab," implying that this had happened only in the eighteenth century. He added, however, that from things found in the soil it was clear that it was the site of a pre-Islamic port.[2] So it would seem that Bushire has a history after all, only very little is known about it and based on the material published so far it would seem that there is only much information for the period after 1800 and even that is meager in view of the abundance of available data.[3]

Modern Bushire is situated at the northern end of a cigar-shaped peninsula of quaterny sandstone, about 21 km long by 6 km broad in the widest part, running parallel to the main land and joined to it in the middle by mud flats (*sabkha, sabakhzar*) of about 30 km wide, known as the *Mashilah*, which in winter, especially with high winds, was turned into a reed-grown swamp across

1 G.N. Curzon, *Persia and the Persian Question*. 2 vols. (London, 1892), vol. 2, p. 230

2 Mirza Hasan Khan E'temad al-Saltaneh, *Mer'at al-Boldan* 4 vols in 3. ed. 'Abd al-Hoseyn Nava'i and Mir Hashem Mohaddeth (Tehran: Daneshgah, 1368/1989), vol. 1, p. 479.

3 The few studies that have some information on the earlier history of Bushire include Stephen R. Grummond, *The Rise and Fall of the Arab Shaykhdom of Bushire: 1750-1850 (Iran, Persian Gulf)* (unpublished dissertation, Johns Hopkins, 1985); Thomas Ricks, *Politics and Trade in Southern Iran and the Gulf, 1745-1765* (unpublished dissertation, University of Indiana, 1975); Iraj Afshar Seystani, *Negahi beh Bushehr*. 2 vols (Tehran, 1369/1990); Ahmad Eqtedari, *Athar-e Shahrha-ye Bastani-ye Savahel va Jazayer-e Khalij-e Fars va Darya-ye 'Oman* (Tehran, 1348/1969).

which ran a caravan road to the main land. This created the impression that Bushire in fact was an island.[4]

WHAT'S IN A NAME: RISHAHR OR BUSHIRE?

The origin of the name Bushire is unclear. Popular etymology has it that the name means Abu Shahr or Father of the City, which is very doubtful. A. Houtum Schindler has suggested that the name is a contraction of Bokht Ardashir (Ardashir has delivered).[5] Given the location of the village of Rishahr on the peninsula other scholars believe that another town that Ardashir created, Rev Ardashir, was the origin of the name. According to Hamzeh, an early Islamic source, Rev Ardashir was called Rishahr in his days, about which more later. Tomaschek has argued that both the names of Bushire and Rishar are derived from the name Hieratis, mentioned by Arrian, which Tomaschek identifies as the Elamite term *raivatis*, meaning 'rich, shining.' Likewise, Hüsing has argued that Rishahr is not a bastardization of Rev Ardashir, as other have argued, but of the Elamite word, *ris-hair* meaning 'great' a term often used to denote the goddess Kiririsha, who was worshipped in the Elamite temple at Liyan, an Elamite settlement, which was situated on the Bushire peninsula.[6]

Whatever the origin of its name may be, the Bushire peninsula clearly was already inhabited in Elamite times. Inscriptions found date back to the 8th century BCE and are part of the remains of the ancient Elamite settlement of Liyan.[7] This may have been the same site as Mesambria, an Achaemenid site, which was visited by Nearchos around 332 BCE. Arrian described the landing site as a peninsula with many gardens and orchards. The peninsula was also an important Sassanian site. In fact, Williamson has argued that the Sasanian town of Rev Ardashir most likely was situated on the Bushire peninsula. He admits that much of the literary historical evidence (Istakhri, Muqaddasi, Ibn Balkhi, Hamdollah Qazvini) proves that its location was in Arrajan,[8] but he points out that (i) Baladhuri and Tabari independently locate Rishahr in the district of Tawaj of the Kura (province) of Shahpur in Fars; (ii) Tawaj was located on the Shahpur River, north-east of Bushire and 160 km from the supposed location in Arrajan; (iii) there are no important Sasanian sites at the alleged Rishahr site in Arrajan; and (iv) the largest archeological site on the Persian Gulf littoral, apart from 'Abbasid Basra, is on the Bushire peninsula. Finally, there is no Rishahr in Arrajan anymore, although there is one on the Bushire peninsula.[9]

---

4 See Lorimer, *Gazetteer*, pp. 330-39 for a detailed description of the peninsula and its 30 small villages.

5 Curzon, *Persia*, vol. 2, p. 231.

6 G. Hüsing, "Elamisches," *ZDMG* 66 (1902), p. 792; W. Hinz, *Cambridge Ancient History* (Cambridge, 1961), pp. 663-64. Rishar allegedly was founded by Luhrasp and embellished with Sasanid constructions under Ardashir; this story was also related by Mirza Hasan Khan E'temad al-Saltaneh, *Mer'at*, vol. 1, p. 479, referring to Mostoufi, *Nuzhat al-Qulub*, p. 129.

7 L. van den Berghe, *Archeologie de l'Iran ancient* (Leiden, 1959), pp. 165-74; Eqtedari, *Athar*, pp. 138-201.

8 For a detailed discussion see Heinz Gaube, *Die südpersische Provinz Arrajan/Kuh-Giluyeh von der arabischen Eroberung bis zur Safawidenzeit* (Vienna, 1973).

9 A. Williamson, *The Maritime Cities of the Persian Gulf and their Commercial Role from the 5th Century to 1507* (unpublished dissertation Oxford, 1971), pp. 38-41.

BUSHIRE IN PRE-ISLAMIC PERSIA

Whether Rashar was in Arrajan or at modern Rishahr or both we may never know, but there certainly was a major Sasanian population center on the Bushire peninsula, in fact the largest on the Persian coast. Partho-Sassanian pottery of a wide range and in large quantity is found there and the area of mounding covers a surface of 450 ha. The pottery, which dates from a period between 300 BCE and 750 CE, covers the entire area of 450 ha, which, according to Williamson, indicates a permanent habitation of at least 50,000 people. The two largest mounds are found near Rishahr and near Haleyla and both overlook sheltered anchorages of the island. The largest mound is at Rishar, which also has the remnants of an old fort, built on top of the Sasanian site. No Islamic pottery was found there. Below the fort are the remains of a jetty more than 100 meters into the sea and almost five meters wide. The presence of Sasanian pottery at the land end of the jetty suggests that it is of pre-Islamic origin. At the Haleyla mound no remains of a jetty was found, but there is a now a silted creek lined with mounding that may have served as inner harbor. Williams suggests that it is "the channel running from the river to the sea called Heratemis" where Nearchus anchored. Between Rishahr and Haleyla many smaller mounds are to be found, most likely houses of the rich as the presence of private wells also suggests. There are further remains of walls and irrigation channels that indicate the main areas of cultivation, which clearly were not sufficient to feed a large population. This means that like in later periods most of its food supplies were imported. There were hardly any signs of settlement on the northern part of the peninsula, although there may have been at its northern point, the current site of modern Bushire. At the eastern and highest part of the peninsula there are signs of defensive works, a fort of 150 m^2 with four watch towers facing inland. The size of the inhabited sites facing natural anchorages, the jetty and creek, as well as the presence of pottery from India and Mesopotamia suggest long-distance maritime contacts.[10]

THE FALL OF BUSHIRE

The Bushire peninsula lost its dominant maritime function after the Arab conquest of Persia due to reasons that are as yet not very well understood. The likely reason for this must have been the destruction caused by the Arab invaders, who had destroyed or reduced in importance many urban centers in Bushire's hinterland. This combined with subsequent insecurity inland as well as the move of the capital of the new Arab Empire to Damascus under the Ummayads may have been responsible for the reduction of Bushire to a minor port of only some local distributive importance. Similarly, the rise and greater success of other ports on the northern littoral of the Persian Gulf in early Islamic times such as Siraf (and later Kish and Hormuz) may be ascribed to the felt need for a secure port for vessels coming from the Indian Ocean at a greater distance from Basra, given the major upheavals in the Tigris-Euphrates delta (the Kufa revolts in the 680-90s CE; the Zanj rebellion in 869-79 CE) and the head of the Gulf in general (Carmathian revolt in the 930s CE).[11] This need for security as determined by structural upheaval and insecurity in Fars, the hinterland of the ports on the Persian littoral, explains why the location of its major ports slowly moved from the upper part of the Persian Gulf (from Bushire to Siraf) to its lower part and off-shore (from Kish to Hormuz).

10 Williamson, *The Maritime Cities*, pp. 31-37.

11 A. Mez, *Die Renaissance des Islams* (Heidelberg, 1922), pp. 461-80; Hamdallah Mostoufi, *Nuzhat al-Qulub*. tr. G. Le Strange (Leyden - London 1919) pp. 114-5; Le Strange, G. *The Lands of the Eastern Caliphate* (London 1905 [1966]), pp. 256-58.

As of the end of the thirteenth century there is no doubt that the inhabited site on the Bushire peninsula was known as Rishahr,[12] although the single mention of the name of Bushire also occurs at that time. This earliest mention of the town of Bushire is by Yaqut, also in the 13th century,[13] although some think that it is a copyist's error of Rishahr.[14] Yaqut mentions Bushire as being on a peninsula, and opposite to it, on the mainland, was Rishar or Rashar of Tawwaj.[15] The former indeed must have been Bushire, for, according to Mostoufi, Tawwaj was a town in present day Shabankarah district, which is very near to Bushire.[16] However, it is impossible to ascribe this description to either location. Both Rishahr and Bushire are situated on the same peninsula, and the geographical names usually referred to both the settlements and the peninsula. Thus, there was and is ample cause for confusion in, for example, Portuguese sources when referring to Rishahr.[17] Also, when reference is made to one site the source may actually be referring to the other. For example, when Nader Shah established his naval base at Bushire and renamed it Naderiyeh he actually referred to Rishar, whose old medieval fort was reconstructed at that time.[18] It is therefore quite likely that the name of Rishar was used to refer to another nearby port on the same peninsula without making a distinction between the two. In fact, Mar'ashi wrote in the eighteenth century that Bushire was the name the common people gave to Rishahr, thus confirming that Rishahr in fact was Bushire.[19]

BUSHIRE UNDER THE SAFAVIDS

Information on Rishahr becomes somewhat more copious as of the sixteenth century due to its interaction with the Portuguese on Hormuz. Duarte Barbosa may have mentioned Bushire as Bascarde or Baxeal around 1516, or, more likely, it is an error for Raixal (Rishahr).[20] During Pêro Albuquerque's exploration of the head of the Persian Gulf in 1514 looking for Bahrain he arrived at Rishahr. Its chief, Mir Abu Eshaq (Mirbuzaca) had seized 20 *terradas* that belonged to the king of Hormuz, the vassal of the king of Portugal. He therefore forced him to return the vessels. Pêro Albuquerque feared that Mir Abu Eshaq's Rishahr might develop as a naval power in the Persian Gulf, which could mean that Esma'il I would have a naval force to strike a blow against Hormuz, or even try to control the open sea, which was one of the reasons for Afonso Albuquerque to sail to

12 E. Quatremère. *Mémoire Géographique et Historique sur l'Egypt et sur quelques contrées voisines* (Paris, 1811), p. 284; A.T Wilson, *The Persian Gulf* (London, 1928), pp. 73-74.

13 Yaqut, *Mu'jam al-Buldan* ed. F. Wüstenfeld (Leipzig, 1866-73 [1924]), vol. 1, p. 503.

14 Wilhelm Tomaschek, *Topographische Erläuterung der Küstenfahrt Nearchs vom Indus biz zum Euphrat* (Vienna, 1890), p. 62; Paul Schwarz, *Iran in mittelalter nach den arabaischen geographen* 4 vols. (Leipzig, 1896-1921), vol. 3, p. 127.

15 Le Strange, *The Lands*, p. 211, not to be confused with Rishahr near Arrajan. Ibid., 270-1; see also Minorsky, V. tr. *The Hudud al-'Alam* (London 1937), p. 378.

16 Mostoufi, *Nuzhat al-Qulub*, p. 115; Gaube, *Die südpersische Provinz Arrajan*, p. 90 also thinks that these remarks do not refer to Rishahr in Arrajan.

17 A. Hotz, "Cornelisz Roobacker's Scheepsjournaal Gamron-Basra (1645); de eerste reis der Nederlanders door de Perzische Golf" p. 387; see also Eqtedari, *Athar*, p. 144.

18 VOC 2546 (24/10/1740) (Naderiyeh).

19 Mohammad Khalil Mar'ashi Safavi, *Majma' al-Tavarikh* ed. 'Abbas Eqbal (Tehran, 1328/1949), p. 39.

20 Duarte Barbosa, *The Book of Duarte Barbosa* translated by M. Longworth Dames, 2 vols. (London, 1918-21), vol. 1, p. 81.

Hormuz.[21] That was one of the reasons why Afonso Albuquerque came to Hormuz in early 1515 to prevent this from happening. During his stay at Hormuz in 1515, Afonso Albuquerque received various officials from other neighboring rulers, such as from Mir Abu Eshaq, the Safavid governor of Rishahr, who allegedly promised to pay tribute to king Manuel I, if Albuquerque would help him conquer certain places and lands. Albuquerque gave an evasive reply stating that this had to be discussed with king Manuel I and there the matter rested.[22] Mir Abu Eshaq was later that year indeed involved with a Safavid attempt to seize Bahrain, which failed to materialize, because the Portuguese declined to supply vessels to transport the 6,000 troops.[23]

Rishahr remained an active player in the upper part of Persian Gulf. In 1531, Badr al-Din, the governor of Bahrain, complained about the activities of Shah 'Ali Soltan son of Mir Abu Eshaq, the governor of Rishahr. The port of Rishahr had grown rich due to the smuggling of spices and Shah 'Ali Soltan had been building vessels and also had captured some Bahraini *jalbehs*. He put his own men on them and Badr al-Din suspected him of wanting to invade Bahrain. Shah 'Ali Soltan had at that time 12 fustas, each with a crew of 20 men armed with arquebuses. He further had a garrison of 70 men at Rishahr, while he controlled Khark Island and thus the supply of pilots needed for the navigation into the Shatt al-Arab. In April 1534, Shah 'Ali Soltan, governor of Rishahr (rey de Raxel), who according to Portuguese sources was tributary to Hormuz, rebelled and was preying on the shipping lanes. Mohammad Shah II, king of Hormuz, therefore asked the captain of Hormuz, António da Silveira to get rid of him and his vessels. In 1534, he sent Jorge de Castro with two galiots and two fustas with 100 men, all good musketeers. But the *vedor* or the financial superintendent of Hormuz believed that this force was too weak and he sent another five vessels and 100 men. They ran into contrary winds and after 20 days were out of water. A landing party of rowers and slaves with 20 Portuguese therefore went ashore to find water, which they did. What they also found was major trouble. The few people who lived there had fled, but later that same day some 300 armed Arabs arrived who killed many of the landing party and captured about 50 of them. Jorge de Castro then decided to return to Hormuz. The *vedor* then sent a force under Francisco de Gouveia to Rishahr, who told its chief that he had come to make him obey the king of Hormuz once again. He was willing to do so, on condition of not having to pay his tribute arrears, which was accepted,

---

21 Brás Afonso de Albuquerque, *Comentários do grande Afonso de Albuquerque, capitão geral que foi das Indias orientais em tempo do muito poderoso Rey D. Manuel, o primeiro deste nome* 4 vols., translated into English by Walter de Gray Birch as *The Commentaries of the Great Afonso DAlboquerque, second viceroy of India*. 4 vols. (London, 1875), vol. 4/25, pp. 115, 117; Albuquerque, Afonso. *Cartas de Afonso de Albuquerque, seguidas de documentos que as elucidam* 7 vols. eds. Raimundo António de Bulhão Pato and Henrique Lopes de Mendoça (Lisbon, 1884-1935), I, p. 347; Correia, Gaspar. *Lendas da India* ed. Rodrigo José de Lima Felner 4. vols. in 8 parts (Coimbra, 1860-66), II, p. 388; Góis, Damião de. *Crónica de felicíssimo rei D. Manuel*. 4 vols. (Coimbre, 1949-55), III/65, p. 245; Ronald Bishop Smith, *The First Age. Of the Portuguese Embassies, Navigations and Peregrinations in Persia (1507-1524)*. (Bethesda, 1970), pp. 31-32; Castanheda, Fernão Lopes. *História do descobrimento e conquista da Índia pelos Portugueses*. 2 vols. (Porto, 1979), III/128, pp. 803-04; III/136, p. 822; Barros, João de. *Da Ásia* de João de Barros e de Diogo de Couto. Nova ed. 24 vols. (Lisboa, Na Regia Officina Typografica, 1777-1788 [reprint: Livraria S. Carlos, 1973-1975]), 2ª-X-I, p. 401. It is likely that Mir Abu Eshaq had taken the Bahraini ships as a result of Safavid designs on Bahrain as is clear from the discussion with the Portuguese embassy in 1515.

22 Albuquerque, *Cartas*, II, pp. 253-55 (the messenger was Khvajeh 'Ala al-Din Mohammad [Coje Abaelidim Mahamet]); see also Ibid., *Cartas*, I, pp. 347, 369-76 (although his information on Bahrain was better than before), III, p. 165, VI, pp. 322, 335, 353, 362; Bishop, *First Age*, pp. 57-58; Albuquerque, *Commentaries*, vol. 4/41, p. 180; Castenheda, *História*, III/153, p. 365; Góis, *Crónica*, IV/11, p. 253.

23 Albuquerque, *Cartas*, vol. 7, p. 166.

provided he returned the men taken captive. As a result a peace agreement was sealed between the two parties.[24]

The peace did not last long. In early 1539, Hasan Soltan Rishahri and his brother Shah 'Ali Soltan, both sons of Mir Abu Eshaq rebelled against Shah Tahmasp I. The emirs of Fars, led by Qadi Khan Dhu'l-Qadr, were ordered to take Rishahr. According to Barros, it was a town of 2,000 families and its houses were all built with stone as were its walls. Moreover, according to Fasa'i, the town was well-armed and well provisioned and its fort had a deep moat filled with sea water. From its remaining ruins it is clear that the fort "is roughly rectangular, having sides of 300 and 390 meters and surrounded by a ditch of 28 to 30 metres wide, cut at least three and half metres through bedrock. Its eroded mudbrick walls survive as mounding which still rises up to 12 metres above the moat."[25] The Safavid troops, who were said to number more than 12,000 could not do much against these defenses. They had no vessels and, moreover, they were harassed by local Arab groups that Hasan Soltan had incited against them. To break the stalemate Qadi Khan, on behalf of Shah Tahmasp I, asked the captain at Hormuz for naval support in mid-1539. The Portuguese, when it was rumored that Hasan Soltan had asked for Ottoman assistance (even though the Ottomans did not control Basra yet), sent Martim do Carvalhal with some vessels, who effectively cut off Rishahr from the sea in October-November 1539. An additional reason was that the Portuguese were worried about Tahmasp I's regular diplomatic relations with the Indian kingdoms of the Deccan, many of which were Shi'ite and they therefore may have wanted to have him indebted to them. This three-month blockade led to famine in the besieged town where allegedly 5,000 people died, for the available food was only given to the soldiers. According to a Portuguese report, people ate children and dogs to stay alive. Hasan Soltan offered Martim do Carvalhal 12,000 *xerafins* if he would allow two *terradas* to land with food. When he refused Hasan Soltan surrendered in February 1540 and the fortress was leveled with the ground. As instructed Qadi Khan, who died en route, took Hasan Soltan to court where he was executed.[26] This 16th century fort must have been built on top of the ancient fort at Rishahr, which, according to Williamson, is of pre-Islamic origin as it has been built in the midst of a Sasanian site, while there is no Islamic pottery in the beach section.[27] It certainly was not built by the Portuguese as many have written or by the Dutch as one source has

---

24 Correia, *Lendas da India*, III, p. 557-60; Castenheda, *História*, VIII/74-76, pp. 693-96; João de Barros. *Da Ásia*. de João de Barros e de Diogo de Couto. Nova ed. 24 vols. (Lisboa, Na Regia Officina Typografica, 1777-1788 [reprint: Livraria S. Carlos, 1973-1975]), 4ª-III-xv, p. 168; Ibid., 4ª-IV-xxvi, p. 522-26; Andrade, Francisco d'. *Chrónica do muyto alto e muyto poderoso rey destes reynos de Portugal dom João III* 4 vols. (Coimbra, 1796), II, pp. 555-57. Rishahr produced much wheat, barley, rice, vegetables, fruits, potherbs, butter, some mediocre fabrics as well as good horses that were exported to Goa.

25 Williamson, *The Maritime Cities*, p. 34.

26 Qazvini Ghaffari, Qadi Ahmad. *Tarikh-e Jahanara* (Tehran 1343/1964), p. 294 (In 945 or 946); Shirazi, 'Abdi Beyg. *Takmelat al-Akhbar*, ed. 'Abdol-Hoseyn Nava'i. (Tehran, 1369/1990), p. 90; al-Qomi, Qadi Ahmad ibn Sharaf al-Din al-Hoseyn al-Hoseyni. *Kholasat al-Tavarikh*, 2 vols., ed. Ehsan Eshraqi. (Tehran, 1363/1984), vol. 1, p. 289; Fasa'i, *Farsnameh*, vol. 1, p. 395; Rumlu, Hoseyn Beyg. *Ahsan al-Tavarikh*. ed. `Abdol-Hoseyn Nava'i (Tehran 1357/1978), p. 287; Schürhammer, G. *Die zeitgenössischen Quellen zur Geschichte Portugiesische-asiens und seiner Nachbarländer, 1538-1552* (Rome, 1962), p. 69, no. 1028 (15/12/1542); Castenheda, *História*, IX/28, pp. 939-40; Barros, *Ásia*, 4ª-IV-xxvi, pp. 522-26; Jean Aubin, "La politique iranienne d'Ormuz (1515-1540)," *Studia* 53 (1994)," pp. 35-40; Couto, *Década* 7ª, IV-viii, pp. 334-339; Thomaz, Luís Filipe F. R. "La présence iranienne autour de l'océan Indien au XVIe siècle d'aprés les sources portugaises de l'époque," *Archipel* 68 (2004), pp. 87, 99-101.

27 Williamson, *Maritime Cities*, p. 34.

it.[28] In 1734, on the same site a new fort was built by Mohammad Latif Khan that became known as Naderiyeh. In Qajar times, the Persian government used "a ditch 70 to 100 feet wide" at the fort for agricultural purposes using forced labor. It also used the fort, which was locally known as Qal'eh-ye Bahman Shah, for military purposes and the British-Indian force that occupied Bushire in 1857 stormed and took it in that year.[29]

This sack and destruction of Rishahr in 1540 signaled its end as an independent player in the upper Persian Gulf. Henceforth a less adventurous Safavid official governed the town and although the port lost much of its local political importance it still continued to function as a local trading town. Nevertheless, initially the Portuguese kept an eye on the small port, because they believed that without their control things might get out of hand once again.[30] Due to the lower customs duties at Rishahr (5% against 11% at Hormuz) some merchants with the connivance of the customs authorities of Hormuz, avoided calling at the island of Hormuz and sailed to Basra via Safavid ports such as Rishahr.[31] The presence of a factor of the king of Hormuz in Basra and Jolfar and a factor of at least one captain of Hormuz in Rishahr undoubtedly facilitated smuggling.[32] This even continued when in 1547 the Portuguese banned trade with Basra.[33] D. Álvaro de Noronha, captain of Hormuz (1550-1553) also was involved in smuggling. He had an agent in Rishahr, who officially was there to gather information on Ottoman activities, but in reality he acted more as his commercial agent and traded with Basra on his behalf.[34] In 1550 the *ouvidor* or justice of peace of Hormuz reported that although Goa had banned trade with Basra, the Moslems of Bahrain, Qatif and Rishahr did it anyway.[35]

Rishahr also was of economic importance to Hormuz and other towns on the Persian Gulf such as Basra, because food supplies to Hormuz were brought in from, among others, Rishahr and Bardestan.[36] For that reason, vessels from Bahrain, Kish, Rishahr, etc. with wheat and other food supplies paid a lower rate (5%) customs duty at Hormuz, and sometimes did not pay the official

---

28 Wilson, *The Persian Gulf*, pp. 73-74; Barbara English, *John Company's Last War* (London, 1971), pp. 87-88.

29 Lorimer, *Gazetteer*, pp. 336-37.

30 P.S.S. Pissurlencar, ed. *Regimentos das fortelezas da India (séc. XVI-XVII)* (Goa, 1951), p. 185. The total cost of the Reyshahr operation had been 8,000 *pardaus*. D. João de Castro, *Obras Completas de D. João de Castro*, (henceforth *Obras*), eds. Armando Cortesão e Luís de Albuquerque (Coimbra, Academia Internacional de Cultura Portuguesa, 1976), vol. 3-118, p. 113 (01/01/1546); *As Gavetas da Torre do Tombo, Gavetas I-XXIII*, 12 vols., edited by A. Silva Rego (Lisbon: Centro de Estudos Históricos Ultramarinos, 1960-77) XV-3510, pp. 39-40 (24/11/1550).

31 Djanirah Potache, "The Commercial Relations between Basrah and Goa in the Sixteenth Centry," *Studia* 48 (1989), p. 151, n. 26. For the customs rates of the kingdom of Hormuz see Floor, *Persian Gulf*, chapter one.

32 Luís Matos, ed. *Das relações entre Portugal e a Pérsia 1500-1758. Catálogo bibliográfico da exposição comemorativa do XXV centenário da monarquia no Irão* (Lisbon: Fundação Calouste Gulbenkian, 1972), p. 188 (13/03/1545); San Luis Francisco de Saraiva, *Obras completas do cardeal Saraiva* (d. Francisco de S. Luiz) patriarcha de Lisboa, precedidas de uma introduccão pelo Marquez de Rezende. 10 vols. Antonio Correia Caldeira ed. (Lisbon, 1872-1883), vol. 6, pp. 220-22.

33 *Gavetas* XV, 3510, pp. 39-40 (24/11/1550); Couto, *Década* 7ª-VII-xi, pp. 145-154.

34 Simão Botelho, *Cartas*, pp. 31-32 (30/01/1552).

35 Schurhammer, *Zeitgenössische Quellen*, p. 307, no. 4539 (24/11/1550).

36 Albuquerque, *Cartas*, in Rodrigo José de Lima Felner ed. *Subsidios para a historia da India portugueza* (Lisbon, 1868), I, pp. 377-78; Pedro Teixeira, *The Travels*. tr. William F. Sinclair (London 1902 [1991]), p. 29. There were many who tried to evade these duties and instructions were given to punish the wrong-doers. António da Silva Rego ed., *Documentação para a história das missões do padroado português do Oriente* 12 vols. (Lisbon, 1947-58), vol. 3, p. 390.

rate at all.[37] This attraction of Rishahr did not change and Teixeira observed around 1600, "We passed the shoals of Kane, and beyond them the fortress of Rexel, famous for the abundance, and good quality, of bread-stuffs, fruit and vegetables in its territory." [...] "a deep river of fresh water has its mouth there."[38] Rishahr was also a possible ally of the Portuguese against the Ottoman threat. When in 1547 the Ottomans took Basra the captain of Hormuz corresponded with the governor of Rishahr (Reixel) as well as with the chief of the Jazeyer and the former ruler of Basra to prepare a common plan of action.[39] It would also seem that the king of Hormuz paid 'protection money' or *moqarrariyeh* to the chief of Rishahr (Rei de Raixel), although as of 1568, if not earlier, this amount was added to that of the Safavid Shah as a means to safeguard the commercial traffic going to and fro Basra.[40]

RISHAHR BECOMES BUSHIRE

Although the Portuguese continued to use the term Raixel (Rishahr) throughout the Safavid period, as of the late sixteenth century the name of Bushire also begins to be used with increasing frequency. John Newbery reports in May 1581, "wee were at Abousher, which is a Castle,"[41] which clearly indicates the location as being Rishahr. The same name (Abuscier) was also used by the Venetian consul Balbi in 1586.[42] Crowther and Steele examined various ports in the Persian Gulf in 1614, amongst which Bushire but decided on Jask as the most convenient port for the English to trade as did Robert Sherley, who preferred Bandar 'Abbas. The main reason was that Jask was not "not so much in danger of the Portuguese at a headland," whereas the other choices were in such danger (Bandar 'Abbas, Bostaneh [?], Bahrain and Rishahr).[43] Bushire thus was already a port of some local importance by the turn of the seventeenth century, for the Safavid naval force, contributed by coastal Arab chiefs, used to harass Portuguese shipping around 1610 consisted of some 1,200 vessels. Of these, 100 were permanently based in Rishahr to attack shipping going to Basra.[44] The Dutch captain Roobacker mentions the flat promontory of Abier or Boecheer in 1645.[45] By that

37 Castro, *Obras*, vol. 3-608, p. 459 (08/10/1546), 3-608, p. 460 (08/10/1547); Schurhammer, *Zeitgenössische Quellen*, p. 220, no. 3368 (08/10/1547). There also was smuggling of pepper and other merchandise, including by the captain of Hormuz, Luís Falcõa. *Gavetas* XIII, 2675, pp. 202, 205, 209-10, 215 (1544?); Matos, *Das relações*, p. 196; Schurhammer, *Zeitgenössische Quellen*, p. 222, no. 3409 (20/10/1547).

38 Teixeira, *Travels* pp. 23, 25, the fresh water river is the Khor Soltani, a large creek with a shallow bar in the 19th century.

39 Schurhammer, *Zeitgenössische Quellen*, p. 239, no. 3646 (25/01/1548); Castro, *Obras*, vol. 3-686, p. 506f. (25/01/1548)

40 Floor, *Persian Gulf*, p. 73.

41 John Newberie, "Two Voyages of Master J.N., One into the Holy Land; The other to Balsara, Ormus, Persia, and backe thorow Turkie," in Purchas, Samuel. *Hakluytus Posthumus or Purchas His Pilgrimes*. 8 vols. (Glasgow 1905), vol. 8, p. 457.

42 Guglielmo Berchet, *La Republica di Venezia e la Persia* (Turín, 1865 [1976]), p. 286.

43 Saldanha, *Précis*, vol. 1, p. ii; Miles, *Country*, p. 206.

44 *Documentos Remetidos da India ou Livros das Monções* (cited as *DRI*) eds. R.A. Bulhão Pata and A. da Silva Rego 12 vols. (Lisbon, 1880-1972), *DRI* II-205, p. 100 (15/03/1611); *DRI* II-224, p. 142 (26/02/1612); *Arquivo Português Oriental* ed. Joaquim Heliodoro da Cunha Rivara 6 vols. (Nova Goa, 1857-76 [New Delhi, 1992]), *APO* 6-1083, pp. 911-13 (09/02/1613); William Foster ed., *Letters Received by the East India Company from its servants* 6 vols. (London, 1896-1602), II, p. 146; Saldanha, *Précis*, vol. 1, p. ii.

45 Hotz "Cornelis Cornelisz Roobacker's Scheepsjournaal," pp. 363, 387.

time the name Bushire also appears on European nautical maps.[46] But many sources still continue to call the port Rishahr, such as Thevenot,[47] or as in a Persian geographical text of the 1670s where Rishahr (but not Bushire) is mentioned as a port where "mostly vessels from India come to anchor and the merchants from the various parts come there to buy."[48]

It is therefore not surprising that the Portuguese had already considered Rishahr as an alternative port to Kong. It would seem that there was a peace agreement concluded by Luís Martins with the governor of Rishahr regarding the division of booty, prizes, etc.[49] According to Portuguese sources, it was the governor of Rishahr (Raxel) who in 1634 offered his town as an alternative port, where the entire trade of "Persia, Bassora and Arabia" would come together, alleging the shah's support.[50] The Carmelites at Shiraz learnt at the end of January 1635 that "the Portuguese Factor *had removed their commerce from the port of Kung,* [italics in original], and there had already come many vessels to this port of Rascel [?Rishire] ... [which] *is halfway between Shiraz and Basra* [? and italics in original]."[51] However, one year later the Portuguese abandoned Rishahr and returned to Bandar-e Kong, because "the Devil has woken up so many robbers at that port, and for other reasons too they are compelled to cease from coming again: and for this cause they have made peace with the Khan of Bandar Kung, where formerly they were coming and they will continue to come in future."[52] However, in mid-1646 the Portuguese once again came to Bushire where they tried to sell their goods unsuccessfully. For the Carmelites report that the Portuguese "did not land goods at Bandar Rascel [=Rishahr], because the 'Sultan' there had been sent for by the king of Persia."[53] This suggests that the governor of Bushire played an important role in trade, even trying to control it for his own pecuniary benefit. A letter from the governor of Bushire, Da'ud Soltan, written in 1645 to the Dutch confirms his interest and involvement in trade matters, while he made it clear to the Dutch in Basra that he wanted to attract European trade to his port, which was also a center of pearl diving.[54]

Bushire vessels had regular trade connections with Basra where they shipped, for example, Omani bread sugar, textiles, pepper and other goods.[55] In 1686, Sultan Akbar son of Aurangzib ar-

46 See for various examples B.J. Slot, *Les origines du Koweit* (Leiden, 1991), plates 7, 14-18, 23.

47 J. de Thevenot, *The Travels of M. de Thevenot into the Levant* (London, 1686 [1971]), vol. 2, p. 151.

48 Mohammad Mofid Mostowfi-ye Yazdi, *Mokhtasar-e Mofid*. 2 vols. ed. Seyf al-Din Najmabadi (Wiesbaden: Reichert, 1989), p. 278.

49 *Boletim da Filmoteca Ultramarina Portuguesa* (cited as BFUP), 50 vols. (Lisbon, Centro de Estudos Históricos Ultramarinos, 1955-1989), *BFUP* 12, no. 86, pp. 450-51 (30/11/1634). .

50 *Diario do terceiro conde de Linhares* 2 vols. (Lisbon, 1937-43), vol. 1, pp. 10 (18/02/1634), 29 (25/03/1634).

51 Anonymous. *A Chronicle of the Carmelites in Persia and the Papal mission of the seventeenth and eighteenth centuries*, 2 vols. (London, 1939), vol. 2, p. 1116. Earlier the Carmelites had reported that the Portuguese had "a new route for their goods at a port of Persia, [called Rascel, which probably is Reyshahr = Bushire] ... about 8 days' distance from Shiraz: and the 'patron' of the port is a person of this town, called Bahram Baig, who formerly was Daruga (governor) of Shiraz and our very great friend." Anonymous, *Chronicle*, vol. 2, p. 1116.

52 Anonymous, *Chronicle*, vol. 2, p. 1116.

53 Anonymous, *Chronicle*, vol. 2, p. 1137.

54 NA, Collectie Geleynssen no. 280 e, Basra Diary (16/08/1646); Willem Floor-Mohammad Faghfoory, *The First Dutch-Iranian Commercial Conflict* (Costa Mesa: Mazda, 2004), Doc. 5.

55 VOC 1732, van der Putt/Basra to Wichelman (03/04/1706), f. 409-10; Ibid., idem to idem (05/10/1706), f. 411-13; VOC 1747, Basra to Casteleyn (?/11/1706), f. 543-45; Hermann Gollancz ed. *Chronicle of Events between the years 1623 and 1733 relating to the settlements of the Order of Carmelites in Mesopotamia*. (Oxford, 1927), p. 377 (vessel to Rig in 1674); Teixeira, *Travels*, p. 29.

rived at Bushire where he was royally received.[56] Goods from India and the Red Sea usually reached Basra via Bandar 'Abbas and Bandar-e Kong, or some other Persian Gulf ports such as Bushire and Bandar-e Rig.[57] In addition to trade, vessels also called on either Bushire or Bandar-e Rig for pilots to guide them to Basra.

Bushire was part of the Dashtestan district (*olka*) and its governor (*soltan*) resided usually at Zireh.[58] Following the unification of the customs administration of the Persian littoral in 1668 there was a *shahbandar* at Bushire, who was a Persian. Ships needed his pass to be able to leave. He also had a number of 'Persian' servants with him.[59] In 1674, Bushire was described as being situated on a point of land extending into the sea to the west, at the end of a large plain. The town was surrounded on the west by a river, which was navigable for large boats; sand on the other side was embellished by woods and palm-groves. Most of the inhabitants were Arabs, the rest were Persians; and the port paid heavy dues to the shah of Persia.[60] At that time Rishahr was deserted, but for some people.[61]

One of the reasons for the lack of security in the upper Persian Gulf (apart from Portuguese-Omani hostilities) was the enmity that existed between the Arabs of Khark, Bandar-e Rig, Dowraq and Bushire who went every year to Bahrain to take control over the pearl fisheries, and who opposed the 'interests' of the Huwalah or Hula Arabs at the lower part of the Persian Gulf such as those of Nakhilu.[62] Apart from ethnic enmity the main reason for their conflict was economic.

> The Arabs of Talanga [Lingeh], Chareque [Charak], Chyrou [Chiru], Kailo [Nakhilu], Aalu [Asalu?], Cheylo [Shilau], Kangon [Kangun], Verdostan [Bardistan], Monkailé [Nakhilu islet], Rishahr, Bushire, Bandar Rig, and Kharg, were all engaged in civil war with one another, and had armed more than eight hundred large dhows, which controlled al the sea from the Persian Gulf to Basra. The sea-route was therefore very perilous, for these Arabs gave no quarter to one another when they met. ... as all of these Arabs live mostly by rapine and deride the power of the Shah of Persia, recognizing only the authority of their sheikhs, who are as great thieves as themselves.[63]

The sheikh of Nakhilu told Carré that, "these Arabs from Kharg, Bandar Rig, Durack, and Bushire, go every year with fleets of armed vessels to the island of barem [Bahrein], where to our preju-

---

56 Miles, *Countries*, p. 218.

57 On the Basra-Sind trade see also William Foster ed., *The English Factories in India 1618-1669*. 13 vols. (London, 1906-27), *English Factories* 1634-1636, pp. 130-31, 243; and pp. 168, 255, 713 for Surat junks sailing to Basra.

58 Seistani, *Negahi*, vol. 2, pp. 604-18.

59 Abbé Carré, *The travels of Abbé Carré in India and the Near East (1672-74)*, 3 vols. (London: Hakluyt, 1947), vol. 3, pp. 833-35.

60 Carré, *Travels*, vol. 3, p. 835.

61 Carré, *Travels*, vol. 1, p. 94.

62 Carré, *Travels*, vol. 1, p. 101 The Nakhilu Arabs were 3,000 men strong and had some 400 vessels. Ibid, vol. 1, p., 103 and they did not recognize any authority, Ibid., vol. 1, p. 111. For the Portuguese-Omani hostilities see Floor, *The Persian Gulf*, pp. 371-75, 383-86, 395-98, 407-24, 469-75. On the early history of the Nakhilu Arabs see Willem Floor, "Who were the Niquelus?" in *The Portuguese in Hormuz 1507-1622* eds. Ruy Manuel Loureiro and Dejanirah Couto (awaiting publication).

63 Carré, *The Travels*, vol. 3, p. 824.

dice they try to make themselves masters of the pearl-fishery."[64] Because of the war there was no trade, which meant reduced revenues. In March 1674 the shah therefore sent messengers, via the governor of Shiraz, to all coastal sheikhs, ordering them to come to Bushire where the governor would attend to terminate the fighting. The reason for the choice of Bushire was that allegedly all Arabs along the coast were friends were allies and friends of Bushire. The governor of Shiraz arrived in Bushire on April 7, 1674.[65] There is no information available how and whether this conflict ended temporarily. What is known is that the enmity continued and led to renewed fighting later.[66]

BUSHIRE IN THE FIRST DECADES OF THE 18TH CENTURY

Bushire remained one of the many small Persian Gulf ports and fishing villages until the end of the 1740s, be it of some regional commercial importance. In 1703 it is referred to as Bandar Boscerum, or the port of Bushire, where some European merchants were shipwrecked.[67] The chiefs of Bushire, such as Sheikh Rahma in 1707, owned vessels and also were engaged in trade with Basra and other ports.[68] In the first decade of the eighteenth century, vessels from Bandar-e Kong, Masqat, Bandar-e Rig, and Bushire frequented Basra.[69] Some 20 years later, the port is described as follows: "Bowchier is also a maritime Town. It stands on an Island, and has a pretty good Trade, both by Sea and Land."[70] Its commercial importance must indeed have been of some significance, for the Afghans took the trouble to conquer Bushire in 1724.[71] However, it was not the only rival port of Bandar 'Abbas, for Sheikh Hazin, around 1720, called Kong the best harbor of the province of Fars, which was an exaggeration.[72] A French commercial report, dated, not 1699 as suggested by its insertion between two dated reports, but rather the 1730s because it refers to the late Shah Soltan Hoseyn (d. 1727), mentions as one of the possible sites for a French East Indies Company's factory in "Congo, Bender Bouchir, or at Bender Rik……. Bender Bouchir seems to be the most attractive of these; it is indeed quite deep in the Gulf, but it is 12 days closer to Shiraz and Isfahan, and much closer to Basra where we also may trade."[73] However, it were the English who, in 1727, were the first to contemplate placing one of their staff in Bushire, not yet as an alternative factory for moribund Bandar 'Abbas, but to speed up correspondence with Basra and Europe.[74]

---

64 Carré, *The Travels*, vol. 1, p. 101. According to A. Aba Hussain, "A Study of the History of the Utoob," *Al-Watheeka* 1 (1982), p. 6, the 'Persians' incited the Hulas to attack the 'Otobis and other tribes that lived on or near Bahrain, for which opinion he does not offer any historical evidence.

65 Carré, *The Travels*, vol. 3, pp. 828-29.

66 See below.

67 Gollancz, *Chronicle*, pp. 125, 447.

68 VOC 1763, Oets/Basra to Casteleyn/Gamron (23/08/1707), f. 294 ("Zjeeg Rhameth of Bandaer Bousjier" charged Jan Oets 460 *mahmudis* or Dfl. 195:10 for this short trip to Basra).

69 VOC 1732, van de Putt/Basra to Casteleijn/Gamron (25/01/1706), f. 579 (six trankis from Bushire); Ibid., idem to idem (09/11/1705), f. 414; also Ibid., idem to idem (29/04/1706), f. 409 (15 trankies).

70 Alexander Hamilton, *A New Account of the East Indies*. 2 vols. in one. (London, 1930 [Amsterdam 1970]), p. 59 [first published in 1727]

71 Anonymous, *Chronicle*, vol. 1, p. 577.

72 *The Life of Sheikh Mohammad Ali Hazin*, ed. & tr. F.C. Belfour (London 1830), p. 100. On the relative position of Kong see Willem Floor, *The Persian Gulf*, chapter 7.

73 Du Mans, *Estat de la Perse*, p. 371.

74 VOC 2088, Dagregister Gamron (07/03/1727), f. 3413vs.

Bushire also continued to have its share of the various political and military events that took place in the upper part of the Persian Gulf. In 1718, when Masqat was at war with the Safavids and had taken Bahrain, the Dutch report that a Masqat ship coming from Bahrain had arrived at Bushire and its chiefs were invited ashore and well treated. Then the ship and its vessels was attacked and taken by the Bushire Arabs and all the Omanis were killed.[75] The attitude of the Arabs of adjacent Dashtestan had been rather sympathetic towards the Omanis reason why Lotf 'Ali Khan, the general charged with the retaking of Bahrain, took punitive action against them.[76] A decade later Bushire was itself the target of an Arab attack. On October 11, 1729 news reached Basra that rebellious Arabs threatened Bushire, whose inhabitants had left in their boats to seek safety elsewhere.[77] The source does not indicate which Arabs attacked Bushire, but in view of later developments and the movements of Arab tribes at that time they were most likely the Hulas.

BUSHIRE BECOMES A NAVAL BASE AND THRIVES

Fortunately there is relatively much information available for the period between 1737 and 1750, when the *Verenigde Oost-indische Compagnie* (VOC or Dutch East Indies Company) had a trading station in Bushire. It is therefore possible to shed some light on the history of Bushire during that period, despite the fact that the Dutch documents concerning this period and location are incomplete and thus the story of Dutch activities in Bushire cannot be told to its fullest extent.[78]

Bushire's importance increased significantly as of 1734, when Tahmasp Khan (the later Nader Shah) selected it as the base for his naval operations against Bahrain and Basra (see below). The choice of Bushire probably was determined by its proximity to both military objectives as well as the availability of supplies of grain in its hinterland. For Bushire, apart from being a naval base also constituted a source of food and other supplies for the Basra and Masqat invasion force. Nader's admiral, Mohammad Latif Khan, had bought two British ships from private owners in Bushire in 1734, which once again confirms that the town had acquired already commercial importance before Nader Shah decided to include the town in his strategic plans. Mohammad Latif Khan left for Bushire on January 7, 1735 to prepare ship building activities and the naval attack on Basra. He repaired the old medieval fortress of Rishahr a few miles outside Bushire, which was renamed Bandar-e Naderiyeh.[79] Despite the increased importance of Bushire this did not mean that it had become the most important port in the Persian Gulf. This was and would remain for another two decades Bandar 'Abbas. All naval operations against Masqat and Makran started from there. Even many of those activities at the other side of the Persian Gulf were planned from there. Most of the

75 VOC 1913, Dagregister Gamron (19/03/1718), f. 324.

76 VOC 1897, f. 202.

77 VOC 2168, Extract uijt het Bassouras Dagverhaal (01/10/1728-07/01/1730), f. 409. The English also had intended to burn 'Asalu and to make a threatening naval demonstration at Bushire in 1727, after Arabs from 'Asalu had badly treated the crew of an English ship. Gombroon Diary 27/07, 38/06 and 30/06/1727.

78 For information on the activities of the VOC elsewhere in Persia during this period see Willem Floor, *Hokumat-e Nader Shah* (Tehran: Tus, 1367/1988).

79 Floor, "Navy," p. 39. Ibid., "A Description of the Persian Gulf and its inhabitants in 1756," *Persica* 8 (1979), p. 171 [163-186] or chapter one. As discussed above the *qal'eh* had not originally been a Portuguese fort, which had been abandoned in the seventeenth century as many believe, see, e.g., Ahmad Eqtedari, *Athar-e Shahrha-ye Bastani-ye Savahel va Jazayer-e Khalij-e Fars va Darya-ye `Oman* (Tehran, 1348/1969), p. 180.

naval crews and its captains also appear to have hailed from the lower Gulf area rather than from Bushire.[80]

The Dutch had no intention at all to start trading activities in Bushire and they were therefore surprised when the issue was raised with them in 1734. The initiative came from Mohammad Latif Khan, the man whom Nader Shah had appointed as admiral of a fleet that he had to put together in the Persian Gulf.[81] On July 18, 1734 Mohammad Latif Khan had come to Bandar 'Abbas for a short stay. On July 25 he already left for Bushire with two vessels, which he had taken from Sheykh Rashid of Basidu (Qeshm Island). Before he left, Mohammad Latif Khan invited the Dutch to come and trade in Bushire, for he intended to build a new town and citadel there. His main base of naval operations was in Bushire and he hoped that the presence of the Dutch in that port also would give him access to technical know-how about ship building as well as to necessary naval supplies, including ships. The Dutch gave a non-committal reply and they hoped that he would not raise the issue again, for they believed that it would mean the end of all trade in Bushire, if Mohammad Latif Khan would stay in that town.[82]

However, Mohammad Latif Khan went to Basra on May 30 1735, where his attack was repulsed by the local forces assisted by two English vessels. Mohammad Latif Khan had more success in Bahrain, which he took unopposed in 1736, when Sheikh Jabbareh was absent in Mecca. He appointed a commander for the fort at Manama, Bahrain's chief town, and sailed away.[83] This action needs some explanation. Bahrain had been seized by the Safavids in 1602, but in 1718 the Omanis had seized the island and kept it until 1721, but due to the civil war they were not able to hold onto it. They handed the island to the Persian authorities it was then transferred to Sheikh Mohammad Majid of Naband, of the Al Harami tribe. At the end of 1722, Sheikh Jabbareh al-Nassur of Taheri, also of the Al Harami tribe took possession of the island on behalf of the Safavids.[84]

Although the Dutch were not interested the issue remained alive among Persian officials. On December 19, 1736 Mohammad Latif Khan sent Carel Koenad, the VOC director at Bandar 'Abbas a letter in which he now officially invited the Dutch to come and trade in Bushire by sending a merchant with merchandise there.[85] Koenad replied that the governor-general might approve his proposal to establish a VOC factory at Bushire, if this happened under Mohammad Latif Khan's protection.[86] On March 20, 1737 Mohammad Latif Khan followed up on his letter when he was in Bandar 'Abbas. He talked with the VOC interpreter about a possible Dutch move to Bushire. He wanted to make space for the Dutch in its castle or allow them to build a factory there. One of the admiral's captains, an Englishman named Cook, who commanded the ship that he had previously owned but had sold to Nader Shah, said that much profit was to be made in Bushire, and that it was

---

80 See chapter one.

81 For more particulars about Mohammad Latif Khan and the fleet that he was trying to put together see chapter one or Willem Floor, "The Iranian Navy during the Eighteenth Century," *Iranian Studies* 20 (1987), pp. 31-53; see also Ibid., *Hokumat-e Nader Shah* (Tehran, 1367/1988), index. He was at that time, governor of Dashtestan, Kazerun and Zoelunad [?] as well as supervisor (*opziender*) of all sea ports. VOC 2323, f. 531 (13/06/1734).

82 VOC 2323, Hey to Batavia (22/09/1734), f. 206.

83 VOC 2448, f. 822; Lockchart, *Nadir Shah*, p. 108; Mohammad Kazem Mervi, *'Alamara-ye Naderi* ed. Mohammad Amin Riyahi 3 vols. (Tehran, 1369/1990), vol. 3, pp. 939-41.

84 VOC 1983, f. 150; Floor, *The Persian Gulf*, pp. 202-03, 418-24. Sheikh Jabbareh was confirmed as governor of Bahrain by Shah Tahmasp II in May 1730. VOC 2254, Gamronsch Dagregister (29/05/1730), f. 46.

85 VOC 2417, f. 3677 (08/01/1737).

86 VOC 2417, Koenad to Mohammad Latif Khan and his *nazer*, Mirza Hasan (29/12/1736), f. 403-33.

safer than in Basra. The Dutch were not certain what to do, the more so given uncertainty about the peace with the Arabs in Basra.[87]

In May 1737, Mohammad Taqi Khan, Nader Shah's most trusted collaborator, governor-general of Fars and commander of the invasion force to Oman, also pressed the Dutch to open a trading station in Bushire. He argued that such a move was both in the interest of the shah and the Dutch. If the VOC agreed to open factory at Bushire, this would stimulate trade there, so that merchants in and around Hoveyzeh, Bandar-e Rig, Khark, and those of Lar, Shiraz and surrounding areas would be inclined to trade there instead of Basra. For the shah this would mean that his revenues would increase and he also would be grateful to the Dutch. To show how serious he was Mohammad Taqi Khan gave the Dutch a *ta'liqeh* (a decision) on May 21, 1737 (20 Moharram 1150) granting them free trade at Bushire, where they could maintain a staff and a factory, at any place between the town and the Naderiyeh fortress. The VOC council at Bandar 'Abbas deliberated the matter, whether it should accept the offer or not. Because the VOC factory at Basra suffered decreasing profits, while its staff was exposed to extortion by local officials, the council decided to send a ship to Bushire with merchandise to see how trade prospects were there. If these were good and after having gained solid foothold at Bushire the Basra factory could be transferred in case the situation there deteriorated further.[88]

The Dutch sent the assistant Jacob Schoonderwoerd to lead this mission. He had little experience in dealing with the local population and did not want to go, but he was not given a choice. Schoonderwoerd had not been the first choice, but junior merchant Nicolaas Duyt, who had worked in Mokha (Yemen), and who knew Arabic and Arabs, had refused to go and the council agreed with his rather flimsy arguments. In addition, one clerk was sent, David Buffkens who knew the country and the people well. A junior-mate, Isaac Willemsz, was also sent to make a precise and detailed description of the depths, banks etc. of the bay of Bushire. Finally, as broker, Naghas Natta was sent along, who had lived in Bushire for two years.[89]

Schoonderwoerd left on July 11, 1737 with the small vessel de *Boucher*. One of his tasks was to test whether such small vessels of 100-130 feet in length might sail to Bushire. He was instructed on his arrival to fire salutes at the approach of Nadiriyeh castle, as was customary. The town authorities then would send some servants to the beach to send vessels to pilot the Dutch vessel into the bay of Bushire. On coming to anchor at Bushire Schoonderwoerd had to fire salutes again. There he was instructed to see Mohammad Rafi'a (Mhamed Rafie), the agent (*vakil*) of Mohammad Taqi Khan Shirazi, and Hasan 'Ali Beyg (Hassan Alie Beek), the deputy-governor (*na'eb*) of Dashtestan. He had to inform them of the reason for his arrival and refer them to the requests by Mohammad Latif Khan and Mohammad Taqi Khan. Schoenderwoerd was further instructed to locate a good house, well situated for trade and drinking water. As far as trade was concerned he had to follow the market and try to buy copper, paisas, red copper in pieces, and Persian *mahmudis*, to which end

---

87 VOC 2417, f. 3825 (23/03/1737). Mohammad Latif Khan was also the builder of the Naderiyeh castle, and in a letter dated May 7, 1736 Mohammad Taqi Khan, governor-general of Fars, referred to Bushire as Bandar-e Naderiyeh, see VOC 2416, f. 1053 (01/06/1736). About the problems in Basra see chapter four and Longrigg, *Four Centuries*, pp. 156-57.

88 VOC 2448 (resolution 26/05/1737), f. 369-73; VOC 2584, f. 2563 (18/11/1741).

89 VOC 2448 (21/06/1737), f. 437-447 (includes a list of the merchandise sent on this first voyage). Schoonderwoerd held the function of deputy-law enforcement officer (*fiscaal*).

he had a pricelist with him as guidance. If he was not able to sell Schoonderwoerd had to make it known that he would move to Basra to sell his goods.[90]

Schoonderwoerd arrived at Bushire on August 18, 1738 after a difficult voyage of 38 days. After his arrival at Naderiyeh nobody came to see him after he had fired salutes and so the broker went ashore to announce their arrival. He returned in the evening with the news that there were no officials present in Bushire, because they had all been summoned by Mohammad Taqi Khan. Hasan 'Ali Beyg, the deputy-governor (*na'eb*) of Dashtestan was at Zireh (Ziera), at about five German miles (38 km) inland and so was his brother Hoseyn Khan Beyg (Hossain chan beecq). The broker had been friendly received by the chief merchant, Sheikh Mohammad Reza Shushtari or simply Hajji Reza (Sjeeg Mohammad Reza Sousterie). The entire Dutch group was welcomed at Bushire and a caravanserai was allocated to them. Schoonderwoerd wrote that the allocated house was sober, but solid. It was situated at 60 paces from the beach, close where the vessel was anchored. There were only 6-7 rooms for storage, but Schoonderwoerd believed that he could manage with his staff. He would have preferred to have a larger house, but this was not available. For, given the fact that he had to receive Armenian and other merchants, the present house was somewhat small.[91]

The bay of Bushire was full of banks and shoals and no ship, not even a small one, could pass them. The only one that could was a one-master sloop which did not draw more water than a *tranki* (a small oared vessel). Ships therefore had to anchor between Naderiyeh, at four miles from Bushire, and the town itself. There vessels could sail as far as two boat lengths from the shore, where there still was four fathoms of water, and there was no surf. Bushire was a healthier place than Bandar 'Abbas and well supplied with people and small merchants. These came to the market at Bushire mostly to barter, because white money was very scarce. On a daily basis many vessels came to Bushire from the Arab coast (Qatif, Bahrain), Basra, and even from Mokha and Malabar. However, it was difficult to get life necessities, firewood and water. Firewood cost 2 *mahmudis*, sometimes 2.5 to 3 *mahmudis* per *mann* of 108 lbs. Those traders coming from Masqat had bought wheat at 7.5 to 8 *mahmudis* without watching its quality, whether barley was mixed with it or not; if fact, wheat was never for sale totally pure. Schoonderwoerd bought a sample of opium that was said to be better than that of Bengal.[92]

As to trade, Schoonderwoerd reported that there was much old copperware for sale at 8.5 to 9 *mahmudis* white money per 7.5 lbs; wheat was scarce and was sold at 6.5 *mahmudis* white money per *mann-e hashemi* of 108 lbs.[93] As to business customs of Bushire he wrote that these were peculiar. The weight used in trade was the *mann-e Tabriz*, which had to be equal with 18 *mahmudis* copper money or 180 *dogas*. One *doga* was 4 *methqal*, thus in all 720 *methqals*. The pound used by the VOC was 106 ½ lbs., and therefore a Bushire *mann* was 6 ¾ lbs. and thus lighter than had been stated in

90 VOC 2448, Instruction to Schoonderwoerd (03/07/1737), f. 482-494. Batavia did not have high hopes for the establishment of the Bushire factory and assumed a wait-and-see attitude. Coolhaas, *Generale Missieven*, vol. 10, p. 230 (31/01/1739).

91 VOC 2448, (24/08/1737), f. 1500-07, 1548.

92 VOC 2448 (23/11/1737), f. 1508-1515. The proper sounding of the bay had led to the selection of a vessel *De Valk* that did not draw much water, which in 1745, therefore, could be hauled ashore at Bushire for repairs. VOC 2680, f. 33 (10/08/1745). According to the Dutch, Bushire was "one of the best ports in the Persian Gulf. A ship drawing 12 to 13 feet of water can very easily with high tide be brought completely as far as the houses." Willem Floor, "A Description of the Persian Gulf and its inhabitants in 1756," *Persica*, vol. 8 (1979), p. 172 or chapter two.

93 VOC 2448, f. 1504 (24/08/1737). The term 'white money' refers to good silver money, i.e., which had not been debased, whereas the term 'black money' refers to bad or debased money, which was exchanged at a discount, in this case of 50%.

his instructions. Another weight in use was the *mann-e hashemi* which equaled 16 *mann-e Tabriz* or about 108 lbs. He tried, but failed to convince the local merchants to adopt different weight system. Schoonderwoerd therefore decided that he would verify the weight with copper coins and calculate the *mann* at 6 lbs.[94] That was a sensible approach, but this was only possible if one's measure was working, which, however, broke in early 1738. Schoonderwoerd reported that "the weights cannot be repaired in the bazaar here, because the smiths do not have the skill; therefore send me nine pieces of 50 lbs stones."[95]

Trade in the beginning was not so good and, in fact, never became very thriving. The English had sold their goods quite cheap in 1736 and moreover had accepted in payment 40% in black money for some of their textiles. Cinnamon did not sell well, while mace was totally unknown. The fabrics that Schoonderwoerd had brought were considered to be odd designs and merchants were hesitant to buy them. Wheat, which he had to buy for Batavia, was scarce, because the authorities bought much of it for the Masqat expeditionary force.[96] He later reported that "in trade one always reckons by white money with a content of 50% black, so that 100 mahmudis actually means 150 mahmudis."[97]

It took some time before Schoonderwoerd met with the local officials. One of the first ones he met was the *shahbandar* of Bushire, Mirza Mehdi. Later, unexpectedly, Sheikh Madhkur (sjeeg Maskoer) arrived. Schoonderwoerd described him as "a kind of chief merchant, who is engaged in commerce on a daily basis and who has good credit."[98] Schoonderwoerd also witnessed a row between Sheikh Madhkur and Hajji 'Ali, apparently a newly appointed *shahbandar,* who departed for Siamael (or Summael) 20 German miles from Bushire, to Hasan 'Ali Beyg. Later he would meet the latter, who was the *na'eb* of Dashtestan and arrived at Bushire on December 27, 1737.[99] According to Niebuhr, specifically referring to Sheikh Naser b. Madhkur,

---

94 VOC 2448, f. 1507 (23/11/1737).

95 VOC 2476, f. 1104 (12/01/1739).

96 VOC 2448 (23/11/1737), f. 1508-1515. For details on the profits by commodity since Schoonderwoerd's arrival until March 1738 see VOC 2448, f. 1889 (30/04/1738); see also VOC 2448, f. 164 (31/12/1737 + 31/01/1738), which also has a table comparing prices between Basra and Bushire.

97 VOC 2448 (21/04/1738), f. 2438.

98 VOC 2448 (23/11/1737), f. 1508-1515; VOC 2448, (24/08/1737), f. 1500-07; VOC 2448 (18/02/1738), f. 2404-07. According to a Dutch source, Sheikh Madhkur's father was called "Gamier," perhaps Khamir (meaning 'red, reddish brown,' referring to his hair?), VOC 2476, f. 676. Both Ricks, *Politics*, p. 176 and Ahmad Abu Hakima, *History of East Arabia 1750-1800* (Beirut, 1965), p. 34 holds that Sheikh Naser was the governor of Bushire as of 1736, which is not borne out by Dutch sources. From this and the following it is clear that the head of the al-Madhkur family, which family would hold sway in Bushire until 1850, was not as yet the uncontested chief of the port. This would only happen under Sheikh Naser b. Madhkur as of 1748, although Sheikh Madhkur had laid the foundation for this development. According to Fasa'i, *Farsnameh*, vol. 2, p. 1321, Sheikh Naser had moved from Rishahr to Bushire in 1738. He called him the builder (*bani*) of Bushire. His source probably is Mohammad Ebrahim Kazeruni, *Tarikh-e Banader va Jazayer-e Khalij-e Fars* ed. Manuchehr Setudeh (Tehran 1367/1988), p. 47, according to whom, Sheikh Madhkur had come from Oman to Rishahr, where he lived in huts made palm tree wood, branches and reed and was engaged in fishing. He had some nephews with him who were good at ship building and sailing ships, who were engaged as skippers on vessels of Nader Shah's fleet, which was the key to the later success of the lineage.

99 VOC 2448, Schoonderwoerd to Koenad (21/04/1738), f. 2438; VOC 2511, Resolution Gamron (27/04/1740), f. 482 also mentions Hajji 'Ali as *shahbandar* of Bushire and Hasan 'Ali Beyg as *na'eb* of Dashtestan; see also VOC 2546, Schoonderwoerd to Koenad (12/12/1740), f. 1887 (*soltan*). Hadje Mhamet Alie is still mentioned as *shahbandar* in 1745. VOC 2705, f. 413. Siamael probably is the village of Samal which is situated in Dashtestan at about 24 miles (thus not 20 German miles, which may be a mistake) east of Bushire. Lorimer, *Gazetteer*, p. 388.

> The Arabs inhabiting the district of Abu Schaehhr are not of the tribe of the Houle. There are among them three eminent families; the two first of which have been, from time immemorial, settled in this country. The third, named *Matarisch*, came lately from Oman, where they were employed in fishing, entered into an alliance with the other two, and found means to usurp the sovereign authority, which they have now held for several years.[100]

The other two families were Shambe and Aumher, whose origin was unknown, because they had lived for such a long time in Bushire, according to Niebuhr. According to the Dutch and a Persian chronicle, the al-Madhkur family belonged to the Omani Al Abu Moheyr tribe.[101] The Matarish also seem to actually have existed (unless it is a printer's error, which seems likely), although no direct link with the Al Madhkur has been suggested. The only indirect and inferred link is the one by Wellstead who reported that the al-Madhkur were from Abu Dhabi.[102] The Dutch report and Ghaffari's chronicle, which are contemporary, have more credibility, however. The more so, since the Al Abu Moheyr, under their chief Sheikh Amir Mahin, were already living in the Bandar Deylam area in 1702, and most likely already much earlier; they still had contacts with their relatives in Oman at that time.[103] In fact, in 1602-03, Sheikh Musa Abu Moheyr assisted Emamqoli Khan with men and vessels to prevent a Portuguese invasion of Bahrain.[104] The bitter enmity that existed between the al-Madhkur of Bushire and the Hula Arabs may date from the mid-16th century, when a group of Arabs settled at Nakhilu (i.e. the Hula Arabs), because they had been ousted from Oman after they had lost the battle for the pearl grounds against their main rivals the *Alimoeiros* [Āl Moheyr?].[105]

Schoonderwoerd was also confronted with a reality of Bushire that would be one of its main drawbacks, as it was for all other locations where merchants operated in Persia, viz. the ubiquitous presence of a variety of officials and officers, who preyed on everybody. His first such encounter was soon after his arrival when Schoonderwoerd met with the *sardar*, a son of Mohammad Taqi Khan; he was a troublesome person, who demanded presents from everybody. Schoonderwoerd was forced to give him his only two chairs. Worse, due to his presence trade had come to a total standstill until

---

100 Carsten Niebuhr, *Travels through Arabia and other Countries in the East* 2 vols. (Edinburgh, 1792), vol. 2, pp. 145-46. See also Lorimer, J. G. *Gazetteer of the Persian Gulf* (Calcutta, 1915 [1970]), p. 110.

101 See Floor, "Description," p. 170 (Abou Mehair) or chapter one. This is also borne out by Abu'l-Hasan Ghaffari Kashani, *Golshan-e Morad* ed. GholamReza Tabataba'i-Majd (Tehran, 1369/1990), p. 275 (Sheikh Sa'dun Abu Moheyri); Fasa'i, *Farsnameh*, vol. 2, p. 1321 (Sheikh Naser son of Sheikh Madhkur Abu Moheyri) and Government of Bombay, *Selections*, pp. 542, 545 (Beni Mohair), 364 ("Shaikh Nassir of the Bomeheere Tribe").

102 Government of Bombay, *Selections*, p. 94 (the Matarish live at "Aboo Heyle" on the lagoon of al-Khan near Sharjah); J. R. Wellstead, *Travels to the City of the Caliphs along the Shores of the Persian Gulf and the Mediterranean*. 2 vols. (London, 1840), vol. 2, pp. 133-36.

103 Mohammad Ebrahim b. Zeyn al-'Abedin Nasiri, *Dastur-e Shahriyan*. ed. Mohammad Nader Nasiri Moqaddam (Tehran, 1373/1995), p. 154.

104 Molla Jalal al-Din Monajjem, *Ruznameh-ye `Abbasi ya Ruznameh-ye Molla Jalal*, ed. Seifollah Vahidniya (Tehran, 1366/1967), p. 215.

105 Francisco Rodrigues Silveira, *Memórias de um soldado da India*. ed. A. de S.S. Costa Lobo (Lisbon, 1987), pp. 45-46.

he left for Shiraz on February 21, 1738 taking Sheikh Madhkur with him. "For a week now no vessel had come to Bushire, while normally 10 to 20 of them came and went." [106]

Meanwhile, the VOC council at Bandar 'Abbas was worried about the safety of Schoonderwoerd's group and their merchandise. When in 1737 Mirza Taqi Khan launched his conquest of Oman, Sheikh Jabbareh retook the island of Bahrain, except for the fort. He had joined a general uprising of the Hulas against the Persians after the defeat the Persian navy had suffered against the Omani fleet.[107] As a result, Bahrain had been totally ruined for the Hula Arabs had ravaged and plundered it without leaving anything. They had abandoned the island afterwards. A royal grab had come from Bahrain to Bushire, reportedly to fetch gun-powder and balls to assist the governor (*soltan*) of the island.[108] The rebelling Hula Arabs also held Basidu on Qeshm Island and Kong (from which they later were ousted) and Koenad therefore instructed the Basra factory to send the ship *de Adriana* directly to Bushire for the staff's protection given that there was much merchandise at its factory.[109] As a result of the general insecurity that prevailed at the head of the Persian Gulf, trade was and remained bad in Bushire.[110] Schoonderwoerd could not sell the remainder of his iron and sugar stock, due to the ruin of Bahrain and the insecurity of navigation to Qatif.[111]

Wheat was expensive and difficult to get at 8 *mahmudi*s per *mann* of 108 lbs. Much of it was shipped to Oman for the Persian army, despite the fact that wheat was sold in public and not kept exclusively for the army. There was also export to Qatif, Basra, Mokha, etc. The price was expected therefore to rise even further, although the harvest had been good, because the locusts that had blackened the skies had not devoured it to everybody's amazement. The rebelling Hula Arabs between Bushire and Bandar 'Abbas also preyed on shipping in that area where they had taken, for example, a vessel belonging to Sheikh Madhkur of Bushire, which transported wheat for the army in Oman. In June 1738, Hasan 'Ali Beyg, the *na'eb* of Dashtestan, had therefore asked Schoonderwoerd to transport grain to Masqat, because Persian vessels were seized by pirates due to the insecurity that prevailed in the Gulf. Meanwhile, due to his involvement with the growing army operations, Sheikh Madhkur gained in importance. In early August 1738, Mohammad Taqi Khan sent a very flattering letter to Sheikh Madhkur in which he cancelled all fiscal contributions, ordinary and extraordinary, that he owed as recompense for his services. However, Schoonderwoerd observed that this exemption served as excuse for his demand for 400 men to replenish Mohammad Taqi Khan's fleet that was without crews. As a result, local officials had already started to recruit men. There was also a lull in piratical and looting activities during the summer. Not much was heard anymore about the robberies on the beaches, for it was said that the Hula Arabs had been told to lay low by Sheikh Jabbareh (Sjeeg Sjabara). But it was all for appearance's sake, for Sheikh Jabbareh (Sjeeg Thabaar) arrived at Qatif in November 1738, although it was unknown why. It was said that he wanted to retake Bahrain, where allegedly the entire royal fleet had concentrated to relieve the island from the Hula threat.[112] Because of these developments Koenad had written to Schoonderwoerd asking him whether there was cause to abandon Bushire? He replied that there were no reasons to do so and he

106 VOC 2448, Schoonderwoerd to Koenad (23/11/1737), f. 1508-1515; VOC 2448, Schoonderwoerd to Koenad (18/02/1738), f. 2404-07, 2411.

107 VOC 2448, f. 884-85; VOC 2510, f. 1097.

108 VOC 2467, Schoonderwoerd to Koenad, (17/08/1738), f. 1066.

109 VOC 2476, Schoonderwoerd to Koenad (08/08/1738), f. 183-84.

110 VOC 2476, Schoonderwoerd to Koenad (14/06/1738), f. 1045.

111 VOC 2467, Schoonderwoerd to Koenad (17/08/1738), f. 1058.

112 VOC 2476, f. 183-84 (08/08/1738); VOC 2476, f. 1045 (14/06/1738); VOC 2467, f. 1058, 1063, 1066 (17/08/1738); VOC 2476, f. 1047, 1050-51, 1065-69, 1077 (14/06/1738); VOC 2476, f. 1097 (12/11/1738).

therefore had decided to stay. To show that things were not as bad as they seemed Schoonderwoerd also reported that he had bought 2,592 lbs. or 24 *mann-e hashemi* of wheat.[113]

But there were still problems, if only because trade had come to a standstill. The *na'eb* of Dashtestan and the *na'eb* of Kazerun (Cazaroen) had bought grain for the *beygler-beygi*'s army. When they made a three-day's visit to Bushire at the end of September 1738 they sold the grain again and distributed it among the merchants.[114] The governor (*soltan*) of Dashtestan, Soltan 'Ali Beyg, arrived at Bushire with troops at the end of December 1738. As a result, firewood became very expensive, viz. 4-5 *mahmudis* per *mann-e hashemi* due to transportation problems.[115] Life was expected to become much cheaper in Bushire once the *soltan* had left, for he collected all firewood that was brought there overland. He did the same in case of most life necessities, which were stopped at the castle by his servants to feed his troops.[116] It was not clear whether these troops were to be ferried to Bahrain or not. Rumor had it that Bahrain was under siege and was hard pressed. Its deputy-governor or *vakil*, Mohammad Amin Beyg (Mhamed Amien beecq) had arrived in Bushire, but therefore could not go there. Hasan 'Ali Beyg, the *na'eb* of Dashestan was kept imprisoned by the *soltan*, for reasons unknown.[117] In late July 1738, Soltan 'Ali Beyg left Bushire. It was said that he would attack Qatif and Hasa. This news gained some credence, because the sheikh of Qatif had sent on July 24, 1738 ten beautiful horses to Shiraz with the request to be left alone. Others said that these troops were to attack Masqat.[118] The fleet referred to was that commanded by Mirza Taqi Khan's son, Mirza Reza, who had been sent as commander of the pearling fleet to Bahrain, but he was not able to achieve anything.[119] This fleet possibly also had been intended to attack the Arabs at Qatif, who had supported the Hulas in their attack of Bahrain.[120] However, setbacks in Oman and Makran made further Persian operations against the Hulas at Bahrain impractical. When, therefore, Sheikh Qasem b. Jaber of 'Asalu of the Al Harami tribe came to Sheikh Jabbareh's assistance the fort of Manama fell into their hands. The latter's brother Mohammad b. Jaber took control of the island after Nader Shah's death in 1747 until he was ousted by Sheikh Naser of Bushire and Mir Naser of Bandar-e Rig in 1752.[121]

Peace did not return to Bushire and trouble raised its head for the VOC. For Mohammad Taqi Khan arrived at Bushire on September 17, 1739 with 12,000 men. He stayed at the Naderiyeh

---

Sheikh Jabbareh had been ousted from Bahrain in 1737 and returned in 1738/39 to retake the island. Government of Great Britain, *Selections*, pp. 24-25.

113 VOC 2476, f. 1084 (29/10/1738); VOC 2476, f. 1093 (12/11/1738).

114 VOC 2476, Schoonderwoerd to Koenad (01/10/1738), f. 1082. This distribution probably was forced upon the merchants, a custom known as *tarh*.

115 VOC 2476, f. 1104 (12/01/1739); VOC 2477, f. 297 (06/05/1739).

116 VOC 2510, f. 875 (07/06/1739).

117 VOC 2476, f. 1106 (12/01/1739); VOC 2510, f. 116 (25/12/1739).

118 VOC 2510, f. 883, 985 (03/08/1739). In March 1739, Schoonderwoerd had given presents to Sheikh Madhkur, the *shahbandar* Hajj 'Ali, the *vakil* Mohammad Amin Beyg and to Soltan 'Ali Beyg. VOC 2477, f. 513 (21/04/1739). In December 1738, Sheikh Madhkur was referred to as the *darugheh* of Bushire, which function normally was held by somebody else. Whether this is a mistake or temporary tenure of that office is not clear, but it seems unlikely that the chief local notable would also act as the beach guard (*strandwacht*), as the term was translated into Dutch, so he must have been the person in charge of this guard. VOC 2477, f. 567. In fact, in 1740 the *darugheh* of Bushire was Hajji Beyg. VOC 2511, f. 667 (17/03/1740), f. 1118 (16/05/1740). For the meaning of the term *darugheh* see Willem Floor, *Safavid Government Institutions* (Costa Mesa, 2003), pp. 115-22.

119 VOC 2511, f. 992.

120 VOC 2511, f. 206; VOC 2476, 1097-98.

121 Government of Great Britain, *Selections*, pp. 24-25; Niebuhr, *Reisebeschreibung*, p. 505.

castle and sent one of his servants, Ahmad Beyg *yasavol-bashi*, to visit Schoonderwoerd.[122] This time the governor-general did not make outrageous demands of the Dutch. However, Sheikh Madhkur who so far had not interfered with Dutch trade complained about the VOC broker to Mohammad Taqi Khan. He claimed that as a result of the broker's actions many Banyans had already left Bushire, which was a great loss to him. To prevent that he would make more and worse trouble Schoonderwoerd gave him a present. But it was to no avail. Two days after Mohammad Taqi Khan's departure Schoonderwoerd was very surprised when the provisional commander of the royal fleet, Mohammad Qasem Beyg, sent someone to arrest the VOC broker, allegedly at Mohammad Taqi Khan's orders. Schoonderwoerd engineered the release of the broker through the payment of 50 *tumans*. He believed that Sheikh Madhkur and Agha 'Abdi were behind this move. The latter was the chief broker in Bushire, both for Mohammad Taqi Khan and all imported Persian commodities.[123] Schoonderwoerd wrote to Koenad to ask for an order (*ta'liqeh*) to confirm the position of his broker (*dallal*) as the official VOC broker, because Aqa 'Abdi had an official royal order to act henceforth as broker for the VOC.[124]

In 1740, it seemed that the same problems would not occur again. Militarily things were also quieter. Rumors abounded about what was going to be done about the insecurity. In May 1740 there was information that the royal fleet would sail to Bushire where the new *darya-beygi*, Mir 'Ali Khan (Mier Alie Chan), who had been *beygler-beygi* of Kerman in 1731 would take over the command of the fleet. Rumor also had it that the fleet would attack the Arabs of Hasa near Bahrain, while others said it would attack Basra.[125] Such news led to all kinds of preparations and as a result pack animals were pressed and firewood became expensive. Trade continued, however, and old copper sold very well at 10 *mahmudis* and even at 12.5 to English ships with Banyans.[126] Later in the year wheat became scarce. The notables of Bushire asked the Dutch not to buy too much wheat to avoid causing problems for the poor. Schoonderwoerd considered this a reasonable demand and he complied with the request.[127] Occasionally, supplies were later still scarce in Bushire, such as in 1746.[128]

Sheikh Madhkur and Aqa 'Abdali had become more reasonable and had apologized to Schoonderwoerd after they had received a letter from Mohammad Taqi Khan.[129] This had nothing to do with the presents that Schoonderwoerd had distributed among the town's officials, including to Sheikh Madhkur.[130] For when merchants came to the VOC house to buy goods the clerk of Sheikh Madhkur also came to calculate the fiscal duties. This led to an altercation when the Sheikh's clerk wanted to interfere with business and therefore beat the VOC porters. Sheikh Madhkur who was next door also arrived and then beat the VOC interpreter, Buffkens, with a stick. Schoonderwoerd was very angry about this behavior and wanted to complain to the governor in

122 VOC 2510, f, 910 (31/09/1739), f. 910-22. In October 1740, the newly appointed castellan (*kotval*) of Naderiyeh castle was Hoseyn Khan Beyg (Hossein Chan beecq). VOC 2546, f. 314 (Oct. 1740).

123 VOC 2510 (31/09/1739), f. 911, 916, 919, 922-23.

124 VOC 2510, f. 948 (29/11/1739). For the same problem elsewhere in Persia, see Willem Floor, "Dutch Trade in Afsharid Iran (1730-1753)," *Studia Iranica* 34 (2005), pp. 46, 53-55.

125 VOC 2511, f. 142, 206 (31/07/1740).

126 VOC 2511 (05/04/1740), f. 1094-95.

127 VOC 2546, f. 1335 (18/09/40).

128 VOC 2705, f. 571, 593 (salaries masons) (28/08/1746).

129 VOC 2511 (05/04/1740), f. 1101.

130 VOC 2511, f. 667 (03/07/1740). Presents were given to Sheikh Madhkur, Hasan 'Ali Beyg, the *darugheh* Hajji Beyg and the *shahbandar* Hajji 'Ali.

Shiraz. Sheikh Madhkur's action did not sit well with the community at large, for the population of Bushire demonstrated against him and he was then forced to publicly ask forgiveness. The next day all merchants came to ask the same. Thus, Schoonderwoerd was proud to report that "we got now double satisfaction." Nevertheless, he asked for an order that instructed Sheikh Madhkur not to interfere with VOC trade, because otherwise, Schoonderwoerd feared, he would do it again. Before the VOC ship left for Bandar 'Abbas all merchants declared that they stood guarantee for Sheikh Madhkur's good behavior.[131] Thus, trade in Bushire was not a very stimulating affair. Profits were disappointing and trade conditions were not favorable. The local chief notable of Bushire, although professing to be committed to the promotion of trade in reality wanted to promote his own interest as attested by Sheikh Madhkur's interference with the activities of VOC staff. Schoonderwoerd repeated his request that Koenad obtain and send official instructions ordering the sheikh not to interfere with trade.[132]

There was also interference with the Dutch by the local authorities, just as they did in Bandar 'Abbas. Schoenderwoerd was forced to allow the VOC ship that had called on Bushire to transport troops to Nakhilu to suppress the mutiny of the Hula Arab crews of the royal fleet.[133] One of the reason that the Persian authorities wanted to make use of VOC ships was that the "mangoese and ghinoese arabs at Jifzeritt and keytz [Jazirat al-Kish; the island of Kish] had promised to subjugate themselves to me [Emamverdi Khan], and on sight of VOC ships will do so quicker."[134] Sheikh Madhkur acquired an important role in the suppression of the mutiny. He had been ordered to come to Shiraz on January 28, 1741 where he was instructed to go to the Hula rebels and induce them to return to their ships.[135]

In 1741, Schoonderwoerd had rented a new house from Hajji Sarraf.[136] When he wanted to move to the new house Sheikh Naser prevented that with all kinds of excuses. Schoonderwoerd therefore asked the governor of Fars, Hatem Khan to intervene. Although he also had received pertinent decisions (*ta'liqehs*) from Mohahmmad Taqi Khan for the VOC's native servants, he still expected trouble.[137] These events, including the troubles it had itself with the Persian authorities, led the council at Bandar 'Abbas to worry about a possible attack of the Dutch factory at Bushire. Schoonderwoerd, however, did not think that the Persians would go so far. However, to flee from there and take VOC merchandise and cash with him, as had been suggested by Bandar 'Abbas, he

131 VOC 2546, f. 1337-43 (18/09/40). One year later, the Dutch mention that the customs of Bushire were collected by Sheikh Madhkur, which implies that either the *shahbandar* was in his employ or that he was the *shahbandar*. Since the Dutch mention a separate *shahbandar* it is clear that Sheikh Madhkur must have been especially charged to collect [part of?] these revenues to be used for a specific purpose. VOC 2584, f. 1535 (31/07/1741).

132 VOC 2546, f. 1154, 1883-84 (12/10/40).

133 VOC 2546 (08/10/1740), f. 1347. For the Dutch text of the official order see VOC 2546, f. 1849-51 (24/10/1740). Sheikh Madhkur had to provide the food supplies. VOC 2546, f. 1153-54 (24/10/1740). On the mutiny itself, see chapter one

134 VOC 2546 (received 30/10/1740), f. 1760. Probably the Arabs from Moghu and Ganaveh, both Persian Gulf coastal settlements, are meant here. See chapter two.

135 VOC 2546, f. 1391 (31/01/1741) (he had borrowed 40 *tumans* from the Dutch before he left to Shiraz). At the end of 1740 'Ali Beyg was still *soltan* of Dashtestan, VOC 2546, f. 1886 (12/10/1740) and his *na'eb* was Hoseyn Khan Beyg. VOC 2546, f. 1391 (31/01/1741). But there were changes. By June 1741, Mohammad Baqer Beyg had become *soltan* (VOC 2584, f. 1446 (18/06/1741), while by September 1741 it was Soltan Hasan was the *vakil* or deputy. VOC 2584, f. 1556, 2443 (15/09/1741). Mohammad Baqer Beyg was the head of the royal militia and the royal *jelowdar* in Bushire. VOC 2584, f. 1432.

136 VOC 2584 (16/09/1741), f. 1662.

137 VOC 2584 (21/11/1741), f. 1577, 1478-81.

considered impractical. It could not be done in secret, because it would become known and the authorities would then prevent it. Burying the Company's cash was also impossible, because it would be found in case of pillage of the factory. The VOC domestic staff would know about it. A factor that also played a role in all this was that the situation in Basra was much worse. Schoonderwoerd reported in November 1741 that the leading families from Basra were all in Bushire, due to the rebellion there.[138]

One year later, Schoonderwoerd finally found a new house with the help of Sheikh Madhkur. However, his son Naser, who had replaced his father now that he was at the court of the governor of Shiraz, prevented them from moving in. On his return and in his presence, Sheikh Madhkur scolded Sheikh Naser and forced him to apologize in public. Mohammad Taqi Khan to show his support had volunteered to put the VOC flag on the house to distinguish it from the Moslem houses. He also granted freedom of imposts to all eleven VOC native servants. Schoonderwoerd told them that the Bushire factory was a temporary one and that they might all be recalled any time. The fact that the profit made at Bushire in the period of 1740-41 was only Dfl. 8,068, which was even less than the previous year may have induced him to make that cautionary remark.[139] The profits also remained disappointing in the subsequent years, although in 1745 there seems to have been some improvement. Sales at Bushire and Basra were even higher than at Bandar 'Abbas, but the two first factories had higher overhead (sea risk, fiscal duties). Profit in Bushire in 1743 was even as high as 160%.[140] However, such an improvement was followed again by a disappointing year, which the VOC agent Cornelis Bijleveld, who had succeeded Schoonderwoerd in 1744, ascribed to continuous extortion of money, pearl fishing and dirty tricks by the Armenian merchant Mazok and the EIC broker Aqa 'Abdi, in addition to the excessive purchasing price for old copper at 17 *mahmudis* per 6 ¾ lbs. The VOC also lost money on the sale and export of rupees.[141] It was also in 1744 that Sheikh Madhkur was replaced by Sheikh Naser as chief (*stadsregent*) of Bushire.[142] The last few years of the Dutch Bushire factory seem to suggest that financially the factory did better. However, not much is known of what happened in the port, due to lack of documents pertaining to Bushire. For example, in 1748, the factory in Bandar 'Abbas received from Bushire Dfl. 17,858, further 45,161 lbs. of old copperware and 4,839 lbs. in copper cakes. Later they received another Dfl. 42,125 in Surat rupees

138 VOC 2584, f. 2754-55 (19/11/1741); VOC 2584 (25/11/1741), f. 1478-81.

139 VOC 2593 (31/10/1742) f. 1711vs, 1709r-verso.

140 VOC 2680, f. 83, 109-11 with details (10/08/1745).

141 VOC 2705, f. 81-82, 89-90, 130 (31/07/1746); VOC 2705 (21/7/1746), f. 81-82 (profit Bushire is disappointing). For a comparison of prices in Bandar 'Abbas and Bushire see VOC 2680, non-foliated (26/03/1745). Schoonderwoerd went to Bandar 'Abbas to replace Emmanuel de Poorter on 20/04/1744 as deputy-director. VOC 2680, Resolution Gamron (25/07/1744), non-foliated. Bijlevelt was from Zierikzee and had arrived in Bandar 'Abbas in 1732 as a young sailor (*hooploper*; at fl.7/month), became assistant in 1734 (fl. 16), and junior merchant in 1740 (fl. 40). VOC 2517, f. 2224; VOC 2546, Resolution Gamron (23/03/1741), f. 665-67. Bijleveld was assisted by F. Kuypers. VOC 2705, f. 130, 200 (31/07/1746). Bijleveld was recalled to Batavia in 1751 and was temporarily replaced by junior-merchant Abraham Haganeus [?]. VOC 781, f. 226 (15/06/1751). As of May 1753 until the end in November 1753, Jan van der Hulst was chief of the Bushire factory assisted by assistant Nicolai. VOC 2824, Cornelis Bijleveld and Jan van der Hulst (Bushire) to Batavia (25/03/1753), f. 71; VOC 2885, Khark to Batavia (05/08/1756), f. 5.

142 VOC 2680, Resolution Gamron (27/03/1745), unfoliated (see report on Bushire dated 08/11/1744). At that time Hajji 'Ali was *shahbandar*, the customs clerk was Molla 'Abdol. At that time (1745), the Carmelites established a mission at Bushire, but this was not permanent due to a lack of priests. Anonymous, *Chronicle*, vol. 1, p. 614.

and Naderis. This indicates that trade had improved, but that probably was a temporary effect that was also noticeable in Bandar 'Abbas.[143]

There was a continuing coming and going of officials, such as Hatem Khan, *beygler-beygi* of Fars, who had to recruit 100 sailors at Bushire, because Nader Shah wanted a navy at whatever cost.[144] These new sailors had to go with Sheikh Naser to Bandar-e Kong.[145] The new navy indeed was being built in Bushire, for in the second half of 1741 Nader Shah had issued orders to that effect. The timber to make the ships from came all the way from Mazandaran on men's shoulders in sixty days. To get timber was not the only problem that this shipbuilding project had to cope with. Other necessary materials (ropes, rigging, and iron) were also difficult to get hold of, while there was a severe shortage of qualified craftsmen to build ships. Nader Shah therefore asked the Dutch and English Companies in December 1741 to send him carpenters and shipbuilding materials, who replied that they did not have any.[146] Nevertheless, a large number of craftsmen were employed at Bushire. For example, in 1742 the Moghul ambassador Sayyed 'Ataollah arrived at Bushire where his ship was boarded by officials from that town. They told him that 500 skilled workers were working day and night to build large ships.[147] Bushire's importance clearly had received an economic boost from the establishment of the shipyard-cum-naval base.

However, the relative prosperous and quiet situation of Bushire was about to end. All of a sudden a rebellion broke out among the Arabs in the Bushire area, which was supported by a powerful Sheikh beyond Bahrain, who may have been the chief of the Banu Khaled as Slot has suggested. The rebels took the town of Bushire, plundered it and then seized three ships of the royal fleet. The Persian authorities in Bandar 'Abbas prepared a strong force to suppress the rebellion; it was commanded by Sardar Khalij Khan. Qalij Khan had arrived in Bandar 'Abbas on December 24, 1746 with close to 4,000 men. The purpose of his visit was unknown at that time, although it was suspected that he would go to 'Oman to subdue the Arabs.[148] Khalij Khan was not in a hurry to carry out this task; he first extorted goods from merchants at Bandar 'Abbas before departing for Bushire. After his arrival there he was unable to do much as shortly thereafter he was recalled by Nader Shah. Rather than facing the unpredictable wiles of his king Khalij Khan did what many generals were doing at that time, he rebelled. This news reached Bandar 'Abbas in March 1747 via the captain of a vessel coming from Jolfar that had been sent to bring Khalij Khan back. Officially it was given out that the general had arrived, but in private the captain reported that Khalij Khan had rebelled and had contacted rebels in Lar. He further reported that a rebellion among the troops

143 VOC 2748 f. 66-67 (10/10/1748).

144 VOC 2583, f. 166 (22/01/1742).

145 VOC 2583, f. 1506 (1741). Hasan Soltan was *na'eb* of Dashtestan; VOC 2583, f. 1556 (1741).

146 On the genesis of this fleet see chapter one. The Persians even asked the *motasallem* of Basra twice to hand over an English ship that was lying in Basra. An English ship lying in the roads of Bushire was almost taken by force by the Persians, but its captain was able to prevent this. Jean Otter, *Voyage en Turquie et en Perse* 2 vols. (Paris, 1748), vol. 2, pp. 134, 142.

147 RiazalIslam, *Calendar of Documents on Indo-Persian Relations*. 2 vols. (Tehran–Karachi, 1982), vol. 2, p. 351.

148 VOC 2705, Gamron to Batavia (31/07/1746), f. 426; VOC 2705, van der Welle to Batavia (28/02/1747), f. 538-39. Qalij Khan (Galieds Chan) was governor of the lower lands (Garmsirat), admiral and *sardar*. His first advisor was Mohammad Soltan (Mhamet Sulthoen) and his deputy (*na'eb*) was Mirza Baqer (Miersa Bager). VOC 2705, f. 725. Governor of Gamron was Mohammad Soltan (Mhamet Sulthoen). VOC 2705, f. 270.

in Oman was imminent, which indeed occurred shortly thereafter, under the leadership of Qalich Khan.[149]

As a result of the worsening situation at Bushire due to the outbreak of the rebellion and the oppression of the local authorities the Dutch had withdrawn their staff and goods from Bushire to Basra, which at that time was relatively quiet.[150] Ahmad Pasha, who had become governor of Basra again had put an end to the rebellion of the Marsh Arabs against Hoseyn Pasha in 1741, who were led by Sheikh Sa'dun b. Milan (Sjeeg Sadoen ben Milaan). The latter's forces robbed and plundered people and places where they could and as a result food prices rose sky-high in Basra. The threat of the Arabs rose to such a level that the Dutch at Basra, after having buried their cash in the factory, boarded an English ship in the river to be in a safer place. They returned to Basra when Ahmad Pasha arrived in April 1741 in the port city. Ahmad Pasha not only imposed himself militarily on the Arabs, but also fiscally on the city, because he levied a sum of 10,000 *qorush* (45,000 *mahmudis* or Dfl. 19,125) on Basra in 1741. But the result was that relative peace returned to Basra until Ahmad Pasha's death in 1748.[151] Meanwhile, in Bushire, Salim Khan, the newly appointed admiral of the fleet, who had remained loyal to Nader Shah, had taken control of four ships. As a result, he ensured relative peace and quiet and the Dutch returned at his request, although only after Nader Shah's death.[152] Salim Khan left Bushire and the fleet in 1747 or 1748, because no funds were made available anymore for the upkeep of the fleet. He probably also left to join the fray of the succession war. The remaining ships of the royal fleet became the property of each of their captains, who all were from different tribal groups and unwilling to work together. It even looked as if fights would break out between them, although this did not happen. In fact, "the ships, gallivats, and dingis remained lying there being abandoned by their captains and sailors,"[153] which later were appropriated by Naser Khan. The rule of Nader Shah had totally broken down as rebellions also had broken out in other parts of Persia and this was fact was shortly thereafter formalized when it became known that Nader Shah had been murdered on June 9, 1747 signaling the end of his reign.[154]

---

149 VOC 2705, Gamron to Batavia (20/02/1747), f. 539; VOC 2724, Gamron to Batavia (22/12/1747); Slot, *'Arab al-Khalij*, p. 311 (referring to Gombroon Diary 30/03, 02/04, 05/04, 10/04 and 16/04/1747); see chapter two.

150 Coolhaas, *Generale Missieven*, vol. 11, p. 710 (31/12/1748).

151 VOC 2583, f. 974, 1048-60, 1103, 115-17; VOC 2511, f. 1035; Colhaas, *Generale Missieven*, vol. 10, p. 939 (05/12/1742); Longrigg, *Four Centuries*, pp. 156-57. This relative peace did not end extortion by government officials such as in 1742 by Rostam Aqa, deputy-governor of Basra who took Dfl. 1,350 from van Suchtelen, the VOC chief in Basra. VOC 3092, f. 24.

152 Coolhaas, *Generale Missieven*, vol. 11, p. 711 (31/12/1748); According to Lorimer, *Gazetteer*, p. 128 in 1747, at the invitation of the *Sardar*, the Dutch re-established their factory at Bushire which they had closed. Mr. Belvelt (=Bijleveld) came from the Dutch factory in Basra with a supply of sugar, sugar-candy, camphor and some spices.

153 VOC 2705 (1746) f. 200 (*shahbandar* there was Hadje Mhamet Alie, f. 413); VOC 2680, f. 161 (28/2/1747); Floor, "Description," p. 170; Slot, *'Arab al-Khalij*, pp. 311-12, referring to Gombroon Diary 03/05, 04/05, 07/05 and 26/05/1747).

154 For the situation in Persia in general at that time and the breakdown of central authority see Michael Axworthy, *The Sword of Persia- Nader Shah from Tribal Warrior to Conquering Tyrant* (London, 2006), chapters nine and ten.

POLITICAL DEVELOPMENTS AFTER THE DEMISE OF THE AFSHAR REGIME

The death of Nader Shah in 1747 failed to bring the hoped for peace, necessary to enable economic growth and trade. The inter-tribal fights and local political instability in most of the coastal areas were a major obstacle to achieve that objective. Following the death of Nader Shah the various petty Arab chiefs in the Persian Gulf tried to take advantage of the power vacuum, amongst whom Sheikh Naser who was able to reinforce his local position. As we have seen Sheikh Naser, as his father Sheikh Madhkur before him, was not the governor of Bushire, because he was but the most important notable, who had extended his influence through trade, political contacts and services as well as relations with the fleet through the supply of crews and what we would call technical assistance nowadays. For the Persian admiral and his Persian officers, who were all land lubbers, needed Arabs captains and crews to sail the ships, for both linguistic and technical reasons. Sheikh Madhkur was still the chief of Bushire in 1745, although Sheikh Naser was mentioned as the new chief, without explanation whether that meant that he had replaced his father.[155] It may be that Sheik Madhkur had become old, but certainly not decrepit, for he was still wily and alive enough in 1747 to take two creditors of the VOC to the cleaners.[156] He probably died shortly thereafter for he is not mentioned in the, granted incomplete, sources anymore. In 1747, the *shahbandar* or customs-agent of Bushire was an Armenian, Khvajeh Malek (Coja Mellesk), who was an agent for the *shahbandar* of Bandar 'Abbas, who was Mohammad 'Ali Beyg. When the latter fled that port after a quarrel with the *sardar* of Fars in 1748, Sheikh Naser saw his chance. He plundered Khvajeh Maleks' house and declared himself *shahbandar* in that same year.[157] It would seem that due to absence of officials from the central government Sheikh Naser as the leading notable of the town by default took over effective control of the government. In addition to his local influence as leading notable, he now also was *shahbandar* by the use of force as well as the commander of a number of ships and vessels, also by default. In 1747 or 1748 Salim Khan the governor of Bushire and admiral of the fleet had left Bushire. Thus, as of the end of 1748 it would seem that Sheikh Naser held uncontested authority in Bushire. To bolster his position *vis à vis* the Persian government Sheikh Naser had become a Shi'ite, for which he was hated by his fellow Sunni Arabs.[158] According to the Dutch, Sheikh Naser like other sheikhs in the region believed that he was independent and that after Nader Shah there would be no new king of Persia. He therefore demanded money from the VOC staff in Bushire, who had just returned from Basra.[159] Initially Sheikh Naser played his cards carefully by taking no sides in the internal strife in Persia, while continuing to reinforce his powerbase in Bushire and its hinterland. For example, Sheikh Naser held Molla 'Ali Shah's family, who had sent a ship to Bushire in 1749 to take them back, but the latter refused to return them, unless the soon to be expected governor appointed by Ebrahim Shah (r. 1748-49) authorized this.[160]

155 VOC 2680, non-foliated (26/03/1745). Hajji 'Ali was still *shahbandar*; the customs clerk was "Molla Abdoel" and there was still the *darugheh* (*derrego*) or beach guard. VOC 2680, non-foliated (08/11/1744).

156 VOC 2724, f. 110 (1747). This short observation in Dutch records, which mention a much lower amount (see below), may refer to the alleged payment of 6,000 *tumans*, which is not recorded in the surviving VOC Bushire documents, by Dutch merchants in mid-June 1747 mentioned in English sources. Ricks, *Politics*, p. 128

157 Ricks, *Politics*, p. 90; Grummon, *The Rise*, pp. 69-70.

158 Floor, "Description," p. 172; Lorimer, *Gazetteer*, p. 110.

159 VOC 2766, Basra to Batavia (30/06/1749), f. 63. In 1747, Sheikh Naser extorted Dfl. 1993:18:3 from Cornelis Bijleveld. VOC 3092, f. 24.

160 Grummond, *The Rise*, p. 71. Molla 'Ali Shah's family was held hostage at Bushire as a result of the rebellion that had broken out in Dashtestan, and when the rebels took Bushire they also seized Molla 'Ali Shah's wife and children. Gombroon Diary (22/04/1747) and (22/05/1747).

SHEIKH NASER OF BUSHIRE BECOMES INDEPENDENT

However, two years later Sheikh Naser asserted himself. He went so far as to arrest 30 tax collectors who had been sent by Shah Esma'il III in January 1751, thus clearly announcing his political independence. The fact that the tax collectors were sent to the Sheikh confirm that he was the de facto power in Bushire.[161] He also had fostered ties with the Dashtestan tribes, who in 1751 appealed for his help against the tax demanded by Esma'il III.[162] The claim on Bushire was 35,000 *tumans*, or 5,000 more than demanded from Bandar 'Abbas and 10,000 more than Bandar-e Rig, indicating the relative and greater importance of Bushire than the other major ports on the Persian side of the Persian Gulf.[163] Sheikh Naser of Bushire and other coastal chiefs who had refused to pay taxes to Esma'il III nevertheless thought it prudent to leave to the islands. Sheikh Naser was leaving to Khark, while Sheikh Hatem of Taheri was going to Bahrain.[164] The reverse side of the coin was that in the absence of a strong central power other outlying peripheral centers also wanted to assert themselves, for Sheikh Naser was not alone in doing so. Bushire therefore had to face other contenders for regional power. There was, for example, the loose Hula confederation of Jolfar, Lengeh, Taheri, and Kangan. By 1751, the Hulas were challenging the position of the Hulas of Charak, who were supported by the governor of Bandar 'Abbas. To the north of Bushire were the Banu Ka'b in Khuzestan, and beyond Basra, the 'Otobis of Kuwait both of which had expansion plans. Closer to home Bushire was vying for control of trade in the upper part of the Persian Gulf with Bandar-e Rig, for both ports made efforts to attract merchants. Bushire had the better cards in that it had been Nader Shah's naval base and shipyard, while it also had a better location for ships. According to the Dutch, Bandar-e Rig "does not have such a good harbour as Boucheer. The ships have to remain lying in the roadstead, which is passably well. However, a small long island which is lying precisely in front of the town occasions that one may only bring a few ships there, for on the banks which lie between the said island and the shore there is only 7 to 8 feet of water above them when there is high tide."[165] But trade was bad at Bushire and Cornelis Bijleveld the head of the VOC factory wanted to leave "this bad Arab place" and asked for a transfer to Bandar 'Abbas, "because as long as there was no king in Persia there was nothing useful to be done here for the Hon. Company."[166]

BUSHIRE AND BANDAR-E RIG TAKE BAHRAIN

Emboldened by his success in refusing to pay taxes to the warlord controlling Shiraz and other parts of Persia as well as the de-facto possessor of part of the royal fleet Sheikh Naser believed that he

161 Grummond, *The Rise*, p. 72.

162 Grummond, *The Rise*, p. 76, n. 26.

163 Grummond, *The Rise*, p. 75, n. 25.

164 Ricks, *Politics and Trade*, pp. 198-99 referring to F. R. Gombroon VI (04/12/1750 and 04/01/1751).

165 Floor, "Description," p. 173. See also the first three chapters in this publication.

166 VOC 2824, Bushire to Batavia (17/04/1751), f. 1. Von Kniphausen and van de Hulst in Basra noted that Bijleveld was always complaining that they did not send him enough merchandise. However, they put the blame on him, because he had been authorized to take one-fourth of the cargo of any VOC ship going to Basra and so far he had never done so. They were reluctant to send goods with a tranki, because the Arabs in the area were fighting with one another. The authorities in Bushire also had imposed a contribution of Dfl. 1,000 on Bijleveld. VOC 2824, Basra to Batavia (11/01/1753), f. 15-16.

had the major part of the means to seize Bahrain. Its revenues were estimated at 80,000 rupees, of which 30,000 from date trees. In 1764 Niebuhr estimated the revenues at 100,000 rupees or 5,000 *tumans*.[167] What Sheikh Naser lacked, however, was manpower, because he could not field more than 400 armed men. Although the chiefs of the two ports were rivals he decided to ally himself with Mir Naser from neighboring Bandar-e Rig and fellow-Shi'ite, who could muster 500 men. In the second half of 1751, Sheikh Naser and Mir Naser of Bandar-e Rig attacked Bahrain to oust the Harami Hulas from the island. However, the Bahrain expedition failed in September 1751 and the two Naser's fled back home.[168] The Hulas now took the offensive even going so far as to invite Sheikh Naser's enemy, Molla 'Ali Shah of Bandar 'Abbas to join them against Bushire. On September 26, 1751 Molla 'Ali Shah had a meeting with the EIC at Naband to discuss the prospect of the Hula chiefs coming to Bandar 'Abbas. They had intimated that they wanted Molla 'Ali Shah's support against Bushire and Bandar-e Rig. The EIC Agent advised Molla 'Ali Shah to refuse any cooperation with the Hulas, because the English feared that this only would result in more insecurity in the Persian Gulf. On September 30, 1751 Sheikh Hatem of Taheri and Sheikh Chaueed of Jolfar arrived in a *tranki* at Bandar 'Abbas. They were followed by 12 more large *trankis* with a force of 3,000 men. During the first week of October the two sides were engaged in talks. The result was that Molla 'Ali Shah married the second daughter of Sheikh Hatem and appointed Sheikh Chaueed of Jolfar as his deputy at Bandar 'Abbas. The English warned Molla 'Ali Shah that this was bad for trade and his authority. Moreover, that the governors of Lar and Fars would not accept this and cause trouble for him. As a result Molla 'Ali Shah back-pedaled a bit and after some more and heated talks reached a compromise. Sheikh Hatem left with one additional gallivat[169] and four months of supplies to Bushire.[170] He was followed by Sheikh Chaueed who left on October 18, 1751 with a token force consisting of one Persian ship, one gallivat, a dinghy[171] and some *trankis*.[172] The allied force arrived at Bushire in November 1751, but had to lift its siege by December 1751, having been totally ineffective and returned to Bahrain, where they had their families and possessions.[173]

This did not put an end to the fighting for reports reached Bandar 'Abbas in mid-May 1752 that Bushiri and allied forces were attacking and pillaging the coastal settlements as far as Taheri. The Bushire force consisted of two ships, four gallivats and many *trankis* and demanded that Sheikh Hatem and his Hula allies pay an old debt of 100,000 rupees (5,000 *tumans*), in which it was successful. Ricks has suggested that the debt may have been lost income due to Bushire's failure to seize Bahrain from the Hulas in 1751, but this seems highly unlikely, because neither Bushire nor Bandar-e Rig had a prior relationship with Bahrain.[174] This success led to a renewed Bandar-e Rig-Bushire allied attack on Bahrain between the summer of 1752 and the end of 1753 with three ships and three gallivats. This time the attack was successful with little loss for the attackers. The

---

167 Grummond, *The Rise*, pp. 74-75, n. 23; Niebuhr, *Beschreibung*, p. 332.

168 Grummond, *The Rise*, p. 76, n. 27; Floor, "Description," p. 170. For higher estimates see Appendix I.

169 An armed vessel, with sails and oars and small draught of water; it was also used on the West coast of India. The term may be a bastardization of the Portuguese term 'galeota', i.e. galiot or galley.

170 Ricks, *Politics and Trade*, p. 213, referring to FR. Gombroon VI (25/09/1751), p. 30. See also chapter three in this publication.

171 Originally a small rowing boat or skiff, sometimes even a warboat; later often as a utility boat attached to a large vessel. In the Persian Gulf and Mekran Coast it seems to have been a rowing boat of varying size, small and larger, often use for warlike purposes. The word has been derived from the Hindi, *dingi* or *dengi*.

172 A very common large vessel, with sails and oars, used in the Gulf and adjacent sea.

173 Grummond, *The Rise*, p. 76-77, n. 28-29; Amin, *British Interests*, p. 28.

174 Ricks, *Politics and Trade*, p. 221 (FR. Gombroon VI (16/07/1751), p. 111).

Harami Hulas of 'Asalu, who controlled Bahrain, withdrew from the island, probably because the other Hulas, such as those of Taheri were fighting amongst themselves. Once the allies had seized the island, Mir Naser (or his two sons Mir Hoseyn and Mir Mohanna) was able to induce Sheikh Naser to return to Bushire and then held Bahrain for himself; he did not pay Sheikh Naser anything, and was not even "willing to refund the cost he had made for this exploit." This was the cause of the enmity between the chiefs of Bandar-e Rig and Bushire.[175] Sheikh Naser would hold Bahrain until 1783, although his position was attacked by the Ka'b in February 1761 and by the Hulas in September 1767 (see below).

Mir Naser therefore had to keep most of his men on Bahrain to hold the island. Mir Naser's neighbor, Qa'ed Heydar chief of Ganaveh, seeing that Bandar-e Rig was weakly defended attacked the town. Mir Naser had to abandon Bahrain to come to the relief of Bandar-e Rig and thus was able to repel those of Ganaveh just in time. The Haramis of 'Asalu then immediately returned and re-established control over Bahrain, which they held without being challenged for two years. Sheikh Naser of Bushire then approached the 'Otobis of Kuwait to assist him regaining Bahrain, by promising them the right to fish for pearls without having to pay taxes. As most of the 'Otobis were pearl divers this was a great incentive for them to agree to participate in the attack of Bahrain in 1753. Their combined fleet consisted of two ships and two gallivats. The Haramis were supported by other Hulas and Molla 'Ali Shah (with one gallivat) and put up such a fierce defense that during a sortie from the fort the Hulas surrounded 200 Bushiris and killed them all, despite the fact that they had surrendered.

Sheikh Naser being weakened significantly by this loss then focused on splitting the force allied against him. After six months he was able to induce Sheikh Hatem of Taheri (he had held Bahrain prior to those of 'Asalu) to defect and join him in exchange for an annual payment of 14,000 rupees from the revenues of Bahrain. The Haramis of 'Asalu, who thus had lost a major part of their defensive force, surrendered to Sheikh Naser and were allowed to leave the island.

> In this manner the chief of Boucheer became master of Bahrehn, where he has placed one of his brothers with 30 to 40 men, who receive a monthly pay from the islanders. For the rest, the island yields him less than one-quarter of the revenues, which it yielded before that time. [For] the Etoubis did not pay the usual imposts according to the agreement for the[ir] diving, while the Houlas also do not pay anything on account of the claim they pretend to have on the possession of the whole island. So that only the people of Bahrain and Qatif remain from whom he collects these imposts. What is more, the pearl divers both from the Etoubis and the Houlas, who during four months stay within sight of the island and dive, come ashore daily and ruin all tammer [date] bearing trees and gardens which stand near the beach so that their owners get nothing thereof and cannot pay their duties. They [therefore] abandon their land and flee to Catieff, Bassora or [somewhere] en route. Sjeek Nassier is unable to prevent these maraudings, because these are partly done by his allies partly by the Houlas, whom he has to respect. Moreover, he has no force or vessel there which strikes fear into these nations.[176]

175 Floor, "Description," pp. 170-71; Niebuhr, *Beschreibung*, p. 331. Perry states that the sons of Mir Naser overtook Naser and took control, but were soon ousted by the Hulas, when were ousted by Sheikh Naser. Perry, *Karim Khan*, p. 151.

176 Floor, Description," p. 171-72 or chapter one. According to the English, Sheikh Naser carried out a devastating attack on Taheri in 1754. Gombroon Diary 09/05/1754.

THE DUTCH WITHDRAW FROM BUSHIRE

In the year of his triumph, the conquest of Bahrain, Sheikh Naser also suffered a setback, for the Dutch abandoned their factory in Bushire. In 1747, the governor-general of the VOC had decided to separate the Basra factory from the Persia directorate, and to place Bushire under the director of the Basra factory, subject to the approval of the XVII, the managing directors of the VOC.[177] Initially, the XVII were not convinced about the wisdom of the change, for what difference did it make?[178] They finally agreed to the change, although they still were skeptical, and thus formally Bushire became part of the Basra operations.[179] The change made sense in so far that trade in Bushire was directly linked with that of Basra and much less so to that of Bandar 'Abbas. This in fact had been one of the reasons for the establishment of the Bushire factory. If sales could not take place at Bushire the goods might be sent to Basra, or as happened in 1753 to Bandar-e Rig.[180] With the establishment of the Dutch factory on the island of Khark in October 1753, the governor-general also decided to consolidate VOC operations in the head of the Persian Gulf by closing down the factories in Basra and Bushire, much to the chagrin of the local authorities. The VOC Resident at Basra, Tido von Kniphausen, had been declared *persona non grata* by the Ottoman authorities in January 1753, because he was alleged to have interfered in local government affairs as well as to have had relations with Moslem women. After payment of a large sum of money von Kniphausen was released and departed from Basra. En route to Batavia he stopped at Bandar-e Rig, where Mir Naser formally invited the VOC to settle on Khark Island. Given the fact that in 1752 Mir Naser had invited the English to come and establish a factory at Bandar-e Rig, it is likely that a similar invitation had been extended to the Dutch at that time.[181] It is also quite likely that the disagreement with Bushire and the loss of his share in the revenues of Bahrain had caused Mir Naser of Bandar-e Rig to invite the Dutch and English to Khark and Bandar-e Rig. The acceptation by the Dutch was a major coup for him, which greatly antagonized Sheikh Naser of Bushire. Sheikh Naser must have had some idea of what changes might take place in VOC institutional arrangements in the upper Persian Gulf, because first Jan van der Hulst (von Kniphausen's deputy) and then "the rest of the staff of the Dutch Company after the lapse of some months secretly and unexpectedly escaped from Basra."[182] Van der Hulst, who had arrived in Bushire on March 19, 1753, took over as head of the Bushire factory and he knew about von Kniphausen's plan to establish a factory on Khark and to return by the end of 1753 to make that happen.[183]

---

177 VOC 779, f. 200 (24/06/1747)

178 VOC 331, non-foliated (11/10/1749).

179 VOC 332, non-foliated (27/09/1751); VOC 781, f. 226 (15/06/1751).

180 In 1751, Bushire sent Dfl. 28,991 in 22,000 rupees to Bandar 'Abbas. VOC 2787, f. 42 (17/02/1751). In 1753, the VOC Bushire factor was still trying to sell part of cargo of *de Batavia* in Bushire, if not successful he intended to try and do so at Bandar-e Rig. VOC 2843, f. 19 (01/10/1753). Bandar 'Abbas also received Dfl. 45,049 from Bushire in that year. VOC 2843, f. 41 (01/10/1753).

181 For the history of the Dutch factory on Khark and the events in Basra see chapters four and five.

182 Anonymous, *Chronicle*, vol. 1, p. 692; VOC 2843, Gamron to Batavia (01/10/1753), f. 40 (the amount was 4,000 zelottes).

183 VOC 2824, Bushire to Batavia (25/03/1753), f. 71-73 (Bijleveld after having unloaded one-third of the cargo of *de Anna* moved to Bandar 'Abbas. Earlier he had asked permission to move to Basra, but this had been refused by Schoonderwoerd. Goods ordered by Batavia were not available due to the troubles upcountry and the continuous hard winter rains that were still falling at that time); VOC 2824, van de Hulst (Bushire) to Batavia

When von Kniphausen returned to the upper part of the Persian Gulf he called on Bushire in October 1753. He did not yet announce that the Bushire factory was to be closed, but everybody must have felt that there was change in the air. Sheikh Naser, who was an enemy of Mir Naser of Bandar-e Rig, did not like that the Dutch were going to establish themselves on Khark, because he believed that this would hurt the economic interests on Bushire and thus his own interests. Also, he feared that once the Dutch were safely established on Khark that they would cast eyes at Bahrain, which he held at that time. In fact, he as well as the EIC staff strongly believed that the Dutch and Mir Naser were aiming to capture the Persian import trade and planning to jointly take Bahrain.[184] Sheikh Naser therefore sent a courier to the Pasha of Baghdad in secret with the message that Mir Naser would not really assist the Dutch in their action against Basra, while, at the same time, he offered the Pasha his own ships to be used against the Dutch. The Pasha therefore felt encouraged and wrote to Mir Naser that if he provided support to the Dutch and allowed them to stay on Khark he would attack him overland. As soon as the Dutch learnt about Sheikh Naser's secret anti-Dutch activities they decided to discontinue their factory in Bushire. Under protection of two of their ships they moved all their merchandise and took it to Khark. According to the English, the Dutch resident there "destroyed his house and garden at that port before leaving it, but his action seems to have been due to a difference with Shaikh Nasir." However, the latter denied all allegations made by von Kniphausen and asked the Dutch to remain in Bushire. Von Kniphausen refused because of the ill-will that Sheikh Naser bore the VOC, leaving aside the fact that he had orders to close the Bushire factory. Meanwhile, Sheikh Naser denied that he had written to Baghdad and had offered his assistance to the Pasha and begged the Dutch to maintain their factory in Bushire. However, the Dutch refused given his anti-Dutch sentiments and activities. As a result, Sheikh Naser tried to foment trouble for the Dutch by trying to incite the chiefs of the ports on the littoral against the Dutch. He told them that the Dutch were infidels, who, like the Portuguese in the past, wanted to dominate the entire Persian Gulf. His efforts bore no result, however. This was partly due to the fact that the Dutch did their best to maintain friendly relations with these chiefs, partly "due to the strife among the sheikhs and chiefs of the Gulf. There are not two among them (who do not rule over more than 300 men) who agree and live in friendship with one another."[185]

The Dutch then established their factory on Khark Island in November 1753, despite Sheikh Naser's threats. Additional reasons given for their departure were that merchants were continuously subjected to violence and extortion. In Bushire there was no merchant who was allowed to buy merchandise with a value of more than 100 rupees without the permission of Sheikh Naser. As soon as goods were imported into Bushire the Sheikh did not allow merchants to buy these or even to let them come to the Dutch factory before he himself or his agent had inspected the merchandise. He then would offer a price for the goods above which nobody else dared to bid. The merchants therefore were forced to make a deal with Sheikh Naser. The latter would allow Moslem and Armenian merchants to buy between one-third and one-fourth of the goods at the price that he had bought them, while for the remainder they had to pay prices that were 20-30% higher. Finally, Sheikh Naser never paid for the goods that he had 'bought' before he had received payment himself for the same goods that he had resold. Thus, the Sheikh in effect invested no money, but only acted

(25/03/1753), f. 76-77 (asked to be recalled, because he suffered from inflammation of his eyes and feared for the total loss of his eyesight).

184 Grummond, *The Rise*, p. 87, n. 48.

185 VOC 2684 (01/11/1755), f. 8-9; Saldanha, *Précis*, vol. 1, p. 91 (Bombay, 17/10/1754); Niebuhr, *Beschreibung*, p. 332; , Amin, *British Interests*, p. 145; Lorimer, *Gazetteer*, p. 1207.

as an undesirable intermediary, appropriating part of the profit himself.[186] The Dutch also had become disenchanted with Sheikh Naser, because of his demand for an annual fixed payment or guarantee of revenue in return for Dutch imports exempt of custom duties.[187] Moreover, Bushire had failed to produce the expected results because it was not as good a transit port as the Dutch had been hoped. The latter argument was a poor one, because the goods from Khark had to be and were shipped to the Persian mainland through one of the Persian Gulf ports, principally Basra or Bushire.

Thus ended the Dutch presence in Bushire, which had never been a great financial success. Although they had been invited, if not urged to come there, their stay had not always been an easy one. That they had to depart from Bushire, because of the unfriendly and grasping activities by Sheikh Naser, was a sign of the unsettled times in which everybody in the Persian Gulf area had to operate. As is clear from the events discussed in what follows, relations between the Dutch and Sheikh Naser did not remain hostile and only a few years later they would trade again and have friendly relations.[188]

SHEIKH NASER INITIALLY PRO, LATER ANTI MIR MOHANNA

By that time the establishment of the Zand regime in Shiraz in 1753 had started to create some measure of stability in the upper Persia Gulf covering the area of Basra, Bushire and Bandar-e Rig. However, the march of Azad Khan on Shiraz caused panic and anxiety among the coastal chiefs and their people. When he took Shiraz in 1754 the inhabitants of Bushire and Bandar-e Rig fled to Khark with their goods and merchandise as did the Armenians of those parts. The latter already constituted a community of 100 persons on Khark with their own religious. Among them were 10 wealthy merchants who traded with Surat, Bengal and Coromandel. Banyans and Persian merchants also came. Although they wanted to start building houses they could not because of the demand of labor and materials for the construction of the Dutch fort.[189]

In August 1754 the chiefs of Dashtestan decided to oppose Azad Khan with their 10,000 badly armed peasants. According to the Dutch the only obstacle, however, that could stop the Afghans was a very narrow pass where 10 men could stop an army of 1,000 by throwing rocks. By October 1754, Mir Hoseyn and Sheikh Naser of Bushire were already for two months in the mountains awaiting Azad Khan's arrival. However, due to lack of food and pay many of their 'soldiers'

186 VOC 2824, Vertoog van den tegenwoordigen staat der regering en negotie te Bassora en Boucheer, f. 62-63. The Sheiks of Bushire continued with this practice also when the EIC was established there. The same policy also prevailed in Masqat, see Floor, *Persian Gulf*, p. 367.

187 Ricks, *Politics and Trade*, p. 317.

188 In fact, according to an anonymous contemporary source, Sheikh Naser had at first tried to obtain Dutch support to obtain their protection for his possession of Bahrain. The Dutch refusal to help him may have added to their differences. "Le Cheh de Boucher qui dans le commencement de l'entreprise [i.e. the Dutch occupation of Khark] n'avoit rien oublié pour le faire ce honer, met aujourd'huit dans son usage, pour rentre non seulement en amitié avec les Hollandois mais encore pour se procurer leurs protection faisant a cet Effet diverses deputations accompagnés des presents er cela pour l'assurer la possession des Iles de Barin et de Calif [sic; Qatif] qui lui appartienent. Ces deux Iles qui ne sont que depuis deux ans au Cheh de Boucher prevoyant la Chose possible, n'oublie rien de son coté por tacher de mettre dans son partie Msr. Le Baron de Kniphausen devenue le Commandant de Karek." NA, Stadhouderlijke Secretarie, no. 1.29.5, Extrait s'une L'Ettre [sic] de Bassora du 20 aout 1754, not foliated.

189 VOC 2864, Khark to Batavia (01/11/1754), f. 17-18.

returned one by one. Nevertheless, sufficient men had stayed behind, for in October 1754 these local Persian Gulf forces, including those of Bushire and Bandar-e Rig, with 4,000 match-lock men defeated Azad Khan with his 15-17,000 men in the battle of Khisht. Towards the end of November 1754 Mir Hoseyn and Sheikh Naser of Bushire returned home.[190]

Naser had allied himself with Karim Khan because he needed the support from that side to cover his back, if he wanted to maintain his position in the Persian Gulf *vis à vis* other contenders (Hulas, Bani Ka'b, Tangesir Arabs) and keep Bahrain. He further depended on Shiraz as the major market of all goods landed in Bushire as well as his own goods, for he was after all also a merchant.[191] Unfortunately, trade was bad in 1754. This was not only due to Azad Khan's attack of Shiraz, but local troubles, the start of the winter and the rainy season also made that by February 1755 no caravans had yet come to Bushire, Bandar-e Rig or Bandar-e Deylam. Trade at Basra was not much better, where the sugar that the English had imported in 1754 still had remained unsold.[192]

The interlude of battle had not lessened Sheikh Naser's antagonism for Bandar-e Rig and its new chief Mir Hoseyn. This hostility was not only due to the conflict about Bahrain; Bushire also just had lost the presence of the Dutch factory, while Bandar-e Rig had acquired its establishment on Khark and thus felt that it had scored a major success. The arrival of the EIC in Bushire would have offset this loss since not only would it mean the arrival of EIC ships, but also of more private English and other country traders as well as Persian merchants.[193] Sheikh Naser therefore supported Mir Mohanna against his older brother and in his attempt to take over Bandar-e Rig in December 1754. Although initially successful, Mir Mohanna then was defeated by opposing neighboring sheikhs and imprisoned. Talks with the EIC representative Francis Wood in March 1755 at Bushire led to no result, while he, moreover, moved to Bandar-e Rig and established a factory there.[194] A conflict between Bushire and Bandar-e Rig might have broken out for the control of the trade to and fro Shiraz, if the English factory at Bandar-e Rig would actually have functioned. Sheikh Naser had already supported a loose collation of Dashtestan chiefs in April, 1755 to oust Mir Hoseyn from Bandar-e Rig and put Mir Mohanna his place again, knowing full well that the latter had no interest in trade. This attempt failed due to the judicious and targeted handing out of presents by Mir Hoseyn and, as a result, Sheikh Naser and Mir Mohanna had to flee back to Bushire.[195]

But Sheikh Naser need not have worried despite some negative facts. In Bandar-e Rig, Ganaveh and Deylam the local chiefs only levied 3% or less on imports. Although these towns were better situated than Bushire as far as transportation to Shiraz was concerned, Bushire boasted of the presence of a few wealthy Persian merchants. These had a large share in caravans coming from

190 Roschan-Zamir, *Zand-Dynastie*, pp. 32-33; Perry, *Karim Khan*, pp. 58-59; VOC 2864, Khark to Batavia (01/11/1754), f. 17-18; see also chapter three.

191 Grummond, *The Rise*, p. 92.

192 VOC 2864, Khark to Batavia (27/02/1755), f. 38.

193 Grummond, *The Rise*, p. 83, n. 41.

194 On these discussion and subsequent events see chapter four in this publication. Trade had been bad in 1754, because due to the political troubles, winter and rainy season no caravans had come to Bushire, Deylam and Bandar-e Rig for a couple of months, and thus trade had come to a halt. VOC 2864, Khark to Batavia (27/02/1755), f. 38. Another reason for this relationship between Sheikh Naser and Mir Mohanna may be due to that fact, according to Mohammmad 'Ali Sadid al-Saltaneh, *Sarzaminha-ye Shomali-ye Peyramun-e Khalij-e Fars va Darya-ye 'Oman dar sad saleh-ye pish 1324-1332* ed. Ahmad Eqtedari (Tehran, 1371/1992), p. 47, that Sheikh Naser through his mother was related to Mir Mohanna.

195 VOC 2864, Khark to Batavia (31/05/1755), f. 41-43.

upcountry and therefore other Persian merchants were wont to stick to them to get their share of that trade as well.[196] Moreover, the fraternal strife in Bandar-e Rig ending with the murder of Mir Naser and the war in Persia, which led to imprisonment of Mir Mohanna, guaranteed the predominance of Bushire which did its utmost to attract merchants by a welcoming behavior. However, prior to that time Sheikh Naser did not cease to make trouble for the Dutch, and even had wanted to attack Khark. Several times he had prepared vessels that had gone to the outer roads of Bushire, but each time these had to return due to contrary winds. Sheikh Naser finally abandoned that plan after he had seen the effective help that the Dutch had given to Mir Hoseyn of Bandar-e Rig. It did not mean that he also abandoned his hostile acticivities against the Dutch, because he also allegedly tried to have von Kniphausen murdered. The Dutch used a request for a physician by Karim Khan in September 1755 as an opportunity to complain about Sheikh Naser's behavior, who publicly stated that he had raised the duties on Dutch goods to 10% to force merchants not to buy anything at Khark. The Dutch received assurances from Karim Khan that he would try to correct this situation and if not, he wrote, that they were allowed to take steps themselves to make Sheikh Naser see sense. Shortly thereafter, the two sides made up, so that as of 1756 the Dutch marketed most of their goods through Bushire.[197]

Despite these hard facts, Sheikh Naser certainly would have tried later to launch a new attack on Bandar-e Rig. However, fate intervened. The conflict about the chieftainship of Bandar-e Rig and Bushire's role therein was put on a back-burner, because Karim Khan once again summoned the chiefs of Dashtestan and their troops to Isfahan in September 1755. Once the Dashtestan troops had arrived in Isfahan, they, after two months or so, started to complain, because of the long duration of their service and the bitter cold of the winter to which they were not accustomed. Their service there was made even less attractive by the unsatisfactory compensation they received from the cash-strapped Karim Khan. Probably around February 1756 they demanded to be released, which Karim Khan refused, because they constituted the bulk of his force at Isfahan, while his major rival Mohammad Hasan Qajar was expected to attack him soon. The two parties were brought at loggerheads when shortly thereafter messengers from Shah Esma'il III arrived in Isfahan making public that Karim Khan had to evacuate Isfahan and return to Shiraz, where, if he accepted Esma'il III as his sovereign, he would be made *beygler-beygi* of Fars, but if he refused then no favor would be shown to him or his supporters. "Which terms being made publick all the Arabs in general and the people of Destastoon (not thro' Loyalty but fear) declared for Isshmael Shaw." This public outcry led to a four-day mutiny - the Dashtestani troops took up positions in the Bidabad, 'Abasabad and Bagh-e Jannat quarters of Isfahan - which Karim Khan had to suppress by using armed force. However, although the two sides settled the conflict and Karim Khan granted a general pardon, he could not rely on the Arab troops anymore as he found out when he faced Mohammad Hasan Khan Qajar at Golnabad. The Dashtestani riflemen refused to fight and as a result Karim Khan was defeated. "Careem Caun Zand finding himself thus deserted by the only people he depended upon, left the City with about eight hundred veteran Soldiers" in March 1756, and returned to Shiraz bent on revenge of the coastal Arabs. However, for the time being he had to wait what his rival Mohammad Hasan Khan Qajar would do in Isfahan, who entered that city on April 1, 1756. The latter "was so far from treating the Arabs as they expected, that he suffered his soldiers to strip and plunder them of all they had, Shaik Nassier of Busshier remains in prison, the Caun having insisted on his rendering account of the Kings Ships and paying also 5,000 Tomaaunds for the last three year's revenues of

196 VOC 2885, Khark to Batavia (27/09/1755), f. 5-7.

197 VOC 2864, Khark to Batavia (31/05/1755), f. 44; VOC 2885, Khark to Batavia (27/09/1755), f. 6; VOC 2885, Khark to Batavia (09/12/1755), f. 11; Grummond, *The Rise*, pp. 89-90. See also chapter four.

Bahreen, but Meer Hossain and his Brother Manna in Consideration of their known poverty were permitted to return."[198]

Three Dashtestan leaders, amongst whom Sheikh Naser, were imprisoned for one year in Isfahan, while the rest were let go. Bushire also suffered because all merchants abandoned the town when the news of Sheikh Naser's imprisonment was received. The merchants feared that they would have to pay his ransom and therefore left, some of whom settled on Khark with their families. One of the latter was a very wealthy merchant, Aqa Ebrahim, who was reputed to possess five lakh of rupees.[199] Due to these set-backs, Sheikh Naser's forces were so weakened that he was less able to protect the island of Bahrain or to maintain his fleet properly. The fleet that he had 'inherited' from Nader Shah was in total disrepair except for one ship, and its armament was lying about. He lacked both men and supplies to make use of them. In 1756, Bushire was not able to organize "even 12 vessels and 70 able-bodied seafaring men anymore. The town is passably filled with Persian merchants, retailers and craftsmen, although none of them are able-bodied and even less fit to be used at sea."[200] This weakness of Bushire became very clear when Mir Mohanna began his attacks on caravans after July 1756 with the result that trade suffered, including that of Bushire. The general decline of the economic welfare of Bandar-e Rig after 1754 had driven Mir Mohanna to piracy and brigandage, a path from which he would not return.

The decline of Bandar-e Rig and Bushire resulted in increased commercial activity in the ports of Deylam and Ganaveh. The chiefs of these two ports exerted themselves to attract merchants and their caravans to come and trade. They also induced the VOC to sell its goods there and showed the Dutch much friendship. When on April 19, 1756 two sailors arrived there, who were deserters, the chief of Deylam detained them and handed them over to the Dutch on condition that they would not be punished. Von Kniphausen, therefore, sent them to Batavia in irons to be judged there. Similarly at Ganaveh, where in the night of May 4, 1756 four soldiers had gone in a stolen native gallivat found no welcome. Its chief arrested the men, handed them and the gallivat over to the Dutch without any condition of pardon.[201]

The financial contribution that Karim Khan imposed on the disobedient chiefs of the littoral in 1756-57 as well as their long imprisonment did not much to improve the situation, of course. It was only in September 1756 that Karim Khan was able give his attention to the coastal areas and then he stayed there for seven months to collect revenues, tribute, promises of loyalty and hostages. They revolted in October and only gave in after having been defeated and forced to do so by 'Ali Khan Shahsevan in December. All coastal chiefs had to pay contribution and supply troops in accordance with their fiscal assessment.[202] On January 11, 1757 somebody from Taheri arrived in Bandar 'Abbas reporting that Karim Khan had imposed the following taxes: on Sheikh Hajar of Kangan 4,000 *tuman*s and 400

---

198 Saldanha, *Précis*, vol. 1, p. 100 (Rig, 03/05/1756); VOC 2885, Khark to Batavia (05/08/1756), f. 8-11; Perry, *Karim Khan*, pp. 62-63, 65; Roschan-Zamir, *Zand-Dynastie*, pp. 35-36.

199 VOC 2885, Khark to Batavia (05/08/1756), f. 10, 20-21; VOC 2885, Gamron to Batavia (08/09/1756), f. 3.

200 Floor, "Description," p. 172.

201 VOC 2885, Khark to Batavia (05/08/1756), f. 22-23. Von Kniphausen was worried about this spate of desertions within one month and to prevent further desertions he constituted a military court with the captain-lieutenant and lieutenant of Khark's garrison. Soldier Johannes Bloon, who was the instigator of the desertion and the theft of the vessel as well as a recidivist was sentenced to be shot, the others were sentenced to unspecified military punishments. Ibid., f. 24.

202 Ricks, *Politics and Trade*, pp. 258-61 referring to F. R. Gombroon VIII (13/01/1756); Perry, *Karim Khan*, pp. 119-20; Fasa'i, *Fasrnameh*, vol. 1, pp. 597-98.

soldiers; Sheikh Alaq of Nakhilu 6,000 *tumans* and 600 soldiers; Sheikh Hatem of Taheri 8,000 *tumans* and 800 soldiers. In return the chiefs received Zand protection and confirmation of their government and the right to agricultural taxes and customs revenues. Sheikh Naser of Bushire had to pay 3,000 *tumans* to retain his post of *shahbandar*, governor and the title and function of deputy admiral to Molla 'Ali Shah. The coastal population complained about this imposition in vain. By April 1757 the Zand army had left the Bandar-e Rig area (Deh Kohneh), but not before imposing 1,000 *tumans* on Bandar-e Rig and 3,000 on Bushire and appointing Mir Mohammad in place of Mir Mohanna. Karim Khan then marched on the Ka'b to resolve that issue.[203]

Karim Khan also talked about attacking Bushire and other coastal towns to punish them for some infraction, but instead he went to Yazd. However, the road to Shiraz and Isfahan was closed for seven to eight months due to the hostilities between Mohammad Hasan Khan Qajar and Karim Khan during the end of 1757 and the beginning of 1758 so that there was no trade. Mir Mohanna remained under arrest from which he was released in July 1758 at the intercession of one of Karim Khan's influential officers, Mohammad Beyg, the chief of Khormuj, who had married Mir Mohanna's sister. On the promise of the payment of a sum of money Mir Mohanna was released and also reinstated as chief of Bandar-e Rig. On his return Mir Mohanna killed his half-brother, Mir 'Ali and two cousins. He also made friendly overtures to the Dutch, who responded positively and also remained friendly towards him.[204]

Because Mir Mohanna's attacks, including on neighboring chiefs, increased Sheikh Naser of Bushire together with other Dashtestani chiefs joined forces in August 1760 to attack Bandar-e Rig. However, dissension among them led to abandonment of the planned attack. Nevertheless, Mir Mohanna was now in trouble with all his neighbors and therefore remained close to Bandar-e Rig.[205] This war also had its impact on other parts of the Persian Gulf. Mir Mohanna continued his marauding and seized a caravan with a value of 20,000 rupees. Having become rich he became bolder and effectively stopped trade between Bushire and Shiraz and defeated the chief of Deylam. Sheikh Sa'dun of Bushire could not interfere, because war had broken out between him and Sheikh Salman of the Bani Ka'b.[206]

---

203 Ricks, *Politics and Trade*, pp. 263-64 referring to F. R. Gombroon IX (11/01/1757; 07/02/1757; 25/02/1757; 04/04/1757 and 26/04/1757).

204 VOC 2968, Khark to Batavia (15/11/1758), f. 16-18 (von Kniphausen sent a present to Karim Khan with a value of Dfl. 1,745); VOC 2968, Khark to Batavia (18/05/1758), f. 23; Perry, "Mir Muhanna," p. 89; Ricks, *Politics and Trade*, p. 260; Grummond, *The Rise*, p. 93.

205 VOC 3027, Khark to Batavia (01/10/1760), f. 3-4.

206 VOC 3064, Khark to Batavia (30/09/1761), f. 26-28. Given the enmity between Sheikh Naser and Mir Mohanna and the latter's piratical activities against Bushiri merchants it is interesting to read that there was a lote tree (*sadr, konar*) in Bushire, known as *konar-e Mohanna*, which allegedly was the place where Mir Mohanna gathered his troops. The people of Bushire, who as we have seen had suffered much at his hands, allegedly considered this a holy site. Given the reality (Mir Mohanna never had an army camp in Bushire), it is more likely that the tree was known for another and kinder Mir Mohanna. Sayyed Ja'far Hamidi, *Nahzat-e Abu Sa'id Ganaveh'i* (Tehran, 1360/1981), pp. 132-33; Ya Hoseyni, *Mir Mohanna*, pp. 145-46. A possible candidate for the other Mir Mohanna is Mir Mohanna-ye Musavi-ye Emamzadeh'i, who died in the early Qajar period, and was a scion of a prominent family of sayyeds in Bushire. Faqih, *Zaval*, pp. 17-18.

THE KA'B AT WAR WITH ALL THEIR NEIGHBORS

The Ka'b are an Arab tribe that had moved from the area at the confluence of the Tigris and Euphrates towards Qobban in the sixteenth century and by the end of Nader Shah's reign they also had taken over southern Khuzestan, where Dowraq, became their capital. Although in the past the Ka'b had paid taxes to both Ottoman and Persian authorities they stopped doing so by the mid-eighteenth century, if not earlier. It was this 'oversight' that induced Karim Khan Zand to try and get tribute from Shaikh Salman, like he had done to other similar sheikhdoms in southern Fars (see chapter four). He had won the succession war that had erupted after Nader Shah's death, and he aimed to make all previous Safavid territories subject and tributary again to his central government based in Shiraz. In 1757, Karim Khan therefore invaded the territory of the Ka'b. The latter vacated their fort at Dowraq and flooded their land. Karim Khan, having been held up there for three months and not having been able to cross the canals, then had to cope with an outbreak of plague in his army. He beat a hasty retreat leaving his artillery behind, now acquired by the Ka'b.[207] This attack also triggered a more outward looking if not expansion policy by Sheikh Salman or Soleyman, the paramount chief of the Ka'b.

Apart from disobedience to their overlords (the Ka'b lived on lands claimed by both the Ottomans and the Zands) and petty robberies at sea and land against travelers, the Ka'b with four gallivats had in vain tried to take Bahrain in February 1761. Except for some vessels that they had seized they returned empty-handed. Sheikh Sa'dun of Bushire, who governed Bahrain, with the help of his allies the 'Otobis of Kuwait, in retaliation attacked Ka'b territory with one ship, three gallivats and 30 other vessels. While this force was blockading the Shatt al-Arab four of Sheikh Salman's gallivats left the estuary via another passageway and attacked Bushire. They set fire to two ships that were lying in the roadstead and seized a few others. They then returned to their home base without encountering any opposition. Thus, Sheikh Salman was able to bring the war to a stalemate, so that 'Ali Aqa, the *motasallem* of Basra, wanted to make peace between the warring parties. Sheikh Salman sent back a haughty reply, which angered the *motasallem* to such an extent that he declared himself for Sheikh Sa'dun. When Soleyman Pasha ordered 'Ali Aqa to collect taxes from the Ka'b he marched with a large army overland via Qobban to Dowraq and finally besieged Sheikh Salman in his capital by the end of July 1761. 'Ali Aqa also had asked the EIC agent Douglas to assist his 14 *trankis* with the *Swallow* to which he agreed. However, when the ship arrived at Dowraq the Ottoman forces were withdrawing on September 30, 1761, having been bought off with presents to Soleyman Pasha, "when his fort was near falling into the hands of Ali Aga, the General of the Turkish Army" and thus the *Swallow* also returned to Basra.[208]

This war also had consequences for other parts of the Persian Gulf. Mir Mohanna had begun his marauding after Sam Khan had lifted the siege of Bandar-e Rig on May 21, 1761. Since that time he had not only forced Qa'ed Heydar from Ganaveh, but he also had plundered two rich caravans on the Bushire-Shiraz route, which carried merchandise with a value of 20,000 rupees. As a result of this success Mir Mohanna had become a rich man and he could reinforce himself. His marauding increased in frequency and went further away so that during the summer of 1761 no caravans plied between Bushire and Shiraz. This would have a negative impact on trade if this

---

207 Willem Floor, "The Rise and Fall of the Banu Ka'b," *IRAN* 2006, pp. 278-315.

208 VOC 3027, Khark to Batavia (22/06/1761), f. 4-5; VOC 3064, Khark to Batavia (30/09/1761), f. 25-26; VOC 3062, Khark to Batavia (01/10/1761), f. 31 (Sheikh Soleyman kept the best of his lands and goods as the result of his peace agreement); Saldanha, *Précis*, vol. 1, pp. 215-16 (Basra, 09/04/1767); John Perry, "The Banu Ka'b: an amphibious state in Khuzistan," *Le Monde iranien et l'Islam* 1 (1971), pp. 136-37; Floor, "The Rise," p. 283.

was allowed to continue. Sheik Sa'dun of Bushire was unable to protect the roads to Bushire alone, because of his war with the Banu Ka'b. The leading chiefs of Dashtestan did not interfere and allowed Mir Mohanna to continue with his marauding unimpeded. Karim Khan did not act either, despite rumors that he would send an army, and therefore Mir Mohanna took heart. Although so far he had kept his gallivats at Bandar-e Rig, he now tried to see how far he could go. In September 1761 he sent a few of his smaller vessels out on the sea, which took two unarmed ships from Bushire. Another of Mir Mohanna's successes was his defeat of the chief of Deylam, who for some time at the request of Sheikh Salman of the Banu Ka'b had sought refuge on Khark.[209] Despite the conflict with the Ka'b, Bushire kept a close watch at the doings of Mir Mohanna. As soon as Sheikh Sa'dun had learnt about Mir Mohanna's attack against the Dutch on Khark in March 1762 he, without having even been asked for his assistance, sent a fleet of 10 vessels and 350 men under command of his brother, Sheikh Gheyth to Khark, where they arrived on April 6. Qa'ed Heydar of Ganaveh with 100 men and Sheikh 'Ali b. Hoseyn of Charak with 50 sailors, both enemies of Mir Mohanna, accompanied the relief force, which later was joined by Sheikh Sa'dun himself in a well-accoutered ship to give the final blow to Mir Mohanna together with the Dutch. The Bushire force left in May 1762, having received Dfl. 37,733 for the Bushire force plus presents for Sheikh Sa'dun.[210]

In May 1762 Sheikh Salman had taken advantage of the situation in Basra caused by the death of Soleyman Pasha of Baghdad by blockading the Shatt al-Arab under the pretext that he wanted to protect the merchants who wanted to go to Basra. In reality, he wanted to become independent and to draw the Basra trade to Qobban and Dowraq, in his own territory. The EIC reported that "Shaik Suliman has blocked up Bussorah River with his Gallivats, declaring he would let no Boats go up or down." The obsolete and immobile Ottoman galleys were out of their league and unable to stop the Ka'b interference with trade. To cover his back, Sheikh Salman asked the Dutch to send him somebody to intercede with Sheikh Sa'dun to make peace with him. Because of Sheikh Salman's influence, the Dutch sent senior assistant Tam to Qobban, who was able to bring this about and also went to Bushire to finalize the peace negotiations between the two parties. Trade resumed again, because until then no Bushiri vessels had dared to go to Basra.[211] Sheikh Sa'dun was only too happy to make peace with Sheikh Salman, because he was under great pressure by the marauding of Mir Mohanna. The peace agreement had barely been concluded, when in February-March 1673 Mir Mohanna attacked Bushire three times, but he failed to take Bushire, which bolstered Sheikh Sa'dun's position.[212] It was at that time that the EIC decided to establish a factory at Bushire.

---

209 VOC 3064, Khark to Batavia (30/09/1761), f. 26-28.

210 VOC 3093, Khark to Batavia (21/08/1762), f. 59-64; VOC 3092, Khark to Batavia (19/10/1762), f. 14-15.

211 VOC 3092, Khark to Batavia (19/10/1762), f. 38-54; Perry, "The Banu Ka'b," pp. 131-52; Lorimer, *Gazetteer*, pp. 1217-18. Sheikh Salman had blocked the Basra River with his gallivats, "declaring that he would let no Boats go up or down." Saldanha, *Précis*, vol. 1, p. 156 (Bombay, 02/09/1762). 'Ali Pasha also asked Sheikh Salman to obey the Soltan's rule and although he withdrew his gallivats from the Shatt al-Arab, they still sailed into the Gulf itself, but allowing vessels from Khark and Bushire to proceed to Basra unhindered. VOC 3092, Khark to Batavia (19/10/1762), f. 38-42; see also chapter four.

212 See chapter four in this publication on these events.

THE EIC MOVES TO BUSHIRE

The English had started to look for an alternative to Bandar 'Abbas already in 1750, but despite several proposals, which all were rejected by Bombay and London, the English remained at Bandar 'Abbas. It was only in 1760, due to the perceived Dutch success at Khark, the growing insecurity and oppression in Bandar 'Abbas and hence sharply falling trade results, and the capture and destruction of the British factory at Bandar 'Abbas by the French in 1759 that made the EIC abandon that port.[213] Looking for other ports meant that the English had to find a new entrepot with good security, low cost, etc. for the Europeans knew well that Persian Gulf was one market area. Douglas, the EIC Agent at Bandar 'Abbas, was instructed to sail in 1761 to Basra and to review all the islands on his way as to the suitability for an English factory. On his return journey Douglas did not visit Bandar-e Rig, which was no real alternative port because there were no merchants there. He called on Bushire, however, where he had a discussion with Sheikh Naser at the latter's invitation. The proximity of Shiraz, the new center of power in Persia, made Bushire a better choice for trade than Bandar 'Abbas, because it was closer. To make sure that the EIC was aware of his interest Sheikh Naser gave Douglas a letter for Bombay formally inviting the EIC to establish a factory in Bushire. In his letter to the EIC, Sheikh Naser referred to an earlier invitation he had sent and to which he had received no reply. He hoped that the EIC would establish a factory at Bushire, for its goods and that of its servants "shall be exempt from paying Customs." Sheikh Naser pointed out that all roads to Persia led through Bushire and that merchants from all over came there to trade. Moreover, "Bushire is in entire security, quiet and flourishing, and the roads for the Caravans are quite free from molestation."[214] The EIC Agent reported on 13/02/1761 that between Basra and Bushire there was no place where inland trade was carried on except at Bushire at that the nearby islands were all uninhabited except for Quish [Kish] and Bussel [sic; ?]. However, he did not make a recommendation to move to Bushire. It was only in early 1762, after having been prodded by Bombay, that he proposed that a trial voyage should be made to Bushire.[215]

Douglas argued that to settle on any of the barren islands required naval assistance, which was costly. Bushire was a secure place under Sheikh Naser, who acknowledged Zand rule and therefore favored trade. Moreover, "That as three parts of the Town was surrounded by water & that towards the land with a wall & mounted with good cannon he thought the expenses could not be great." It was full of merchants, who seemed to enjoy complete liberty of trade. "The Agent mentioned one conveniency attending Bushire, that a Person there need have no connections or caress any one but the Shaikh himself." According to Douglas, he had an excellent character and wanted the EIC to settle there to which end he had written an invitation letter.[216] The Agent therefore proposed to send one person with a small lot of goods to make a trial of the market. Bombay decided to have the Agent himself or another leading staffer assess the prospect of the Bushire market to determine whether to settle there. The council at Bandar 'Abbas, however, tended to prefer to send a vessel there occasionally rather than have a fixed residence.[217] One year later Sheikh Naser again wrote a letter to the EIC at Bandar 'Abbas reminding the Agent that Bombay had written him

213 For these earlier proposals and the decision to abandon Bandar 'Abbas see chapter three in this publication.

214 Saldanha, *Précis*, vol. 1, p. 153 (Sheikh Naser's letter is dated 11 Rabi II 1175 or 09/11/1671). For Douglas's mission objectives see Ibid., vol. 1, p. 144 (Bombay, 01/05/1761).

215 Saldanha, *Précis*, vol. 1, p. 154 (Bombay, 05/05/1762).

216 Saldanha, *Précis*, vol. 1, p. 151 (Bombay, 30/01/1762); Lorimer, *Gazetteer*, p. 93; Niebuhr, *Reisebeschreibung*, p. 505 (the wall was in bad shape and had some towers).

217 Saldanha, *Précis*, vol. 1, p. 151 (Bombay, 30/01/1762), 152 (Bombay, 01/02/1762).

that he would come to discuss terms of settling here, but that this was a long time ago. He also reminded the Agent that he had written Bombay that all goods would be exempt from Customs.[218] Nevertheless, Bushire was not put forward as the alternative to Bandar 'Abbas due to the dislike the EIC had taken to Persia. In April 1762 the EIC decided to move its entire Persian operation from Bandar 'Abbas to Basra, a decision that was carried out in February/March 1763.[219]

TRADE AGREEMENT BETWEEN THE EIC AND KARIM KHAN

To audit the activities at its factory at Basra, Bombay had appointed William Andrew Price as "Provisional Agent of Persia" in January 1763. Because sales of English woolens had risen considerably in the upper Persian Gulf and in particular at Bushire, which gave rise to the fear that the Dutch might start trading in that commodity again, Bombay also instructed Price to call on Bushire en route from Bombay to Basra. Another consideration was that about half of the trade at Basra was re-exported to the Persian market and it was therefore considered of commercial interest to keep an EIC foot in the Persian market. This, moreover, had the additional advantage that the EIC could maintain the right to its privileges in Persia. Finally, Sheikh Naser of Bushire had already invited EIC by letter in 1761 and in 1762 promising every desirable privileges and encouragement if the EIC would open a factory there.[220]

Price did not know that the EIC factory at Bandar 'Abbas had already been abandoned in March 1763 and thus called on that town on March 24, 1763. "His vessel fired several Guns, and burnt a number of blue Lights," but no boats came to his ship the *Tartar*. The next morning he rightly assumed that the factory had been abandoned and he therefore raised the Dutch ensign and fired a gun. Then people came from the port and he learnt from a servant of the EIC factory that the English had abandoned and burnt their factory and had pillaged the town and then had left for Basra. Price declined the friendly invitation from the Persian governor to come ashore and sailed to Qeshm. There, to his great surprise, Molla 'Ali Shah provided him with a pilot and sent him some fowls and almonds as a present.[221]

Price reached Bushire on April 7, 1763 to arrange for the establishment of a factory "in order more particularly to introduce the vend of Woollen Goods into the Kingdom of Persia." A son of Sheikh Sa'dun who was in charge of the town during his father's absence and that of his father's brother Sheikh Naser, visited him on board and invited him ashore on April 17, 1763. He discussed with Price the conditions of EIC trade at Bushire, which led to negotiations. The son of Sheikh Sa'dun had a major problem with the EIC demand that only it would be allowed to sell woolens in Bushire. He allowed the EIC, however, to confiscate any woolens that were brought clandestinely to Bushire. To ensure Sheikh Sa'dun's agreement who was at some distance from Bushire at that time the linguist Stephen Hermit was sent to talk to him and an agreement was reached on April 12, 1763. As a result the EIC was allowed to trade at Bushire exempt from customs duties.

218 Saldanha, *Précis*, vol. 1, p. 157 (received at Bandar 'Abbas on 09/09/1762); see also Ibid., vol. 1, p. 156-57 (Bombay, 26/10/1762).

219 Saldanha, *Précis*, vol. 1, pp. 162-63 (Bombay, 22/01/1763); Amin, *British Interests*, pp. 49-50; The Agent's intention to withdraw from Bandar 'Abbas had already been approved in 1761. Saldanha, *Précis*, vol. 1, p. 150 (Bombay, 03/11/1761). For details about the implementation of this decision see chapter three.

220 Amin, *British Interests*, p. 71. For an extract of Price's instructions, which make no reference to Bushire, see Saldanha, *Précis*, vol. 1, pp. 162-64 (Bombay, 22/01/1763), but see Ibid., vol. 1, p. 165 (Bombay, 20/04/1763).

221 Saldanha, *Précis*, vol. 1, p. 165 (Extract Journal of Andrew Price, 24 and 25/03/1763); Lorimer, *Gazetteer*, p. 1779.

Furthermore, the Company was allowed to levy a duty of 3% on all imports and exports on those trading under EIC protection. Art. 9 of the agreement with Sheikh Sa'dun stated when Bushire merchants bought goods from EIC protected persons they had to pay the EIC factory to which end a representative "is to attend at the weight and delivery of all goods so sold.' Art. 11 stipulated that none of the sheikh's subjects were to buy goods from English vessels. Although Price had instructions that the EIC resident also had to levy consulage of 1%, he decided to drop this demand as being impractical for the moment. It was further agreed that the EIC would give the Sheikh of Bushire a list of all goods sold to merchants so that he might levy customs from them.[222] On April 22, 1763 Price, before he sailed to Basra, appointed B. Jervis, who was with him on the *Tartar*, to be the first EIC Resident at Bushire. Jervis had 1 artillery officer, 7 soldiers and artillery people for the protection of the factory as well as a *sarraf* or money changer, because he would be paid in different coins. Jervis had instructions to discourage the Dutch at Khark from selling woolens, e.g. by selling a large quantity at low profit.[223]

Price reported that Bushire was 14 days from Shiraz and 30 from Isfahan and that entire stretch of country was under the secure control of Karim Khan Zand and thus extremely well situated for the sale of woolens. The people of Bushire were different from most in the Persian Gulf, "being of a mercantile turn and have several vessels of their own and as the Shaik has two ships two Gallivats and some Trankies" the risk of oppression was considered low. Also landing woolens in Bushire would have an upward pressure on sales in Basra. Price opined that for loading and unloading *trankis* were no good, in particular in bad weather. He therefore suggested to make available "a vessel of about 100 tons Burthen with a deck and Pique sail like the Dutch luggege [sic] Boats at Surat" and to put 8-10 carriage guns on it for protection in case of transport of surplus cash.[224]

Price, who only later realized that Sheikh Sa'dun was subordinate to Sadeq Khan, brother of Karim Khan and governor of Shiraz, therefore instructed Jervis to get the former's confirmation of the recently obtained privileges, so that they would have validity not only at Bushire. Jervis sent his linguist Stephen Hermit accompanied by Lt. Durnford to that end to Shiraz who returned on August 1, 1763. Sadeq Khan had confirmed the privileges.[225] Soon thereafter via a letter from

222 Saldanha, *Précis*, vol. 1, pp. 165-67 (Bushire, 20/04/1763); Ibid., vol. 1, pp. 167-69 (Bushire, 22/04/1763); Lorimer, *Gazetteer*, p. 1779. For the text of the agreement see C. U. Aitchison, *A Collections of treaties, engagements and sanads relating to India and neighbouring countries*, 4th ed. vol. XII, pp. 33-34 and Appendix III. The Dutch were upset by the establishment of this new factory, which they believed to be disadvantageous for their Khark operation. They also reported that the new agreement was just a confirmation of the one already agreed upon one year earlier. VOC 3123, Khark to Batavia (08/05/1763), f. 6-7. The demand for consulage may have been brought about by the fact that the English ambassador at Istanbul had obtained consular *barat* for the EIC Agent at Basra. Saldanha, *Précis*, vol. 1, pp. 180-82 (Constantinople, 09/1764). This new situation also meant that EIC could demand consulage against which the pasha of Baghdad opposed himself having been paid by merchants to do so. The EIC argued that the consulage was beneficial for merchants as their goods were protected en route and not any longer exposed to chicaneries at the "shahbandari in the Gomrok." Henceforth they would be landed the EIC's Lathy, cleared upon sale without any charge but the 2% consulage and trade would be freer. The EIC would pay the government of Basra the 7% duties it was entitled to. Ibid., *Précis*, vol. 1, p. 186 (Basra, 31/03/1765).

223 Saldanha, *Précis*, vol. 1, p. 166 (Bushire, 20/04/1763). According to Niebuhr, *Reisebeschreibung*, p. 506, Jervis had devoted his life to science in his youth and continued to do so in his leisure time. He spoke Persian and also read and wrote it rather well; he also collected Persian manuscripts. Niebuhr also remarked that there were two Carmelite monks at Bushire, one of which styled himself as the bishop of Isfahan. The Carmelites had re-established themselves at Bushire in 1764. Anonymous, *Chronicle*, vol. 1, pp. 663, 695.

224 Saldanha, *Précis*, vol. 1, p. 169 (Bushire, 20/04/1763).

225 Saldanha, *Précis*, vol. 1, p. 172 (n. p.; n. d. [Bushire, September 1763?]); Ibid., vol. 1, pp. 171-72 (Bushire, 17/08/1763). In Basra the situation was once again in turmoil. The Bedouins had cut all communications with

Bushire dated August 27, 1764 it was reported that Karim Khan the real power in Persia had confirmed his brother's grant. In fact the monopoly for woolen goods was even extended to all Persian ports.[226]

The EIC was allowed to build a factory and any number of related ordinary houses at Bushire or at any other port on the Persian coast with as many guns as it wanted, but not larger than 6 lbs. EIC trade was exempt of all import, export and inland duties at Bushire and other ports. The Sheikh of Bushire as chiefs of other Persian ports would not charge more than 3% export duty on English goods bought by Persian merchants. The EIC was granted the monopoly of import of woolens into Persia, excluding all other nations. Governors had to assist the EIC in recovering lawful debts in Persia, failing that the EIC was authorized to take its own measures realize the same. EIC trade was free and unhindered throughout Persia. Native merchants were not allowed to purchase goods from English ships at any Persian port without prior permission from the EIC chief. English vessels that were wrecked or stranded should be salvaged free-of-charge by the local authorities. The English and those under their protection enjoyed freedom of religion throughout the kingdom. Deserters, soldiers and slaves, were to be handed over by the Persian authorities on condition that they would not be punished for the first two offenses. The linguist, broker and other EIC servants were free of Persian taxation and under EIC jurisdiction. A plot of land would be assigned as burial place, and that if the EIC wanted a garden a piece of royal land would be gratis assigned to it or it might be rented at a fair price, in case of private property. The former EIC house and garden at Shiraz would be restored to the EIC. In return the EIC was required not to support or protect enemies of the Persian ruler, not ask for cash but mainly barter for Persian goods, for which reasonable prices had to be paid, as well as to sell mainly to certain principal Persian merchants and men of credit, which London did not like, because it gave Persian merchants also a kind of monopolistic position *vis à vis* the EIC. The EIC furthermore had to treat Moslems well, should not harbor rebels, but hand them over on the understanding that these would not be punished for the first two offenses. Finally, the EIC should not support enemies of the shah of Persia.[227]

The EIC thus was exempt from all import and export duties. However, Amin is wrong to interpret the phrasing that the export duty charged at Bushire should not be higher than 3% that this percentage also included the inland duties. This is what English may have wanted to believe, based on their experience in India, but this was neither meant nor even possible yet in the Persian context. Given the fact that the inland duties were farmed out to different tax officials these would have to agree with it, while it would even be possible that the inland duties would have been higher than 3% on arrival in Bushire. In that case, following Amin's argument the EIC could have asked for a refund of any amount higher than the 3% export duty. This, of course, did not happen and the

Baghdad and Shushtar due to a conflict with the Pasha of Baghdad. In the lower Gulf conditions also were in uproar due to a rebellion that had broken out against the Imam of Masqat. VOC 3123, Khark to Batavia (08/05/1763), f. 8. Risso, *Oman & Muscat*, pp. 45-46.

226 Saldanha, *Précis*, vol. 1, pp. 171-72 (Bushire, 17/08/1763); Ibid., vol. 1, p. 178 (Bombay, 08/10/1764); Saldanha, *Précis*, vol. 1, p. 178 (Bombay, 08/10/1764). For the text of the grant made by Karim Khan see Aitchison, *Collection*, vol. X, p. 33 and Appendix III.

227 For the text see Aitchison, *Treaties*, 4th ed. Vol. XII, pp. 34-36 and Appendix III; for a summary see Lorimer, *Gazetteer*, pp. 1780-81. Amin, *British Interests*, p. 75. As to art. 6 Bombay said they preferred free trade rather than forcing merchants to trade only with sheikh; the same for art. 1, which it considered unnecessary; also it did not meant to have any limitations as to whom they could sell. Saldanha, *Précis*, vol. 1, p. 174 (Bombay, 24/01/1764).

EIC did not even raise the issue.[228] Amin also assigns too much importance to Karim Khan's grant. Apart from the fact that rights within the Persian context were not always respected by the same person who had granted them there is also the fact that the reality in the Persian Gulf was a bit different than Amin implies. He, for example, rightly states that the monopolistic character of the agreement was something totally new, but it was not "successfully implemented" as he stated. His proof for this success is that he claims that between 1763-69, when the EIC withdrew from Bushire, only English woolens were sold. However, already prior to 1763 no other woolens but English ones were sold in the Persian Gulf. The Dutch had stopped selling woolens as of 1755 and the French, if they had sold them at all, did so in such small quantities that there is no trace of them in the published sources.[229]

KARIM KHAN WANTS ENGLISH NAVAL SUPPORT

During his meeting with Hermit and Durnford, Sadeq Khan the governor of Shiraz, had made it clear that Karim Khan needed naval support to deal with the maraudings of Mir Mohanna. He therefore had asked for naval assistance, in particular, for a guard-ship to be stationed there permanently for which he would pay 22,000 Rs/year via an assignment on the customs revenues.[230] When Price forwarded the newly obtained treaty he had therefore added: "Nothing now remains to secure our trade on a solid footing but the reduction of Meer Mahanna, Governor of Bandareek, who having it in his power to stop the caravans, coming from Shyrash or at least greatly intimidate them. The Persian, some months ago, sent an army against him the Shaikh of Bushire ordered to join them but as it's said he has private intelligence with Meer Mahanna who having also his port open the Persians have hitherto been able to do little of consequence."[231] In response to Sadeq Khan's request for naval support Price instructed Jervis to inform Sadeq Khan that EIC vessels were not of the right build and capacity to operate against Bandar-e Rig. Because he did not want to sound too negative after having received such a favorable new agreement Price suggested that the Persian government pay for the cost of an EIC ship to be stationed in the Persian Gulf, which would have a positive impact and trade and cost the EIC not a penny.[232] Since Sadeq Khan had not replied to Price's proposal Bombay said it could not decide on the matter, but even if three guard-ships were needed, it would only agree to it if Shiraz paid all the expense of Rs 35,000 excluding wear and

228 Amin, *British Interests*, p. 75. The same issue was raised in the second half of the nineteenth century, based on similar arguments, and the matter dragged on for decades and was finally only resolved by the reform of the entire customs system of Qajar Persia. See Willem Floor, *A Fiscal History of Iran in the Safavid and Qajar Period* (New York: Bibliotheca Persica, 1999), pp. 373-400.

229 Amin, *British Interests*, p. 74. For Dutch imports of woolens see chapters three and five. In 1757 one French ship that entered the Gulf reportedly had "about ten pieces of broad cloth on board." Saldanha, *Précis*, vol. 1, p. 124 (Bushire, 28/02/1758). For trade by the French East Indies Company see, e.g., Louis Dusaulchoy, *Considérations sur les Indes Orientales et leur commerce* (Paris: L.M. Cellot, 1789) and Ray Indrani, "Trade in Basra in the Mid-Eighteenth Century," in Lakshmi Subramanian ed. *The French East India Company and the trade of the Indian Ocean: a collection of essays by Ray Indrani* (New Delhi, 1999), pp. 203-14.

230 Saldanha, *Précis*, vol. 1, pp. 171-72 (Bushire, 17/08/1763) and Ibid., vol. 1, p. 172 (Basra, n.d. [September, 1763]).

231 Saldanha, *Précis*, vol. 1, p. 172 (Basra, [September] 1763). For details on Mir Mohanna's marauding see chapter four.

232 Amin, *British Interests*, p. 76.

tear and conversion losses, which would make the sum much higher than Price had calculated.[233] Karim Khan informed the EIC that he would be down in the littoral in November-December 1764 to march against Mir Mohanna and he therefore asked the EIC for naval assistance to prevent him from escaping. He also agreed to pay for two cruisers to be stationed at Bushire at Rs 40,000/year for the protection of trade "and had also made an offer of delivering to the Honble. Company the Town and Goverment of Bunderik if agreeable to us."[234] Bombay did not agree to station guard-ship at Bushire "at present"; however, if the resident thinks that occasionally it is to advantage of EIC then he may provide assistance, but not hold a vessel over, thus causing inconvenience to the Company and its trade.[235]

According to the Dutch, despite the attractive new agreement that Karim Khan had granted, Sheikh Sa'dun caused the English many problems. He forced them to sell their goods to him and then resold them to the merchants. The English did not like this, which led to disputes between them to such an extent that Sheikh Sa'dun even told them in early 1764 that they either accept his conditions or they had better leave. The EIC resident then had to accept a few disadvantageous conditions such as that he had to share part of the profit of the goods that he imported on commission from Bombay and Bengal for his own private account. This gave rise to daily bickering. The EIC also had not yet constructed its fort, which Buschman, the Dutch chief of Khark, believed they would not built anyway. He furthermore believed that Karim Khan would not allow it, because he had informed him about the conditions under which the English had to trade in Surat and had also sent him a detailed letter about the monopoly that the new agreement with EIC included and what it would mean to trade with Persia.[236] Despite these problems, commercially the Bushire residency seemed to be a success. During 1763-65, the EIC sold 750 bales of woolen goods equal to about 20% of the entire sales of EIC in Asia. Moreover, with the departure of the Dutch from the Persian Gulf in 1766 after the fall of their factory on Khark the EIC was in very strong commercial position, because there were no European competitors anymore vying with them for the Persian Gulf market. However, the expected positive trade prospects did not materialize due to the difficulties that arose between the EIC and Karim Khan, which led to the EIC withdrawal from Bushire in 1769.[237] The cause of these difficulties were the EIC conflict with the Ka'b and the bad timing of the reluctant naval EIC assistance given to Karim Khan, about which more later.

THE *ISLAMABAD* AFFAIR

It was shortly after the decision not to station a guard ship at the head of the Persian Gulf that the murder of Captain Sutherland and his offers as well as the plundering of his ship the *Islamabad* took place and there was nothing the EIC could do. In the 1760s the Persian Gulf had become a dangerous place and this was not only due to the piracy of the Banu Ka'b and Mir Mohanna. The Hula Arabs were traditionally also engaged in this activity, but they had limited themselves to at-

233 Saldanha, *Précis*, vol. 1, p. 174 (Bombay, 24/01/1764).

234 Saldanha, *Précis*, vol. 1, p. 178 (Bombay, 08/10/1764). For the text of the grant made by Karim Khan see Aitchison, *Collection*, vol. X, p. 33, for a summary see Lorimer, *Gazetteer*, p. 1780.

235 Saldanha, *Précis*, vol. 1, p. 184 (Bombay, 04/12/1764).

236 VOC 3156, Khark to Batavia (30/09/1764), f. 24-26. Buschman did not know why the EIC linguist had been twice to Karim Khan. He assumed it was about the dispute with Sheikh Sa'dun or about the commission that had been established at Shiraz to the great disadvantage of traveling merchants and its inhabitants, who generally had a commissionaire to whom they sent those goods that they were not able to sell in Bushire.

237 Amin, *British Interests*, pp. 79, 125.

tacking native shipping. It therefore came as a major surprise that a group of Arabs, who had been hired as sailors at Basra to replace those of crew who had died during the voyage from Bengal and at Basra, murdered Captain Sutherland and his officers of the *Islamabad* and took the ship's cargo on 6 February 1765. Of the rest of the crew (all, but one, Indians), who had gone to Moghu in a longboat to fetch water and provisions, one was killed and some wounded on their return to the *Islamabad*. They therefore fled and went to a town a league south of Moghu where the local sheikh stripped them of everything including the long boat. After the murder of Captain Sutherland the Arab perpetrators plundered the ship of its money and pearls and went to the island of Kish (Khisht), where they killed one of the Armenian merchants who were passengers on the ship. The sheikh of Kish, when he learnt that they were murderers and pirates, arrested them and their goods, and sent them ashore in a small boat to the mainland.[238]

Jervis learnt of the murders and the act of piracy on March 6, 1765 when the survivors of the long boat arrived at Bushire. He sent an express letter to Basra, which arrived there only at March 26. As Jervis had suggested the Agent at Basra sent him the brig *Tartar* to see whether he might recover the stolen money, without endangering the vessel or its cargo, of course. However, more than one month of time had passed and thus nothing could be done by the *Tartar*, which seems to have not even gone further than Bushire. The reason for this may have been that meanwhile Nasir Khan of Lar having learnt about this booty had sent a force under Sheikh 'Abdollah of Hormuz to Kish, who took the plunder from the sheikh of Kish. Nasir Khan in his turn then was seized by Karim Khan when his troops took Lar in April 1765. Nevertheless, the Company did not make any claim for restitution from him, although the value of cargo was 40,000 rupees, half belonging to English and the other half to Armenian and other merchants. The ship itself had been taken to Masqat by the crew and passengers assisted by pilots from Kish.[239]

KARIM KHAN ATTACKS THE KA'B

In the letter to the EIC in which he had granted the Company new privileges Karim Khan had also indicated that he could not any longer to afford the problem that Mir Mohanna posed and he therefore wanted to put an end to Mir Mohanna.[240] However, rather then coming down himself to the coast, as he had intimated, Karim Khan sent one of his generals to Ganaveh to initiate operations against Mir Mohanna. He also asked for English naval assistance, which between June 2 to July 11, 1765 was reluctantly given, poorly executed and badly coordinated with the Persian invasion force (see chapter four). This experience became a cloud that hang over EIC-Zand relations and led to the EIC withdrawal from Bushire in 1669. Karim Khan had much counted on the English support, because he himself was fully engaged with the expedition against the Ka'b.

---

238 Saldanha, *Précis*, vol. 1, pp. 184-85 (Bushire, 06/05/1765). In a note to this letter the Agent gave as his comments that the village on the island of Kish (Khisht) had no defenses and only a trifling force. He therefore believed that it could be easily taken by the *Tartar*.

239 Saldanha, *Précis*, vol. 1, p. 187 (Basra, 31/03/1765); Ibid., vol. 1, p. 226 (Basra, 09/10/1767); Perry, *Karim Khan*, p. 121.

240 Amin, *British Interests*, p. 72 greatly exaggerates when he writes that Karim Khan was "impressed by the rising power of the British in India." I doubt whether he had any inkling of this and the fact that he was making the same noises to the Dutch only indicates that he was looking for a partner with naval power to deal with Mir Mohanna. The problem with the Banu Ka'b was less of an issue for him than Amin suggests, which Karim Khan therefore did not mention in his letter, and which he took care of with his own land forces.

For instead of coming to the littoral Karim Khan attacked Dowraq, the capital of the Ka'b and then had moved to Qobban in the spring of 1765. How had this Persian attack on the Ka'b come about? On October 12, 1763 the Ka'b had landed a number of men at the Dawasir (Dawasha) area, who drove the inhabitants away and carried off the dates. Shaw, the EIC Agent at Basra, had a stake in those groves, whose produce served as repayment of a debt and he therefore wanted to use force against the Ka'b to protect his claim. The *motasallem* and the janissaries, however, advised against this. They did not want trouble with the Ka'b and the *motasallem* therefore sent a letter to Sheikh Salman per his *mum-bashi* (or chief of the lighting department) that same day of October 13. Although there was no reply, meanwhile the Ka'b had fled and had left the dates there as well as many of their effects on October 17. Shaw wanted the *motasallem* to give an order to the inhabitants to deliver the dates to the *Swallow*, but he replied that he was the outgoing governor did not have so much power. He suggested addressing Hajji Yusof (Hodgee Esuf) in whose hands the government was now. Hajji Yusof agreed with Shaw's request and immediately sent 100 soldiers with orders for the inhabitants to give the dates. Meanwhile, 'Ali Pasha of Baghdad was en route towards Basra with an army intending to punish the Ka'b. Because he did not consider his force strong enough 'Ali Pasha requested agent Price to support him with the *Tartar* and the *Swallow*, "which it was judged necessary should be complied with."[241] 'Ali Pasha thanked Price for his cooperation. He called the Ka'b insolent and he hoped that the EIC would continue to support the governor of Basra with its ships against Sheikh Salman's hostilities. 'Ali Pasha had intended to march on Hoveyzeh, but in view of the events mentioned above he had decided to march to Basra by land, "depending on the assistance of your ships" by water to block the mouth of the river. "You will have full power to take, burn and destroy whatever you may meet belonging to the Chaab, in short make yourselves master of the Gallivats, as they will no doubt endeavour to escape by sea."[242] Price replied on October 19 that he had sent the ships as requested; he had even unloaded one ship [the *Swallow*] that was ready to sail for India.[243] There were some inconclusive encounters with Ka'b gallivats in their attempt to block the Khur Musa and Jarrahi. 'Ali Pasha had not advanced at all, because the Ka'b withdrew into the marshes. Shaikh Salman then sought and obtained peace without further fighting, and thus the EIC vessels returned to Basra.[244]

Despite the peace, the Ka'b were still felt to be a major nuisance. In 1764 'Omar Pasha, the new governor of Baghdad, therefore proposed to Karim Khan Zand that they should carry out a joint pincer-movement attack on the Ka'b, whom he considered to be his, if rebellious, subjects. The *motasallem* of Basra, Soleyman Aqa, would provide troops, supplies and vessels to support the Persian troops. Karim Khan accepted the proposal, because he had unfinished business with the Ka'b and he now also had the time, because he was finally the uncontested master of most of Persia having finally eliminated all his major rivals. At the end of 1764 therefore Zand troops moved into Dashtestan and entered Ka'b territory in April 1765. Because the Zand troops were too strong for them the Ka'b fled. They were difficult to find in the marshes, however. As the Zand army advanced,

---

241 Saldanha, *Précis*, vol. 1, pp. 169-70 (Basra Diary October 1763), 216 (Basra, 09/04/1767). Hajji Yusef was one of the debtors of Shaw hence his interest to be of service to him, see Ibid, *Précis*, vol. 1, p. 173 (Bombay, 24/01/1764); Perry, "The Banu Ka'b," p. 138; Floor, "The Rise," p. 284.

242 Saldanha, *Précis*, vol. 1, p. 170 (Ali Bashaw to Andrew Price, rec. 18/10/1763).

243 Saldanha, *Précis*, vol. 1, p. 171 (Basra, 19/10/1763). Bombay did not agree with keeping the *Swallow* at Basra. Ibid., vol. 1, pp. 173-74 (Bombay, 24/01/1764).

244 Saldanha, *Précis*, vol. 1, pp. 169-70 (Basra Diary October 1763), 216 (Basra, 09/04/1767). Hajji Yusof was one of the debtors of Shaw hence his interest to be of service to him, see Ibid, *Précis*, vol. 1, p. 173 (Bombay, 24/01/1764); Perry, "The Banu Ka'b," p. 138; Floor, "The Rise," p. 284.

the Ka'b hopped from island to island, each time staying one step ahead of it. They abandoned Dowraq, which Karim Khan destroyed, and then moved towards the Shatt al-Arab, followed by the Zand army. The latter waited for the Basra force to arrive; meanwhile, the Ka'b had taken refuge on "an Island [Abadan] below the River call'd Dwiack" [Dowraq], where they were expected to defend themselves fiercely and only to flee as a last resort. When the Zand army arrived at Haffar, a village between the Karun and the Shatt al-Arab, it found it abandoned, so they built a fort there. Sheikh Salman had already secured an asylum for himself and his people where Karim Khan could not get him. When Sadeq Khan Zand moved to Abadan island with one of the largest of the vessels supplied by the *Vali* of Hoveyzeh, the Ka'b did not defend the place, but took to the open sea, where the Zand troops, having no maritime experience or vessels, could not follow them. [245]

Several soldiers of Karim Khan's army had been seen at Minawi on the other side of the river. When in early May, 1765 the *motasallem* had a discussion at Ma'gil (Maygill), a village on the Shatt al-Arab north of Basra, with the Montafeq sheikh the English believed that it probably was about Karim Khan having sent his people to demand the Ka'b's money and effects that they had deposited with the Montafeq sheikh.[246] Meanwhile, due to the commotion caused by the Persian invasion and warlike preparations at Basra there was neither trade nor money in that port. Indeed preparations to assist the Persian force had been made. Messengers had arrived from Baghdad with a request from 'Omar Pasha to assist the Persian army against the Ka'b with vessels; he would sent from Baghdad "5-600 Barratalys" (regular, but locally raised infantry) to join Karim Khan's forces. As a result, the *qaputan basha*'s gallivats had been prepared to go against the Ka'b, but they were a sorry lot from which the English expected little action. 'Omar Pasha also authorized the *motasallem* to deal with the EIC Agent in this regard as he saw fit. The EIC informed the *motasallem* that it would help with the *Fanny Snow*, because the Company felt that Ka'b gallivats might attack English trankis and other vessels. Immediately rumors started to circulate in Basra that the Ka'b would try to set fire to the *Fanny Snow*, because they could easily deal with the *qaputan basha*'s gallivats. Mowlna Hoseyn (Moulna Hosein) in the name of the *motasallem* promised to insure the *Fanny Snow*, which Captain Parkinson valued at Rs 20,000, on condition that if Ka'b gallivats were taken he would get "1*s*. of the value exclusive of what he is to have for his trouble." The *motasallem* would send 3,000 musketeers as soon as the *baratalis* from Baghdad had arrived. On May 10, 1756 people of the *qaputan basha* complained to the *motasallem* that they had received neither pay nor provisions although order to go on expedition. The *qaptan basha* then resigned his post and Mostafa Pasha was appointed in his stead. During that time, Karim Khan's force of 5,000 has crossed the river Euphrates at Meezza [?] and had taken a granary belonging to the Ka'b. An English vessel reported that Sheikh Salman had 12 gallivats with his women and effects lying at the entrance of the Shatt al-Arab and had stopped all navigation with Basra; three of the gallivats did all kinds of mischief to Sheikh Dervish's lands, burning and destroying villages near the river banks as well as taking women and plunder. On May 11, 1756 the *motasallem* came with a considerable force at the Creek's mouth and reviewed the *baratalis* that had arrived yesterday from Baghdad. Just as the *motasallem* had embarked in the evening of May 10 a letter arrived from Karim Khan expressing his dissatisfaction about his tardiness and to ask where the promised troops and vessels were. He also wrote that he had decided not to wait any longer and to march away immediately. The *motasallem* convened his officers and the result was that the expedition was called off; the soldiers were allowed to return and

245 Saldanha, *Précis*, vol. 1, p. 190-92 (Basra Diary, 01-11/05/1765); Floor, "The Dutch," p. 185; Perry, *Karim Khan Zand*, pp. 163-64, 169; Niebuhr, *Beschreibung*, p. 320; Ghaffari, *Golshan-e morad*, p. 257; Olivier, *Voyage*, vol. 6, pp. 109-10.

246 Saldanha, *Précis*, vol. 1, p. 190 (Basra Diary, 01-11/05/1765).

the *baratalis* were unloaded from the vessels. The *motasallem*, however, remained encamped at the creek's mouth.[247] The *motasallem* did not have his army ready, so he excused himself and sent two vessels only. Niebuhr states that the Ka'b had bribed him, while the East India Company's agent reported that he really wanted to supply the troops and vessels but had problems in doing so.[248]

Thus, after six weeks, the Zand army returned in May 1765 just as the *motasallem* of Basra was embarking his promised troops. The returning Zand army devastated the Dowraq area, and most importantly the major irrigation dam at Sabla, but not the date groves. Sheikh Salman then opened negotiations to avoid further destruction of his lands, and made peace with Karim Khan Zand in July 1765. He paid a large sum as a present, sent one of his sons as a hostage to Shiraz and promised to pay an annual tribute of 3,000 *tumans*.[249]

THE KA'B AND THE EIC AT WAR

Although Karim Khan had withdrawn from the campaign against the Ka'b having obtained his objective, to wit: the nominal obedience of Sheikh Salman by the payment of tribute, the Ottomans had obtained nothing. Therefore, a short while after the departure of the Zand troops, 'Omar Pasha of Baghdad ordered his *motasallem* of Basra, Soleyman Aqa to attack the Ka'b. He intended to do so with his own troops and the vessels of the *qaputan-bashi*. Because they did not consider their force strong enough to face the Ka'b they both requested Wrench, the EIC Agent at Basra, for the assistance of the *Fanny Snow*, then the only English ship at Basra. Captain Parkinson was induced to accompany the Ottoman force as did the EIC Agent's sloop. The two forces were lying opposite one another "on this side of the river with the camp of the Mussalim, [...] and a few shot were some times exchanged." Nothing much further happened; only the Ka'b seized three of the *qaptan-pasha*'s vessels (*teknes*) and later sailed daringly in face of the Ottoman fleet, then plundered some villages and seized some vessels, while the Anglo-Ottoman force did nothing. Then, three weeks after the start of the operation, the two parties reached a kind of agreement, including the payment of a nominal tribute, and each returned to their homes at the end of May 1765.[250]

The war with the Ka'b showed the limits of the use of force in the Persian Gulf as the Dutch and also the English had already experienced earlier at Khark. Given the fact that the European forces were well-armed, but not appropriately equipped, they fared badly in all of their engagements with the coastal Arabs. First they lacked a sufficient number of men on the ground with adequate arms to gain and keep any advantage they might have gained. Second, their vessels, although well-armed, were too unwieldy to match the more nimble, shallower and better crewed Arab gallivats, *batils* and dingis in the shallow water of the Gulf. Third, the Arabs made optimal use of their mobility and thus made more effective use of their resources. Four and finally, the Arabs, although less well-armed were better motivated than the European forces and were not their inferiors in fighting skills.

---

247 Saldanha, *Précis*, vol. 1, p. 190-92 (Basra Diary, 01-11/05/1765).

248 Floor, "The Dutch," p. 185; Perry, *Karim Khan Zand*, pp. 163-64, 169; Niebuhr, *Beschreibung*, p. 320; Ghaffari, *Golshan-e morad*, p. 257; G.A. Olivier, *Voyage dans l'Empire Othoman, l'Egypte et la Perse*. 6 vols. (Paris: Agasse, 1802-07), vol. 6, pp. 109-10.

249 Perry, "The Banu Ka'b," pp. 139-40; Floor, "The Rise," p. 284.

250 Saldanha, *Précis*, vol. 1, p. 216 (Basra, 09/04/1767); Niebuhr, *Reisebeschreibung*, p. 586; Lorimer, *Gazetteer*, p. 1219; Perry, "The Banu Ka'b," pp. 139-40; Floor, "The Rise," p. 285.

In the war with the Ka'b the English had to deal both with the Turks and Persians, as the Ka'b territory straddled both states. Their performance in that war thus had a great impact on their relations with those states and the perception that those states had of English capabilities. After the EIC had moved its main factory in the Persian Gulf to Basra and moreover experienced a thriving trade it had a stake in the maintenance of peace and stability in that area, which the Ka'b threatened. In fact, the EIC was afraid that the Ka'b would overrun Basra, in which case all the Turks would be killed, which would result in the closure of the road to Baghdad and thus would end trade. It was for that reason that in the view of the English the Ka'b had to be destroyed.[251] The Ottomans had the same considerations as the English and as nominal overlord of the province of Basra they launched three campaigns against the Ka'b between 1761 and 1765, which all ended in disaster.

The peace did not mean that the Ka'b stopped their raiding activities and they continued to pressure Basra. However, the English never thought that they themselves would ever become the target of Ka'b attacks, despite their naval assistance to the Basra governor and their shelling of Ka'b vessels. The English at Basra were therefore stupefied when, on the night of July 18, the Ka'b attacked with six gallivats and seized the *Sally* in the Shatt al-Arab. The next day when they were hauling their prize to Qobban they met the Bushire's resident's sloop and the *Fort William*, which had just come from Khark sailing to Basra, which they then also took. The EIC asked the *motasallem* to intervene as the Ka'b were his subjects and EIC traded under his protection, and thus the EIC could not contact the Ka'b directly. He immediately sent a letter to the Ka'b and a letter exchange followed but Sheikh Salman would not release the vessels, because he had a claim on the EIC concerning dates on land at Ma'gil that had been taken from his subjects by Shaw/Price. He also wrote a reply to a letter sent by Wrench, the EIC agent, reminding him that it was the English who had attacked him first, who apparently did not want peace with him. Wrench continued to pressure the *motasallem* to obtain the release of the seized vessels, but he was convinced that only the use of naval force would have any effect. The *motasallem* was willing to march by land if the EIC would join his force by water to attack the Ka'b gallivats and prevent them from escaping. He proposed that the EIC received half of what would be taken from the Ka'b except for the three vessels in Sheikh Salman's possession which were the Company's. The EIC decided to provide assistance, because alone the *motasallem* could not do anything in which case all maritime traffic to and fro Basra would be hostage to the Ka'b. Wrench asked Bombay for naval support, in particular gallivats that could sail up the creek. The Ka'b released Captains Phillips and Holland plus all their officers. Sheikh Salman had first insisted that the Agent sent him a Treaty of Friendship to be continued on the old footing between them, which was agreed to. Sheikh Salman further informed the EIC that he only would release the vessels when Bombay had confirmed the treaty. However, that looked very unlikely as EIC cruisers that were under way to Basra were to attack the Ka'b as soon as they had arrived, while 'Omar Pasha also had promised his support. Because the destruction of the Ka'b was believed to be in the interest of trade and the Turks could not do that without EIC naval support, Wrench argued that the Company should not let this opportunity pass.[252] He further argued that Sheikh Salman had no claim at all on the lands at Ma'gil and Sillik. [?] Shaw had bought these from the real owner and the relevant documents were there to prove this. Sheikh Salman might have received the *miri* tax in the past from some of these lands, but that was a right that the Porte assigned on somebody on an annual rotating basis and that in itself did not constitute a right to ownership.[253]

251 Saldanha, *Précis*, vol. 1, p. 205 (Basra, 24/08/1766); see also Amin, *British Interests*, p. 85.

252 Saldanha, *Précis*, vol. 1, pp. 192-94 (Basra, 14/08/1765).

253 Saldanha, *Précis*, vol. 1, pp. 194-95 (Basra, 09/1764).

Bombay was very much upset about the capture of the three vessels and decided that punishment was needed to send a strong signal in the interest of trade that such a thing would not be tolerated. In March 1766 it sent the *Bombay*, grab, the *Success*, ketch, the *Dolphin* and the *Tyger* schooners, the *Wolf* gallivat and the *Fame* storeship with 50 European infantry, 15 artillerists, 150 sepoys, 25 lascars under the command of Captains Lesley Baillee and John Brewer. Bombay gave instructions that it insisted on the restitution of all EIC vessels and goods as well as ample satisfaction of expenses incurred. If the Ka'b would accept this Wrench was allowed to discuss this further with Sheikh Salman promising that the EIC would not interfere with his affairs as long he would not trouble English trade again in the future. Bombay actually assumed that Sheikh Salman might agree to these demands and conclude a treaty. In that case if the government of Basra wanted EIC support against him Wrench had to explain that since they had been unable to help the Company to recover its rights they could not expect the EIC to help them in helping them to resolve their quarrels. If the Ka'b refused to give satisfaction Wrench had to inform the *motasallem* that in response to 'Omar Pasha's request the EIC fleet had come to join theirs to destroy the Ka'b. If the Ottoman force would not be ready to begin operations nor to hand over Hajji Yusof's assets Wrench was instructed to tell the captains of the EIC fleet to proceed alone against the Ka'b without waiting. The outcome of the operation was never in doubt for a moment, for Bombay further informed Wrench that after the operation against the Ka'b had been completed he was authorized to do something about the recovery of the cargo of the *Islamabad* if that would be possible.[254] Meanwhile, in February 1766, the Ka'b had plundered all the villages above and below the town of Basra and it was feared that they would attack the town itself. This news had just arrived at Bushire when the EIC fleet arrived at Bushire on March 10 en route to Basra, whither it sailed on March 13.[255]

On arrival at Basra Wrench instructed the fleet to join the *motasallem*'s camp and further sent the *Tartar* and the *Wolf* into the Haffar River. Lieutenant Dutton and some boats had previously reconnoitered the Jarrahi and he had observed the English prizes "with only their lower Masts in" as well as some Ka'b gallivats lying near a recently built fort. The EIC fleet consisting of the *Success*, the *Dolphin* schooners, the *Wolf*, gallivat, the *Protector*, launch, the *Bombay*, grab with 3 armed trankeys arrived in the Haffar River on April 26. Baillie had wanted to attack, but without assistance from the *motasallem*'s land force he could not do anything. He had immediately written to the governor to join forces with him, who wrote that he was waiting for reinforcements from Baghdad. Nesbitt therefore had to return, also because his supplies were getting low, which the *motasallem* had not readied either as promised.

Meanwhile, Wrench allowed Captain Baillie to take sick leave. He also was aware that the *motasallem* was not going to take any action until reinforcements from Baghdad would have arrived. Wrench therefore did three things; he sent a letter to Karim Khan requesting him not give refuge to the Ka'b, if they would flee into his lands; a letter to which he received no reply. Wrench also sent a letter to Jervis, the EIC resident at Bushire, instructing him to talk to Sheikh Sa'dun, the Sheikh of Bushire "for sending his Fleet and Forces to join Us, & talk to the Shaik fully on this subject, but on no Account to make any promises or engagements in regard to Our assisting them against Meermanna, being positively Ordered by Our Superiors to preserve an Amicable understanding with him, unless his Conduct he had given any Just Cause to violate that Friendship." So far Mir Mohanna had behaved in a most friendly fashion towards English vessels. In addition to the orders from London not to interfere with Mir Mohanna there also was the fear that the Basra Agent had that if the EIC fleet would assist the Bushire fleet and Zand army against Khark that

254 Saldanha, *Précis*, vol. 1, pp. 195-96 (Bombay, 05/01/1766).

255 Saldanha, *Précis*, vol. 1, p. 198 (Bombay, 21/07/1766).

Sheikh Salman "would immediately Embrace that Opportunity of getting out with his Gallivats & sending away his most valuable, Effect &c.," leaving aside the fact that Mir Mohanna had reinforced the Dutch fort on Khark. This was to be expected as the EIC had refused to collaborate with Karim Khan with regards to a joint operation against Mir Mohanna, in exchange of which he had promised redress from the Ka'b. Given EIC refusal to accept this offer Sheikh Sa'dun could not go against his overlord's wishes and give aid to the EIC. It is, of course, questionable whether the Bushire fleet would have made a real contribution given its poor performance so far, in particular at Khark (see chapter four)

Wrench also contacted 'Omar Pasha of Baghdad and informed him that the Bombay fleet was already two months at Basra and no Ottoman help had been given. The problem of supplies from and coordination of operations with the *motasallem* continued to bedevil the campaign, from the very beginning until the end. The cooperation with the *motasallem* was ineffective; he promised boats, pilots, and supplies, but did not deliver, while the English from their side showed little understanding or interest in the *motasallem*'s constraints and objectives. The English wanted this to be a quick efficient campaign in view of the heat, which made their people sick, while their vessels were in need of repairs and therefore they wanted it to be over with by the end of June at the latest. Wrench therefore informed both 'Omar Pasha and the *motasallem* that the fleet would not stay beyond July 1 and after that date the EIC would consider the war with the Ka'b to be their war. Moreover, they had to pay for the all of the fleet's expenses, "which if they'r willing to Comply with, the Fleet must of Course be kept for the Security of this place otherwise We must come to a Resolution of withdrawing the Consequence of which would be the Turks could never remain the Masters of this place any longer; the Arabs would Govern it, and the Turks would fly to Bagdat."

In the third week of May, Sheikh Salman had twice written to Wrench offering to come to an accommodation. The latter had sent as a reply what the English demands were (direct negotiations with Sheikh Salman and full compensation of the Company's loss and expenditures), but he had little hope that this would lead to anything. Wrench believed that Sheikh Salman's letters were a mere ploy to gain time. However, if Sheikh Salman was seriously interested in reaching an agreement Wrench would not such an opportunity slip by, because he believed that an accommodation between the Ka'b, the Ottomans and the English was of vital importance, "otherwise it would be to little purpose our Continuing at Bussora tho' in Peace with the Chaub, while it is Somuch in his Power to interrupt the Commerce of the Place, and on the One hand his demands would be so Extravagant that the Turks could not possibly comply with them & on the other, they are so determined to reduce him; having recd the grand Signor positive Orders on this head that between both we can Entertain very little hopes of a Mediation taking place."[256]

Although the troops from Baghdad were still delayed the EIC force started its operations on May 17 by sailing into the Jarrahi. Captains Nesbitt and Brewer reconnoitered the rivers and found a large number of vessels near a newly constructed fort called Mansureh (Mansure), 40 miles inland. They attacked, destroyed the vessels, but failed to get the fort. This was due to the difficulty of the terrain and the lack of people to drag the guns over 7 miles from the place where they had landed. The English therefore withdrew in the evening and asked the *motasallem* for coolies. He sent a few men, but then desisted amd requested tjhat all operations be halted, because he had received news that Mahmud Kahya (Mahmoud Kiya) was approaching with troops. He therefore suggested halting all operations until the latter had arrived. Meanwhile 'Omar Pasha informed the Agent that he agreed to pay 1,000 *tumans* per month for the fleet until June 30. To speedily settle the Ka'b issue he would come either himself or one of his principal officers. On June 25 Mahmud Kahya arrived from

256 Saldanha, *Précis*, vol. 1, pp. 199-201 (Basra, 29/05/1766).

Baghdad with 1,500 men. The Agent asked him about the payment of Hajji Yusof's debt, to which he replied that nothing could be done until the enemy had been defeated. Then, after 20-30 days, "he would pay it off by Separating the Lands among the Sons and obliging them to pay off the whole in proportion & for discharging the sum allowed; for the Charges of the Fleet he gave a Note for 600 Toms in part thereof on the Customs." After some dispute between the *motasallem* and Mahmud Kahya who would be the commander of the troops, the *motasallem* ordered the *qaputan-basha* to go with his galleys to Qobban with the *Wolf*. The Ka'b immediately abandoned the fort, while "a whole Tribe of Chaubs principal Musquetiers having Fledd to Mahmoud Kia with their families for protection as well as to their Ships." From the defectors the Turks and English learnt that the Ka'b were divided among themselves and Sheikh Salman only kept control by keeping "their chiefs continually within his Sight & on the least Suspicion commits the most horrid Barbarities." The attacking force thus believed that on their appearance that the people would abandon Sheikh Salman. The *motasallem* promised to march shortly as he was waiting for some horse from the Montafeq, which was agreeable as the Agent was ill. When contacting Karim Khan to obtain permission to attack Ka'b, Karim Khan refused to reply. The EIC was told that Karim Khan did not want to hear EIC's name, because he was angry about the naval support that Jervis had promised him against Mir Mohanna in 1765 and that had not come. Moreover, the Bushire Resident wanted to have a cruiser in the roads being afraid that Mir Mohanna would attack the EIC because of the assistance of the *Tartar* in attacking him. Thus, "there is as much to fear from the Khaun as Meer Mahanna unless some Methods are taken to reconcile affaires."[257]

The Turks asked the EIC to maintain the blockade for they wanted to continue the war. On August 19 Lyster asked Mahmud Kahya for the monthly payment, who said that he was unable to do so, because the coffee ships had not yet arrived and the great want of money, but he promised to pay. He was, however, willing to transfer certain revenues on dates to the Agent with an estimated value of 1,080 *tumans*. Sheikh Ghanem, Sheikh Salman's eldest son, had invited Captain Nesbitt on the August 23rd at 1 mile from the lower fort. The meeting was a trap, or so the English claimed, for the Sheikh "who spoke so impertinently" that Nesbitt was sure that he wanted to kill the English who pre-emptied this by killing many of the Arabs, of which three sheikhs. The EIC party also suffered two dead and seven wounded. Sheikh Ghanem was "dangerously wounded." The Ka'b then set fire to the *Sally* and the *Fort William* when Nesbitt wanted to board them at high tide.

The Agent was upset that Nesbitt had agreed to such a meeting so far away from the reach of the EIC vessels and to take on him the charge to discuss peace without permission. Nesbitt left Qobban on August 30 to join the fleet and Mahmud Kahya near Dowraq. He was itching for action, but could not do much as he and his men were under constant fire by the Ka'b from behind their redoubts, being only half a cannon-shot's distance from the Ka'b fort. On September 13, the Ka'b had attacked the EIC vessels and gallivats with 1,000 men, but they were beaten back with heavy loss, according to the English. The Turks pursued them on horse and foot and made prisoners, before they reached the safety of the fort. On September 14 the Ka'b made a night raid and burnt nine of the 12 Basran galleys, among which the one of the *qaputan-basha*, and killed some of the crew. They also had lost all their powder and most of their ammunition. They had not put scouts and thus were surprised. On the Ka'b side everything was not pleasant either for two Ka'b sheikhs surrendered and were welcomed with robes of honor by the *motasallem*. Having arrived at the fleet near Dowraq on the 23rd September Wrench learnt the next day that an attack had been made on the Ka'b redoubts, which ended disastrously. The *motasallem* then had proposed to Brewer to attack the redoubts and so it was agreed. The latter was so gung-ho that he had decided that if Turkish

257 Saldanha, *Précis*, vol. 1, pp. 200-03 (Basra, 30/07/1766).

assistance was not forthcoming he would attack himself. On September 23 Brewer had enough of the inaction and ignoring advice to the contrary frontally attacked the Ka'b fort with his less than enthuastic troops. They ran into the Ka'b defenses and came under cross-fire from two Ka'b forts and then were ridden down by Ka'b cavalry supported by Ka'b foot. The result was a rout of the EIC force, which suffered 18 killed, amongst whom Brewer and two other officers, 23 dangerously wounded, while all field pieces were taken with 23 boxes of ammunition. The Ka'b attacked the remaining EIC vessels, but were repulsed with loss of life. The Agent then decided to withdraw the EIC force leaving only 6 gunners with Mahmud Kahya for shooting shells.[258]

On October 7, 1766 news arrived that an ambassador from Karim Khan had arrived with a letter to the *motasallem* demanding the Turks and English to leave his country and not any further attack the Ka'b, his subjects and that Sheikh Salman had been appointed governor of Dowraq. However, "they wou'd oblige him to make full reparation for all the Damages which he had Committed on the English & Turks." Soleyman Aga, the *motasallem,* did not want to be the cause of war with Persia, but the English told him that "We had nothing to do with the Persians nor shou'd we be refer'd to them for redress of our grievances & Losses that it was by their Instance we came here & on their Acct." However, the Turks withdrew on October 10, and thus the English after having initially regrouped near Qabban withdrew as well. On October 14 they saw a boat with a representative of Mahmud Kahya pass heading for Bushire with a letter for Karim Khan. Thus on October 17, 1766 it was decided to withdraw until such time as orders would arrive from Baghdad as well as answers from Karim Khan. Mahmud Kahya asked the fleet to stay with the same financial arrangement. The English told him that they first wanted to be paid for the previous period, that Hajji Yusof's debt be settled, and that the losses suffered had to be recompensed by the Turks not the Persians. Bushire informed Basra that Karim Khan was upset with the EIC. He was also still incensed at the English because of their bad performance at Khark in June-July 1766, whom he therefore blamed for the failure of that campaign. Karim Khan there did not allow the name of the English to be mentioned in his presence. It was also further reported from Bushire that the Ka'b had claimed protection from Karim Khan supported by large presents. Wrench wrote Jervis that if, because of this, the Bushire agency would be in danger he would immediate send him a vessel for their protection or to withdraw the entire factory. If Karim Khan asked them about the EIC involvement Bushire had to reply that the Company only assisted the Turks against the Ka'b, who had caused loss to the EIC, and who now wanted satisfaction for those losses.[259] The result of the punitive campaign was the loss of seven Basrene vessels as well as of three East India Company ships with their cargo; many men were killed and wounded; and many guns, as well as reputations, lost.

EIC NEGOTIATES WITH KARIM KHAN TO REDUCE THE KA'B

The Ka'b threat to Basra seemed more imminent than ever before. The Ottoman governor of Basra therefore made a new agreement with the EIC to protect the city and its trade in particular against the Ka'b for a payment of 1,000 *tumans* per month so that the *Success* would stay. Given the fact that trade flourished and that the compensation was ample the EIC agreed. Moreover, the disastrous 1765 campaign had stiffened EIC resolution to defeat the Ka'b, it was now also a case of English honor.[260]

258 Saldanha, *Précis*, vol. 1, pp. 206-08 (Basra, 23/10/1766).

259 Saldanha, *Précis*, vol. 1, pp. 208-12 (Basra, 23/10/1766).

260 Saldanha, *Précis*, vol. 1, p. 210 (Basra, 23/10/1766).

The Pasha had sent an embassy to Karim Khan's court which returned on March 13, 1767 together with Aghasi Khan (Agasy Caun) as ambassador of Karim Khan to the EIC and the Ka'b. Messrs. Lyster and Skipp went to the *motasallem* to hear the ambassador who made it known that "Carim Caun had sent him to require of the Chaub to deliver up all such property as he had taken from us, for which purpose he should immediately send a person to demand the same, which should he not immediately comply with, it would plainly prove he had no intentions of being subject to either power." In that case he would take appropriate steps. Also, Karim Khan would be personally answerable for the EIC losses and that if the Ka'b did not pay the EIC had to give a list of its losses and send somebody to his court at Shiraz. This position was quite reasonable and not hostile towards the English at all, an impression that the Basra Agency had tried to create. In reply the EIC stated that Karim Khan was a friend; that the Company had not engaged in the war as a principal, but had assisted the Turkish government. As the seizure had taken place on Turkish soil the EIC had asked the Turks for restitution. If the goods might be returned through the good offices of Karim Khan the EIC would gladly accept this. The ambassador also brought a letter from Karim Khan which he handed over in the EIC Factory on March 17. The ambassador further sent a letter to Sheikh Salman to demand restitution, who replied with evasive responses, disputing the amount of the losses and asked for a person to be sent to him. The ambassador therefore decided to go there in person and asked the EIC for a detailed list of the losses. He left on March 23 and returned on March 29. Aghasi Khan reported that rather than bring about reconciliation with the Turks and Ka'b he had been met with insults, and thus his mission for Karim Khan had been complied with. He would make one final try via a messenger demanding restitution of the English goods and their return at the Haffar, where in exchange receipts would be given, else he would return to Shiraz and report to his master. The messenger returned with no satisfactory reply and the ambassador plus the *salam aghasi* left to Baghdad on April 8, but not before insisting that the EIC send a representative to Shiraz. He gave a letter of introduction to Mr. Skipp.[261]

Three days after the arrival of Aghasi Khan (March 16, 1767) a letter from Bombay arrived in which Wrench was given instructions not to pursue hostile operations against the Ka'b, "but in conjunction with the Turks or Persians, at the same time we still think amicable measures the best to be pursued if it is possible to bring him by that means to suitable terms of accommodation, which from the Tenor of his Sons letter to Captain Nesbitt there seems reason to hope." Wrench therefore was ordered to try and get "an immediate and categorical answer, which should he refuse of decline treating, and you should have no prospect of brining affairs to a speedy issue, solely with the Turks, the only eligible method which seems then to be left, is to make a direct application to Carim Caun for his assistance likewise." Bombay was aware that this was against the sentiments and orders of London (dated 22/03/1765), hence the emphasis that Wrench was only to contact Karim Khan if a speedy settlement directly with the Ka'b was impossible. As to the demand that the Ka'b should categorically state whether they were to return the English properties or not, Basra argued, that this instruction had been complied with through the ambassador, who had demanded the same and in a more peremptory manner. Because the ambassador "was not only sent by the Caun but also by the English between whom his master had now become Umpire." Basra could not of course have refused Karim Khan's offer of mediation, although this was a deviation from Bombay's orders. Although Bombay did not want a continuation of the violence against the Ka'b, but rather a peaceful solution to the conflict, it was nevertheless very much upset about the disastrous campaign against the Ka'b and therefore immediately sent reinforcements consisting of: the *Defiance*, the *Salamander*, a bomb ketch, the *Eagle*, a snow and a merchant ship with part of the provisions. On these vessels a complete

261 Saldanha, *Précis*, vol. 1, p. 220 (Basra, 16/04/1767).

company of infantry under two officers, 30 artillerists and 75 sepoys were transported as well as six months of provisions to make the blockade of the Shatt al-Arab an effective one. On the face of it the blockade was effective and made an impression on all parties concerned (Ottomans, Persians, Ka'b), although as later would appear it was a rather futile and costly effort.[262]

Bombay realized that Karim Khan might only agree to provide his assistance against the Ka'b provided the EIC would help him against Mir Mohanna. In the instructions to the Agent at Basra Bombay therefore stated that this should be avoided, although if that were the price to be paid the Company was willing to do so as the Ka'b matter was of the greatest importance. George Skipp was sent to Shiraz with the following list of essential conditions for an agreement:

1. A confirmation of Sadoo Caun's [Sadeq Khan] Grants for settling at Bushire expressly mentioning therein that we may be at liberty to build any such Fort or factory there or elsewhere as we may think proper and mount on it what cannon we please.
2. That an annual sum at least from 20 to 24,000 Rupees be stipulated to be paid to the Honble Company from the Rent of Baneen or Customs of Bushire to defray the expense of keeping a Cruizer always in the Gulph.
3. A grant of any one of the Islands in the Gulph such a one as may be judged by us best calculated for the purpose in case of their being desirous to settle on an Island.
4. That ample satisfaction be made us for all our losses out of the booty which may be taken from the Chaab whose Vessels must either be bestroyed or delivered up to us or at least security given that they shall never again be employed against us.
5. That one-half of all plunder or Booty of what nature soever taken from Meer Mhanna be delivered up to us.
6. In case of our undertaking an expedition against Meer Mahanna jointly with carim Caun and proving successful at Carrack, he may be permitted to keep possession of it provided he will engage not to deliver it up to any European power whatever except the English in case our Hon'ble masters should chuse to settle there.

Bombay further stipulated that the return of field pieces taken from the Ka'b should also be demanded, "whether we act with Turks or Persians or jointly." Skipp was further instructed to try and insert any other clause beneficial to EIC trade such as the export of raw silk from Gilan. Despite the fact that Skipp was sent to Shiraz, Bombay was still skittish about talking to Karim Khan (given London instructions not to do so) and instructed him that if he had to have to contact with Karim Khan, "which we wish you to avoid," he was allowed to give a present of maximum 10,000 rupees. Because the Basra Agent had written that he feared that if the EIC would take action against the Ka'b without permission from Karim Khan that he might take action against EIC property at Bushire, Skipp was ordered to take preventive measures, in case of a breakdown of negotiations, and to try to conclude the Ka'b affair as soon as possible.[263]

262 Saldanha, *Précis*, vol. 1, pp. 213-15 (Bombay, 18/01/1767); Ibid., vol. 1, p. 220 (Basra, 16/04/1767); Lorimer, *Gazetteer*, pp. 1790-91.

263 Saldanha, *Précis*, vol. 1, pp. 213-15 (Bombay, 18/01/1767).

In April 1767, Henry Moore had become the new Agent at Basra. He was a somewhat bizarre and mercurial person and not at all in favor of dealing with Karim Khan as he was very hostile towards Persians. The reason for this attitude was that he favored dealing with the Turks and to make Basra the EIC center of trade in the Persian Gulf. Thriving trade in Bushire interfered with that objective. He also believed that the objectives concerning the Ka'b could be achieved without the need to have recourse to Karim Khan. Moore even wrote that the only reason that he had sent Skipp to Shiraz was that he wanted to avoid the ire of his superiors.[264] He therefore had modified Skipp's instructions from Bombay, which he did not consider as "terms all of which must be positively be insisted upon." It was therefore left to Skipp's discretion to obtain the best terms. However, if Skipp believed that he really had discretion Moore added some really hard terms that Skip had to insist upon.

> The conditions of granting him the assistance he may want against Meer Mahanna, must be either to destroy the Chaub or procure for us-
>
> A firm and lasting peace between the Chaub on one part , the Turks and us on the other restitution in money of all he has taken from the English and the sum of One hundred thousand Rupees at least for the expences to which he has put the Company- Secondly
>
> Either to compel the Chaub to give up to the Turks the territory of Gaban, and reside entirely at Doorack, or to remain neuter & let the Turks endeavour the recovery of their own territories.
>
> Should the Caun propose our being neutral in the disputes between the Turks and the Chaub; you are by no means to come into it as neither our interest nor our honour will admit of it.

Moore, using Bombay's arguments against itself, further wrote that he could not return the *Defiance* because he had been forced by circumstances to negotiate with Karim Khan, who would insist that the EIC help him against Mir Mohanna, in which case nothing could be done without the *Defiance* and the *Salamander,* a bomb ketch. He also piously added that Skipp, of course, had to avoid if possible the subject of support against Mir Mohanna, but he had little hope on that score.[265] Thus, Skipp was given much leeway, or a rope to hang himself as is clear later, how to reach an agreement with Karim Khan.

The terrain in Persia, both at Shiraz and Bushire was not a very welcoming either. After the failed naval support activity against Mir Mohanna in June 1765, London had forbidden the resident of Bushire to correspond with Karim Khan about new privileges or settlements without prior permission or to deputy anybody to represent him at the Zand court; he was of course allowed to have contacts concerning normal trade matters.[266] Bowyear wrote that his predecessor Jervis, before reception of these orders, had sent the Linguist to Shiraz with a written request that Sheikh Naser be removed about which he expected trouble, "as the Government has been in the Family for ages." Sheikh Naser's son demanded 1,000 Rs more per year in rent for the factory and Sheikh Naser sent for the EIC broker from Shiraz. "The first he knows will be disagreeable for us to Comply with and the last Impossible." Bowyear therefore wrote him a polite letter to improve relations.[267] Another

264 Amin, *British Interests*, pp. 94-95.

265 Saldanha, *Précis*, vol. 1, pp. 218-19 (Basra, 14/04/1767); Ibid., vol. 1, p. 220 (Basra, 16/04/1767).

266 Saldanha, *Précis*, vol. 1, pp. 198-99 (London, 02/05/1766).

267 Saldanha, *Précis*, vol. 1, p. 204 (Bushire, 02/08/1766); Lorimer, *Gazetteer*, p. 1793.

problem was that a conflict between Sheikh Naser and Karim Khan had broken out that affected trade negatively.

CONFLICT BETWEEN KARIM KHAN AND BUSHIRE.

The negotiations between the EIC and the Zand court as well as trade were also impacted by a conflict that had broken out in early 1767 with Sheikh Naser of Bushire over tax payments. According to the EIC resident at Bushire:

> Ever since the death of Nadir Shah, this family [the al-Madhkur] has enjoyed unmolested the revenues of this port and bahreen without paying for 20 years past that tribute due on their phirmands … and for which some merchants do imagine they will be called upon to account for, nor will excuses or outward obedience any longer pass with the Khan without a present in proportion to the amount due to the Khan.[268]

Because Sheikh Naser refused to give in, Karim Khan incited the chiefs of the Tangesir and Dashtestan to attack and lay siege to Bushire. On February 8, 1767 Bushire reported that Zaki Khan with about 6,000 men had entirely destroyed Kangan (Congoon), which was a punishment for its disobedient behavior in 1765 (see chapter three). It "was suddenly surrounded by his troops, who sacked it and after massacring the oldest and the infirm inhabitants took away the rest as prisoners to Shiraz." Among the prisoners was Sheikh Hajar, who together with his core retainers, who also had allegedly been involved in piracy, was executed.[269] Zaki Khan had given orders "for every merchant with their families to leave Bushire, and that all of them had been prohibited under the most severe penalties from trading there, or exporting any specie in future, which had occasioned an entire stagnation of all business." The Resident had written Skipp in Shiraz to get the order revoked, but the roads leading from Bushire were strictly guarded so that without permission from Zaki Khan no messenger could pass. He also had allowed the government of Tangesir "to take up arms against the Shaik and that the Caun had demand 4000 Tomaunds annually from the Government of Barreem and Bushire, which they supposed would be complied with."[270] As a result Shirazi merchants withdrew their agents from Bushire. In April 1767, the EIC shipped woolen cloth for Bushire to Basra to reduce their risk, "whilst the army under Zaki Khan (Laikey Caun) continued in the Dashtatoun province."[271] By May 1767 Bushire was under siege by the Zand army. In August/September 1767 Naser's only son went to Shiraz with gifts to get the siege lifted. Sheikh Naser offered to pay 1,000 *tumans* which was refused.[272] Sheikh Naser's change of heart may have been brought about by the attack of Bahrain by the Hulas, which, although unsuccess-

268 Grummond, *The Rise*, p. 95.

269 Anonymous, *Chronicle*, vol. 1, p. 668; Perry, *Karim Khan*, p. 158.

270 Saldanha, *Précis*, vol. 1, p. 222 (Bombay, 03/09/1767); Lorimer, *Gazetteer*, p. 1793. The blockade was very effective, for the Carmelites write "that without help (we have had) from the sea we should have all died of starvation." Anonymous, *Chronicle*, vol. 1, p. 668.

271 Saldanha, *Précis*, vol. 1, p. 218 (Basra, 09/04/1767).

272 Anonymous, *Chronicle*, vol. 1, 668; Grummond, *The Rise*, p. 97. The Carmelites who had settled in Bushire in 1764, reported that they had baptized 21 persons by 1765, but no Moslems. Afterwards the Carmelites occasionally visited Bushire. Anonymous, *Chronicle*, vol. 1, 668-89, 695.

ful required that he had to rapidly resolve his problem with Karim Khan.[273] By December 1767 he agreed to Karim Khan's demands and the Zand troops retreated in January 1768, while his son was sent to Shiraz to stay at Karim Khan's court as a hostage for his good behavior. The incident did not hurt Sheikh Naser's standing at court. In 1768 Sheikh Naser participated in a naval blockade of Bandar-e Rig and in 1769 he was confirmed as governor of Bushire and Bahrain and received the title of admiral (*darya-beygi*). It showed also that Bushire without a secure hinterland (i.e. support of Dashtestan tribes) had no chance in challenging the Zand regime in Shiraz.[274]

SKIPP'S FIRST MISSION TO SHIRAZ

Skipp arrived in April 1767 in Shiraz. Although Karim Khan had asked that the EIC send an envoy to him he ignored Skipp totally and refused to see him. At the beginning of August Moore instructed Skipp to leave by the end of that month and on arrival to move all the Company staff and property from Bushire to Basra, while at the same time seizing as many vessels as possible belonging to Karim Khan and the Sheikhs of Bushire and Bahrain. At the instructions of Basra, Bowyear had on return of Skipp to ship all EIC goods aboard "and seize all the gallivats and ships belonging to Carem Caun, the Shaik of Barreem and the Shaik of Bushire." After that he had to sail to Basra.[275] Bombay was upset about this news and realized that the EIC might be at war with Karim Khan as a result of this action and it could not reach the Resident in time to forbid it, because they lamented this decision.[276]

Fortunately, the fact that Skipp was making preparations to depart from Shiraz drew the attention of Karim Khan, who did not allow him to leave for he now wanted to talk to him. Karim Khan made it clear that he would not allow the English or the Turks to attack the Ka'b, who were his subjects. However, he was willing to come to an accommodation. Instead of war Karim Khan proposed that the Ka'b pay the full value of English losses, provided that the EIC supported him against Mr Mohanna, for which help he offered a remuneration of 500,000 rupees and the island of Khark.[277]

The result of Skipp's mission was that Karim Khan withdrew his support from the Ka'b and gave the EIC a free hand, but unassisted by the Turks, to attack the Ka'b at a time and place of their choosing. Although Karim Khan claimed that he detested the Ka'b he prevaricated as to the question of the transfer of the Ka'b fleet to the EIC. He maintained that to do so was not honorable, as he was the protector of the tribe. Apart from the fact that Karim Khan probably would not have been able to deliver on such a promise, he probably also preferred the Ka'b to keep their gallivats to be used if need be against the Ottomans and other possible enemies, such as the English. The issue of the gallivats was thus left vague. Karim Khan only promised to destroy the Ka'b and repay the EIC 10-fold if they would attack again. Also he promised to pay the remuneration of five lakh of rupees as soon as the EIC had its naval squadron ready to move against Mir Mohanna. Moore instructed Skipp to temporize because of this impediment. Skipp therefore promised Karim Khan naval support subject to approval by Bombay. Moore did not have faith in Karim Khan's promises,

273 Grummond, *The Rise*, pp. 77-78; Perry, Karim, *Karim Khan*, pp. 151, 157, 163.

274 Grummond, *The Rise*, p. 98; Anonymous, *Chronicle*, vol. 1, p. 668.

275 Amin, *British Interests*, p. 95; Saldanha, *Précis*, vol. 1, p. 222 (Bombay, 03/09/1767); Anonymous, *Chronicle*, vol. 1, p. 668.

276 Saldanha, *Précis*, vol. 1, p. 223 (Bombay, 03/09/1767).

277 Amin, *British Interests*, p. 95.

whom he described as "by far too wavering and capricious to have the least reliance on his promises." He felt so strong, because the EIC's most important point the handing over of the Ka'b's gallivats was not acceded to. Moore further argued that if Bombay approved the Khark action why not then also insist on a combined action against the Ka'b and finish them? As long as the Ka'b had their gallivats they presented a danger to Basra and its trade. Nothing could be expected from the Turks, because they had been cowed by Karim Khan's threats. Moore would therefore try to get at least Qobban for them or try to influence Karim Khan in their favor. Meanwhile, Moore's position was weakened by Mir Mohanna's continued piratical activities, for in September 1767 he exacted 380 bales of 550 bales of coffee as customs. As a result, nobody dared to sail from Masqat to Basra and the EIC therefore promised to provide convoy, if possible.[278]

DISASTER STRIKES EIC AT HORMUZ

Because of the confusion created by the different reactions by London and Bombay to Moore's ideas the latter pursued his own policy. He, for example, kept two ships at Basra to continue the blockade against the Ka'b. While following the completion of the negotiations with Karim Khan and awaiting Bombay's reaction he decided to use the EIC's idle naval force at Basra for some action. Although nothing had been done about the *Islamabad* affair for two years Moore believed that it was the right time to show the flag and impress the natives with English power. The result was what Lorimer rightly has called "an appalling catastrophe, the most serious that has ever befallen a British operation in the Persian Gulf."[279] Moore and his council without any authorization decided to send one of Bombay's largest ships, the *Defiance* to Hormuz to "convince him [Karim Khan] of our power, we convince him of the consequence of our Alliance: we give him a testimony how willing we are to be his friends if his mistaken friendship for the Chaub and ignorance of his own interests does not prevent our being so." The *Islamabad* event had almost been forgotten. Moore had to look for the details of the affair in his archives to give his unauthorized operation a sheen of legitimacy. In 1766, Bombay indeed had looked favorably on a possible operation to deal out punishment for the murder of Sutherland c.s. and the plundering of his ship, but only after the Ka'b had been chastised and if a favorable opportunity offered itself.[280]

Moore who intensely disliked Karim Khan now uncharacteristically cited the fact, allegedly mentioned by Skipp on August 4, 1767 that the ruler of Persia wanted the EIC to reduce Sheikh 'Abdollah, Karim Khan had told Skipp that the EIC could keep all vessels that it would seize there and thus "it is not therefore reasonable to imagine Carim Caun would be in the least disgusted at our demanding restitution of the *Islamabad* treasures, nor at the same time as Allies to Carim Caun, insisting upon the delivery up of the Chaub's ship and Gallivats to him." Moore believed that the current force available was enough to do that task. The *Defiance* or the *Bombay* Grab with a schooner or gallivat were sufficient to blockade the Haffar, which meant that all other vessels would be inactive for the next three months, unless used for this expedition. Moore preferred to settle problem with Sheikh 'Abdollah by treaty, if he would agree to (i) ample restitution the value of the cargo of the Islamabad was, according to Sutherland's broker, more than 4 lakh of rupees, exclusive of this we demand 100,000 Rs for the Company and 40,000 Rs for the captors; (ii) the surrender of all ships and vessels lying at Hormuz; and (iii) release of the island of Hormuz to the

278 Saldanha, *Précis*, vol. 1, pp. 224-25 (Basra, 05/10/1767).

279 Lorimer, *Gazetteer*, p. 1795.

280 Saldanha, *Précis*, vol. 1, pp. 225-26 (Basra, 09/10/1767); Lorimer, *Gazetteer*, p. 1794.

EIC or to whomever Karim Khan wants to give the government. If he refused the squadron had to seize all vessels and the person of the sheikh himself. If the island were taken by force it had to be handed over to those commissionaires that would be appointed, while inventories had to be made of all stores that had to be loaded on the vessels and immediately shipped to Basra. When Karim Khan had appointed proper people to take charge of the island the EIC representatives would hand it to them, if not they were to depart to Basra; no garrison was to be left there. Karim Khan therefore should be properly informed of the EIC designs concerning the island. It was also reported that part of the *Islamabad* booty was on the island of Kish, which the squadron had to check out on their return and demand its sheikh for an account of it.[281] Available information indicated that Sheikh 'Abdollah was at Hormuz in "his fort [which] was all in pieces, and not one of his Gun carriages but what was useless: that his gallivats were all in very bad order that our ships could go within hail of the fort, and that if they were to go, the Fort could not hold out two hours." Bombay argued that as good relations existed with Karim Khan the factory at Bushire did not need any naval protection. It further submitted that although Sheikh 'Abdollah was not the murderer or thief he nevertheless was a fence, because he had not returned the stolen goods.[282]

Once having achieved its objective at Hormuz, the squadron had to demand satisfaction from the Sheikh of Khark "for his taking our armed boat in the month of May last on her return from Muscat for his cruelty to our people, and for his insolence in saying the English were not equal to his shoes." The value of boat and contents was estimated at 10,000 Rs. "We would therefore by every military exaction, have the Shaik of that place convinced of his insolence: we would have all his Gallivats taken the Shaik seized, and be made to pay as largely, as so poor a Shaikdom will admit-we would then have him brought a prisoner to Bushire and there be disposed of as Carim Caun may think proper."[283]

With these orders the cruiser the *Defiance*, the bomb-vessel the *Salamander* and the gallivat the *Wolf* under the command of Messrs. Lyster and Bowyear left Basra in mid-October. The expedition ended in a disaster when on November 15, 1767 the *Defiance* blew up just off Qeshm and sank with more than 300 men on board, including the commanders of the operation. The other EIC vessels were considered to be too few in number compared to the enemy force and therefore went to Bandar 'Abbas. According to the few survivors, the ship blew up due to the carelessness of the gunner and the steward, "who had a candle down in the after hold drawing Arrack off which took fire."[284]

Bombay immediately sent its largest ship the frigate the *Revenge* to replace the *Defiance* with orders to do nothing. It was not that Basra was without naval protection, because in February 1768, Moore reported that the Haffar was blockaded by two schooners, one gallivat and some small Turkish vessels, with which they hoped to keep things quiet until the return of the *Bombay* grab.[285] London had disapproved of the plan for dealing with the *Islamabad* affair, before it was aware of the disaster that had taken place. It commented that on the face of it the plan regarding Hormuz sounded very attractive, but there was nothing on paper. London argued that Moore in acting the way he wanted would expose the Company to major problems. The idea of the handing out of passes was not in the interest EIC either, London argued, in fact it considered it destructive. If Mir

281 Saldanha, *Précis*, vol. 1, pp. 226-28 (Basra, 09/10/1767).

282 Saldanha, *Précis*, vol. 1, p. 226-27 (Basra, 09/10/1767).

283 Saldanha, *Précis*, vol. 1, p. 228 (Basra, 09/10/1767).

284 Saldanha, *Précis*, vol. 1, p. 229-30 (Basra Diary 1767), with a report on the events, which may also be found in toto in Lorimer, *Gazetteer*, pp. 1795-96.

285 Saldanha, *Précis*, vol. 1, p. 232 (Basra, 06/02/1768).

Mohanna would respect them it would only for a short while and then he or others would start to attack anyway. This would result in many complaints and the EIC fleet will have to be kept in the Gulf the entire year and see what happened in Basra. Also, the directors scoffed at the idea to go to Hormuz to take it for Karim Khan, who Moore reported was displeased by this step as the Sheykh was his subject and should therefore not be touched. Also, Moore had no authority from Bombay to do something about Hormuz. London also raised the question of the attractive distribution of the expected spoils at Hormuz and asked on what it had been based? In short, the directors concluded that Moore had no agreement and Karim Khan would never allow it, while it was highly unlikely that sheikh 'Abdollah had so much money as he intimated. For if he had he would have had a better force to protect it than the small one he had.[286] In fact, after the disaster had taken place Skipp reported in April 1768, "With respect to Shaik 'Abdollah the vakeel from [the] time of my first arrival till now has not requested our assistance against him, or indeed mentioned him to me." As might be expected, Karim Khan was annoyed by the Company's action, which added to the tension between the two sides.[287]

SKIPP'S SECOND MISSION TO SHIRAZ

In November 1767 Bombay accepted Karim Khan's terms as very advantageous and scolded Moore for not having settled with Karim Khan based on the proposed offer. It instructed Basra that if the offer was still open to accept it immediately, in which case Skipp had to be sent "with the utmost expedition" to Shiraz to conclude a treaty that included special measures to insure that while the EIC fleet was at Khark and Hormuz for reducing respectively Mir Mohanna and Sheikh 'Abdollah the Ka'b could not take action against Basra. If the offer was not valid anymore then Basra had to try to conclude the matter on the most advantageous terms, and not to make war on Karim Khan or to form an alliance with Mir Mohanna or somebody else against him, in fact Bombay forbade it. Karim Khan had to give a peremptory order to that effect or have a sufficient force ready for that purpose. Bombay further instructed Basra that in the agreement with Karim Khan mention should be made of the annual quantity of woolens that he would buy from the EIC and at what price and the same had to be done for raw silk from Gilan, goat hair from Kerman and copper that would be supplied to pay for the woolens.[288]

Skipp did not leave immediately and only departed on February 7, 1768 for Shiraz.[289] Meanwhile, Bombay had berated Moore for proposing to form an alliance with Mir Mohanna against Karim Khan. It sent a number of vessels to Bushire for the Khark operation and informed Moore that it disapproved of his order to begin hostilities against Karim Khan and destroy the town and vessels lying there and expressed its astonishment that he even had given such orders. Also, Bombay did not understand Moore's proposal to ally itself with Mir Mohanna when on June 29 he had described him in very negative terms and then on July 16 had changed his mind all together describing Mir Mohanna in positive terms saying that he never had injured the EIC forgetting that he had destroyed the Bandar-e Rig factory and chased the resident away, while he also had described him as "the scourge of the Gulph." Contrariwise Karim Khan has never injured the EIC and he was not of an unsteady character as Moore had described him. When the operation at

286 Saldanha, *Précis*, vol. 1, p. 244-46 (London, 02/03/1768).

287 Lorimer, *Gazetteer*, p. 1797.

288 Saldanha, *Précis*, vol. 1, pp. 231-32 (Bombay, 17/11/1767).

289 Saldanha, *Précis*, vol. 1, p. 232 (Basra, 06/02/1768).

Khark turned out to be successful Bombay wanted to keep the island; the Dutch had only rented it and thus they had no just claim to it, the more so since the EIC would not seize it, "but by virtue of a grant by Carim Caun." Therefore Bombay instructed Moore to keep a naval force there as large as he deemed necessary. Bombay understood that Karim Khan wanted to stand security for the Ka'b so that they would not molest the EIC in the future. Furthermore, that after having acted jointly with Karim Khan against Mir Mohanna the former did not want the EIC to start new hostilities against the Ka'b, unless provoked thereto. Also, that if the EIC would conclude a treaty with Karim Khan along those lines it would agree to keep one guard vessel in the Gulf, but only on condition that he paid for the expense in no uncertain terms. Bombay stipulated that these cost were 62,440 rupees for a first rate and 40,099 rupees for a second rate per year. In the treaty with Karim Khan, if it were to be concluded, Bombay insisted that it also should be stated that the EIC is "to have the exclusive right to trade in his Dominions, without particularly naming any other Europeans whatsoever."[290]

Sheikh Sa'dun returned from Shiraz having had a positive discussion with Karim Khan. But despite this positive sign, "there are impediments to the trade of [sic] still subsisting and which Cerim Caun says shall not be taken off until the English negotiations are over." Skipp second visit to Shiraz started better than his first one. He had almost immediately an interview with Karim Khan and it did not take long before Skipp reached an agreement with him on April 17, 1768. Karim Khan agreed and gave an undertaking that he (i) would pay 15,000 *tumans* once Khark was taken, (ii) would be responsible for any damage caused by the Ka'b, and (iii) gave a copy of his orders to the Ka'b not to attack the EIC or the Turks. The Ka'b agent at his court was sent to Sheikh Salman to convey this order. Karim Khan further promised free trade once it was clear that EIC really would assist him. He also had still some points to settle with the sheikh of Bushire, before he would open the road between Bushire and Shiraz. Skipp then promised that the EIC would send a force to take Khark. While waiting for the papers the Sheikh of Bushire and his allies urged Karim Khan to reject the EIC's assistance and they offered to undertake the action themselves, but he had not full confidence in it. Skipp reported on April 16 that a few days prior to that date Sheikh 'Abdollah's brother of Hormuz had come. He supported the Sheikh of Bushire's proposal and offered his help as well. Karim Khan, however, declared if the EIC performed the service he would grant it all the privileges. If he had not accepted this Skipp argued the sheikhs' proposal would have accepted and the EIC would have had nothing. He further emphasized that Karim Khan had not requested EIC help against Sheikh 'Abdollah or even mentioned him. Karim Khan now also accepted last year's present to him, which he earlier had refused. He was satisfied now. Skipp had not informed Karim Khan about Moore's proposed peaceful solution, for he argued that had to come from Mir Mohanna. He therefore suggested to Moore that he urge him to do so, provided that he would come in person to Shiraz. Karim Khan would be willing to spare his life if the EIC interceded for him, adding that Karim Khan "is far from being of a cruel disposition."[291]

It was decided to implement the part concerning Khark in the new agreement immediately to which end a large EIC fleet was already present in the Persian Gulf. The operation against Khark was started on May 19 and "ended in an ignominious failure" on May 29, 1766.[292] Skipp stayed for another three months in Shiraz after the failed attack on Khark and tried to come to an agreement with Karim Khan. However, chances were worse than ever, because Moore did not want an agreement with Karim Khan, but one with Mir Mohanna against Karim Khan. Moreover,

290 Saldanha, *Précis*, vol. 1, pp. 234-35 (Bombay, 15/01/1768); Lorimer, *Gazetteer*, p. 1798.

291 Saldanha, *Précis*, vol. 1, pp. 237-39 (Shiraz, 16/04/1768); Lorimer, *Gazetteer*, p. 1798. For the text of Karim Khan's undertaking, see Saldanha, *Précis*, vol. 1, pp. 239-40 (14/04/1768).

292 Lorimer, *Gazetteer*, p. 1799; for details of the Khark operation see chapter four.

he had developed an antipathy against Skipp, which made collaboration impossible. Basra decided on September 6, 1768 "of having nothing further to do with the Caun, his perfidious and injurious treatment of us [being] the cause of it." It further ordered Skipp to leave Shiraz and annul all commitments. Even when Karim Khan made a new proposal by the end of August they were not interested to change their mind nor that he sent troops to Ganaveh opposite Khark, for this was but a mere blind. On his arrival in Basra in October 1768 Skipp was suspended of his duties and sent to Bombay to account for his breach of trust and breach of orders in commercial matters.[293]

THE EIC WITHDRAWS FROM BUSHIRE

Although these EIC decisions should have made the Persian Gulf a safer place this actually did not happen. Mir Mohanna to show off his prowess and disdain for both the English and Karim Khan attacked an English ship in August 1768, when Skipp was still at the Zand court in Shiraz. On Skipp's return to Basra, Moore decided to reduce the EIC's risk at Bushire by reducing the value of its stock held there to a value of 5,000 rupees in case the failed negotiations might lead to a break with Karim Khan. In addition, Moore sent word to Masqat that vessels sailing to Basra might be at risk, reason why he ordered an EIC squadron to cruise between Basra and Bardestan to prevent any further piratical activities by Mir Mohanna. The two-vessel squadron was in such a bad state of repair and undermanned that the laying up of the smaller vessels was considered to enable the larger one to function normally. A few days before the arrival of a Persian force at Ganaveh, to be ferried across to Khark by EIC vessels, Moore, in June 1768, ordered the squadron to return to India, where it arrived in August. The failed invasion of Khark was of no great consequence, although further contributing to bad blood between Karim Khan and the English. Even the fact that on January 29, 1768 Mir Mohanna was expelled by his subjects and shortly thereafter executed in Basra did not change that (see chapter three) EIC behavior after Mir Mohanna's expulsion from Khark in January 1769 was not very helpful either. Moore ordered the EIC fleet to blockade Khark and demand that its new chief, Hasan Khan, put it under EIC protection. Although Hasan Khan was not very enthusiastic to obey Zand rule and thus welcomed an English barrier between him and Karim Khan, he balked at the idea when Moore also demanded that he surrender Mir Mohanna's fleet in compensation for EIC losses. Hasan Khan rejected EIC protection now claiming that he was a faithful subject of Karim Khan and would oppose any English action against Khark. Moore fearing that he did not have enough military force to impose himself on Hasan Khan then returned to Basra.[294]

In February 1768, J. Morley, the EIC Resident at Bushire on his own authority decided to withdraw from Bushire after Moore's decision to blockade Khark, whose possible consequences greatly alarmed him. The Resident's argumentation was that given the losses the EIC had suffered a claim should be made on Karim Khan; this is also what people at Bushire thought and therefore he had ordered withdrawal of all staff and goods from Bushire, a decision approved by Moore. Morley told Sheikh Sa'dun that the EIC had sent for him from Basra and he had to go immediately. Sheikh Sa'dun tried to dissuade Morley, who insisted and Sheikh Sa'dun then said that Karim Khan would take it out on him, for he had just received orders from Zaki Khan not to allow Morley to depart until he had orders from Shiraz, "imagining our fleet might be employed against Carrack." Morley expressed surprise, since the EIC was happy with the end of the pirate's career, which had been

293 Lorimer, *Gazetteer*, p. 1801.

294 Amin, *British Interests*, p. 100.

detrimental to trade and now that the island was in Karim Khan's hands it was no more of English concern. He then allowed Morley to go. When the hospitalized people were ferried aboard Morley heard that Sheikh Sa'dun had set a guard at the factory and did not allow any of the EIC effects to be taken away and Morley therefore went again to see Sheikh Sa'dun. He excused himself stating that he had received new orders from Zaki Khan not allowing the EIC to depart at all, failing to do that his father would be the sacrifice of the Khan's ire. He expected the messenger sent to Shiraz with information regarding Khark to be back soon. He promised Morley that if he stayed until the messenger returned or the 11 February he would not impede his departure, despite contrary orders of Zaki Khan. Since with the wounded the EIC had some 100 people ashore it was impractical to board them under these circumstances Morley accepted his word. Meanwhile he continued preparing for departure and later indeed left.[295]

London was upset about the disastrous campaign against the Ka'b and its follow-up, which it blamed "in a great measure to want of knowledge and experience in those who transacted this disagreeable undertaking." As to the Ka'b disaster, London blamed the commanders of the operation, who had landed their force in a very bad wet place, where marching was very difficult, which was too far away from its target and thus it was very difficult to bring up the artillery. Also they did not wait for the Ottomans to arrive before attacking, although the latter had sufficient troops, contrary to the situation of the English force. London further blamed Karim Khan who claimed that the Ka'b were his subjects and that he would take care of the problem. However, he did not do anything. Even when Skipp went to see him, he was treated very indifferently, and when he was about to leave Karim Khan all of a sudden wanted to deal, promised to pay for the cruisers, but also wanted a joint attack against Hormuz. Given his treatment of the EIC in general up to that time, and in particular that the EIC was not allowed to export cash to Bushire etc. London berated Bombay that "you should have withdrawn our staff and effects immediately." London argued that if Karim Khan really wanted to treat with the EIC he would have to send people to us, which would be advantageous for us. The Ka'b then would have seen that Karim Khan had no power over the EIC, nor that he could do the Company any harm. Then, or so believed London, Bombay could have decided to do whatever it wanted, make an agreement, of what nature, or not at all, but from a position of strength.[296] London was not pleased with the Ottoman authorities either and instructed Bombay to remind them that they were in arrears with the payments for the hired ships. Bombay had to remain friendly with the government of Basra, but if the arrears were not paid it had to withdraw the fleet. Finally, London repeated once again that it disapproved of Bombay's involvement in local politics and gave instructions not to get involved with expeditions, alliances with or against Arabs, unless it was for friendship, because in case of disputes each side had to defend his own interest.[297]

The result of Moore's policy, clearly supported by London, but in defiance of Bombay, was that he had not achieved his objective of bringing more security to the upper part of the Persian Gulf,

295 Saldanha, *Précis*, vol. 1, pp. 250-51 (Bushire, 04/02/1769). To outsiders, such as the Carmelites, the reason for English withdrawal from Bushire seemed to be: "out of a point of mere pique, because the Persian government had not allowed them [the EIC] to construct, as they claimed for their security, a fort at Bushire." Anonymous, *Chronicle*, vol. 1, p. 673. This is an observation of some interest because Wilson, *Persian Gulf*, p. 179 implies that such a factory had been built, which was clearly not the case in 1772, the date of the Carmelite report. It would seem that the English factory in Bushire was only built in the nineteenth century, because no eighteenth century source reports its existence, as far as I know. The English indeed had a factory in Bushire, but this was a house rented from Sheikh Naser. To have a large fort also would not have made any sense for the single EIC servant staying in Bushire after 1778.

296 Saldanha, *Précis*, vol. 1, p. 243-44 (London, 02/03/1768).

297 Saldanha, *Précis*, vol. 1, p. 247 (London, 02/03/1768).

in particular for Basra, neither by reaching an agreement with Karim Khan, as Bombay wanted, nor by challenging him, as London and Moore himself wanted. The EIC did not have sufficient military force (in numbers and equipment) to impose itself on Persia or the coastal Arabs, while Moore's sabotage of efforts to reach an agreement with Karim Khan cost the EIC dearly. Bombay therefore was furious and not convinced at all by Moore's arguments for the justification of the withdrawal from Bushire. In fact, it attributed this as well as the failed negotiation to Moore's enmity toward Karim Khan. After all, so argued the Council, given the importance it attached to the purchase of Gilan silk as well the sale of woolens the departure from Bushire was incomprehensible, because the best place to do so was at Bushire, at least "before the trouble between the Caun and Shaiks of that Place."[298]

Bombay did not appreciate London's support of Moore nor its observations on the situation in the Persian Gulf. It pointed out that apart from the fact that Bushire was the best place to sell woolens and buy raw silk, Persian merchants did not go to Basra because of the bad treatment they received there. It was easier for merchants to get it from the Russians up north. Bombay therefore wanted to make this clear so that London understood the importance of having a trading station in Bushire. The Council explained in a letter to the directors that in the head of the Persian Gulf the Persian market was supplied via three routes: (i) via Hoveyzeh and Shushtar; (ii) by sea via Bushire or Bandar-e Rig; and (iii) via Baghdad, in case the former was insecure, because the Ka'b or "Bennalim [?] Arabs" plundered caravans. The export duty from Basra to Shushtar was also believed to be high. Apart from maritime risk, freight cost, an export duty of 3-5% and an import duty of 8% at Bushire and Bandar-e Rig was levied. At that time, the Baghdad route was less secure than the other two, while the river duties from Basra to Baghdad were estimated to amount to at least 20%. Therefore, about one-third of woolens imported at Basra reached the Persian market. Thus, or so Bombay concluded, Persian merchants could easily afford to pay the higher price at Bushire where they experienced less hassle. Given these arguments Bombay felt that the EIC was obliged to re-open its factory there. Therefore it submitted that it liked to have a fortified factory like at Bandar 'Abbas, at Bushire or any other port, because Basra was getting less and less secure.[299]

Bombay was not only annoyed with London, but so much more with Basra that it appointed a committee to study whether the Basra operation should not be transferred to Bushire or be reduced to a Residency. The members of that commission were Messrs. Wrench, Jervis and Martin, who but for the last one had extensive experience in the Gulf. They also consulted with Skipp and Morley, who had just returned from the Gulf and submitted their report on November 3, 1769. In it they recommended the establishment of a fortified factory at Bushire, which would be as secure as

298 Saldanha, *Précis*, vol. 1, p. 255 (Bombay, 24/04/1769); Ibid., vol. 1, pp. 258-59 (Bombay, 31/10/1769); Amin, *British Interests*, p. 100.

299 Saldanha, *Précis*, vol. 1, pp. 262-63 (Bombay, 03/11/1769). This pattern was not new for it was also observed around 1740 that merchants from Shushtar, Hoveyzeh, Dowraq etc. came to trade in Basra. VOC 2511, f. 1027. In 1757, the EIC Basra agency reported that the result of the Zand campaign against Dowraq had a negative impact on trade at Basra, because the Zands "having plunder'd all the bordering places and lying so near us in Basra, prevented the Despool [Dezful], Haviza, and Doorach Caphilas [*qafilah* or caravan] from coming which We frequently have at that Season of the Year and the Persia Market takes off." Ricks, *Politics and Trade*, p. 339 referring to F. R. Gombroon X (14/09/1757). Other contemporary observers also confirm the EIC report. Parsons, *Travels*, p. 155; Raynal, *A Philosophical and Political History*, vol. 1, pp. 305-06. This situation had not changed 20 years later; see Saldanha, *Précis*, vol. 1, p. 423 (Report on the Commerce of Arabia and Persia by Samuel Manestry and Hardford Jones, 1790).

Basra and better situated for the trade, in particular of woolens. The commission also believed that if raw silk was taken in payment Karim Khan would consume 2 to 3 lakh of rupees in woolens.[300]

The directors in London had become so worried about the security situation in the Persian Gulf that they in 1769 asked the English government for naval assistance. The Company's resources were overtaxed due to the conflict with Heydar 'Ali of Mysore and the looming conflict with the French in India and thus could not spare more ships and men to deal with the situation in the Gulf. After long negotiations the English government and the EIC reached an agreement and fleet of the royal navy was sent to the East to assist the Company in India and the Gulf. The commander of the fleet Sir John Lindsay was also named plenipotentiary for the Gulf and charged:

> To negotiate, transact and conclude all or any treaty or treaties of peace or commerce, and all leagues offensive or defensive with all or any princes nobles or potentates, powers or states, within or bordering upon the Gulph of Persia.

However, when Lindsay's fleet arrived in India in 1770 the seemingly critical situation for the Company had become entirely diffused. Peace had been concluded with Heydar 'Ali, the French threat in Bengal was not really considered that much of a threat anymore and with the death of Mir Mohanna and the truce with the Ka'b the Persian Gulf was also at peace. Lindsay therefore decided not to undertake any military action against the Ka'b or Karim Khan. He did not even try to conclude an agreement with them, although he was empowered to do so, but only sent a reconnaissance ship to the Gulf to verify that all was peaceful. When this was confirmed he forgot all about the Gulf as he had other, more important issues to deal with in India.[301]

Meanwhile, Sheikh Naser was keenly interested in the EIC returning to Bushire and he asked passing EIC ships to sell their cloth, which they did not do in view of strict orders from Basra, which did not want to have anything to do with Persia. Nevertheless, in September 1769, the Basra Agency decided not to organize a convoy for the coffee fleet from Masqat, which was at war with Karim Khan (see below). Although this decision was against the Basra Agency's sentiments, it thus obeyed Bombay's orders. In 1770, Bombay moreover instructed Basra to communicate to Sheikh Naser, who had many times invited the EIC to return, that if Karim Khan would request such a return in writing a European envoy would be sent to discuss the matter with him. If this would happen then Mr. Morley of the Basra Agency was to go to Shiraz with the same instructions as Skipp had received, minus those dealing with Khark, but plus the demand for the return of the *Speedwell* and its cargo that Mir Mohanna had taken in 1768.[302] Basra sabotaged this opening towards Persia by replying that "We have delayed sending a mission to Shiraz, because we do not have the necessary presents nor a good linguist to accompany Morley. Can you send both?"[303] The delaying tactics were effective, because in August 1770 London forbade a return to Bushire, because this would only lead to expenses and new perpetual disputes. Also, the Company directors doubted that the move would result in an increase of the sale of woolens, despite the drop in sales of this commodity in Basra. They therefore instructed that no embassy was to be sent to Karim Khan to discuss a factory at Bushire.[304]

---

300 Lorimer, *Gazetteer*, pp. 1803-04.

301 Amin, *British Interests*, pp. 101-05.

302 Lorimer, *Gazetteer*, p. 1804.

303 Saldanha, *Précis*, vol. 1, pp. 265-66 (Basra, 31/08/1770).

304 Saldanha, *Précis*, vol. 1, pp. 264-65 (London, 24/08/1770).

TURMOIL IN THE PERSIAN GULF

The situation in the Persian Gulf had become so uncharacteristically peaceful by the autumn of 1770 that Basra submitted that having two cruisers would be more than sufficient for its needs. Moreover, Hoseyn Khan, who had expelled Mir Mohanna, wrote to the Agent offering friendship and assistance to EIC ships and a factory at Bandar-e Rig to which a polite reply was given, to wit: that the Company was unable to settle at that time at Bandar-e Rig.[305] However, this idyllic interlude did not last long, for reality struck back in 1771. Khark gallivats at Karim Khan's orders had sailed southward "to make prices [sic] without exception which they could master." The Basra Agency had given this piece of intelligence little attention, but the information proved to be true. On 22 June, 1771 three gallivats off Kangan (Congoon) seized the *Britannia Galley*, owned by a private Englishman, and a country ketch from Gogo [?] under English colors, besides a Botella ketch and sundry boats from Masqat. The pirates tried to bring them to Khark but a strong NW wind drove them to Bahrain, and when the wind turned they sailed to Bandar-e Rig where they arrived on June 27. The *Britannia* got stuck on the bar at Bandar-e Rig, but half of her goods were unloaded and sold on the coast. Moore heard about it on July 9 and immediately sent the *Resolution*, the *Expedition* and the *Dolphin* to Khark and Bandar-e Rig. Moore wrote to Hoseyn Khan demanding the release of the vessels and its cargos. The EIC ships had orders in case of refusal to recover them or failing that to destroy all Khark gallivats. If all else failed they had to sail to Masqat and give warning and escort English vessels in convoy and then cruise near Khark. On July 12 the squadron sailed away, but did not find the vessels. They arrived on July 14 at Bandar-e Rig and the linguist went ashore with Moore's letter. When he did not return immediately Commander Inu sent the two other ships to Bushire to get information on the whereabouts of the vessels. He received an unsatisfactory answer from Mir Hoseyn and returned to Basra. On his arrival, the linguist was received by Mir Hoseyn's *vakil* and then taken to 2-3 of Karim Khan's people. They demanded the letter, but he refused as it was for Mir Hoseyn. They threatened to take it by force but did not. The next morning Mir Hoseyn arrived from Khark. In public he threatened to attack the EIC squadron, but in private he told the linguist that it was all Karim Khan's fault. He wanted to be friends with the English and was ready to make an alliance. If they would not molest him he would give them Khark and denounce Karim Khan. He also maintained that the *Britannia Galley* had attacked first and that he would give her back when she returned to Bandar-e Rig, which he did not. He had maltreated the English crew, who were given no shelter from the sun and hardly any life necessities. The captain and the first officer had been sent to Shiraz; the former was said to have died. Part of the crew was sent to Bushire and the rest was handed to the Basra Agency by Mir Hoseyn. The latter wrote a letter to Moore blaming Sheikh Naser of Bushire for the hostilities, who was its sole promoter. The EIC linguist reported that Mir Hoseyn was usually drunk; his people were poor and mutinous and only with great difficulty was he able to control them. He had 10 gallivats and some boats. One of the gallivats had 10 guns, another 8 and the rest each 6, mostly 6-pounders. "They are extremely well built, carry 60 to 80 men, and the largest does not draw water above five feet water." The fort was entirely neglected and was falling apart in several places. Usually there were only 30-50 men there, but when the EIC ships had arrived men were transported from Bandar-e Rig in boats at night. Karim Khan's people were there to receive the pirated goods, while the officers had been sent to Shiraz, showing that he was behind these deeds. Moore therefore wrote to Karim Khan on July 15 asking why he had give orders for the hostile acts, but no reply was expected.

305 Saldanha, *Précis*, vol. 1, pp. 267-68 (Basra, 15/10/1770).

Basra therefore asked Bombay for a naval and land force to destroy all Khark gallivats and any forts and places in the Persian Gulf, which might offer to protect them; also all places or islands from which Karim Khan drew revenues and any gallivats under his orders, including the Khark fleet of 10 gallivats, the Bushire fleet of 7-8 gallivats, two ships and boats, the Ka'b fleet of 14-15 gallivats and the Hormuz fleet of about 12 gallivats. This was the only way to do trade in the Gulf, according to Moore, for the Ka'b fleet was also out at sea and the Bushire fleet was expecting orders any day from Shiraz to initiate piratical activities as well. When Commander Farmer went to Bushire the sheikh warned him to leave immediately or be detained with its crew. The sheikh claimed that he did so out of fear of Karim Khan's people at Bushire, which the English believed given his humane treatment of, for example, the crew of the *Britannia Galley* who had been sent to Bushire. Moore submitted that given the strength of the Persian fleet, the EIC fleet should consist of one large ship for battering with one or more of the first and second rates; one bomb vessel and about 10-12 small craft to run after the gallivats into shoal water. The land force should consist of 500 Europeans at least, a train of artillery and 1,500 to 2,000 sepoys. The expedition should not stop at Masqat but sail unexpectedly into the Gulf and take and destroy first all Hormuz gallivats and then all others that they would encounter. Mir Hoseyn's proposal to take Khark did not merit any credence, Moore opined. He could only subsist by piracy; whether Sheikh Naser was the instigator or not Mir Hoseyn was the executor.[306]

In November 1771 London when learning of this plan immediately nixed it and instructed Basra to resolve the issue by negotiations. The proposed plan was much too expensive in view of the possible advantages to be gained. If peaceful means did not work then Basra could apply for naval protection from ships of the royal navy available in India under the command of Lindsay. At the same time, Bombay instructed Moore to organize convoys at Masqat and protect these when sailing to Basra.[307] Although an understandable step, the decision not to return to Bushire cost the EIC dearly. It put an effective end to direct country trade between India and Bushire and had a downward effect on the sale of woolens in the Persian Gulf. This negative impact was further reinforced by the decline of Basra trade due to a series of events after 1773, about which later.[308] London's decision was understandable, because the EIC was in a difficult position in the Persian Gulf by 1770. During 1764-1770 it had lost on all fronts (face, soldiers, ships, and lots of money). It had neither been able to punish the Ka'b nor Mir Mohanna, or to contain their piratical activities. Furthermore, it had been unable to obtain the island of Khark, it had withdrawn from Bushire and was in conflict with Karim Khan and, as a result, it had not even been able to ensure secure trade in the Gulf. In fact, after a brief peaceful lull in 1770, security had become worse, due to EIC inability to impose itself on its various enemies. In fact, these had even started to attack English ships, something that was highly exceptional. The EIC's attempts to take punitive action in these cases only had ended in disaster (loss of life, ships, and money). Amin takes partial exception to this conclusion and argues that the EIC had been able to protect trade effectively between 1766 and 1770, while it also had prevented by its presence that the Ka'b or Karim Khan had taken Basra. Unfortunately, the facts do not bear him out, as discussed above. True, most ships reached their destination unhindered because of EIC convoys, but the cost of protection became so high that it was Bombay not Karim Khan that sought an accommodation to get better security in the Gulf and a relief of the burden of protection. Despite that protection English and other shipping still suffered from piratical activi-

306 Saldanha, *Précis*, vol. 1, pp. 268-71 (Basra, 31/08/1771).

307 Lorimer, *Gazetteer*, p. 1807. For the presence and role of the English royal navy in India at that time see Amin, *British Interests*, pp. 103-04.

308 Amin, *British Interests*, p. 107.

ties. Furthermore, if English presence had really been a deterrence, as Amin claims, why then did Karim Khan attack Basra in May 1775 in full knowledge of the fact that three weeks prior to his attack the EIC had successfully driven back Ka'b vessels that were intending to join his invasion army? It was not the Persians or the Ka'b that ran at Basra, but the English when they saw the size of the invasion army.

THE PERSIAN-OMANI CONFLICT.

I have already referred to a Persian-Omani conflict several times and thus this should be explained. In 1769 Karim Khan and the Imam of Masqat, who was supported by the Banu Ma'in of Hormuz and Qeshm, fell out for reasons that are not clear. There had not been any interference by Oman into Persian affairs, apart from giving support to Sheikh 'Abdollah in 1760 to take Qeshm. Given the fact that Karim Khan demanded that the Imam of Masqat return a Persian ship that he already had since 1767-68 as well as payment of the arrears of the annual tribute, which formerly had been paid to Nader Shah, it seems likely that this conflict was just the result of his policy to re-establish the tributary relationships of the Persian kingdom such as these had been under Nader Shah. As the latter had occupied parts of Oman between 1737 and 1747, while its Imam had been tributary to the Persian ruler, it was but natural that he also wanted to re-instate this tributary relationship. As to the Imam's purchase of the *Fath Rahmaniyeh*, Karim Khan argued that it was one of the ships of Nader Shah's fleet, and that it had been illegally sold by Sheikh 'Abdollah of Hormuz, who was a Persian subject. Karim Khan had in vain tried to subdue the Bani Ma'in 1767 and thus addressing the Imam of Oman, an ally of Sheikh 'Abdollah, was an indirect way to get at also the latter. Also, Karim Khan needed a fleet if he wanted to subdue the coastal Arabs and thus getting possession of this 'Persian' ship might strengthen one of the constituting elements of this fleet, most likely that of Bushire. The Omanis countered that they had bought the ship from Sheikh 'Abdollah of Hormuz in exchange for a few gallivats and some cash; that they had repaired the ship at great cost and that they had owned it for a long time and would not give it up. As to the tribute the Omanis argued that in the case of Nader Shah they had no choice, because they had dreaded him; Karim Khan, however, they despised. Nader Shah was a conqueror; Karim Khan was but the *vakil* of three provinces. They would answer him with canon and ball.[309]

The conflict with Masqat added to the insecurity in the Persian Gulf, for Karim Khan had ordered 'his fleet' to attack the Omanis when the Imam had refused to agree to his demands. Although Bombay realized that this would increase insecurity it gave explicit instructions to its staff in Basra that they were not allowed to interfere in this conflict. They only were allowed to offer convoy to those vessels with an English pass. This neutral attitude had positive results, for two EIC vessels were well received at Bushire, when they called on that port.[310] The result of the Persian-Omani conflict was a wave of attacks by Hoseyn Khan of Bandar-e Rig on all vessels, in particular Omani ones. For example, two large Masqat boats laden with coffee belonging to the Suree Arabs[311] were taken by Persian gallivats; the crew was sent to Kuwait in a small boat. Therefore, despite his

309 Saldanha, *Précis*, vol. 1, pp. 260-61 (1769-70); John Porter, *Remarks on the Bloachee, Brodia and Arabian Coasts* (London, 1781), p. 12 (The Imam "who was also to pay him [Nader Shah] a yearly Clout, which as he has not fulfilled for some years past, is the occasion of the present War between them.")

310 Saldanha, *Précis*, vol. 1, pp. 259-60 (05/11/1769).

311 Probably refers to the Arabs from the Sur district on the coast of the Gulf of Oman, in N.E. Oman, i.e. the Qavasem.

tough talk, the Imam held up "the Beneshroff [?] and Suree coffee fleet."[312] The EIC refused to provide protection through convoys, although it allowed other ships to follow English protected ships if they could keep up. The Company felt that Oman had strong enough a fleet to provide protection all by itself to its coffee fleet. Moore, the EIC agent proposed Bombay to make an alliance with the Imam of Masqat against Karim Khan, which Bombay rejected because it preferred to come to an accommodation with the latter.[313]

Sheikh Naser supported Karim Khan against Masqat in 1770 and made occasional forays in the southern part of the Persian Gulf. In retaliation Masqat sent a fleet of several ships and gallivats with 5,000 men to Bushire in 1770 to demand restitution of property taken by the Persians, but the Omani fleet never reached its destination, because it was dispersed and not being able to assemble at the point of rendez-vous returned to Masqat.[314] To bring the message home to the Imam, Karim Khan had ordered an invasion army of 18,000 men under his brother Zaki Khan to gather at Lengeh in 1773. He hoped to find vessels there to ferry his troops to Oman; to that end he had sent couriers to the chiefs of the various Persian ports ordering them to send vessels, food supplies and soldiers to Bandar 'Abbas and Lengeh.[315]

Although Sheikh 'Abdollah of Hormuz was an ally of the Imam of Masqat, Zaki Khan in particular counted on his vessels, because his son was held as a hostage in Shiraz. This had come about when in 1766 a Zand army under Hajj Aqa Mohammad Ranani had subdued Bandar 'Abbas and by subterfuge had taken Sheikh 'Abdollah of Hormuz and his family prisoner. Arrived in Shiraz he promised obedience and loyalty to Karim Khan and was allowed to return. As a guarantee for his good faith he had to leave behind his son Mohammad as a hostage. Sheikh 'Abdollah therefore intimated his willingness to provide the service demanded. When Zaki Khan heard that Sheikh 'Abdollah had a beautiful daughter he asked for her hand. Sheikh 'Abdollah agreed to the marriage proposal. He invited Zaki Khan for the marriage to Hormuz and then detained him and his party and was able to arrange for a prisoner swap, i.e. his son for Zaki Khan and his men.[316] Leaderless and without vessels the army at Lengeh waited for both. Karim Khan therefore put pressure on the Ka'b, the Ottomans and the English to provide him with transportation. Karim Khan also ordered English and Ottoman ships to assist him against Masqat else he would attack Basra. Moore therefore wrote to the Pasha of Baghdad asking him to mobilize troops and send them down to Basra for its defense.[317] Karim Khan put further pressure on the EIC by making EIC naval assistance against Masqat a condition for the release of Messrs. Green and Beaumont, who had been taken prisoner by him in 1773 (see below) and who were kept at Bushire. Karim Khan gave some of the pearls, which were part of the cargo of the *Tyger* to the commanders of the gallivats; the rest he kept himself or-

312 Saldanha, *Précis*, vol. 1, pp. 260-61 (1769-70). The Suree Arabs are the Qavasem.

313 Risso, *Oman & Muscat*, pp. 57-58, 80.

314 Government of Bombay, *Selections*, p. 173; Lorimer, *Gazetteer*, p. 412; Miles, *Countries*, p. 271 writes that this took place in 1772.

315 Nami, *Tarikh*, pp. 174-76; Fasa'i, *Farsnameh*, vol. 1, p. 612; Parsons, *Travels*, p. 207; Sadid al-Saltaneh, *Bandar 'Abbas*, p. 734 (with the text of the order); Perry, *Karim Khan*, p. 160.

316 Saldanha, *Précis*, vol. 1, pp. 285-86 (Basra, 23/04/1774); Risso, *Oman & Muscat*, p. 58; Nami, *Tarikh*, p. 176; Perry, *Karim Khan*, p. 160 (the new governor of Bandar 'Abbas became Sheikh Mohammad Bastaki, who had to supply 3,000 *mann* of dates and 5,000 *mann* of grain to Zaki Khan's army). Sheikh 'Abdollah later offered his beautiful daughter to Nasir Khan of Lar, who declined. Sadid al-Saltaneh, *Bandar 'Abbas*, p. 613.

317 Saldanha, *Précis*, vol. 1, pp. 282-83 (Basra, 20/02/1774); Perry, *Karim Khan*, p. 159.

dering the fleet of the coastal Arabs (initially mostly Sheykh Naser's and Hoseyn Khan of Khark's vessels) to continue hostilities against the English and to transform the *Tyger* into a gallivat.[318]

The vessels of the coastal Arabs, who were supposed to support the Zand operation, were not made available by their chiefs. The gallivats of Bandar-e Rig and the seized English ship the *Tyger*, commanded by Mir 'Ali, joined by three gallivats and an old ship of the Bushire fleet were lying at Kangan (Congoon) in December 1773 and despite Zaki Khan's insistence refused to proceed against the Omani fleet, so that the English expected that probably nothing would happen between the two sides. When ordered to prepare his fleet, the Sheikh of the Ka'b had scuttled his gallivats and showed them to Karim Khan's messenger as proof that they were unfit for service.[319] At the end of 1773 the Imam, supported oddly enough by his old enemy Sheikh Rashed of Jolfar as well as by Sheikh 'Abdollah's gallivats, attacked the Persian army at Lengeh with three large and three small ships and many smaller vessels such as dinghies. They plundered the army camp and thereafter burnt two gallivats at Bandar Abbas.[320] Several coastal Arab chiefs, who had gallivats, then also turned pirate attracted by the confusion. The EIC ordered its and EIC-protected ships not to call anymore on Bushire. Bombay made it clear, however, that it did not want any action against Persian property on ships under its convoys, but Moore in Basra wrote that this pacific approach only gave rise to the belief that EIC was weak. He in fact had argued that the EIC should ally itself with the Imam of Masqat, Mir Hoseyn Khan of Rig and other willing coastal chiefs against Karim Khan, but he was overruled.[321]

Karim Khan, who continued the pressure on Omani vessels, allegedly also had sought naval assistance from Heydar 'Ali of Mysore. Messrs. Beaumont and Green informed Basra that Heyder 'Ali had sent an ambassador to Karim Khan with presents to reach a settlement in the Persian Gulf for trading, to propose marriage between their children and in return promised his support of his ships. It seems Karim Khan had rejected the marriage idea, but had promised Bandar 'Abbas to Heyder 'Ali, which was of little consequence considering the opposition that he was likely to get from Sheikh 'Abdollah of Hormuz. Apparently nothing came of this proposed alliance with Mysore as nothing is heard about it anymore. But it is also possible that the relationship with Heydar 'Ali may have been misunderstood, as Perry has argued. At that time, the Pasha of Baghdad had promised two ketches to support Karim Khan against Masqat, but nobody expected that he would actually do so.[322]

318 Saldanha, *Précis*, vol. 1, pp. 278-79 (Muscat, 01/12/1773).

319 Saldanha, *Précis*, vol. 1, pp. 279-81 (Basra, December 1773); Ibid., vol. 1, p. 284 (Basra, 23/04/1774). The unwillingness of the various coastal chiefs to engage their vessels against the Omanis may have to do with the fact that Persian vessels were still allowed to come and trade unmolested in Masqat, provided ready cash was paid for the merchandise. Parson, *Travels*, p. 207. Nami, *Tarikh*, pp. 175-76, however, claims that such vessels were plundered after having been duped to come to Omanis ports.

320 Saldanha, *Précis*, vol. 1, p. 280 (Basra Diary, 01-23/12/1773); Risso, *Oman & Muscat*, p. 58; Lorimer, *Gazetteer*, p. 412. Sheikh Rashed's support may have been due to the fact that his relatives in Lengeh, under their chief Sa'id b. Qazib al-Huwali, who paid allegiance to him, whom he therefore had to protect and, moreover, because they may have felt imposed upon by the Persian army. Risso, *Oman & Muscat*, p. 69, n. 28. It may also have been at that time that the Qavasem occupied Qeshm and its neighboring islands (see chapter three).

321 Saldanha, *Précis*, vol. 1, pp. 286 (Basra, 23/04/1774).

322 Porter, *Remarks*, pp. 12-13; Saldanha, *Précis*, vol. 1, pp. 286-87 (Basra, 23/04/1774); see also Risso, *Oman & Muscat*, p. 59, citing a letter from the Imam of Masqat to Bombay asking the EIC not to allow the Persian to buy any timber or ships, because these would be used against his and English ships going to Basra. The Imam further asked Bombay (received 06/11/1774) to write to Heydar 'Ali Khan of Mysore not to give any ships to Karim Khan. In 1775, the Imam had one Mysore vessel bound for Basra seized and another Mysore vessel ran aground

It was at that time that Sheikh Naser once again, like in 1767, balked at the idea of paying 4,000 *tumans* for his governorship of Bushire and Bahrain. He may have been encouraged by the absence of any punitive action against the coastal chiefs for not providing naval assistance to Zaki Khan. However, he was mistaken that Karim Khan would also turn a blind eye against this rebellious act. He did not and incited the chiefs of the littoral against Bushire, which proved to be effective. This time Sheikh Naser went in person to Shiraz to settle the problem and he made such a good impression that Karim Khan made him his envoy to Masqat and admiral of the Persian fleet with orders to wage war on Masqat or make peace with Imam as he saw fit. Sheikh Naser returned to Bushire on 17/08/1774 and then left to Oman. According to Lt. John Porter, who had received this information from inhabitants of Masqat,

> Carim Cawn [at] the beginning of last Month sent Embassadors with presents to the Imaum requesting him to return the Ship he had taken, and to make good the losses they had met with, by sending a certain Number of Arms, &c. of different kinds, to the Value of the losses he had sustained by the War, and on these terms [he] was willing to make peace; the Imaum it seems would not return anything he had taken, and did not chuse to make peace, unless the Cawn would pay him so much more than the Value of what he had taken, as his expence in fitting the Fleet out came to: He has given the Embassadors one of his largest Ships and a Gallivat to carry them back, with a present of less Value than that received by him.[323]

Although Sheikh Naser had not gone beyond Khur Fakkan to meet with the Imam's *vakil* as intended, because the Imam refused to listen to what he considered to be disgraceful terms that were offered, the Imam, nevertheless, seemed to be willing to come to an accommodation, for he released the requested Persian effects that he had seized at the outbreak of hostilities. The Imam wanted to be on friendly terms with the Persians, but he was not willing to pay an annual tribute. He further intimated that the Masqat ships would continue to sail to Basra and that anybody who wanted to interfere with them did so at his own risk.[324] However, this was but talk and bluster, for shortly thereafter Masqat sought peace promising to pay 200 *tumans* present and an annual tribute.[325]

But this does not seem to have been accepted by Karim Khan, for in October 1775, when the Zand army was besieging Basra, the Imam sent a fleet to its relief at Basra government's request. This fleet actually was the normal annual coffee fleet, only larger and better armed, which is an indication how hard-pressed the Omanis were that they risked capture and destruction to sell their coffee. However, without the promised support from the Ottomans, limited provisions and uncertain supply lines, the battered Omani fleet had to withdraw in November 1775. The relief to Basra was thus only temporary and the town fell into Persian hands on April 16, 1776. It was because of this Persian success and its fall-out that the Imam of Masqat was willing to come to agreement,

---

on the Omani coast. Karim Khan allegedly asked 'Omar Pasha of Baghdad to allow passage of Persian troops to march through Ottoman territory to Masqat, who refused stating that he needed to ask the Porte for permission to do so. Golestaneh, *Mojmal*, p. 337; Perry, *Karim Khan*, pp. 270-71.

323 Porter, *Remarks*, P. 12

324 Saldanha, *Précis*, vol. 1, pp. 285-86 (Basra, 23/04/1774); Ibid., *Précis*, vol. 1, pp. 288 (Basra, 01/10/1774); Lorimer, *Gazetteer*, pp. 1809, 1822; Risso, *Oman & Muscat*, p. 58.

325 Perry, *Karim Khan*, p. 160.

including an annual tribute, given the importance of trade with Basra for Masqat.[326] Moreover, Karim Khan had ordered Sheikh 'Abdollah of Hormuz and Sheikh Rashed of Jolfar to seize all Omani vessels and to interdict the transportation of food supplies (rice, wheat) to Oman. It is not known whether Sheikh Rashed, not a Persian subject after all although an enemy of the Imam and once again at war with him at that time, heeded this order, but Sheikh 'Abdollah did. He took one a dhow belonging to one of his own people but with goods from Masqat, because Karim had ordered to seize all Masqat property and cut off all its communications with the Persian Gulf. Mir 'Ali of Bandar-e Rig also had received an order to sail as a privateer, but he had declined to do so.[327] That the Persian-induced action was effective is clear from the fact that the Imam did not use his assembled fleet in 1776 against prime Persian targets such as Basra, Bushire or Bahrain. However, one year later the situation had changed 180 degrees showing the fragile nature of the agreement and how volatile the political situation in the Gulf was at that time. One of the first hostile actions was that Sheikh 'Abdollah of Hormuz was taken aboard one of the Imam's ships in November 1777 and taken as a prisoner to Masqat. The Imam thus had better control over the Straits of Hormuz (although this was contested by the Qavasem of Jolfar), while he concluded an agreement with the Ottomans, who paid him an annual subsidy, formally for his help in 1775, but in fact to ensure his naval assistance against Persia.[328] Prior to his imprisonment Sheikh 'Abdollah had "attempted to take two or three Bushire Dows the Bushire People have lately in return made a capture of one of the Ormuse Dows but it is thought she will be given up." The conflict seems to have been settled by the return of at least one of the vessels in February 1788 to Bushire.[329] It was further reported in July 1780 that the conflict between Bushire and Jolfar still persisted, which had been caused by the capture of the *Expedition*, a Bushire vessel under EIC protection, which the Qavasem claimed had flown an Omani flag. In 1780, some of Sheikh Rashed's people came to Bushire to propose peace to Sheikh Naser, "but having no authority to restore the *Expedition*, and other Restitutions that were demanded, they returned without effecting anything."[330] Although the Qavasem would make peace with Bushire thereafter, while the Persian-Omani conflict disappeared almost unnoticed, the Omani-Qavasem conflict remained as contentious as before and dominated the shipping lanes at that time.[331]

326 Saldanha, *Précis*, vol. 1, p. 299 (Bushire; 06/05/1776); Risso, *Oman & Muscat*, p. 80. The impact on the 'Otobis was also significant. The English reported that "the Inhabitants [of Kuwait] were so intimidated at the progress of the Persians that they were preparing to abandon that Town and retire with their best effects into the desert." For the size of the Masqat fleet, see Parsons, *Travels*, p. 206f.

327 Saldanha, *Précis*, vol. 1, p. 301 (Bushire, [08/1776]). The EIC therefore asked for a royal decree to be allowed to ship rice from Bombay to Basra. Risso, *Oman & Muscat*, p. 72, n. 47.

328 Risso, *Oman & Muscat*, p. 61; Saldanha, *Précis*, vol. 1, pp. 305-06 (Bushire, 06/01/1778); Lorimer, *Gazetteer*, p. 1825.

329 Saldanha, *Précis*, vol. 1, pp. 305-06 (Bushire, 06/01/1778); see also Ibid., vol. 1, p. 306 (Bushire, 15/02/1778); Lorimer, *Gazetteer*, p. 1825.

330 Saldanha, *Précis*, vol. 1, p. 316 (Bushire, 15/07/1780). According to Risso, *Oman & Muscat*, p. 73, n. 55 the release of the *Expedition* had already occurred in 1779, which contradicts the letter from Bushire and so her data must refer to the discussions that took place in 1779 as to the ships's release.

331 For the Omani-Qavasem hostilities see Risso, *Oman & Muscat*, pp. 61-62.

BASRA: THE KA'B AND THE PERSIAN SIEGE.

In October 1768, the Ka'b were building forts on both sides of the river and the Turks were unable to check that. The EIC decided not to take action against the Ka'b, partly induced by the fact that the Pasha of Baghdad's debt for the lending of the EIC ships had not yet been recovered. Moreover, the *motasallem* had recently died; it was suspected of poison. As a result, Basra was a place in turmoil.[332] Because Basra was threatened in 1769 by the Montafeq the new *motasallem* asked the Ka'b to help him defend the city. Sheikh Ghanem, who had succeeded his father, Sheikh Salman, in 1768, agreed to do so provided the EIC promised free passage. The Company's agent did so and later even decided to end its futile blockade. Five Ka'b gallivats and two armed boats came to Minawi with 100 men in each to assist Turks in defending Basra and its surrounding villages against the Montafeq. The *motasallem* gave each *nakhoda* a robe of honor. Sheikh Ghanem also wrote to the petty chiefs of the Montafeq in charge of sundry posts around Basra to cease all hostilities immediately and decamp. If not he would destroy them and their possessions. The "Benichaali" [Banu Khaled?] Arabs were also marching to help the government of Basra as reportedly was the pasha of Baghdad. Soon thereafter the Montafeq withdrew. It was said to join Sheikh 'Abdollah, who had been joined by the "Hazace" [?] Arabs under Sheikh "Ahmood" [Mahmud?].[333]

By 1773 the EIC started to lose interest in the Persian Gulf. Up to that time exports from Bengal to Basra and Bushire had helped sustain the flagging financial situation of the Bengal directorate. However, with the arrival of Warren Hastings as governor-general of India the deficit situation had been transformed into a surplus one, while trade with China had become much more profitable for the EIC than with the Persian Gulf. On top of that was the added disaster that befell Basra in March 1773, when the city and its hinterland were anew stricken by the Plague. Tens of thousands of people died and trade in Basra came to a complete halt. The EIC staff therefore decided to temporarily leave Basra and go to Bombay to wait there until the situation became normal again.[334]

This escape from the plague turned into a partial disaster for the EIC. In April 1773, the Basra staff left in two vessels the *Tyger* and the *Drake*. Near Hormuz four gallivats from Bandar-e Rig boarded the *Tyger*. The crew jumped over board and was later taken in by the *Drake*, but Messrs. Green and Beaumont were taken prisoner. The *Drake* tried to overtake the gallivats but to no avail. The gallivats sped away in shoal water; the *Drake* had to wait till the next tide to pursue them, which was useless and thus continued to Bombay. The two prisoners were taken to Shiraz; Green was released to Bushire and returned to Basra on 19 September 1774; Mr Beamont was released on 22 April 1775 and thus was imprisoned for two years.[335]

After the devastation of the plague, which killed much of the city's economic and human capital, trade could not pick up, because the Ka'b started attacking Basra. At the end of July 1773, when the plague was over in Basra, the Ka'b (now under Sheikh Barakat, son of 'Othman), who also had been stricken by the plague but less so, immediately attacked and plundered two quarters of the town and burnt the *qaputan basha*'s house with some of his boats. The governor of Basra had to buy peace at a high price, which was paid for by the survivors of the plague.[336] To prevent future Ka'b

---

332 Saldanha, *Précis*, vol. 1, pp. 247-48 (Basra, 30/10/1768).

333 Saldanha, *Précis*, vol. 1, p. 260 (1769-70); Perry, *Karim Khan*, p. 150; Abdullah, *Merchants*, p. 51.

334 Amin, *British Interests*, pp. 108-09

335 Saldanha, *Précis*, vol. 1, pp. 270-71 (Muscat, 05/05/1773).

336 Perry, *Karim Khan*, p. 170; Lorimer, *Gazetteer*, p. 1221; Anonymous, *Chronicle*, vol. I, p. 673; Abdullah, *Merchants*, p. 53.

attacks the government of Basra asked for help from the Montafeq who then helped themselves by plundering the city. When the EIC staff returned in January 1774 they found a totally devastated city that in Moore's view needed years to recuperate. The city did not get that time, because when in April 1774 the *motasallem* of Basra executed a Ka'b tribesman, they again attacked the city and plundered and burnt several bazaars. The East India Company helped the government of Basra against the Ka'b.[337] Because of the expected Persian invasion force the EIC decided to move its goods on the *Drake*. However, the *motasallem* asked the English not to do so as this would give the wrong signal to the market and people of Basra. Moreover, Karim Khan's chief aim was to ruin Basra so as to force the EIC to settle at Bushire. By moving its goods now the EIC would bring about Karim Khan's objective without having sent a single soldier. At that time, April 1774, the Ka'b had promised support to both the Zands and Ottomans. A representative of the Sheikh of the Ka'b came to Basra, after having been assured that the EIC would not interfere with him, and promised the *motasallem* "not to lend the Persians any assistance, but to quit Doorack with his Galivats and people as soon as he received certain intelligence that they had marched from Schiras." Despite this commitment the Ka'b later captured an Ottoman vessel around April 10, which was rescued by the English. They then withdrew all their tribesmen from Basra on April 17, which was perceived as a threatening gesture, the more so since the Ka'b fleet was lying in the Haffar in attack mode, while other Arab chiefs in the Gulf "with gallivats or boats have lately turned Pirates, and greatly interrupt the trade to this place." Indeed, midwinter Ka'b raids showed the weakness of the Basra government.[338]

The finishing touch to Basra's fall was provided by courtesy of Karim Khan. His timing was well-chosen, because Basra had still not recovered from the plague. Karim Khan wanted to take advantage of this opportunity and laid siege to the city in April 1775 that lasted more than one year. On 16 March, 1775 some 30,000 Zand troops were at Suweyb commanded by Sadeq Khan Zand. The Ka'b supported the Zand army with their vessels; the *qaputan basha* had an equal number, but these were not equal in effectiveness to the Ka'b vessels.[339] Because of the cooperation with the Ka'b, the Zand army now had the fleet that they lacked to move around in the marshes and canals. Parsons, a member of the East India Company's staff at Basra, then suggested putting a boom in the channel to Basra to deny the Ka'b access, and this worked for a time.[340]

Moore had tried London to support his plea to assist the government of Basra against the Persian attack. However, London was not interested to do so and in fact considered abandoning its factory in Basra altogether due to the disappointing sales results during the last few years. Bombay likewise was not interested in opposing Karim Khan given the importance of Persia as a market for its woolens. Moreover, Bombay had always been in favor of reaching an agreement with Karim Khan and had already decided in February 1775 to do so. Besides, it also feared for increased attacks of English shipping in the Persian Gulf by Persian privateers. Finally, the timing for the request for military assistance could not have been worse as Bombay needed all its naval resources to battle the

---

337 Saldanha, *Précis*, vol. 1, p. 291 (Bombay, 01/02/1775); Abraham Parsons, *Travels in Asia and Africa* (London, 1808), p. 162; Abdullah, *Merchants*, p. 36.

338 Longrigg, *Four Centuries*, p. 188; Saldanha, *Précis*, vol. 1, pp. 284-86 (Basra, 23/04/1774).

339 Longrigg, *Four Centuries*, pp. 190-91. For the reasons for the Persian attack see Perry, *Karim Khan Zand*, pp. 170-74; Roschanzamir, *Zand-Dynastie*, pp. 71-72.

340 Perry, *Karim Khan Zand*, pp. 174, 177; Nami, *Tarikh*, pp. 134-39; Hedayat, *Rawzat al-safa*, vol. IX, p. 79; Parsons, *Travels.*, p. 166.

Marathas. It therefore wanted the two cruisers at Basra for its own use in India and ordered Moore to return them forthwith.[341]

Moore assisted the government of Basra with the two EIC cruisers to oppose the Persian attack indirectly. In mid-March 1774 they had successfully attacked Ka'b gallivats that were sailing in the Shatt al-Arab to join the Persian army at Qorna. The EIC vessels burnt one Ka'b gallivat and took another, while the rest was scattered. This action bolstered the resolve of the government and people of Basra to put up a stiff resistance. However, it also made the EIC the target of any future Persian attack and Moore therefore wrote to Bushire to inform Sheikh Naser of this event, to report whether those of Bushire and Khark would join the Persian army and to send any cruiser that might come to Bushire to Basra to assist the Basra Agency. But when on April 11, 1774 he saw a large Persian army with 60 sails coming to Basra Moore and his council all of a sudden decided to immediately withdraw the EIC staff and ships from Basra and thus he left that same day. In spite of the absence of English arms the Basrenes defended themselves bravely against the Persian army and held out until April 1776.[342] Garden, the visiting member of the council at Bombay, strongly condemned Moore's attack on the Ka'b gallivats, because the Company ships were an inadequate force to face the Persian gallivats; "the three Merchants Vessels being so miserably Equip'ed, that they are not capable of the least defence." By choosing sides, in affair in which he had no business, Moore had endangered Company property on board the ships. Garden qualified the action as madness.[343] Sadeq Khan was in command of the Persian invasion force that attacked Basra and laid siege to the city, while the Persian fleet was under the command of Sheikh Naser of Bushire, who had supplied 14 gallivats and 50 armed boats, while the Ka'b had supplied 14 gallivats. The departing EIC vessels and the Persian fleet exchanged some fire during five hours in the Haffar. Later Sheikh Naser wrote that the EIC vessels had fired first.[344]

THE EIC RETURNS TO BUSHIRE.

In December 1773 the EIC staff returned to Basra, where they arrived in January 1774. En route to Basra the EIC ships arrived at Bushire. Sheikh Naser wanted to talk to the Agent about Messrs. Green and Beaumont. Mr. Abrahams went ashore with a letter for Karim Khan. Agha Kuchek, Sheikh Naser's agent remained on board to guarantee Mr. Abraham's safety, who bought sugar from the English. Sheikh Naser invited the EIC to settle at Bushire and was very polite.[345] After having settled the problem of the payment of tribute in Shiraz Sheikh Naser had returned to Bushire (see above) and he was going to take Messrs. Green and Beaumont with him. Moreover, he had instructed Sheikh Sa'dun, his brother, to prepare the English factory for the two gentlemen. It is not clear

341 Amin, *British Interests*, pp. 112-13.

342 Saldanha, *Précis*, vol. 1, pp. 291-92 (Basra, rec. at Bushire 30/03/1775); Ibid., vol. 1, p. 294 (Bushire, 23/04/1775); Ibid,., vol. 1, pp. 296-97 (Bushire, 30/04/1775); Lorimer, *Gazetteer*, p. 1811; Amin, *British Interests*, pp. 113-14; Perry, *Karim Khan*, pp. 174-77. Moore had informed the *motassalem* already in April 1774 that he could not assist him in the defense of Basra, while he had urged the Pasha of Baghdad to send troops to Basra and prepare its defense. Saldanha, *Précis*, vol. 1, p. 284 (Basra, 23/04/1774). Before his return to Bombay he wrote to the *motasallem* that he regretted that he had not been able to help him more. Ibid., vol. 1, pp. 297-98 Bushire, 18/07/1775).

343 Saldanha, *Précis*, vol. 1, p. 293 (Bushire, [22/04/1775]).

344 Saldanha, *Précis*, vol. 1, pp. 292 (Bushire, 22/04/1775); Ibid, vol. 1, p. 293 (Bushire, [22/04/1775]); Ibid., vol. 1, p. 295 (Bushire, 23/04/1775).

345 Saldanha, *Précis*, vol. 1, pp. 279-81 (Basra, December 1773).

whether the release of Green-Beaumont was due to Sheikh Naser's influence or to Khvajeh Sarkis (Coja Sarguise), an Armenian merchant. "He bears a most execrable character, but has a most unaccountable influence over the Vackeel [Karim Khan]." Moore had promised him 5,000 rupees if he exerted himself for the release of the two imprisoned Englishmen. Karim Khan made no other move towards the EIC, while the number of coastal Arab chiefs attracted by Karim Khan's promise of plunder if they joined his war with Oman increased. To put pressure on Karim Khan Moore, without any authorization, instructed all English vessels to boycott Persian ports, because the Ka'b and other Arab coastal chief interfered with trade thus hurting EIC interests.

> As Carim Caun and his subjects therefore seem determined on distressing us as much as is in their power, we think it would be absurd in us, whilst we wait your further orders, to keep up the communication which we hitherto have done between our vessels and the places belonging to him- the trade carried on there increase his revenues, benefit his subjects, and at the same time run the risk of our ships lying in Ports, whose friendship at least is not to be relied upon.

Moore also had almost confiscated a cargo of Persian goods on the *The Four Friends*, but for the strong prohibition by Bombay to bring about a rupture with Karim Khan.[346]

Messrs. Green and Beaumont reminded Sheikh Naser on his return from Khur Fakkan on 17 August 1774 that he had promised to release them. However, Sheikh Naser claimed that he dare not face Karim Khan's wrath in doing so, and he finally only released Green to carry his proposal for an EIC settlement at Bushire to Basra. Sheikh Naser proposed that the EIC send a European or Armenian merchant to Bushire to act as temporary resident as before until London's final decision would arrive allowing trading to resume; in return Sheikh Naser undertook to return the *Tyger* with its stores, to be answerable for any piracy that might occur in the future "be remitted on our trade either by the Bunderrick or Genova Gallivats" and to return Mr. Beaumont. Moore replied on 23 September 1774 and rejected the proposal, because he had instructions from Bombay not to make any agreement until Green-Beaumont had been set free. Basra felt confident in pursuing this policy, because it argued that Sheikh Naser's move had only been occasioned by the effect of the English boycott of Persian ports.[347]

In February 1775 Bombay decided to try and settle the differences between Karim Khan and the EIC. It was sick and tired of the substantial financial and other consequences of the hostile situation, and more in particular the need to maintain a large armed fleet in the Persian Gulf at high cost, the continued imprisonment of Beaumont and the prevalence of piracy. It believed that the cause of the problem with Karim Khan was Moore's enmity for him, who seems to have acquired a similar dislike for Moore. Bombay did not expect the same benefits that he had offered in the past, but the Basra Agency had to seriously do something about it and Moore was ordered to set aside his resentment so that the Company could do without the cruisers in the Gulf. For the bad terms on which the Company was with Karim Khan "has always been assigned by the Agent and Council as their reason for keeping Cruizers in the Gulph," and the high cost incurred was detrimental to the EIC. Moore and his council were also enjoined to strictly adhere to any agreement that was reached with Karim Khan. They therefore were instructed to try to come to an agreement with

346 Saldanha, *Précis*, vol. 1, pp. 285-86 (Basra, 23/04/1774); Lorimer, *Gazetteer*, pp. 1809-10, 1822. Khvajeh Sarkis probably is the same person who came to Khark in June 1765 to urge the Dutch to join the attack on Mir Mohanna (see chapter four).

347 Saldanha, *Précis*, vol. 1, pp. 288 (Basra, 01/10/1774).

Karim Khan, which needed to include the release of Beaumont. Such an agreement furthermore might include the obligation of a factory in Bushire, which, however, was against the direct orders of London. Bombay therefore added a cautionary note that "In case an establishment at Bushire should take place, the property of the Company must be limited to a very moderate sum, that no ill consequences may result from it."[348]

The Council of Bombay chose one of its members, Robert Garden, as their envoy to Persia as he was going to Basra on private business. En route to Basra, Garden arrived at Bushire on April 7 with his three unarmed ships and hearing that the Persian fleet and army were at Basra and that Moore had attacked the Ka'b vessels he decided not go there despite instructions from the Agent to do so. Garden contacted Sheikh Sa'dun, brother of Sheikh Naser to obtain the release of Beaumont and an agreement with Karim Khan. The Sheikh could not do anything, but he informed Karim Khan about the EIC's intentions, viz. to settle the rift, to which end Garden had given him a letter on April 11. Sheikh Naser had told Beaumont on the eve of his departure for Basra that Mr. Moore was the cause of the present war. On April 15 Moore and his council arrived at Bushire and informed Garden on what had occurred until then. Garden then wrote a second letter to Karim Khan requesting that he instruct his troops to respect EIC property at Basra, while he wrote a similar letter to Sheikh Naser who was at that time with the Persian forces at Basra. Garden received a positive reply from Karim Khan on April 24. Beaumont was set free and the *Tyger* would be returned as soon as it would be back from Basra. Karim Khan further put all the blame for their differences on Moore. Garden took lodging in the old EIC factory and raised the flag.[349]

Sheikh Naser wrote to Garden expressing his great delight and that "Bushire and my house are your's." As to Moore, he wrote that he had incessantly written him during the past two years not to persist in his resentment, but he did not listen. Arrived at Basra, at Karim Khan's orders, Sheikh Naser had wanted to talk to Moore to try and settle the conflict between Karim Khan and him. To that end he had ordered his gallivats to anchor at a considerable distance from the English ships, but they weighed anchor and bore down on them and immediately fired upon them. Sheikh Naser was able to restrain his own men; others under Mir 'Ali, however, had accused him of cowardice and had fired back. They later complained to Sadeq Khan that if Sheikh Naser would have given the order to attack they could have taken the English ships.[350] Sheikh Naser returned with his gallivats from Basra on June 30, 1776 as did all other sheikhs such as Ma'sum Khan (Masoon Caum) of Ganaveh and Mir 'Ali of Bandar-e Rig. Merchants came to the EIC factory led by Sheikh Naser, who "is too much of a Merchant himself for us to expect any assistance from in regard to the prices we sell for, for as he takes a third part of whatever Goods are brought from the Factory, it is evidently his interest to join the Merchants for getting them as cheap as possible."[351]

348 Saldanha, *Précis*, vol. 1, pp. 289-90 (Bombay, 11/02/1775).

349 Saldanha, *Précis*, vol. 1, p. 290 (Bombay, 11/02/1775); Ibid., vol. 1, pp. 293-95 (Bushire, 23/04/1775). For the text of the reply Karim Khan to Garden. Saldanha, *Précis*, vol. 1, p. 297; Lorimer, *Gazetteer*, p. 1812. Moore also brought two Ottoman vessels with him which he took with him en route to India and delivered them to the Imam of Masqat at the *motasallem*'s request. Parsons, *Travels*, p. 178

350 Saldanha, *Précis*, vol. 1, pp. 296-97 (Basra; rec. 03/05/1775); Parsons, *Travels*, p. 178.

351 Saldanha, *Précis*, vol. 1, pp. 301 (n.d. [August 1766]).

WAS BASRA'S LOSS BUSHIRE'S GAIN?

The fall of Basra had consequences that went beyond the interests of the city itself and it even affected the relations between Karim Khan and Oman, for example (see above). However, more importantly, the Persian occupation incapacitated Basra as an international seaport for quite some time. Not only had trade been dead during the one-year siege, but during the Persian occupation Basra had been cut-off from its hinterland and thus could not perform its normal role as a hub by forwarding imports and receiving exports. Moreover, due to the Turkish-Russian war of 1768-1774 demand for Indian goods was in a slump. Furthermore, merchants were oppressed and open to extortion as a result of which most of them withdrew from Basra and settled in Zubara, which by 1770 had become a flourishing town, a development that ironically was accelerated by the Persian siege and occupation of Basra.[352]

Basra was not the only port that suffered from the Persian occupation. Ironically, so did Bushire, despite the fact that some authors have argued that Sheikh Naser had supported the siege with 20 gallivats, partly undoubtedly to destroy Basra and draw its trade towards Bushire. However, trade at Bushire was bad as well and the EIC suffered an operational loss, although less than at Basra in 1777. Here the EIC had returned in May 1776 and was open for business one month later. However, the situation was not conducive to trade, while due to the behavior of 'Ali Mohammad Khan, the Zand governor of Basra, the EIC was forced to close its factory there, while appealing to Karim Khan for redress. This had the desired result so that by March 17, 1777 when the positive reply was received the EIC factory was opened for business once again, while another advantageous decree from Karim Khan was received in June 1777. Unfortunately, there was not much business to write home about. The Company directors in London, ignorant of the redress and advantages granted by Karim Khan, therefore had decided on July 4, 1777 to abandon the Persian Gulf altogether and withdraw all its operations from Basra and Bushire. However, they also realized that Karim Khan would not permit it to withdraw its staff from Bushire and therefore London decided to close down the Basra factory whose staff, but one, had to go to Bushire. Later the staff there also had to be reduced to one person. These orders dated July 4, 1777 only arrived at Bombay almost one year later, i.e. on April 30, 1778. Because at that time war with France was likely and indeed broke out thereafter, Bombay decided on August 2, 1778 not to implement the order, given the importance of Basra for overland communications with the Levant and onwards to London. However, it withdrew most of its staff leaving only a skeleton staff of one person in both Basra and Bushire, who, in case that one of them died, could replace the other. This situation was continued until the end of the eighteenth century.[353]

Because of the slump in trade from which both Basra and Bushire experienced the little trade that still existed suffered from interference by the governments of Bushire and Basra in the late 1770s. "At Bushire we are almost as much exposed to Oppression as we are at Bussora. The Shaikhs there interfere too much in the Trade of the Place; and the few Merchants with any Property who are there, are too much in a Combination to admit of our drawing any great Commercial Advantages from it wretched indeed as is the Situation in Bussora at Present it is much superior in Point of Trade

---

352 Amin, *British Interests*, pp. 106-07; Abu Hakimah, *History*, pp. 71-74; Kelly, *Persian Gulf*, p. 26.

353 Saldanha, *Précis*, vol. 1, pp. 298-99 (Bushire, 06/05/1776); Ibid., vol. p. 302 (Basra, 22/09/1776); Ibid., vol. 1, pp. 302-03 (Basra, 23/02/1777); Ibid., vol. 1, p. 304 (Bombay, 04/07/1777); Ibid., vol. 1, pp. 304-05 (Bombay, 02/08/1778); Amin, *British Interests*, pp. 115-16; Kelly, *Persian Gulf*, p. 53 briefly explains how this system of overland mail worked. Basra and Bushire also became separate residencies. Saldanha, *Précis*, vol. 1, pp. 304-05 (Bombay, 02/08/1778); Lorimer, *Gazetteer*, pp. 1813-14. For the text of Karim Khan's order of March 17, 1777 see Saldanha, *Précis*, vol. 1, p. 303.

than Bushire."[354] To alleviate some of the worst cases the EIC had recourse to Karim Khan with whom it had friendly relations. For example, the EIC complained about an infraction committed against the EIC at Basra, about which Karim Khan immediately sent a peremptory order.[355] He also ordered the Ka'b to restore goods taken from Bushire merchants in August 1777, which actually took place on February 5, 1778.[356] As a result, according to the somewhat optimistic Carmelites, in 1778 Bushire was "a now much frequented port."[357] The withdrawal of the Persian occupation force from Basra in March 1779 did not bring the hoped for improvement in trade. Moreover, Basra continued to suffer from depredations caused by the Ka'b.[358] The conflict between the Ka'b and Bushire that had lain dormant during the Persian siege and occupation of Basra had erupted again as a result no boat from Bushire could sail to Basra in 1777. Although matters seem to have been patched up between the two sides in 1778, the Ka'b continued to support elements hostile to Sheikh Naser of Bushire; in 1779 they even showed support for the Tangestani seizure of Bushire (see below).[359]

The 1770s thus ended on a negative note for Sheikh Naser of Bushire, for it had been a bad ending of the decade. It had started so well. Despite the conflict in 1774 about the payment of tribute, Karim Khan had much appreciated Sheikh Naser's abilities and had appointed him as his point man for solving the Masqat crisis. This had been followed by his successful participation in the siege of Basra and the re-establishment of the EIC factory at Bushire. Having these good relations with the Zand ruler and being his naval arm in the northern Persian Gulf had enabled Sheikh Naser to build up a fleet of his own. In 1765 he had only one ship, three gallivats, and two *batils*.[360] In 1769 he had two ships, 7-8 gallivats, besides many boats. During the siege of Basra in 1775 he had 20 gallivats each with 8-10 guns and a number of merchant vessels of 40-80 tons, which could be used for naval purposes.[361] On land he had good relations with the people of Ganaveh and 'Asalu, for example, which came in good stead given the enmity of the people of Tangesir and Bandar-e Rig. In 1778, the Carmelites even qualified Bushire somewhat optimistically as "a now much frequented port."[362] Unfortunately, the aftermath of the siege and occupation of Basra had been bad for trade and thus for Sheikh Naser and the economy of Bushire. This was further aggravated by the loss of Bahrain in 1777 to the 'Otobis. In 1778 the Qavasem joined Sheikh Naser in trying to recover Bahrain.[363] During this difficult period the long-awaited death of Karim Khan occurred on March 2, 1779. Because the latter had not taken effective steps to ensure a peaceful transfer of power to a designated successor his immediate family members started to fight among each other to claim his throne. Zaki Khan emerged as the strong man from this squabble, but he was challenged by his

354 Abu Hakima, Ahmad. *History of Eastern Arabia. The Rise and Development of Bahrain and Kuwait* (Beirut, 1965), pp. 99-100.

355 Saldanha, *Précis*, vol. 1, pp. 302-03.

356 Saldanha, *Précis*, vol. 1, p. 305 (Bushire, 06/01/1778); Ibid, vol. 1, p. 306 (Bushire, 15/02/1778).

357 Anonymous, *Chronicle*, vol. 1, p. 702.

358 Floor, "Rise and Fall," p. 286.

359 Grummond, *The Rise*, pp. 104-05; Lorimer, *Gazetteer*, p. 1850.

360 A very popular vessel in the Gulf as in W. India, often described as a kind of small dhow with a square flat stern and a long grab-like head. It was in particular used as a warboat and slave ship.

361 Lorimer, *Gazetteer*, p. 1822.

362 The Carmelites had a small house there without a church, for there were only 7 to 8 Catholics at Bushire. Anonymous, *Chronicle*, vol. 1, 702. In 1765, there had been as many as 35 Catholics in Bushire and two friars who also served Khark. Ibid, vol. 1, 710. These Catholics must have dwindled, if not left (certainly the friars), for in 1772 the opening of missionary activities at Bushire was discussed again. Ibid, vol. 1, 717.

363 Miles, *Countries*, p. 275.

half-brother Sadeq Khan, who laid siege to Shiraz. Zaki Khan then sent a messenger to the besiegers, informing them that if they did not leave he would kill their wives and children. This had desire result the army dispersed and Sadeq Khan had to flee. However, because of his subsequent behavior he was killed by his own officers.[364] At that time, the fight over control over the shipping lanes in the Persian Gulf also began between various coastal settlements; in particular the war between the Imam of Masqat and the Qavasem under Sheikh Saqar b. Rashed.[365]

RA'IS BAQER KHAN TANGESIRI OCCUPIES BUSHIRE

After the death of Zaki Khan (Jackey Caun) on June 14, 1779 Ra'is Baqer Khan (Reis Bagur Caun) of Tangesir, "his instrument in ill-treating Sadoo Caun's women, escaped from the camp." On June 28 Bushire received information that he had had arrived at Bandar-e Rig. On June 29, Ra'is Hamid (Reis Hamet), the commander of the Tangesir troops, although blind, raised 2 to 3,000 men to meet Baqer Khan. However, instead he led them to Bushire at Baqer Khan's instructions. The conditions for an attack Bushire looked promising. Sheikh Naser was at Jedda and the city wall was only half finished. Sheik Hamid had further received information from Tangesiris in Bushire that two Bushiri gallivats had just left to convoy Sheikh Naser from Masqat. However, the information about gallivats was wrong. They were about to depart, but were too late for the tide. However, it made no difference.

It is not clear why the Tangesiris attacked Bushire at that time. It may have been all due to happenstance; if Sheikh Naser had known that Karim Khan would have died he would not have gone to Masqat. Moreover, Baqer Khan had given his promise to protect Bushire on the eve of his departure. The reason cannot have been simply the existing enmity between Sheikh Naser and Baqer Khan, although that was, of course the driving force. It may well have been that Baqer Khan spoke the truth, when on July 1 he publicly stated that he had fled out of fear of Sadeq Khan's wrath and felt more secure in Bushire than in Tangesir. Given the fact that the English reported that Baqer Khan had been Zaki Khan's "instrument in ill-treating Sadoo Caun's women" his choice of Bushire as a refuge becomes understandable. Whatever the reason for the attack, the Tangesiris had prepared their decision to invade and occupy Bushire well in advance, indicating that this was no spur of the moment decision. They had been about to make two earlier attempts during the cold season (i.e. November-March), but their spies had told them each time that the inhabitants were ready for them, but not this, the third time.[366] Also, the manner in which the occupation of Bushire was accomplished shows that the Tangesiris were careful in its implementation rather than a headlong mad rush to take the town, because they wanted to be sure that their risk was low. "Reis Hamet first sent 3 or 4 successive parties into the Town who having all informed him the gates were open, the wall unguarded and everybody asleep, he was in Town before any one knew of his coming except some of his people residing here who betrayed the place by giving notice of this carelessness and who fired the Town the moment of his entrance but since its restoration they have every one turned out of it."

Beaumont, the EIC Agent, reported that at two in the morning of June 30 he was woken with the news that these bandits had seized the town. There was hardly any opposition, for only 12-

364 Roschanzamir, *Zand-Dynastie*, pp. 80-86.

365 Miles, *Countries*, pp. 274-75, 279.

366 The reason cannot have been simply the enmity between Sheikh Naser and Baqer Khan, although that was, of course, part of the driving force.

15 people were killed on either side. The town wall had been left unguarded and all were asleep that night. Sheikh 'Ali and most of Sheikh Naser's people were more concerned with saving the Sheikh's family and effects on the gallivats where they fled with 203 merchants and 300 men than in defending the town. Those remaining behind then lost heart. The town was set fire to and burnt until the morning; some 1,000 huts were burnt. Sheikh Sa'dun remained in his house with almost 200 men with muskets and did not venture outside, although 50 men could have taken the town. There were plenty of men willing to fight, but there was no commander. Thus a town of 10,000 lost to a handful of men. Fear had blown up the number of attackers and later people were astonished how few had in fact taken the town. After the takeover the streets were empty and the enemy did not plunder or hurt anyone. A frightened Sheikh Sa'dun left his house to swear with Reis Hamet that neither side would do anything until the arrival of Baqer Khan. When Sheikh Sa'dun thus had been secured some Arabs appeared to the assistance of Bushire and killed 4-5 Tangesiris at the watering place. Then learning about the situation in the town they cursed Sheikh Sa'dun for his cowardice.

On July 1 Baqer Khan entered Bushire with 200 men. He promised that all persons and property would be safe and sacred. The people were forced to surrender their arms and were put to work to complete the fortifications. The population (Moslems, Armenians, Indians) were forced to petition 'Abdol-Fath Khan (Abdul Fatee Caun) to confirm Baqer Khan in his government. On July 2 the two Bushiri gallivats in the roads sailed away to search for Sheikh Naser. On July 3 all inhabitants were expelled from the town and stripped of everything to make room for Tangesiri families. "A few of whom including the Cauns and Reis Hemets were armed previous to this of one Meer Ally's Captains having come here and demanded the late Shaik Ises family and his son they were delivered to him" and he returned to Bandar-e Rig on July 5. Mir 'Ali of Bandar-e Rig had advised Baqer Khan against this move. Everybody also expected that he as soon as he had returned to Bandar-e Rig he would march on Bushire with those of Ganaveh to relieve Bushire.

On July 9 three messengers arrived from 'Abdol-Fath Khan in Shiraz commanding Baqer Khan to restore everything that he might have taken, to restore the town to Sheikh Sa'dun, leave Bushire immediately and return with the messengers to Shiraz. Baqer Khan had no intention to heed these order, for he forced the merchants to pay him the customs arrears of 30-40,000 rupees and the EIC also had to pay by giving presents to him and his principal men with a value of 3-4,000 rupees. "He likewise plundered and destroyed to the foundation every house belonging to the Arabs in revenge for the hostilities committed by their Tribe in his country, for they no sooner heard that he had fallen upon Bushire than making Shaik Nassir's cause their own they acrose [sic], pillaged, laid waste, and all in their power depopulated Tankseer and other villages under his Government sparing neither age nor sex and continuing these barbarities till Shaikh Nassir's arrival put a stop to it."

For indeed Bushire's allies had arrived, because the moment the capture became known *chapars* or express messengers from Shiraz were sent to all parts between Congoon and Gombroon to assist the allies against the rebel they also were offered troops from Shiraz which they declined, as these soldiers were apt to prey on those they are supposed to help. The allies had struck camp near Tangesir and by mid-July these amounted to almost 3,000 men consisting of Arabs, people of Dashtestan, and many from Bandar-e Rig and Ganaveh commanded by "Meers Ally Gunnos and Heyder." Finding that the whole area was arming against him and readying to attack by sea and land and fearing that Shiraz troops would arrive shortly as well, being shut up in a place with not more than 500 men with no escape possible and fearing that his own men would abandon him, because their families were exposed to the advancing Arabs, made Baqer Khan decide to leave Bushire. One day later he sent boats with his plunder to two forts near the sea; the value of the booty was 3 or 4 lakhs rupees, mainly belonging to Sheikh Naser; he only had plundered the notables. In the morning of July 11 Baqer Khan peaceably left to the joy of the inhabitants of Bushire to Tangesir taking the messengers with him, after some of his rabble had broken open a few shops in the bazaars and stripped them. Thus ended the 11-day occupation of Bushire.

On July 12 two gallivats from Bandar-e Rig and on July 15 one from Ganaveh came to Bushire's assistance and Sheikh Sa'dun went to the allied camp at the request of the Arabs to sanction their operations. Ma'sum Khan (Masoon Caun) of Ganaveh joined them on July 22 from Shiraz. On July 26 the three gallivats went to meet Sheykh Naser. "The 31th accompanied by Shaik Sagur of Alharam with his two Galivats and Shaik Nassor of Barein with his own and the two Bushire Gallivats making together a fleet of 9 gallivats and 5 or 6 Dows. One of the Imaun's ships came with the Shaik as far as Alharam when she sailed for Zebarra. But 2 Dows laden with Bushire property having separated from the fleet off Gombroon for want of water were taken by Kishme by the Gallivats belonging to Shaik Abdallah of Ormuse."

Sheikh Nassur engaged the Khan of Bardestan to assist him with 1,000 men, who joined the allies at the beginning of August 1779, and on August 7 Sheikhs Naser, Saqr (Sagur) and Nassur joined them and the whole fleet and land force of ca. 4,000 men with 5-6 large cannons laid close siege to Baqer Khan in his main fort. "On receiving news that near 200 men in 7 boats were came from Taury [Taheri] (between Congoon [Kangan] and Alharam) to the assistance of Bagur Caun [Baqer Khan] and were landed at his Fort near the sea the 12th, three Gallivats sailed thither to intercept their return and stop the landing of further reinforcements. It is certain that Bagur Caun depended much on the succour from the Caub whom he solicited soon as he got possession of Bushire." Although the Ka'b were engaged in war with their neighbors and were hurting they sent a tranki with 50 men, which arrived at Deylam at the end of July, but on learning that Baqer Khan had left Bushire it returned to Dowraq.

A few days later Baqer Khan left his fort and consulted with Ma'sum (Masoon) Khan, Mir 'Ali and others. On the 24th on promise of these leaders he went to visit Sheikh Naser promising to return the next day and throw himself at his mercy and surrendering his forts and people to him. When he did not come it was suspected he wanted to escape, while he also used that occasion to transport provisions into the fort. On the 26th he again came to Mir 'Ali and gave a false account of the plunder he had taken and at that time those of Ganaveh demanded his blood and Sheikh Naser gave permission. They cut off his head when he was with Mir 'Ali and with him 15 of his people were killed and another 25 made prisoner, having been saved by the Sheikh; they were his chiefs and some of his best men. The day thereafter his small fort and another at Haram were given up to Sheikh Naser, and on August 29 Sheikh Hamet in the large fort surrendered.

Beaumont was right when he commented: "To the Arabs the Bushire merchants are indebted for the preservation of their property as well as for the sudden retreat of Bagur Caun for their quick invasion of his country left him no secure place to convey the effects to had he plundered the Town and obliged him to hasten to the protection of Tankseer."[367] After matters had settled down the allies returned to their homes, while Sheikh Naser continued to hold the Tangesir forts. After the death of Zaki Khan, the fight among the Zand contenders for the throne, Sadeq Khan versus 'Ali Morad Khan, had broken out, which continued into 1780, a fight ultimately won by 'Ali Morad Khan in 1782.[368] Meanwhile, life continued such as that the English had just completed a new factory in 1780, which had suffered much damage due to "the uncommon violence of the rains

367 Saldanha, *Précis*, vol. 1, pp. 308-312 (Bushire, 30/08/1779).

368 Roschanzamir, *Zand-Dynastie*, pp. 87-93.

here this year."[369] The internal troubles in Persia also left their mark on the situation in the Persian Gulf. From the observation made by Beaumont in Bushire it would seem that everybody wanted to settle a score with everybody else.

> From these troubles [among the Zands] this Gulph is in great Confusion. The Imaum continues at war, with Shaik Reshed. Shaik Abdulla of Ormuse, is at war, with the people of Charack as is also Shaik Sagur of Alharam, with the Tamia People, which latter Place, the Former has lately burnt. The Zebarra, and [315] Grain People, are at war, with the Chaub, and Bunderick was a few days ago accidentally consumed by fire. Some of Shaik Rashed's People came here not long ago, proposing to make a Peace with Shaik Nassir but having no authority to restore the Expedition, and other Restitutions that were demanded, they returned without effecting anything.[370]

Travel between Baghdad and Basra as well as via the Shatt al-Arab towards Bushire had become practically impossible in 1783, because of the marauding of the Banu Ka'b and the enmity between Kuwait and Bushire. The French biologist Michaux left on May 23 with 17 Bushiri boats who were met at the river's entrance by 30 boats from Kuwait. During the panic that followed he was able to escape and return to Basra. In September the British consul offered Michaud passage on a boat that was going to Masqat. The consul believed that he would have no problem because he was a friend on the sheik of the Ka'b. On September 9 Michaud left and the next day they were held up by the Ka'b gallivats. They were plundered and most of their possessions taken. Michaux was set free on September 18, and received his money and two guns, but his scientific equipment was gone. He took passage on a boat of the British consul and reached Bushire on September 21. Michaux noted that the dangers that he had been exposed to on his journey to and from Basra did not exist in Persia and he contrasts that with the security on the roads from Bushire to Resht.[371]

Thus it would seem as if Bushire was a rather peaceful place compared with its neighbors, due to the fact that it lived in peace with most of them. This also was due to the considerable power base that Sheikh Naser had been able to build. As a result, he had been able to easily oust and subjugate Baqer Khan his Tangesir enemy, thanks to his solid relationship with the Arabs between Ganaveh and 'Asalu, who had supported him as well the government in Shiraz. At the same time, Baqer Khan had not been alone and also had supporters, such as the Banu Ka'b, some of the Hulas and in particular those of Taheri. Moreover, as earlier and subsequent events showed to-day's ally could be tomorrow's foe and thus these alliances proved to be short-lived. Grummond therefore seems to be correct in stating that Naser's grip on the upper Persian Gulf began to slip as of 1782.

---

369 Saldanha, *Précis*, vol. 1, pp. 312 (Bushire, 16/09/1779); Ibid., vol. 1, p. 313 (Bushire, 05/02/1780); Ibid., vol. 1, p. 315 (Bushire, 15/07/1780),

370 The description of the occupation of Bushire is entirely based on Saldanha, *Précis*, vol. 1, pp. 315-16 (Bushire, 15/07/1780); see also Lorimer, *Gazetteer*, pp. 1846-51.

371 E.-T. Hamy, "Voyage d'André Michaux en Syrie et en Perse (1782-1785) d'après son journal et sa correspondance." *Neuvième Congrès International de Géographie, Compte Rendu Des Travaux du Congrès*, vol. 3 (1911), pp. 27-30.

SHEIKH NASER LOSES BAHRAIN

In that year hostilities broke out again with the 'Otobis. Part of its Khalifa branch had abandoned their 'Otobi kinsmen in Kuwait in 1766 and had settled at Zubara, where slowly the remainder of the Al Khalifa joined their brethren in the following decade. Zobara received an economic boost, when Karim Khan had invaded Basra in 1775, because many merchants from Basra as well one sheikh of Kuwait and his people migrated there, "and the power, wealth, and influence of the Bemni Khaleefa rapidly increased," because it became a center for the pearl and part of the India trade.[372] This development was to the detriment of Basra and Bushire and as a result Sheikh Naser between 1777 and 1801 in vain tried to reduce Zubara. Jealous of its rising star Sheikh Naser attacked Zubara in 1776 and 1777 but to no effect, and after some quiet period warfare erupted again in 1782. In that year the Al Khalifa turned the tables on Sheikh Naser for his repeated attacks on Zubara by attacking Bahrain, trying to take advantage of the confused conditions prevailing in Persia at that time. Their attack forced Sheikh Naser to withdraw into the fort and to look on as the Al Khalifa plundered and destroyed the town. When they returned to Zubara the attackers took the Bushire gallivat with them, which had come for the annual tribute. Bushire collected a fleet, supported by Bandar-e Rig, Ganaveh, 'Asalu and Dashtestan and attacked the 'Otobis in September 1782. The fleet with 2,000 Dashtestani Arabs sailed under Sheikh Mohammad, Sheikh Naser's nephew, to Zubara, and blockaded the sea lanes of Zubara and Bahrain. The 'Otobis were unable to do something about this and suffered economically. They therefore asked Mir Guneh (Meer Gunneeh) of Bandar-e Rig to intercede, promising to return the plunder taken at Bahrain. Sheikh Naser declined the offer, while the mediation by Sheikh Rashed of Jolfar was also in vain. Realizing that negotiations failed to produce his objective the Bushiri commander decided to storm the fort at Zubara. The Bushire force had barely landed when a much greater force than they had expected made a sortie from the fort and attacked them with such vehemence that the Bushiri troops dropped their arms and fled to their gallivats. Sheikh Mohammad was killed as were some important Bahrainis. The lack of vessels prevented the Zubara Arabs from attacking Bahrain, which unbeknownst to them was done on the same day by the 'Otobis of Kuwait. They sacked and plundered the town and forced the garrison to seek refuge in the fort. Sheikh Naser wanted revenge and went with Sheikh Rashed to 'Asalu to mobilize forces for a new attack. There was some skirmishing and Sheikh Rashed captured a boat belonging to the 'Otobis and killed 18 of its crew, but otherwise not much progress was made. Sheikh Naser therefore returned to Bushire on June 12, 1783. En route he dispatched a letter to his son at Bahrain informing him of his defeat, charging him to defend the island until help would arrive. This letter was intercepted by an 'Otobi fleet of Kuwait which was en route to the relief of their Al Khalifa fellow-tribesmen. Realizing that Bahrain was defenseless the 'Otobis immediately set course for Bahrain, where on July 23, 1783 they took its main fort and became the masters of the island. The Zubara Arabs on learning this news immediately sent auxiliaries to help secure Bahrain. The Bushiri garrison had surrendered, however, and with Sheikh Rashed arrived on August 5, 1783 in Bushire.[373]

Sheikh Naser wanted to retaliate and immediately contacted Shiraz for assistance. In September 1783, 'Ali Morad Khan promised Sheikh Naser 6,000 men to retake Bahrain, but his promised troops did not arrive. Despite 'Ali Morad Khan's failure to provide timely military sup-

372 Abu Hakima, *History*, pp. 71-74.

373 Government of Great Britain, *Selections*, pp. 140-41, 363-65; Abu Hakima, *History*, pp. 112-14; Grummond, *The Rise*, pp. 111-12. Some Zubara Arabs returned to Basra after the Persian occupation, see Saldanha, *Précis*, vol. 1, p. 308 (Basra, 28/05/1778). From the above it is clear that Slot, *'Arab al-Khalij*, p. 383 is wrong in arguing that Sheikh Naser's military activities were initiated by the Zand authorities.

port to Sheikh Naser the latter sent presents to him when he declared himself king in 1784. Sheikh Naser also tried to mobilize support from the Qavasem and the Banu Ma'in for another expedition against Bahrain. On February 12, 1785 he left Bushire to travel overland to Kangan for a meeting with Sheikh Rashed of Jolfar and Sheikh 'Abdallah of Hormuz in that town. His fleet of vessels from Bushire and Bandar-e Rig left on February 21, while a small force (not the 6,000 promised) from Shiraz had already arrived at Kangan. However, the unexpected death of 'Ali Morad Khan in February 1785 led to the deferment of the expedition to retake Bahrain. Sheikh Naser therefore had to accept the loss of Bahrain and did not try anymore to regain the island. His last connection with the island was in 1799, when the 'Otobis sought his support against Masqat and to that end paid him one-year's tribute, because "they were desirous becoming subject to the King of Persia." It is interesting that the Imam of Masqat had sent four ships, 60 buggalows and armed gallivats to reduce the 'Otobis and take Bahrain "in compliance with the application of the Beglerbeg of Fars," who was Sheikh Naser's superior. When he learnt about the payment of tribute by the 'Otobis to Sheikh Naser, the Imam, during the absence of Sheikh Naser from Bushire, seized Khark. He circulated the rumor on the island that Sheikh Naser had fled and that his cousin Sheikh Ghanum had been appointed governor. Therefore all Bushiris had to be sent back from Khark to Bushire, otherwise Sheikh Ghanem would consider them rebels, in which case he would confine their women, while the fort had to be entrusted to him. The people of Khark therefore transferred the fort to the Imam, who then wrote to the governor of Fars that in view of the small number of people living there he had seized Khark to prevent the 'Otobis from taking it. He offered to pay five-years' revenue if the island was given to him. In the summer of 1798 the 'Otobis also helped Sheikh Naser in his conflict with his nephew Sheikh Ghanem retake Bushire, while they also took the island of Khark for him. Thereafter, it was seized by the Imam of Masqat, but at the end of July 1800 it was again retaken by the 'Otobis for Sheikh Naser.[374]

SHEIKH NASER DEFECTS TO THE QAJARS

In 1785 a new power struggle broke out in Persia after the death of 'Ali Morad Khan, which was won by Ja'far Khan Zand and thus provided some stability for the time being. In the spring of 1786, Ja'far Khan Zand, his nominal overlord, led an army to Bushire to punish Sheikh Naser who had refused to pay the annual *pishkesh* and had given protection to his rival Rezaqoli Khan. Sheikh Naser who was 80 years old at that time decided to oppose him. When Ja'far Khan had reached Kazerun friends mediated in the conflict and for one lakh of rupees Sheikh Naser was left undisturbed and on December 17, 1786 Ja'far Khan and his army left Kazerun and returned to Shiraz.[375] When Ja'far Khan was murdered in January 1789 his eldest son Lotf 'Ali Khan was in Lar with part of the army that rebelled against him. He fled to Bushire where Sheikh Naser promised help. He together with Mir 'Ali Khan Hayat Davudi of Bandar-e Rig were able to mobilize an army and put Lotf 'Ali Khan on the throne after three months, assisted by a rebellion among his opponent's

374 Grummond, *The Rise*, pp. 112-13; Government of Great Britain, *Selections*, pp. 141, 173, 365-66; Saldanha, *Précis*, vol. 1, pp. 342 (Bushire, 27/09/1798) 354-55 (Basra, 17/12/1798), 382 (Bushire, rec. 28/08/1800). Kelly, *Persian Gulf*, p. 30 rightly points out that this temporary payment of tribute made it easier for the Al Khalifah to scare off other 'suitors.'

375 Saldanha, *Précis*, vol. 1, pp. 319-20 (Bushire, 25/10/1786); Ibid., vol. 1, p. 322 (Bushire, 05/01/1787); William Francklin, *Observations made on a tour from Bengal to Persia in the years 1786-7* (London, 1790), p. 344. Ja'far Khan also issued an edict granting the EIC free trade in Persia. For the text see Saldanha, *Précis*, vol. 1, p. 335 (18/01/1788), see also another edict promising protection of English trade, see Ibid., p. 326 (September 1788).

supporters. However, before his force left Bushire Sheikh Naser died on April 11, 1789, and he was succeeded by his son Sheikh Naser II. On April 22, 1789 Lotf 'Ali Khan marched to Shiraz accompanied by Sheikh Naser II, whose brother remained in charge of Bushire. Two years later, however, Sheikh Naser II actively opposed the Zands. When Lotf 'Ali Khan was betrayed by his grand vizier Hajji Ebrahim in August 1791 he first fled to Bushire, but Sheikh Naser refused him entry. In fact, Sheikh Naser was said to have been part of the conspiracy against Lotf 'Ali Khan and he publicly had declared his allegiance to the Qajars. Lotf 'Ali Khan then went to the Sheikh Naser's enemy Mir 'Ali of Bandar-e Rig to regroup and launch his campaign to regain the throne. Sheikh Naser then attacked Lotf 'Ali Khan with 2,000 men but he was defeated. Nevertheless he continued to harass him. The reasons for Sheikh Naser's defection are uncertain. Perhaps because Lotf 'Ali Khan had offered the EIC the port of Khark, which implied that the Company would withdraw from Bushire thus hurting Sheikh Naser's revenues, or that Naser II felt that he could profit from Lotf 'Ali Khan's fall.[376] It should also not be ruled out that this was pay-back time for the Zands, who had failed to support Bushire in its bid to regain Bahrain in 1783 and 1785, or because Sheikh Naser had allegedly advised his successor, Sheikh Naser II, not to support Lotf 'Ali Khan.[377] Another and related reason may have been that Lotf 'Ali Khan was said to have confiscated much of Sheikh Naser's wealth when he died.[378]

Whatever the reason for his defection, Sheikh Naser took steps to establish control over Dashtestan and the neighboring parts. Lotf 'Ali Khan was supported by those of Khist and Bandar-e Rig. Mir 'Ali Khan, who was not in a position to resist, being weak in health due to a wound, was forced to deliver up Bandar-e Rig at the demand of Sheikh Naser and to return "to his ancient government of Genowa. Meer Gunnoss the former Governor of Bundereeg who was deprived of the Government by Lutf Ali Khan has again been put in possession of it, in consequence, by the Sheikh." This change of hands at Bandar-e Rig was followed by an attack by a force of 300 men on Khark that was still in the hands of Mir 'Ali Khan. Because he was in the strong former Dutch fort Mir 'Ali Khan was able to resist the Bushire attack. Mir 'Ali Khan has also been able to send men and supplies to the fort. Moreover, the attackers were unskilled in the art of siege warfare. Sheikh Naser II in person led an expedition against Khisht from January-June 1792, which seemed an easier target as it was defended by a small fort, but it was governed by Leal [?] Khan. The latter was a courageous man and a supporter of Lotf 'Ali Khan so there was little chance of success. All trade with Shiraz was stopped.[379] The attack on Khisht failed, whence he returned on June 27, but Sheikh Naser II had more and unexpected success at Khark, where fate handed him an easy victory. Mir 'Ali Khan had died about that time and thus Khark quietly came into the possession of Sheikh Naser II. Agha Mohammad Khan had ordered Sheikh Naser to come to Shiraz and although he did not want to go he had no choice.[380]

The establishment of a new central government in Persia did not mean that peace and quiet returned to the Persian Gulf. At that time, for example, a new conflict had broken out between the governor of Basra and the Ka'b, because the former had destroyed the principal part the Ka'b fleet in

---

376 Saldanha, *Précis*, vol. 1, pp. 327 (Bushire, 11/05/1789); Ibid., vol.1, p. 328-29 (Bushire, 01/06/1792); Fasa'i, *Farsnameh*, vol. 2, pp. 690, 648; Roschanzamir, *Die Zand-Dynastie*, pp. 104, 106; Brydges, *Dynasty*, CXIX-CXX; Grummond, *The Rise*, pp. 115-16.

377 E'temad al-Saltaneh, *Mer'at*, vol. 1, p. 484.

378 Edward Scott Waring, *A Tour to Sheeraz* (London, 1807), p. 7.

379 Saldanha, *Précis*, vol. 1, pp. 328-29 (Bushire, 01/06/1792). Grummond, *The Rise*, p. 117 has Zul Khan instead of Leal Khan.

380 Saldanha, *Précis*, vol. 1, pp. 329 (Bushire, 27/07/1792).

September/October 1791. As a result the Ka'b erected batteries on the banks of the Shatt al-Arab to stop vessels leaving Basra and claim compensation in cash or vessels for their losses. When at the end of December 1791 the coffee fleet left Basra, they were accompanied by the Basra fleet commanded by the *qaputan basha*. The engagement that took place between the two sides was inconclusive. The Ka'b withdrew from their batteries to Dowraq, the coffee fleet continued their voyage into the Gulf and the Basra fleet returned.[381]

THE TRADE OF BUSHIRE

In 1763 the EIC decided to establish a trading station at Bushire, although it was abandoned in 1768, but re-established seven years later. At first one cargo per year was sent there, consisting of 60-100 bales of cotton fabrics, iron, sugar and muslins. After 1777, the EIC lost interest in trade with Persian Gulf, because of bad trade results, economic malaise in Gulf, and very good opportunities elsewhere in the East. Also, English private trade declined, while Arab trade increased, as evidenced by the decline of trade in Basra and Bushire and the growth of several Arab ports. By the 1780s, the importance of Bushire had been reduced considerably.[382] The town was described in1787 as follows:

> Boushier is a small town near the mouth of a river. It is the residence of a Shaik Nasser. The bazar, or market-place, is well supplied with provisions and fruits, as well as coarse shawls, and other cloths. The surrounding country, which is naked, and without verdure, exhibits a dreary and unpleasant prospect. The only curiosities I saw there, were two large brass guns, which had been cast in Goa, and were now lying dismounted without the town: the caliber of one of them will receive a ball of forty-two pounds. Many other brass guns, of a large bore, lay neglected on the sand, by the river side; for the Persians hardly know how to use them. An old ship of the line, which belonged to the famous Nadir Shaw, has been rotting, for these fifty years past, in the middle of the river.[383]

Despite the fact that the bazaar was well supplied, in 1787, according to Francklin, "little business is carried on, owing to the ruinous state of Persia; caravans come frequently to this place from Shiraz, and bring the commodities of that city, which are exported to various parts of India."[384] The manner of trade favored those big merchants, who had friendly ties with Sheikh Naser, who himself participated in trade, the same way that his father had done before him. According to the EIC Agents at Basra, writing in 1790 about Bushire:

> Its Government partakes more of the Arabian, than the Persian form and nature. The Shaik or Governor, is induced by motives of self Interest, to favor and protect in their Persons and Property as well as the Resident Merchants as the Strangers that frequent the Port, and this protection was during the Life times, of the late

381 Saldanha, *Précis*, vol. 1, pp. 327-28 (Basra, 10/01/1792).

382 Amin, *British Interests*, pp. 137-39.

383 Thomas Howel, *Journal of the Passage from India* (London, 1789), pp. 20-21; see also Francklin, *Observations*, p. 39.

384 Francklin, *Observations*, p. 39.

> Shaik Nassir and Iaafer Khan Government of Schyras; from which, nothing but the unfortunate Assassination of Iaafer Khan could have extricated him with Impunity. The duties levied at Bushire, on Importation are very moderate, but it is impossible to state them with precision, since they are frequently varied, according to the Commercial Importance of the Importer, and according to the peaceful or confused state of the interior parts of the Empire. During the Government of the late Sheikh Nassir, the freedom of the Market suffered some degree of restraint, for the Shaik himself being engaged in Commerce considered himself entitled on the arrival of Vessels and foreign Merchants, to a preference, and to have the refusal of their Importations. This Evil was however in some Measure alleviated, by the Shaikh's uniformly inviting the principal Merchants of the place, to take shares in the Purchases which he made; and therefore was only felt more severely, by the British Resident and the inferior order of Merchants.[385]

This attitude towards trade may explain why Howel reported that in 1787 Sheikh Naser refused to supply a pilot the ship he was on "unless we employed him up the Euphrates, because he shares in the hire of the pilots. We refused, sailed the ship out of the harbor and took a pilot at Khark Island by firing a gun, a signal for a pilot. Thus, he lost the customary profits on the pilotage of the harbor."[386] Khark was the location where pilots usually were hired, but Howel's captain decided to do without one.

From 1780-90, the EIC only sold £ 2,608 in woolens, with a loss of about 5%. This, combined with the annual expenses of the factory of £1,400/year, yielded an annual loss of £1,800. Sales never yielded more than £7,000/year, in 1788 being as low as £93.[387] In 1780/81-1790 the EIC only sold 667 bales of woolens of all kinds at Bushire, incurring a loss of £1,232 over the decade.[388] In short, by the end of the 18th century trade with Persia had become totally insignificant and a loss-maker. The only reason that the EIC remained in the Gulf, as discussed above, was to secure the communication lines with Europe due to the war with France.

By 1790, the trade of Bushire was mainly with India. Imports of goods from Bengal (sugar candy, iron, planks, and indigo from Masulipatnam), were decreasing in importance by 1790. They were "suited to and designed for the Bussora, Bagdad, Aleppo and other Northern Markets." Imports from Surat were insignificant, while it imported sugar (crystal and candy), spices, coffee, metals and other items via Masqat that were transported by Masqati boats to Bushire. Because apart from EIC vessels that went to Bushire and Basra, most other ships (Bengal, French and Dutch) only sailed to Masqat. China and glassware was often imported by the EIC from Bombay. Exports to India consisted of an inconsiderable quantity of "old Copper Drugs, Rose water, dried Fruits &." The remainder of exports was to Masqat and Basra and consisted of "to the former in raw Silk, Cotton, Drugs and Dried fruit and to the latter inconsiderable quantities of grain and Dried Fruits." Because the value of these exports were not enough to pay for the imports to make up for the current account deficit, Bushire exported to India "Venetian Sequins, and different sorts of Persian Silver Coin," but because of the fluctuating rate of exchange exporters preferred to be paid

---

385 Saldanha, *Précis*, vol. 1, pp. 422-23 (Report on the Commerce of Arabia and Persia by Samuel Manestry and Hardford Jones, 1790).

386 Howel, *Journal*, pp. 22-23.

387 William Milburn, *Oriental Commerce* 2 vols. (London, 1813), vol. 1, p. 129.

388 Charles Issawi, *The Economic History of Iran*, 1800-1914 (Chicago, 1971), p. 83.

in gold and silver bars. Also, due to the loss of Bahrain, "less Intercourse has subsisted between the Inhabitants of the Opposite Shores of the Gulph."[389]

Bushire continued to maintain its position as the most important port on the Persian littoral, which partly was due to Sheikh Naser's support of the victorious Qajar party. According to Manesty and Jones in 1790, "The Port of Bushire is now the only one, of Importance; on the Persian side of the Persian Gulph. [...] The present Shaikh Nessr, who succeeded his Father, in the Government of Bushire in the Month of April 1789, has not yet engaged in commerce, but it is probable that the Advice of his confidential Servants, may early induce him to tread in the footsteps of his Father."[390] By 1800, Bushire was still the main port of entry for goods entering southern Persia, but there was a shift in emphasis of the economy from the south to the north. John Malcolm reports that "The trade of this city [Shiraz] has much decreased since it ceased to be the Seat of Government. It will, however, always maintain some importance as a place of trade, while Bushire is the chief port in the Gulph,"[391] However, it would take a few decades before Bushire acquired its status as the main import terminus for Persia.

CONCLUSION

The available evidence shows that the Bushire peninsula was inhabited since Elamite times. It further shows that it was an important port in Sasanian times, if not earlier, whose role declined following the fall of the Sasanids due to structural changes in its hinterland. When Rishahr lost its leading role as an international port in the 7th century, it would seem that it probably was reduced to the role of a secondary distributive port, a role it would have until the mid-18th century. The name Rishahr seems to have been the name by which the educated class knew the island, whereas the common people called it Bushire. There is no real information available on Bushire until the beginning of the 16th century. According to Portuguese sources, Rishahr played an important maritime and military role in the Upper Gulf. It provided pilots to those vessels going to Basra, supplied food to Basra, Hormuz and other markets within the Gulf area, served as a regional distribution port, while it further tried to carve a role out for itself as a local power. When the Portuguese first met the Rishahris in 1514 they were preying on vessels from Bahrain and Mir Abu Eshaq, the chief of Rishahr, even had designs on Bahrain itself. In 1515 he tried to ally himself with the Portuguese, asking them to provide naval support to seize Bahrain. When the Portuguese demurred he tried to achieve the same objective with troops of his nominal overlord Shah Esma'il I in that same year. The operation failed to achieve its objective, but it set an example that would be followed for the next 200 years in the Persian Gulf. I.e. in the absence of strong states on the mainland with a pronounced and unchallenged presence in the commercial and security situation of the Persian Gulf by default the latter was determined by the various petty chiefs living on the littoral of the Persian Gulf. Since none of the latter was strong enough to impose himself on other similar chiefs or control the traffic in the Persian Gulf itself they would either join forces with like-minded chiefs or serve as unwilling instruments for the mainland states in the execution of a half-hearted and poorly supported policy

389 Saldanha, *Précis*, vol. 1, p. 423 (Report on the Commerce of Arabia and Persia by Samuel Manestry and Hardford Jones, 1790).

390 Saldanha, *Précis*, vol. 1, pp. 422-23 (Report on the Commerce of Arabia and Persia by Samuel Manestry and Hardford Jones, 1790).

391 A.T. Wilson, "Some Hitherto Unpublished Dispatches of Captain John Malcolm", *Journal of the Central Asian Society* 16 (1929), p. 25.

to impose themselves on the Gulf. The mainland states considered the Europeans with naval power present in the Gulf merely a foreign variety of the many pretty chiefs who did their bidding, if and when they could enforce it. The Europeans had no easy time of it, for despite their superior firepower the better maneuverability of the low-bottom rowing vessels of the local chiefs gave the latter an edge over the Europeans as the Portuguese, the Dutch and the English found out to their chagrin and cost. In the second half of the 18th century, when control of the mainland states over their littoral was almost non-existent and constantly challenged, Europeans, in particular the English, after the Dutch had abandoned the Gulf in 1766, were forced to assume a greater role of protecting sea routes against their will. It not only was a costly undertaking, but also one that was successfully challenged by the coastal chiefs. As a result the English had to play a role that should have been exercised by the Ottoman and Zand states. Those who claim that Europeans had imperialist designs in the Persian Gulf are mistaken, for the increased role of the Europeans there was due to the failure of the mainland states (Ottoman Empire, Zand Persia) to provide protection and security to those who they claimed were their subjects, while at the same time ruining the local commercial and maritime operators, engaged in the long-distance trade.

AFTERWORD

After all the details about the political, military and commercial developments in the Persian Gulf, in particular concerning the three Persian ports (Bandar 'Abbas, Khark, and Bushire), let's have a look at the broad outline to see if we can make sense of it all. First, some context, to better understand the developments that were taking place in the Gulf. Commercially speaking the Persian Gulf during the period discussed was of no great importance anymore, certainly not to the European Companies. In fact, they had been losing money since 1722 (this certainly held for the Dutch), and voices to withdraw from the Gulf altogether were already raised in the 1740s. Trade with the Gulf consisted mainly in the import of chintz, muslins, piece goods, woolens, sugar, sugar candy, Chinaware, ginger, spices, and metals. The main exports were Kerman goat hair, dried fruit, asafetida, rose water, copper, and a variety of drugs supplemented by specie, which was the most important export commodity.[1] The main trade problem of the Persian Gulf was not the limited range of products traded, but that its trade figures were small as were its profits compared with other parts of Asia. Also, the countries adjacent to the Gulf had very few goods suitable goods for export; in fact, the bulk was in specie, which was often adulterated. For the EIC, however, it was one of the few areas where it could sell its woolen cloth and the EIC therefore continued to trade there because it had the statuary obligation that 10% of its goods sold had to be of English origin. Between 1750 and 1770, the EIC sold about 16% of its total exports to the East in the Gulf. The most important product being woolen goods; for the same period it represented one-third of EIC goods sold in Gulf.[2] More importantly, the country trade was even more significant than official EIC trade. Between 1750 and 1760, private merchants brought some £400,000 annually to Bandar 'Abbas and Basra, or five times more than the EIC.[3] When the sales of broadcloth plummeted and were of no importance anymore the EIC decided to withdraw from the Gulf in 1777, also because it was losing money and getting a lot of headache in exchange.

The situation for the Dutch was not that much different. The Company directors had already wanted to withdraw at the end of the 1740s, but private interests in Batavia connected with the production of sugar there pressed for a continuation of VOC operations in the Persian Gulf. When even the sale of surplus sugar from Batavia was not profitable anymore Batavia complied, too late, in 1765 to execute the 1762 orders from the VOC directors to withdraw from the Gulf. The VOC had concluded that it could also sell its main exports to the Gulf

1 Floor, *The Economy*, pp. 181-95; Amin, *British Interests*, p. 128; Ives, *Voyage*, p. 199.

2 Amin, *British Interests*, pp. 119-20.

3 Amin, *British Interests*, p. 133.

(sugar, pepper and spices) in Surat and in Masqat. For many Asian traders the Gulf trade still was profitable, although the cost of doing business had increased due to growing insecurity. Many European and Indian merchants therefore sold their goods at Masqat and from there these would be forwarded in smaller ships in convoy. In this way these European and Indian merchants, who had larger and more expensive ships in operating terms, saved time and money (shorter voyages; less lay-overs and thus less wages to pay and other overhead, and finally less risk). The comparative advantage of Arab and Persian traders thus was, apart from having the same and/or similar linguistic, religious, cultural backgrounds, that they were able to serve a dwindling and volatile market more effectively with small vessels moving smaller quantities of goods.[4] Hardford-Jones, who had spent more than a decade in Basra and Southern Persia at the end of the eighteenth century, in 1800 commented on this issue as follows:

> In my opinion, it is not because the Native Merchants in India want the Spirit of Enterprise, that they decline to engage in the Trade of the Gulf, but because the Trade, in most of its branches, except those which are peculiarly adapted to the Speculations of the Arabs wants the degree of Profit which would make it worth their Notice. Where there is Honey there always be Flies.[5]

Thus, commercially the Gulf area had become less and less interesting for most foreign players, whether Indian or European, although there were of course always merchants who found it profitable to trade. Although all authors agree that Gulf trade was in decline, its causes have been misunderstood by authors such as Amin and Kelly. Amin argues that:

> Indian trade constantly drained the Persian reserves of gold and silver to the great benefit of the British who had assumed political and economic control in India. The effect of this trade on the Gulf itself was very profound. Indeed, it was an important factor in the impoverishment of Persia and the Ottoman provinces in the area. Had this trade been transacted by Persian merchants and by subjects of the Sultan, the harm of the local economies might have been minimized. Unfortunately, it was carried on mainly by Indian, Armenians, Europeans, and Arabs of the Gulf.[6]

Amin is wrong, because he clearly does not understand the mechanics of trade. The reason that Persian Gulf countries had to export specie to pay for their imports from India was because they themselves had not enough exportable commodities. Thus, to pay for their imports, instead of offering merchandise in barter, they had to pay in cash. Where did this cash come from? Not from the agricultural taxes, the main source of government income, as money was scarce in Iraq and Persia. No, the money was imported from the Levant and Russia where Middle Eastern (Armenian, Greek, Moslem, Jewish, and Indian) merchants sold their exportable goods (Persian raw silk and Indian cottons mostly) for which they were paid in broadcloth and/or cash. It is the latter that

---

4 I am not convinced by Risso, *Oman & Muscat*, p. 201 that the long terms of credit demanded were an additional advantage to Omani merchants as long credits had been the norm in the Gulf trade for a long time already, which all merchants, including the European Companies had to grant, see Floor, *The Economy*, p. 118. In addition to Omani traders and vessels the 'Otobis of Kuwait and their vessels also played an important role in the Gulf trade at that time. Abu Hakima, *History*, pp. 165-66.

5 Risso, *Muscat & Oman*, p. 201.

6 Amin, *British Interests*, p. 141.

served to finance the imports from India. This phenomenon of a current account deficit with India had been characteristic for Persian Gulf trade from the very beginning of the arrival of European trade and even prior to that, and it remained that way until well into the twentieth century. Thus the export of specie does not explain anything about the decline in trade. The nationality of the merchant had nothing to do either with the export of cash. The same amount of specie would have left the Gulf if all merchants had been Persian and Ottoman subjects. Thus, the problem of Gulf trade was not India or English traders; it was the political organization of the economies of Iraq and Persia.[7] Kelly has identified the following causes for the decline of the Gulf trade:

> piracy, the extinction of the Dutch settlement of Kharaq, the ravages of the plague in Turkish Arabia, the siege and capture of Basra, the dearth of specie in 'Iraq and Persia, and the civil wars that raged in Persia from 1779 onwards. [He also argues that] the Company hastened the demise of its own trade by cutting down its purchases of raw silk and Kirman wool.[8]

Kelly is also wrong, because what he sees as causes of the decline in trade are but its symptoms. Piracy, while certainly not helpful, did not stop trade, it only raised its transaction costs. The demise of the Khark factory had nothing to do with the decline in Gulf trade; prior to its fall the Dutch had already decided to close the factory due to its disappointing and falling commercial results. The dearth of specie in Iraq and Persia was structural in nature and even existed when trade was booming and thus had nothing to do with the decline in trade, as pointed out above. Clearly the 1773 plague was damaging, but then it was not the first time that the plague had struck Basra and with the same devastating impact. Each time the port had rebounded and was back in business soon thereafter. However, this time the plague was followed by the Persian siege and occupation (1775-79) one might counter. True, but the 1690 plague followed by the Persian occupation (1694-1700) did not have the same disabling impact. Moreover, Gulf trade continued also after 1775, but now it was mainly captured by Masqat and Kuwait. Therefore, the main cause of the decline of trade must be sought in the way the political and economic system functioned in Iraq and Persia, where, in the case of the latter, the succession war certainly was such a cause. The EIC, of course, did not hasten the demise of its Gulf trade by not buying raw silk and Kerman wool anymore. They did so because they could not get enough of it, and of a quality and at a price that were competitive with those acquired by others and thus the EIC did the right thing and discontinued the export these commodities. Moreover, this decision was not just based on the export of these two items, which really were of no great importance within overall EIC trade, but rather on the overall picture of the Gulf trade in the 1770s, which looked dismal and was a money-losing operation. As to what I consider to be the real causes for the decline of Gulf trade I refer the reader to the beginning of chapter one.

Politically the governments in the countries on the northern littoral of the Gulf were unable to impose themselves on the coastal sheikhdoms that had started to assert themselves after 1747. These not only held the Zand regime and the Ottoman government (Pasha of Baghdad) at bay, but also vigorously engaged the rising Arab states and ports from the other side of the Gulf (Oman, Jolfar, Kuwait, and Zubara). This growing independence of the self-assertive old sheikhdoms as well as of the new ones (Jolfar, Kuwait, Bahrain after 1783) also led to warfare and piracy contributing to the growing insecurity in the Gulf. When the central governments in Shiraz and Baghdad (via

7 On these issues see Willem Floor, *The Economy of Safavid Persia* (Wiesbaden, 1999) and Ibid. *A Fiscal History of Iran* (New York, 1999).

8 Kelly, *Persian Gulf*, p. 56.

its deputy-governor in Basra) wanted to take action to destroy or control these independently acting sheikhdoms they found that they were unable to do so. First, they lacked the political and military capability to enforce their authority on a sustained basis, i.e. they were sometimes able to pacify the area for a few months, but were unable to maintain an occupation army in the area to keep things quiet after the initial pacification. Second, the pacification was often rendered ineffective by the fact that the sheikhs and their followers either fled into their marshes (Banu Ka'b) or fled to the islands (e.g. to Hormuz, Qeshm, Khark) and thus could not be reached and brought to justice or under control. Third, the central governments were unable to establish a naval force that was able to impose itself on the Banu Ka'b, Mir Mohanna, Sheykh 'Abdollah and the others. Fourth, these governments therefore were forced to blackmail the Dutch and English Companies into providing naval support, which these Companies did as a last resort and very reluctantly. The directors of these Companies wanted their servants to avoid any involvement in local political conflicts, which, as previous experience should have taught them, was impossible, if they wanted to continue to trade in the Gulf. Fifth, to their great surprise the well-armed European Companies were defeated by their Arab opponents, which led to the loss of life, merchandise, military supplies, ships and face. Despite these defeats European agents and commentators continued to repeat the old belief that with a few ships and troops they could easily conquer Khark or destroy the Banu Ka'b and each time they found that to be wrong, although they did not change their tune. Sixth, although the EIC finally remained as the sole European trader in the Gulf the nature of the Company had changed. Because of its territorial gains in India the EIC was being transformed from a trading company into a government. By the 1770s, its interest in the Gulf was not of a commercial nature anymore, but that of a state looking after the interest of its subjects. For its tax payers (Indians, Arabs) who continued to trade with the Gulf complained about the insecurity there and said that if nothing was done to protect them they could not pay their taxes anymore. For, if there was no security, then the other Asian traders (Omanis, Persians, Ottomans, Kuwaitis, etc.) also suffered and thus could not buy their Indian products and it were these Asian merchants, not English ones as is so often maintained, who freighted the bulk of merchandise leaving and entering the Gulf by the end of the eighteenth century. In short, the EIC was forced to intervene in the Gulf and protect shipping, because the states whose duty it was to do so had abandoned this responsibility; in fact, they had totally washed their hands of it. Neither the new Qajar government in Persia, nor the Ottoman governor in Baghdad was able, willing or even interested to take any pro-active steps to bring security to the Gulf. In short, the growing role of the English in the Gulf in the nineteenth century was not due to an English interest in the Gulf (in fact it had none whatsoever), but because its Indian commercial interests demanded it in the absence of any government (Omani, Ottoman or Qajar) involvement in the Gulf. Thus, the power vacuum created by the inability and/or lack of interest by the states adjacent to the Gulf to establish security forced the English to reluctantly assume that role rather than its often touted imperialist interests. Thus, if people (historians, readers, politicians, etc.) from the Gulf States complain about the growing English presence after 1800 they in fact complain about their own forebears, who failed to do establish a secure environment for trade, foreign and local.

Finally, was the eighteenth century the period of English influence in the Gulf as Wilson has submitted? There is no denying that the English dominated the sea lanes. Especially the country trade by English merchants flourished, while the EIC also did good business between 1750 and 1770. The high cost of maintaining its expensive infrastructure (factory with a large administrative and military staff and guard vessel in the roads) in the Gulf was financed by the consulage revenues paid by ships sailing under English protection. However, the number of EIC ships and troops sent into the Gulf increased significantly after 1750, and in particular after 1760, which were engaged in several military operations against Gulf Arabs, and this was a money-losing operation. Thus, it would seem as if the English role in the field of commerce, freight and the use of violence was really significant and influential. However, what was the result of these activities? Trade by the 1770s was a deficit operation and the EIC directors understandably wanted to withdraw from the Gulf altogether. The only reason the EIC maintained a one-man presence at all in both Basra and Bushire was fear of Karim Khan's negative reaction against the remaining English trade, but in reality to secure fast communications with Europe. Substantial English military presence disappeared completely from the Gulf after 1775. It did not pay to have it there; all EIC military operations either had achieved no result or had resulted in disaster and defeat at great cost to the Company. Thus, despite all these military actions the English failed to achieve any advantage for themselves. While the English were withdrawing, the coastal Arabs (Omanis, 'Otobis, Qavasem, Banu Ma'in, Banu Ka'b, and the chiefs of Bushire and Bandar-e Rig) were the ones who really had gained influence in the Gulf, politically, militarily and commercially. If the presence and influence of any group characterized the eighteenth century in the Persian Gulf then it was that of coastal Arabs, because they more than anyone else had determined the nature of political and mercantile life in the Gulf. It is because of this reason that I chose the title for this book, because the eighteenth century was not the century of the growth of English but of Arab influence.

APPENDIX I
The Bahrain Project of 1754

In 1754 the VOC embarked on what to the English looked like a new commercial and strategic policy in the Persian Gulf. This alleged new policy greatly disturbed the VOC's biggest competitor, the EIC, as well as some local chiefs in the Gulf. However, despite English and locals apprehension there was no new Dutch plan for the Gulf. There was only a re-arrangement of Dutch factories or trading stations – a slimming down of the level and size of VOC operations rather than an expansionist trade policy. English and local apprehensions were partly inspired by the somewhat flamboyant and self-assertive behavior of Baron von Kniphausen, the VOC chief on Khark island. Partly, they were led by what they themselves would have liked to do if they had been in von Kniphausen's position. However, it was never the official Dutch intention to embark upon an expansionist trading and territorial policy in the Gulf.

In fact, the VOC directors were increasingly worried about the continued Dutch presence in the Persian Gulf. Since the fall of the Safavid state in 1722 trade results had gone from bad to worse owing to the political instability and impoverishment of Persia. Especially during the reign of Nader Shah (r. 1736-1747) the Dutch had been exposed to extortion of money and forced 'loan's of ships. The VOC remained in Persia not so much because of the trade profits, but because of the large debt which the state of Persia owed to the VOC. During the last days of the siege of Isfahan in 1722 Shah Soltan Hoseyn had borrowed more than 2.9 million guilders or 70,000 *tumans* from the VOC to pay is troops. Under the Afghan occupation new 'loans' had increased this debt. Moreover, the VOC still had some hope for improvement of the economic situation of Persia. To offset the decrease of trade with Persia the VOC had opened a factory in Basra in 1724, which yielded reasonable profits. However, here also the VOC was troubled by demanding local authorities and dishonest VOC servants. The factory at Bushire, opened in 1738, never became a success. Already in 1741, the governor-general of the VOC in Batavia had given orders to close down the factory in Isfahan. However, the VOC director in Bandar `Abbas did not implement this order out of fear for retaliation by Nader Shah. Nevertheless the Isfahan factory had a low-key position after that time and only a caretaker was in charge of it.

When in November 1753 the Dutch settled on the island of Khark and constructed a fort the English feared that the Dutch would seek further (territorial) expansion and would challenge the English position in the Persian Gulf. The English, therefore, felt that a countermove should be made to which end they established a factory in Bandar-e Rig just opposite Khark island. The fact that this factory was destroyed by Mir Mohanna and that he was believed to have done so as a result of Dutch meddling, only served to increase English fears and apprehension about Dutch intentions.

Sheikh Naser the chief of Bushire rightly felt that the Dutch fort on Khark was built as a protective measure against local chiefs such as himself. The English resident in Basra was right when he commented that the Dutch factory on Khark "will I imagine be rather a Fort than a Factory and when too late, Meer Nassir may perceive, he has Introduced a new Government instead of a merchants factory on his Island." Although von Kniphausen in his letters to Batavia stressed the friendly relations which he had with the local chiefs, he mentioned on one occasion that the local neighboring chiefs feared and respected the Dutch. Von Kniphausen's interference in 1755 with the fight between Mir Hoseyn and his younger brother Mir Mohanna for the succession to the chieftainship of Bandar-e Rig may have increased local apprehension about Dutch intentions. Anyway, the English were not the only one to suspect the Dutch of having intentions to seize Bahrain. Sheikh Naser of Bushire, who had recently conquered Bahrain also feared that the Dutch intended to displace him in Bahrain. The fact that Sheikh Naser's position in Bahrain was not such a strong one at that time and that the Dutch had closed their factory in Bushire added to his fears. Von Kniphausen, when reporting Sheikh Naser's fears to Batavia, indignantly rejected the latter's accusations.[1]

However, those fearing Dutch intentions were partly right. At the time von Kniphausen was reporting these fears, which he said were preposterous, he sent a detailed proposal for the conquest of Bahrain in a private letter to Jacob Mossel, the governor-general of the VOC in Batavia.[2] In view of the fact that the official correspondence denies such a plan, while in a private letter a detailed plan of action is submitted, it must be assumed that von Kniphausen had discussed such a project with Mossel prior to his return to the Persian Gulf. This seems likely, because Mossel was the main supporter and promoter of the Khark project in the High Government. It would therefore appear that Mossel had in principle agreed to the conquest of Bahrain, provided that the action against Basra and the establishment of a factory on Khark proved to be successful. This may explain why von Kniphausen submitted a detailed proposal for the conquest of Bahrain instead of merely suggesting such an action. By treating the Bahrain project as a private matter Mossel, moreover, would be able to consider its merits and acceptability and ask for additional information, if necessary, before putting the Bahrain Project before the High Government. Apparently the proposal sent to Mossel was acceptable to him (and this underscores the foregoing suppositions), for as soon as Mossel received it he presented it formally to the High Government. Mossel in fact was so enthusiastic about the Bahrain Project that without consulting the High Government or waiting for its approval he had started to recruit soldiers for the expedition against Bahrain.[3]

In view of the importance and the far-reaching consequences of the Bahrain Project, the High Government decided that the discussion about it should be postponed so that everybody would have ample time to study the proposal. On Friday April 21, 1755 the High Government met in secret session to deliberate the merits of the Bahrain Project.

During this session the various members of the High Government gave their views. Mossel's objective was clear. He argued that Persia owed the VOC the enormous sum of Dfl. 1,730,595. Mossel saw no other way to collect this debt than by seizing Bahrain. That such an undertaking might be successfully undertaken was borne out by the outcome of the action against Basra. The

1 VOC 2864, Khark to Batavia (01/11/1754), f. 9.

2 VOC 2864, Project aengaande het bemachtigen van tEijland Bahrehn bij T.F. von Kniphausen en J. van der Hulst, Karreek, November 1, 1754; for a translation of this proposal see below.

3 VOC 2864, Khark to Isaac Sweers (08/01/1756), not foliated (inserted between folios 53 and 54 of the Kareek section of VOC 2864).

justification for the selection of Bahrain as the target was agued by Mossel by referring to John Ovington's *A Voyage to Surat in the year 1689*.[4] In this travelogue the revenues from the pearl banks of Bahrain for the Shah of Persia were estimated at 50,000 ducats per year, exclusive of the 100,000 ducats which the Shah's servants were able to pocket. The view of this independent observer tallied with von Kniphausen's estimate of the official revenues, Mossel pointed out. He concluded his arguments by stating that the VOC would not have to fear political or military retaliation by Persia or local Arab chiefs, for Persia was a divided chaotic country, while the coastal Arabs were also divided and weak. To clinch the matter, Mossel further pointed out that the execution of the Bahrain Project would be in complete agreement with official VOC policy in such matters. The VOC directors would undoubtedly approve of the undertaking, just as they had done in 1728 when the VOC director in Bandar `Abbas had been willing to take possession of the island of Hormuz. At that time, the High Government had rejected this plan, but the VOC directors had allowed the director in Bandar `Abbas to proceed with his plan.[5] In view of this precedent the VOC directors should consider the Bahrain Project to be in the interest of the Company, Mossel argued. He also proposed that the High Government's decision of June 29, 1753 that the factory in Bandar `Abbas be abandoned when the factory of Khark island was established should be carried out forthwith in view of the secure position which the Dutch now enjoyed on Khark.

The second man in the High Government, the director-general van der Parra, opposed Mossel. He considered it disadvantageous for the VOC to seize Bahrain. Furthermore, the Company should not close down the factory in Bandar `Abbas, where trade had shown an upsurge with reasonable profits during the last two years. Moreover, an important part of sales at Bandar `Abbas consisted of (Dutch) manufactured goods and woolens, which was very much appreciated by the VOC directors. In view of the fact that there were not many VOC factories that sold manufactured goods, van der Parra believed that closing down the Bandar `Abbas factory was not in the interest of the VOC. Besides, leaving Persia would be tantamount to relinquishing the possibility of collecting the huge debt which Persia owed the VOC. Van der Parra, therefore, submitted that the Bahrain should be rejected and that the factory in Bandar `Abbas should not be closed down.

Van der Parra was supported by a majority of the High Government, viz. six other members. Mossel was supported only by one member, who considered it to be high time that an action like the Bahrain project be undertaken and that the factory in Bandar `Abbas should be closed. He therefore declined to take any responsibility for a negative decision by the High Government when the directors would let them know their displeasure. Two other members took an intermediate position. They argued that one might carry out the Bahrain Project, but that the VOC should continue to trade in Bandar `Abbas until such time that the Bahrain project had been carried out.

In view of the strong opposition against the Bahrain Project, Mossel concluded the secret session by having it recorded that the majority was against it and that the proposal was therefore rejected. However, he stated that he did not want take any responsibility for this decision. For in doing so, he argued, the VOC had allowed to slip through its hands a unique opportunity of collecting Persia's debt to the VOC. Mossel further pointed out that the English and the French would undoubtedly take a different view of this matter and if that happened the VOC would be left in the lurch. This plea, however, did not make the majority change its mind.[6] As a result of the High

4 John Ovington, *A Voyage to Suratt in the year 1689* (London, 1696). Mossel used the French translation by J.P. Nicéron, *Voyages faits à Surate et en d'autres lieux de l'Asie* 2 vols. (Paris, 1725).

5 On these events see Willem Floor, *The Afghan Occupation of Safavid Persia 1721-1729* (Paris, 1998), pp. 339-60.

6 VOC 2848, secret resolution by the High Government (Batavia, 11/04/1755), f. 1144-48.

Government's decision Mossel in a secret letter communicated to von Kniphausen the negative view of Batavia to the Bahrain Project.[7]

Notwithstanding the lack of Dutch enthusiasm for playing the role attributed to them, the English and the coastal chiefs in the Persian Gulf continued to believe that the Dutch had grand designs for the political and commercial control of the Gulf. The English Resident in Basra, for instance, wrote to London that he feared that the Dutch would also become masters of "Barreen and all the pearl fisherys, [the great treasure of this Gulph] will soon follow, for that, in My Humble Opinion is that the Dutch have chiefly in view; and their rule, will be compleat in the Gulph."[8] Since the English not only suffered a set-back in Bandar-e Rig, where their factory was destroyed by the local chief, Mir Mohanna, but also were very much annoyed at the Dutch success of establishing themselves at Masqat- "one of the most important trade centers in the Gulf whose rulers had hitherto refused to allow any European to open a factory on their territories"[9] – the EIC decided to adopt a more active policy in the Gulf. The English Company's servants were strongly ordered to defend English interests in the Gulf and provide precise information on Dutch activities.[10]

This continued and indeed increased apprehension on the part of the English was, ironically, a waste of energy. There never had been a Dutch master-plan to encroach upon the English position through the seizure of strategic territories in the Persian Gulf and by extending Dutch trade to Masqat. In fact the Masqat voyages were completely unconnected with the Bahrain Project and had originated not with Mossel or von Kniphausen, who opposed them, but with the VOC director in Bandar `Abbas, who had no knowledge of the eventual plans for Bahrain (as is detailed in chapter three).

Mossel did not accept defeat in the Bahrain matter. He wrote privately to von Kniphausen and permitted him to write directly to the VOC directors in Amsterdam to enlist their support for the project and in this way to override the High Government's rejection. Von Kniphausen and his deputy, Jan van der Hulst, therefore sent a copy of the Bahrain Project proposal to Isaac Sweers, the first advocate of the VOC.[11] In their letter von Kniphausen and van der Hulst pointed out that many had opposed the Khark project, but against expectations it had been carried off and made into a success. The VOC, therefore, had to continue its actions and seize Bahrain, or else it would be lost to the Dutch. Here they implied that if the Dutch would not take it the English would, an old ploy that had often worked in the past to induce the directors to agree to commercial and/or military action or to excuse expenditures made. Von Kniphasuen and van der Hulst wrote that unexpectedly a majority within the High Government had opposed the Project. These objections were not based on facts, they pointed out, for the conquest of Bahrain was an easy task. Only one European ship with 300 soldiers well supplied with ammunition would be able to do the job. To lend credence to this contention von Kniphausen and van der Hulst gave the following example. When they were still in Basra, Bahrain had been much better supplied with defensive forces and ammunition that it was at their time of writing the Bahrain Project proposal. However, even Mir Naser of Bander-e Rig had been able to conquer Bahrain with only 250 Arabs, whom he had transported on one decrepit Persian so-called 'man-of-war' and on some smaller vessels, and equipped with only one

7 VOC 1009 (secret), Batavia to Khark (22/04/1755), f. 5.

8 Amin, *British Interests*, p. 145.

9 Amin, *British Interests*, p. 145, note 3. On Dutch relations with Masqat see chapter six.

10 Amin, *British Interests*, p. 146.

11 VOC 2864, Khark to Isaac Sweers (08/01/1756), not foliated (inserted between folios 53 and 54 of the Kareek section of VOC 2864).

keg of English gun-powder.[12] Besides, the fact that the Dutch had been able to force the Pasha of Baghdad to repay the money extorted from them and that they had been holding Khark with only 60 Europeans for a period of two years was, according to von Kniphausen and van der Hulst, another point underscoring the justification for their proposal and the guarantee of its success. To underline this, von Kniphausen and van der Hulst drew attention to the fact that the natives of Khark would certainly kill the Dutch, if they saw a chance to do so, while the neighboring local chiefs rather feared and respected the Dutch on Khark. These hard facts, they argued, would take away any basis for the objections against the Bahrain Project.

Moreover, the advantages of the project were self-evident so that the only worry the directors might have would be the question of whether they would enjoy the peaceful possession of Bahrain. To set the minds of the directors at ease von Kniphausen and van der Hulst pointed out that in Asia the natives had not so far dared undertake anything against the VOC, unless encouraged by neglect, bad policy or tyranny. In the Persian Gulf the Portuguese had been able to hold the island of Hormuz for a very long time, in spite of the fact that they were hated. The natives had been unable to expel the Portuguese until the English had assisted them. But the situation in 1756 was different from that of 1622, von Kniphausen and van der Hulst pointed out. Persia had been in total chaos after Nader Shah's death in 1747. The country had no navy anymore, for of the 18 three-masters that Nader Shah had built only two were still afloat in 1756. These two ships were badly supplied with sails, rigging and ammunition and lacked experienced crews. Moreover, they might only be able to equip the equivalent of one VOC sloop with these.[13]

The strongest Arab ruler was the Imam of Masqat, but he would be unable to do anything. The Imam did not receive any revenues from his African possessions (Mombassa) any more and lacked the power to do anything about it. His rule in Mombassa was only nominal. Even in Oman itself some towns and area did not acknowledge him. His navy did not amount to much and consisted of one three-master with which he shipped slaves from Africa each year. He also had two gallivats, but these were so badly equipped that the Sangian pirates[14] even dared to show themselves off Masqat notwithstanding the fact that they had neither cannons nor guns. The other Arab chiefs in the Persian Gulf were all independent and had many vessels at their disposal. But these were sewn vessels, so that even an unarmed European vessel could sink them with their bow. Finally the Ottoman naval force in the Gulf did not amount to much, so that militarily speaking there was nothing to fear.

Von Kniphausen and van der Hulst drew attention to the fact that the VOC by seizing Bahrain would command the largest pearl fisheries in the world. By taking Bahrain the Dutch would preempt the English, who also had designs upon the island. However, since the High Government was afraid to take the risk and preferred to do nothing this was exactly what was going to happen. They reminded Sweers of the proposal by the English Agent in Bandar `Abbas in 1750 and they intimated that the English were still undecided about what to do. As proof of continued English interest in Bahrain von Kniphausen and van der Hulst cited the fact that a few months earlier an English brig had twice been to the island and had only been engaged in making maps of the island

12 On these events see chapters one and seven.

13 On Nader Shah's navy see chapter one.

14 These are the Sangharas or Sanganis of Okhamandal, in the western extremity of Kathiawar. These people, together with their neighbors the Vaghers and a miscellaneous crowd of outlaws whom they harbored, scoured the Arabian Sea, even attacking English men-of-war, until they were exterminated by a number of expeditions from Bombay.

and its surrounding territory.[15] As final proof of English interest in Bahrain it as brought to Sweers's attention that the English had some men-of-war under construction in Bombay. They implied that these were to be used for military action against Bahrain.

In view of the above arguments von Kniphausen and van der Hulst asked the directors' permission to proceed with the preparations for the conquest of Bahrain. They suggested that it would be best if a ship be sent directly from the Netherlands to the Persian Gulf, since ships from Batavia could only arrive in the Persian Gulf by the end of June or July. Von Kniphausen and van der Hulst were convinced that with a well-supplied ship together with their own gallivat and a sloop at Khark, Bahrain was for the taking.

Van der Hulst also wrote to one of the members of the Council of Seventeen, Jan Calkoen, burgomaster of Amsterdam. In his letter van der Hulst argued that after having acquired possession of Khark Island they had to proceed to take Bahrain, which would even be more profitable than Khark. He included a copy of both the Bahrain Project and the letter to Sweers and hoped for Calkoen's approval of the Project. Van der Hulst also wrote that he would shortly make a trip to Qatif and would visit Bahrain en route. In this way he would be able to give an even better account of the situation of the island.[16] This piece of information probably referred to The Description of the Persian Gulf and its Inhabitants which von Kniphausen and van der Hulst drew up shortly thereafter (see chapter two). This description was a kind of intelligence report that showed the High Government that there was nothing to fear from the local chiefs in the Persian Gulf area.

All these endeavors came to nought, however, for the VOC directors agreed with the majority of the High Government. The directors, after having deliberated the pros and cons of the Bahrain Project, had come to the conclusion that it was not advisable to embark on this scheme. The VOC already had too many establishments in Asia and the directors therefore preferred that the ones which they possessed should perform better rather than acquiring new ones, which, moreover, were often disadvantageous and their possession always of an uncertain nature.[17]

Herewith ended Dutch interest in Bahrain, but not in its most covered asset, viz. pearls, for that was the next subject in which von Kniphausen tried to get the VOC interested.[18]

PROJECT CONCERNING THE CAPTURE OF THE ISLAND OF BAHRAIN (BAHREHN) ADDRESSED TO HIS EXCELLENCY, THE HONORABLE AND WIDELY COMMANDING GENTLEMAN JACOB MOSSEL

Because the United East Indies Company possesses Khark (Ghareek) the island that is the best situated in the Gulf and which certainly will become the most important center of trade in the Gulf within a few years, it would be very easy for the United East Indies Company to seize the island of Bahrain, which is the richest and most profitable place in the Gulf.

---

15 Von Kniphausen probably refers here to the voyage made by Wood towards the end of 1755 to make an inquiry into the various possible new locations for the EIC. Wood had not much to say about Bahrain. "I can get no better intelligence relating to the island of Bahreen, than its being a place held in superstition by the Hoolah Arabs, and that it is very fertile. Abounding with springs and fresh water, but that both the Air and Water are extremely unwholesome according to the account of several Persons who have been formerly Inhabitants of that Place." Lorimer, *Gazetteer*, p. 838.

16 VOC 2864, van der Hulst/Khark to Jan Calcoen/Amsterdam (08/01/1756), not foliated.

17 VOC 334, XVII to Batavia (19/10/1758), section of Karreek, not foliated.

18 See appendix II

The said island is situated on the southern side of the Gulf about thirty [German] miles from here. It is more fertile than all other islands in the Gulf. Its inhabitants earn their living by producing plenty of wheat, barley, rice, dates and all other kinds of tree fruits and even kapok. The circumference of the island is more than 21 [German] miles and it is cultivated and inhabited all over. One finds there more than 300 villages, both big and small ones.

The inhabitants are very faint-hearted and defenseless and only capable of agriculture and weaving. This is the reason why they have always been ruled and subjected by others.

In the days that the Portuguese flourished in Asia they had built a fortress on Bahrain, which is still in good repair.[19] In it one still finds 21 of their big metal pieces, however, without their mountings. The revenues [of the island] made good the total costs of the Portuguese in the Gulf. After the conquest of Hormuz (Ormus) the Persians also conquered and possessed Bahrain until about 31 years ago when the Imam of Masqat (Mascatte) conquered it and expelled them.[20]

Shah Soltan Hoseyn [r. 1694-1722] [then] waged a war on the Imam and took Bahrain from him and from that time onwards Bahrain has been governed by a duke appointed by him. After his death an Arab sheikh of the Hulas expelled the Persians and ruled over the island. The latter was in turn driven away by Mir Naser (Mir Nassier) about 5 years ago and he in turn was forced to leave the island one year later by the aforementioned Hulas. About three years ago Sheikh Naser (sjeek Nassier), supported by some Arabs of the caste of the `Otubis (Etoubis), tried to seize Bahrain. However, after having been there for a few months and been unable to accomplish anything he was able to cause discord among the said Hulas. After having bought one of their sheikhs with the promise of an annual present of 20,000 rupees the often mentioned Hulas fell out with one another and left the island. In this manner Sheikh Naser acquired control of the island, which is now garrisoned by his brother with two remaining gallivats of Nader Shah's (Nadier Schah) fleet with 40 to 50 men.

Sheikh Naser although nominally possessing Bahrain is unable to collect the revenues that pertain to the island. The pearl fishers, who have to pay, per *beseel*,[21] 25 rupees to the rulers of Bahrain do not pay anything, because they belong to different Arab castes against whom Sheikh Naser is unable to use force. The inhabitants of Bahrain are also unable to pay their taxes on their fields in full, because all the abovementioned pearl fishers plunder the date and other tree fruits and even fell the trees. Sheikh Naser is unable to prevent this, because on his own he is too weak, having not more than 100 able-bodied men.

Under these circumstances there should not be anything easier than to seize the said island for the Hon. Company. Because it is part of the Persian kingdom we could make use of the pretext that we have taken it to pay [from its revenues] the money that the kingdom owes to the factory of Bandar `Abbas (Gamron).

The inhabitants of the island will be happy to be ruled by the Hon. Company, because they will then be rid of and protected against the maraudings of the Arab pearl fishers and the crews of [passing] trankis, [a fact] which already has become clear to the inhabitants of Khark, who in former times were plundered by all passing Arab vessels. Since our presence here they have not suffered the least trouble either from strangers or from our own people, which is praised by them in particular.

---

19 On this fort see Monique Kevran, *Bahrain Through the Ages* (Manama, 1988).

20 Von Kniphausen is not entirely correct with his data. For a discussion of these events see Floor, *Persian Gulf*, pp. 418ff.

21 Probably *beseel* is derived from *bisalho* (Portuguese) meaning package.

We know from officials who have received the revenues and taxes of the Bahrain fields in the days of Nader Shah that these amounted to 240,000 rupees of good[22] money, excluding that which the ruling governor had extorted from the pearl fishers. About this nothing definitive can be said, but it certainly was not a small amount, for all those who have governed there have left very rich after a short period.

If the Hon. Company will conquer Bahrain it will become the uncontested owner of the entire Gulf and of the best pearl fishing [banks] in all of Asia. The occupation of Bahrain and Khark will not consume the revenues of Bahrain by far, even if it were governed in the most wasteful manner, while the inhabitants will not be heavily burdened [with taxes] at all.

Once we have secured the island a garrison of 100 soldiers will be sufficient to hold it, while 50 European sailors, distributed over 2 to 3 gallivats can collect duties from the pearl fishing [activities].

With regard to this point Your Excellency's attention is drawn to the fact that sloops or small European vessels are by not as useful for war or to enforce respect as gallivats. For one cannot row or sail as close to the wind and with so little wind as the native vessels, while [European vessels] also require deeper water. For a gallivat as is required here in the Gulf, of 50 feet length and drawing 4 feet of water, is easily navigated with 8 Europeans and 12 to 15 Kaffirs or African slaves, which one can buy at choice for 100 to 120 rupees [each].

In case Your Excellency will approve the proposal of the undersigned, which appears to be both easy and profitable for the Hon. Company, Your Excellency is kindly advised first to send in the month of May a ship with timber from Tinkang[23] and some 6 to 8 poles of 50 feet length which [will be used] as masts and yard arms for the gallivats as well as 3 to 4 good European carpenters with a crew of 120 sailors. They, assisted by native carpenters, will be able to build gallivats in 1 to 2 months. Further equipment and other necessities may be obtained here, with the exception of guns to which end twenty-one 2, 3, and 4-pounder pieces may also be sent here.

If Your Excellency sends another ship in the month of April or June with a two-masted vessel, both manned with 200 sailors and 120 to 150 soldiers, in view of the mortality rate during the voyage, which ship is proportionally supplied with ammunition, the undersigned then do not doubt that the Hon. Company can easily, and without great loss of men, conquer Bahrain.

However, as soon as we start with this plan the Company's factory in Bandar `Abbas has to be closed down or has to be put in a better state of defense to be covered in case of Persian chicanes.

For the rest Your Excellency may be assured that this project will not suffer any difficulties, [for] you may well believe that those who make such proposals would certainly think twice before recommending such an affair, if they were able to foresee any important obstacles, on the negative result of which their life, honor and fortune depends.

Your Excellency will never again meet with such a favorable time to do something for the [advantage of] Hon. Company in this Gulf. The Persian kingdom is in such anarchy that from that side one has to fear nothing. With regards to the Arabs, they all live in discord with each other and are unable to prevent our plan.

Khark, November 1, 1754
T. F. von Kniphausen
Jan van der Hulst

---

22 'Good', i.e. unadulterated money as against 'bad' money.

23 Tinkang is probably Ting Ang or Ting Chang in the Gulf of Tonkin.

Project to send a ship directly to Persia, if the plan for [the conquest of] Bahrain be approved, to which end one may employ:

One ship of 150 feet, mounted with guns and provisioned just like [all other] departing ships. Further,

150	sailors
150	soldiers
3	bombardiers
6	gunners
2	master carpenters
2	junior carpenters
2	gunsmiths

As cargo:

5 *hoed*[24] of forge coal

As much iron as is required for its under-layer

30,000 lbs of lead in pieces

600 pieces of perpets[25] selected as follows; to be taken in lots of 25 pieces:

5 p. scarlet
4 p. dark-green
2 p. grass-green
4 p. dark-blue
2 p. olive
2 p. cinnamon-brown
2 p. ash-grey
2 p. black
2 p. violet

400 pieces of Liege serge[26]	selected as above
100 pieces of Kroonrassen[27]	selected as abov
100 pieces of Imperials[28]	selected as above
50 pieces of Ras de Morocko[29]	selected as above

24 A *hoed* is an old Dutch measure of capacity. For coal one *hoed* was equal to 1,172 liters.

25 Perpets (English rendering) or *perpetuanen* (Dutch) literally means 'perpetual.' Therefore this kind of fabric was also called *sempiterne*. It is a kind of serge, originally made in Portugal, but later in particular in Great Britain.

26 Serge (from Latin '*sericus*'; Italian '*sergia*': silken) was originally the name of a silken fabric; later it as used to refer to a thin, twilled fabric. The serge referred to here originated from the city of Liège (Belgium).

27 *Kroonras* or crown-rash (Eng.) is a kind of *ras* (from Italian *raso*) or a woolen fabric. Crown means here 'first quality.'

28 Imperial is a kind of high-quality woolen fabric.

29 *Ras de Morocko* is a *ras* produced in or destined for Morocco.

300 pieces of cloth andasti[30] selected as above
30 pieces of cloth Mahoud or Poetsacky[31] selected as above
30 pieces of cloth Begras[32] among which
- 5 p. scarlet
- 10 p. crimson
- 5 p. crimson-violet
- 5 p. hair colored
- 3 p. dark-green
- 2 p. grass-grey

50 pieces of Sieburg[33] serge, to wit
- 12 p. scarlet
- 8 p. crimson
- 2 p. crimson-violet
- 10 p. dark-green
- 6 p. grass-grey
- 4 p. ash-grey
- 4 p. olive-colored
- 4 p. cinnamon-colored

100 pieces of broadcloth
25 pieces of kalmenken[34] with small stripes for a try-out
10 pieces of goudmoor[35] of which
- 5 p. on crimson
- 3 p. on grass-grey
- 1 p. on violet
- 1 p. on light-blue

10 pieces of silver moor, to wit
- 5 p. on crimson
- 2 p. on grass-green
- 1 p. on violet
- 1 p. on violet

20 pieces of velvet of which
- 6 p. crimson
- 2 p. pink
- 4 p. grass-green

---

30 *Andasti* is a term that I have been unable to identify.

31 *Mahoed* is from the Persian word *mahut* or broadcloth. The term *poetsacky* is unknown to me.

32 *Begras* from the Persian *bakras*; a kind of waterproof woolen fabric of which hats and cloaks were made.

33 The serge referred to here originated from the town of Siegburg in Germany.

34 *Kalmenk* is a twilled, satiny, thin woolen fabric. In English it was known as *calamanco* or lastings.

35 *Moor*, from the French moiré, is a kind of watered fabric, in this case with golden and silver patterns.

1 p. dark-green
3 p. violet
2 p. dark-blue
1 p. light-blue
1 p. orange-yellow

Ammunition
2,000 lbs. of fine powder
4,000 lbs of gun-powder
2 mortars of a diameter of 6 to 8 inches with their accessories and
100 bombs
6 iron or metal 8-pounders
10 iron or metal 6-pounders, [both] with their gun carriages and accessories
4 iron or metal 3-pounders
10 iron or metal 2-pounders, with their gun carriages and accessories

For each piece of gun
100 balls, round, long, chain-balls and slide-long ones
300 matchlocks, grenadier [type] with iron rammers and bayonets
20 blunderbusses with side fuses
100 pair of pistols
1,000 hand grenades
3 copper drums
2 fifes
100 grenadier caps
100 cartridge-pouches [type] grenadier
300 common cart-ridge pouches
100 fine grenadier sabers with copper hilts and guards
300 common ones with iron hilts

Equipment
1 bellows, anvils, bickers, side-sticks and kinds of smith's tools
2 chests with all kinds of both ship's and home carpentry tools
1 chest with such medicines that are not to be had in these parts
10 rolls of sailing-cloth
40 rolls of Flemish linen
10 leaguers of spirits for victuals.

Khark, in the fortress Mosselstein, January 8, 1755
T.F. von Kniphausen
J. van der Hulst

APPENDIX II
Pearl Fishing in the Persian Gulf in 1757

The initiator of the Dutch factory on Khark Island the baron von Kniphausen did his utmost to make this new venture of the VOC a success. Apart from the fact that he personally would profit from a successful commercial operation he also had to show a profitable turnover of the Khark factory, because of the criticism by the VOC directors, who in fact would have preferred to close down the factory. Since trade during the first years was rather disappointing von Kniphausen tried to find ways and means to make more profit for the VOC.[1] To that end he proposed to conquer Bahrain in 1754, for that would have meant that its rich pearl banks would have fallen into Dutch hands. However, both the High Government in Bata as well as the VOC directors in Amsterdam turned down this proposal.[2] Undaunted von Kniphausen continued to plan new schemes to make the Khark factory a profitable undertaking. He probably thought that if the VOC did not want to conquer Bahrain it surely would not say no to pearls. Already in 1753 von Kniphausen had drawn the High Government's attention to pearls as a possible export commodity of which he said that these were in fact the best that the Persian Gulf had to offer and on which at least 50% profit could be made.[3] To make sure that pearls could an important item for VOC trade von Kniphausen engaged a few pearl divers and on the basis of their catches made a calculation, which showed, so he said, that such an operation could be profitably managed from Khark.[4]

---

1 For the commercial results of the Khark factory see chapter five.

2 See Appendix I.

3 See chapter four.

4 The EIC servant Francis Wood reported after his visit to Khark in 1756 that "Mynheer Kniphausen constantly employed eight or ten small trankeys with divers (whenever it happens to be a Calm day) in fishing for pearl of which there is great abundance round about the Island, he send Coffree Slaves in each boat who receive all the oysters the divers take up and deliver them to Mynheer just the same as they come out of the Sea, so that unless a man could be present to see them opened (which is always done in private) there is no judging what success he has in this particular branch." Saldanha, *Précis*, vol. 1, p. 99 (03/05/1756); see also Lorimer, *Gazetteer*, p. 131.

In his detailed proposal[5] von Kniphausen outlined the advantages for the VOC as well as pointing out that he would like to try a new invention, viz. the diving bell.[6] For von Kniphausen believed that the use of this bell would enable him to obtain richer pearl catches.

The High Government, which as much as von Kniphausen wanted the Khark factory to show a profit, agreed to the scheme and at von Kniphausen's request sent him glass diving bells in 1758.[7] Unfortunately, Batavia had forgotten to include the directions of use, despite the fact that von Kniphausen had explicitly asked for them. Disappointed von Kniphausen reported to the High Government that the diving bells could not be made use of.[8] It is unknown what happened with them and whether they in fact were ever used. Von Kniphausen left Khark in November 1759 and his successors never wrote anything about a continuation of the pearl fishing scheme.

The VOC directors for once took a positive position with regards to a proposal by von Kniphausen and wrote that they had high hopes about the eventual revenues. They also expressed their surprise about the omission of the directions of use for the diving bells and commented that "the Residents could not make use of them, of course."[9] This was the end of the last of von Kniphausen's brainwaves and so another interesting chapter in VOC history was closed.

It must be pointed out, however, that von Kniphausen was neither the first VOC servant in the Persian Gulf to draw the Company's attention to pearls as an export commodity nor was he the first to test the feasibility of the pearl market by actually fishing for pearls.

In fact, pearl fishing in the Gulf and especially around the island of Bahrain had attracted the attention of the VOC already from the beginnings of its commercial activities in the Gulf. Although the VOC started to trade with Persia in 1623 it was not until 1643 before the Company took an active interest in pearls from the Persian Gulf. For it was only in May 1643 that Carel Constant, the director of VOC trade in Persia, decided to obtain information about the pearl trade.

> I intend to send merchant Walckaert together with junior merchant Costerus, who are experienced in the Arab and Persian languages, one of these days to Congo and Barain with a sum of 25,000 laris to discover precisely once and for all the mystery of the pearl trade. They have been instructed to examine everything very thoroughly and if they find some good lots to buy them. For if these places are never visited one can hardly start a proper trade in this market. I have sent with these

5 See below.

6 "Pearl oysters have been found near this island, but as they lie in considerable depths, not less than 13 or 14 fathom water, the divers (who were not very expert at the business) had not met with much success, at the time we were there. Some pearls of considerable value however had been found, particularly one, very handsome and large, which the *Baron* was so polite as to present to Mr. *Doidge*. It had a *Lusis Naturae* upon it, strongly resembling the face of a human foetus in the early months of pregnancy. The *Baron* was very inquisitive about the diving-bell, and some other late discoveries made in *England* for enabling men to keep a long while under water; and desired Mr. *Doidge* to think of him on this article. He gave me also communication to buy, and send him out from *England* the following books and instruments [list not reproduced]... as Captain *Tovey*'s new instrument for levelling cannon &c. and any other invention for the bomb. ... And such other instruments as tended to illustrate any art or science, or could be of service to him in his new settlement." Ives, *Voyage*, pp. 215-16.

7 VOC 1012, Batavia to Khark (25/04/1758), f. 130.

8 VOC 2986, Khark to Batavia (15/11/1758), f. 20.

9 VOC 334, XVII to Batavia (30/09/1760), section Carreek, not foliated; VOC 334, XVII to Batavia (24/09/1761), section Carreek, not foliated.

> abovementioned merchants an intelligent Banyan merchant to assist them, who knows these various places as well as the pearl trade.[10]

Constant had collected as much information as possible about the pearl trade to prepare his two merchants as thoroughly as possible. In his instruction to them he wrote about the pearl trade as follows:

> About July 1 the pearl fishers go with their boats from Barain, Congo, Catifa[11], and Iulfar[12] to sea, where the diving takes place. When they have gathered an important quantity they go with their oysters to a certain island, which is situated at about 10 to 12 [German] miles from Barain. Here the gathered oysters are opened in the presence of the *nachoda*[13] of the boats and a supervisor especially appointed for that purpose. These pearls are taken out and handed over to the supervisor, who takes them into custody under the seal of the nachoda. Then they go out to sea for a second trip to gather more oysters; they continue this in the same manner until the third catch has been hauled in, which is at about the beginning of or mid-September, when these pearl fishers return each to their home base (although mostly to Barain), where they try to sell the fished pearls at the highest possible price, which are then taken away by sellers from different parts.[14]

This first venture into the pearl trade was no success for the VOC, for Costerus who apparently had been sent alone to buy pearls in Bahrain had been attacked by Arab pirates near Cabo Nabaas[15], who had taken all his money, viz. 32,000 *mahmudis*. Out of fear for retaliatory action by the VOC the leader of the pirates returned the money to the VOC a few days later. Only 1,300 *mahmudis* were missing, for that amount had already been distributed among his men.[16] Constant decided to forget pearls for the time being, since all his attention was demanded by the conflict that had arisen between the VOC and the Persian government, a conflict that would lead to the outbreak of hostilities in 1645.[17]

It was only in the early 1660s that the VOC again took an interest in pearls. A Banyan merchant was sent to Bahrain to buy pearls there in 1662, while in the following years the situation in Bandar-e Kong was investigated. The fact that one of the merchants at the Bandar `Abbas factory had previous to his stay in Persia served in Tutikorin, which was famous for its pearl banks, also kept this interest in Bahrain pearls alive. However, both he and the director, Hendrik van Wijck,

10 VOC 1164, Gamron to Batavia (20/05/1653), f. 821vs.

11 Qatif.

12 Jolfar or Ra's al-Khaymah.

13 *Nakhoda* or captain of a sea-going vessel.

14 VOC 1164, Gamron to Batavia (20/05/1643), f. 821 vs; VOC 1164, Instructie voor den Coopman Henrick Walckaert tot incoop van paerelen (Gamron; 22/05/1643), f. 823r-vs.

15 Probably Cape Naband.

16 VOC 1167, Gamron to Batavia (23/11/1643), f. 908.

17 On this conflict see Willem Floor and Mohammad Faghfoory, *The First Dutch-Persian Commercial Conflict: the attack on Qeshm Island, 1645* (Costa Mesa, 2004).

died in 1666 before a proper reconnaissance of the pearl trade had been made. This was the second time that the VOC lost interest in pearls from the Gulf.[18]

In 1690 the VOC again turned to pearls as a possible export commodity. What was new this time was the fact that merchant Jacob Hoogcamer left Bandar-e Kong on July 19, 1690 to stay in the vicinity of Bahrain and to fish for pearls himself instead of buying them from pearl trader. This was done with the explicit objective, just as von Kniphausen would do 67 years later, to see whether it would be profitable for the VOC to be engaged in pearl fishing. Hoogcamer reported as follows about his experience:

> The pearls here are mainly divided into three grades and are referred to as *cabessa*[19], *bariga*[20], and *pe*.[21] The *cabessa* [grade] is sold at 130, 140 up to 150 *mahmudis* at a certain weight of 3.5 grains[22], being less than one half of an ounce, or a heavy Arab *matttical*,[23] but only after these [pearls] have been mixed with a few that are yellow, black or dull. The *bariga* [grade] is sold for 60 to 70 *mahmudis* at the same weight and under the same abovementioned condition. The *pe* [grade] weighs 2.5 grains and if more it is not included in the abovementioned price. For in that case they are weighed and assayed separately. The abovementioned pearls are not less than 24 times assorted to establish their true value according to their size.[24]

Although Hoogcamer had been able to make a profit of 77 ½ *mahmudis* during his pearl fishing trip he advised the VOC directors to buy pearls if they wanted to invest their money in that commodity. He had found that it was not easy to make money as a pearl fisher. He estimated that out of 10 boats hardly one was able to make a profit. Moreover, the divers were an untrustworthy lot, who had tried to steal pearls throughout the trip.[25]

This last but one effort did not result in VOC follow-up activities in the pearl trade. That this lack of interest had nothing to do with pearls as a commodity, but rather with the conditions prevailing in the Persian Gulf, is shown by the fact that the VOC took an active interest in pearls in other parts of Asia.

---

18 VOC 1252, Gamron to Batavia (19/01/1665), f. 718-19; see also VOC 1240, Gamron to Batavia (30/08/1662), f. 1412vs; VOC 1245, f. 369 vs (1663); VOC 1245, f. 1093 vs (1663).

19 From the Portuguese word *cabeça* (head). The three-fold division and nomenclature was also used for other commodities such as silk.

20 From the Portuguese word *barriga* (belly).

21 From the Portuguese word *pé* (foot).

22 One grain (in Dutch *greijn*) weighed 0.065 gram.

23 *Mattical* or *methqal* weighs 4.6 grams.

24 VOC 1476, Hoogcamer/Congo to XVII (15/11/1690), f. 603r-vs.

25 VOC 1476, Hoogcamer/Congo to XVII (15/11/1690), f. 603r-vs; VOC 1476, Extract brief Gamronsen raad to Batavia (19/11/1690), f. 607; for a list of the pearls acquired by Hoogcamer (their weight and prices), VOC 1476, Memorie tot wat prijzen en wat quantiteijt and wat qualiteijt de paarlen etc. (09/01/1691), f. 604-05.

Report Concerning Pearl Fishing in the Persian Gulf and in particular Around The island of Khark

[33] The most important [areas] where one engages in pearl fishing range from Cape Musandam[26] as far as Bahrehn and Catif. Not inconsiderable quantities of pearls are also found near various islands on the other [i.e. Persian] side of the Gulf, particularly around the islands of Hesch[27], Schaib[28] and Karreek. [34]

There are three kinds of pearl oysters. The first kind the Arabs call *machaar*.[29] These oysters have a small, hollow, thin shell. It is seldom that one does not find one or more pearls in them, although they are for the greater part *stampaarlen* (seed pearls)[30] or somewhat bigger. This kind of oyster is found on the banks near Bahrehn and is the kind that the Arabs most look for. Because diving for this kind of oyster makes at least good the expense of the diving operation

The second kind of pearl oysters is called *siddeff*.[31] It has a large, flat, thick shell and has very beautiful mother-of-pearl; some have a diameter of not less than 7 to 8 inches. [However] out of every 100 of these [shells] there are hardly 5 to 6 [that contain pearls], if they contain anything at all. Nevertheless this kind produces the largest and most perfect pearls.

The last kind of [pearl] oysters is called *simi*[32] and is [as yet] (as far as the undersigned knows) unknown to the naturalists. These [oysters] are being found at depth of 15 to 18 fathoms. The oysters are attached to trees or shrubs of a coral-like material just like fruit, while one is unable to discern whether the vegetation produces the oysters [35] or that the oysters only attach themselves to such a shrub. This [kind of] oyster has a very beautiful pink color on the outside when they are hauled fresh from the sea, which color is lost shortly thereafter due to drying and mortification. Concerning the contents of this kind [of oyster] it is similar to that of the said *siddeff* kind. These latter two kinds [of pearl oysters] are found near Rig and Little Kareek[33] in rather large quantities, although the former in smaller quantities.

The pearl divers throughout the Gulf are Arabs who live on its shores. They are able to dive to depths of 3 to 8 fathoms. Very few among them dare to dive to depths of 12 to 18 fathoms. If this happens it is done as an act of daring for very good recompense once in a while.[34]

From the middle of May until the end of September [pearl] fishing is carried out here.[35] However, one has to exclude the month of the Moslem fast and some days prior to and after the

26 Ra's Musandam.

27 Kish Island.

28 Abu Sho`eyb.

29 *Mahharah* (pl. *mahhar*). It is the most prolific source of pearls; it is found all over the Gulf. Lorimer, *Gazetteer*, p. 2223.

30 *Stampaarlen* or seed pearls; a Dutch/English term that has no single Arabic equivalent.

31 *Sadayfiya* (pl. *sadayfi*); occurs mainly round the islands of Sheikh Sho`eyb, Henderabi and Kish. It does not often yield pearls, but those which it produces are ordinarily large and of fine quality. Lorimer, *Gazetteer*, p. 2223.

32 *Zanniya* (pl. *zanni*). According to Lorimer, *Gazetteer*, p. 2222, this is the second kind of oysters. The pearls that it produces are few and of inferior quality. The finest pearls of this kind are found in the same area as those of the *sadifi* kind.

33 Big Karreek is Khark, little Karrek is Kharqu. The Dutch already observed in 1645 that pearls were fished round Khark and Kharqu when some 150 to 160 barques (small vessels) were engaged in pearl fishing. Hotz, "Cornelisz. Roobacker's scheepsjournaal," p. 362.

34 On the depth of diving see Lorimer, *Gazetteer*, p. 2229 and note.

35 On the pearl fishing season see Lorimer, *Gazetteer*, p. 2228.

end [of this period] so that 90 to 100 days are left for diving. A hired diver gets 50 to 60 rupees for diving in addition to board and those who row the vessel and who have to haul that which the diver has gathered [**36**] earn 25 to 30 rupees.

Another and the most common agreement (very few and none of the best divers are willing to agree to the abovementioned) amount to [the following], viz. an owner of a vessel engages 6 to 8 divers and as many sailors. He then equips himself with ropes and provisions for the whole monsoon and departs to go fishing. All oysters that are fished during the day are opened towards the evening in the presence of the crew. That which is found therein is kept in a piece of linen, which is sealed with wax each day until the end of the fishing season. Then the whole lot is sold in the presence of everybody on Barehn or Catiff. From the proceeds first the expenses are deducted, then [the remainder] is divided into five parts, of which the said owner receives one. The remaining four [parts] are divided among the crew, a diver getting twice as much as a sailor.[36]

The undersigned considered it a good idea to try out this island's pearl fishing, for it appeared to him that its inhabitants cannot dive, yet are finding [pearls] at the lowest tide [**37**] and are able to gather pearls and oysters. Last year he therefore gave orders to engage divers ashore and had them come here. This has not been without difficulties, because most of the divers and especially the best ones are not allowed to leave by the sheikhs and are always kept in debt to them.[37]

Having hired the said diver and having equipped himself properly the undersigned had them dive each day around the islands. However, he found that unless he was present himself on the vessels there was no profit in it. For the sailors are constantly lying still and do not row, while the divers do not dive deeper than 2 or 3 fathoms and hardly dive more than 5 to 6 times per day.[38] It would be very impractical with these people to induce them to greater industry with force and beatings by a European. (Meanwhile the undersigned is assured by this experiment that the [pearl] fishing around these 2 islands will yield considerable profits if other means were used). This [**38**] may be evident to Your Excellency from the fact that these lazy and badly working divers, nevertheless have made good their expenses. The experts value the pearls that are sent herewith at 865 rupees, while the costs for the sailors, divers, vessels and their sustenance amounted to 854 rupees, which makes it even. The undersigned believes that if one might have divers from the coast of Coromandel, Ceylon or Tutucorijn[39] (of whom it is said that they dive to greater depths [than is done here]) come hither, we would be able to realize noteworthy profits through them, for then the Europeans who are engaged on the gallivats may be used as rowers without extra costs.

Another way, which in the opinion of the undersigned may be used as well at no fewer costs and may be with as much profit from pearl fishing, would consist of having some glass diving bells sent from the fatherland for a test. Your Excellency will be well aware of the fact that this invention has appeared a few years ago in England and has been used with much success [in diving for] sunken ships. These [diving bells] not only enable (according to what the English newspapers [**39**] have reported) someone who uses them to reach deep water, but also to stay under water for a considerable time, and to do the required task there. All these items promise substantial profits for pearl fishing[40], for one might also reach such deep places that the Arabs have never fished. It is clear that

36 For the division of the proceeds see Lorimer, *Gazetteer*, pp. 2232-33, 2235.

37 For the indebtedness of the divers see Lorimer, *Gazetteer*, p. 2233.

38 See also Lorimer, *Gazetteer*, pp. 2230-31.

39 Tutikorin, town in S. India and famous for its pearl banks.

40 For a contemporary list of pearl prices see VOC 2885 (Gamron; 28/12/1756), f. 48. A short summary of this list is produced herewith: 1 pearl of 1 *alba* costs 1.5 *mahmudis*; of 2 *albas* 4 *mahmudis*; of 3 *albas* 12 *mahmudis*; of 5 *mahmudis*; of 10 *albas* 300 *mahmudis*; of 20 *albas* 2,200 *mahmudis*; of 30 *albas* 6,700 *mahmudis*; of 40 *albas*

there one may find the best harvest [for] the diver does not have to immerse quickly because of lack of air and would have the time to search properly and would be able to fill large baskets with oysters. In this way he might do more than 4 of the best divers. These reasons have induced the undersigned to add to the [annual] order [from Batavia] six of these bells with clears directions for their use in the expectation of Your Excellency's favorable approval.

T. von Kniphausen
In the fortress of Mosselsteijn
Kareek, October 15, 1757

10,000 *mahmudis*; of 50 *albas* 25,000 *mahmudis*; of 60 *albas* 56,000 *mahmudis*; of 70 *albas* 96,000 *mahmudis* and of 72 *albas* 105,000 *mahmudis*. The price of pierced pearls was in general two-third's of the abovementioned prices. The word *alba* probably is from the Arabic *habbah* or 'grain, barley corn' which weighed ca. 0.05 gram.

APPENDIX III
Royal Decrees

From *A Collection of Treaties, Engagements and Sanads Relating to India and Neighbouring Countries*, by C.U. Aitchison, 1933

Articles of Agreement with Shaik Sadoon of Bushire, 12 April 1763

ARTICLE 1.

No customs duties to be collected on goods imported or exported by the English; and, in like manner, only three per cent. to be taken from the merchants who buy or sell to the English.

ARTICLE 2.

The importance and sale of woolen goods to be solely in the hands of the English; and if any person whatever attempts to bring woollen goods clandestinely, it shall be lawful for the English to seize them. This Article to take place in four months from the date hereof.

ARTICLE 3.

No European nation whatever its to be permitted to settle at Bushire so long as the English continue a factory there.

ARTICLE 4.

The brokers, linguists, servants, and others of the English are to be entirely under the protection and government of the English; nor is the Shaik, or his people, in any shape to molest them, or interfere in their affairs.

ARTICLE 5.

In case any of the inhabitants become truly indebted to the English and refuse payment, the Shaik shall oblige them to give the English satisfaction.

ARTICLE 6.

The English to have such a spot of ground as they may pitch upon for erecting a factory, and proper conveniences for carrying on their commerce to be built at the Shaik's expense. They are to hoist their colours upon it and have twenty-one guns for saluting.

ARTICLE 7.

A proper spot of ground to be allotted to the English for a garden, and another for a burying ground.

ARTICLE 8.

The English, and those under their protection, not to be impeded in their religion.

ARTICLE 9.

Soldiers, sailors, servants, slaves, and others belonging to the English, who may desert, are not to be protected or entertained by the Shaik or his people, bit, *bona fide*, secured and returned.

ARTICLE 10.

In case any English ships sell to or buy from the country merchants apart from the factory, a due account thereof is to be rendered to the English Chief for the time being, for which purpose one of his people is to attend at the weight and delivery of all goods so sold, which is to be done at the public Custom House.

ARTICLE 11.

If through any accident an English vessel should be drove on shore in the country belonging to the Shaik, they shall not in any respect be plundered; but, on the contrary, the Shaikh shall afford the English all the assistance in his power for saving them and their effects, the English paying them for their trouble.

ARTICLE 12.

The Shaik shall not permit his subject's to purchase any goods from English vessels in the road, but only on shore.

THE
SEAL OF
SHAIK SADOON

Royal Grant From Karem Khan, King Of Persia, 1763

The Great God having, of his infinite mercy, given victory unto Karem Khan, and made him Chief Governor of all the kingdoms of Persia, and established under him the peace and tranquillity of the said kingdoms, by means of his victorious sword, he is desirous that the said kingdom should flourish and re-obtain their ancient grandeur by the increase of trade and commerce, as well as by a due execution of justice.

Having been informed that the Right Worshipful William Andrew Price, Esq., Governor-General of the English nation in the Gulf of Persia, is arrived with power to settle a factory at Bushire, and has left Mr. Benjamin Jervis, Resident, who, by directions from the said Governor-General, has sent unto me Mr. Thomas Durnford and Stephen Hermit, linguist, to obtain a grant of their ancient privileges in these kingdoms, I do, of my free will and great friendship for the English nation, grant unto the said Governor-General, in behalf of his king and Company, the following privileges, which shall be inviolably observed and held sacred in good faith:-

That the English Company may have as much ground, and in any part of Bushire, they choose to build a factory on, or at any other port in the Gulf. They may have as many cannon mounted on it as they choose, but not to be larger than six pounds bore; and they may build factory houses in any part of the kingdom they choose.

No customs shall be charged the English on any goods imported or exported by them at Bushire, or any other port in the Gulf of Persia, on condition, that at no time they import or export other persons' goods in their names. They may also send their goods customs free all over the kingdom of Persia; and on what goods they sell at Bushire, or elsewhere, the Shaik or Governor, shall only charge the merchants an export duty of three per cent.

No other European nation, or other persons, shall import any woolen goods to any port on the Persian shore in the Gulf, but the English Company only; and should any one attempt to do it clandestinely their goods shall be seized and confiscated.

Should any of the Persian merchants, or others, become truly indebted to the English, the Shaik or the Governor of the place, shall oblige them to pay it; but should he fail in his duty herein the English Chief may do his own justice and act as he pleases with the debtors to re cover what owed him or them.

In all the kingdom of Persia the English may sell their goods to, and buy from whomever they judge proper; nor shall the Governor, or Shaik, of any ports or places, prevent their importing or exporting any good whatever.

When any English ship or ships arrive at any ports in the Gulf of Persia, no merchants shall purchase from them clandestinely, but with the consent and knowledge of the English chief there resident.

The English, and all those under their protection, in any part of the kingdom of Persia, shall have the free exercise of their religion, without molestation from any one.

Should soldiers, sailors, or slaves desert from the English in any part of Persia, they shall not be protected or encouraged, but, *bona fide*, delivered up, but not be punished for the first or second offence.

Wherever the English may have a factory in Persia their linguist, brokers, and all their other servants, shall be exempt from all taxes and impositions whatever, and under their own command and justice, without any interfering therein.

Wherever the English are they shall have a spot of ground allotted them for a burying ground; and if they want a spot for a garden, if the king's property, it shall be given them gratis; if belonging to any private person they must pay a reasonable price for it.

The house that formerly belonged to the English Company at Schyrash I now re-deliver to them, with the garden and water thereto belonging.

Articles Desired By The Khan, 1763

That the English, according to what was formerly customary, shall purchase from the Persian merchants such goods as will answer for sending to England or India, provided they and the Persians shall agree on reasonable prices for the same, and not export from Persia the whole amount of their sales in ready money, as this will impoverish the kingdom and in the end prejudice trade in general.

That the English, wherever they are settled, shall not maltreat the Musselmen.

What goods are imported by the English into Persia they shall give the preference in sale of them to the principal merchants and men of credit.

The English shall not give protection to any of the king's rebellious subjects, nor carry them out of the kingdom, but deliver any up that may desert to them, who shall not be punished for the first or second offence.

The English shall at no time, either directly or indirectly, assist the king's enemies.

All our Governors of provinces, sea-ports, and other towns are ordered to pay strict obedience to these orders, on pain of incurring our displeasure, and of being punished for their disobedience or neglect.

Dated in Schyrash, the 23rd of Seerhoja 1176, or the 2nd of July 1763.

Translation Of A Firman From Jaffir Khan, 1788

In the name of the Almighty and Glorious God!

This is exalted Firmana. *After compliments, -* And as we are always desirous that the merchants of Coflas,[1] who have occasion to pass backwards and forwards in our dominions, should do so in safety, that they should sleep in the cradle of security and confidence, and that they should transact all their business, as far as in us lies, without trouble or vexation. –

Therefore the high, exalted Firmana has been issued forth, containing the strictest mandates to all Governors and Commanders of our towns and castles, to all our Sirdars, and to all our Riotdars,[2] who receive customs on the roads, that they do show every favour to all persons employed by the English nation in our dominions for the purpose of merchandize, whether it

1 From the Arabic word *qafilah* or caravan.

2 Printer's error for *rahdar* or road guards.

be for importation, or exportation, and that they be constantly vigilant in protecting them, and moreover that these our above-mentioned servants, upon no account or pretence whatsoever, require any customs, presents, or money from the Agents of the English nation, but that it may so happen that from a confidence is us, and from a full persuasion of not receiving any insult or vexation, they, the English, may be induced to pass backwards and forwards and to trade in our dominions. And whenever they shall have disposed of the goods and merchandize which they may import for sale, they shall have full liberty to make their returns according to their own wishes.

And it is therefore necessary that our most honoured friend, the English Balios[3] at Bussora. Should perfectly understand that in this way our favour is equal in magnitude to whatever he can hope or desire, and it is moreover necessary that in order to make trial thereof he should encourage his nation to trade into Persia, and he has again our word that they shall do so in the fullest and most perfect security.

Again, whatever goods or merchandize the English nation shall import for sale there shall be no restrictions put upon the sale thereof, but after their Agents shall have completed the sales and fulfilled the design of their journey, they shall have every protection granted them on their return, and again upon our royal word there shall be no impositions or vexations practised upon the English nation in Persia, it is our will that from this day they be abolished and forgotten.

And being persuaded of the sincerity of our most honoured friend the Balios, we accept of his offer of services and request of him to purchase immediately such rarities as are procurable at Bussora, favouring us at the same time with the amount cost thereof, in order that we may order the same to be repaid to the person who shall be sent with them.

Let our friend, therefore, on all occasions rest satisfied of our favour and protection. Let him on all occasions make known to us his wishes and wants, and let the above for ever remain a compact between us.

Written on the eighth of the second month of Rabbee, in the year of Hijree one thousand two hundred and two, answering the 18th January 1788.

THE
REFUGE OF
SUPPLICANTS
JAFFIR, THE SON OF
MAHOMED SADUCK

Source: C.U. Aitchison, *A Collection of Treaties, Engagements and Sanads Relating to India and Neighbouring Countries* (Calcutta, 1933), vol. XIII, pp. 32-36.

3 *Balios* is from the Venetian word *bailo*, meaning, inter alia , consul, which was Turkicized into *balyuz*.

BIBLIOGRAPHY

Archives

Nationaal Archief (cited as NA) in The Hague, the Netherlands.

Aanwinsten 1889, nr. 23 B.
Collectie Alting nr. 68
Collectie Geleynssen nr. 280 e
Collectie de Hochepied nrs. 100, 104, 108
Legatie archief Turkije nrs. 168, 596, 691, 721, 784
Staaten-Generaal nr. 7005, Lias Turkije
Stadhouderlijke Secretarie, nr. 1.29.5

VOC archief: Archief Oost-Indisch Comité nrs.10, 71, 78.
COC 811, Resolutions of the High Government
Hooge Regering Batavia, nrs. 789, 873
Outgoing letterbook of the Gentlemen XVII (331-336)
Overgekomen Brieven (1149-3365)
Outgoing letterbook and resolutions of the High Government (779-1015)

Published Books and Articles

Abdullah, Thabit A.J. *Merchants, Mamluks, and Murder. The Political Economy of Trade in Eighteenth-Century Basra* (Albany, 2001).

Aitchison, C.U. *A Collections of treaties, engagements and sanads relating to India and neighbouring countries*, 4th ed. (Calcutta, 1909), vols. X, XII.

Amin, Abdul Amir. *British Interests in the Persian Gulf* (Leiden, 1967).

Anonymous. *A Chronicle of the Carmelites in Persia*. 2 vols. (London, 1939).

Asaf, Mohammad Hashem. *Rostam al-Tavarikh* ed. Mohammad Moshiri (Tehran, 1348/1969).

Axworthy, Michael. *Sword of Persia: Nader Shah, from Tribal Warrior to Conquering Tyrant* (London, 2006).

Barros, João de. *Da Ásia*. de João de Barros e de Diogo de Couto. Nova ed. 24 vols. (Lisboa, Na Regia Officina Typografica, 1777-1788 [reprint: Livraria S. Carlos, 1973-1975]).

Carré, Abbé. *The travels of Abbé Carré in India and the Near East (1672-74)*, 3 vols. (London: Hakluyt, 1947).

Coolhaas, W. Ph., van Goor, J. and Schooneveld-Oosterling J.E. eds. *Generale Missiven van Gouveneur-Generaal en Raden aan Heren XVII* 11 vols. (The Hague, 1960-1985).

Davies, Charles E. *The Blood-Red Arab Flag. An Investigation into Qasimi Piracy 1797-1820* (Exeter, 1997).

Dunlop, H. *Bronnen tot de geschiedenis der Oostindische Compagnie in Perzië* (The Hague, 1930).

Dusaulchoy, Louis. *Considérations sur les Indes Orientales et leur commerce* (Paris: L.M. Cellot, 1789).

Eqtedari, Ahmad. *Athar-e Shahrha-ye Bastani-ye Savahel va Jazayer-e Khalij-e Fars va Darya-ye 'Oman* (Tehran, 1348/1969).

E'temad al-Saltaneh, Mirza Hasan Khan. *Mer'at al-Boldan* 4 vols in 3. ed. 'Abd al-Hoseyn Nava'i and Mir Hashem Mohaddeth (Tehran: Daneshgah, 1368/1989).

Fasa'i, Hajj Mirza Hasan Hoseyni. *Farsnameh-ye Naseri*, 2 vols. Mansur Rastegar-e Fasa'i (Tehran, 1378/1999).

Fattah, Hala. *The Politics of Regional Trade in Iraq, Arabia and the Gulf 1745-1900* (Albany, 1997).

Floor, Willem. "A Description of the Persian Gulf and its inhabitants in 1756," *Persica*, vol. 8 (1979), pp. 163-86 (reprinted here as chapter two).

__, "Pearl fishing in the Persian Gulf in the 18th century," *Persica*, vol. 10 (1982), pp. 209-222 (reprinted here as Appendix II).

__, "Dutch trade with Masqat in the second half of the 18th century," *African and Asian Studies*, vol. 16 (1982), pp. 197-213 (reprinted here as chapter six).

__, "First Contacts between the Netherlands and Masqat," *Zeitschrift der Deutschen Morgenlandische Gesellschaft* 132 (1982), pp. 289-307.

__, "The Revolt of Shaikh Ahmad Madani in Laristan and the Garmsirat (1730-1733)," *Studia Iranica*, vol. 8 (1983), p. 63-93.

__, "The Bahrein Project of 1754," *Persica*, vol. 11 (1984), pp. 129-148 (reprinted here as Appendix I).

__, "Masqat Anno 1673," *Le Moyen-Orient et l'Océan Indien* (1985), pp. 1-69.

__, "Dutch East India Company's Trade with Sind in the 17th and 18th centuries," *Moyen-Orient & Ocean Indien*, vol. 3 (1986), pp. 111-144;

__, "The Iranian Navy during the Eighteenth Century," *Iranian Studies* 20 (1987), pp. 31-53 (reprinted here as chapter one).

__, *The Commercial Conflict between Persia and the Netherlands, 1712-1718*, Durham University, Occasional Papers no. 37. (1988).

__, *Hokumat-e Nader Shah* (Tehran: Tus, 1367/1988), translated by Abu'l-Qasem Serri;

__, "The Decline of the Dutch East Indies Company in Bandar 'Abbas, 1747-1759," *L'Ocean Indien & Le Moyen-Orient*, vol. 6 (1989), pp. 45-80 (part of chapter three).

__, "The Dutch and Khark Island, 1753-1770, A Commercial Mishap," 24 (1992) *IJMES*, pp. 441-460 (reprinted here as chapter five).

__, "The Dutch and Khark Island, The adventures of the Baron von Kniphausen," in: Européens en Orient aux XVIIIe siècle. *Moyen Orient & Ocean Indien* (1994), pp. 157-202 (reprinted here as part of chapter four).

__, *The Afghan Occupation of Persia, 1722-1730* (Paris- Cahiers Studia Iranica, 1998);

__, "New Facts on Nader Shah's Indian Campaign," in: Kambiz Eslami ed. *Iran and Persian Studies. Essays in Honor of Iraj Afshar.* (Princeton: Zagros, 1998), pp. 198-219.

__, *The Textile Industry in historical perspective 1500-1925* (Paris, 1999).

__, *The Economy of Safavid Persia* (Wiesbaden, 2000).

__, "Dutch Trade in Afsharid Iran (1730-1753)," *Studia Iranica* 34 (2005), pp. 43-93.

__, *The Persian Gulf 1500-1730. The Political Economy of Five Port Cities* (Washington DC, 2006);

__, "The Rise and Fall of the Banu Ka'b – A Borderer State in Southern Khuzestan," 44 (2006) *IRAN*, pp. 277-315.

Francklin, William. *Observations made on a tour from Bengal to Persia in the years 1786-7* (London, 1790)

Gaube, Heinz. *Die südpersische Provinz Arrajan/Kuh-Giluyeh von der arabischen Eroberung bis zur Safawidenzeit* (Vienna, 1973).

Ghaffari Kashani, Abu'l-Hasan. *Golshan-e Morad* ed. Gholamreza Tabataba'i (Tehran, 1369/1990).

Golestaneh, Abu'l-Hasan b. Mohammad Amin. *Mojmal al-Tavarikh* ed. Modarres Razavi (Tehran, 2536/1977).

Government of Great Britain, *Selections from the records of the Bombay Government* No. XXIV-New Series (Bombay, 1856).

Grummond, Stephen R. *The Rise and Fall of the Arab Shaykhdom of Bushire: 1750-1850 (Iran, Persian Gulf)* unpublished dissertation Johns Hopkins University (Baltimore, 1985).

Hakima, Ahmad Abu. *History of Eastern Arabia 1750-1800. The Rise and Development of Bahrain and Kuwait* (Beirut, 1965).

Hamilton, Alexander. *A New Account of the East Indies.* 2 vols. in one. (London, 1930 [Amsterdam 1970]).

Hamy, E.-T. "Voyage d'André Michaux en Syrie et en Perse (1782-1785) d'après son journal et sa correspondance." *Neuvième Congrès International de Géographie, Compte Rendu Des Travaux du Congrès*, vol. 3 (1911), pp. 1-38.

Hazin, Sheikh Mohammad Ali, *The Life of Sheikh Mohammad Ali Hazin*, ed. & tr. F.C. Belfour (London 1830)

Heeres, J.E. and Stapel, F.W. eds. *Corpus Diplomaticum Neerlando-Indicum* 6 vols. (The Hague, 1907-55).

Horsburgh, James. *India Directory or Directions for Sailing to and from the East Indies* 4th edition (London, 1836).

Hotz, A. ed. "Cornelisz. Roobacker's scheepsjournaal, Gamron-Basra (1645)," *Tijdschrift v.h. Koninklijk Aardrijkskundig Genootschap* 20 (1879), pp. 289-405.

Howel, Thomas. *Journal of the Passage from India* (London, 1789).

Indrani, Ray. "Trade in Basra in the Mid-Eighteenth Century," in Lakshmi Subramanian ed. *The French East India Company and the trade of the Indian Ocean: a collection of essays by Ray Indrani* (New Delhi, 1999), pp. 203-14.

Ives, Edward. *A Voyage from England to India in the Year MDCCLIV ... also A Journey From Persia to England* (London, 1773).

Kelly, K. B. *Britain and the Persian Gulf, 1795-1880* (Oxford, 1968).

Khalifehzadeh, 'Alireza. *Bandar Deylam va Haft Shahr-e Liravi* (Bushire, 1382/2003)

Faqih, Khorshid. *Zaval-e Dowlat-e Holand dar Khalij-e Fars ba Zohur-e Mir Mohanna Bandar-e Rigi* (Bushire, 1383/2004).

Le Strange, G. *The Lands of the Eastern Caliphate* (London 1905 [1966]).

Lockhart, Laurence. "The Navy of Nadir Shah," *Proceedings of the Iran Society* vol. 1/1 (London, 1936), pp. 3-18.

__, *Nadir Shah* (London, 1938).

Longrigg, S.H. *Four centuries of modern Iraq* (Oxford, 1925).

Lorimer, J.G. *Gazetteer of the Persian Gulf* 2 vols. (Calcutta, 1915).

Meilink-Roelofsz, M.A.P. "Een Nederlandse Vestiging in de Perzische Golf," *Spiegel Historiael* (1967), pp. 80-88.

Miles, S.B. *The Countries and Tribes of the Persian Gulf* (London, 1969).

Moqtader, Sarlashkar *Kelid-e Khalij-e Fars* (Tehran, 1333/1954).

Mostoufi, Hamdallah. *Nuzhat al-Qulub.* tr. G. Le Strange (Leyden - London 1919).

Nami, Mirza Mohammad Sadeq Musavi. *Tarikh-e Giti-gosha* ed. Sa'id Nafisi (Tehran, 1363/1984).

Niebuhr, Carsten. *Beschreibung von Arabien, aus eigenen beobachtungen und in lande selbst gesammleten nachrichten abgefasset nachrichten* (Kopenhagen: N. Möller, 1772).

__, *Travels through Arabia, and other countries in the East* 2 vols. (Edinburgh, 1792).

__, *Reisebeschreibung nach Arabien und andern umliegenden Ländern* 3 vols. in one with continuous pagination (Zürich, 1992).

Nurbakhsh, Hoseyn. *Bandar-e Lengeh dar Sahel-e Khalij-e Fars* (Bandar 'Abbas, 1358/1979).

__, *Jazireh-ye Qeshm va Khalij-e Fars* (Tehran, 1369/1990)

Nur-Darya'i, Ahmad. *Marasem-e Ayini va Fulklur-e Mardom-e Bandar-e Kong* (Tehran, 1384/2005).

Parsons, Abraham. *Travels in Asia and Africa* (London, 1808).

Perry, John R. "The Banu Ka'b an amphibious state in Khuzistan," *Le Monde iranien et l'Islam* 1 (1971), pp. 131-52

__, "Mir Muhanna and the Dutch. Patterns of Piracy in the Persian Gulf," *Studia Iranica* 2 (1973), pp. 75-95.

__, *Karim Khan Zand, A History of Iran, 1747-1779* (Chicago, 1979).

Plaisted, Bartholomew. *A Journal from Calcutta in Bengal, by Sea, to Bussera: from thence across the great Desart to Aleppo ... In the Year 1750* (London, 1757).

Porter, John. *Remarks on the Bloachee, Brodia and Arabian Coasts* (London, 1781).

Raynal, Abbé G.T.F. *A Philosophical and Political History of the Settlements and Trade of the Europeans in the East and West Indies* 4 vols. (Dublin, 1779).

Ricks, Thomas Miller. *Politics and Trade in Southern Iran and the Gulf, 1745-1765.* unpublished dissertation Indiana University, 1975.

Risso, Patricia. *Oman & Muscat an early modern history* (New York, 1986).

Roschan-Zamir, Mehdi. *Zand-Dynastie* (Hamburg, 1970).

Sadid al-Saltaneh, Mohammad 'Ali. *Bandar 'Abbas va Khalij-e Fars* ed. Ahmad Eqtedari (Tehran, 1342/1963).

Saldanha, J. A. *The Persian Gulf Précis* 10 vols. (Gerards Cross: Archive Editions, 1986).

Sestini, D. *Viaggio da Constatinopoli a Bassora* (n. p., 1786).

Seystani, Iraj Afshar. *Nehagi beh Bushehr* 2 vols. (Tehran, 1369/1990).

Shirazi, 'Ali Reza. *Das Tarikh-i Zendije des Ibn 'Abd al Kerim Ali Riza von Shiraz* Ernst Beer ed. (Leiden, 1888).

Slot, Ben J. *The Arabs of the Gulf, 1602-1784: an alternative approach to the early history of the Arab Gulf States and the Arab peoples of the Gulf mainly based on sources of the Dutch East India*

Company (Leidschendam, 1993) translated into Arabic by 'Ayidah Khuri muraja'at Mohammad Mursi 'Abdollah as *'Arab al-Khalij, 1602-1784: fi daw' masadir Sharikat al-Hind al-Sharqiyah al-Hulandiyah* (Abu Dhabi, 1995).

Wijnandts van Resandt, W. *De Gezaghebbers der Oost-Indische Compagnie* (Amsterdam, 1944).

Williamson, A. *The Maritime Cities of the Persian Gulf and their Commercial Role from the 5th Century to 1507* (unpublished dissertation Oxford, 1971).

Wilson, A.T. *The Persian Gulf* (London, 1928).

Ya Hoseyni, Sayyed Qasem. *Mir Mohanna - ruyaruye inglisiha va holandiha dar khalij-e Fars* (Bushire, 1375/1994).

INDEX

C

D

E

K

L

M

S

T

U

V

W

Y

Z

www.ingramcontent.com/pod-product-compliance
Ingram Content Group UK Ltd.
Pitfield, Milton Keynes, MK11 3LW, UK
UKHW050135171225
466058UK00006B/32

9 781933 823188